S0-COM-090

FORTRAN:

A Practical Approach
with Style and Structure

Third Edition

Wilfred P. Rule

Northeastern University

Prindle, Weber & Schmidt
Boston, Massachusetts

© Copyright 1980 by Prindle, Weber & Schmidt,20 Providence Street, Boston, Massachusetts 02116.All rights reserved. No part of this book may be reproduced or transmitted in any form or by any means, electronic or mechanical, including photocopying, recording, or any information storage and retrieval system, without permission in writing from the publisher.

Prindle, Weber & Schmidt is a division of Wadsworth, Inc.

Library of Congress Cataloging in Publication Data
Rule, Wilfred P.
  FORTRAN, a practical approach with style and structure.

  Includes index.
  1. FORTRAN (Computer program language) I. Title.
QA76.73.F25R84   001.64'24   80–11159
ISBN 0–87150–290-9

Designed by Helen Walden and the production staff of Prindle, Weber & Schmidt. Composition and artwork by Jay's Publishers Services, Inc. Printed and bound by The Alpine Press, Inc.

Cover photo is a section of a microcircuit chip, and is reprinted courtesy of International Business Machines Corporation.

Preface

This edition of *FORTRAN: A Practical Approach with Style and Structure* is the result of the experience of two previous editions and the feedback from students and instructors who used the book. This information has been combined with current coverage of Fortran 77 and programming style and structure.

Overall, the book remains true to the basic goals stated in the previous edition:

It is specifically designed for undergraduate students who have no experience in computer programming. It is not a guide or outline to computer programming, but on the contrary is a descriptive, detailed presentation of:

(a) the basic principles of computer programming; and

(b) a typical computer language called FORTRAN.

One of the main features of the text is the number and variety of sample programs used to supplement the formal presentation of the text matter. The illustrations and case studies assist in the mastery of the mechanics of the computer language, but more importantly, they develop a feel for the tremendous potential of the computer.

The text sets a moderate pace, bringing key concepts in gradually so that students can build skill and confidence before moving into more advanced topics. Correct style and structure are provided in every example so that no poor programming habits are developed in learning elementary concepts. Style and structure are formally and thoroughly covered in Chapters 8 and 16 respectively.

Beyond these chapters, the text's organization is based on Chapters 1 – 9 providing the essentials of FORTRAN and the remaining chapters being worked in to suit course goals and student needs. A chart of chapter dependencies is given below.

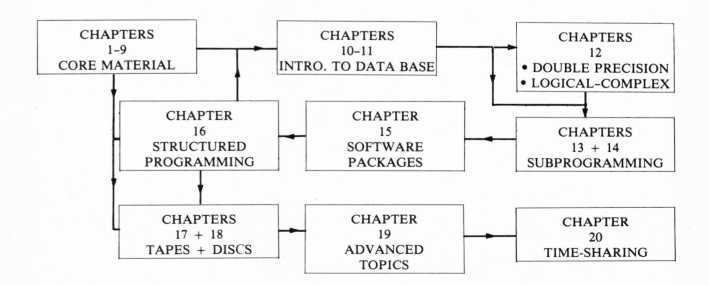

The material has several features to build student interest and abilities and to make key concepts accessable.

1. Quizzes are provided in Chapters 1 – 10 and 13 that give questions and short programming problems for students to check their progress. The answers to these quizzes are given at the end of the quiz.
2. Almost every chapter has review exercises for reinforcing important points and work in FORTRAN.
3. "Additional Applications" sections follow most chapters to illustrate how FORTRAN can be used to solve real-world problems in such areas as business, engineering, social sciences and many others.
4. The appendices provide a guide to programmable statements in FORTRAN IV and FORTRAN 77, a guide to system dependent statements and a key to various flowcharting conventions.
5. Key FORTRAN statements are listed on the end papers (inside covers).

Finally, I would like to thank the following reviewers for the advice and help they provided: Weston Beale (Indiana University), Geneva Belford (University of Illinois), William F. Brown (Ball State University), John Buck (Indiana University), Mario J. Casarella (Catholic University), G. Ford (Arizona State University), Louise Hay (University of Illinois), Bernard E. Howard (University of Miami), Gregory W. Jones (Utah State University), L. Levine (University of Wisconsin), Michael Murphy (University of Houston), David Petrie (Cypress College), E. H. Rogers (Rensselaer Polytechnic Institute), Lester Smith (Ohio State University), Sanford H. Stone (San Diego State University), David Thuente (Indiana-Purdue University), Frank D. Vickers (University of Florida), Vernon Vinge (San Diego State University), Jay Wolf (Ohio State University).

Contents

Contents

1 Introduction to Digital Computers

It is important that you approach Chapters 1 and 2 of this text in the correct frame of mind. These are very special chapters in that they attempt to give you a quick exposure to what computers are all about, in the form of an **overview.** The amount of information in these chapters is considerable, but it is being presented for *background* information only! Each topic covered now will be covered again (and in considerable detail). On the second time around, however, you will have a better idea of how any one topic relates to all the others. That is the purpose of an overview. Read these first two chapters somewhat casually and do not expect to master the subject at this time.

This overview takes a quick look at the various hardware components that constitute a digital computer. This is followed by a brief description of how these components contribute to the overall operation of the computer system. Finally, we touch upon the important parts of a set of instructional commands (computer language) that a programmer uses to coordinate and direct these computing activities. We want you to see how the whole system works before getting down to the sometimes drab details associated with any one of its parts.

1.1 Correct Focus

Many students feel that the only important part of computer programming is learning the various elements of the computer language. As part of the overview, we will show that this is just not true. As it turns out, learning the language is the easy part. There will be little hassle involved in learning the various commands that comprise the FORTRAN language. The challenge lies in combining these individual commands (**instructions**) into a logical sequence (a **program**) that efficiently and correctly solves the problem at hand.

You are being given a warning: *learning the elements of a computer language is relatively easy. Learning how to combine these elements into an efficient program can be difficult.*

As part of the overview approach, we will try to focus your attention on this hidden obstacle. Accordingly, we will emphasize the general strategy or game plan associated with writing complete programs, rather than the individual statements. This will give you some idea of how each instruction contributes to the functioning of the total program.

1.2 Basic Operations

The operations that a computer is capable of performing can be grouped into a surprisingly short list.

1. INPUT/OUTPUT
2. ARITHMETIC
3. LOGIC/CONTROL
4. SPECIFICATION

This list identifies all the operations a computer is capable of performing. All programs, no matter how complicated they may appear, can be resolved into some combination of these basic operations.

The list is being presented to make your dealing with the computer more organized and it should be used in the following way. When writing a program, it is not uncommon to become confused as to what to do next. The organized approach we are promoting suggests that when this happens, you return to this list. Attempt to get things started again by classifying which basic operation should be accomplished next.

Each of these operations is implemented by a specific piece of computer hardware. For example, all computers have one or more input devices, such as a card reader, a terminal or some other unit. There must also be some output device, possibly a printer or a typewriter. Other important hardware items include a unit that adds, subtracts, multiplies, and divides. Collectively these components are what make up the total computer system.

In writing a program we are in effect lining up this equipment in a sequence appropriate to solving the problem. FORTRAN uses a list of key words or symbols such as READ, WRITE, +, – to identify which piece of equipment is needed next. If we issue the instruction READ, we are in effect signalling that the input device is needed. (Actually the instruction involves more than the word READ, but those details will be covered shortly.) If the instruction that follows uses the symbol + or –, the appropriate arithmetic hardware will be activated.

In the next few pages we will describe each of the four basic operations in more detail. Try to get a feel for what each operation accomplishes and the key words or commands associated with that operation.

1.3   Input/Output   Basic Commands: READ/WRITE

During the execution of a program, there are times when the programmer will want to *give* new information to the computer — provide a fresh set of data values, for example. On other occasions, the programmer might want to *receive* information (such as the results of a calculation just performed) from the computer. *Two-way dialogue* or communication is a part of every program and is accomplished by INPUT/OUTPUT instructions.

You will soon be dealing with a program that computes the volumes of a number of cylinders. The radius and height of each cylinder represent *input* to this program. The computed volume will represent *output.* Assume the radius and height of each cylinder is punched on a card and these cards are stacked in the card reader. Each time we want the computer to accept a new card (defining a new cylinder) we issue the instruction READ.* Later, after all calculations are complete, we will issue the instruction WRITE to obtain output.

---

*This represents a substantial simplification of the actual process. Because many people will be using the computer at any given time, all your data cards are read when your program is submitted. They are used to build what's called an "input file." Each time a READ command is executed, the information associated with one of your data cards is taken from this "input file."

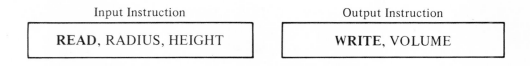

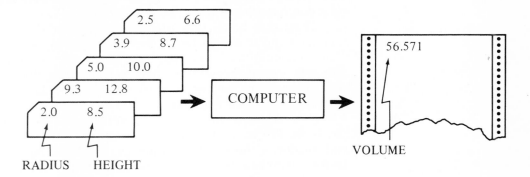

Figure 1.1
Input/Output Operations

1.4 | Arithmetic   Basic Commands: + – * /

Computers have electronic circuitry (hardware) that adds, subtracts, multiplies and divides. These pieces of equipment are activated in FORTRAN by the symbols +, –, *, /. These symbols are preferred to the words ADD, SUBTRACT, MULTIPLY and DIVIDE so that FORTRAN will have an algebraic likeness or similarity. Each symbol identifies a specific operation (electronic component) available to accomplish the mathematics of the problem being solved.

Take a look at the following set of instructions. They are presented to show that a computer program does *not* have to be complex and intimidating. You should have little difficulty understanding how the computer would respond.

Program
```
READ, X, Y, Z
ANS1 = X + Y + Z
ANS2 = X*Y/Z
WRITE, ANS1, ANS2
```

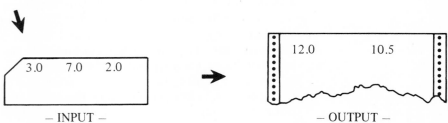

Three values are read from input. A sequence of add operations is specified producing what appears to be answer 1. A second sequence of mathematics (multiplication of X by Y; then division by Z) is stipulated producing a second answer. These answers are then displayed (sent to output).

1.5 | Logic/Control   Basic Commands: IF   GO TO   STOP

As a program is running, it is sometimes necessary to test for special conditions. For example, we may test to see if a person has worked over 40 hours and therefore overtime is authorized. Other tests may be less routine in nature. It may be necessary to test a value to avoid division by zero. Consider the last calculation of the sample program just written:

$$ANS2 = X*Y/Z$$

This calculation must be avoided whenever Z takes on the value zero. The result would be an infinite number, which causes a result that cannot be computed.

LOGIC/CONTROL operations are used to handle these special situations. The LOGIC operation is used to do the testing. The CONTROL group, often called **branching instructions**, permits the interruption of the normal program operation for the purpose of doing something special, like jumping to an alternate set of instructions.

The words IF, STOP and GO TO identify instructions that are part of the LOGIC/CONTROL group.

Example:

IF (HOURS. GT. 40.0) GO TO 8

Meaning:

Test the value of HOURS, and if the value is greater than 40, take special action . . . GO TO instruction 8.

Example:

IF (Z. EQ. 0.0) STOP

Meaning:

Test the value of Z, and if it has a value of 0, stop the program.

In these examples, the control statements (STOP and GO TO) will only be executed when the conditions specified in the logic or IF statement are satisfied. Using an IF test to *selectively* execute a statement can be applied equally well to other types of statements:

Example:

IF (LINES. LT. 100) WRITE, A, B, C

Meaning:

Test the value of LINES; if it is less than 100, execute the WRITE statement generating another line of output.

Example:

IF (DIST. LT. 200.) RATE = 4.25* TIME

Meaning:

IF the value of DIST (distance) is less than 200, compute the rate using the equation RATE = 4.25 times TIME.

1.6 | Specification   Key Word: FORMAT

INPUT/OUTPUT, ARITHMETIC and LOGIC/CONTROL statements are the *action* instructions in FORTRAN. All program logic consists of some combination of these statements. A final group of statements, SPECIFICATION statements, are more passive in nature. They supply supportive information, usually administrative details, needed while performing one of the action statements.

Fortunately, the only specification statement you will initially be involved with is the **FORMAT statement**.

The word FORMAT means layout or arrangement, and a FORMAT statement is used to support or assist a READ or WRITE activity. For example, consider the READ statement used in the previous example programs:

READ, X, Y, Z

Now consider a READ statement that reads a student's name and her average score on a series of exams:

READ, NAME, AVRAGE

How does the computer know that one card contains three numbers, while the other contains two values, a name and a number? The computer does *not* know and should be told by a FORMAT statement. How the FORMAT statement is linked to the READ statement will be covered later. The layout of a data card, however, is one of those administrative details handled by statements in the SPECIFICATION group.

1.7 | Summary

Unless you use an organized, structured approach to programming, you may find it a chaotic, confusing activity. In the near future, you are going to get hung up in a program and not know what to do next. You do not have many options. You can read or print (INPUT/OUTPUT). You can do more calculations (ARITHMETIC). You can test (LOGIC) and possibly jump to another part of the program (CONTROL). One way to reduce confusion is to learn to classify the basic operations as described in the preceding paragraphs.

1.8 | Combining Statements

It is important that you learn how to write complete programs as soon as possible. As the first step in that direction, the following examples suggest how individual statements can be combined to accomplish a specific task. You should be able to recognize most of these statements and may even be able to follow a good deal of the logic being used.

| **Programming Example** Which Number Is Larger? | Given two numbers punched on a data card, determine and report which is the larger. |

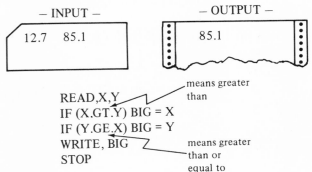

The first statement reads the data card and defines X and Y. An IF test asks, "Is X greater than Y?" If the answer is yes, the memory location BIG is given the value of X. A second IF test determines if BIG should be given the value of Y. The contents of BIG is sent to output and the program terminates.

Programming Example
Honors List

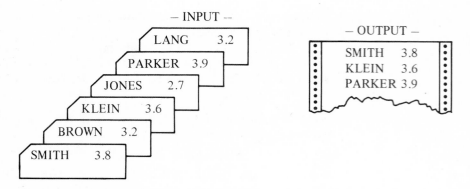

Each card in a data deck gives the name and scholastic average of a group of high school students. Write a program to print the names of all students with a 3.5 average or better.

```
8   READ, NAME, AVRAGE
    IF (AVRAGE. GE. 3.5) WRITE, NAME, AVRAGE
    GO TO 8
```

Note: We have given the READ statement an identifying number (a label) so that the GO TO statement can pass control back to it, thus establishing a repetitive loop.

Programming Example
Different Pay Rates

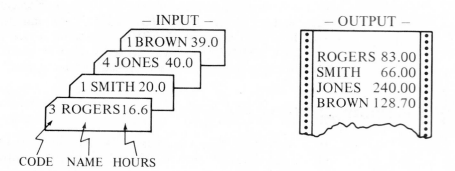

Each data card gives the name and hours worked by an employee. The first number on the card indicates which hourly rate should be used for this person (see pay rate table below). Determine and report the amount due each individual.

Rate Table:

RATE	AMOUNT
1	3.30
2	4.40
3	5.00
4	6.00

```
12   READ, CODE, NAME, HOURS
     IF (CODE. EQ. 1) PAY = 3.30* HOURS
     IF (CODE. EQ. 2) PAY = 4.40* HOURS
     IF (CODE. EQ. 3) PAY = 5.00* HOURS
     IF (CODE. EQ. 4) PAY = 6.00* HOURS
     WRITE, NAME, PAY
     GO TO 12
```

Discussion: While there are four arithmetic statements to compute PAY, only one will be executed for each data card, namely, the one associated with the value of CODE on the card. Statement 12 is numbered so that control can be passed back to the top of the program and, thereby, repeat the logic over and over until we run out of data cards.

Programming Example
Number Search

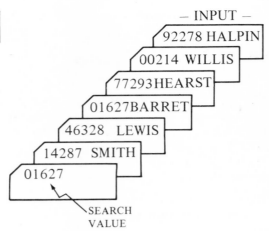

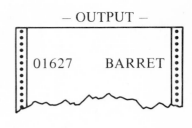

The card at the front of the data deck shown contains a student identification number. We want to know the name of the student assigned this number. Read the remaining cards, which tell the name associated with each ID number in active use. When the number is found, print the student's name. NSERCH will be used to hold the identification number we are searching for and IDNO will hold the number on each of the main body data cards.

```
      READ, NSERCH
  5   READ, IDNO, NAME
      IF (NSERCH. NE. IDNO) GO TO 5
      WRITE, IDNO, NAME
      STOP
```

means not
equal to

Discussion: This is a typical search activity. A search quantity is read from the first card. A loop is established to read the remaining cards. As long as the identification number, IDNO, on each new card does not match the one we are looking for, NSERCH, the GO TO statement will be executed. When a match is made, control passes to the WRITE statement and the program terminates.

1.9 | Review

1. What are the four basic groups of statements (operations) in FORTRAN?

Answer: *ARITHMETIC*
                  INPUT/OUTPUT   SPECIFICATION   LOGIC/CONTROL

2. What words or symbols are used in FORTRAN to call out these operations?

Answer: *INPUT/OUTPUT ——— READ, WRITE*
          *ARITHMETIC ——————— + – * /*
          CONTROL ——————— IF, GO TO, STOP
          SPECIFICATION ——— FORMAT

3. Is it difficult to learn the details of any one of these statements? Is it the important part of FORTRAN?

Answer: *Language structure of individual statements is not difficult. Combining statements into a logical program is what is important.*

4. Is there a fixed sequence in which FORTRAN statements should appear? For example, should a READ statement always be followed by an ARITHMETIC statement?

Answer: *Just as there is no fixed sequence in which chess pieces are moved, there is no fixed sequence of statements in writing a program.*

5. Examine the program segment that follows. It is used to arrive at a student's grade based on his/her performance in the homework assigned and the exams taken:

```
5   READ,HW1,HW2,HW3,HW4,HW5,HW6
    HWAVE=(HW1+HW2+HW3+HW4+HW5+HW6)/6.0
    READ,EXAM1,EXAM2,EXAM3,FINAL
    EXAMS=(EXAM1+EXAM2+EXAM3)/3.0
    GRADE=.20*HWAVE+.30*EXAMS+.50*FINAL
    WRITE,HWAVE,EXAMS,GRADE
    GO TO 5
```

5a. Describe the input to this program.

Answer: *For each student there are two cards. The first gives 6 homework scores. The second gives the scores of three exams and the score achieved in the final exam.*

5b. In computing the grade, (a) how much did the homework count? (b) How much did the final exam count?

Answer: (a) *20%*   (b) *50%*

5c. Could the second READ statement be moved up one line, that is placed before the computation of the homework average?

Answer: *YES*

5d. Could the WRITE statement be moved up one line, placed before the computation of GRADE?

Answer: *NO*

6. Assume a company pays its employees $4.80 an hour for up to forty hours of work each week and $7.20 for all overtime hours. Analyze the program that follows. Explain how there can be two arithmetic statements that compute PAY. Won't that cause trouble?

```
5   READ,HRSMON,HRSTUE,HRSWED,HRSTHU,HRSFRI
    TOTAL=HRSMON+HRSTUE+HRSWED+HRSTHU+HRSFRI
    PAY=TOTAL*4.80
    IF(TOTAL.GT.40)PAY=40.0*4.80 + (TOTAL-40.0)*7.20
    WRITE,TOTAL,PAY
    GO TO 5
```

Answer: The first arithmetic statement computes PAY for a normal work week (40 hours or less). An IF test then checks for the special condition of an overtime situation. If overtime is detected, the second PAY calculation is applied. When the WRITE statement is reached, the correct value of PAY will be printed.

1.10 | Hardware Organization

We now take a closer look at the computer's hardware components and how they are interconnected.

All computers have at least one input device. A large computer facility, however, may have many input units. There could be two or three card readers, four or five magnetic tape drives and the potential of linking up to virtually hundreds of terminals. As a beginning programmer, you will probably be involved with *one*

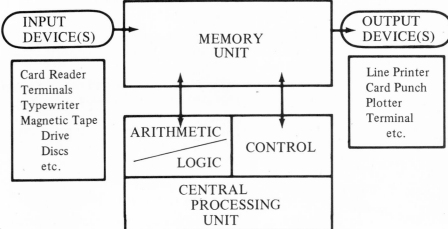

Figure 1.2
Organization of a Digital Computer

input device only. For some, this will be the card reader; for others, input will be via a terminal. In either case, it will appear to you that there is only one input unit in active operation, namely, the one you are using. Whether dealing with cards or with the terminal, the basic input command is READ. As we progress, we will make a relatively easy transition to deal with all the other input devices such as magnetic tapes and disks. We will still use the command READ, but in an expanded form to incorporate all other means of input.

One final point of clarification. Input is not just the presentation of a problem's data values. It also includes providing the logic to solve the problem (the FORTRAN instructions). Thus, the input device is used to place in memory an *instruction* set and a *data* set in a form compatible with high speed operations. We will discuss this form later, but for now consider it as an electronic image of what was on a card, if card input is used.

The **memory unit** is the name given to the device used for the internal storage of information. It is capable of storing massive amounts of information in a relatively small space. For example, it must hold all the information associated with your program as well as all the other programs that are running along with yours. This unit must not only have a large capacity to store information, it must also have the ability to retrieve any specific piece of information *directly*. This feature is called **random access**.

The Central Processing Unit (the CPU) is the most active of all the hardware components. It is subdivided into two major units, the **arithmetic/logic unit** and the **control unit**. The arithmetic unit is the portion of the CPU where all arithmetic operations (adding, subtracting, multiplying and dividing) are performed. If it occurs to the reader to wonder if the arithmetic unit can perform high-order mathematics such as computing trigonometric values, taking roots of equations or evaluating logarithms, the answer is that it can, but not directly. Such high-order operations are accomplished by a clever combination of the basic operations of add, subtract, multiply and divide. We will get to that shortly.

The arithmetic unit has another feature, namely, the ability to determine if one number is larger than another or whether the result of a calculation is zero, negative or positive. This feature is used by the LOGIC/CONTROL group of operations to provide the decision-making instructions described earlier.

The control unit is the boss or supervisor of all activities. Its job is to sequentially fetch your instructions (the program) from memory and interpret the operation required. Depending upon the instruction, the control unit activates the appropriate hardware and coordinates the movement of information involved. This could be the activating of an input device and the coordinating of the transfer of information into memory. It might involve transferring information from

Figure 1.3
A total computer system
Photo courtesy I.B.M. Corporation

memory to the arithmetic unit for numeric processing and transferring the result back to memory. In any event, this is part of the internal processing in which the programmer is seldom directly involved.

Finally, output is achieved on any of several devices capable of conveying to the programmer the values stored in specific memory locations. A common output device is the **line printer**. **Terminals** are equally popular and have both an input and output capability. Terminals allow the programmer to interact with the computer more directly than when cards are used.

Figure 1.3 shows the impressive layout of the total computer system.

We have discussed the general layout of the hardware that constitutes a computer system. Programming will be more meaningful to you if you are aware of the equipment you are controlling and understand (even superficially) how it works. Read the next few pages with this limited objective in mind.

1.11 | Input Unit

We have mentioned that all information presented to the computer falls into two categories: instructions, followed by data values. The instructions must be presented in a rather rigid, fussy form (otherwise they are undecipherable by the computer). If input is to be by cards, the programmer can obtain specially printed cards that display the required layout or form each instruction must have. The cards are taken to a typewriter-like machine called a **keypunch**. As you type on this machine, a pattern of punched holes is imposed on the card, and typing appears across the top. The typing is for you to read. The holes are for the computer (card reader) to interpret.

At the appropriate time we will reference operating instructions for this keypunch and go into more detail on preparing these instruction cards.

After the instruction cards are prepared, the data values are keypunched, forming what we call the **data deck**. These two groups of cards are presented (all in one batch) to a card reader. The card reader uses some high speed electronic device, such as a series of photoelectric cells, to detect the pattern of punched holes and convert them into an electronic image for transmittal to memory.

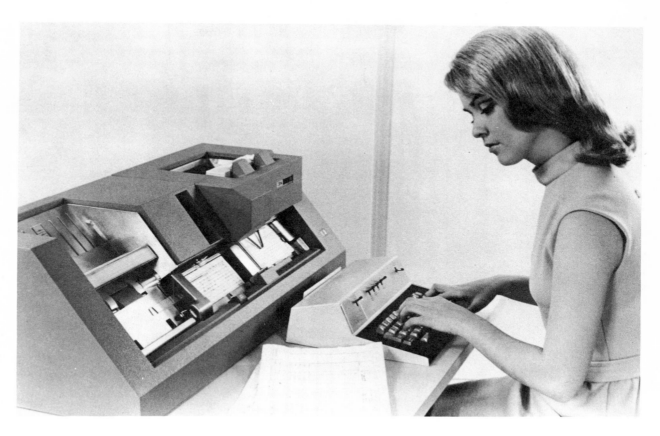

Figure 1.4
An IBM-029 keypunch
Photo courtesy I.B.M. Corporation

Figure 1.5
The card reader
Photo courtesy Control Data Corporation

The alternative to this "batch card operation" is input via terminals. The mechanics are very much similar in that the instructions are typed on the keyboard line by line. As each line is typed, a pattern of electronic pulses is generated and either sent directly to the computer or transmitted acoustically over the telephone. As each line of information is transmitted, the computer builds a file of information until all instructions are received.

Figure 1.6
A typical CRT terminal
Photo courtesy Control Data
Corporation

The entry of data values on terminals is accomplished as follows. Each time a READ instruction appears in your program, the terminal signals a request for input (usually by displaying a question mark). You then type the data associated with that READ statement. When this line is entered on the terminal, the computer picks up processing the program just as if a data card had been read.

The real advantage of a terminal is that it has both input and output capabilities. Each time a WRITE instruction appears in your program, the values you are asking for by this statement are displayed before you. This provides immediate "turn around" of information and allows for rapid two-way communication that becomes almost conversational in mode.

The more exotic input devices are **magnetic tapes** and **discs**. The tape is made of the same material as a home tape recorder except of higher quality. The long plastic tape is covered with a thin coat of brown or black iron oxide and wrapped on large reels. Information is recorded on the tape in the form of a pattern of magnetic spots that is retained by the iron oxide. Information can be "packed" much more tightly on the tape. One tape is the equivalent of over 100 boxes of cards. A box contains 2000 cards. Because the information is coded magnetically it can be processed at much higher rates than information punched on cards.

Magnetic discs use a similar technique for storing information. These units resemble a group of large phonograph records stacked as in a 1950 vintage juke box. The discs are covered with the same iron oxide (organized in concentric tracks) as used on tapes. Information is stored on each track in the form of a

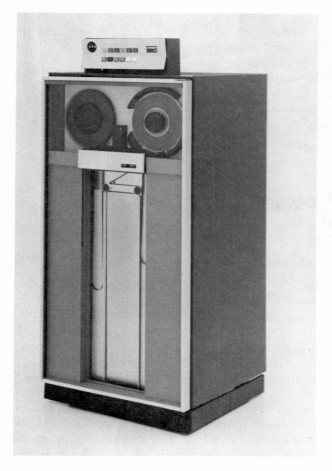

Figure 1.7 Magnetic Tape Drive
Courtesy I.B.M. Corporation

Figure 1.8 Magnetic Disc Drive
Courtesy I.B.M. Corporation

string of magnetic spots imposed on the iron oxide surface. Either side of any disc in the stack is available for almost instantaneous reading. This is because each side is equipped with its own movable "reading head" somewhat like the tone arm on a phonograph. The discs are continuously rotating at very high speed. Any portion of the discs can be reached directly by one of the reading heads, which give what is called **direct access**. Tapes must, of course, be read sequentially.

1.12 | The Output Device

As is the case with input, there are many different devices that may serve as output units. Very often one sees a computer writing answers on an electronic typewriter. Although electric typewriters are used by computers to print brief, coded, technical messages to the computer operator, they are far too slow to be used for general program output. Many students' programs can be completely run in the space of time it takes to type one character on an electric typewriter.

For that reason high-speed **line printers** have been developed to handle printed output. A line printer will print a whole line of approximately 132 characters in less time than it takes to typewrite one character. (Each output device may have a different line size. Consider the value 132 as typical.) A line printer will fill a 60-row page of computer output paper with answers in half the time it takes to type one line of output on the typewriter.

Figure 1.9
The High Speed Line Printer
Courtesy Control Data Corporation

If output is needed on cards, there does exist a device, the **card punch**, which will punch answers on cards. Although faster than an electric typewriter, it is many times slower than any other output device discussed here. It is used only when absolutely necessary.

Magnetic tapes, discs, and drums are much more efficient input/output devices. The electromagnetic design of these units permits an exceptionally rapid transfer of information to and from internal memory. For this reason, information supplied by slower input/output units (card input for example) is often transferred to a disc before being sent to internal memory.

1.13 How Memory Is Organized

The **memory unit** is where the computer stores instructions and data brought from the input unit. It is here that intermediate answers are stored pending their use in later computations. It is here that the final output is stored ready to be sent to the output unit for printing when requested by the programmer.

The memory unit is organized into tens of thousands of elements known as **memory locations**. It serves as a useful learning device if the student will think of each memory location as a post office box, one for each variable in the program. Each box has the following features:

1. It can store a number (input value, output value or intermediate calculation).
2. It can be assigned a name (as in algebra) to be used each time the contents of the box are needed.

Thus, the instruction

$$X = 4.5$$

in fact says, "Store the value 4.5 in a memory location." It further says, "Allow the programmer to reference that memory location by a label or name of his or her choosing (by the name X)."

The instruction

$$Y = X + 2.0$$

says, "Add 2.0 and the value stored in memory location X together; store the result in a new memory location and label that location Y."

Some operations change the contents of a memory location while others do not. Take the READ and WRITE operation, for example:

READ, X, Y   (Contents of X and Y change)
WRITE, X, Y   (Contents do not change)

The READ instruction is specifically designed to bring in fresh data from input replacing the old values. The WRITE statement merely asks for a display of the contents of memory locations X and Y, not a change in their value. Actually, a copy of the contents of locations X and Y is made and sent to output.

In similar fashion, the instruction:

$$Z = X + Y$$

does not change the contents of X or Y. It merely requires a copy of the contents of locations X and Y to be made and sent to the arithmetic unit. It is only the contents of memory location Z that will be changed by the above operations.

It will be useful to adopt the practice of portraying each memory location as a labelled box with its present value written inside, such as

X   Y
8.3   2.1

As each instruction is encountered, you update the contents of each box. Keep track of the contents of memory location X and Y as the following typical instruction is issued.

$$Y = 3.6$$

Result:

X   Y
8.3   3.6

Note that by storing a new value in location Y the former value has been destroyed.

Consider the effect of this instruction:

$$X = Y$$

Result:

X   Y
3.6   3.6

The instruction says, "Get a copy of the contents of memory location Y and store the copy in memory location X." A new value is stored in memory location X, displacing or destroying the original value. The contents of memory location Y are unchanged.

Any one of the memory locations discussed above consists of a connected series of small elements each capable of storing a zero or a one. Figure 1.10 (a) shows one of the original designs that utilizes small donut-shaped cores (about the size of a pinhead) made of soft iron. The iron cores are connected by thin wires and each core can be magnetized either clockwise (CW) or counter-clockwise (CCW), thereby storing a zero or a one.

Magnetization	Value Represented
CW	0
CCW	1

Figure 1.10(a) Magnetic Cores

Figure 1.10(b) Bubble Memory

Any individual string of cores can be accessed directly, thereby providing the random-access feature mentioned previously. This explains why numbers are stored in binary form (0's and 1's) and not in decimal form.

Figure 1.10 (b) shows a recent design innovation called "bubble memory." The small chip in Figure 1.10 (b) is divided into *one million* domains that may or may not contain a bubble. An individual bubble can be moved into or out of a specific domain by the action of a magnetic field. The presence of a bubble corresponds to the value one. The absence corresponds to the value zero.

We are seldom interested in dealing with a single bubble or single core of memory. For this reason, several of these binary elements are usually grouped together for the purpose of storing a single decimal digit or alphabetic character. An even more practical arrangement is to group many of these binary elements to form a unit (it is called a "word") that can hold a number of decimal digits or alphabetic characters.

The next section describes how the binary number system is used to represent both decimal quantities and alphabetic information.

1.14

Number Systems

The conversion of numeric values from decimal to binary for internal storage takes place almost automatically. Most programmers are not and need not be aware of what is going on. A programmer should, however, be at least familiar with the binary system of number representation.

Reading a decimal string of numbers and reading any other string is really quite similar. Consider the string of digits in Figure 1.11 as might appear on an old-fashioned desk calculator, i.e., as a decimal string. It is immediately interpreted as six *thousand,* four *hundred,* thirty-seven. Through years of drilling, it has become second nature to recognize the six as being in the thousands position, the four in the hundreds position and so on.

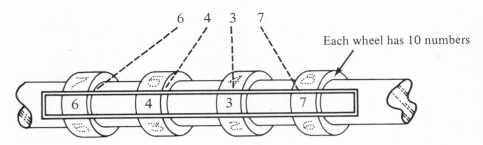

Figure 1.11
Decimal Number Representation

Realize that each digit is contributing something to the final answer. To determine each digit's contribution, you multiply the digit by some power of 10 (which is the base of the system). The power depends on where the digit appears in the string. You then add up all the individual contributions. This will be easier

$$6437_{10} = \boxed{6} \times 10^3 + \boxed{4} \times 10^2 + \boxed{3} \times 10^1 + \boxed{7} \times 10^0$$

$$= \boxed{6} \times 1000 + \boxed{4} \times 100 + \boxed{3} \times 10 + \boxed{7} \times 1$$

Figure 1.12
Interpreting Decimal Numbers

$$= (6437)_{10}$$

to understand if we move out of a base 10 system into some other, let us say a base 8 system.

If the wheels of our desk calculator had only 8 possible positions, we would number them 0 through 7 and be forced into the octal number system. The number 6437 in octal has the following meaning:

$$6437_8 = \boxed{6} \times 8^3 + \boxed{4} \times 8^2 + \boxed{3} \times 8^1 + \boxed{7} \times 8^0$$

$$= \boxed{6} \times 512 + \boxed{4} \times 64 + \boxed{3} \times 8 + \boxed{7} \times 1$$

$$= 3072 \quad + 256 \quad + 24 \quad + 7$$

Figure 1.13
Interpreting Octal Numbers

$$= 3359_{10}$$

Again, each digit contributes something to the final answer; only this time you multiply by some power of 8 (the new system base).

Note that in a discussion involving various number systems, it is necessary to show what system a number is being written in. Here the subscript 8 reminds the reader that the system is to be interpreted according to the octal system.

Having reached this point, we are now ready to handle binary numbers. If, for some reason, our wheels had only two positions, we would label them 0 and 1. Consider the pattern (binary string) shown in Figure 1.14. It represents the decimal number 19.

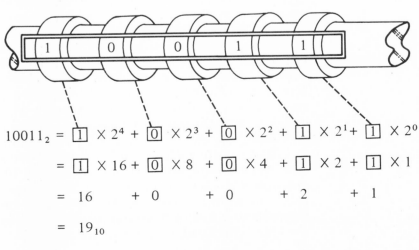

$$10011_2 = \boxed{1} \times 2^4 + \boxed{0} \times 2^3 + \boxed{0} \times 2^2 + \boxed{1} \times 2^1 + \boxed{1} \times 2^0$$

$$= \boxed{1} \times 16 + \boxed{0} \times 8 + \boxed{0} \times 4 + \boxed{1} \times 2 + \boxed{1} \times 1$$

$$= 16 \quad + 0 \quad + 0 \quad + 2 \quad + 1$$

Figure 1.14
Binary Representation

$$= 19_{10}$$

A final point about memory. Even though storage of all information is confined to a form using the numeric digits 0 and 1, this does not restrict the computer in any way. It can store all kinds of information such as letters of the alphabet as well as special characters, such as the period, comma, dollar sign, etc. This is done by simply coding all such nonnumeric characters into two or three digit numbers. For example, an A can be represented by a 41, and B by 42, and C by 43, and so on. The numbers are then converted to binary and stored as a string of zeros and ones.

As a quick exercise, determine the decimal value of the following binary numbers:

Exercise		Answers	
a. 1000	c. 1011	a. 8	c. 11
b. 1010	d. 1111	b. 10	d. 15

1.15 Machine Language Vs. FORTRAN

In the discussion of the design of the memory unit, the point has been made that all information stored in memory must be in binary form. This means that instructions as well as data values must ultimately be transformed into binary form before they can be stored in memory.

Don't panic. Just as data values are expressed in decimal form and somehow internally converted to binary, instructions will be handled in a similar way. When a student writes her first FORTRAN program, it will contain instructions such as:

$$X = Y + Z$$

These instructions will be read and converted to a form acceptable to the computer by a special program called the **compiler**. It is like a translator in that it converts instructions written in FORTRAN into instructions that the machine can understand. These are called **machine language instructions**. A single FORTRAN statement may require a whole series of basic operations to be performed. For each basic operation, a machine language instruction will be generated by the compiler. Each of these instructions is converted to a string of binary digits automatically. All of this is not your problem; it is the compiler's.

Please add, however, two new terms to your expanding computer vocabulary: *source* program and *object* program. A computer program written in a higher level language such as FORTRAN is referred to as the **source program**. Its translated or machine language equivalent is called the **object program**.

All FORTRAN programs must be translated (compiled) before they can be executed. During compilation, the computer is under the control of the compiler. Your FORTRAN statements will be read one after another. If you have issued the instruction READ, that instruction will be converted to the appropriate machine language code. If you have issued the instruction STOP, that instruction will be translated into machine language. When *all* statements in your program have been properly translated into machine language, the compiler is released and control passes to the first statement in your program (now in machine language). This marks the beginning of an entirely different phase of operations. Your instructions take over control of the computer, i.e., they are executed.

Now when a READ instruction is reached, information associated with one of your data cards will be transferred to internal storage. When a STOP instruction is encountered, the computer will terminate the execution of statements in your program. As you can see, compilation and execution are two distinctly different operations.

All computer programming languages that require compilation before being usable by the computer are referred to as **compiler languages**. FORTRAN, the language presented by this book, is by no means the only compiler language. It is the most widely used language in the fields of mathematics, science, engineering, statistics and probability, etc. Its name is derived from the words *FOR*mula *TRAN*slation. COBOL, the *CO*mmon *B*usiness *O*riented *L*anguage, is another very popular Compiler Language. It is designed for use in bookkeeping and accounting applications. Nothing would be gained by attempting to list all other compiler languages in use today. There are many different languages, each designed with some specific application in mind.

1.16 | Hardware Vs. Software

A brief word about two frequently used terms. The computer itself is physically comprised of nuts, bolts, cabinets, wires, resistors, transistors, cores, etc. Just as one might suspect, these items are referred to as its **hardware**.

The arithmetic unit is able to obey an ADD instruction because there are electronic circuits physically wired into it that enable it to add. The computer's ability to add is "a part of its hardware capability."

The basic philosophy of computer design is, however, to provide no more hardware than is absolutely necessary. This places a large responsibility on the programmer. We are constantly taking a minimal configuration of hardware and somehow combining these basic operations into a sequence of instructions that accomplishes any and all tasks assigned. This is where the concept of software comes in.

The Concept of Software

Each computer is equipped with a large group of prerecorded programs that extend its capabilities above and beyond those provided by the hardware. These capabilities include its ability to raise to a power, to take sines and cosines, to find roots, to take logarithms, and to compile source programs into object programs, naming just a few. These prerecorded programs are what is referred to by the term **software**.

The idea of accomplishing some high-order mathematics by combing a sequence of basic operations can be shown by the application of the relatively obscure formula shown below.

$$\text{Sin}(X) = X - \frac{X^3}{3 \cdot 2 \cdot 1} + \frac{X^5}{5 \cdot 4 \cdot 3 \cdot 2 \cdot 1} - \frac{X^7}{7 \cdot 6 \cdot 5 \cdot 4 \cdot 3 \cdot 2 \cdot 1}$$
$$+ \frac{X^9}{9 \cdot 8 \cdot 7 \cdot 6 \cdot 5 \cdot 4 \cdot 3 \cdot 2 \cdot 1}$$

Note: X must be in radians

This formula would have exceptionally limited application except for one thing. Look at the operations needed to evaluate the equation. Addition, subtraction, multiplication and division are needed. Raising to a power can be accomplished by repetitive multiplication. Do you see what this means? We can obtain the sine value by writing a small block of code that calls the basic operations (hardware capabilities) we already have! The ability to compute the sine becomes a software feature. This block of code (software routine) is but one of many that are organized into a software library and supplied by the computer manufacturer. Each of these library functions is as available to the programmer as readily as any of the hardware components. We use names like SIN or COS to evoke a particular software routine in the same way we use + and − to evoke a particular hardware component. For the moment, however, it is only important to recognize the term "software" and know how it relates to the term "hardware."

Review Exercises

1.*A digital computer is superior to a desk top calculator because it has a large memory unit. What type of information is stored in memory? (a) Numbers (b) Instructions (c) Both of these (d) None of these

2. The first information read by the computer is a list of instructions on how to solve the problem. What is this list of instructions called?

3.*What does the term "CPU" mean and what is the function of this unit?

4. Name the two most common means of input.

5.*Name four basic arithmetic operations that are performed by hardware components in the arithmetic unit.

6. Can the computer make logical decisions? If so, describe how this is accomplished.

7. Give an example of when the computer would have to make a logical decision.

8.*How is information recorded on cards?

9. The information punched on a card may also appear typed at the top of the card. Does the computer look at this typed line?

10. How is information stored on magnetic tape or discs?

11.*Which is faster, card input or magnetic tape input?

12. The line printer has an approximate capacity of 132 characters. What does this mean?

13. Why does memory use binary numbers? Why not decimal?

14. Describe what happens inside the computer as a result of the statement

$$Z = A + 6$$

15.*Are the contents of memory location A modified as a result of the above statement?

16. Are the contents of memory location Z affected by the statement?

17. What are "cores" used for and why are they associated with the binary number system?

18.*Express the number 5 in binary.

19. What is an octal number?

20. Describe the difference between a FORTRAN program and a MACHINE LANGUAGE program.

21.*Each FORTRAN statement must be processed by "the compiler." Why?

22. What is the source program?

23. What is the object program?

24. Why does FORTRAN use symbols such as +, −, *, / instead of the words ADD, SUBTRACT, MULTIPLY, and DIVIDE?

25.*During the compiling of your program, describe what happens when a READ instruction is reached.

26. Why is the typewriter seldom used as an output device?

27. What is the function of a FORMAT statement?

28. Where does the name FORTRAN come from?

29. Why is software preferred over hardware and what does the term "minimal hardware configuration" mean?

30. The text indicates that learning the various commands of a computer language is not the important part of programming. What is the important part?

31. What is meant by the term *compiler language*?

2 | Programming- General Description

The purpose of Chapter 1 was to provide general background material relative to the concept of digital computation and to describe some of the internal design and organization of a digital computer. Included in the chapter was a classification of basic operations that the computer is capable of performing, a look at some of the individual FORTRAN instructions and a partial explanation of what a complete program looks like.

Chapter 2 will amplify these latter topics. We will look at several other programs to see how they are constructed and how they are physically presented to the computer. It is still too early to expect that all the parts to this puzzle will fit together right before your eyes. You should continue to read for *general understanding only*! Most of the material presented at this time will be formally discussed in subsequent chapters.

More specifically, the purposes of this chapter are:

1. To reinforce your understanding of the terms *compilation* and *execution,*
2. To continue an introductory presentation of the components of a complete computer program, and
3. To describe the difference between integer and real numbers used by the computer.

2.1 | Compilation vs. Execution of a Program

It is important to realize that the computer must be given a *full* set of instructions, which must be translated and stored, before any single instruction can be executed. A computer receives instructions in the same way a tourist receives directions from a policeman. The policeman might say something like this, "Walk to the end of this block. Turn right. Walk another two blocks, and the bus station will be directly in front of you."

The tourists are in a situation where they must (1) receive a full set of instructions, (2) understand each instruction, and (3) memorize the sequence in which they were given. Then and only then can an attempt be made to obey (execute) the first instruction. A similar set of conditions prevails when a program is presented to the computer.

The Stored Program Concept: All instructions of a program are stored in the computer's memory before any of them are executed.

If a program is presented to the computer in the form of punched cards, it has the appearance of a single deck called the **program deck**. This program

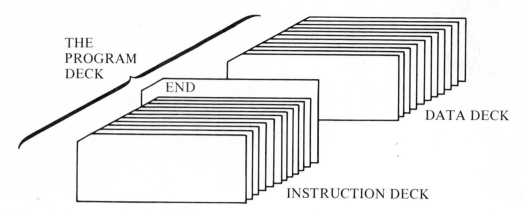

Figure 2.1 The Program Deck

deck has two subdivisions: the *instruction* deck followed by the *data* deck. The instruction deck will contain a sequence of instructions to be followed in the solution of the problems, and the data deck will contain those variable quantities (usually numbers) that are to be used in the computations. If the program deck is fed to the computer through the card reader, the first action taken by the computer is to cause the reading of the contents of the entire instruction deck. At this time the computer is being controlled by the compiler, which is serving as a translator. Each FORTRAN instruction is being translated into machine-language instructions.

We must somehow mark the end of the instruction deck; otherwise, the compiler will start processing data cards believing they contain FORTRAN instructions. This is done by placing a card at the end of the instruction deck that contains the one word "END."

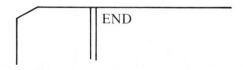

When the END card is detected, the compiling process is terminated and the computer releases the compiler. Control passes back to the first instruction of your program (now in machine language form) commencing the *execution* of the program.

From this discussion the student should conclude that processing of a computer program in fact occurs in two distinct phases: **compilation** followed by **execution**. Compilation describes the reading, translating and storing of instructions in the computer's memory. By the way, if you write any of your FORTRAN statements incorrectly (make a grammatical error), the compiler will indicate the nature of the error. If the error is not serious, it will attempt to fix it and go on.

If there are no errors, compilation continues until the END card is detected. The program then goes into execution. The computer goes back to your first instruction (now in memory and now in machine language) and starts *obeying it*.

2.2 | Another Sample Program

The following programming example is used to provide additional information concerning:

    1. Deck configuration.
    2. Sequential processing of statements.
    3. Use of statement numbers.
    4. Branching using the GO TO statement.

Programming Example Write a program to compute the volume of a cylinder, given its radius and height.

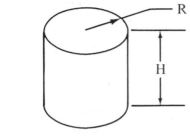

Suggested Variables:

RADIUS = Radius of cylinder
HEIGHT = Height of cylinder
AREA = Area of cylinder
VOLUME = Volume of cylinder

Volume = Area × Height
       = $\pi R^2 \times H$

The program for this is as follows:

		READ, RADIUS, HEIGHT
		AREA = 3.14 * RADIUS ** 2
		VOLUME = AREA * HEIGHT
		WRITE, VOLUME
		STOP
		END

The logic of this program starts by reading the radius and height of the cylinder from data and storing these two values as RADIUS and HEIGHT. The programmer has elected to compute the area of the cylinder's base as a separate calculation defining a quantity called AREA. The statement:

    AREA = 3.14 * RADIUS ** 2

needs a little explanation, since we are here introducing a new symbol. The single asterisk means multiply. A double asterisk means raise to a power. The statement says, "Evaluate the expression on the right of the equal sign which involves raising the contents of memory location RADIUS to the power 2 and multiplying the result by 3.14. Store the value thus obtained in a memory location and label it AREA." The volume is then computed by multiplying AREA by HEIGHT, and a WRITE statement displays the value obtained.

    To run this program on the computer, five statements must be punched on statement cards (or entered as separate lines on the terminal). These five cards plus the END card are then assembled into the instruction deck. A single data card forms the data deck. (A card in the data deck is called a **data card**). It contains the value of the radius and height of the cylinder whose volume is to be computed. The combined program deck is then placed into the card reader.

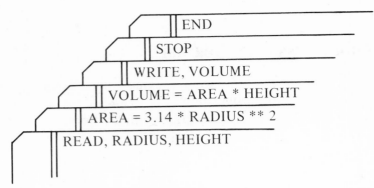

Figure 2.2 Typical Instruction Deck

After the instruction deck is read and compiled, the computer commences execution.

The first statement executed is the READ statement. Very often a student will want to put a data card immediately after the READ statement. "After all," he asks, "doesn't the computer need that data card as soon as it is told to read it?" The answer is, "No, it doesn't, because all instructions are stored in the computer's memory before the READ statement (or any other statement) is executed." By the time the READ statement is executed, all instruction cards have been processed during the compilation of the instruction deck. Any remaining cards should be data cards waiting to be processed by the execution of a READ command. *The instruction deck is consumed during compilation. Cards in the data deck are processed during the execution phase.*

Let us get on to something else.

In what order are instructions executed? Without giving it a moment's thought the answer comes, "Why, they are executed in the same order they appear in the instruction deck! First one first, second one second, last one last!"

Correct. But to put it in a single word, they are executed *sequentially*.

Another Computer Concept: Except when obeying branching (CONTROL) instructions, the computer will always execute instructions sequentially.

Control instructions are very important in programming. They allow us, for example, to return to an earlier part of a program in order to repeat the execution of a certain group of statements. This is referred to as **setting up a loop in the program**. The most elementary control instruction is the GO TO statement.

Suppose it was desired to compute the volume of three different cylinders. One not too clever approach to that problem would be to rewrite the program as follows:

Instructions	Meaning
READ,RADIUS,HEIGHT	Read the 1st data card.
AREA=3.14*RADIUS**2	Compute the 1st area.
VOLUME=AREA*HEIGHT	Compute the 1st volume.
WRITE, VOLUME	Print the 1st volume.
READ,RADIUS,HEIGHT	Read the 2nd data card.
AREA=3.14*RADIUS**2	Compute the 2nd area.
VOLUME=AREA*HEIGHT	Compute the 2nd volume.
WRITE, VOLUME	Print the 2nd volume.
READ,RADIUS,HEIGHT	Read the 3rd data card.
AREA=3.14*RADIUS**2	Compute the 3rd area.
VOLUME=AREA*HEIGHT	Compute the 3rd volume.
WRITE, VOLUME	Print the 3rd volume.
STOP	Stop execution.
END	

Three data cards would be required in the data deck, one for each cylinder, and three answers would be printed on the line printer.

The program involves essentially three repetitions of the same four instructions. Although it is only a mild annoyance to be required to punch three duplicates of each instruction, the situation would be intolerable if the volume of 250 cylinders were to be calculated. The GO TO statement is designed to remove that annoyance by allowing the program to be written like this:

5	READ, RADIUS, HEIGHT
	AREA = 3.14 * RADIUS ** 2
	VOLUME = AREA * HEIGHT
	PRINT ~~WRITE~~, VOLUME
	GO TO 5
	END

The original program has been modified by first labelling the READ instruction with an identifying number, in this case the number 5, and by inserting the GO TO 5 statement after the WRITE instruction. The number 5, called a statement number, is a label and nothing more. It has no numerical significance and is never used in the mathematics of calculating the volume. In programs where many statements must be numbered, their numbers do not have to be in numerical order. Statement numbers are used whenever there is a need to mark the intended destination of a branching instruction such as the GO TO.

There are two restrictions on the use of statement numbers, both logical and easy to remember:

1. None may be greater than 99999. (This is because they must be able to fit into the 5 spaces allowed for them on the instruction card).
2. There may be no duplicate statement numbers within one program. (This is for the same reason that there may not be two rooms numbered alike in the same building. A person told to "Go to Room 5" would not know where to go if there were more than one room numbered 5. A computer told to "GO TO 5" would likewise be "confused" if there were more than one statement labelled 5 in the program.)

In summary, statement numbers:

1. Are not required on all statements.
2. Order is unimportant.
3. No duplicates are allowed.
4. None can be greater than 99999.
5. None can be less than 1.
6. Must *be integer numbers.*

Inserting the GO TO 5 statement in our cylinder program modifies the execution of statements as follows. The statements,

```
5   READ,RADIUS,HEIGHT
    AREA=3.14*RADIUS**2
    VOLUME=AREA*HEIGHT
    WRITE,VOLUME
```

are executed sequentially as before. The next statement is GO TO 5. This branching statement stops sequential execution of instructions and sends the computer back to the statement labelled 5:

    5   READ,RADIUS,HEIGHT

The computer executes this instruction, causing the reading of another data card. Because this is *not* a branching instruction, the computer resumes sequential execution of the following statements:

    AREA=3.14*RADIUS**2
    VOLUME=AREA*HEIGHT
    WRITE,VOLUME

Again the GO TO 5 statement is reached, and the program branches back to the READ statement. This process is repeated over and over until the data deck is depleted. When the computer attempts to obey a READ instruction and finds no data cards left in the data deck, it automatically stops execution.*

Sequential Execution *Without* Branching	Sequential Execution *With* Branching
READ,RADIUS,HEIGHT ↓ AREA=3.14*RADIUS**2 ↓ VOLUME=AREA*HEIGHT ↓ WRITE,VOLUME ↓ STOP	5 READ,RADIUS,HEIGHT ↓ AREA=3.14*RADIUS**2 ↓ VOLUME=AREA*HEIGHT ↓ WRITE,VOLUME ↓ GO TO 5
Result: Only one pass through program.	Result: As many passes through program as there are data cards.

The next two illustrations try to suggest the actions taking place inside the computer as your program is being processed. Figure 2.3 describes the compilation of the program (when the computer is being told how to solve the pro-

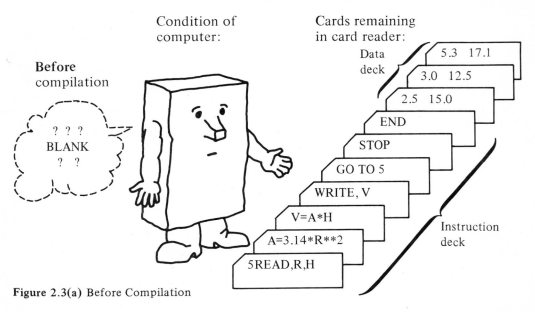

Condition of
computer:

Cards remaining
in card reader:

Before compilation

? ? ?
BLANK
? ?

Data deck

5.3   17.1
3.0   12.5
2.5   15.0
END
STOP
GO TO 5
WRITE, V
V=A*H
A=3.14*R**2
5READ,R,H

Instruction deck

Figure 2.3(a) Before Compilation

*Stopping a program by allowing it to run out of data cards is considered to be about as clever as stopping a car by allowing it to run out of gas. At this point in the text, however, it is the only stopping technique that could reasonably be presented.

After
compilation

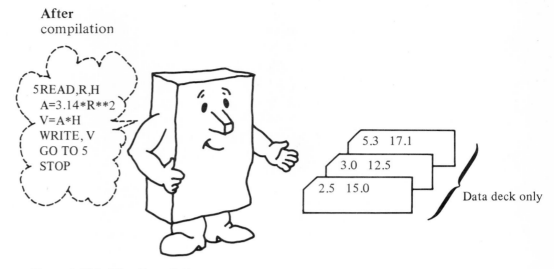

Figure 2.3(b) After Compilation

blem). This is when the instruction deck is consumed. Figure 2.4 describes what is going on during the execution phase. It shows the state of various memory locations as each instruction is being executed. The number of cards in the card reader and the status of the line printer are also shown at each step in the program. Because of space limitations, the various variable names have been abbreviated to a single letter.

INSTRUCTION JUST EXECUTED	CONDITION OF MEMORY LOCATIONS		CARDS REMAINING IN CARD READER	RESULTS APPEARING ON LINE-PRINTER
READ, R, H	R [2.5◄A [ ]	H [15.0◄V [ ]	5.3 17.1 / 3.0 12.5	
A=3.14*R**2	R [2.5] A [19.6◄	H [15.0] V [ ]	5.3 17.1 / 3.0 12.5	
V=A*H	R [2.5] A [19.6]	H [15.0] V [294.0◄	5.3 17.1 / 3.0 12.5	
WRITE, V	R [2.5] A [19.6]	H [15.0] V [294.0]	5.3 17.1 / 3.0 12.5	◄ 294.0
GO TO 5	R [2.5] A [19.6]	H [15.0] V [294.0]	5.3 17.1 / 3.0 12.5	294.0
READ, R, H	R [3.0◄A [19.6]	H [12.5◄V [294.0]	5.3 17.1	294.0
A=3.14*R**2	R [3.0] A [37.5◄	H [12.5] V [294.0]	5.3 17.1	294.0

V=A*H	R [3.0] A [37.5] H [12.5] V [468.8] ◄	5.3 17.1	294.0
WRITE, V	R [3.0] A [37.5] H [12.5] V [468.8]	5.3 17.1	► 294.0 468.8
GO TO 5	R [3.0] A [37.5] H [12.5] V [468.8]	5.3 17.1	294.0 468.8
READ, R, H	R [5.3] ◄ A [37.5] H [17.1] ◄ V [468.8]		294.0 468.8
ETC.	*ETC.*	*ETC.*	*ETC.*

Figure 2.4 The Execution Phase

2.3   FORTRAN Instruction Cards and Coding Forms

Figure 2.5 shows a typical card used to present information to the computer. It consists of 80 vertical columns, each of which may contain a pattern of punched holes thereby representing a letter, a number or one of the other characters used in FORTRAN.

This particular card shows the keypunched appearance of the digits 0 through 9, the 26 letters A through Z, and the other special characters. Collectively, these are referred to as the **FORTRAN character set.** A keypunch machine is used to impose the desired pattern of punched holes in response to entries made at its typewriter-like keyboard.

Notice that digits are represented by a single punched hole in the column, letters by a double hole punch, and only selected special characters involve a triple punch. At the top of each column, the keypunch types the character represented in the column so that the programmer can verify that the card has been punched correctly.

These cards will be used to prepare both statement cards and data cards. If a card is to contain a FORTRAN statement, however, specific columns on the card are reserved for each part of the FORTRAN statement. For example, the statement number (if any) must appear in the first five columns of the card. To help the programmer meet these location requirements, most computer facilities make available what is called a **FORTRAN statement card.** These cards are overprinted with lines that divide the 80 columns into zones. Each zone has a title or label to remind the programmer what information belongs in this zone (see Figure 2.6).

As we said, columns 1–5 are used for statement numbers. If a statement needs to be numbered, the number should appear in this zone, otherwise leave the zone blank. Columns 7–72 on the card are used to contain the actual FORTRAN statement. The computer looks here for the instruction you are issuing. Columns 73–80 are ignored by the compiler. This zone provides room on the card for any special (identifying) information the programmer might want on each card. One possibility is your initials and a three-digit identification number. These characters would prove useful if the cards got out of order or got mixed up with someone else's cards.

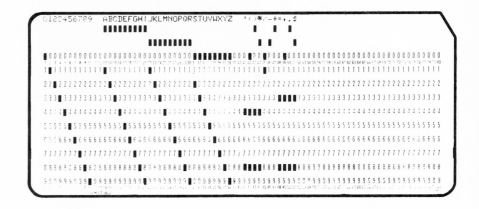

Figure 2.5 Character Representation on an 80-Column Card

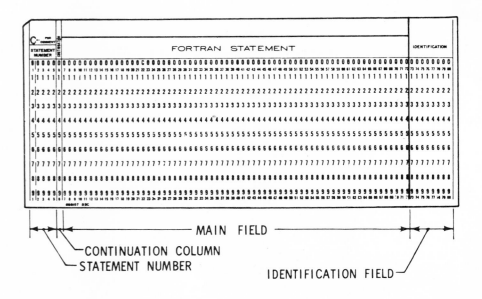

Figure 2.6 The FORTRAN Statement Card

Column 6 is known as the **continuation column**. It is used whenever it is necessary to continue a long statement onto one or more (continuation) cards. All statement information *must* be confined to columns 7–72. If more than one card is needed to express a long statement, it is necessary to punch a character other than a blank or zero in column 6 of each additional card used. (The latest FORTRAN standards require the compiler to accommodate at least nine continuation cards.) If, for example, a statement is so long as to require three continuation cards, one possibility is to put a 1 in column 6 of the first continuation card, a 2 in column 6 of the second continuation card, and so on. Another appealing technique is to put a plus sign, +, in column 6 of each continuation card. This tends to suggest that the information on this card is needed in addition to that on the previous card to complete the statement. Please note that no character is punched in column 6 of the first card of a long statement.

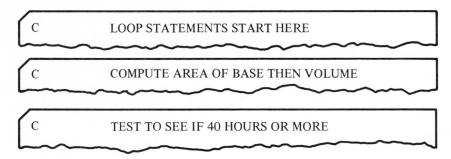

Figure 2.7 Typical Comment Statements

One last detail. In a program deck, it is desirable to insert cards containing English language comments that make the program easier to read and understand. We might precede each segment of FORTRAN code with a brief description of what the code is trying to accomplish. Such carefully chosen and properly placed comments can greatly ease the job of understanding a program written by someone else or one that has been on the shelf for several months. The computer would try to interpret such English language comments as FORTRAN statements if it was not told otherwise. A "C" in column 1 signals that the card contains one of these comments and the computer is thereby advised to ignore this card during compilation. The card is then called a **comment card.**

2.4 | Spacing Not Critical

Spaces typed within any given field on an instruction card are permissible and have no effect on the compilation of the contents of that card. From the computer's point of view the statement:

$$AREA = 3.14 * RADIUS ** 2$$

Many Imbedded Blanks

is equivalent to the statement:

$$AREA=3.14*RADIUS**2$$

as long as neither statement begins before column 7 nor extends beyond column 72. From the programmer's point of view, it is desirable to place spaces in statements wherever it makes the statement more legible.

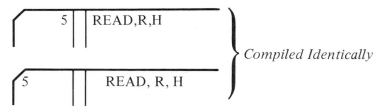

When writing a FORTRAN program out in long hand, FORTRAN coding forms are available to assist in proper spacing (see Figure 2.8). Each line on the coding form corresponds to a single instruction card. These forms show, for example, which statements are too long to fit on one card. Their greatest usefulness, however, comes when it is time to type the program onto cards at the key-

Form X28 7327 3
Printed in U.S.A.
FORTRAN CODING FORM
Program
Coded By
Checked By
Date
Page ___ of ___
Identification
73 80
C FOR COMMENT
STATEMENT NUMBER
Cont.
FORTRAN STATEMENT
1 5 6 7 10 15 20 25 30 35 40 45 50 55 60 65 70 72

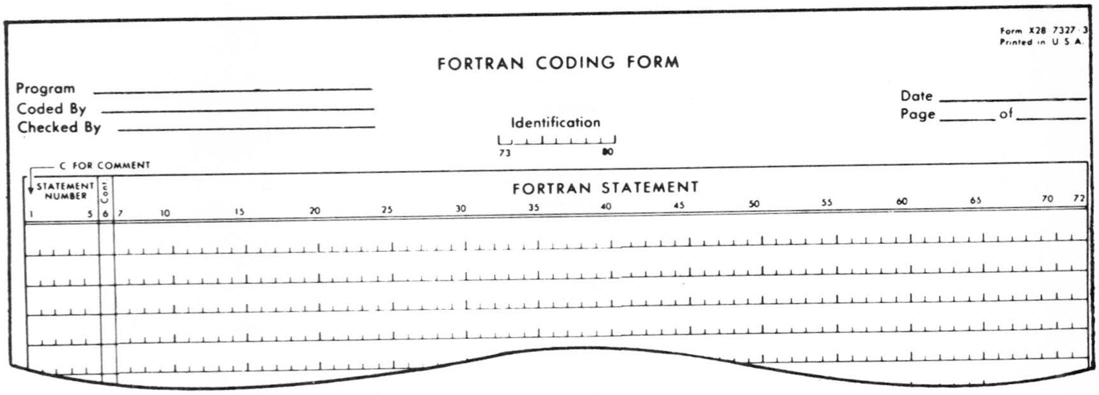

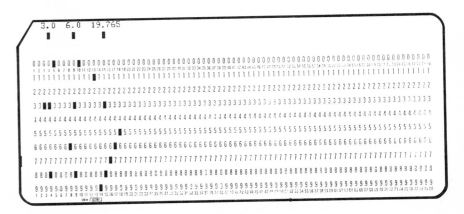

Figure 2.8 The FORTRAN Coding Form

punch. Unlike on a typewriter, the portion of the card that has just been punched is not visible to the operator. He depends upon an indicator on the keypunch to tell him into which column he will next punch. If he is distracted or otherwise loses his place while punching a card, he need only glance at the indicator and see that he is aligned on (for example) column 43. He then looks on his coding form and finds what character should be punched in column 43 and has found his place again.

Before leaving this section, it should be pointed out that the column restrictions just discussed pertain to *statement* cards only, that is, cards that make up the instruction deck. These restrictions do *not* apply to cards in the data deck.

2.5 Data Cards

The 80 columns of a data card can be divided into whatever zones the programmer finds appropriate to hold the input values. The compiler allows data to be presented in two basic forms. One form is called "free format," where the only requirement is that one data value be separated from another by at least one blank column. The other form requires the programmer to tell exactly where each piece of data is located on the card by providing a FORMAT statement. When the FORMAT statement is not supplied, each time a data card is processed the card must be scanned and a search made for the information that would have been provided by the FORMAT statement.

Figure 2.9 shows a typical data card. You should remember that the computer sees only the holes punched into the card. It does not see the overprinting

Figure 2.9 A Typical Data Card

on the card. For that reason, there would be no harm whatsoever in using a FOR-TRAN statement card to hold data.

2.6 | Integer vs. Real Constants

It is now necessary to become embroiled in a sticky, sometimes confusing aspect of computers, namely, that they can do arithmetic in *two* different ways. One method is called **integer arithmetic** and is used only when whole numbers are involved (numbers that have no fractional or decimal part). Integer mathematical operations have the feature of being exceptionally fast. This speed is achieved by the special way in which integer numbers are stored and by the fact that all integer calculations (like a division operation) are terminated as soon as the decimal point in the answer is reached. (There is not supposed to be anything after the decimal point, so why keep on calculating?) You will soon see that this represents a considerable saving of time.

The alternate and more common form of arithmetic is called **real arithmetic,** which is long and time-consuming. Let us see why. Assume you are computing the average number of cars passing a dangerous intersection. You observe 40 cars in a 3-minute period of time. The average rate is:

$$\frac{40}{3} = 13.3333333333333333333333333333333333\ldots\text{cars/minute}$$

This answer is clearly a number with a fractional part. It is called a **real number.**

Even if every core or bubble in memory is committed to storing this unfortunate (but not uncommon) value, some inaccuracy is inevitable. Therefore, each memory location that is to hold a real number must be relatively large to keep the inaccuracy (the part of the number that gets chopped off) as small as possible. The more digits we retain in memory, the smaller the inaccuracy. Some computers store real numbers to an accuracy as high as 15 to 20 decimal digits.

13.333333333333	33333333333333...
15 digits Retained	Remainder lost (Truncated)

If real numbers are stored to this accuracy, consider what effect this has on a typical arithmetic operation such as multiplication. Fifteen (or more) digits of the first number must be multiplied by each of the 15 digits of the second number. That is a relatively long process, and even then some inaccuracy is still present. This is a typical feature of real numbers and real calculation.

Constants vs. Variables

Recall one of the arithmetic statements used in the last programming example:

AREA = 3.14 * RADIUS ** 2

The quantities RADIUS and AREA may take on several different values during the execution of the program and are, therefore, called **variables**. On the other hand, 3.14 and 2 are obviously **constants**. The computer, however, recognizes two distinctly different forms of constants (integer constants and real constants) and two different forms of variables (integer and real). The remainder of this section demonstrates when the integer form is used and when the real form is necessary.

An account number at a bank, a telephone area code, a student ID number, the ZIP code in a mailing address are all typical examples of integer numbers. These numbers never get involved in complicated arithmetic. We might sort mail by ZIP code number or count the number of students who have better than a 3.5 scholastic average, but we would never divide one of these numbers by another producing an answer with a fractional component. *Integer calculations have an important but somewhat specialized use in computer programming.*

By way of contrast, consider the problem of computing the interest earned in a savings account or the price-to-earnings ratio of a stock. Clearly, you would not want to perform these calculations in the *integer* mode. These calculations should be performed in the *real* mode using *real* numbers (those with a fractional component.)

Real calculations are easy to recognize because they are typical of the arithmetic you deal with on a day-to-day basis. These calculations are more frequently associated with involved or complicated arithmetic operations compared to integer quantities.

If a real number was stored as an integer, the fractional or decimal part would be lost. For example, storing the real value 5.75 as an integer (in an integer memory location) would result in losing its decimal portion. It would be stored as 5. On the other hand, the integer value 5 *could* be stored as a real value without any loss of accuracy. It would be stored as

```
|5.00000000000000|
|15 decimal digits |
```

For that reason, the novice programmer is tempted to conclude that for the sake of simplicity he should use real numbers only. This would be an unfortunate mistake. As you get deeper into programming, the need for high speed integer mathematics becomes more obvious. Integers will be used for "loop control" (counting how many times you have gone around a given loop in the program); for "deck control" (counting how many data cards have been read); and for "subscript control" (providing a subscript for a subscripted variable). In each case, the need for integer arithmetic is very important.

When writing arithmetic expressions, the way in which we distinguish a real from an integer constant is by the presence or absence of the decimal point.

| no decimal point | decimal point present |
| CONSTANT IS *INTEGER* | CONSTANT IS *REAL* |

Other examples are as follows:

Integer numbers	Real numbers
+28374	3.14159
–19	–29.003176
0	0.0
–87132	+6431000.

As you can see, a plus or minus sign may be attached to any constant. If there is no sign, the value is considered as positive. Notice that commas are not allowed:

```
ILLEGAL   87,132,000   ILLEGAL
              V commas not allowed
```

The following table outlines the rules governing the writing of integer and real constants.

Constants		
	Integer	Real
Rules	1. NO DECIMAL POINT 2. No commas 3. No letters 4. + – allowed but no other special character 5. For size limitations see computer manual.	1. MUST HAVE DEC-IMAL POINT 2. No commas 3. No letters except E (discussed in Chapter 4) 4. + – . allowed but no other special characters 5. For size limitations see computer manual.
Valid Examples	–1 2164 +13 0 9 108	–1.000004 2164.798 +13.2 0.0 9. 108.54
Invalid Examples	–1. (decimal point 31,000 (comma) 71E (letter)	1 (no decimal point) $108.54 (special character $) 7B. (letter)

Rule 5 speaks of a "size limitation." This gets back to the internal design of memory. Each computer uses a different number of binary elements for the storing of a real or integer number. The more elements used, the larger a number may be held by that memory location. Remember, this was called the computer's **word size**. Computers having a relatively small word size must limit the number of digits (and maximum value) a constant may have. The limits are different for each model and make of computer.

When a constant is more than 7 or 8 digits in length, you could be in trouble. Check with your instructor or see appendix A of this text entitled "System Characteristics." All systems impose a limit to the magnitude of a real number. On some machines a real value may be as large as 10^{75} or as small as 10^{-75}. On other systems the limit is 10^{32} to 10^{-32}. Realize that you should not normally be generating numbers outside this range, unless, of course, you do something wrong (such as divide by zero.) It is by no means imperative that you know the exact value of the size and magnitude limitation of your computer. You should, however, be aware that these limitations do exist.

2.7 Developing a Program's Algorithm

When setting up a problem for solution on the computer, it is important that you go about the task in a methodical and orderly fashion. You should develop a very fixed, very controlled approach to the solution of each and every problem you are assigned. If you rely on a *random* method, your chances of success will be diminished substantially.

Ultimately, the solution of any problem will take the form of a computer program. Writing the program (FORTRAN code), however, is one of the relatively trivial aspects of breaking the problem down into a well-defined connected series of easy-to-understand steps. This series of steps is called an **algorithm.** An algorithm defines in outline or schematic form how the problem is to be solved. It frequently takes the form of a block diagram where each step is expressed in simple English (not FORTRAN.) Developing correct and efficient algorithms is a very important and sometimes difficult aspect of programming.

It is easy to become overwhelmed while solving a problem. There are many reasons for this. You may not understand the original statement of the problem sufficiently well. You may not have spent enough time analyzing the problem and breaking it down into more manageable (simpler) parts. You may not be sure of the data values involved or have used uninformative variable names to represent them. If you are like most beginning students, you will be trying to solve the problem all at once (proper code, correct logic, deck construction, equations, and so on).

All these difficulties can be avoided if you learn to tackle the problem one step at a time. Strategy comes first, details later. At various points in this text, we will identify a methodical and structured procedure for solving a problem. In Chapter 8 we tabulate these various recommendations, providing a precise and efficient approach to developing a program's algorithm.

This is such an important part of your learning that we will use the following technique each time one of these special topics or recommendations is presented.

The specific recommendation will be stated below the heading "Programming Style." An explanation of the recommendation will appear immediately to the right.

Programming Style:
Resist the Temptation to Start Writing FORTRAN Code Immediately

There are many steps needed to properly analyze a computer problem. Writing FORTRAN code is the last step, not the first.

Unless a problem is very short, there are many steps needed to properly construct an algorithm to solve the problem. Jumping in and starting to write FORTRAN code immediately (with the idea of straightening things out later) is a bad mistake. The time it takes to track down faulty logic and make several rounds of corrections will far exceed the time to develop the program algorithm correctly the first time.

The proper way to start a problem is to:

1. Spend a reasonable amount of time to get a clear understanding of the definition of the problem,
2. Familiarize yourself with the input to the problem and make sure it is compatible with the problem definition,
3. Attempt a hand calculation of the problem to define the logic and equations involved.

In the next programming examples, we introduce a number of recommendations, each concerned with getting a proper start in the development of a reasonably complex algorithm. Here are the first two recommendations.

Programming Style:
Problem Statement — Don't Start Until You're Sure

The first step in developing a program's algorithm is to make sure you understand what problem you are solving. Read the problem statement carefully — two or three times, if necessary. Do you understand all aspects of the problem? Has the problem been defined clearly enough? A problem that is clearly understood is well on the way to being solved.

Programming Style:
Get a Firm Grasp on the Problem's Input

Part of a problem's definition is its input. The input and problem statement must be compatible. Organize your input as to name, type and meaning (by table or comment statements) so that these details will not distract you when developing the problem's logic.

The next programming example shows the importance of these suggestions.

Programming Example
Blood Donor

Each card in a data deck gives information on possible blood donors. It gives:

1. the donor's name
2. the blood type (a number code is used)
3. donor's telephone number
4. the distance the donor lives from the hospital

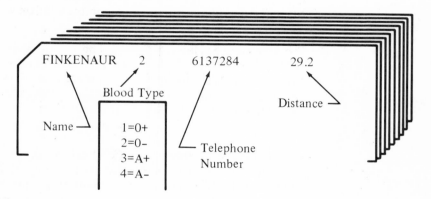

First Request:

Write a program to search the data deck for all people with 0– blood who live within 50 miles of the hospital. Report the name and telephone number of all donors that meet these requirements.

Second Request:

This program would be more general if it could be used to search for any type blood and if the distance limitation was allowed to be variable. To permit these improvements, assume that on each run of the program a card is placed at the front of the existing data deck. It contains two values telling what type of blood to search for this time and at what maximum distance.

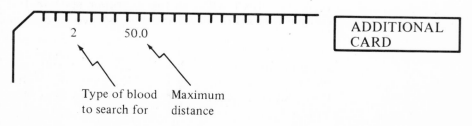

The complete data deck will now appear as follows:

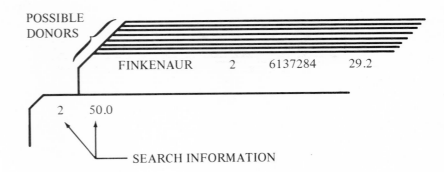

This is obviously not a trivial problem. It is not intended to be. Go back and read the problem statement (several times, if necessary). As you read, concentrate on understanding the problem and not on how to solve it (that comes later). Until you gain a degree of proficiency, limit yourself to a "one-step-at-a-time approach" and in a relatively fixed pattern or sequence. Do not try to do everything at once.

If you find the "Second Request" difficult to handle, try the simpler version of the problem first. Think about searching just for 0– blood at a distance of 50 miles from the hospital. Now try to generalize your understanding to handle the improvements that were suggested. Does the extra card at the front of the data deck (containing the search information) bother you? If the answer is "No" you are ready to move on to the next step.

Get a firm grip on the input data. Make sure the input is consistent with the problem definition. If there is no conflict, spend some time to come up with descriptive variable names for storing the data. Read these names over a couple of times so that you will not be distracted by having to look up a name while writing the general logic. Record all names in one place for easy reference. Any one of three techniques is recommended. These are shown in Figure 2.10. Some programmers like to set up a *table* that lists all the variables and gives a brief explanation of what each one means. An equivalent procedure is to make a *sketch* of the data deck displaying the same information appearing in the table. A final alternative is to use a series of *comment statements* at the beginning of the program describing each variable. This is the most popular method because it is an integral part of the program and does not involve an extra (external) item. Look at these methods and adopt whichever one appeals to you the most.

METHOD #1   Table

FIRST CARD:
1   IWANT   desired blood type
2   BIGEST   maximum distance
REMAINING CARDS:
1   NAME   donor's name
2   IHAVE   donor's blood type
3   NUMBER   telephone number
4   DIST   travel distance

Figure 2.10 Documenting Input Value

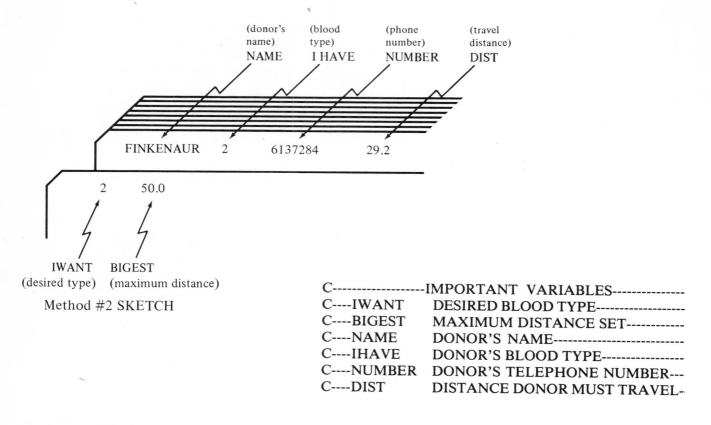

(donor's name) NAME   (blood type) I HAVE   (phone number) NUMBER   (travel distance) DIST

FINKENAUR   2   6137284   29.2

IWANT (desired type)   BIGEST (maximum distance)

2   50.0

Method #2 SKETCH

```
C-----------------IMPORTANT  VARIABLES--------------
C----IWANT      DESIRED BLOOD TYPE------------------
C----BIGEST     MAXIMUM DISTANCE SET-----------
C----NAME       DONOR'S NAME------------------------
C----IHAVE      DONOR'S BLOOD TYPE----------------
C----NUMBER     DONOR'S TELEPHONE NUMBER---
C----DIST       DISTANCE DONOR MUST TRAVEL-
```

Figure 2.10 (continued)

METHOD #3   COMMENT Statements

Now it is time to start thinking about how to solve the problem, but only in the most general terms. We want to identify those steps needed in the solution of the problem. This technique forces the programmer to subdivide the problem into smaller and therefore more manageable parts.

Programming Style
Pseudocode first:
• Identify the steps
• Subdivide problem

Attempt to break the problem down into simpler (more manageable) parts. Express these parts or modules in English, not FORTRAN. Think of the logic that would be used if the problem was to be solved by hand. Express each step clearly and in detail. (You don't have to be brief and to the point at this stage). Number the steps and show how each can be reached. We call all this **pseudocode**.

An example of pseudocode is seen in Figure 2.11.

About this time the more advanced students are saying, "I could have the program written, keypunched and run in the time it takes to do all this." That is probably true, but what happens when the problems really get hard? We are trying to establish good habits and a style of programming that will stand up when the going gets rough.

The program follows.

Notice that statement numbers in the program correspond to steps in the pseudocode. Notice also that comment statements with blank lines are used to clearly

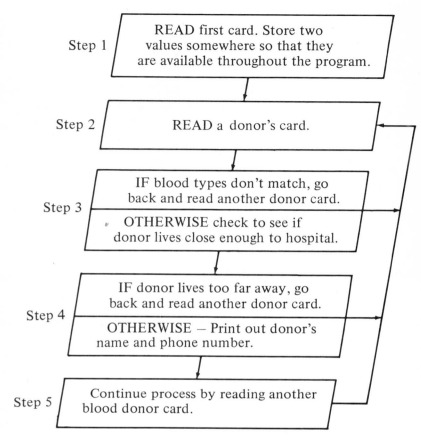

Step 1 READ first card. Store two values somewhere so that they are available throughout the program.

Step 2 READ a donor's card.

Step 3 IF blood types don't match, go back and read another donor card.
OTHERWISE check to see if donor lives close enough to hospital.

Step 4 IF donor lives too far away, go back and read another donor card.
OTHERWISE — Print out donor's name and phone number.

Step 5 Continue process by reading another blood donor card.

Figure 2.11 Pseudocode

```
C
C...     PURPOSE - SEARCH A DATA DECK FOR THE POSSIBLE BLOOD  ..
C..              DONORS WHOSE BLOOD TYPE AND PROXIMITY TO    ..
C..              THE HOSPITAL ARE AS SPECIFIED ON A LEADING  ..
C..              DATA CARD.                                  ..
C.............................................................
C
C               -----IMPORTANT VARIABLES-----
C
C   --IWANT      BLOOD TYPE BEING SEARCHED FOR            --
C   --BIGEST     MAXIMUM DISTANCE FROM THE HOSPITAL       --
C   --NAME       NAME OF BLOOD DONOR                      --
C   --IHAVE      DONOR BLOOD TYPE                         --
C   --NUMBER     DONOR TELEPHONE NUMBER                   --
C   --DIST       DISTANCE DONOR LIVES FROM THE HOSPITAL   --
C
C               READ FIRST CARD.......SET SEARCH VALUES
C
  1 READ,IWANT,BIGEST
C
C               .....LOOP STARTS HERE....
C
C
  2 READ,NAME,IHAVE,NUMBER,DIST
C
C       IF BLOOD TYPE DOES NOT MATCH
C                  TERMINATE PROCESSING THIS CARD
C
  3 IF(IWANT.NE.IHAVE) GO TO 2
C
C               CHECK DISTANCE REQUIREMENTS
C
  4 IF(DIST.GT.BIGEST) GO TO 2
C
C               SEARCH SUCESSFUL - PRINT NAME AND PHONE
C
    WRITE, NAME,NUMBER
C
  5 GO TO 2
C       .............LOOP ENDS HERE....................
C
    END
```

separate various blocks of code. Any technique that makes a program easier to follow is of value.

The following programming example shows how to deal with a table.

Programming Example
Car Insurance

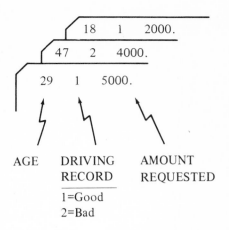

Age	Good Driving Record	Poor Driving Record
Under 25	27.50	42.86
25 or Older	20.80	30.00

Rate Table
(cost per thousand)

AGE   DRIVING RECORD   AMOUNT REQUESTED

1=Good
2=Bad

The cost of automobile insurance is based on two factors; age and driving record. The rates for drivers under 25 are shown in the top line of the rate table. The figures given are the cost for $1,000.00 of insurance coverage. Drivers with good driving records pay substantially less than those with poor records.

Each data card gives the age and past driving record of an applicant. The last value on the card is the amount of insurance coverage requested. Write a program to compute the charge to be made for the coverage requested.

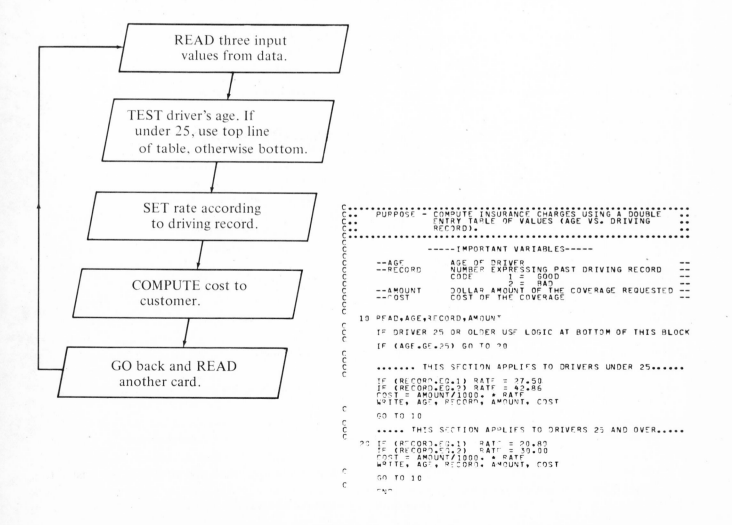

```
C...  PURPOSE - COMPUTE INSURANCE CHARGES USING A DOUBLE   ..
C..             ENTRY TABLE OF VALUES (AGE VS. DRIVING      ..
C..             RECORD).                                    ..
C
C             -----IMPORTANT VARIABLES-----
C
C   --AGE        AGE OF DRIVER                               --
C   --RECORD     NUMBER EXPRESSING PAST DRIVING RECORD       --
C                CODE       1 =   GOOD
C                           2 =   BAD
C   --AMOUNT     DOLLAR AMOUNT OF THE COVERAGE REQUESTED    --
C   --COST       COST OF THE COVERAGE                        --
C
  10 READ,AGE,RECORD,AMOUNT
C
C      IF DRIVER 25 OR OLDER USE LOGIC AT BOTTOM OF THIS BLOCK
C
       IF (AGE.GE.25) GO TO 20
C
C      ....... THIS SECTION APPLIES TO DRIVERS UNDER 25......
C
       IF (RECORD.EQ.1) RATE = 27.50
       IF (RECORD.EQ.2) RATE = 42.86
       COST = AMOUNT/1000. * RATE
       WRITE, AGE, RECORD, AMOUNT, COST
C
       GO TO 10
C
C      ..... THIS SECTION APPLIES TO DRIVERS 25 AND OVER.....
C
  20   IF (RECORD.EQ.1)  RATE = 20.80
       IF (RECORD.EQ.2)  RATE = 30.00
       COST = AMOUNT/1000. * RATE
       WRITE, AGE, RECORD, AMOUNT, COST
C
       GO TO 10
C
       END
```

Flowchart:

READ three input values from data.

TEST driver's age. If under 25, use top line of table, otherwise bottom.

SET rate according to driving record.

COMPUTE cost to customer.

GO back and READ another card.

Review Exercises

1. Describe the difference between compilation and execution.

2.*Does the computer execute each instruction immediately upon receipt or does it wait until all instructions have been received before executing any one of them?

3. How is your program ultimately stored in memory?

4.*What is the last card in the instruction deck?

5. What type of cards follow the instruction deck?

6. Describe what happens if the following instructions are given to the computer:
   a. READ , X
   b. Z = X * X
   c. WRITE , Z
   d. STOP

7.*Is it true that the computer normally executes instructions in the order in which they are given, i.e. sequentially?

8. What is the purpose of a branching instruction?

9.*Must all statements be numbered?

10. Why should any statement be numbered?

11.*Can two statements have the same number?

12. On a FORTRAN statement card, what are the following zones used for:
    a. Columns 7–72
    b. Columns 73–80
    c. Columns 1–5
    d. Column 6

13. What is a "comment card"?

14.*Do the zones described in question 12 apply to data cards or can data appear in any column (1 through 80)?

15. Describe the difference between integer and real numbers. Which would more likely be used to store the velocity and acceleration of a particle in free-fall?

16. Give two examples of an invalid integer constant.

17. Are constants restricted in their size? Why?

18.*What type of memory location would be used to store the flight number of an aircraft?

19. Is it true that the computer performs its arithmetic to an infinite degree of accuracy and, therefore, there is never any error in its answers?

20. Which of the following are valid real constants:
    a. $108.54   b. 16   c. 1,167.2   d. 1.06×10^5

21.*The program deck consists of two parts. Name these two parts.

22. Give your understanding of what each of the following "Programming Style" recommendations mean.

Programming Style:
Problem statement —
Don't start
until you're sure

Programming Style:
Get a firm grasp
on the problem's
input

Programming Style:
Pseudocode
first:
● Identify the steps
● Subdivide problem

23. What is pseudocode and why is it used?

24. In writing a program you can sometimes make the mistake of writing the same variable name in several slightly different ways. How can this be avoided?

25.*What does the term "word size" mean? Do all computers have the same "word sizes"?

26. There is an upper limit on the magnitude of a real variable (10^{32} or 10^{75} for example.) Under what circumstances could a number this large be generated?

27. What is the purpose of a "coding form"?

28. Are blanks allowed within a statement field?

29. What does the term "algorithm" mean?

30. What are some of the reasons a student will sometimes become overwhelmed while attempting to solve a problem?

31. When writing pseudocode, why are the steps written in English and not FORTRAN?

32.*The last card of the instruction deck is shown below. What is wrong with the way in which this instruction is presented?

| END |

33. You have written a FORTRAN program in which several statements have been written incorrectly. Describe how the compiler will handle this situation.

34.*A program is said to contain a loop. What does the term "loop" mean?

35. A program is being compiled and the END statement is reached. Describe what happens next.

36.*A statement is very long and will not fit on one card. Describe how to handle this situation.

37. What are some of the steps to be followed when initially formulating the algorithm to solve a problem?

Please note that the numerous programming examples at the end of each chapter are purely supplemental. They are intended to show the many ways in which the information learned in that particular chapter can be applied. Many areas of interest are covered. Select for study *only* those problems that parallel your area of interest. By all means, do *not* expect to follow each and every program presented.

Additional Applications

> **Programming Example**
> Unit Cost

When purchasing an item sold by weight at the supermarket, it is sometimes difficult to know which item is the best buy:

Item 1	18 oz.	$1.15
Item 2	2 lbs.	$2.18
Item 3	1 lb – 6 oz.	$1.80

To help the consumer, the government requires that all items sold by weight be labelled with a *unit cost* figure (price per pound).

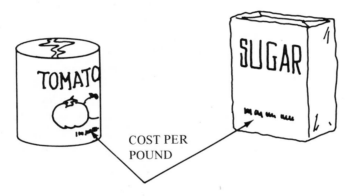

Each card in a data deck gives the name and weight of an item (pounds followed by ounces.) The last two values give the total cost and an inventory number (a number used to identify the product).

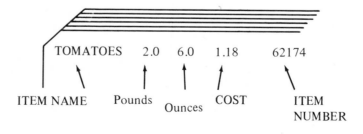

Write a program to:

1. convert the weight to pounds,
2. compute the unit cost (cost/pound),
3. generate the output suggested.

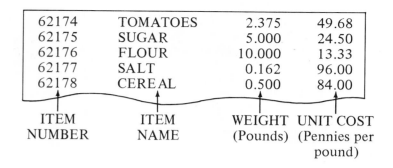

ITEM NUMBER	ITEM NAME	WEIGHT (Pounds)	UNIT COST (Pennies per pound)
62174	TOMATOES	2.375	49.68
62175	SUGAR	5.000	24.50
62176	FLOUR	10.000	13.33
62177	SALT	0.162	96.00
62178	CEREAL	0.500	84.00

```
C..........................................................
C.... PURPOSE - COMPUTE ...PRICE PER POUND... VALUE FOR  ..
C....            STANDARDIZED LABELLING OF FOOD PRODUCTS  ..
C..........................................................
C
C              -----IMPORTANT VARIABLES-----
C
C      --NAME        NAME OF FOOD PRODUCT              --
C      --POUNDS      FIRST WEIGHT FIGURE (LBS)         --
C      --OUNCES      SECOND WEIGHT FIGURE (OZS)        --
C      --COST        COST OF ITEM (DOLLARS)            --
C
C              COMPUTED QUANTITIES
C
C      --WEIGHT      WEIGHT IN POUNDS                  --
C      --UNIT        UNIT COST OF ITEM                 --
C
C              LOOP STARTS HERE
C
10 READ, NAME, POUNDS, OUNCES, COST, ITEMNO
C
C              CONVERT WEIGHT TO TOTAL POUNDS
C
   WEIGHT = POUNDS + OUNCES / 16.0
C
C              COMPUTE COST IN CENTS PER POUND
C
   UNIT = COST * 100. / WEIGHT
C
   WRITE, ITEMNO, NAME, WEIGHT, UNIT
C
   GO TO 10
C
C              LOOP ENDS HERE
C
   END
```

Programming Example
Credit Request

A bank allows customers to borrow money automatically up to a certain limit, and that limit depends on the individual's credit rating.

The first card in a data deck gives the account number of someone asking for credit. The remaining cards identify all active accounts at this bank. Each card gives:

1. the number of an active account,
2. who that number belongs to,
3. any loans already made to that person,
4. that individual's credit rating.

Rating	Maximum Loan
1	$10,000.00
2	5,000.00
3	2,500.00
4	1,000.00

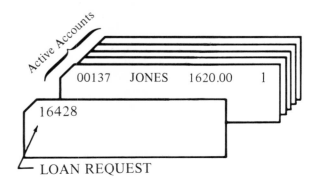

Search the data deck for that particular account number. Determine how much credit has already been extended. Determine how much additional credit can be extended based on this individual's credit rating. The sketch below will establish what variable names will be used in the program. We intend to write the program with full documentation. This means it is going to be a fancy presentation to show what extremes we will go to for the sake of clarity.

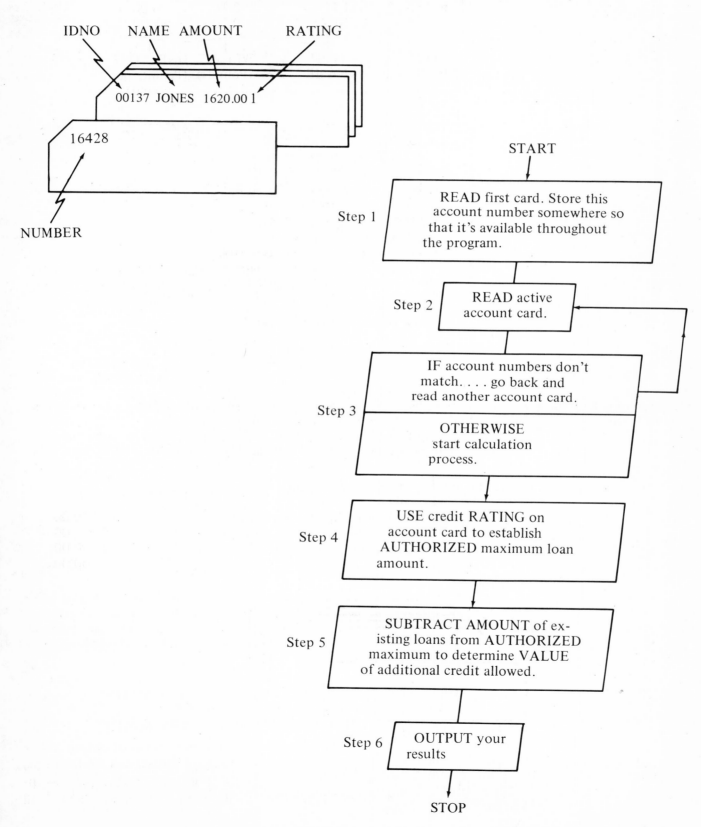

```
C.............................................................
C..    PURPOSE - SEARCH FOR A SPECIFIC ACCOUNT NUMBER AND   ..
C..              DETERMINE HOW MUCH ADDITIONAL CREDIT CAN    ..
C..              BE EXTENDED TO THAT PERSON.                 ..
C.............................................................
C
C                  -----IMPORTANT VARIABLES-----
C
C      --NUMBER      ACCOUNT NUMBER OF APPLICANT         --
C      --IDNO        INDIVIDUAL ACTIVE ACCOUNT NUMBERS    --
C      --AMOUNT      AMOUNT OF CREDIT ALREADY EXTENDED    --
C      --RATING      NUMBER CODE OF CREDIT RATING         --
C      --AUTHOR      MAXIMUM TOTAL CREDIT AUTHORIZED      --
C      --VALUE       AMOUNT OF ADDITIONAL CREDIT          --
C
C    1 READ, NUMBER
C
C                SEARCH MODULE STARTS HERE
C
     2 READ, IDNO, NAME, AMOUNT, RATING
C
     3 IF(IDNO.NE.NUMBER) GO TO 2
C
C          STATEMENT ABOVE CAUSES LOOPING UNTIL CORRECT
C                        RECORD LOCATED
C
C                CALCULATION PHASE
C
       IF(RATING.EQ.1)AUTHOR=10000.00
       IF(RATING.EQ.2)AUTHOR= 5000.00
       IF(RATING.EQ.3)AUTHOR= 2500.00
       IF(RATING.EQ.4)AUTHOR= 1000.00
C
     5 VALUE = AUTHOR - AMOUNT
C
     6 WRITE, NUMBER, VALUE
C
       STOP
       END
```

Programming Example Number Game	The first card in a data deck gives four digits that are to be stored as N1, N2, N3, and N4. Each remaining card contains four digits (GUESS1,GUESS2,GUESS3, GUESS4) and represents an attempt to guess the value of this four-digit number.

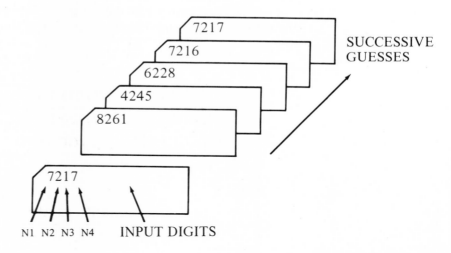

    The object of the game is to guess the number in the least number of tries. After each try, you will be told if your first digit is too high, too low or correct. The same information will be given for the other three digits. (This game would have to be played on a terminal so that the player could get this information prior to making the next guess.)

    Statements such as:

WRITE, 'YOUR FIRST DIGIT TOO HIGH — TRY AGAIN'
WRITE, 'YOUR SECOND DIGIT IS CORRECT'
WRITE, 'YOUR THIRD DIGIT TOO LOW — TRY AGAIN'

will be used in this program and demonstrate a different form of output available within a WRITE statement. A message (character string) can be included in any line of output along with the contents of memory locations, if any. Each character string is contained within quotation marks so that it will not be mistaken for a variable name.

```
C...  PURPOSE - NUMBER GAME...GUESS THE FOUR DIGIT NUMBER...
C..            ON THE FIRST CARD (UNKNOWN TO YOU) IN THE   ..
C..            LEAST NUMBER OF TRIES                       ..
C...
C
C            -----IMPORTANT VARIABLES-----
C
C  --N1,N2,N3,N4        FOUR DIGITS TAKEN FROM LEADER CARD
C  --GUESS1,GUESS2      FOUR DIGITS REPRESENTING A GUESS
C  --GUESS3,GUESS4         OF THE ORIGINAL NUMBER
C
C         .....READ CORRECT NUMBER.....
C
   READ, N1, N2, N3, N4
C
C            READ CARD REPRESENTING A GUESS
   READ, GUESS1, GUESS2, GUESS3, GUESS4
C
C          CHECK FIRST DIGIT
C
   IF(GUESS1.GT.N1) WRITE,' YOUR FIRST DIGIT TOO HIGH'
   IF(GUESS1.LT.N1) WRITE,' YOUR FIRST DIGIT TOO LOW'
   IF(GUESS1.EQ.N1) WRITE,' YOUR FIRST DIGIT CORRECT'
C
C          CHECK THE SECOND DIGIT
C
   IF(GUESS2.GT.N2) WRITE,' YOUR SECOND DIGIT TOO HIGH'
   IF(GUESS2.LT.N2) WRITE,' YOUR SECOND DIGIT TOO LOW'
   IF(GUESS2.EQ.N2) WRITE,' YOUR SECOND DIGIT CORRECT'
C
C          CHECK THE THIRD DIGIT
C
   IF(GUESS3.GT.N3) WRITE,' YOUR THIRD DIGIT TOO HIGH'
   IF(GUESS3.LT.N3) WRITE,' YOUR THIRD DIGIT TOO LOW'
   IF(GUESS3.EQ.N3) WRITE,' YOUR THIRD DIGIT CORRECT'
C
C          CHECK LAST DIGIT
C
   IF(GUESS4.GT.N4) WRITE,' YOUR FOURTH DIGIT TOO HIGH'
   IF(GUESS4.LT.N4) WRITE,' YOUR FOURTH DIGIT TOO LOW'
   IF(GUESS4.EQ.N4) WRITE,' YOUR FOURTH DIGIT CORRECT'
C
   GO TO 4
   END
C...............................................................
```

The program as presently written has no means of normal termination in that there is no STOP statement in the program. One possible improvement would be to substitute the following statements in place of the present "GO TO 4" statement.

	IF(GUESS1.NE.N1) GO TO 4
	IF(GUESS2.NE.N2) GO TO 4
	IF (GUESS3.NE.N3) GO TO 4
	IF (GUESS4.NE.N4) GO TO 4
C	
C	ALL DIGITS ARE CORRECT
	WRITE, 'YOU HAVE FOUND THE CORRECT NUMBER'
C	
	STOP
	END

This book is written for students who are *not* heavily involved in mathematics as well as for those who are. To that end, examples that require a degree of mathematical sophistication will be presented, but usually at the end of each chapter, and will be labelled with double asterisks. Each student should decide if that problem is appropriate to his or her career objectives.

Programming Example
Quadratic Equation**

Write a program to find the two roots of the quadratic equation, assuming only equations with real roots are to be solved:

$$3x^2 + 6x + 1 = 0$$

After reading the statement of the problem, the programmer should recall the following equation that will yield the desired roots.

$$x = \frac{-b \pm \sqrt{b^2 - 4ac}}{2a}, \quad \text{where: } \begin{aligned} a &= 3 \\ b &= 6 \\ c &= 1 \end{aligned}$$

This equation will in effect direct the writing of the FORTRAN code.

```
C.............................................................
C..  PURPOSE - DETERMINE ROOTS TO A SPECIFIC QUADRATIC    ..
C..            EQUATION.                                   ..
C.............................................................
C
C              ESTABLISH INITIAL VALUES
C
   A = 3.0
   B = 6.0
   C = 1.0
C
C              COMPUTE VALUE UNDER RADICAL
C
   Z = (B**2-4.0*A*C)
C
C              COMPUTE TWO ROOTS
C
   XONE = (-B+Z**0.5) / (2.0*A)
   XTWO = (-B-Z**0.5) / (2.0*A)
C
C              PUBLISH RESULTS
C
   WRITE, XONE, XTWO
C
   STOP
   END
```

It is basically incorrect to write the program logic as shown above. The constants 3.0, 6.0 and 1.0 belong in the data deck, not the logic deck. When possible, write a *general* program. This means referencing variables by name, not by specific value. Rewrite this program so that it can solve several quadratic equations, not just the one shown.

```
C.............................................................
C..  PURPOSE - MORE GENERAL SOLUTION OF QUADRATIC EQUATION..
C.............................................................
C
C              READ INITIAL VALUES
C
 5 READ, A, B, C
C
C              COMPUTE VALUE UNDER RADICAL
C
   Z = (B**2-4.0*A*C)
C
C              COMPUTE TWO ROOTS
C
   XONE = (-B+Z**0.5) / (2.0*A)
   XTWO = (-B-Z**0.5) / (2.0*A)
C
C              PUBLISH RESULTS
C
   WRITE, XONE, XTWO
C
C              REPEAT LOGIC
C
   GO TO 5
C
   END
```

Programming Example Linear Interpolation** A sometimes troublesome calculation is to enter a table with a value that lies between the table listings. Finding the sine of 39.67 degrees from the accompanying table would be a typical example. Since the need to interpolate applies to trig tables, log tables, tax tables and the like, it might be appropriate to computerize the procedure. Write a program to accomplish linear interpolation between two tabular entries.

Before you start this problem, make sure you really understand the concept of **linear interpolation**. Values in the table represent known points on a curve — in this case the sine curve. Interpolation involves approximating the curve between the two closest known points with a straight line. Computing Y on this straight line for the input X value is accomplished by proportions and approximates the Y value on the curve.

Degrees	sin
0°	.0000
1°	.0175
2°	.0349
3°	.0523
4°	.0698
5°	.0872
6°	.1045
7°	.1219
39°	.6293
40°	.6428
41°	.6561
42°	.6691
43°	.6820
44°	.6947
45°	.7071

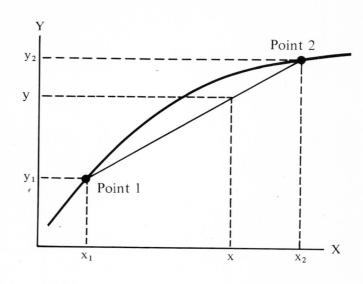

The next sequential step in the solution is to *clearly define the data values* you will be dealing with. Having a weak or marginal understanding of these values will complicate matters later on when you attempt to set up your equations.

X	Input to the table
X1 Y1	Table values immediately above input value
X2 Y2	Table values immediately below input value

Select a sample set of input data values and show how they will be presented to the computer. Do not use complicated input to start with. Use the simplest values possible.

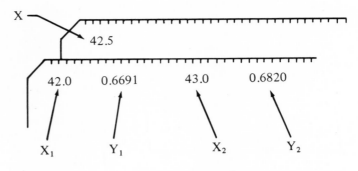

SAMPLE TEST DATA

After completing these initial two steps in the problem solution, if the logic is still not clear. . .try a hand calculation.

Programming Style
If you're having difficulties, deal with a specific example — generalize later

Don't handle too many abstractions at once. Most students find it easier to define the logic of a problem if they deal with a specific example first. When this is completed, the algorithm can be made more general.

As you do the calculation, mentally talk out the steps you are taking. To demonstrate this, determine the sine of the angle 42.5°.

Input:
$X_1 = 42.0$ $Y_1 = 0.6691$
$X = 42.5$ $Y = ?$
$X_2 = 43.0$ $Y_2 = 0.6820$

1. I must first determine the change in X and the change in Y of the value listed in the table:

$$\Delta X = X_2 - X_1 \qquad \Delta Y = Y_2 - Y_1$$
$$= 43.0 - 42.0 \qquad\qquad = 0.6820 - 0.6691$$
$$= 1.0 \qquad\qquad\qquad = 0.0129$$

2. The input value 42.5 lies what fraction of the distance between the table values:

$$\text{fraction} = \frac{42.5 - 42.0}{43.0 - 42.0} = \frac{1}{2}$$

3. I must now add ½ the change in Y to the initial table entry.

$$Y = Y1 + \tfrac{1}{2}\Delta Y$$

$$= 0.6691 + \frac{0.0129}{2} = 0.67555$$

Notice that each step in the solution is a little easier to see when a specific example is being worked. Steps taken in this solution will suggest factors that must be accounted for in the general solution. There will be a close parallel between this solution and the pseudocode solution.

The final FORTRAN code can now be written as the last step in this slow but methodically developed algorithm.

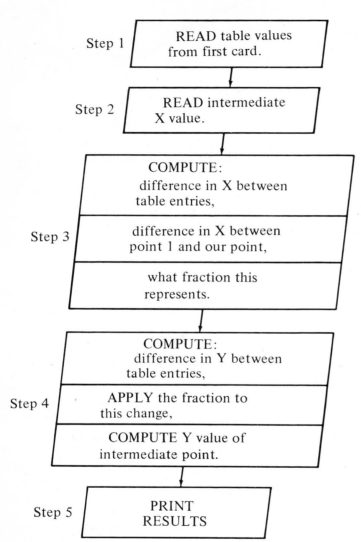

Step 1 — READ table values from first card.

Step 2 — READ intermediate X value.

Step 3 — COMPUTE:
difference in X between table entries,
difference in X between point 1 and our point,
what fraction this represents.

Step 4 — COMPUTE:
difference in Y between table entries,
APPLY the fraction to this change,
COMPUTE Y value of intermediate point.

Step 5 — PRINT RESULTS

```
C............................................
C..  PURPOSE - FACILITATE LINEAR INTERPOLATION OF VALUES ..
C..            FROM A TABLE.                              ..
C............................................
C
C              -----IMPORTANT VARIABLES-----
C
C     --X        INPUT VALUE TO THE TABLE           --
C     --X1       TABLE VALUE JUST ABOVE INPUT VALUE  --
C     --Y1       TABLE VALUE JUST ABOVE INPUT VALUE  --
C     --X2       TABLE VALUE JUST BELOW INPUT VALUE  --
C     --Y2       TABLE VALUE JUST BELOW INPUT VALUE  --
C
      READ, X1,Y1,X2,Y2
      READ, X
C
C              COMPUTE IMPORTANT FRACTION
C
   3  DELTX = X2 - X1
      XDIFF = X - X1
      FRACTN = XDIFF / DELTX
C
C              APPLY FRACTION TO Y VALUES
C
   4  DELTY = Y2 - Y1
      YDIFF = FRACTN * DELTY
      Y = Y1 + YDIFF
C
      WRITE, Y
C
      STOP
      END
```

3 | Arithmetic Assignment Statements

The next three chapters cover some of the details of the FORTRAN instructions used thus far. We delay the presentation of broad *program development* concepts until these details are out of the way. Your reading should become more deliberate and you should strive to gain a complete understanding of the topics presented. The overview phase has been completed. Adjust your approach to these chapters appropriately.

3.1 | General Form

Take a look at the following equations:

$$Y = 2X - 12 \qquad\qquad 2X - Y = 12$$

| Explicit | | Implicit |

Both express the same relationship between X and Y, but the equation on the left is more direct in showing how to compute Y for any given value of X. It is called the *explicit* form of the equation. FORTRAN arithmetic assignment statements must have this same "explicit" form. (If an arithmetic statement is to be generated from a mathematical equation, the equation must be in the explicit form (or converted thereto) prior to constructing the FORTRAN statement.)

The right-hand portion of the statement must explicitly define how the basic arithmetic capabilities of the computer are to be combined to determine a desired value. A single variable name must appear to the left of the equal sign (replacement symbol). It tells where in memory the single numerical value thus obtained should be stored.

$$Y = \underbrace{2.0 * X - 12.0}_{\text{expression}}$$

single variable name ⟶

replacement symbol

Arithmetic Assignment Statement

General Form:
    Variable Name = Expression
Example:
    $Z = 3. * X ** 2. + 6. * X - Y - 12.$
Invalid Example:

| $X - 3.4 = Y$ | IMPROPER FORM |

Note that the expression is a sequence of constants, previously defined variables, operational symbols and other parameters that define what operations are to be performed. In interpreting an expression, the compiler first looks at the operational symbols to determine what hardware component to use. It then looks to the left and to the right of each symbol to determine which constants or variables are to be involved in that particular operation. As you will soon see, however, the computer does *not* perform operations in the order of their appearance (left to right) in the arithmetic statement.

3.2 | Operational Symbols

Figure 3.1 shows a complete list of operational symbols allowed in FORTRAN. Each of these symbols has been used in previous programs.

+	ADDITION
−	SUBTRACTION
*	MULTIPLICATION
/	DIVISION
**	EXPONENTIATION

Figure 3.1 FORTRAN Arithmetic Operators

Parentheses may also appear in arithmetic statements, but observe that they are not included in the list of operational symbols. The parentheses symbols, ( ), convey the operation of multiplication in mathematics, but not so in FORTRAN. Parentheses have a special clarifying function, the details of which we will describe now.

3.3 | Rules of Interpreting Expressions: Hierarchy of Operations

The purpose of any arithmetic statement is to express an equation in a proper and correct form to the computer. The FORTRAN standards demand specific rules for translating (evaluating) expressions, but allow each compiler to implement these rules in whatever way is most efficient for that particular computer. Accordingly, each compiler uses a different (and rather complex) *algorithm* for expression evaluation. The description that follows represents an oversimplification of that process. It is intended to make the interpretation process more meaningful from a programmer's point of view.

Sometimes the arithmetic statement and the equation it represents are almost identical in appearance.

Equation: Arithmetic Statement:
$y = 6x^2 - 4x + 1$ Y = 6. *X**2 − 4. *X + 1.

At other times, the FORTRAN statement will be different. There are two reasons for this. One obvious reason is that the arithmetic statement must appear on *one continuous line* (across the top of a card), while the equation does not. As a result, parentheses sometimes will be needed in the arithmetic statement that were not needed in the equation. The second reason is that the compiler gives preference to some operations (they will be accomplished first) while ignoring all other operations. Let us take a specific example.

Equation: Arithmetic Statement:

$$y = \frac{x + 6}{b - c}$$ $$Y = (X + 6.)/(B - C)$$

To solve this equation, the computer must at some time perform the operations of addition, subtraction and division, but *the order in which these operations are performed is important.* That is, in this equation addition and subtraction must take place first. Then and only then can division be initiated. Parentheses are needed to convey to the computer this desired sequence of operations.

This example calls attention to two things:

1. the order in which mathematical operations are accomplished is important; and,
2. parentheses can be used to force certain operations to be performed before others.

All that remains is to learn in what sequence the computer normally performs mathematical operations and then to learn how to use parentheses to force an alternate sequence should it be necessary.

As we said before, the computer does *not* perform mathematical operations in the order in which they appear in an equation. Certain arithmetic operations take precedence over others. (There is a hierarchy of operations.) Stated briefly, all exponentiation is accomplished first. Next, any multiplication or division will be handled. Finally, addition and subtraction are undertaken.

1st	RAISING TO A POWER	**
2nd	MULTIPLICATION and DIVISION	* and /
3rd	ADDITION and SUBTRACTION	+ and –

Figure 3.2 Hierarchy of Operations

A more detailed explanation is as follows:

The statement is scanned by the computer from left to right at least three times before processing is complete. Unless directed otherwise (by using parentheses), the operation of raising to a power (exponentiation) is accomplished on the first pass. All other operations are ignored. On the second pass, multiplication and division are performed in the order of their appearance (from left to right). Finally, addition and subtraction are accomplished on the third pass.

Consider the following arithmetic statement:

$$Y = X + 6. / B - C$$

Look familiar? It is the same arithmetic statement discussed at the top of the page, but formed without parentheses! On the first scan, the compiler is looking for any exponentiation to be performed. None is required. On the second scan, it looks for any multiplication or division. When the "/" symbol is reached, the constant 6 will be divided by B. On the final or third sweep, addition and subtraction are accomplished. This means that the normal sequence of operations will interpret this statement to represent the equation:

$$y = x + \frac{6}{b} - c$$

This is clearly not the intended equation, and, therefore, parentheses are needed.

evaluated next ↗

$$Y = (X + 6.) / (B - C)$$

evaluated first ↘

Parentheses force the compiler to handle the equation in parts. *Expressions inside parentheses are handled first. If there are several levels of nested parentheses, the expression in the* innermost *set of parentheses is evaluated first (inside out sequence).* An expression inside parentheses is treated as a separate entity. It is "cleared out" as if it was the only expression present. In the above example statement, it will take three scans to clear the expression inside the left pair of parentheses. Another three scans are needed to clear the expression inside the right pair of parentheses. Finally, three more scans are required to process the expression as a whole.

In clearing the first expression, addition becomes the first operation to be performed. In clearing the second expression, subtraction takes place. In processing the expression as a whole, division takes place. This is a sequence that correctly expresses the equation we had in mind.

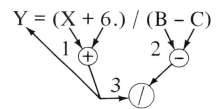

Forced Sequence of Operations

Omission of either or both sets of parentheses will result in an incorrect equation.

FORTRAN arithmetic statement		Equivalent algebraic equation
$Y = (X + 6.)/B - C$	⟶	$y = \dfrac{x + 6}{b} - c$
$Y = X + 6./(B - C)$	⟶	$y = x + \dfrac{6}{b - c}$
$Y = X + 6./B - C$	⟶	$y = x + \dfrac{6}{b} - c$

To express an equation, the following procedure is recommended:

1. Write the equation on *one continuous line.*
2. Include any parentheses that were part of the original equation.
3. Simulate the scanning (translating) process performed by the compiler as the statement is presently written.

Each time the normal hierarchy of operations is contrary to what is needed by your equation, add extra parentheses to force the proper sequence.

Are parentheses needed to make the arithmetic statement on the right properly express the equation on the left?

Equation	Statement
$y = x^{1/3} + 4.6$	$Y = X ** 1.0/3.0 + 4.6$

Remember, the answer is best found by "playing computer." As the statement now stands, the first operation to be performed is exponentiation (raising to a power). The compiler looks to the left and to the right of the double asterisk to see what numbers are involved: X and 1.0. Hold it! That is not the correct power, it should be one-third. This suggests that parentheses are needed, namely to get the computer to divide one by three prior to raising to a power.

$$Y = X ** (1.0/3.0) + 4.6$$

Are parentheses needed in this example?

Equation	Statement
$y = \dfrac{6}{x^2 - 1}$	$Y = 6.0/X ** 2.0 - 1.0$

Without parentheses the first operation will be raising to a power and the value of x is squared (no trouble as yet). On the second sweep, the divide symbol is recognized and 6 will be divided by X square. That is not what we want, so parentheses are needed.

$$Y = 6.0/(X ** 2.0 - 1.0)$$

3.4 When in Doubt

Since parentheses are used for clarifying an expression, a good rule to follow is: *If there is any doubt as to how an expression will be read, use parentheses!* The presence of redundant parentheses does not affect the final result. The arithmetic statements:

$$Y = A / B * X \quad \text{and} \quad Y = (A / B) * X$$

both result in the equation

$$y = \frac{a}{b} * x$$

Programming Style
Parenthesize if it
makes it clearer

When writing complex arithmetic expressions, some programmers will only use those parentheses demanded by hierarchy considerations. That is a mistake. If additional parentheses will make the expression clearer and easier to read, those parentheses should be used.

3.5 Test Data

The compiler can tell if you have a missing left or right parenthesis (unpaired set). It cannot, however, tell how many pairs of parentheses are needed by your particular equation. You are on your own. For this reason, it is important to test each statement with sample data values. Look at the equation and come up with a combination of input values that allows you to solve the problem in your head.

For the statement:

$$Y = (X - 6.)/(B - C)$$

the test data might be:

$$X = 7 \quad B = 1 \quad C = 0$$

These values should give the result, Y equals 1.

Later, a more exhaustive range of input values should be used to make sure your equations will work under all sets of circumstances.

A program that is run without at least *three* sets of test data should be viewed with suspicion. Note, however, it is not the number of data sets that make for a good test but the *variation* of the data and the way it covers the range of the program variables.

Programming Style Test data are essential to every program ‖	Just because a program has been compiled successfully and has given output values in no way guarantees the output to be correct. It must be verified using test data.

3.6 | Two Operational Symbols

When evaluating any portion of an expression, the compiler looks to the left and to the right of any operational symbol to see what numerical values are involved. These values are called the **operands**. It expects to see a constant or a variable on either side — not another operational symbol.

6. * B	A * – B
Allowed	Not allowed

Two operational symbols may not appear together. As shown in Figure 3.3, parentheses are used to separate adjacent operational symbols.

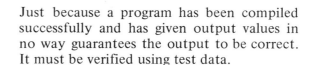

Not Permitted	A * – B	Permitted	A * (– B)
	C / – D		C / (– D)
	10. ** + X		10. ** (+X)

TWO OPERATIONAL SYMBOLS TOGETHER:
NOT PERMITTED

Figure 3.3 Adjacent Operators Prohibited

It should be noted that the operational symbol for raising to a power, **, is considered a single symbol, even though two characters are used to denote it.

3.7 | Many Programming Examples

Not all programmers are required to deal with long, complicated equations resulting in wild arithmetic statements. For these people, the simple examples in the following table should be studied to firm up their understanding of the very important material just presented. More complex examples are presented in Figure 3.5 but are intended for math/science majors only.

STATEMENT:	MEANING:
Y = A*B/C	$y = \dfrac{ab}{c}$
Y = A/B * C	$y = \dfrac{ac}{b}$
Y = A/(B * C)	$y = \dfrac{a}{bc}$
Y = A · B	Not allowed – "·" is an improper OPERATING SYMBOL
Y = A(B + C)	Not allowed – missing OPERATIONAL SYMBOL
Y = A * – B	Not allowed – two operational symbols appearing together
Y = (X – 6.) ** 0.5	$y = \sqrt{x - 6}$
Y = X ** 2. – 6. * X + 1.	$y = x^2 - 6x + 1$
H = X * Y * Z/A * B * C H = (X * Y * Z)/A * B * C	$h = \dfrac{xyzbc}{a}$

Figure 3.4 Example Arithmetic Statements

To test your understanding of this material, take this quiz and check your answers with those at the end of the quiz.

Quiz#1   Understanding Arithmetic Statements

Part 1: Indicate which arithmetic statement is correct for each of the following algebraic equations:

1. $y = \dfrac{x^2 - 10}{\sqrt{x}} - 6$

2. $y = x^2 - \dfrac{10}{\sqrt{x} - 6}$

3. $y = \dfrac{x^2 - 10}{\sqrt{x} - 6}$

4. $y = x^2 - \dfrac{10}{\sqrt{x}} - 6$

(a) Y=X**2–10./X**0.5–6.
(b) Y=(X**2–10.)/X**0.5–6.
(c) Y=X**2–10./(X**0.5–6.)
(d) Y=X**2–10./(X–6.)**0.5
(e) Y=(X**2–10.)/(X**0.5–6.)

Part 2: Examine the following arithmetic statements and indicate any errors they may contain:

5. A = (B**3 + 4.)/–3.
6. Y = 5.(X**2.5 – 1.)–4.
7. X – Y = 3.*(X**2./3.)
8. Y = A/(B + C)**4 + D)

(a) Unpaired parentheses
(b) Missing operational symbol
(c) General form incorrect
(d) Two consecutive operational symbols
(e) Valid statement

Part 3: Indicate the *minimum* number of parentheses needed to express the following equations:

9. $y = x^2 - \dfrac{6}{x}$

10. $y = \dfrac{1}{x} + \dfrac{1}{a}$

11. $y = (x-1)^{2/3} + \dfrac{1}{x} 2 + 1$

12. $y = x^{3-z} + \dfrac{11}{a^2 + b^2} - 2$

(a) None
(b) One pair
(c) Two pairs
(d) Three pairs
(e) Four pairs

Part 4: For each of the following arithmetic statements, show the algebraic equation it represents:

13. X=H**2-70./H+5.

14. X=H**2-70./(H+5.)

15. X=(H**2-70.)/(H+5.)

16. X=(H**2-70.)/H+5.

Answers: 1. (b), 2. (c), 3. (e), 4. (a), 5. (d), 6. (b), 7. (c), 8. (a), 9. (a), 10. (a)

11. (c), 12. (c), 13. $x = H^2 - \dfrac{70}{H} + 5$, 14. $x = H^2 - \dfrac{70}{H+5}$,

15. $x = \dfrac{H^2 - 70}{H+5}$, 16. $x = \dfrac{H^2 - 70}{H} + 5$

The table that follows represents more difficult arithmetic statements and is intended for math/science majors.

Math/Science Majors Only	
Statement:	Meaning:
H=X*Y*Z/(A*B*C) H=(X*Y*Z)/(A*B*C)	$h = \dfrac{xyz}{abc}$
X=(Y*(Z-6.2)/(Y+1.))**2.	$x = \left(\dfrac{y(z-6.2)}{(y+1)}\right)^2$
Z=A**X/Y**2-B*C+1.	$z = \dfrac{a^x}{y^2} - bc + 1$
Z=A**X/Y**(2.-B)*C+1.	$z = \dfrac{a^x c}{y^{(2-b)}} + 1$
Z=A**X/(Y**2.-B)*(C+1.)	$z = \dfrac{a^x}{y^2 - b}(c+1)$

Figure 3.5 More Complex Example Statements

Equation:	Statement:
$y = \left[\dfrac{c^2 + b}{\dfrac{t}{c} - 6}\right]^2 - 1$	Y=((C**2+B)/(T/C-6.))**2-1.
$y = \dfrac{\dfrac{x^{-2}}{c+1}}{x^2 - c} - 6$	Y=(X**(-2.)/(C+1.))/(X**2-C)-6.
$y = \left[\dfrac{c^{a+b} - 1}{(x^2 - 6)^2}\right]^{1.4}$	Y=((C**(A+B)-1.)/(X**2-6.)**2)**1.4

Figure 3.5 (continued)

One of the examples in this table is the statement:

$$X=(Y*(Z-6.2)/(Y+1.))**2.$$

As can be seen there are two inner pairs of parentheses and one outer pair. In processing this statement, the inner parentheses will be cleared first. That is, 6.2 is subtracted from Z and 1 is added to Y. In clearing these inner parentheses, each expression is treated as a separate entity and is scanned three times looking first for exponentiation, then multiplication or division, and so on. At this point, the following values have been determined:

$$Z - 6.2 \quad \text{and} \quad Y + 1$$

Next, the outer parentheses are cleared (again three sweeps). Y is multiplied by "Z – 6.2" and then division by "Y + 1" takes place. We now have:

$$\frac{y(Z - 6.2)}{y + 1}$$

Finally, with all the parentheses cleared, the remainder of the statement is scanned three times in the usual left-to-right fashion.* The only activity is on the first sweep where exponentiation is accomplished.

$$X = \left(\frac{Y(Z - 6.2)}{y + 1}\right)^2$$

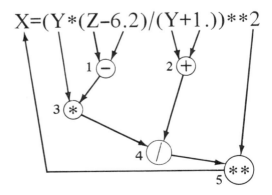

*There is one exception to the "left-to-right" processing of operations at the same hierarchy level. Consecutive exponentiation operators are evaluated from right to left. Y=X**4**2 is equivalent to Y=X**(4**2).

3.8

Naming Variables

In this chapter, the majority of equations have been written using single-letter variable names. When dealing with one equation having no more than two or three variables, single-letter variable names are possible. As soon as a problem takes on any level of complexity, an improved method of naming variables is needed. It is absolutely essential that the programmer be able to quickly recognize each variable in a program. Figure 3.6 gives two possible representations of each of several equations. One uses highly descriptive variable naming, the other uses single-letter descriptions. Obviously, descriptive variable naming is preferred.

Descriptive Variable Naming:		
Equation	Single Letter Naming (DISCOURAGED)	Descriptive Naming (PREFERRED)
$a = \frac{1}{4}\pi d^2$	A = 1./4.*P*D**2.	AREA = 1./4.*PI*DIAM**2.
$v = \frac{4}{3}\pi r^3$	V = 4./3.*P*R**3.	VOL = 4./3.*PI*RAD**3.
$s = \frac{1}{2}at^2$	S = 1./2.*A*T**2.	DISP = 1./2.*ACC*TIME**2.

Figure 3.6 Descriptive Variable Naming

The rules for naming a variable are presented as follows. Notice the method used to distinguish *real* from *integer* variable names.

Rules Governing Variable Names:

1. Names must not exceed *six* characters in length.
 2. All characters must be *letters* or *digits*.
 3. The *first* character must be a *letter:*
     a. If it is an I, J, K, L, M, or N, the variable is an *integer* variable.
     b. If it is any other letter, the variable is a *real* variable.

A variable name is used not only to identify where in memory a value has been stored, but also to convey *how* the value is stored. Because real and integer numbers are stored differently, the variable name must identify the mode of storage. *Integer* numbers are stored as you might expect, as a simple string of digits. *Real* numbers are stored in a more complex form: a string of digits representing a mantissa and a second string representing an exponent.

The variable name identifies:
1. An address
2. A mode of storage

The compiler uses variable names when processing arithmetic statements in the following way. The statement:

$$A = 6.5$$

means, for example, "Store the value 6.5 in a memory location. Store the value in the real mode. Identify the address of this memory location by the name A."

The statement:

$$A = B + C$$

means, "Obtain copies of the memory locations B and C. Interpret the contents of these memory locations as REAL numbers. Add these numbers and store the results in a memory location to be called A."

This somewhat elaborate explanation has been given to help in the interpretation of the following statement:

$$N = N + 1$$

It means, "Fetch a copy of the integer value stored at the address associated with the name N. Add 1 to this value and store the results of that calculation back in the memory location identified by the name N."

This example clearly shows that the symbol = does not have the traditional meaning of "*is equal to.*" In FORTRAN, the symbol = is called the **replacement operator** and is understood to mean "is to be replaced by." For that reason, the statement N = N + 1 is interpreted to mean, "Replace the value stored in N with its former value plus 1."

The following table illustrates some correct and incorrect variable names. It should be studied to reinforce the rules just presented.

Correct Variable Names	Incorrect Variable Names	
Integer Variables	Integer Variables	
ITEM	K–5	(illegal character used)
MONEY	NUMBERS	(too many characters)
JOB	L(6)A	(illegal characters used)
LINE	6N	(first character not a letter)
N6	VALUE	(incorrect first letter)
Real Variables	Real Variables	
DIA4	VELOCITY	(too many characters)
TIME	ASUM$	(illegal character used)
B1	NUMBER	(incorrect first letter)
ACC	4B	(first character not a letter)
	A60.	(illegal character used)
	X–RAY	(illegal character used)
	LENGTH	(incorrect first letter)

When groups of variables are related to one another, they may be given similar names. For example, the value of the velocity of a projectile may be computed at ten-second intervals for one minute. These values may be given the names:

$$\text{VEL0} \quad \text{VEL10} \quad \text{VEL20} \quad \text{VEL30} \quad \text{VEL40} \quad \text{VEL50} \quad \text{VEL60}$$

Here the names are similar but not identical.

3.9   Explicit Type Statements

It is possible to circumvent the "I,J,K,L,M, or N" restriction in naming variables. When necessary, we can call a variable by whatever name we want. FORTRAN permits variables to be defined in two ways: implicitly or explicitly. The implicit definition you already know: using the first letter of a variable to indicate its type. Whenever we wish to override this method, we use what is known as a **type statement:**

```
INTEGER   X, Y, ABLE, DERIV
REAL    M, N, ITEM, MONEY
```

These statements start with the word INTEGER or REAL and then list all the variables that are to be considered integer or real regardless of what letter they start with. This is called **explicit definition** and is allowed on most systems.

The type statements like the ones shown above must appear early in the source program so that the type statement precedes the first use of any of the variables being declared. It is a good idea to make these type statements the first statements in your program.

Once the type of a variable has been declared in a program, you cannot change it in the middle of the program.

Programming Style Use highly descriptive names, and display them clearly	Highly descriptive variable names are one of the trademarks of a well-written program. They have been shown to reduce the error count in programs as well as the time required to track down errors. Once variable names have been selected, list them in a table or sketch for easy reference to insure their proper use. (See Figure 2.10 on page 37 for the suggested methods of documentation of variable names.)

3.10 | Real and Integer Mode Calculations

Chapter 2 described the difference between integer and real numbers and the effect this difference has on the way in which these numbers are stored. This difference appears again in attempting to manipulate numbers in an arithmetic assignment statement.

The expressions shown in the following table result in typical real calculations. These calculations are performed to a high degree of accuracy because of the possibility of a fractional component. The result is a real number, which must be stored in a real (floating point) memory location to preserve the fractional component. This mode of calculation is more common than the alternate: integer mode calculation.

Real Mode Calculations	
Expression	Result
4.08*2.2	8.976
3.69/3.	1.23
4.08*2.2+3.69/3.	10.206
10.9–2.*.45	10.0

An **integer calculation** is a simpler truncated version of the above in that digits to the right of the decimal point are dropped irrespective of their value. The result of this mode of calculation is an integer value. Because of the fact that digits to the right of the decimal point are truncated, some strange results occur when integers are divided. Even if the result of a division operation was supposed to be 8.99999, the value would be truncated to 8. Furthermore, this truncation can occur more than once in the evaluation of an integer expression. Several examples of integer mode calculations are shown in the following table.

Integer Mode Calculations	
Expression	Result
5+3	8
2*6	12
33/5	6
3/2	1
4/3+5/4 = 1 + 1 =	2
16/3*(6/4+1/2) = 5*(1+0) =	5

A final comment. Expressions in an arithmetic assignment statement should be written in a consistent mode. The expression should be real or it should be integer. Mixing modes in an expression should be avoided.

Quiz#2   Understanding Arithmetic Statements

Part 1: Answer the following questions.

1. In the following statement, two expressions would be described as "inner expressions" and one expression as an "outer expression." Identify these expressions:

$$Y = 6.0*((X-3.1)**2.+(X**1.4/3.0))**0.5$$

2. In the statement shown in question 1, which operation will be performed first? Second? Third?

3. Are the expressions identified in question 1 all written in a consistent *mode*? What is that mode?

4. Are real and integer values stored in the same way?

5. Describe the way in which the contents of memory locations X and C are affected by the statement:

$$C = X + 5.0$$

6. The statement:

$$A = B + C$$

causes the computer to "Obtain a copy of memory locations B and C. The contents of these memory locations are interpreted as real numbers." What does this mean?

7. The statement:

$$N = N - 2$$

shows that the symbol = does not have the traditional meaning "is equal to." Describe what it does mean.

8. If N has the value 16 when the statement in question 7 is executed, describe in detail how the statement is interpreted.

9. The following variable names are identical except for one character.

TIME10   TIME20   TIME30   TIME40

Does that mean each variable will still be assigned a different location in memory?

10. When defining the mode of a variable, which definition overrides — the implicit or explicit definition?

Part 2:

11. Write a program that will determine which way a beam will rotate when two weights are placed on the beam as shown.

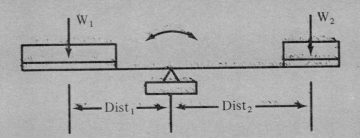

The program should print one of the following three messages:

```
BEAM WILL ROTATE CLOCKWISE
```

```
BEAM WILL ROTATE COUNTERCLOCKWISE
```

```
BEAM WILL BALANCE
```

12. The magnitude and location of two weights are given on separate data cards. How will this affect the program?

34.5   7.89   (card 2)
WEIGHT$_2$ DISTANCE$_2$
123.4   12.34   (card 1)
WEIGHT$_1$ DISTANCE$_1$

13. The following variable names have been selected to represent the values shown. Are the names used acceptable? If not, why?

Name		Meaning
WT–1	WT–2	Weight one and two
DISTONE	DISTWO	Distance from fulcrum
MOMNT1	MOMNT2	Moment produced by each weight

Answers:

1. Y=6.0*((X–3.1)**2.+(X**1.4/3.0))**0.5

   INNER   INNER

   OUTER

2. First: Subtraction X–3.1
   Second: Exponentiation X**1.4
   Third: Division $X^{1.4}/3.0$

3. Yes; real

4. No

5. X is not affected
   C changes—takes on the value of X+5.0.

6. The string of digits at each memory location is interpreted as a mantissa portion that is to be raised to an exponent portion of this word of memory.

7. The equal sign is a replacement operator.
   The variable on the left is to be replaced by the quantity (expression) on the right.

8. Fetch a copy of the contents of memory location N (the value 16). Subtract 2 from this value and store the result thus obtained (the value 14) in memory location N.

9. Yes

10. Explicit definition.

```
11. C   PURPOSE-DETERMINE WHICH WAY BEAM WILL
    C              ROTATE.
    C
    C              – IMPORTANT VARIABLES –
    C   – WT1        MAGNITUDE OF WEIGHT 1
    C   – DIST1      DISTANCE FROM FULCRUM
    C   – MOMNT1   MOMENT CAUSED BY WEIGHT 1
    C
    C   – WT2        MAGNITUDE OF WEIGHT 2
    C   – DIST2      DISTANCE FROM FULCRUM
    C   – MOMNT2   MOMENT CAUSED BY WEIGHT 2
    C
        REAL MOMNT1, MOMNT2
    C
        READ,WT1,DIST1
        READ, WT2,DIST2
    C
        MOMNT1=WT1*DIST1
        MOMNT2=WT2*DIST2
    C
        IF (MOMNT1.GT.MOMNT2) WRITE, 'BEAM WILL ROTATE COUNTER-
       + CLOCKWISE'
        IF (MOMNT1.EQ.MOMNT2) WRITE, 'BEAM WILL BALANCE'
        IF (MOMNT1.LT.MOMNT2) WRITE, 'BEAM WILL ROTATE CLOCKWISE'
    C
        STOP
        END
12. Two READ statements are needed.
13. WT-1 and WT-2 are illegal (dash not allowed)
    DISTONE is illegal (too many characters)
    MOMNT1 and MOMNT2 must be declared as REAL.
```

Review Exercises

The left-hand column contains numbered questions or examples. The right-hand column contains lettered answers or comments. One or two items in the right-hand column can apply to any given item in the left-hand column. Read the numbered question and choose the correctly lettered answer(s).

Part A Identify the following FORTRAN quantities:

1. *0.
2. 0.6
3. A3
4. *13
5. A1.
6. 23
7. *23.
8. NUM
9. VALUE
10. *3,582.

(a) Real constant
(b) Real variable
(c) Integer constant
(d) Integer variable
(e) Unacceptable

Part B Most of the following integer names are unacceptable. Indicate in each case the error(s), if any.

11.* 1-6

12. 6I

13.* I6

14. VALUE

15.* MVALUES

16. LOGF

17.* (X)

(a) Valid name – acceptable

(b) Invalid – too many characters

(c) Invalid – illegal character

(d) Invalid – incorrect first character

(e) None of these

Part C Most of the following real names are unacceptable. Indicate in each case the error(s), if any.

18. ZTWO

19.* Z2

20. 2Z

21.* 2/Z

22. Z2,3

(a) Valid name – acceptable

(b) Invalid – too many characters

(c) Invalid – illegal character

(d) Invalid – incorrect first character

(e) None of these

Part D Each of the following FORTRAN statements contains at least one error. Indicate the error(s).

23. Y=(A+3.)/X**-2

24. Y=X**2/3.+M

25.* I=(X-Y) (B+7.)

26. Y=(A3,7-B2)/(B67)

27. P=π*R**2

28.* Y=((W+X)/(Y2+Z-1)

29. Y-1.=C

30.* 2.=A+B**2/3.

(a) Mixed mode

(b) Missing operational symbol

(c) Invalid variable name

(d) Unpaired parenthesis

(e) None of these

Part E Given: J = 10; K = 2; X = 10.; Z = 2. Indicate the result of the following FORTRAN calculation:

31. I = J/K + 2/3

32.* B = J/K + 2/3

33. I = X/Z + 2./3.

34. Y = X/Z + 2./3.

35.* I = J/Z + 2./3

36. I = J/K * (5/3*6/4)

37. Y = J/K * (B/3*6/4)

38.* Y = X/Z * (3./10.)*3.

(a) 5

(b) 5.0000

(c) 4.5

(d) 5.6666

(e) Not allowed

Part F What is the minimum number of parentheses needed to express the following equations in a FORTRAN arithmetic statement?

39. $Y = \dfrac{X^2 - 6}{X + 1} - 1$

40.* $Y = \dfrac{1}{2}(X - 6) + \dfrac{X}{2}$

41. $Y = X^2 - \dfrac{6}{X} + 1$

42. $Y = X^{-3} - 6X^{-2} + 3$

43. $Y = 10 - \dfrac{a}{b}\sin(90° - C)$

44.* $Y = \sqrt{b^2 - 4ac}$

(a) None

(b) One pair

(c) Two pairs

(d) Three pairs

(e) Four pairs

Part G Provide a brief response to the following questions:

45. Describe the normal hierarchy of performing arithmetic operations.

46.*Parentheses are not included in the table of arithmetic operators. Why?

47. There are two reasons an equation and its arithmetic assignment statement are different. What are these reasons?

48.*If an arithmetic statement has several nested expressions (one expression contained within another), which expression is evaluated first?

49. If several pairs of redundant parentheses are used in a statement, will this have a detrimental effect?

50. What is to be gained by using test data on a program?

51.*Two operational symbols cannot appear together. How do you avoid this?

52. In the statement

$$Z = A**X/(Y**2.-B)*(C+1.)$$

describe the sequence in which arithmetic operations are performed. How many scans are needed to completely process the statement?

Additional Applications

| Programming Example Computing Interest | A bank is offering 5% interest rates on all deposits. The following illustrates the increase in value a $1,000.00 account would experience over a four-year period. |

$$\text{TOTAL} = \boxed{\text{PRINCIPAL}} \, (1 + \boxed{\text{RATE}} \,)^{\text{NO. OF YEARS}}$$

1st year	$1,000.00	$(1 + 0.05)^1$ =	$1,050.00
2nd year	$1,000.00	$(1 + 0.05)^2$ =	$1,102.50
3rd year	$1,000.00	$(1 + 0.05)^3$ =	$1,157.63
4th year	$1,000.00	$(1 + 0.05)^4$ =	$1,215.51

Write a program to produce a similar table of values for each of the different interest rates represented in the data deck (one value per card).

Input:

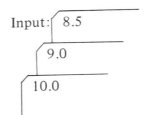

8.5
9.0
10.0

Output:

CALCULATION FOR 10.0 PERCENT
YEAR 1 $1100.00
YEAR 2 $1210.00
YEAR 3 $1331.00
YEAR 4 $1464.10

```
C.....................................................
C...     PURPOSE - COMPUTE GROWTH OF $1,000.00 OVER FOUR YEAR ...
C...           PERIOD AT VARIOUS INTEREST RATES              ...
C.....................................................
C
C            ---IMPORTANT VARIABLES---
C
C      --RATE     INTEREST RATE READ FROM DATA            --
C      --VALUE1    VALUE OF PRINCIPAL AT END OF YEAR ONE   --
C      --VALUE2    VALUE OF PRINCIPAL AT END OF YEAR TWO   --
C      --VALUE3    VALUE OF PRINCIPAL AT END OF YEAR THREE --
C      --VALUE4    VALUE OF PRINCIPAL AT END OF YEAR FOUR  --
C
C      READ RATE FOR THIS PASS.....TRANSFER TO OUTPUT
C
   10 READ, RATE
      WRITE,' CALCULATION FOR ',RATE,' PERCENT'
C
C      APPLY INTEREST EQUATION
C
      VALUE1 = 1000.00*(1.0 + RATE/100.)**1
      VALUE2 = 1000.00*(1.0 + RATE/100.)**2
      VALUE3 = 1000.00*(1.0 + RATE/100.)**3
      VALUE4 = 1000.00*(1.0 + RATE/100.)**4
C
C      OUTPUT ALL VALUES
C
      WRITE, ' YEAR 1  $', VALUE1
      WRITE, ' YEAR 2  $', VALUE2
      WRITE, ' YEAR 3  $', VALUE3
      WRITE, ' YEAR 4  $', VALUE4
C
      GO TO 10
C
      END
```

Programming Example
Right Triangle

Given: 2 sides of a right triangle. Required: Compute the length of the hypotenuse.

Governing Equation

$$\text{Hypotenuse} = \sqrt{(\text{SIDE 1})^2 + (\text{SIDE 2})^2}$$

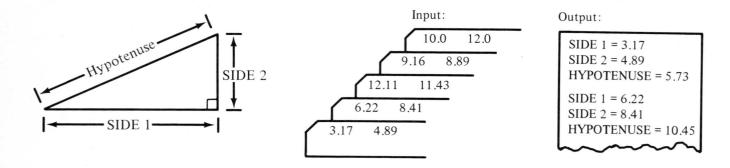

Input:

10.0	12.0
9.16	8.89
12.11	11.43
6.22	8.41
3.17	4.89

Output:

```
SIDE 1 = 3.17
SIDE 2 = 4.89
HYPOTENUSE = 5.73

SIDE 1 = 6.22
SIDE 2 = 8.41
HYPOTENUSE = 10.45
```

Note: The presentation of how to obtain a message (character string) as part of a line of output is discussed in the programming example on page 45 entitled "NUMBER GAME".

```
C.....................................................
C..   PURPOSE - COMPUTE THE HYPOTENUSE OF RIGHT TRIANGLE   ..
C..            GIVEN TWO SIDES OF THE TRIANGLE.            ..
C.....................................................
C
C           ---IMPORTANT VARIABLES---
C
C    --SIDE1     ONE SIDE OF TRIANGLE (READ FROM DATA)   --
C    --SIDE2     ONE SIDE OF TRIANGLE (READ FROM DATA)   --
C    --HYPNUS    HYPOTENUSE OF THE TRIANGLE (COMPUTED)   --
C
   10 READ, SIDE1, SIDE2
C
C           ......APPLY EQUATION.........
C
      HYPNUS = (SIDE1**2 + SIDE2**2)**0.5
C
      WRITE, 'SIDE 1 =', SIDE1
      WRITE, 'SIDE 2 =', SIDE2
      WRITE, 'HYPOTENUSE = ', HYPNUS
C
C                 REPEAT LOGIC FOR REMAINING DATA CARDS
      GO TO 10
C
      END
```

Programming Example
Temperature
Conversion

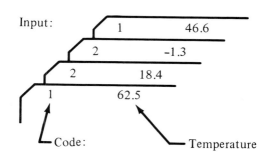

Input:

1	46.6
2	-1.3
2	18.4
1	62.5

Code: ⌐   Temperature

The temperatures at various weather stations are being reported by the data cards shown. Unfortunately, some of the temperatures are in degrees Fahrenheit and others are in degrees Centigrade. The first digit on the card tells what value is being reported (1=°Fahrenheit, 2=°Centigrade). Write a program to report all

Governing Equations: Output:

$$F = 1.8C + 32.0$$
$$C = \frac{5}{9}(F - 32.0)$$

```
FAHRENHEIT=62.5 CENTIGRADE=17.5
FAHRENHEIT=65.1 CENTIGRADE=18.4
FAHRENHEIT=29.7 CENTIGRADE=-1.3
FAHRENHEIT=46.6 CENTIGRADE= 8.0
```

temperatures in both degrees Fahrenheit and degrees Centigrade (Celsius). This program will give output as shown above.

```
C.......PURPOSE - READ TEMPERATURES IN DEGREES FAHRENHEIT OR.
C..              DEGREES CENTIGRADE. REPORT TEMPERATURES IN ..
C..              BOTH FORMS.                                  ..
C.......................................................
C
C               -----IMPORTANT VARIABLES-----
C
C     --CODE    A CODE TELLING WHICH TEMPERATURE IS GIVEN  --
C                  1 = FAHRENHEIT      2 = CENTIGRADE
C     --VALUE   TEMPERATURE AS PROVIDED ON THE CARD         --
C     --CENTGD  COMPUTED TEMPERATURE (DEGREES CENTIGRADE)   --
C     --FARNHT  COMPUTED TEMPERATURE (DEGREES FAHRENHEIT)   --
C
      INTEGER CODE
C
   10 READ , CODE, VALUE
C
C               WHICH TEMPERATURE REPORTED
C
      IF (CODE.EQ.2) GO TO 20
C
C               VALUE IS IN DEGREES FAHRENHEIT
C
      CENTGD = 5. / 9. * (VALUE - 32.0)
      WRITE, 'FAHRENHEIT = ',VALUE,'CENTIGRADE =', CENTGD
      GO TO 10
C
C               VALUE IN DEGREES CENTIGRADE
C
   20 FARNHT = 1.8 * VALUE + 32.0
      WRITE, 'FAHRENHEIT = ',FARNHT,'CENTIGRADE = ', VALUE
C
      GO TO 10
C
      END
```

| **Programming Example** Volume of Tray | A baking pan is to be made from a piece of sheet metal 17″ by 22″ in size. A square cut is to be made at all four corners and the piece folded as shown. The resulting dimensions of the pan are shown in the illustration. Two possible values of X (the square cutouts) are being considered. Read these values from data. |

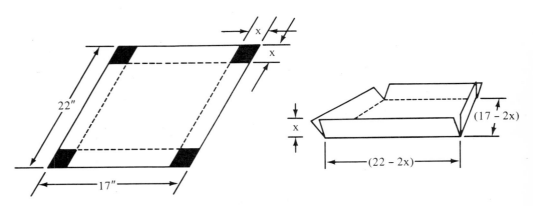

Determine and report which value of X produces the larger volume baking pan.

Input: Output:

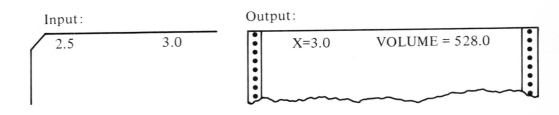

```
   2.5              3.0
```

```
X=3.0        VOLUME = 528.0
```

```
C.....................................................
C..  PURPOSE - COMPUTE TWO VOLUMES....REPORT THE LARGER  :
C.....................................................
C..........................................
C
C            -----IMPORTANT VARIABLES-----
C
C     --X1,X2      SIZE OF EACH SQUARE CUTOUT            --
C     --VOL1       VOLUME OF PAN USING CUTOUT SIXE X1    --
C     --VOL2       VOLUME OF PAN USING CUTOUT SIXE X2    --
C
      READ, X1, X2
C
      VOL1 = (22.-2.*X1) * (17.-2.*X1) * X1
      VOL2 = (22.-2.*X2) * (17.-2.*X2) * X2
C
C            REPORT LARGER VALUE ONLY
C
      IF(VOL1.GT.VOL2) WRITE, ' X= ',X1, ' VOLUME = ', VOL1
C
      IF(VOL2.GE.VOL1) WRITE, ' X= ',X2, ' VOLUME = ', VOL2
      STOP
      END
```

Programming Example Stock Report	Computers provide an important management tool by their *report generating* activity. Assume a company has some of its assets invested in the stock market. Each stock owned is represented on a data card forming the deck shown. The first card indicates 200 shares of Chrysler purchased at $15.75 per share and now selling for $14.50.

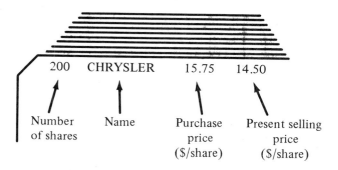

200	CHRYSLER	15.75	14.50
Number of shares	Name	Purchase price ($/share)	Present selling price ($/share)

Management needs up-to-date reports to evaluate the performance of their stocks. In a subsequent example, we will generate this whole report (headings and all). For the moment, consider the problem of generating each line in the middle of the report.

			STOCK REPORT			
NAME OF SECURITY	NO. OF SHARES	PUR-CHASE PRICE	TOTAL COST	TODAY'S PRICE	TOTAL VALUE	PROFIT (LOSS)
ALCOA	40	130.00	5200.00	138.75	5550.00	350.00
DISNEY	20	75.00	1500.00	125.00	2500.00	1000.00
DOW CHEM	100	38.65	3865.00	48.65	4865.00	1000.00
IBM	80	43.41	3472.00	42.45	3396.00	-76.80
MONSANTO	45	83.75	3768.75	38.70	1741.50	-2027.25
TEXACO	60	62.50	3750.45	93.47	5608.20	-2562.40
TOTALS			54521.90		53751.05	-770.85

These lines contain 7 values, 4 of which are read from data. This means that 3 calculations are necessary: the *total cost* to purchase a given stock, its *present total value,* and the *profit or loss* of this particular stock.

```
C...........................................................
C..    PURPOSE - GENERATE DETAIL LINE FOR STOCK REPORT SHOW-..
C..             ING HOLDINGS, PROFIT OR LOSS INFORMATION    ..
C..             FOR EACH STOCK.                             ..
C...........................................................
C
C                      -----IMPORTANT VARIABLES-----
C
C     --NAME       NAME OF STOCK                            --
C     --NUMBER     NUMBER OF SHARES HELD                    --
C     --PRICE      PURCHASE PRICE ($/SHARE)                 --
C     --VALUE      PRESENT VALUE OF EACH STOCK ($/SHARE)    --
C                  ------COMPUTED VALUES------
C     --TCOST      TOTAL COST OF EACH BLOCK OF STOCK        --
C     --TVALUE     TOTAL VALUE OF EACH BLOCK OF STOCK       --
C     --PROFIT     PROFIT OR LOSS FOR EACH BLOCK OF STOCK   --
C
C     REAL NUMBER
C
    5 READ, NUMBER, NAME, PRICE, VALUE
C
      TCOST = NUMBER * PRICE
      TVALUE = NUMBER * VALUE
C
      PROFIT = TVALUE - TCOST
C
      WRITE, NAME, NUMBER, PRICE, TCOST, VALUE, TVALUE, PROFIT
C
      GO TO 5
C
      END
```

Programming Example
Series Expansion**

It is possible to use the simple mathematics described in this chapter to obtain higher order operations without an additional hardware commitment. Write a program that will read the value of an angle (expressed in degrees) from data. Convert the angle to radians and then use the equations shown to compute the sine, cosine and tangent of the angle.

Input:

Angle	X
26.3	26.3
	57.3

Angle in degrees → Convert to radians

Equation 1

$$\sin(X) = \underset{\text{Term 1}}{X} - \underset{\text{Term 2}}{\frac{X^3}{3\cdot2\cdot1}} + \underset{\text{Term 3}}{\frac{X^5}{5\cdot4\cdot3\cdot2\cdot1}} - \underset{\text{Term 4}}{\frac{X^7}{7\cdot6\cdot5\cdot4\cdot3\cdot2\cdot1}} + \underset{\text{Term 5}}{\frac{X^9}{9\cdot8\cdot7\cdot6\cdot5\cdot4\cdot3\cdot2\cdot1}}$$

Equation 2

$$\sin^2(X) + \cos^2(X) = 1 \text{ or } \cos(X) = \sqrt{1 - \sin^2(X)}$$

Equation 3

$$\tan(X) = \frac{\sin(X)}{\cos(X)}$$

The most substantial part of this program is evaluating the various terms in the series expansion of Equation 1.

```
C...........................................................
C..    PURPOSE - DEMONSTRATE SOFTWARE TECHNIQUES BY COMPUT- ..
C..             ING TRIGONOMETRIC VALUES USING A SERIES     ..
C..             EXPANSION.                                  ..
C...........................................................
C
C                      -----IMPORTANT VARIABLES-----
C
C     --ANGLE      VALUE OF ANGLE READ FROM DATA (DEGREES)  --
C     --X          VALUE OF ANGLE CONVERTED TO RADIANS      --
C     --SINVAL     OUTPUT SINE VALUE                        --
C     --COSVAL     OUTPUT COSINE VALUE                      --
C     --TANVAL     OUTPUT TANGENT VALUE                     --
C                  -------------------------
C
C
      READ, ANGLE
      X = ANGLE / 57.3
C
C              EVALUATE TERMS IN SERIES EXPANSION
C
      TERM1 = X
      TERM2 = -X**3 / (3.*2.*1.)
      TERM3 = X**5 / (5.*4.*3.*2.*1.)
      TERM4 = -X**7 / (7.*6.*5.*4.*3.*2.*1.)
      TERM5 = X**9 / (9.*8.*7.*6.*5.*4.*3.*2.*1.)
C
C              COMPUTE OUTPUT VALUES
C
      SINVAL = TERM1 + TERM2 + TERM3 + TERM4 + TERM5
      COSVAL = (1.0 - SINVAL**2)**0.5
      TANVAL = SINVAL / COSVAL
C
      WRITE, ANGLE, SINVAL, COSVAL, TANVAL
C
      STOP
      END
```

This program is not very efficiently written. There are several improvements that might be considered. The first would be to express the factorial values as a single constant.

Old: New:
Term 2 = –X**3/ $\boxed{(3.*2.*1.)}$ Term 2 = –X**3/ $\boxed{6.}$

Term 3 = X**5/ $\boxed{(5.*4.*3.*2.*1.)}$ Term 3 = X**5/ $\boxed{120.}$

Recommended change

This change does eliminate a substantial amount of repeated calculations without obscuring the method of solution. Such a change is recommended. Let us look at another possible change.

Each term in the numerator, X**9 for example, is obtained by repeated multiplication (X is multiplied by itself nine times). This involves a lot of multiplication:

X**5   (X is multiplied by itself 5 times)
X**7   (X is multiplied by itself 7 times)
X**9   (X is multiplied by itself 9 times)

A small savings could be had by recognizing that the numerator for any new term could be obtained by multiplying the numerator of the old term by –X**2:

TERM5 = TERM4*X**2/72.0

A change such as this is highly questionable in that the basic method of solution is being obscured.

Programming Style:
Avoid tricks: keep
it simple

A clever programmer can devise numerous diabolical techniques to save one or two memory locations a program needs or make the program run a few thousandths of a second faster. If, in the process, the ability to easily follow the program logic is forfeited, the price is too high.

4 Elementary Input/Output/Format Statements

We have not been telling the whole story with regard to input statements. If the READ statement is to be implemented in its most common form, two new parameters must be provided:

READ (5, 12) NAME, NUMBER, ITEM

Device code ⟋   ⟍ Number of supporting format statement

This form of READ statement identifies:

1. which of several possible input devices is to be used — in this case device number 5,
2. an accompanying FORMAT statement that describes the layout of information on the card (or line) being read — in this case statement 12.

4.1 | Introduction to Format Control

It is possible for the system software to search a data card and ultimately determine the layout of information on the card. By layout we mean:

1. how many pieces of information are on the card;
2. how many columns are used to express each datum value;
3. what type of information is contained within this field.

This layout can be expressed much more directly by simple codes contained within a FORMAT statement.

Assume, for example, a data card contains the name of a blood donor in the first 6 columns; the next column holds an integer number expressing the donor's blood type; followed by a telephone number in the next 7 columns.

An appropriate FORMAT statement would be:

12 FORMAT (A6, I1, I7)

The codes within this FORMAT statement are easy to decipher:

Code	Meaning
A6	information is alphabetic, consumes 6 columns on the card
I1	information is integer number, consumes 1 column on the card
I7	information is integer number, consumes 7 columns on the card

Deciphering the codes for real numbers is only slightly more complicated.

4.2 | General Program

A general program is one written to allow its repeated use with different sets of input values. This means that the instruction deck must always reference variable quantities by *name* only and never by specific value. In the data deck, the opposite is true.

The data deck should contain only those specific numbers or alphabetic values that change for each execution of the program logic. Students are sometimes tempted to include the variable name on the data card, but that is wrong.

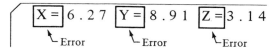

The names X, Y and Z belong in the instruction deck (as part of the READ statement).

One-to-One Correspondence

The specific values appearing in the data deck somehow must be linked to the corresponding variable names in the instruction deck. This is the function of the READ statement and is essentially a matching process. Names following the command READ are matched on a one-to-one basis with the sequential data values appearing on the data card. A corresponding sequence of format codes (appearing in the FORMAT statement) supports this activity. Figure 4.1 illustrates this process.

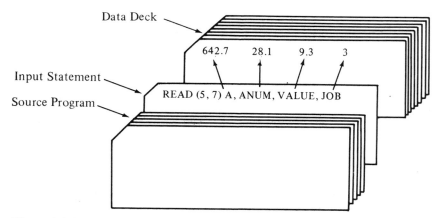

Figure 4.1 Variables in the READ Statement Related to Numbers on the Data Card

The more advanced form of READ statement is used in Figure 4.1. It consists of four parts.

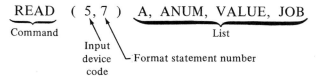

1. LIST. Consider first the list. It contains a series of variable names separated by commas. Notice that these names match in number and mode the numerical values appearing on the data card shown.

When this read statement is executed:

the value 642.7 is stored in memory location A,

the value 28.1 is stored in memory location ANUM,

the value 9.3 is stored in memory location VALUE, and

the value 3 is stored in memory location JOB.

2. COMMAND. The command READ is the executable part of the statement. It directs the processing of a new data card. Data cards are processed in the order of appearance in the data deck. Each execution of a read statement causes the examination and processing of at least one new data card.

3. DEVICE CODE. One of the new parameters is the device code. This number is most important at computer facilities that have more than one input device available. It identifies which specific device to use during this READ operation. If there is more than one card reader, or if input is to be from a tape drive or a disc drive, this number will tell what device to use. Each input device has been assigned a number (a device code) by the computation center. This text uses the number 5 to identify the student card reader. Your instructor will provide the device code you should use.

4. FORMAT NUMBER. The other new parameter is a number that identifies a FORMAT statement appearing somewhere in your program that supplies information to support this read activity.

These two new parameters are enclosed in parentheses and separated by a comma. There should be a **consistency of mode** between:

1. the variable names used in the READ statement,
2. the values appearing on the data card, and
3. the codes used in the FORMAT statement.

Any discrepancy invites trouble.

Programming Style
Mode Consistency:
Double Check

In an input operation, a consistency of mode is needed in three places. The sequence of variable names following the command READ must be consistent with the mode of the values punched on the data cards and must be consistent with the mode declared by the FORMAT codes. This is a frequent source of error and should be checked.

Using an integer name to store a real value or declaring the wrong mode in a FORMAT code will result in errors that may or may not be signalled by the compiler. This is another situation in which you are on your own and should take proper precautions. By proper precautions we mean using extra printouts.

Programming Style
Echo Check
All Input

To be sure input data has been read correctly, insert a temporary WRITE statement immediately after each READ that displays (echoes) each value read. This output statement can be removed as soon as the input has been verified.

4.3 | Codes for Real Numbers

You are familiar with the use of I-codes and A-codes. We now present two others, F-codes and E-codes. These are used to describe the layout of real numbers. In mathematics a real number can be expressed in two ways. When the number is not too large or not too small it is expressed in the following way:

Number	Code
0.05	F 4 . 2
1 6 2 . 7 4 3 9	F 8 . 4
0 . 1 7 5	F 5 . 3
– 9 6 1 . 4 2 8	F 8 . 4

This form is a string of digits with a possible sign at the beginning of the string and a decimal point located somewhere (floating) inside the string. This is called the "Floating Point" form of representing a real number. The interpretation of a typical floating point code is as follows:

F   8   2

Type   Field   Accuracy
       Width   Parameter

The letter F declares that the number is written in the "floating point" form. The next digit specifies the **field width** (the number of columns allowed for the number.) All this is very much similar to the other codes. *Codes representing real numbers require something else — it is called the* **accuracy value.** In addition to the field width, a second parameter is provided to specify the degree of accuracy to which the real number is represented. By this, we mean the number of places provided after the decimal point. On input this value would be used if the decimal point was missing. On output it will have a more important use.

1 4 8 4 9 5 7   F 7 . 3

Implied location of decimal point

Alternate Form

There is an alternate form of representing real numbers sometimes needed by the programmer. You have seen this form used in mathematics to express a very large or very small number:

Scientific Notation	Number
-8.10×10^{13}	$-81{,}000{,}000{,}000{,}000.$
-4.27×10^{-15}	$-.00000000000000427$
3.862×10^{9}	$3{,}862{,}000{,}000.$

mantissa   exponent

This notation uses one or more digits written with a decimal point (called the **mantissa**) followed by the number 10 raised to some power (called the **exponent**).

    This exponent tells how many places the decimal point in the mantissa should be moved to convert to the more standard form. Since FORTRAN statements *must* be written on one continuous line, numbers in scientific notation must be represented in the following way.

Mathematical Notation	Equivalent FORTRAN Representation
$-8.1 \times 10^{13} \longrightarrow$	–8.1E13
$-4.27 \times 10^{-15} \longrightarrow$	–4.27E – 15
$3.862 \times 10^{9} \longrightarrow$	3.862E9

The letter E is used to separate the mantissa from the exponent. It is a substitute for writing the number 10 and a superscript. Numbers may be expressed in this form in the instruction deck and in the data deck. When reading or printing a real value expressed in this form, an E-code is used in the FORMAT statement:

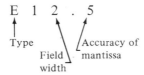

4.4 | Variations in Compilers

A new set of FORTRAN standards has recently been released. They are officially called, "American National Standard Programming Language FORTRAN, X3.9–1978." These standards replace the old set that has been in existence since 1966. Very fortunately, the new standards have made every effort to avoid features that would conflict with the old set. Further, the new features have been added at a minimal increase to the complexity of the language.

Between 1966 and 1978 many computer centers experimented with various "add-on" improvements to the language. These features were implemented in different ways at different installations (because they were not part of the old standards). Free-format input/output is a typical example. A small computer system might not provide any one of these so-called "goodies." The new standards define what is called a "Standard-Conforming-Processor." This will result in a much higher level of uniformity in what is available at your system, and how it is implemented.

When are FORMAT Statements Needed?

Most modern processors do *not* demand the use of FORMAT statements. They merely require that values on the data card be separated by at least one blank space in the same way that names in the list of a READ statement are separated by commas. The FORTRAN 77 standards allow values on the data card to be separated by commas or slashes in addition to blanks. The most common way to implement this "Free-Format" input is by the following READ statement.*

READ (5, *) ITEM, VALUE, X

The use of the asterisk in place of the FORMAT statement number signals the

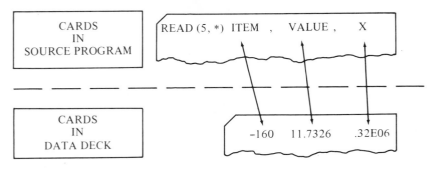

Figure 4.2(a) Free Format Input

*The FORTRAN 77 standards allow the forms:

READ *, ITEM,VALUE,X
READ(UNIT=5,FMT=*)ITEM,VALUE,X

need to call out a routine (algorithm) that searches the card for the information that is not being provided by the format codes.

The more precise form of READ requires the programmer to exercise stricter control over the form in which data values appear on a card and to specify that form in a FORMAT statement.

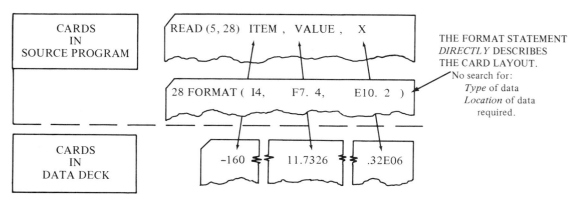

Figure 4.2(b) Input With Format Control

Programming Style
Avoid System-
Dependent Features

Some compilers allow a variable name to be greater than 6 characters in length. Some compilers allow free format using statements other than those permitted by the standards. Avoid using these system-dependent features. They reduce the portability of your program (it will not work on other computing systems).

4.5 | FORMAT Statements: General Form

The FORMAT statement is of the general form:

n FORMAT (coded list)	
28 FORMAT (I4, F7.4, E10.2)	EXAMPLE

where:

n is a necessary identifying statement number;

FORMAT is a declaration of the purpose of the statement; and

(coded list) is a list giving a coded description of each data value appearing on the data card.

As you can see, the computer is very list-conscious. The names in the list of a read statement are matched to numbers or alphabetic values listed on the data card after information in the coded list of a format statement is consulted.

Figure 4.3 shows a typical data card and the format codes to describe the card. The first value on the card is an integer, and the programmer has set aside 4 columns to hold this data value. This is conveyed by the code I4. The code A6 says, "The next data value is alphabetic and 6 columns are needed."

Notice that the word ALCOA and the number 500 do not fill the zone provided for them. The number of columns reserved to hold any variable must be made large enough to hold the largest value that variable will ever have. The use of an I4 code suggests that on some other card there is an integer that requires four columns. The A6 code implies that some stock is represented by a 6-letter name.

FORMAT (I4, A6, F7.2, F7.2, F8.4, E9.4)

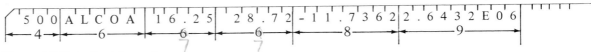

Figure 4.3 Data Card Layout

The remaining values on the card are all real, three in floating-point form and one in E-notation. The first two floating point numbers consume 6 columns each. The last consumes 8. The number in E-notation consumes 9 columns, and the mantissa is expressed with 4 places after the decimal point.

4.6 | Number Codes: Summary

The general form of format number codes is a letter (I, F or E) followed by one or two numbers. The letter describes the mode of the data value; the first number indicates the field width (space provided for this value); the second number is for real numbers only and describes the location of the decimal point.

Code (General Form)

character mode
↳ A w ┐
field width

I w	Fw . d	Ew . d
I = Integer Mode	F = Floating Point Mode	E = Floating Point E – Form
w = Field Width	w = Field Width	w = Field Width
	d = Digits after decimal point.	d = Digits after decimal point

There should be no difficulty determining the mode of a particular data value. The field width must be made large enough to accommodate the biggest value in the set. Do not forget to include a column for the decimal point and for the sign, if any.

4.7 | Repeat Codes

If several data values are of the same form (have the same format code), the FORMAT statement may be written in an abbreviated fashion by using what are called repeat codes.

> READ (5, 7) A, B, C, D, I, J, K
> 7   FORMAT (4F12. 4, 3I6)

Repeat Code ⟋   ⟍ Repeat Code

The number preceding the letter in the code indicates this code (F12.4 or I6) should be repeated as many times as indicated.

The FORMAT statement:

> 7 FORMAT   (4F12.4, 3I6)

is the same as

> 7 FORMAT (F12.4, F12.4, F12.4, F12.4, I6, I6, I6)

Quiz#3   Introduction To FORMAT Statements

Part 1: Answer the following questions.

1. A data card has been prepared as shown. What is wrong with the card?

   SIDE1 = 8.512   SIDE2 = 10.604   HYPNUS = 16.730

2. Describe the error associated with the following input/output statements:

   ```
        READ(5,10)I,J,K
   10   FORMAT (I8,I8,I8)
        WRITE (2,20)I,J,K
   20   FORMAT (F8.2,F8.2,F8.2)
   ```

3. Describe the function of the "ACCURACY PARAMETER" in the following output activity.

   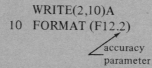

   ```
        WRITE(2,10)A
   10   FORMAT (F12.2)
                    ╱ accuracy
                      parameter
   ```

4. How will the value shown on the following data card be interpreted? Must the decimal point be punched on the card?

   1 2 3 4 5 6 7 8

   ```
        READ (5,10)X
   10   FORMAT (F8.3)
   ```

5. Show how the value read in question 4 would be printed if the following output statement was used:

   ```
        WRITE (2,20)X
   20   FORMAT (E15.4)
   ```

   └┴┴┴┴┴┴┴┴┴┴┴┴┴┴┴┴┴┴┴┴┴┴┴┴┴┴┴┴┴┴┴┴┴┴┴┴┴┴┘

6. What special purpose is the asterisk serving in the following READ statement?

   READ (5,*)A,B,C

7. What is a "REPEAT CODE" and what purpose does it serve?

8. What is the meaning of the term, "system dependent feature"? Give an example.

9. Why should "system dependent features" be avoided?

10. Information pertaining to Federal Income Tax Returns is recorded on data cards as shown below.

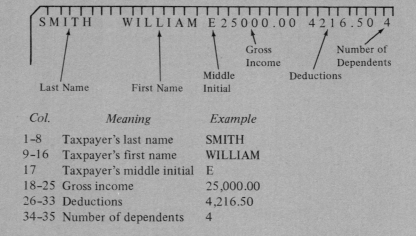

Col.	Meaning	Example
1–8	Taxpayer's last name	SMITH
9–16	Taxpayer's first name	WILLIAM
17	Taxpayer's middle initial	E
18–25	Gross income	25,000.00
26–33	Deductions	4,216.50
34–35	Number of dependents	4

Select appropriate variable names and format codes for the information listed on the card.

Part 2: Writing a program (see data card in question 10).

11. Write a program to compute the TAXABLE INCOME of this taxpayer according to the following equation:

$$\text{TAXABLE INCOME} = \text{GROSS INCOME} - \left\{ \begin{array}{c} \text{LISTED DEDUCTIONS} \\ -\text{ OR }- \\ 15\% \text{ OF GROSS.} \end{array} \right\} - \$750. \times \text{NO. OF DEPENDENTS}$$

Note: After reducing the GROSS INCOME by $750.00 for each dependent, the GROSS INCOME should be further reduced by the value listed in columns 26–33 (the listed deductions) or by 15% of GROSS INCOME. . . *whichever is larger.*

```
C      PURPOSE – COMPUTE TAXABLE INCOME ACCORDING TO GIVEN
C               EQUATION.
C
C               – IMPORTANT VARIABLES –
C
C      – GROSS    GROSS INCOME LISTED ON CARD
C      – DEDACT   ACTUAL DEDUCTIONS AS LISTED ON CARD
C
C      – NODEP    NUMBER OF DEPENDENTS
C      – TAXABL   TAXABLE INCOME
```

Answers:

1. Variable names should not be on data card, only the values 8.512, 10.604, and 16.730.

2. Mode of format codes in output statement not correct. String of digits representing an integer value would be divided into a mantissa and exponent portion if F-code was followed.

3. Only digits up to and including two places after the decimal point will be transferred from memory location A to output.

4. 12345.678   Decimal point need *not* be provided.

5.   1 . 2 3 4 5 E + 0 4
   |_|_|_|_|_|_|_|_|_|_|_|_|_|_|_|_|_|_|_|_|
   ←————— 15 —————→

6. On some compilers, this symbol is used to signal "Free-Format" input or output.

7. 3I4,5F8.2   Causes specific format code to be repeated as many
   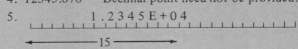 Repeat   times as necessary.
                   Code

8. Feature that is not common to all systems. Variable names greater than 6 characters, for example.

9. Your program will not run on another computer (it is not portable).

10.   READ (5,10)NLAST,NFIRST,MI,GROSS,DEDACT,NODEP
    10 FORMAT (2A8,A1,F8.2,F8.2,I2)

```
11.        READ(5,10)NLAST,NFIRST,MI,GROSS,DEDACT,NODEP
      10   FORMAT (2A8,A1,F8.2,F8.2,I2)
C
           ALLOWD=0.15*GROSS
C
           IF(DEDACT.GT.ALLOWD)TAXABLE=GROSS-DEDACT-750.*NODEP
C
           IF(DEDACT.LE.ALLOWD)TAXABLE=GROSS-ALLOWD-750.*NODEP
C
           WRITE(2,20)TAXABL
      20   FORMAT(F20.2)
C
           STOP
           END
```

4.8 | Spacing Difficulties

When keypunching integer numbers, the number must be carefully positioned within the field specified by its format code. *Blanks on a data card are interpreted as zeros.* Zeros before or after a floating point number have no effect. Zeros inadvertently positioned after I-code and E-code numbers *do* affect their value.

$$\boxed{4\ 2\ .\ 7\ 5\ \ \ }$$

$$\boxed{4\ 2\ .\ 7\ 5\ 0\ 0}\qquad \leftarrow\text{extra zeros}$$

A floating point number can be positioned anywhere within the field specified by its format code. If the number of digits after the decimal point is other than declared by the code, it makes no difference. The number will be interpreted as keypunched. As we said before, this is not true of the other types of numbers (integers and numbers in E-code). Blanks after these numbers have a disastrous effect. These numbers must be right justified in their field.

Assume an integer is to be read according to an I6 code. Consider the following placement of the number:

Integer Mode:

$$\text{Error}\quad \left| \ \ |4|6|\ \ \right| \quad \text{Error}$$
$$\phantom{\text{Error}}\ \ |\leftarrow \text{I } 6 \rightarrow|$$

With the value positioned in the middle of the field, the two blanks on either side of the value will be interpreted as zeros. The number will be decoded as if it had been written as:

$$\text{Error}\quad |0|0|4|6|0|0| \quad \text{Error}$$
$$\phantom{\text{Error}}\ \ |\leftarrow \text{I } 6 \rightarrow|$$

The important point to remember is that *integer values must be right justified in their respective fields.* **Right justified** means the right most digit in the number string is located in the right most column of the field containing the number. This obviously means that the correct way to keypunch our example data value is:

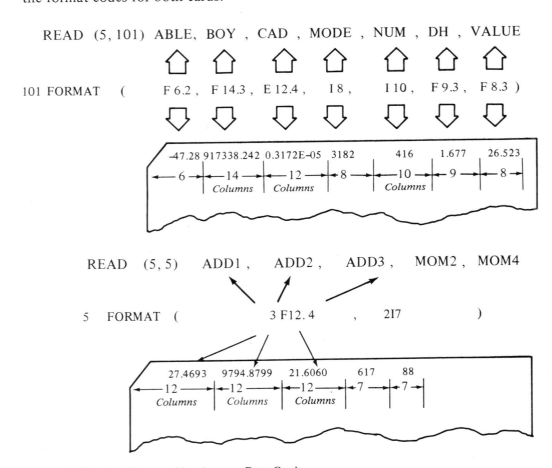

This difficulty can also occur in E-notation. Since the exponent is expressed as an integer, blanks can affect it as we will show in a later chapter. Errors such as these will not be detected by the compiler and can introduce large errors in your solution. We recommend again that you adopt the practice of using an **echo check**. That is, print values you have just read to assure they have been read properly.

This is by no means a complete explanation of these codes, but your understanding of FORMAT control is developing. As an exercise, consider the two relatively complex data cards shown in Figure 4.4. You should be able to write the format codes for both cards.

Figure 4.4 Spacing Between Numbers on Data Cards

For each data value there is a corresponding format code and a corresponding variable name. The names, the codes and the numbers must match in *mode*! If there are eight data values and only seven codes, you can expect difficulties.

4.9 | Output Statements

The advanced form of output statement is similar in form to the expanded input statement. It contains the command WRITE, followed by a pair of numbers, followed by a list of names. This statement appears in a program whenever the programmer wishes to examine the value(s) stored in any memory location(s) at the time the WRITE statement is executed.

WRITE (2, 102) XONE, XTWO, 1, A, JOB, VALUE

Command
Output
Device
Code

Format Statement Number

List

Figure 4.5 An Example Output Statement

Figure 4.6 shows the output printed on a sheet of paper resulting from the execution of the WRITE statement in Figure 4.5. Notice the output contains a series of numbers only. They have been printed as directed by the FORMAT statement:

102 FORMAT (F20.4,F16.3,I12,E20.8,I10,F14.4)

The WRITE statement causes the transfer of values from memory to the appropriate output device. The output device code specifies which output device is to receive these values. In this case, unit 2 has been specified, which is assumed to be the on-line printer.

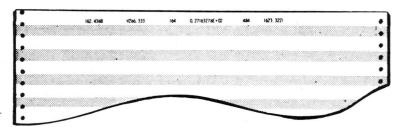

Figure 4.6 Line Printer Output Paper

The names in the list indicate which memory locations are to supply the output values, while FORMAT statement 102 controls how these values are to be converted from their *internal* form to the desired *external* form (the way they are to appear on the output sheet).

Notice again the matching in number and mode of the quantities appearing in:

1. the list of the WRITE statement,
2. the sequence of codes in the FORMAT statement, and
3. the values appearing on the output sheet.

More simply stated, if the printing of six values is desired, there must be six names in the list of the WRITE statement and a FORMAT statement with six codes to match.

Each execution of the WRITE statement causes a new line of output. Each line of output can accommodate 132 characters.* If the list of the output statement is a long list, additional lines will be automatically printed. Each line will conform to the FORMAT statement referenced in the WRITE command. As each memory location in the list of the WRITE command is examined, the corresponding FORMAT code tells how to interpret the sequence of zeros and ones that are stored in that location. An A-code, for example, signals that the binary values should be decoded as alphabetic information. An F-code would mean that the zeros and ones represent a number stored in floating-point form.

---

*The number of characters allowed in a line of output depends upon the device being used. The number 132 is a typical value of most line printers.

4.10 | Overspecify

The format codes used to control the output shown in Figure 4.6 purposely have been given very large field widths. There are two reasons for this. It avoids "over-crowding," and it avoids the possibility of "data overflow."

102 FORMAT (F20.4,F16.3,I12,E20.8,I10,F14.4)

large field width

Assume you have written a format code that just barely accommodates an output value. Later, you find the value is larger than you expected. If a small field width was used, there will not be room for the value. It will cause an overflow. Most operating systems have some way of signalling the programmer that an overflow has taken place. The most common method is to display a string of asterisks in the zone where the data value should appear. If your output contains asterisks where you expected a number to appear, check the field width for that number. It is too small. Overflows are easily avoided by using large field widths.

To understand why, let us examine how the number:

$$1\ 6\ .\ 5\ 1\ 7\ 3\ 9\ 2\ 4\ 6\ 8\ 7\ 5\ 9\ 3$$

would be taken out of memory and sent to output when an F20.4 code is used. The accuracy parameter calls for four digits to the right of the decimal. It, in effect, establishes a cut-off point as suggested below:

1 6 . 5 1 7 3 9 2 4 6 8 7 5 9 3

The parameter also controls which digits are sent to output and which are not. All digits up to and including 4 places after the decimal point will be displayed. The system software will examine digits to the right of the cut-off point to see if rounding should take place. In this case, the first digit after the cut-off point is a 9 and so the number will be presented as follows:

1 6 . 5 7 1 4

←———— 20 ————→

Overspecification of the field width will provide for ample spacing of numbers to avoid a crowded appearance when printing many values on a single line.

4.11 | Column 1

Column 1 of any line of output has a special use. It is called the **carriage control column**. The character in this column is never printed, but rather controls where on the page the line is to be placed. Sometimes we will want double or triple spacing of output lines. We may want to drop to the bottom of a page before printing the line. Frequently, it will be desirable to jump to the top of the next page before a line is printed. All this can be controlled by placing an appropriate character in the carriage control column (column 1).

Usually, we want a line of output to appear immediately after the previous line (single spacing). Having a blank in column 1 accomplishes this (causes the carriage to advance a single line). Any other character in column 1 will give some other "page positioning instruction." Overspecifying the field width of the first format code controlling any line of output usually causes column 1 to be blank.

A safer method is to start all FORMAT statements controlling output with the code "1X." This puts a blank in column 1 and will be explained later.

7 FORMAT (1X, F20.4)

4.12 | Various Forms of Input/Output Statements

There are a number of variations in the input/output statements to which most compilers will respond. The basic input command is READ, but there are several forms (levels) of this statement, as shown below:

Format Controlled:

READ (5, 7) A, B, C
READ 7, A, B, C

Free Format:

READ (5, *) A, B, C
READ *, A, B, C

The top statement is the most advanced form and exercises total control over the input operation. It specifies the input device and the format statement to be used in executing the read command. This form of the READ allows input from more than one device and in more than one form (tapes or discs – not just cards).

The next lower level READ statement specifies the controlling format statement but not the input device code. This level of input statement is frequently used when working on a terminal. The omission of a device code in this case causes the system to *assume* a device, namely, your terminal.

The "free format" versions of these statements use the asterisk in place of a format statement number. You have seen this feature before.

For each level of READ statement, there is an equivalent or corresponding level of output statement:

Format Controlled:

WRITE (2, 9) A, B, C

PRINT 9, A, B, C

Free Format:

WRITE (2, *) A, B, C
PRINT *, A, B, C

A message (string of character constants) may be included in the list of each of these output statements as suggested below.

Format Controlled:

WRITE (2, 9) 'THE ANSWERS ARE', A, B, C
PRINT 9, 'THE ANSWERS ARE', A, B, C

Free Format:

WRITE (2, *) 'THE ANSWERS ARE', A, B, C
PRINT *, 'THE ANSWERS ARE', A, B, C

This text will not dwell on all these variations. An understanding of the top level input/output commands usually allows the programmer to interpret all subordinate commands. Two brief explanations are perhaps appropriate at this time.

The command PRINT comes from an early version of the FORTRAN language when output was predominantly via the line printer. To obtain output on any other device, a different command was used. For output on the console typewriter, the command TYPE was used. To get card output, the command

PUNCH was used. As the number of output devices grew, the situation became unmanageable. A decision was made to create a universal output command, the command WRITE. The device code was then added to specify which of the many devices would be used (the printer, the card punch, etc). This explains the shift in names (WRITE and PRINT).

The 1966 FORTRAN standards required the list of variables to be transferred to output by a WRITE statement to be identified by variable name only:

WRITE (2, 9) A, B, C   variable names only

One of the features of the new standards is that they generally allow an "expression" to be substituted in almost all the instances where previously only a "variable name" was allowed. This means that the statement:

WRITE (2, 9) A + 6., B/2., C + D   expression permitted

is permitted under the new rules.

Quiz#4 FORMAT Statements

Part 1: Answer the following questions.

1. A FORMAT statement must always be numbered.
   True or False?

2. When keypunching both real and integer numbers, the number must always be right justified in the specified field. Is all or part of this true?

3. Which of the two statements that follow is true?
   (a) Each READ and each WRITE statement must have its own FORMAT statement which must immediately follow the READ/WRITE statement.
   (b) A FORMAT statement may be used by more than one READ or WRITE statement and the location of the FORMAT statement is not restricted to being immediately after the READ/WRITE statement.

4. The number of characters allowed in a line of output is the same for all output devices.

5. What will be the value of I,J,K and L if they are read as follows:

   READ(5,10)I,J,K,L
   10 FORMAT(2I3,I1,I4)

   6 1 7 6 0 3 5 9 1 2

6. Overspecifying the "field width" in all format codes avoids two possible difficulties. What are they?

7. What is the special purpose of column 1 of any line of output?

8. The usual output command is the word WRITE. Is this the only output command? Give examples.

9. Is the following WRITE statement allowed by *all* FORTRAN compilers?

   WRITE(2,9)A+1.,B*C,D**2

10. What is the purpose of the "1X" code written in the following FORMAT statement?

WRITE(2,10)A,B,C
10   FORMAT(1X,F8.1,2F10.2)

Part 2: Writing a Program (Roulette: Placing A Bet)

11.–20.

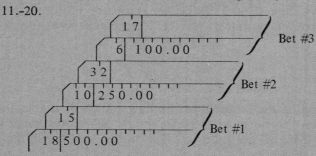

Each pair of cards in the following data deck represent a bet made at the roulette table.

CARD 1

Col.	Meaning	Example	
1–2	Number being played	1 8	← This card
3–10	Amount of wager	5 0 0 . 0 0	describes the bet

CARD 2

Col.	Meaning	Example	
1–2	Winning Number	1 3	← This card tells the winning number

Write a program to read these cards and process the bet. If the winning number comes up, the payoff is 35 to 1.

Answers:

1. True.

2. Integer numbers only.

3. b

4. False

5. I = 617   J = 603   K = 5   L = 9120
   (Note: L not right justified. Blank causes ending zero)

6. Overcrowding; data overflow

7. Carriage Control Column — tells *where* line is to be printed.

8. No. PRINT, TYPE, PUNCH

9. No. Some FORTRAN compilers only allow variable names.

10. Put a blank in the carriage control column.

```
11.  C        PURPOSE-PROCESS CARDS REPRESENTING BET AT A
     C                 ROULETTE TABLE.
     C
     C              — IMPORTANT VARIABLES —
     C
     C        — NUMBER   NUMBER BEING PLAYED
     C        — AMOUNT   AMOUNT OF WAGER
     C        — WINNER   WINNING NUMBER
     C        — PAYOFF   AMOUNT TO BE PAID
     C
              INTEGER WINNER
     C
        10    READ(5,20)NUMBER,AMOUNT
        20    FORMAT(I2,F8.2)
     C
              READ(5,30)WINNER
        30    FORMAT(I2)
     C
              IF(NUMBER.EQ.WINNER)PAYOFF=35.0*AMOUNT
              IF(NUMBER.NE.WINNER)PAYOFF=0.0
     C
              WRITE(2,40)NUMBER,WINNER,PAYOFF
        40    FORMAT(1X,2I6,F14.2)
     C
              GO TO 10
     C
              END
```

Review Exercises

1. Describe the data values being specified by the following format codes:

   (a) I7   (b) F8.2   (c) A4

   (d) E14.4   (e) 3I10   (f) 2A6

2. What do the terms "field width" and "accuracy parameter" mean?

3. How would the following value appear on output if controlled by the codes shown?

       3 . 1 4 1 5 9 2 6 5 3 5 8 9 7 9

   (a) F16.4 |⎵⎵⎵⎵⎵⎵⎵⎵⎵⎵⎵⎵⎵⎵⎵⎵⎵⎵⎵⎵⎵⎵⎵⎵⎵|

   (b) F16.2 |⎵⎵⎵⎵⎵⎵⎵⎵⎵⎵⎵⎵⎵⎵⎵⎵⎵⎵⎵⎵⎵⎵⎵⎵⎵|

   (c) F16.8 |⎵⎵⎵⎵⎵⎵⎵⎵⎵⎵⎵⎵⎵⎵⎵⎵⎵⎵⎵⎵⎵⎵⎵⎵⎵|

   (d) F8.7 |⎵⎵⎵⎵⎵⎵⎵⎵⎵⎵|

4. *What does the presence of a string of asterisks signal in a line of output?

5. Why is it a good idea to use large field widths when printing a line of output?

6. *Describe the carriage control character. What character causes single spacing?

7. What does the term "free format" mean?

8. Show several ways (levels) an input statement may be written.

9. *What is the purpose of the "input device code"?

10. How could you cause output to be sent to a magnetic tape unit or to the console typewriter?

11. What are "repeat codes"?

12. Show several ways (levels) an output statement may be written.

13. In the format statement:

    17 FORMAT (1X,I10,3F8.4)

    what does the first code, 1X, accomplish and why is it being used?

14. What are the *minimum* format codes for the following values:

    63.24 to -123.7178

    164 to -12

    -7.283E5 to -8.416E-12

15. How many columns are there on the line printer? Do all devices have the same character capability (line width)? Are they all available for displaying output values?

16. Assume you are printing 8 real numbers whose ranges are:

$$728.1947 \text{ to } -16.5283$$

Write a FORMAT statement that will cause these values to be spread approximately equally across the output page.

17. When keypunching a data card, is it true that spacing is unimportant as long as the value is punched within the specified field width?

18. What does the term "echo check" mean? What is it used for?

19. What does the term "right justified" mean? Must all input and all output be right justified?

20. What does the term "word size" mean?

21. What happens when a device code is not specified?

22. If you do not provide a FORMAT statement in a READ command, what do you use in place of the statement number?

23. Give an example of a system-dependent feature.

24. Why is it a good idea to overspecify the field width when outputting a group of numbers?

Additional Applications

Programming Example
Hit-and-Run Driver

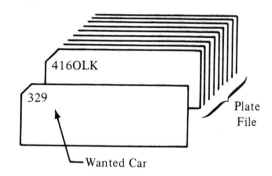

Assume that license plates in your state have a three digit number followed by three letters of the alphabet. Assume further that the victim of a hit and run accident was able to get only the first three numbers of the runaway car (see first card in the data deck). Write a program to search the file of all registered cars and print all those that start with the three digit number of the wanted car.

(1X, I3, A3)

```
C..........................................................
C..   PURPOSE -   READ HEADER CARD AND SEARCH FOR        ..
C..               HIT AND RUN DRIVER.                    ..
C..........................................................
C
C                 -----IMPORTANT VARIABLES-----
C
C        --NUMBER VARIABLE HOLDING THE FIRST THREE NUMBERS   --
C                 OF A LICENSE PLATE
C        --LETTER VARIABLE HOLDING THE LAST THREE ALPHABETIC  --
C                 CHARACTERS OF A LICENSE PLATE
C        --WANTED FIRST THREE NUMBERS OF WANTED CAR           --
C
C        INTEGER WANTED
C
           READ(5,10)WANTED
        10 FORMAT(I3)
C
C                **** SEARCH LOOP FOLLOWS ****
C
        20 READ(5,30)NUMBER,LETTER
        30 FORMAT(I3,A3)
C
           IF(NUMBER.EQ.WANTED)WRITE(2,40)NUMBER,LETTER
        40 FORMAT(1X,I3,A3)
C
           GO TO 20
C
           END
```

Programming Example
Restock the Shelves

A large department store needs a program written to assist in reordering items when the stock level gets low.

Each item the store sells is given a stock number, which appears in columns 1-5 of a data card. The next three numbers on the card tell: 1. NOW — How many units now in stock. 2. LOW — How low the stock should get before reordering. 3. MORE — How many units are ordered when restocking.

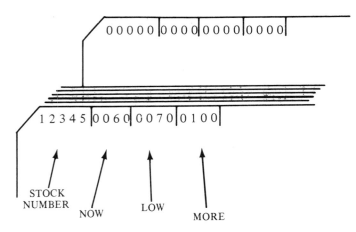

STOCK
NUMBER   NOW   LOW   MORE

Write a program to print out the stock number and order size of all items the store is low on. There is a data card at the end of the data deck containing zeros in all of its fields. Such a card is referred to as a **trailer card**. The program tests for its presence every time it reads a data card in order to detect the end of the data deck.

```
C...................................................................
C..    PURPOSE - CHECK INVENTORY LEVEL OF STOCK....IF STOCK  ..
C..    LEVEL TOO LOW.....REORDER.                            ..
C...................................................................
C
C                   -------IMPORTANT VARIABLES-------
C
C      --NUMBER      STOCK NUMBER OF EACH ITEM                --
C      --LOW         MINIMUM LEVEL BEFORE REORDERING          --
C      --NOW         PRESENT LEVEL OF STOCK                   --
C      --MORE        ORDER SIZE WHEN REORDERING THIS ITEM     --
C
C              ...........INITIALIZATION SECTION..............
C
   10  READ(5,11) NUMBER,NOW,LOW,MORE
   11  FORMAT(I5,I4,I4,I4)
C
C              IS THIS THE TRAILER CARD
C
       IF(NUMBER.EQ.0) STOP
C
C              SEE IF STOCK LEVEL TOO LOW
C
   20  IF (NOW.LT.LOW) WRITE(2,21)NUMBER,MORE
   21  FORMAT(1X,I10,I12)
C
C              CONTINUE SEARCH
       GO TO 10
C
       END
```

**Programming Example
Restock – Different
Method**

It is the responsibility of a store manager to monitor the stock level of the various items in his or her store. The table below shows the reorder point of various items. If the stock on hand falls below the reorder point a replacement order for the amount shown in the table should be made.

REORDER POINTS		
Item Number	Reorder Point	Quantity To Order
0125	100	200
0136	1200	5000
6273	50	100
6281	120	180
6294	4000	7000

The first card in a data deck contains the item number and present stock level of a product that appears to be running low.

Each of the remaining cards in the data deck represents a line in the table of reorder points.

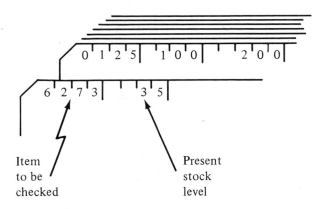

Item to be checked

Present stock level

Write a program to search the table for the item being checked and print one of two messages:

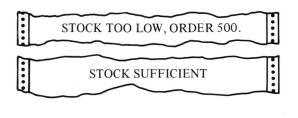

STOCK TOO LOW, ORDER 500.

STOCK SUFFICIENT

```
C......................................................
C..    PURPOSE -   SEARCH TABLE OF REORDER POINTS - INDICATE ..
C..               IF STOCK LEVEL IS SUFFICIENT              ..
C......................................................
C
C              -----IMPORTANT VARIABLES-----
C
C    --CHECK  ITEM NUMBER OF STOCK BEING CHECKED        --
C    --PRESNT PRESENT STOCK LEVEL OF THIS ITEM          --
C
C    --ITEM   ITEM NUMBER OF VARIOUS TABLE ENTRIES      --
C    --LOWEST REORDER POINT OF THIS ITEM                --
C    --MORE   QUANTITY TO ORDER WHEN REORDERING         --
C
     INTEGER PRESNT,CHECK
C
C              READ HEADER CARD --- PICK UP SEARCH VALUE
C
     READ(5,10)CHECK,PRESNT
  10 FORMAT(2I4)
C
C              SEARCH LOOP STARTS HERE
C
  20 READ(5,30)ITEM,LOWEST,MORE
  30 FORMAT(2I4,I5)
C
C
     IF(CHECK.NE.ITEM)GO TO 20
C
C              ITEM WE WANT HAS BEEN FOUND
C
     IF(PRESNT.LE.LOWEST)WRITE(2,*)'STOCK TOO LOW, ORDER ',MORE
     IF(PRESNT.GT.LOWEST)WRITE(2,*)'STOCK SUFFICIENT'
C
     STOP
     END
```

**Programming Example
Cost to Recall**

A large manufacturer of air conditioners may have to recall some units. The malfunction of a welding machine has caused all Model 125 air conditioners manufactured during the latter part of 1982 to have weak supports.

The data deck shown describes all shipments from the plant during 1982.

Write statements that will read the information of these cards. Store the year and month of the shipping date in memory locations called YEAR and MONTH.

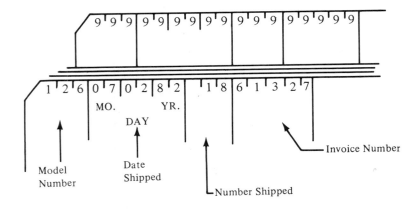

STATEMENT NUMBER			FORTRAN STATEMENT														
1	5	6	7	10	15	20	25	30	35	40	45	50	55	60	65	70	
			INTEGER DAY, YEAR													
			READ(5,7)MODEL, MONTH, DAY, YEAR, NUM, INVOC													
	7		FORMAT(I3, I2, I2, I3, I5)													

The end of the data deck is signalled by a trailer card having 9's in all zones. Write statements that will stop the program when the value 99 appears in memory location YEAR.

			IF(YEAR.EQ.99) STOP							

Write a complete program that will print the invoice number, date of shipment and number of units shipped for all Model 125 units shipped during the last 6 months of 1982.

```
C.........PURPOSE - SEARCH FOR FAULTY AIR CONDITIONERS........
C..                                                          ..
C.............................................................
C
C                   ------IMPORTANT VARIABLES-------
C
C        --MODEL      MODEL NUMBER OF AIR CONDITIONERS      --
C        --DAY        DAY UNITS WERE SHIPPED                --
C        --MONTH      MONTH UNITS WERE SHIPPED              --
C        --YEAR       YEAR UNITS WERE SHIPPED               --
C        --NUM        NUMBER OF UNITS SHIPPED               --
C        --INVOC      INVOICE NUMBER OF SHIPMENT            --
C
         INTEGER DAY, YEAR
C
C               ....LOOP START HERE....
C
   10    READ(5,11)MODEL, MONTH, DAY, YEAR, NUM, INVOC
   11    FORMAT(I3,I2,I2,I2,I3,I5)
C
C                    IS THIS THE TRAILER CARD
         IF(YEAR.EQ.99)STOP
C
C                    IS THIS THE MODEL NUMBER WE ARE LOOKING FOR
         IF(MODEL.NE.125) GO TO 10
C
C                    MANUFACTURED IN 1982
         IF (YEAR.NE.82) GO TO 10
C
C                    MANUFACTURED IN FIRST HALF OF YEAR
         IF (MONTH.LE.6) GO TO 10
C
C        .......FAULTY UNIT LOCATED...........
C
   20    WRITE(2,21) INVOC, MONTH, DAY, YEAR, NUM
   21    FORMAT(1X,I15,I12,I6,I6,I13)
C
C        .......LOOP ENDS HERE.............
C
         GO TO 10
C
         END
```

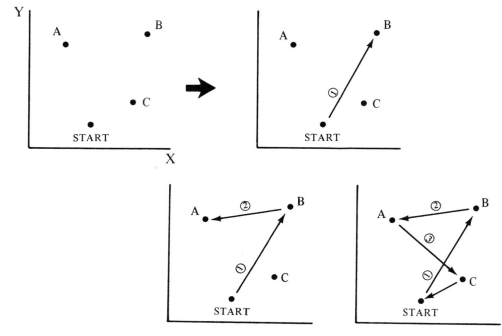

B – A – C SEQUENCE

A truck driver must leave the warehouse and make deliveries at points A, B and C (shown above) and then return to the warehouse.

This program will help the driver determine in what sequence he should travel the route to keep the distance traveled at a minimum.

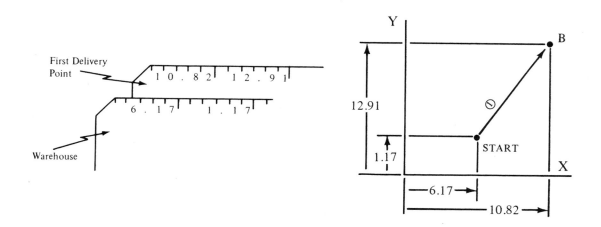

Part A – First Leg

The first two cards of a data deck give the X and Y locations of the warehouse followed by the X and Y locations of the first delivery point.

Write a program to:

    (a) Determine the difference in the X coordinates of these two points.
    (b) Determine the difference in the Y coordinates of these two points.
    (c) Determine the distance separating these point.

```
C.......................................................
C::    PURPOSE -   DETERMINE DISTANCE OF FIRST LEG      ::
C::              OF DRIVER'S ROUTE.                     ::
C.......................................................
C
C               -----IMPORTANT VARIABLES-----
C
C      --X0,Y0  X AND Y LOCATION OF THE START POINT      --
C      --X1,Y1  X AND Y LOCATION OF FIRST DELIVERY POINT --
C
       READ(5,10)X0,Y0
    10 FORMAT(2F6.2)
C
       READ(5,10)X1,Y1
C
       XDIFF=X1-X0
       YDIFF=Y1-Y0
C
       DIST=(XDIFF**2+YDIFF**2)**0.5
C
       WRITE(2,20)DIST
    20 FORMAT(1X,F10.2)
C
```

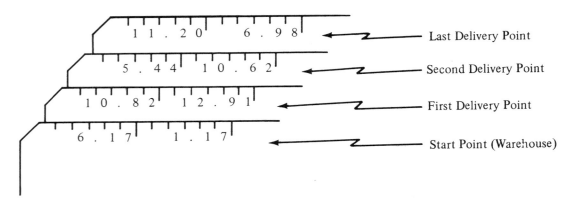

11.20   6.98 ←──── Last Delivery Point

5.44   10.62 ←──── Second Delivery Point

10.82   12.91 ←──── First Delivery Point

6.17   1.17 ←──── Start Point (Warehouse)

Part B:

Expand the previous program to allow the X and Y coordinates of the remaining pick-up points to be added to the data deck. The program should now determine the total distance that must be travelled. *By alternating the sequence of pick-up points, the best route can be found.*

```
C
C                   ---- NEW VARIABLES ----
C
C      --X2,Y2  X AND Y LOCATION OF SECOND DELIVERY POINT --
C      --X3,Y3  X AND Y LOCATION OF THIRD DELIVERY POINT  --
C
       READ(5,10)X0,Y0
       READ(5,10)X1,Y1
       READ(5,10)X2,Y2
       READ(5,10)X3,Y3
C
C               COMPUTE FOUR DISTANCES
C
       DIST1=((X1-X0)**2+(Y1-Y0)**2)**0.5
       DIST2=((X2-X1)**2+(Y2-Y1)**2)**0.5
       DIST3=((X3-X2)**2+(Y3-Y2)**2)**0.5
       DIST4=((X0-X3)**2+(Y0-Y3)**2)**0.5
C
C               COMPUTE TOTAL DISTANCE
C
       DIST=DIST1+DIST2+DIST3+DIST4
C
       WRITE(2,30)DIST
    30 FORMAT(1X,F10.2)
C
       STOP
       END
```

| **Programming Example**
Computing
Resistance** | A data card gives the value of 3 resistors used in an electric circuit. |

120.   300.   50.   2

R_1 R_2 R_3 Which circuit

The total resistance of the circuit depends on the way in which the resistors are joined together (series, parallel, or series-parallel).

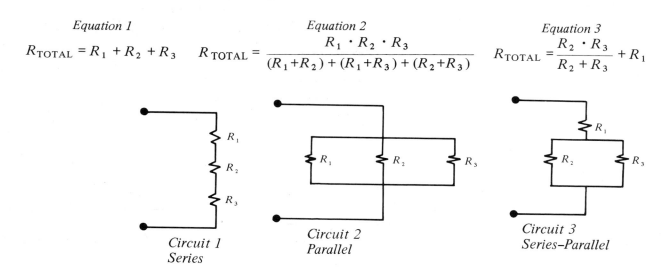

Equation 1

$$R_{TOTAL} = R_1 + R_2 + R_3$$

Equation 2

$$R_{TOTAL} = \frac{R_1 \cdot R_2 \cdot R_3}{(R_1+R_2) + (R_1+R_3) + (R_2+R_3)}$$

Equation 3

$$R_{TOTAL} = \frac{R_2 \cdot R_3}{R_2 + R_3} + R_1$$

Circuit 1
Series

Circuit 2
Parallel

Circuit 3
Series–Parallel

The last value on the data card is the number 1, 2, or 3 and tells which of the three circuits is being used. Compute and report the appropriate total resistance.

```
C..........................................................
C..    PURPOSE - COMPUTE RESISTANCE IN ONE OF THREE POSSIBLE..
C..            CIRCUITS.                                   ..
C..........................................................
C
C                 -----IMPORTANT VARIABLES-----
C
C      --R1,R2,R3    RESISTANCE VALUES                        --
C      --KODE        INTEGER TELLING WHICH TYPE CIRCUIT       --
C      --               1 = SERIES
C      --               2 = PARALLEL
C      --               3 = SERIES-PARALLEL
C      --RTOTAL     TOTAL RRSISTANCE OF CIRCUIT               --
C
       READ(5,10) R1, R2, R3, KODE
   10 FORMAT(3F9.1,I2)
C
C              TEST FOR APPROPRIATE EQUATION
C
       IF(KODE.EQ.1) RTOTAL = R1+R2+R3
       IF(KODE.EQ.3) RTOTAL = R1*R2*R3/((R1+R2)+(R1+R3)+(R2+R3))
       IF(KODE.EQ.3) RTOTAL = R1+R2*R3/(R2+R3)
C
       WRITE(2,20) RTOTAL
   20 FORMAT(1X,F19.2)
C
       STOP
       END
```

5 | Elementary Control Statements

By numerous examples we have shown that the computer processes statements in the order of their appearance. This means that the programmer first exercises control over the sequence in which statements are executed by the order in which the statements appear in the instruction deck. If this "one-after-another" sequence was the only control available, programs would be highly inflexible. Only one straight path of solution would be possible.

5.1 | Control Statements - GO TO

Control statements allow the programmer to interrupt this "one-after-another" processing for the purpose of making the program more dynamic and, therefore, more useful. One of the more common control statements is the GO TO statement:

GO TO n

It contains the command GO TO followed by a statement number that serves as a label.

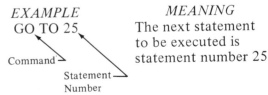

EXAMPLE
GO TO 25

Command
Statement
Number

MEANING
The next statement
to be executed is
statement number 25

The number identifies where in the program control is to be passed when this statement is executed.

Notice that this statement produces an *unconditional* transfer of control. By this we mean there is no testing or decision involved. When this statement is reached, control is *always* passed to the statement identified after the command GO TO. The transfer can be either forward or backward in the program.

A GO TO frequently appears in the bottom of a block of FORTRAN code for the purpose of passing control back to the top of the block, thereby establishing a *loop* in the program.

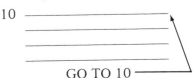

10

GO TO 10

5.2 | Logical IF

More often than not, the transfer of control needs to be *conditional,* that is, based on some decision or test:

– has hours worked exceeded 40?
– has the balance dropped below zero?
– is X greater than 10?

While most programs have a normal path of logic, a *general program* must accommodate all possible variations and alternatives. Conditional control statements, such as the logical IF, allow us to test for these special conditions and transfer control to that point in the program written to handle the particular situation.

A typical example is as follows:

<u>IF</u>	<u>(X. GT. 10.0)</u>	<u>GO TO 5</u>
Command	Control Quantity (Logical Expression)	Dependent Statement

There are three parts to this statement. The command IF identifies the statement and signals a possible interrupt. What follows next is a "logical expression" contained within parentheses. This expression has two possible values, "true" or "false." If the expression is evaluated as true, the dependent statement will be recognized (executed); otherwise, it will be ignored. If the dependent statement is ignored, no interruption takes place and normal processing resumes.

The "true/false" value of the logical expression serves as a control quantity for a two-way branch, that is, to determine which of two statements will be executed next:

true ⟶ execute the statement to the right of the logical IF.

false ⟶ execute the statement below the logical IF.

General Form

IF   (logical expression)   **Dependent Statement**

Some examples are:

IF(X.EQ.3.5)STOP
IF(HOURS.LT.40.)PAY=HOURS*RATE
IF(AVERAGE.GT.90.)WRITE(2,8)NAME
IF(TEMP.LT.32.0)GO TO 12

Observe that the statement appearing to the right of the logical IF is *not* restricted to a control statement. It can be almost any statement. It cannot, however, be another logical IF (or a DO statement, which we will be covering shortly).

It may be helpful to think of the logical expression as a switch placed in front of the dependent statement. If the logical expression is true, the switch is on and the statement becomes part of your program. If the expression is false, the switch is off and the statement is ignored.

5.3 | Constructing Logical Expressions

The symbols used in mathematics to describe the relationship of one quantity to another are shown in the left-hand column of the table below.

Relational Operators

=	.EQ.	equal
≠	.NE.	not equal
>	.GT.	greater than
<	.LT.	less than
⩾	.GE.	greater than or equal to
⩽	.LE.	less than or equal to

In mathematics, we say that one quantity is "greater than" or "less than" or "not equal to" another. For each of these mathematical symbols, the equivalent FORTRAN symbol (relational operator) consists of two letters preceded and followed by a period. You have used symbols such as +, –, *, / to construct arithmetic expressions. The symbols .EQ., .GT., .LT., etc. will be used to construct logical expressions. These symbols are easy to remember and are included in the summary charts on the back cover for easy reference.

It is important that you realize the full potential of the logical IF. It is used in banking problems, calculus problems, aircraft loading problems, medical problems, etc. The following table shows some sample uses to suggest just how versatile the statement is:

Sample IF Statements and Their Uses

Aircraft Loading	IF(WEIGHT.GT.9000.)STOP	Is the aircraft overloaded (cargo weight greater than 9000 lbs.)
Water Treatment	IF(TEMP.LT.32.0)Y=1.68*H	Has the temperature of water dropped below freezing?
Trig Problem	IF(ANGLE.EQ.90.)GO TO 5	Are we dealing with a right triangle?
Missile Control	IF(ALT.LE.0.0)STOP	Is the missile still airborn or has it crashed?
Slope of a Line	IF(Y2.GT.Y1)WRITE(2,8)Y1	Is the slope of a line positive?
Banking Problem	IF(DEBIT.GT.CREDIT)GO TO 6	Is the account overspent?
Medical Problem	IF(PRES.GT.134.)WRITE(2,8)NAME	Is the patient's blood pressure greater than normal?

5.4 | Compound IF Statements

The majority of IF tests are as simple as those suggested thus far. There are occasions, however, when more complex testing is required. These more complicated tests are merely a sequence of simple tests joined together by the .AND. operator or the .OR. operator.

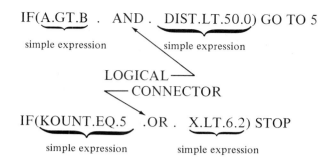

The two most common connectors are .AND. and .OR. When the .AND. operator is used, the two expressions it connects must *both* be true for the compound expression to be true.

IF(TYPE.EQ.3..AND.DIST.LT.50.0) GO TO 5

In this example, TYPE must be equal to 3, and the value of DIST must be less than 50 for the expression to be evaluated as true.

When the .OR. operator is used, the complex expression is true if *either* (or both) of the simple expressions is true.

IF(KOUNT.EQ.5.OR.X.LT.0.0) STOP

The STOP statement will be executed when:

(a) KOUNT equals 5, or

(b) X is less than zero, or

(c) KOUNT equals 5 and X is less than zero.

It is possible to construct even more complex logical expressions. We will cover this later. For the moment, keep your logical expressions as simple as possible.

5.5 | Flow Charts

As the number and complexity of control statements in a program increases, there is a corresponding increase in the number of alternate paths through the program's logic. Attempting to trace each loop and each branch can be an overpowering task for the programmer and for anyone attempting to use the program. We need some sort of "road map" to assure the correct passage of control for each branch in the logic.

Pseudocode diagrams provide a little "path" information, but not in the right form. They are verbose, awkward and difficult to read. A more abbreviated and direct means of symbolically representing the program's algorithm is described below.

Flow charts are schematic diagrams that use a set of symbols (see Figure 5.1) to display in a highly graphical form the executable statements of a program. Each symbol suggests the type of statement being used and shows how control can be passed to and from that statement by one or more arrows connected to the symbol.

The flow chart is in effect a "short hand" representation of the logic originated in the pseudocode. You will soon find it to be an indispensable tool for planning, designing and checking complex programs.

SYMBOL	MEANING	SYMBOL	MEANING
⬭	PROGRAM START/STOP	◇	DECISION STATEMENT
▱	GENERAL INPUT/OUTPUT	▭	PROCESSING STEP
▱	PUNCHED CARD INPUT/OUTPUT	→	DIRECTION OF FLOW
▱	LINE PRINTER OUTPUT	○	CONTINUATION POINT

Figure 5.1 Flow Chart Symbols

Before getting heavily involved in this subject, take a moment to familiarize yourself with the individual symbols.

The oval shows the beginning and end of a program.

Input by cards and output on the line printer are represented by these easily-remembered symbols (a card and a sheet of output paper).

The parallelogram is the generalized input/output symbol. It represents input/output in any form — tapes, cards, disc, terminals.

The diamond represents a decision-making statement, a logical IF, for example.

The rectangle represents a processing step, usually an arithmetic assignment statement.

The direction of flow (possible paths) is shown by lines and arrows.

The small circle is used to connect two points on a diagram that, for some reason, cannot conveniently be connected by lines; for example, when the diagram carries over onto another page.

A well-constructed flow diagram shows much more than just the possible paths through the program. A flow diagram displays each variable name chosen to represent input, output and intermediate values. It indicates each important equation and all decision-making factors. This diagram along with a well-documented program is usually all that is needed to describe even the most complex problem. Read the next programming example and see if you do not agree.

**Programming Example
Volume Discount**

To encourage sales, a wholesale distributor offers its customers a discount if they buy in volume (6 items or more). The larger the order, the larger the discount

Number Purchased	Discount
1–5	no discount
6–10	10%
11–20	16%
21 or more	20%

Discount Policy

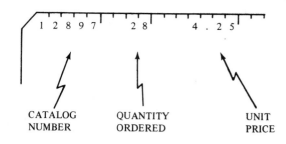

CATALOG NUMBER   QUANTITY ORDERED   UNIT PRICE

(see table above). Each order received is represented by a data card. The card gives the catalog number of the item ordered, number of units ordered, and the unit price (cost before discount). Write a program to determine what discount is allowed for this size order, and provide the information needed for a packing slip that will be shipped with the order.

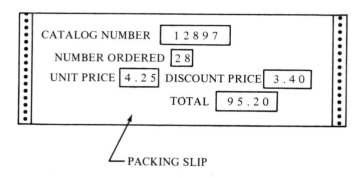

PACKING SLIP

The flow diagram shown on p. 103 suggests that the program starts with a READ statement followed by a series of IF tests that determine which discount level to use. Control passes to one of four statements that sets the appropriate discount rate. After the discount is established, control is transferred to a series of closing statements that compute the total bill, print the output and terminate the program. The numbers placed near a flow chart symbol correspond to a statement number that will be used in writing the program. These tie the program and the chart closer together.

Take a moment and look at the numerous comment statements used in this program. They make the logic easy to follow.

Programming Style
Use Comment Statements: Make Them Meaningful

Comment statements are an important tool to:

(1) provide assistance in reading the program,
(2) isolating and identifying important segments of modules of the program.
(3) showing the program's structure.

Comment statements should be used frequently, but should *not* be direct copies of the FORTRAN code:

```
C   READ X FROM DATA
    READ (5, 12) X
```

Such comment statements are not very meaningful.

Another feature of this program, a *bad* one, is the number of GO TO state-

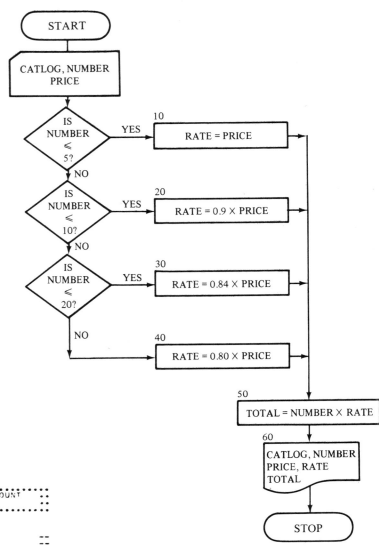

```
C.....................................................
C..    PURPOSE -     TO DETERMINE THE APPROPRIATE DISCOUNT    ..
C..                  WHEN ITEMS ARE PURCHED IN VOLUME.        ..
C.....................................................
C
C         -----IMPORTANT VARIABLES-----
C
C     --CATLOG      CATALOG NUMBER OF ITEM                --
C     --NUMBER      QUANTITY OF ITEMS ORDERED             --
C     --PRICE       UNIT PRICE PRIOR TO DISCOUNT          --
C     --RATE        UNIT PRICE AFTER DISCOUNT             --
C     --TOTAL       TOTAL COST OF UNITS ORDERED           --
C
      INTEGER CATLOG
C
    5 READ(5,6) CATLOG, NUMBER, PRICE
    6 FORMAT(I5,I4,F7.2)
C
C         .....SELECT CORRECT CATEGORY.....
C
      IF(NUMBER.LE.5)  GO TO 10
      IF(NUMBER.LE.10) GO TO 20
      IF(NUMBER.LE.20) GO TO 30
      IF(NUMBER.GT.20) GO TO 40
C
C         .....LEVEL 1 DISCOUNT CATEGORY.....
C
   10 RATE=PRICE
      GO TO 50
C
C         .....LEVEL 2 DISCOUNT CATEGORY.....
C
   20 RATE= 0.90 * PRICE
      GO TO 50
C
C         .....LEVEL 3 DISCOUNT CATEGORY.....
C
   30 RATE= 0.84 * PRICE
      GO TO 50
C
C         .....LEVEL 4 DISCOUNT CATEGORY.....
C
   40 RATE= 0.80 * PRICE
C
C         -----TERMINATION SECTION-----
C
   50 TOTAL = NUMBER * RATE
C
      WRITE(2,60) CATLOG,NUMBER,PRICE,RATE,TOTAL
   60 FORMAT (1X,I16,I20,3F12.2)
C
      GO TO 5
C
  100 STOP
      END
```

ments used. There are 7 of them. Very often this is a signal that the program logic is weak and could be improved.

**Programming Style
Don't Patch Bad
Code: Rewrite It** ▌▌ There are many signals that show that a program's logic is not working out well (excessive GO TO's is one). Making superficial changes to "patch things up" is a mistake. Reexamine the logic. Rewrite the code.

With this recommendation in mind, let us rewrite the program with fewer GO TO statements. Notice that this version of the program has only one GO TO statement. Here the transfer of control is more direct (linear in fashion). This makes a better program.

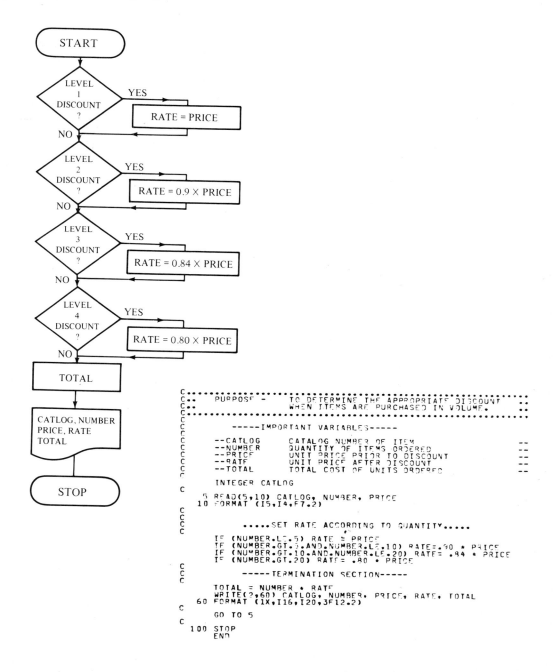

```
C...............................................................
C..    PURPOSE -   TO DETERMINE THE APPROPRIATE DISCOUNT      ..
C..               WHEN ITEMS ARE PURCHASED IN VOLUME.         ..
C...............................................................
C
C         -----IMPORTANT VARIABLES-----
C
C     --CATLOG     CATALOG NUMBER OF ITEM                      --
C     --NUMBER     QUANTITY OF ITEMS ORDERED                   --
C     --PRICE      UNIT PRICE PRIOR TO DISCOUNT                --
C     --RATE       UNIT PRICE AFTER DISCOUNT                   --
C     --TOTAL      TOTAL COST OF UNITS ORDERED                 --
C
      INTEGER CATLOG
C
    5 READ(5,10) CATLOG, NUMBER, PRICE
   10 FORMAT (I5,I4,F7.2)
C
C         .....SET RATE ACCORDING TO QUANTITY.....
C
      IF (NUMBER.LE.5) RATE = PRICE
      IF (NUMBER.GT.5.AND.NUMBER.LE.10) RATE=.90 * PRICE
      IF (NUMBER.GT.10.AND.NUMBER.LE.20) RATE= .84 * PRICE
      IF (NUMBER.GT.20) RATE= .80 * PRICE
C
C         -----TERMINATION SECTION-----
C
      TOTAL = NUMBER * RATE
      WRITE(2,60) CATLOG, NUMBER, PRICE, RATE, TOTAL
   60 FORMAT (1X,I16,I20,3F12.2)
C
      GO TO 5
C
  100 STOP
      END
```

5.6 | Arithmetic IF

There is another type of IF test called the *arithmetic* IF. It uses an *arithmetic* expression instead of a logical expression as the decision making or control quantity.

$$\underbrace{IF}_{\text{Command}} \qquad \underbrace{(B**2-4.*A*C)}_{\substack{\text{Arithmetic}\\\text{Expression}}} \; \underbrace{8,10,7}_{\substack{\text{Statement}\\\text{Numbers}}}$$

(Possible Branch Points)

While logical expressions have two possible values (true or false), an arithmetic IF has three possible values (negative, zero or positive). When an arithmetic IF is encountered, control is passed to one of three possible points (statements), which are identified to the right of the arithmetic expression. If the expression is evaluated and found negative, control is passed to the first of the three statement numbers shown. If the expression is positive, control is passed to the last statement. If the expression is identically equal to zero, control passes to the middle statement number.

The Logical IF Provides a Two-Way Branch   The Arithmetic IF Provides a Three-Way Branch

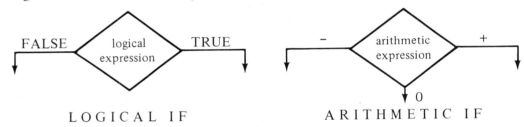

LOGICAL IF   ARITHMETIC IF

Occasionally, the arithmetic IF can be a useful statement. At one time, it was the only IF test in the FORTRAN language. Today, it is considered somewhat outdated because it produces an overly disruptive interruption in the program logic. It is necessary that you be able to recognize this statement and understand how it functions. Its general use is *not* recommended, however.

Given here is an example of an arithmetic IF:

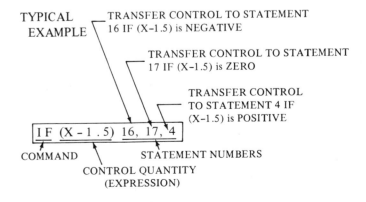

Special Section

One of the important features of the new FORTRAN standards is that they introduce statements that allow a program to be written with a good deal more finesse than was previously possible. By finesse, we mean in a more logical and orderly fashion. Take, for example, the IF tests just described. Using an arithmetic IF produces up to three erratic branches that are difficult to follow. While the logical IF is a considerable improvement, it has its disadvantage: it only allows one statement to be executed if the logical expression is true. If several statements are to be executed, a disruptive branch must be taken.

The IF-THEN-ELSE statement is an extension of the logical IF. It allows a whole group of statements to be executed if the logical expression is "true" and an alternate group of statements to be executed if the expression is "false."

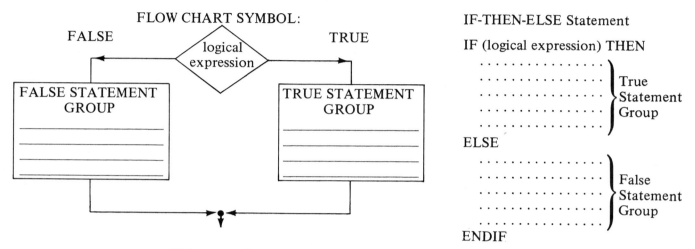

This control statement is somewhat different in that it is written on three separate lines. It consists of the following parts:

(1) IF (logical expression) THEN- the *header* portion used to identify the top of the statement and its type.

(2) ELSE–a separator used to separate the "TRUE" statement group from the "FALSE" statement group.

(3) ENDIF–the terminator to identify the end point of this control statement.

Example Use

Read two values, A and B, from data. Determine which is the larger value and which is the smaller value. Store results as BIG and SMALL.

```
C.................................................
C..   PURPOSE - DEMONSTRATE IF-THEN-ELSE STATEMENT..
C.................................................
C
    5 READ(5,10) A, B
   10 FORMAT (2F8.1)
C
C
      IF (A.GT.B) THEN
C
          BIG = A
          SMALL = B
C
      ELSE
C
          BIG = B
          SMALL = A
C
      ENDIF
C
      WRITE (2,15) BIG, SMALL
   15 FORMAT (1X,F8.1,10X,F8.1)
C
      GO TO 5
C
      END
```

Additional Examples

Example #1

The average of a class on a recent exam is stored in a memory location called AVE. Determine how many points must be added to each student's grade to make sure the class average is at least 65.

```
IF(AVE.GE.65.0) THEN
    ADD = 0.0
ELSE
    ADD = 65.0 – AVE
ENDIF
```

Example #2

A variable called DOLLAR represents a deposit if it is positive or withdrawal if it is negative. Use an IF-THEN-ELSE statement to execute a WRITE statement declaring the type of transaction.

```
IF(DOLLAR.GT.0.0) THEN
    WRITE(2,*)'DEPOSIT. . . . .', DOLLAR
ELSE
    WRITE(2,*)'WITHDRAWAL..', DOLLAR
ENDIF
```

Example #3

Write an IF-THEN-ELSE statement that loads a memory location called Y with the absolute (positive) value of X.

```
IF(X.GE.0.0) THEN
    Y=X
ELSE
    Y= –X
ENDIF
```

Coverage of the more advanced features of the FORTRAN 77 standards will be presented in the later chapters of this text. This particular feature is so important, however, that an exception is being made. If your compiler allows this statement, you should by all means use it. Read sections 16.3 and 16.4 for a more complete explanation of this statement.

5.7 | Common Control Activity: Counting / Deck Control

After you have written a number of programs, you will detect that certain activities keep recurring. The first of these is **deck control**. Almost all programs involve some sort of deck control. This means making sure that the command READ is executed only as many times as there are cards in the data deck. You may be told, for example, there are 40 cards in the data deck (fixed size deck). Another possibility is that a card is positioned at the front of the deck declaring the deck size for this run of the program. Both of these situations involve counting. *Deck control and counting are recurring activities in programming.*

Programming Style
Separate the Familiar
from the Unfamiliar

In establishing a program's algorithm, there are bound to be a number of steps with which you are familiar. They are part of almost any program. Being quick to recognize these steps will help break down the problem and make it more manageable.

Counting algorithms involves a small amount of cleverness in the use of an integer memory location. Assume we must process a data deck consisting of 40 cards. We will show this cleverness by forming an integer memory location called COUNT. As suggested below, we will use three statements to manipulate this counter. There is nothing new about these statements except for the special meaning they are being given by the programmer.

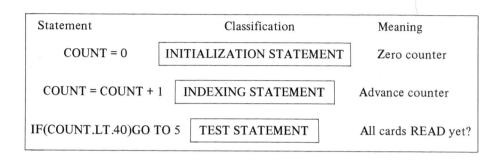

Statement	Classification	Meaning
COUNT = 0	INITIALIZATION STATEMENT	Zero counter
COUNT = COUNT + 1	INDEXING STATEMENT	Advance counter
IF(COUNT.LT.40)GO TO 5	TEST STATEMENT	All cards READ yet?

These statements will be used as shown by the flow chart and program segment shown below.

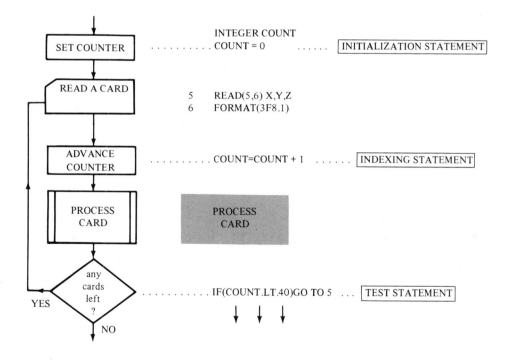

The statement COUNT = 0 is made early in the program and sets the initial value of the counter at zero. The statement:

$$COUNT = COUNT + 1$$

is the key to the counting process. It is called an indexing statement because each time it is executed the contents of memory location COUNT increases by one. This statement is usually placed immediately after the item being counted (in this case the READ statement).

To understand how this statement works, recall the way in which the replacement symbol (equal sign) is interpreted in an assignment statement.

Symbol	Meaning
=	"is replaced by"

Example	Meaning
N=N+1	N is to be replaced by its current value plus 1
KOUNT= KOUNT+5	KOUNT is to be replaced by its current value plus 5 (counting by 5's)
N=N–1	N is to be replaced by its current value *minus* 1

The statement:

$$COUNT = COUNT + 1$$

says, "Fetch a copy of the contents of memory location COUNT. Add one to this value. Store the result thus obtained back in memory location COUNT."

Controlling Output

Frequently we use a counter to control or limit the amount of output a program generates. In a previous program, you were asked to find all blood donors with O-blood living within a specific distance from the hospital. In many situations this could add up to a relatively large amount of output. The following illustration suggests the use of an integer counter called LINES. LINES is used in an indexing statement placed immediately after a WRITE statement to terminate the program after 100 lines of output are generated.

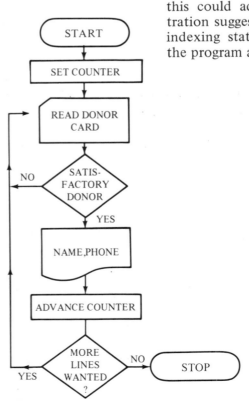

```
      INTEGER TYPE,PHONE
      LINES = 0
    5 READ(5,6)NAME,TYPE,PHONE,DIST
      IF(TYPE.NE.2.OR.DIST.GT.50.0)GO TO 5
    C      SATISFACTORY DONOR FOUND
      WRITE(2,7)NAME, PHONE
      LINES = LINES + 1
    C      TEST FOR SUFFICIENT OUTPUT
      IF(LINES.LE.100) GO TO 5
      STOP
      END
```

Quiz#5 Elementary Control Statements

Part 1: Answer the following questions.

1. Describe the difference between a conditional and unconditional transfer of control.

2. What is wrong with the following IF statement:

    IF(X.GT.10.0)BIG=X,GOTO6

3. Both IF tests that follow are looking for values of X that lie in the range:

    $10 \geqslant X \geqslant 20$.

    Which IF test is correct? Why?

    a) IF(X.GE.10.0.AND.LE.20.)WRITE(2,5)X
    b) IF(X.GE.10.0.AND.X.LE.20.)WRITE(2,5)X

4. A flow chart should begin and end with what symbol?

5. Why is the LOGICAL IF and the IF-THEN-ELSE preferred to the ARITHMETIC IF?

6. You usually need three statements to control a deck counter. What are these statements? Give an example.

7. Write an IF statement to determine if a person's blood pressure (PRESUR) is between 140 and 160. If it is, issue the message, 'BLOOD PRESSURE TOO HIGH'.

8. May a LOGICAL IF be followed by another **LOGICAL IF**?
   EXAMPLE:

    IF(A.GT.B)IF(C.EQ.D)WRITE(2,10)A,C

9. What is the last statement executed if the value of **TEMP** is 125. when the following IF statements are reached?

                IF(TEMP–32.0)1,2,3
        3   IF(TEMP–100.0)3,4,5
        5   IF(TEMP–180.0)6,7,8

    (Do you see why arithmetic IF's must be limited in their use?)

10. A data card gives the length of two sides of a triangle, followed by the length of its hypotenuse. Write an **IF-THEN-ELSE** construct to determine if this is an isosceles triangle (both sides equal).

Part 2: Write a program (Straight line approximation).

11. The first card in the data deck gives five sample prices of gasoline in 1970. The next card gives five sample prices observed in 1980. Determine:

    (a) Average price paid in 1970
    (b) Average price paid in 1980

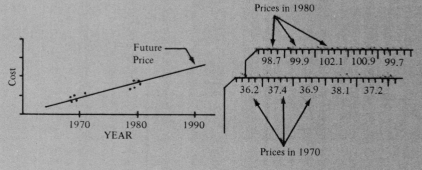

(c) Price we will pay in 1990 as price continues to increase in straight line fashion.

Answers:

1. Conditional transfer involves a decision factor to determine if the specified transfer should take place. IF(A.GT.B)GOTO6. An unconditional transfer involves no decision factor. GO TO 10

2. Only one statement to the right of the logical expression allowed.

3. Statement b

4. ⬭ This symbol shows START and END of program.

5. No wild branching involved. Position of dependent statements better positioned.

6. INITIALIZATION   COUNT=0
INDEXING   COUNT=COUNT+1
TESTING   IF(COUNT.LE.20)

7. IF(PRESUR.GE.140.0.AND.PRESUR.LE.160.0)WRITE(2,*)'BLOOD PRESSURE TOO HIGH'

8. No

9. Statement 6

10.
```
READ(5,10)SIDE1,SIDE2,HYP
IF(SIDE1.EQ.SIDE2)THEN
    WRITE(2,*)'TRIANGLE IS ISOSCELES'
ELSE
    WRITE(2,*)'TRIANGLE NOT ISOSCELES'
ENDIF
```

11.
```
C.............................
C     PURPOSE - STRAIGHT LINE PREDICTION OF 1990 GASOLINE
C               PRICES.
C.............................
C
C                    - IMPORTANT VARIABLES -
C
C     -X1TOX5   INDIVIDUAL GAS PRICES(5 FROM CARD)
C     -AVE70    AVERAGE PRICE 1970
C     -AVE80    AVERAGE PRICE 1980
C     -AVE90    EXPECTED PRICE 1990
C
      READ(5,10)X1,X2,X3,X4,X5
   10 FORMAT(5F5.1)
C
      AVE70=(X1+X2+X3+X4+X5)/5.0
C
      READ(5,10)X1,X2,X3,X4,X5
C
      AVE80=(X1+X2+X3+X4+X5)/5.0
C
      ADVNCE=AVE80-AVE70
C
C     AVE90=AVE80+ADVNCE
C
      WRITE(2,20)ADVANCE
   20 FORMAT(1X,F5.1)
      STOP
      END
```

5.8 | Deck Control (Fixed Size)

The problem that follows asks that you determine how many times the number 5 appears in a data deck consisting of 20 data cards. This is typical of those problems where the entire deck must be examined before a meaningful answer can be given. You cannot be careless about executing the command READ. If you execute the READ instruction more than 20 times, the program will terminate before an answer is printed.

| Programming Example |
| Number of Fives |

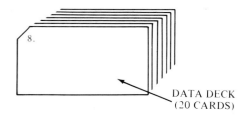

DATA DECK
(20 CARDS)

You are given a data deck consisting of 20 cards. Each card contains a single integer value in column 1. The integer number on each card is supposedly chosen at random, which would suggest that the number 1 appears as often as the number 2 and as often as the number 3, etc. Write a program to determine and report how many times the number 5 appears on these data cards.

This problem forces the programmer to set up two counters. One counter called CARDS will keep track of how many data cards have been read, while another counter, FIVES, will count how many times the number 5 appears on a card.

In this programming example, we are going to discuss another aspect of program style. For some reason, beginning programmers are usually optimistic that everything will go well. Experienced programmers, on the other hand, continually anticipate disaster. They expect things to go wrong and build into a program certain safeguards that will let them know when and why their programs malfunctioned. One way to do this is with extra printouts. While this program calls for only one output value, look at all the output a cautious programmer would generate.

CARD BEING PROCESSED	VALUE READ FROM CARD	CONDITION OF COUNTER
1	8	0
2	1	0
3	5	1
4	2	1
17	4	2
18	7	2
19	5	3
20	3	3
RUN COMPLETE: FINAL RESULT 3		

This output displays the state of the card counter (left-hand column) to verify that it is working properly. The center column displays each number read from data to show if the fives counter (right-hand column) is detecting the number 5 properly. We encourage you to take the same precautions when writing a program. (We have not yet reached the point of producing the fancy headings suggested in this output, but the topic will be covered shortly.)

Programming Style
Program Defensively:
Print — Print — Print   ‖   Of all the recommendations given thus far, this is the most important one. Use extra print statements at every opportunity to monitor the correct behavior of your program. They will help to detect and isolate incorrect code.

We continue to develop the problem solution in a series of gradual steps: pseudocode first, followed by variable name table, flow chart and finally FOR-TRAN code.

Step 1

Variable Names	
NUMBER	Value read from data
CARDS	Card counter
FIVES	Counter recording number of 5's

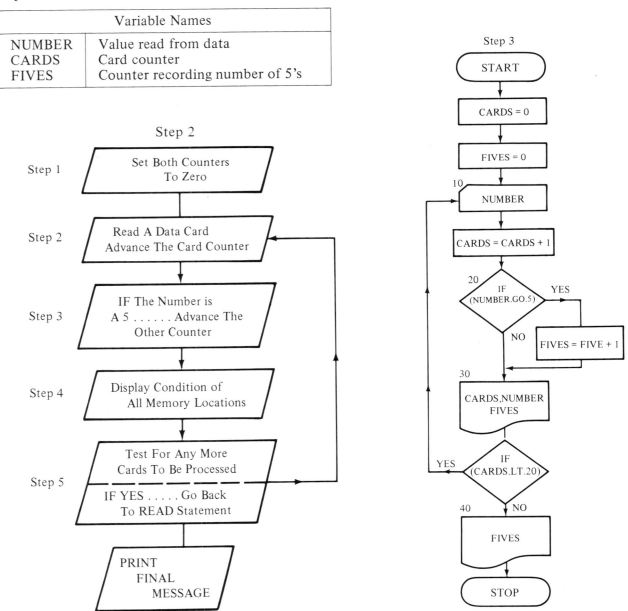

Figure 5.2 Program Development

```
C
C.........................................................
C..    PURPOSE - DEMONSTRATE DECK CONTROL WITH A FIXED SIZED..
C..            DATA DECK.(20 CARDS)                        ..
C..            -------------------                         ..
C..            COUNT THE NUMBER OF TIMES A 5 APPEARS.      ..
C.........................................................
C
C              ----------IMPORTANT VARIABLES----------
C
C      --CARDS      THE CARD COUNTER                       --
C      --NUMBER     VALUE READ FROM THE DATA CARD          --
C      --FIVES      COUNTER RECORDING THE NUMBER OF 5 S     --
C
       INTEGER CARDS, FIVES
C
C                    INITIALIZE BOTH COUNTERS TO ZERO
       CARDS = 0
       FIVES = 0
C
C                    ..........LOOP ENTRY POINT..........
C
    10 READ(5,11) NUMBER
    11 FORMAT(I1)
       CARDS = CARDS + 1
C
C                    TEST FOR THE APPEARANCE OF THE NUMBER 5
C
    20 IF (NUMBER.EQ.5) FIVES = FIVES + 1
C
C                    DISPLAY CONDITION OF ALL MEMORY LOCATIONS
C
    30 WRITE (2,31) CARDS, NUMBER, FIVES
    31 FORMAT (1X,I4,10X,I4,10X,I4)
C
C                    TEST FOR ADDITIONAL CARDS TO PROCESS
C
       IF(CARDS.LT.20) GO TO 10
C
C                    ..........LOOP EXIT POINT..........
C                    ..........ISSUE FINAL MESSAGE..........
C
    40 WRITE(2,41) FIVES
    41 FORMAT(1X,I7)
C
       STOP
       END
```

5.9 | Deck Control (Variable Size)

The counting procedures of the last problem can be modified slightly to permit the processing of *variable* size data decks. One method is to place at the front of the deck a card containing an integer number. This number declares the size of the deck for this particular run and is called a **leader card**. (A leader card was used in the blood donor problem in Chapter 2. It gave the type of blood being

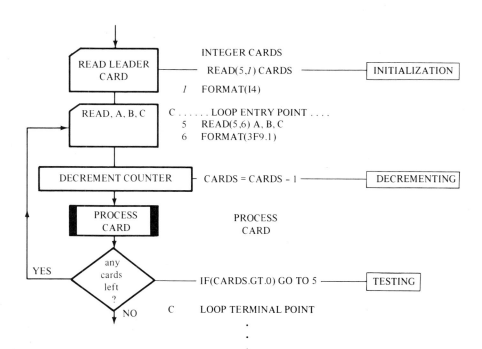

searched for and a maximum distance.) The counting procedure is modified as follows. Instead of setting the initial value of the counter (CARDS) to zero, we set it at the number on the leader card. Each time one of the remaining cards in the data deck is read, we *decrement* (decrease) this counter by the statement:

CARDS = CARDS − 1

Using this approach, the value of the counter tells how many cards are left in the data deck. The processing loop is terminated when the counter reaches zero. This process is suggested by the flow chart on the preceding page.

It was stated in Chapter 1 that the real challenge in FORTRAN is using its commands to solve an exceptionally broad range of problems. The numerous programming examples being presented are for the purpose of developing your problem-solving skill. The next example has many applications. It is called a minimum/maximum search. It uses a leader card and requires deck control.

**Programming Example
Use of a Leader Card**

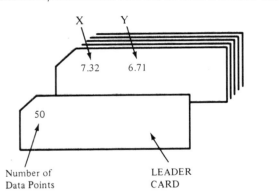

Number of
Data Points

LEADER
CARD

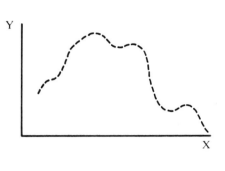

START

10 READ LEADER
CARD

PRODUCE
HEADINGS

SET POINT
COUNTER

20 READ DATA
POINT

ADVANCE POINT
COUNTER

30 DISPLAY DATA
POINT

NO   all
points
yet
?

40   YES
RUN COMPLETE

STOP

We have been asked to plot a series of data points. Each card in the main deck gives the X and Y coordinates of an individual point. At the front of the deck an extra card (a leader card) has been placed containing an integer number telling how many points (data cards) there are to be processed. Search the deck and determine the largest and smallest value of Y to be plotted.

The final solution of this problem is sufficiently involved to warrant a two-part explanation. Read the following partial program that just lists the values of X and Y appearing on the data cards. Answer the questions in the exercise that follows. This will get you involved in the solution but, more importantly, will show the value of extensive program documentation. Write a program segment that will produce a listing of the X and Y values appearing on each data card.

NUMBER OF POINTS IS 50		
1	1.62	3.87
2	1.74	4.02
3	1.79	4.48
4	1.92	4.90
5	2.06	5.21
47	82.61	−19.71
48	83.05	−21.14
49	84.12	−20.03
50	86.72	−18.61
RUN COMPLETE		

```
C*.......PURPOSE - PROVIDE A LISTING OF ALL DATA POINTS........
C..                                                          ..
C.*........................................................
C
C                      ---------- IMPORTANT VARIABLES----------
C
C         --NPOINT         NUMBER OF POINT TO PROCESS            --
C                            (VALUE READ FROM LEADER CARD)       --
C         --X , Y          DATA POINT VALUES                     --
C         --COUNT          INTERNAL COUNTER TELLING WHICH        --
C                            POINT (CARD) IS BEING PROCESSED     --
C
C         INTEGER COUNT
C
   10 READ(5,11) NPOINT
   11 FORMAT(I4)
C
         WRITE(2,*) ' NUMBER OF POINTS IS ',NPOINT
C
         COUNT = 0
C
C                      ..........LOOP ENTRY POINT..........
   20 READ(5,21) X, Y
   21 FORMAT(2F8.2)
C
C                      UPDATE COUNTER
C
         COUNT = COUNT + 1
C
   30 WRITE(2,31) COUNT, X, Y
   31 FORMAT(1X,I9,2F15.2)
C
C                      ANY CARDS LEFT
C
         IF(COUNT.LT.NPOINT) GO TO 20
C
C                      ..........LOOP EXIT POINT..........
   40 WRITE(2,*) ' RUN COMPLETE '
C
         STOP
         END
```

QUIZ#5-A

1. This program uses two different FORMAT statements to describe the input. Why?
2. If the statement:

   COUNT = 0

   was included inside the loop, would that affect the soluion?
3. If the data deck had either one more card or one less card than declared on the leader card, what affect would this have?
4. How must the number 50 (number of data points) be punched on the leader card (in which columns)?

Answers:
1. There are two different types of data cards, the leader card and the cards describing each data point.
2. Yes, it would keep resetting the counter destroying loop control.
3. If there was one less card, the command READ would be executed and there would be no card available. The program would terminate. If there was one card too many, the data point on that last card would not be examined.
4. It might be right justified in columns 1 through 4.

In the program that follows, YBIG and YSMALL will be used to store the largest and smallest value of Y encountered as the various data cards are being processed. The program starts by reading the first value of Y and setting both YBIG and YSMALL to this value. After all, at this point in the solution this value is both the largest and the smallest encountered thus far. A loop is then established that reads the remaining values of Y. Each new value of Y is compared with YBIG and YSMALL. Each time a value of Y is encountered that is smaller than the number stored in YSMALL, YSMALL is redefined. Each time a value of Y is encountered that is larger than the number stored in YBIG, YBIG is redefined.

Clearly, this is not a trivial problem. Accordingly, we will elect to display a considerable amount of intermediate output to see if the program functions properly. As in other programs, the output is a little more elegant than you are capable of producing at this time, but it is not the headings that are important — it is the monitoring process.

NUMBER OF DATA POINTS IS 45				
POINT	X	Y	YBIG	YSMALL
1	1.62	3.87	3.87	3.87
2	1.74	4.02	4.02	3.87
3	1.79	4.48	4.48	3.87
4	1.92	4.90	4.90	3.87
47	82.61	−19.71	189.71	−19.71
48	83.05	−21.14	189.71	−21.14
49	84.12	−20.03	189.71	−21.14
45	86.72	−18.61	189.71	−21.14

RUN COMPLETE: YBIG = 189.71   YSMALL = −21.14

The method of deck control used by this problem and the previous one is not the most reliable. A safer and therefore more popular technique is covered in the next section. It does not involve counting, but instead uses what is called a **trailer** or **sentinel** card.

Programming Style Deck Control By Counting: Use With Caution

Deck control that involves counting requires special precautions. If the deck is one card short or one card over, problems will occur. If the deck size changes, the leader card must be changed.

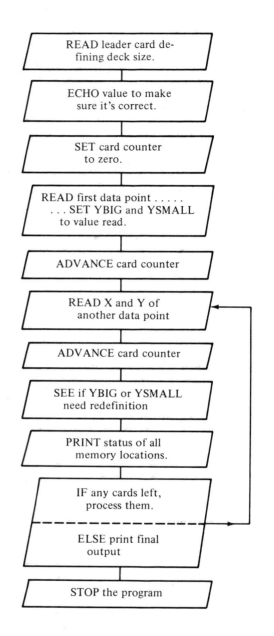

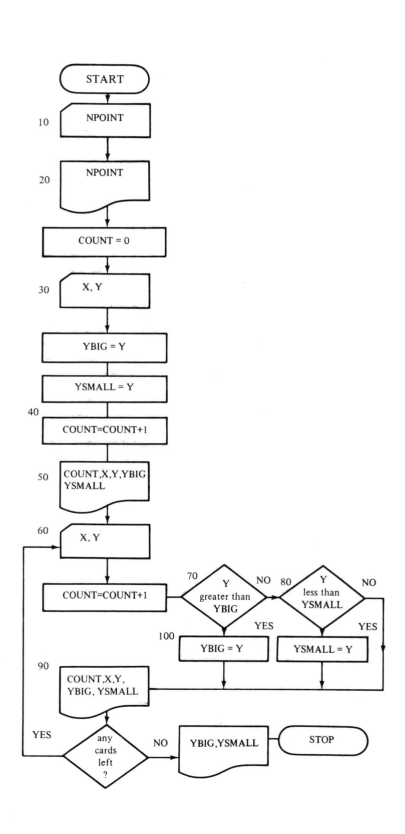

```
C...............................................................
C..     PURPOSE - DEMONSTRATE THE USE OF A LEADER CARD        ..
C..     --------------------------------------------          ..
C..          FIND THE MINIMUM AND MAXIMUN VALUE OF A VAR-     ..
C..     IABLE.                                                ..
C...............................................................
C
C               --------IMPORTANT VARIABLES--------
C
C    --NPOINT      NUMBER OF DATA POINTS               --
C    --COUNT       CARD COUNTER                        --
C    --X  , Y      VALUE OF INDIVIDUAL DATA POINT      --
C    --YBIG        LARGEST VALUE OF Y                  --
C    --YSMALL      SMALLEST VALUE OF Y                 --
C
      INTEGER COUNT
C
C               HOW LARGE IS DATA DECK
C
   10 READ(5,11) NPOINT
   11 FORMAT(I3)
   20 WRITE(2,21) NPOINT
   21 FORMAT(1X,I6)
      COUNT = 0
C
C    ......DEFINE INITIAL VALUE OF YBIG AND YSMALL..........
C
   30 READ(5,31) X, Y
   31 FORMAT(2F8.2)
C
      YBIG = Y
      YSMALL = Y
C
   40 COUNT = COUNT + 1
   50 WRITE(2,51) COUNT, X, Y, YBIG, YSMALL
   51 FORMAT(1X,I6,4F8.2)
C
C           .........LOOP ENTRY POINT..........
C
   60 READ(5,31) X, Y
      COUNT = COUNT + 1
C
   70 IF(Y.GT.YBIG) YBIG = Y
   80 IF(Y.LT.YSMALL) YSMALL = Y
C
C        DISPLAY CONDITION OF ALL MEMORY LOCATIONS
C
   90 WRITE(2,51) COUNT, X, Y, YBIG, YSMALL
C
C        ARE ALL CARDS PROCESSED
      IF(COUNT.LT.NPOINT) GO TO 60
C
C           .........LOOP EXIT POINT..........
C
C           FINAL MESSAGE TO OUTPUT
C
  100 WRITE(2,101) YBIG, YSMALL
  101 FORMAT(2F12.2)
      STOP
      END
```

5.10 | Deck Control (Trailer Card)

The last method of deck control to be covered is the most popular because it does not involve counting. It consists of placing an extra card at the back of the data deck instead of the front. This card is called a "trailer" or "sentinel" card and has the same format as those that precede it. The purpose of this card is to signal the end of the deck, and it is accomplished by putting false (ridiculous) information on the card. By ridiculous, we mean giving a zero for a person's age or a negative social security number. Using this method, there is no need to count the cards in the data deck. It is necessary, however, to test all input. Each time a card is read, it must be tested to see if it contains the false information associated with the trailer card. If it does not, process the card. If the sentinel card turns up, it must not be processed. Use this card to break out of the processing loop.

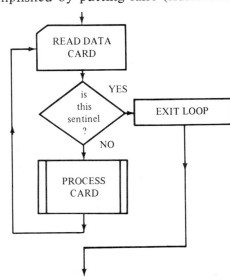

Programming Example
Small Lot Trading

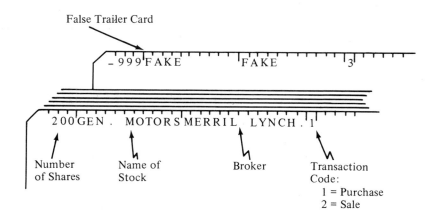

False Trailer Card

Number of Shares

Name of Stock

Broker

Transaction Code:
1 = Purchase
2 = Sale

A large data deck records a series of stock transactions. Each card lists the name of the stock, how many shares were involved, who the broker was and if the transaction was a buy or sell order.

People in finance are interested in what is called "small or odd lot trading," which means a purchase of under 100 shares. It is felt that small investors make this type of purchase while large institutions tend to deal in larger blocks of stock. Determine how many transactions are represented in the data deck. How many of these were "small lot transactions"? What percent of the trading did the small lots account for?

Notice the trailer card at the back of the deck. It lists a negative number where the number of shares should be. It is used to signal the end of the deck.

The problem asks for the total number of transactions represented in the data deck. A counter called CARDS will be used to keep track of how many cards are read. When dealing with a trailer card, you must be careful, however, not to advance the card counter until the card has been tested to see if it is legitimate or not. Students are anxious to get the card counter as close as possible to the READ statement, but testing for the trailer must come first.

A second counter called NSMALL is used to keep track of small lot transactions. The program will be written *with an intentional error* to show the need for extra printouts. Because of the large number of stocks involved, we will follow the correct behavior of our counters for the first ten stocks only (ten lines of printout).

Special Topic

As each card is read, we will be interested in the number of shares and the name of the stock only. Storing the name of the stock presents a small problem. Twelve columns are reserved on the data card to hold the name of each stock, but that is probably too many characters to fit in one memory location. We have mentioned the topic "word size" before. Assume that our computer can hold a maximum of 6 alphabetic characters in any one memory location. Instead of an A12 format code, a 2A6 code will be used. Because there are two A-codes in the format statement, there must be two memory locations assigned to hold this information. We will use memory locations called NAME1 and NAME2. If the space allowed for the name of the stock was longer or the word size was smaller, we would have to divide the name into even smaller parts.

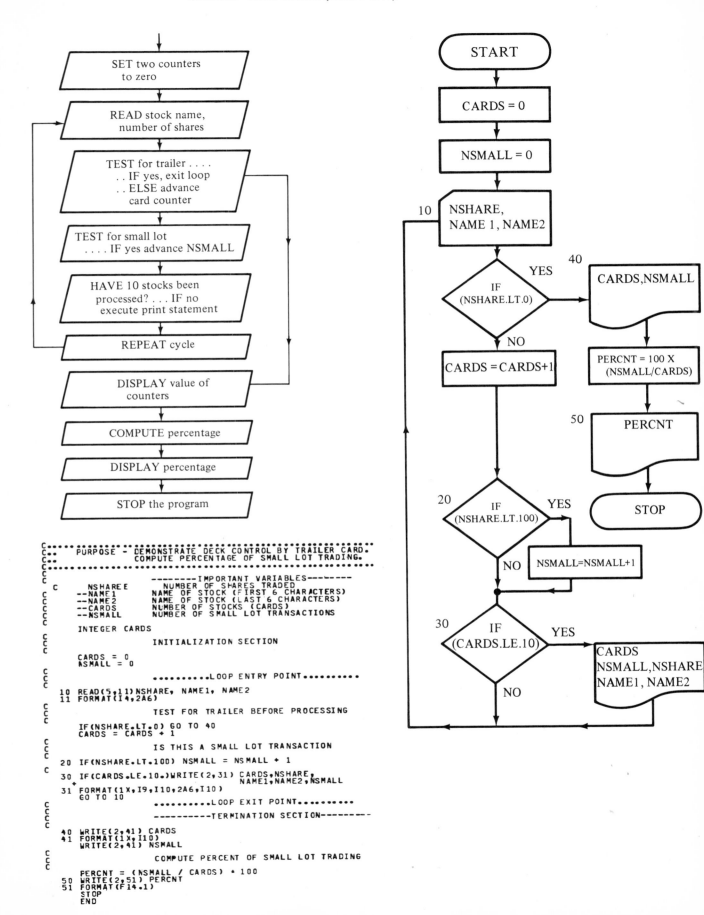

```
C.........................................................
C..    PURPOSE - DEMONSTRATE DECK CONTROL BY TRAILER CARD. ..
C..              COMPUTE PERCENTAGE OF SMALL LOT TRADING.   ..
C.........................................................
C
C                     --------IMPORTANT VARIABLES--------
C    NSHAREE          NUMBER OF SHARES TRADED
C    --NAME1          NAME OF STOCK (FIRST 6 CHARACTERS)
C    --NAME2          NAME OF STOCK (LAST 6 CHARACTERS)
C    --CARDS          NUMBER OF STOCKS (CARDS)
C    --NSMALL         NUMBER OF SMALL LOT TRANSACTIONS
C
      INTEGER CARDS
C
C                     INITIALIZATION SECTION
C
      CARDS = 0
      NSMALL = 0
C
C                     .........LOOP ENTRY POINT..........
C
   10 READ(5,11)NSHARE, NAME1, NAME2
   11 FORMAT(I4,2A6)
C
C                     TEST FOR TRAILER BEFORE PROCESSING
C
      IF(NSHARE.LT.0) GO TO 40
      CARDS = CARDS + 1
C
C                     IS THIS A SMALL LOT TRANSACTION
C
   20 IF(NSHARE.LT.100) NSMALL = NSMALL + 1
C
   30 IF(CARDS.LE.10.)WRITE(2,31) CARDS,NSHARE,
     +                            NAME1,NAME2,NSMALL
   31 FORMAT(1X,I9,I10,2A6,I10)
      GO TO 10
C                     .........LOOP EXIT POINT..........
C
C                     ---------TERMINATION SECTION--------
C
   40 WRITE(2,41) CARDS
   41 FORMAT(1X,I10)
      WRITE(2,41) NSMALL
C
C                     COMPUTE PERCENT OF SMALL LOT TRADING
C
      PERCNT = (NSMALL / CARDS) * 100
   50 WRITE(2,51) PERCNT
   51 FORMAT(F14.1)
      STOP
      END
```

Examination of the output shows everything going well until the final average is printed out. The reported value is 0.0%.

CARD	SHARES	NAME	SMALL LOT COUNTER
1	200	GEN. MOTORS	0
2	75	I.B.M.	1
3	60	U.S. STEEL	2
4	500	SQUIBB	2
5	1000	BAXTER	2
6			
8	400	CHRYSLER	4
9	20	HONDA	5
10	500	MELVILLE	5

TOTAL NO. STOCKS   673
NO. SMALL LOT   206
AVERAGE = 0.0%

The counters are working correctly but the computed value of average small-lot trading is coming out as zero. The error must be somewhere between the printing out of the final counter values and the printout of PERCNT. The trouble is with the statement:

PERCNT = NSMALL/CARDS*100

The first operation performed is the division of NSMALL by CARDS. Notice that both are integer values. The result will be a number less than one, which in integer arithmetic comes out to zero. Avoiding this type of difficulty is covered in the next chapter.

5.11   Computed GO TO Statement

Logical and arithmetic IF's are designed to allow the transfer of control to one, two or even three alternate points in a program. Anything beyond a three-way branch is accomplished by the computed GO TO. It allows transfer of control to an almost unlimited number of points.

GO   TO   (12, 108, 9, 15, 56) , J

Command   Statement Numbers   Selector

The statement consists of the command GO TO followed by a series of statement numbers separated by commas and enclosed in parentheses. All this is followed by a comma and an integer variable. The new standards even allow an integer expression.

This particular statement allows transfer of control to any one of five statements, depending on the value of the integer variable J, which is used as a selector as follows:

If J has the value 1, control is passed to the 1st statement number in the series, i.e., to statement 12.

If J has the value 2, control is passed to the 2nd statement number in the series, i.e., statement 108.

If J has the value 3, control is passed to the 3rd statement number in the series, i.e., statement 9, etc.

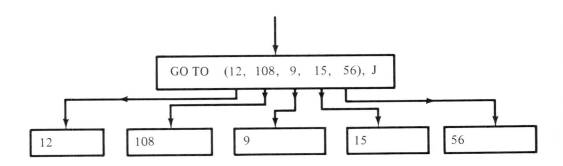

This particular computed GO TO is the equivalent of the following five statements:

IF (J.EQ.1) GO TO 12
IF (J.EQ.2) GO TO 108
IF (J.EQ.3) GO TO 9
IF (J.EQ.4) GO TO 15
IF (J.EQ.5) GO TO 56

Additional examples:

GO TO (103,5,13,4),NUM
GO TO (3,2),JOB
GO TO (4,41,18,32,75,108,109,11,302,5),KING

Name Banner

One popular student pastime is to make large name banners by printing each letter of the name on a separate sheet of output paper.

```
RRRRRRRRRR     UU        UU  LL            EEEEEEEEEEEE
RRRRRRRRRRR    UU        UU  LL            EEEEEEEEEEEE
RR        RR   UU        UU  LL            EE
RR        RR   UU        UU  LL            EE
RR        RR   UU        UU  LL            EE
RR        RR   UU        UU  LL            EE
RR        RR   UU        UU  LL            EE
RRRRRRRRRRR    UU        UU  LL            EEEEEEE
RRRRRRRRRR     UU        UU  LL            EEEEEEE
RR        RR   UU        UU  LL            EE
RR        RR   UU        UU  LL            EE
RR        RR   UU        UU  LL            EE
RR        RR   UU        UU  LL            EE
RR        RR   UU        UU  LL            EE
RR        RR   UUUUUUUUUUUU  LLLLLLLLLLLL  EEEEEEEEEEEE
RR        RR   UUUUUUUUUUUU  LLLLLLLLLLLL  EEEEEEEEEEEE
```

This is done by setting up an algorithm capable of producing any message by having 26 blocks of code as suggested below (one for each letter of the alphabet). Each block consists of many WRITE statements that produce a large letter "A" or a large letter "B".

```
1 WRITE(2,*)'      AAA          2 WRITE(2,*)'BBBBBBBBB      3 WRITE(2,*)'    CCCCC
  WRITE(2,*)'      AAA            WRITE(2,*)'BBBBBBBBBB        WRITE(2,*)'  CCCCCCCC
  WRITE(2,*)'     AA AA           WRITE(2,*)'BBB      BBB      WRITE(2,*)' CCC    CCC
  WRITE(2,*)'     AA AA           WRITE(2,*)'BBB       BBB     WRITE(2,*)'CCC       CCC
  WRITE(2,*)'    AA   AA          WRITE(2,*)'BBB      BBB      WRITE(2,*)'CCC
  WRITE(2,*)'    AA   AA          WRITE(2,*)'BBB     BBB       WRITE(2,*)'CCC
  WRITE(2,*)'   AA     AA         WRITE(2,*)'BBBBBBBBBBB       WRITE(2,*)'CCC
  WRITE(2,*)'   AA     AA         WRITE(2,*)'BBBBBBBBBB        WRITE(2,*)'CCC
  WRITE(2,*)' AAAAAAAAAA          WRITE(2,*)'BBBBBBBBBB        WRITE(2,*)'CCC
  WRITE(2,*)' AAAAAAAAAA          WRITE(2,*)'BBB     BBB       WRITE(2,*)'CCC
  WRITE(2,*)'AA        AA         WRITE(2,*)'BBB      BBB      WRITE(2,*)'CCC
  WRITE(2,*)'AA        AA         WRITE(2,*)'BBB       BBB     WRITE(2,*)'CCC       CCC
  WRITE(2,*)'AA        AA         WRITE(2,*)'BBB       BBB     WRITE(2,*)' CCC    CCC
  WRITE(2,*)'AA        AA         WRITE(2,*)'BBBBBBBBBB        WRITE(2,*)'  CCCCCCCC
  WRITE(2,*)'AA        AA         WRITE(2,*)'BBBBBBBBBB        WRITE(2,*)'    CCCCC
```

In printing a message this way, the computed GO TO is used over and over to pass control to one of 26 different parts of the program to print out the specific letter that is wanted.

Which Department?

In large department stores, the trend is to have centralized check-out areas where items picked up in any of twenty or thirty different departments can be paid for. As the various items are processed, a dollar amount and the department number are recorded. This department number could be used as a selector value in a computed GO TO for the purpose of passing control to that section of a program that credits that particular department for the sale listed.

Approximating a Function

As a final example, a program is presented that must select one of 9 possible equations to solve a problem. A complicated function of Y is approximated by a series of straight lines. Each line approximates Y for a unit interval of X. Between X = 1 and X = 2, Equation 1 should be used. Between X = 2 and X = 3, Equation 2 should be used.

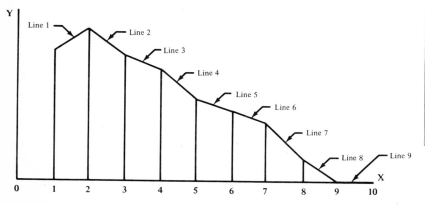

Range	Line	Equation
X = 1 to X = 2	1	Y = 0.65X + 5.10
X = 2 to X = 3	2	Y = −.32X + 7.04
X = 3 to X = 4	3	Y = −2.1X + 12.38
X = 4 to X = 5	4	Y = −1.8X + 11.18
X = 5 to X = 6	5	Y = −1.1X + 7.68
X = 6 to X = 7	6	Y = .66X − 2.88
X = 7 to X = 8	7	Y = −.99X + 8.67
X = 8 to X = 9	8	Y = −.75X + 6.75
X = 9 to X = 10	9	Y = 0

Each equation will require a separate arithmetic statement. There will be nine of these in all, and we number them 1 through 9 to show which equation they represent.

The heart of the program is a computed GO TO:

GO TO (1, 2, 3, 4, 5, 6, 7, 8, 9), J

that transfers control to one of 9 equations depending on the value of the selector quantity.

The selector quantity is formed by the statement preceding the computed GO TO.

J = X

It is obtained by taking the value of X and sending a copy of it to the integer memory location J. Here truncation will take place. If X has the value of 6.293, J will assume the value 6. If X is 2.975, J will be 2.

C			READ X FROM DATA
	100		READ(5,101)X
	101		FORMAT(F12.2)
C			TRUNCATE X-FORM SELECTOR VALUE
			J=X
C			TRANSFER CONTROL TO APPROPRIATE EQUATIONS
			GO TO (1, 2, 3, 4, 5, 6, 7, 8, 9), J
	1		Y=0.65*X+5.10
			GO TO 10
	2		Y=X*(-.32)+7.04
			GO TO 10
	3		Y=X*(-2.1)+12.38
			GO TO 10

Equation of Line 1

Equation of Line 2

Equation of Line 3

	9		Y=O.
	10		WRITE(2,90)X,Y
	90		FORMAT(F20.10,E20.8)
	120		STOP
			END

End Of File Check

The FORTRAN '77 standards provide a very simple means of deck control that eliminates the need for a trailer card. This feature allows an additional specifier in the READ statement:

READ(5,7,END=120)ID,GRADE

Tells where to pass control when end of deck detected

The above statement will cause the transfer of control to statement 120 when the READ instruction is executed if there are no more cards in the data deck.

The new specifier (END=120) produces what is called an automatic "End of File Check."

Quiz#6   Writing Programs

Part 1: Answer the following questions in the space provided.

1. Extra print statements are often added to a program during the early stages of the program's development. Why?

2. If the command READ is executed and there are no more input data cards, what happens?

3. How can the situation in Question 2 be avoided?

4. Is one method of deck control any better than another? Why?

5. When using a 'trailer' or 'sentinel' card to signal the end of the data deck, where should the IF test for this card be located (at the beginning or end of the program)? Why?

Part 2: (Account Numbers No Longer In Use)

6. A bank uses a 6-digit account number to identify its customers. The largest number issued thus far is 617042.

   Each card in the data deck lists all the account numbers that are *still active. This deck has been sorted.*

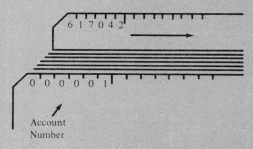

Write a flow chart for a program that will determine which account numbers between 000001 and 617042 are no longer active (not represented in the data deck).

Part 3: (Shipping Charges)

The following table is used to determine shipping charges when cargo of different weights is transported from one part of the country to another.

Weight (lbs)	Number of Zone Changes Rate-per-thousand lb		
	1	2	3
0–199	$ 7.63	$ 9.29	$12.86
200–299	$12.26	$18.87	$21.03
300–399	$20.53	$28.43	$37.51
400–499	$42.67	$54.00	$62.04
500–over	$79.81	$84.15	$96.82

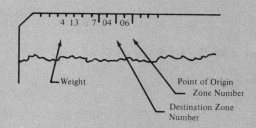

7. Write a flow chart to read the destination and origin zone number of a package (see card above) and determine the number of ZONE CHANGES involved.

8. Line 1 of the table is used for packages weighing between 0–199 pounds. Line 2 of the table is for packages between 200–299, etc.

Write statements that will load a memory location called LINE with a value between 1 and 5 based on the WEIGHT of the package and the table values.

Answers:

1. Check the correct behavior of the program. Was input read correctly? Are intermediate calculations correct? Is the transfer of control as it should be?

2. An *execution* error takes place. The program terminates with a message such as "RAN OUT OF DATA CARDS" or "END OF FILE ENCOUNTERED."

3. Deck control. Header Cards; Counting; Trailer Cards.

4. Use of a TRAILER or SENTINEL card preferred (no counting involved).

5. Early in the program. You do not want to process "False" card in that it may adversely affect some calculations.

6.

7.

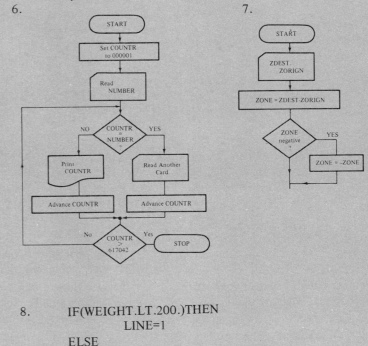

8.

```
        IF(WEIGHT.LT.200.)THEN
                LINE=1
        ELSE
                LINE=WEIGHT/100.
        ENDIF
C
        IF(LINE.GT.5)LINE=5
```

| **Programming Example** Reading the Correct Card | The table of shipping rates presented in Part 3 of the last Quiz has been recorded on data cards (one line per card). |

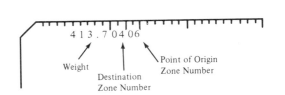

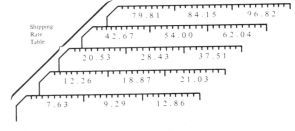

Write a program to read the WEIGHT and ZONE changes of a package (first card). Determine what LINE in the table should be used. Use the value of LINE as a counter to reach the appropriate rate card in the table of shipping rates.

```
C...............................................................
C..   PURPOSE -  DETERMINE SHIPPING RATE FROM DOUBLE           ::
C..             ENTRY TABLE.                                   ::
C...............................................................
C
C                  -----IMPORTANT VARIABLES-----
C
C      --WEIGHT    WEIGHT OF SHIPMENT (READ FROM FIRST CARD) --
C      --ZDEST     ZONE OF DESTINATION POINT                 --
C      --ZORIGN    ZONE OF ORIGIN POINT                      --
C      --LINE      LINE IN TABLE (WEIGHT CATEGORY)            --
C
       INTEGER ZDEST,ZORIGN,ZONE
C
       READ(5,10)WEIGHT,ZDEST,ZORIGN
    10 FORMAT(F8.1,2I2)
C
C               DETERMINE WEIGHT CATEGORY
C
       IF(WEIGHT.LT.200.)THEN
              LINE=1
       ELSE
              LINE=WEIGHT/100.
       ENDIF
C
       IF(LINE.GT.5)LINE=5
C
C               DETERMINE ZONE CHANGE
C
       ZONE=ZDEST-ZORIGN
C
C          MAKE SURE ZONE IS A POSITIVE NUMBER
C
       IF(ZONE.LT.0)ZONE=-ZONE
C
C              READ TABLE CARDS
C
    20 READ(5,30)RATE1,RATE2,RATE3
    30 FORMAT(3F10.2)
C
       IF(LINE.NE.1)THEN
C
C              THIS IS NOT CORRECT CARD
C
              LINE=LINE-1
              GO TO 20
C
       ELSE
C
C              THIS IS CORRECT CARD
C
       IF(ZONE.EQ.1)CHARGE=WEIGHT/1000.*RATE1
       IF(ZONE.EQ.2)CHARGE=WEIGHT/1000.*RATE2
       IF(ZONE.EQ.3)CHARGE=WEIGHT/1000.*RATE3
```

Review Exercises

1.*A logical expression used as the control quantity in an IF test may have two values. What are they?

2. An arithmetic expression used in an arithmetic IF test may have three values. What are they?

3. Provide the symbol used in FORTRAN (relational operator) for each of the symbols used in mathematics shown below.

    a. $=$ d. $<$
    b. $\neq$ e. $\geq$
    c. $>$ f. $\leq$

4.*Answer the following questions as true or false:

   (a) The statement at the right of a logical IF statement can only be a control statement (STOP or GO TO).

   (b) The statement at the right of a logical IF can be any statement allowed in FORTRAN including another logical IF.

   (c) Only one statement is allowed to the right of a logical IF.

5. If you choose to join (compound) two simple logical expressions, what logical connectors are available?

6. What information does a well constructed flow chart provide?

7. Describe the advantages of an IF-THEN-ELSE statement compared to other IF statements.

8. List three reasons that a programmer might want to set up a counter in a program.

9.*You have been told to program defensively. What does this mean?

10. What does the term "word size" mean? Explain the relationship of this term with respect to storing alphabetic information.

11. What is the primary advantage of computed GO TO statements over other control statements?

12.*The statement:

READ(5,10,END=20)ID,GRADE

is allowed by many compilers. What does the END = 20 mean in this statement?

13.*A data card contains two real values that are the X and Y coordinates of a point. Write a program to read this card and determine the distance the point lies from the origin. Construct your own data card.

14. A data card lists four real values. The first three are the length, width, and height (in inches) of a rectangular prism. The fourth real value is the weight (in pounds) of the prism. Write a program to compute and report the density of this object.

Many of the problems that follow can be tested using data decks that are much smaller than suggested.

15. A data deck consists of 100 cards. Each card gives the dollar amount of a deposit or a withdrawal to a checking account. Negative values represent withdrawals. Positive values represent deposits. Determine the number of deposits and the number of withdrawals.

16.*A data deck consists of 100 cards as described in problem 15. Write a program to determine how many withdrawals of over $200.00 appear in the first 50 cards; in the last 50 cards.

17. A data card gives the radius and height of a cylinder. A second data card gives the radius and height of a second cylinder. Write a program to compute and compare the volume of both cylinders but to report as output the volume of the larger cylinder only.

18. The data card shown gives the X and Y coordinates of a point and the radius, R, of a circle centered at the origin. Write a program to determine if the point lies outside, inside, or on the circle. Have the computer print a –1 if the point is outside the circle, or a 1 if the point is inside or on the circle.

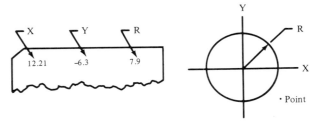

19.*A data card contains four real values which are the X and Y coordinates of point 1 and point 4 as shown.

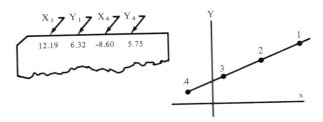

These points form the line 1–4. Write a program to determine and report the X and Y coordinates of points 2 and 3 which divide the line into three equal parts. Check your answer by comparing the distances 1–2, 2–3 and 3–4 which should, of course, be equal.

20. The gas company uses the following rate schedule in billing its customers based on the number of cubic feet of gas used.

First 1000 cubic feet	$2.5¢/\text{ft.}^3$
Next 1000 cubic feet	$2.0¢/\text{ft.}^3$
Remaining 1000 cubic feet	$1.8¢/\text{ft.}^3$

Write a program to read the amount of gas used by a customer and calculate the charge appropriately.

21. Given exam grades (1 per data card) for 25 students, write a program to compute the number of students who failed the exam (received a score of less than 60).

22. A data deck consists of 200 cards, each of which contains two integer numbers representing the roll of a pair of dice. Determine how many times a seven was rolled. Determine how many times a roll of seven is followed by a roll greater than seven; less than seven; equal to seven.

23. Using the data deck of problem 22 determine how many times a pair was rolled (a pair of fours or a pair of sixes for example).

24.*For the data deck in problem 22, how many cards must be read before "box cars" (double six) are rolled?

25. A programming course involves 6 large projects, each of which is graded on a scale of 0 to 10.

$$\overline{\smash{)}\,9\ 9\ 7\ 0\ 5\ 9}$$

Write a program to read these 6 grades and determine the lowest of the 6 grades listed.

Drop this lowest grade and compute the average score based on the remaining 5 grades.

26. If a student received a zero on any of the projects described in problem 25, it is because the project was never turned in. What percentage of the students failed to turn in one or more of the projects assigned? (Use a data deck of 20 cards.)

27. The hyperbolic arc tangent of X may be evaluated by a series expansion:

$$\textbf{ARCTAN} = X - \frac{X^3}{3} + \frac{X^5}{5} - \frac{X^7}{7} + \dots\dots$$

Write a program to read values of x from data (one value per card) and to report as output:

(a) the sum of the first four terms of this series, and

(b) the value of the term $\frac{X^9}{9}$ (which is the first term neglected).

28. Evaluate successive terms in the arc tangent equation of problem 27 until such time as any one of the terms is less than 0.0001. Report the value of the arc tangent and the number of terms used in the evaluation.

Additional Applications

Programming Example
Throw Out Lowest Grade

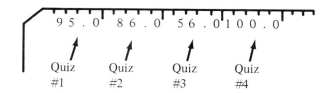

An instructor plans to give four quizzes before the final exam, but with the understanding that the lowest quiz grade will be dropped (quiz average based on best three scores).

Write a program to compute the quiz average based on this agreement.

```
C..........................................................
C..    PURPOSE -   DROP LOWEST OF FOUR GRADES.  COMPUTE QUIZ  ..
C..                AVERAGE.                                   ..
C..........................................................
C
C                     -----IMPORTANT VARIABLES-----
C
C      --LOWEST    LOWEST GRADE OF FOUR QUIZES          --
C      --AVE       AVERAGE GRADE                        --
C
       REAL LOWEST
C
       READ(5,10)QUIZ1,QUIZ2,QUIZ3,QUIZ4
    10 FORMAT(4F5.1)
C
C                  DETERMINE LOWEST SCORE
C
       LOWEST=QUIZ1
C
       IF(QUIZ2.LT.LOWEST)LOWEST=QUIZ2
       IF(QUIZ3.LT.LOWEST)LOWEST=QUIZ3
       IF(QUIZ4.LT.LOWEST)LOWEST=QUIZ4
C
       SUM=QUIZ1+QUIZ2+QUIZ3+QUIZ4-LOWEST
       AVE=SUM/3.0
C
       WRITE(2,20)AVE
    20 FORMAT(1X,F12.2)
C
       STOP
       END
```

Programming Example
Qualifying Events

In order to qualify at a swimming meet, you must participate in three preliminary events. Each of these events involves 6 swimmers. Your time in *each* event must be better than the average time for that event or you are disqualified.

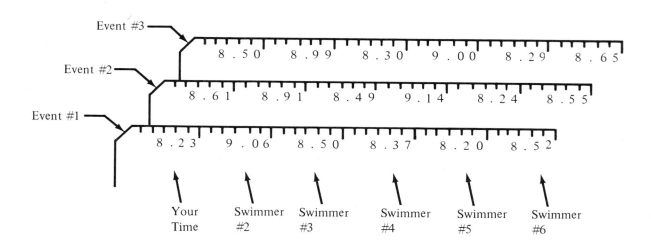

Write a program to see if your time is better than the average time in each of the three events. (Award a point for each successful event. Three points needed to qualify).

```
C...............................................................
C..   PURPOSE -  DETERMINE IF SWIMMER QUALIFIES             ::
C...............................................................
C
C              -----IMPORTANT VARIABLES-----
C
C      --T1,T2,...T6    TIME FOR EACH SWIMMER
C      --AVE            AVERAGE TIME FOR THAT EVENT          --
C      --POINTS         ONE POINT GIVEN FOR EACH EVENT       --
C                       (THREE POINTS NEEDED TO QUALIFY)     --
C
       INTEGER POINTS
C
       POINTS=0
C
       READ(5,10)T1,T2,T3,T4,T5,T6
    10 FORMAT(6F6.2)
C
       AVE=(T1+T2+T3+T4+T5+T6)/6.0
C
       IF(T1.LT.AVE)POINTS=POINTS+1
C
       READ(5,10)T1,T2,T3,T4,T5,T6
       AVE=(T1+T2+T3+T4+T5+T6)/6.0
C
       IF(T1.LT.AVE)POINTS=POINTS+1
C
       READ(5,10)T1,T2,T3,T4,T5,T6
       AVE=(T1+T2+T3+T4+T5+T6)/6.0
C
       IF(T1.LT.AVE)POINTS=POINTS+1
C
       IF(POINTS.EQ.3)THEN
C
           WRITE(2,*)' THIS SWIMMER QUALIFIES'
C
       ELSE
C
           WRITE(2,*)' THIS SWIMMER DOES NOT QUALIFY'
C
       ENDIF
C
       STOP
       END
```

Programming Example
Simple Curve Fit

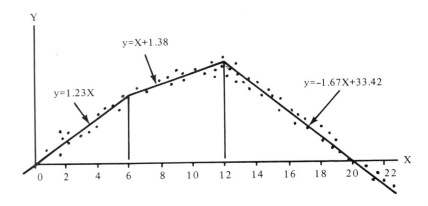

A series of data points have been plotted and between X = 0 and X = 6 they seem to be approximated by the equation:

$$\text{EQ. 1} \quad Y = 1.23 * X$$

Between X = 6 and X = 12, the slope of the curve changes and is better approximated by the equation:

$$\text{EQ. 2} \quad Y = X + 1.38$$

Finally, for values of X greater than 12, the slope turns negative and should be approximated by:

$$\text{EQ. 3} \quad Y = -1.67 * X + 33.42$$

A. Write a program to read a series of X values from input and determine which equation should be used to evaluate Y. Use a series of logical IF tests to make this decision. If X is less than 0.0 or greater than 22.0, do not attempt a calculation.

```
C.......................................................
C..    PURPOSE - READ RANDOM VALUES OF X...SELECT CORRECT ..
C..           EQUATION.                                   ..
C.......................................................
   10   READ(5,11) X
   11   FORMAT(F8.1)
C
C             DETERMINE IF X IN DEFINED RANGE
C
        IF(X.LT.0.0) STOP
        IF(X.GT.22.0) STOP
C
C             TEST TO SEE WHICH EQUATION TO USE
C
        IF(X.LT.6.0) Y=1.23*X
        IF(X.GE.6.0.AND.X.LE.12.0) Y=X+1.38
        IF(X.GE.12.0) Y=-1.67*X+33.42
C
C             REPORT BOTH VALUES
C
   20   WRITE(2,21) X,Y
   21   FORMAT(1X,2F16.2)
        GO TO 10
        END
```

B. Solve this same problem using a series of arithmetic IF's. Make every effort to show the path (logic) branches for the various values of X.

```
C.......................................................
C..    READ RANDOM VALUES OF X FROM DATA                  .
C.......................................................
  100   READ(5,101) X
  101   FORMAT(F6.1)
C
C             TEST TO SEE IF EQUATION 1 APPROPRIATE
C
        IF(X-6.0) 10,15,15
   10   Y=1.23*X
        GO TO 200
C
C             TEST TO SEE IF EQUATION 2 APPROPRIATE
C
   15   IF(X-12.0) 20,30,30
   20   Y=X+1.38
        GO TO 200
C
C             EQUATION 3 IS APPROPRIATE
C
   30   Y=-1.67*X+33.42
C
  200   WRITE(2,201) X,Y
  201   FORMAT(2F16.2)
        STOP
        END
```

Take a minute to compare the two programs just written. Notice that the logical IF is much more direct in selecting the appropriate equation to use.

C. This problem can be solved by a computed GO TO. The integer variable to serve as a selector value can be computed as follows:

$$J = X/6.0 + 1$$

Dividing X by 6.0 and adding 1 makes J equal to 1 when equation 1 is appropriate, makes J equal to 2 when equation 2 is appropriate, and 3 or greater for larger values of X.

```
C
C             READ RANDOM VALUES OF X FROM DATA
C
  100   READ (5,101) X
  101   FORMAT (F6.1)
C
C             FORM SELECTOR VALUE
C
        J=X/6.0+1.0
C
C             APPLY COMPUTED GO TO
        GO TO (10,20,30,30,30,30,30) ,J
   10   Y=1.23*X
        GO TO 200
C
   20   Y=X+1.38
        GO TO 200
C
   30   Y=-1.67*X+33.42
C
  200   WRITE(2,201) X,Y
  201   FORMAT(1X,2F15.2)
        STOP
        END
```

Programming Example IF-THEN-ELSE (Car Insurance Repeated)	Rate Table (cost per thousand)		
Age	Good Driving Record	Poor Driving Record	
Under 25	27.50	42.86	
25 or Older	20.80	30.00	

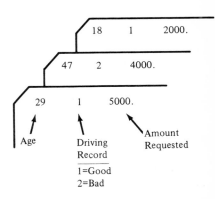

The automobile insurance problem presented in Chapter 2 is repeated below. Write a program to solve the problem, but this time use an IF-THEN-ELSE construct. Include a flow chart to show the program logic.

The cost of automobile insurance is based on two factors, age and driving record. The rates for drivers under 25 are shown in the top line of the rate table. The figures given are the cost for $1,000.00 of insurance coverage. Drivers with good driving records pay substantially less than those with poor records.

Each data card gives the age and past driving record of an applicant. The last value is the amount of insurance coverage requested. Write a program to compute the charge to be made for the coverage requested.

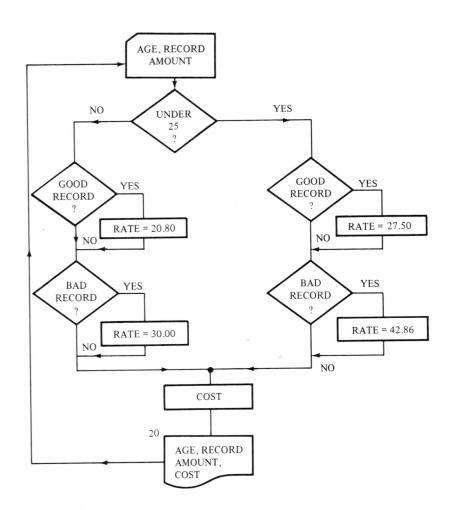

```
C .....................................................
C  PURPOSE - DEMONSTRATE USE OF IF-THEN-ELSE CONSTRUCT.
C .....................................................
C
       INTEGER AGE, RECORD
   10  READ(5,11) AGE,RECORD,AMOUNT
   11  FORMAT(2I3,F8.0)
C
C               TEST AGE CATEGORY
C
       IF(AGE.LT.25) THEN
               IF(RECORD.EQ.1) RATE=27.50
               IF(RECORD.EQ.2) RATE=42.86
       ELSE
               IF(RECORD.EQ.1) RATE=20.80
               IF(RECORD.EQ.2) RATE=30.00
       ENDIF
C
C          COMPUTE AND REPORT COST
C
       COST=AMOUNT/1000.*RATE
C
   20  WRITE(2,21) AGE,RECORD,AMOUNT,COST
   21  FORMAT(1X,2I6,2F12.2)
C
       GO TO 10
C
       END
```

Data Checking

An often-neglected aspect of writing effective FORTRAN programs is the topic of *internal data checking*. The programmer is so involved with attempting to develop the correct logic that other important aspects are sometimes overlooked. The last program is a typical example.

As written, the program logic depends on the value of RECORD being either 1 or 2. If this value is keypunched incorrectly, nothing very dramatic happens. An incorrect answer will probably be generated and may well slip through undetected. Assume RECORD is keypunched as equal to 3 on the last data card. For this card, none of the IF tests will be evaluated as "true" and the quantity RATE is never redefined. *It maintains the value it had from the previous card.* Obviously, the value COST is computed and reported incorrectly. Including the value of RECORD in the output line may cause the error to be detected, but it would be much better to include a "data check" in the program logic as follows:

$$\text{IF (RECORD.NE.1.OR.RECORD.NE.2) GO TO 1000}$$

where statement 1000 provides an *error message.*

Programming Example
Using Arithmetic IFs

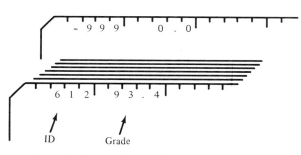

The examination grades of a large class of students are punched on data cards, one to a card. Each card contains a student's identification number and an examination grade. Write a program that will publish a list of all students who failed the exam (scored less than 60%). Include statements that will print out the following information:

highest score_____   lowest score _____

The end of the data deck is signalled by a trailer card that lists a negative ID number.

This problem involves a minimum/maximum search that was covered in this chapter using logical IF's. Demonstrate your understanding of arithmetic IF's by using them to solve this problem. You will probably find the solution a little awkward. Rely heavily on the flow diagram.

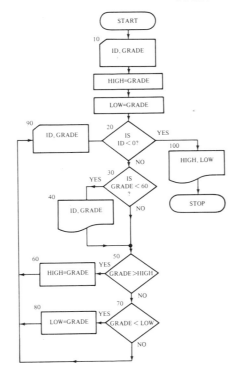

```
C.....................................................
C..    PURPOSE - DEMONSTRATE USE OF ARITHMETIC IF     ..
C..             -FIND HIGH/LOW/FAILING GRADES.        ..
C.....................................................
C              -----IMPORTANT VARIABLES-----
C
C       --ID        STUDENT IDENTIFICATION NUMBER      --
C       --GRADE     STUDENT GRADE                      --
C       --HIGH      HIGHEST EXAM SCORE                 --
C       --LOW       LOWEST EXAM SCORE                  --
C
C     ...............INITIALIZATION SECTION...............
C
      REAL  LOW
C
   10 READ(5,11)  ID,GRADE
   11 FORMAT(I5,F5.1)
      HIGH =GRADE
      LOW =GRADE
C
C     ............. LOOP ENTRY POINT.................
C
   20 IF(ID) 100,30,30
C
C                  PASSING GRADE
C
   30 IF(GRADE-60.0) 40,50,50
C
   40 WRITE(2,41) ID,GRADE
   41 FORMAT(1X,I10,F15.1)
C
C                  REDEFINE HIGH OR LOW IF NECESSARY
C
   50 IF(GRADE-HIGH) 70,70,60
   60 HIGH =GRADE
      GO TO  30
C
   70 IF (GRADE-LOW) 80,90,90
   80 LOW =GRADE
C
   90 READ(5,11)   ID,GRADE
      GO TO 20
C
C     .............LOOP ENDS HERE.................
C
  100 WRITE(2,101) HIGH,LOW
  101 FORMAT(1X,2F15.1)
      STOP
      END
```

> **Programming Example**
> Using Computed
> GO TO**

BELOW	60's	70's	80's	90–100
5	12	23	17	9

Using the same data deck of the previous problem, assume that the teacher giving an exam must report the grade distribution by filling out the table shown above. Write a program that uses a computed GO TO to reach one of 5 counters depending on each student's grade.

The computed GO TO must pass control to one of five blocks (modules) of code in the program that advance one of the counters. If J has the value 1, 2, 3, 4, or 5 control should be passed to the following module:

```
C...MODULE 1...FAILING GRADE...
  1  NBELOW = NBELOW + 1
     GO TO 10
```

If J has the value 9 or 10, control should be passed to the module:

```
C...MODULE 5..."A" GRADE...
  5  NO90S = NO90S + 1
     GO TO 10
```

The computed GO TO statement will be written as follows: for J equal to 1, 2, 3, 4, or 5, control passes to statement number 1. For J equal to 9 or 10, control passes to statement 5. Note that a statement number may appear several times in the choice of transfer points.

A problem will arise if a student scores a very low grade, below 10 points. Such a grade causes J to have the value 0, which is not realistic as a selector quantity. An easy solution is to test for a zero value, and, when one is detected, set J to 1 (to avoid problems with the computed GO TO).

The flow chart and code for the remaining part of this program is now presented.

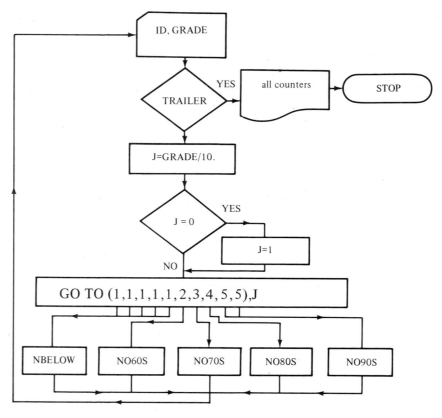

```
                     NO90S=0
                     NO80S=0
                     NO70S=0
                     NO60S=0
                     NBELOW=0
      C
      C                       START PROCESSING GRADES
      C
      100   READ(5,101) ID,GRADE
      101   FORMAT(I4,F5.1)
      C
      C                       IS THIS THE TRAILER CARD
      C
            IF(ID.LT.0) GO TO 200
      C
            J =GRADE/ 10.
      C
      C                       TEST FOR SPECIAL CASE
      C
            IF(J.EQ.0) J=1
      C...........................................................
            GO TO (1,1,1,1,1,2,3,4,5,5) ,J
      C...........................................................
      C
      C          MODULE1.....FAILING GRADES
      C
      1     NBELOW=NBELOW+1
            GO TO 100
      C
      C          MODULE 2.....LOW GRADES
      C
      2     NO60S=NO60S+1
            GO TO 100
      C
      C          MODULE 3.....C  GRADES
      C
      3     NO70S=NO70S +1
            GO TO 100
      C
      C          MODULE 4..... B GRADES
      C
      4     NO80S=NO80S+1
            GO TO 100
      C
      C          MODULE 5..... A GRADES
      C
      5     NO90S=NO90S +1
            GO TO 100
      C
      C                       LOOP TERMINATES HERE
      C
      200   WRITE(2,201) NO90S,NO80S,NO70S,NO60S,NBELOW
      201   FORMAT(5I10)
      C
            STOP
```

6

More On Format Codes

In Chapter 4 you had your first look at FORMAT statements and the codes they use to describe how information is laid out on an input data card or on a line of output. Unfortunately, it is relatively easy to misuse these codes. For example, a student will write the following statements:

```
        READ(5,7) A, B, C, D
    7   FORMAT( F8.1 )
```

and wonder why *four* data cards are consumed each time this READ statement is executed. The difficulty is that the READ statement is calling for the input of four variables (A,B, C and D), but the FORMAT statement specifies the card layout as having a single value located in columns 1 through 8. Even though additional values are punched on the card, they will not be processed, for to do so would be contrary to the specifications provided by the FORMAT statement.

This chapter will take a more thorough look at these codes and some of the complications that can result if they are not used correctly. The much-delayed topic of "Elegant Output" will also be covered.

6.1 | I-Codes

I-codes have the general form:

I w

where "I" identifies the integer mode and "w" specifies a field width. This code, like all the other format codes, tells what type of information is being processed and how many columns are used to specify the value.

When a code such as I6 is encountered in a sequence of format codes, it signals that the next quantity is an integer number and is contained in the next six columns. When constructing I-codes, watch out for these things:

1. Make the field width large enough to hold all the digits and the sign of the number (if any).
2. Make sure the number is right-justified in the field.
3. Make sure the memory location (variable name) associated with this code is *integer* in mode.

Let us see what happens when these rules are not followed.

The specification I5 (controlling output) may be used to print a 5-digit positive integer number or a 4-digit negative integer mode number. The difference exists because all unsigned values are considered positive and on output the plus sign is omitted. If the value is negative, however, the negative sign is written consuming one column of width. If you misuse this code and try to print a 5-digit negative number, an overflow will result. The operating system will signal this overflow, usually by filling the field with asterisks. When you see asterisks in your output, check for insufficient field width.

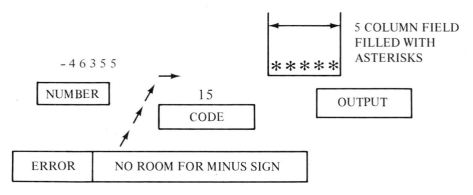

Figure 6.1 One Digit Overflow

The way to avoid an overflow is to use a *large* field width, let us say I9.

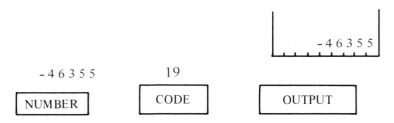

Figure 6.2 Sufficient Field Width

Notice all digits will be printed, and three blank columns will precede the number.

Right Justified

You have been cautioned to position integer numbers so that the extreme right-hand digit of the number is placed in the extreme right-hand column of the field. Numbers so positioned are described as **right justified.** On output, integers are right justified because their position is being controlled by the computer. On input, placement is controlled by the programmer, but the integer must still be right justified.

Range of Values

Each format code results in a specific range of values that can be accommodated by that code. Consider the range associated with an I4 code:

RANGE

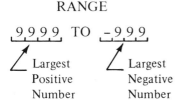

Figure 6.3 Range of Permitted Values

When constructing a format code, you must keep this range limitation in mind.

6.2 | F-Codes

F-codes have the general form:

$$F\ w.d$$

where:

"F" signals that the data item is a floating point or real number:
"w" again defines the field width;
"d" describes the position of the decimal point.

This code is similar to I-codes except for the "d" parameter. This extra value is required because floating point or real numbers are structured differently from integer numbers. Remember that a real memory location must be capable of accommodating a large number of digits after the decimal point to reduce truncation error. As explained in Chapter 2, it is possible for real numbers to be stored to 15- or 20-decimal digit accuracy.

13.333333333333333333

A programmer is seldom interested in displaying numbers to this degree of accuracy. Usually two- or three-digit accuracy is sufficient. This is controlled by the "d" parameter, which tells how many digits are to be displayed after the decimal point. Consider how the above number would appear when printed under the following F-codes:

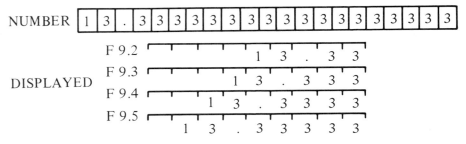

Floating-point numbers require one space for the decimal point and may consume one space for the sign (as described in I-codes).

Each floating-point format code accommodates a specific range of numbers. An F 8.2 code can accommodate the following range of values:

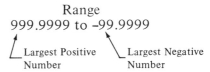

The code F 8.4 consumes the same field width, but because the numbers are written to four-place accuracy, the safe range is considerably reduced.

Range
999.9999 to –99.9999

L Largest Positive   L Largest Negative
  Number   Number

It is often very difficult to predict the size of an output value. This is especially true if the number has been obtained after long or difficult calculations. If the field width is not sufficient to hold the number, overflow will result as explained previously. As before, we recommend specifying a large field width.

6.3 | Truncation vs. Rounding

You will hear the terms "truncation" or "rounding" used to describe how a real number is transferred from memory to output. Consider the transfer of the number:

| 7 | . | 3 | 1 | 4 | 9 | 2 | 7 | 8 | 6 | 3 |

under the control of an F 6.3 code. The cut-off point is between the 4 and the 9.

$$7 . 3 1 4 \mid 9 2 7 8 6 3$$

The printed value may appear in two possible ways:

  7.314   7.315

  TRUNCATION   ROUNDING

Truncation implies a direct transfer of digits. If rounding is used, digits after the cut-off point are allowed to affect (by rounding up) the value being sent to output. In this case, the 9 causes a rounding up of the 4 to a 5.

6.4 | E-Codes

E-codes have the general form:

E w.d

They provide an alternate way of publishing real numbers but with the distinct advantage of *protection from overflow*. When real numbers are published using an F-code, there is always a specific range of values the code can accommodate and therefore there is the possibility of overflow. Not so with E-codes. As long as the field width is a fixed number larger than the "d" parameter, no overflow will take place. All computers have a maximum size (magnitude) of real numbers they can handle. This is usually a very large number. A typical range of magnitudes is 10^{38} to 10^{-38}. Let us see why there is no overflow with E-codes.

The quantity "d" again controls the accuracy to which the number is displayed. This time it controls the number of digits appearing after the decimal point of the mantissa.

Number	As Printed	E-Code
−0.00006275432	−0.6275E−03	E11.4
167,280,000.	0.16728E+09	E12.5
.126	0.1260E+00	E11.4

Having decided on a value of "d", 7 additional columns are needed to complete the number.

> *Four* columns are needed to express the exponent (the E, the sign, and a two digit integer)
>
> *Three* more columns to complete the mantissa (a sign, leading zero, and a decimal point)

If the field width "w" is 7 greater than the accuracy parameter "d", *all* numbers expressed by this code will be accommodated. It is much safer to make the field width larger than the minimum, but the point is that an E-code is a safe one to use if you are not sure how large or how small your data value may be.

The table below shows the way in which the number:
$$-0.12345678 \times 10^4$$
would appear when printed under various E-codes.

Number	As Printed	Code	
−0	*****	E6.4	
.	******	E7.4	Insufficient
1	*******	E8.4	Field Width
2	********	E9.4	
3	*********	E10.4	
4	−0.1234E 04	E11.4	
5	−0.1234E 04	E12.4	
6	−0.1234E 04	E13.4	
7			
8	−0.123456E 04	E15.6	
×	−0.123457E 04*		
1			
0⁴			

*Last digit affected by truncation or rounding

When E-FORMAT numbers are written by the programmer as input values, certain short-cuts in writing the number are allowed. We see below the number 0.16728×10^9 written as output and the equivalent acceptable input forms.

Output Form
(E12.5)
0.16728E 09

Equivalent Acceptable Input Form

.16728E9	.16728E+9	+.16728E09	+.16728E+09

These shorter forms are not recommended for the beginner. One form:

Blank

0.16728E+9 ⟍

will produce an error. The problem in the example shown is that, since the exponent is an integer number, it must be positioned right justified in its field. The blank in the extreme right-hand column of the field will be read as a zero. The exponent will be read incorrectly, causing the number to be:
$$0.16728 \times 10^{90}$$

6.5 | More Than One Unit Record

In the beginning of this chapter it was suggested that the statements:

```
READ(5,7) A, B, C, D
7   FORMAT ( F8.1 )
```

would cause the reading of four data cards. This section will explain why in greater detail. Notice that there are four names following the command READ but only one format code in the FORMAT statement. This is perfectly legal but represents a somewhat advanced technique.

Soon we will be reading massive amounts of input that could easily involve 20 or 30 cards. Because each card has the same layout, the FORMAT statement describes one (so-called typical) card *only*! Under these circumstances, a single READ instruction will cause card after card to be read (until all variables in the list of the READ statement are defined).

Until you gain a degree of experience in dealing with FORMAT statements, it is a good idea to have the number of codes in the FORMAT statement:

1. match in number and mode the variable names in the list of the input or output statement, and
2. match in number and mode the values on the data card or line of output.

You should be aware, however, that a FORMAT statement is assumed to describe one "typical unit record" only (either a data card or a line of output). As many "typical records" as necessary will be used to transfer all the values represented by the variable names appearing in the list of the input/output statement. Whenever the number of variable names exceeds the number of format codes, more than one record will be processed.

It is for this reason that the statements:

```
     READ(5,7) A, B, C, D
7    FORMAT ( F8.1 )
```

cause the reading of four data cards. The fact that you may have keypunched four real values on each card has no effect.

A similar situation applies in the following output command:

```
     WRITE (2,10) A, B, C, D, E
10   FORMAT ( 1X, F8.4 )
```

These statements result in 5 lines of output, each containing a single real number.

6.6 Elegant Output

The ability to get brief messages as part of any line of output

WRITE (2,*)'THE ANSWERS ARE', X, Y, Z

helps considerably in making the output easier to read. It is possible to produce very elaborate output as has been suggested in several previous problems. Page headings, column headings, double and triple spacing, indentation, and alignment of data are typical of what is called "elegant output." In this section we will examine several new format codes that allow the programmer to exercise absolute control over where and how various output values are to be printed.

New Format Codes

Code	Meaning	Example
X-code	skip columns	20X — skip 20 columns
H-code	fixed typing (count involved)	3HTHE — type three characters — THE
'-code	fixed typing	'THE' or *THE*
*-code	(no count involved)	type the characters between symbols
/-code	skip lines or cards	//// — skip 3 lines

Figure 6.5 Additional Format Codes

These new codes have one feature that makes them markedly different from I,F,E and A codes. They do not involve any exchange or interaction with memory. The purpose of these new codes is entirely different, namely, to present the output in a more readable form.

X - code

The X-code is used to skip spaces. The code:

20X

appearing in a FORMAT statement would cause twenty spaces to be skipped. On input this would mean, "ignore the next 20 columns on the card." On output, it would be like hitting the space bar of a typewriter twenty times. If this was the first code in a FORMAT statement, it would result in a 20-column margin. It could also be used to separate one column of data from another by 20 spaces.

/ -code

The /-code causes the skipping of lines or cards. The code:

///

means skip three unit records. If this code was used in a FORMAT statement controlling a READ operation, each slash would mean, "skip a card." On output it means, "skip a line." Each slash is the equivalent of hitting the carriage return bar on the typewriter.

Character Strings

Figure 6.6 shows an example of elegant output. The first two lines of the output are of primary interest. They are used to form titles and headings that assist in reading the numeric data that follows. Obtaining a message in a line of printout is

THE ANSWERS ARE			
I	X	Y	Z
21	5.2305	62.3000	.2847
82	9.2634	12.4819	.7490
8	52.9538	.2849	81.8479
124	0.0362	116.3859	54.3905
56	826.3950	6.3793	7.2933

Figure 6.6 An Example Output Page

by no means a new topic. Consider the statement:

WRITE(2,*)'ANSWER 1 =', X, 'ANSWER 2 =', Y

You should recognize that the quotation marks enclosing the message 'ANSWER 1 =' and 'ANSWER 2=' signal that these character strings are to be included in the line of output.

To obtain the headings shown in Figure 6.6 we will use a similar technique except that the character string will be stipulated *inside* a FORMAT statement so we can tightly control where the desired character string is to be positioned on the page.

To get the line that says "THE ANSWERS ARE" two instructions are needed:

1. skip across the line to somewhere near the middle of the page, and
2. type the words "THE ANSWERS ARE."

There are three ways of issuing these instructions:

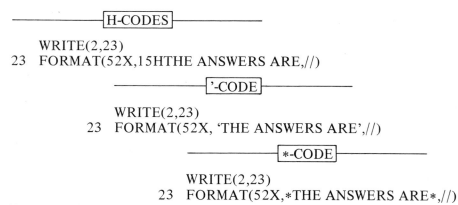

```
                        ┤H-CODES├

        WRITE(2,23)
23   FORMAT(52X,15HTHE ANSWERS ARE,//)

                        ┤'-CODE├

        WRITE(2,23)
23   FORMAT(52X, 'THE ANSWERS ARE',//)

                        ┤*-CODE├

        WRITE(2,23)
23   FORMAT(52X,*THE ANSWERS ARE*,//)
```

Figure 6.7 Code for Character Strings

In each method, the command WRITE is used to get control of the output device. Notice that there are no variable names in the list of this WRITE statement. This is because the line of output can be generated without any exchange with memory. Memory comes into play only when the line of output contains a variable quantity. The contents of this line are fixed.

The first code in each FORMAT statement is a "skipping" code. It indicates that the first 52 columns of the output line are to be blank. The printer is now sitting at column 53 of the output line ready to process the next field, the message. Figure 6.7 shows that there are three ways of defining the message.

The middle set of instructions encloses the message between quotation marks paralleling the techniques used before. The last set of instructions shows that the asterisk can be used in place of the quotation marks.

The quotation mark or asterisk is called a **delimiter** and is used to show where the message begins and where the message ends. The asterisk becomes a very useful delimiter if the message to be printed contains an embedded quotation mark:

SALESMAN'S COMMISSIONS

H-codes

The method of defining the message in the first set of instructions in Figure 6.7 is called a **Hollerith code**. It allows *any* combination of characters in the message. This code starts by giving an exact count of how many characters are in the message string. The letter H defines the type of code being used.

When the code:

15H

is encountered in the FORMAT statement, the computer will copy the 15 characters following the letter H directly onto the next 15 columns of the output line.* The complete Hollerith code is characterized by a numeric quantity followed by the letter H followed by the message to be printed. The number

---

*The serious disadvantage of this method is that a character count is required. If this count is not accurate, an error occurs. For this reason H-codes are less popular than the other methods.

preceding the letter H must be an exact count of all characters in the message including blanks.

Getting the Second Line

The second line of output in Figure 6.6 is like the first in that no exchange with memory is required. This line can be generated by the statements:

```
      WRITE(2,24)
24    FORMAT(20X,1HI,20X,1HX,20X,1HY,20X,1HZ)
```

As usual, the format codes provide an efficient means of describing exactly the various fields needed to obtain the desired line of output:

> 1st field — A blank field of 20 columns.
> 2nd field — A one-column Hollerith field in which the letter I appears.
> 3rd field — A blank field of 20 columns.
> 4th field — A one-column Hollerith field in which the letter X appears.
> 5th field — A blank field of 20 columns.
> 6th field — A one-column Hollerith field in which the letter Y appears.
> 7th field — A blank field of 20 columns.
> 8th field — A one-column Hollerith field in which the letter Z appears.

The remaining lines of output in Figure 6.6 contain numerical values only. The field width for each of these values would be adjusted to make the number fall under the column headings just printed.

6.7 | Combining FORMAT Codes

All the FORMAT codes described thus far (A,I,F,E,X,H,*,',/) may appear in any combination within a single FORMAT statement. Figure 6.8 shows output similar but not identical to that in Figure 6.6. Most of the output contains a mixture

```
                  THE ANSWERS ARE
    I= 21      X=   5.2305     Y=62.7330     Z=    .6486
    I= 82      X=   9.2733     Y=12.9476     Z=   1.1684
    I=  8      X=  52.5321     Y=   .6488    Z=  86.8372
    I=124      X=   8.0357     Y=  7.3857    Z=167.7940
    I= 56      X=537.9386      Y=46.5667     Z=  20.0375
    I=  5                                    Z=   7.3950
```

Figure 6.8 An Example Output Page

of Hollerith fields and blank fields interspersed with the numeric values. These lines are obtained by the statements:

```
      WRITE(2,30)I,X,Y,ZERO
30    FORMAT(14X,2HI=,I3,10X,2HX=,F8.4,10X,2HY=,
     1 F8.4,10X,2HZ=,F8.4)
```

Because there are four variables in the output line, the WRITE statement contains four variable names. Statement 30 controls the format of the line. It starts by skipping 14 spaces and printing, I=. The code I3 is then reached. Because this type of code involves an exchange with memory, the computer consults the list of variable names following the WRITE statement to determine where in memory this integer value is stored. The next two format codes are a blank and Hollerith field respectively. The code F8.4 is the second code that involves an exchange with memory. The second name in the list of the WRITE statement determines where in memory this value is found. The process continues until the output line is complete.

Commas are used to separate the various codes in the FORMAT statement. They make the code easier to read.

6.8 | Carriage Control

In Chapter 4 a brief reference was made to the fact that column 1 of any output line has a special meaning. Whatever character appears in this position will *not* be printed on the output sheet, but rather will be used to control where on the output page the line should appear. Stated another way, it controls how many lines the paper will be advanced before the printout takes place. For this reason the character in column 1 is called "the carriage control" character.

A blank in column 1 indicates the line should be printed on the next available line (advance the carriage one line before printing). By using other characters we can get double spacing, triple spacing, advancing to the middle of a page, advancing to the top of a new page, etc.

Character	Effect
Blank	Paper advances a single line.
0	Paper advances two lines.
1	Paper advances to the first line on the next page.
+	Paper does not advance.

Figure 6.9 Carriage Control Characters

Figure 6.9 shows the four most commonly used control characters and the effect they have on advancing the paper. One of these characters should be made to appear in column 1 of each line of printed output. Again realize that this character will *not* be printed on the output line.

There are three techniques for getting a character into the carriage control column.

        7 FORMAT (1H1, 6F 8.2)
                7 FORMAT(*1*, 6F 8.2)
                        7 FORMAT ('1', 6F 8.2)

In each of the examples, a 1 has been placed in the carriage control position, which will cause the line of output to appear at the top of a new page.

Other carriage control characters are not as standard as those in Figure 6.9. Each computer system has its own set of characters, described in the User's Manual for that system.

6.9 | FORMAT Statements with Internal Parentheses

Internal parentheses are allowed in FORMAT statements to cause the repeating of certain portions of the FORMAT code. For example, internal parentheses are used in the statement:

        6   FORMAT(2F6.2,3(F12.1,I2))

This statement is functionally equivalent to the statement:

    6   FORMAT(2F6.2,F12.1,I2,F12.1,I2,F12.1,I2)

As a second example, consider the statement:

    7   FORMAT(2(I6,F8.3),E10.3)

This statement has the same meaning as:

    7   FORMAT(I6,F8.3,I6,F8.3,E10.3)

Using more than two internal parentheses (parentheses inside of parentheses) is not allowed. For example:

Allowed:

FORMAT (2(I6, F6.3), 10X, 4(I6, F5.1))

Not Allowed:

FORMAT (10X, 4(F12.2, 3(I4, I6)))

6.10 Summary

You are getting very close to having the ability to place output values (numeric, alphabetic or both) anywhere on the output sheet you find appropriate. Most scientific programmers make use of these new format features to generate the clear and "pleasant to look at" output we have shown in several previous programming examples. It is called **elegant output.**

    These new format features have another application. Consider the problem of generating the payroll check shown in Figure 6.10. The usual output paper is removed from the printer and replaced by a series of blank checks. As the programmer, you may not only be required to calculate a person's pay amount, but also be told to place that value in a specific position, namely two lines down from the top of the check and 36 columns in from the lefthand edge of the check. This would be accomplished by statements such as:

WRITE(2,18) PAY
18   FORMAT(1H1,//,36X,F8.2)

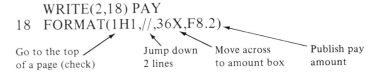

Go to the top   Jump down   Move across   Publish pay
of a page (check)   2 lines   to amount box   amount

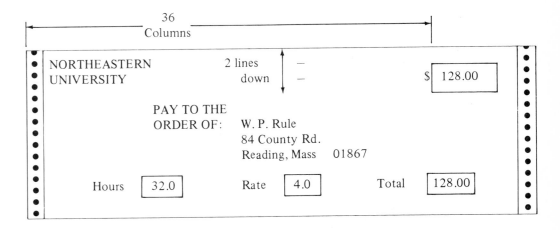

Figure 6.10 Computer Generated Paycheck

The next requirement might be to drop down three more lines and print the employee's name starting in column 11.

WRITE(2,19)NAME1,NAME2
19 FORMAT(///,10X,2A6)

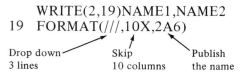

The point is that your understanding of format codes gives you considerable flexibility to meet the vast majority of problems you might be presented with.

Recall some of the elegant output used in previous programming examples. The stock report example on p. 70 is typical. At the time it was first presented, you did not have the ability to:

1. start the report on a new page,
2. center the words "STOCK REPORT" on the top of the sheet,
3. produce the column headings, or
4. spread the individual stock listings evenly across the page.

The situation should be different now. Now you have the ability.

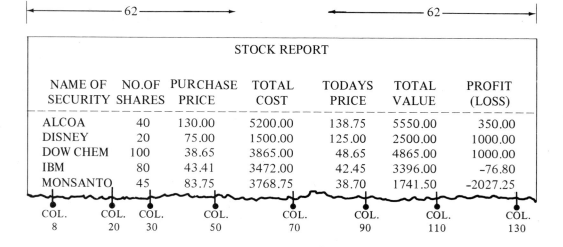

There are two ways of spreading the listing of individual stocks across the output sheet. One uses skipping codes. The other uses large "field widths."

Large Field Widths

Realize that the codes:

    10X,F6.1

and the code:

    F16.1

are very similar with regard to the positioning of a floating point number. The latter code uses a field width that is 10 larger than necessary for the number. It thereby obtains separation of fields and at the same time provides extra protection from overflow. The use of large field widths is recommended.

Quiz#7   FORMAT Codes

Part 1: Answer the following questions.

1. Describe the output generated by the following statements:

          WRITE(2,10)A,B,C,D,E
      10 FORMAT(1X,F12.2)

2. Asterisks in an output field are symptomatic of what problem?

3. What does the term "unit record" mean? On input? On output?

4. What is the first column of any line of output used for?

5. In the following output statement, the letter L has been mistakenly placed in column 1. How will the output be written?

          WRITE(2,10)
      10 FORMAT(*LARGEST VALUE*)

6. Write an output statement whose only function is to go to the top of a page and print the message 'PG.1' on the right of an output page.

7. Write a single FORMAT code that is the equivalent of the codes:

          10X,F6.3

8. What is the most important advantage of E-codes compared to F-codes?

9. What are the three ways of causing a character string (fixed message) to be included as part of a line of output?

10. Define "elegant output." What advantage does it have?

Part 2: Writing a Program

11.

```
*  *  *  *  *  *  *  *  *  *  *  *  *  *  *  *  *  *  *  *  *  *  *
*  *                      CROSS TABULATION                  *  *
*  *            ETHNIC ORIGIN      BY      FAMILY INCOME     *  *
*  *  *  *  *  *  *  *  *  *  *  *  *  *  *  *  *  *  *  *  *  *  *
RACE:    INCOME:
              0-4000   4001-6000  6001-8000 8001-10000   OVER    TOTAL
- - - -I- - - -I- - - -I- - - -I- - - -I- - - -I- - - -I
WHITE   I    40   I    68   I   190   I   270   I   301   I   869
- - - -I- - - -I- - - -I- - - -I- - - -I- - - -I- - - -I
BLACK   I    45   I    82   I   168   I   201   I   210   I   706
- - - -I- - - -I- - - -I- - - -I- - - -I- - - -I- - - -I
SPANISH I    16   I    47   I    84   I   120   I   119   I   386
- - - -I- - - -I- - - -I- - - -I- - - -I- - - -I- - - -I
OTHER   I     3   I     5   I     8   I    24   I    52   I    92
- - - -I- - - -I- - - -I- - - -I- - - -I- - - -I- - - -I
  TOTAL     104      202      450      615      682     2053
```

Write statements that will produce the heading, column heading and the first detail line (listing WHITE incomes) similar to those of the table shown above.

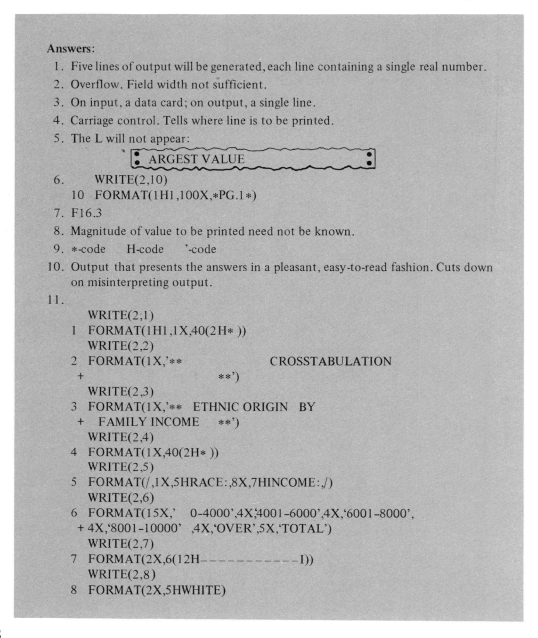

Answers:

1. Five lines of output will be generated, each line containing a single real number.
2. Overflow. Field width not sufficient.
3. On input, a data card; on output, a single line.
4. Carriage control. Tells where line is to be printed.
5. The L will not appear:

> : ARGEST VALUE

6.   WRITE(2,10)
   10   FORMAT(1H1,100X,*PG.1*)

7. F16.3
8. Magnitude of value to be printed need not be known.
9. *-code   H-code   '-code
10. Output that presents the answers in a pleasant, easy-to-read fashion. Cuts down on misinterpreting output.
11.

```
   WRITE(2,1)
 1 FORMAT(1H1,1X,40(2H* ))
   WRITE(2,2)
 2 FORMAT(1X,'**              CROSSTABULATION
  +               **')
   WRITE(2,3)
 3 FORMAT(1X,'**  ETHNIC ORIGIN  BY
  +   FAMILY INCOME    **')
   WRITE(2,4)
 4 FORMAT(1X,40(2H* ))
   WRITE(2,5)
 5 FORMAT(/,1X,5HRACE:,8X,7HINCOME:,/)
   WRITE(2,6)
 6 FORMAT(15X,'  0-4000',4X,'4001-6000',4X,'6001-8000',
  + 4X,'8001-10000'  ,4X,'OVER',5X,'TOTAL')
   WRITE(2,7)
 7 FORMAT(2X,6(12H-----------I))
   WRITE(2,8)
 8 FORMAT(2X,5HWHITE)
```

Review Exercises

1. The following integer values are to be printed as output using an I3 FORMAT code. Show how these values will appear.

Value	Output
76	
1006	
+1	
1234	
–104	

2.*The statements:

```
   READ(5,8)XINIT,YINIT,XFINL,YFINL,NUM
 8 FORMAT(2F8.2,2F10.3,I6)
```

are used to transfer five values from the data card shown to memory.

(a) Do all values lie within their specified field width?
(b) Several values are not right justified in their respective fields. Will this produce an error?
(c) Which values have their decimal points located in the proper column?

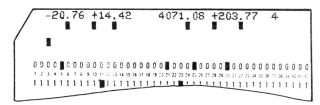

(d) Is improper decimal point location a problem?

(e) Show how these values would appear if printed as output under the control of FORMAT statement 8.

3. Repeat part (e) of problem 2 for the following modified FORMAT statements:

(a) Each field width has been increased by two columns.

        8   FORMAT(2F10.2,2F12.3,I8)

(b) Each field width has been increased by four columns and two additional places after the decimal points have been requested.

        8   FORMAT(2F12.4,2F14.5,I10)

4.*Complete the table by specifiying the range of values the following format code will accommodate:

Code	Range	
I5		to
F8.6		to
F10.4		to
I7		to
E14.4		to

5. Write a program that will print the letter H 15 units high and 15 units wide centered on the output sheet as shown.

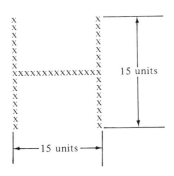

6. All field width specifications should include room for either a plus or a minus sign. True or false?

7. What is meant by the term "carriage control character"? Give two examples.

8.*Which of these two groups of output statements is preferred? Why?

          WRITE(2,20)NAME1,NAME2
        20   FORMAT(///,1X,2A6)

          WRITE(2,20)NAME1,NAME2
        20   FORMAT(///,2A6)

9. How many data cards will be consumed by the following READ statement? Describe the location of A, B and C.

          READ(5,10)A,B,C
        10   FORMAT(//,3F8.1)

10. Describe the line of output generated by the following statements:

          WRITE(2,30)
        30   FORMAT(1H1,///,3X,60(2H_))

11.*In the following output statement, the count of Hollerith characters is in error (it's one too large). What effect will this have regarding the correct syntax of the FORMAT statement?

          WRITE(2,40)
        40   FORMAT(35X,7HOUTPUT)

12. A data deck consists of cards containing a single value of X. This value may be positive or negative and represents DEPOSITS or WITHDRAWALS to a checking account.

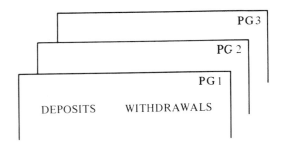

Post these transactions as shown above.

(a) Provide statements to produce the column headings shown at the top of an output page.

(b) Post the individual transaction amount on the left or the right of the page as appropriate.

13. Repeat problem 12 but include the following features. You are to post no more than forty transactions on any one page. If several pages are needed to list all the transactions contained in the data deck, each page is to have its own column headings and each page should be numbered. You will need a page counter and a transaction counter.

14. A fraternity wants a banner made of letters 30 lines tall and 20 characters wide. This is a tedious job of writing 30 pairs of WRITE/FORMAT combinations to obtain the desired output. Write the statements necessary to obtain the top two lines of the output wanted.

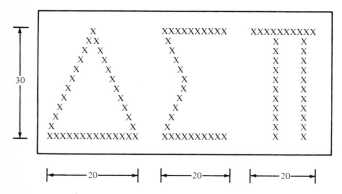

15. A video terminal is used to display the flight number of arriving and departing aircraft. Write statements to obtain the top two or three lines of this output.

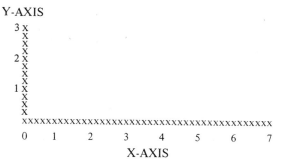

16.*The output of a program is to consist of several lines of output and a graph plotting this output. The graph is to be plotted by hand, but the X and Y axes of the graph are to be machine generated through the use of appropriate Hollerith codes. Write the statements needed to print the X and Y axes shown.

```
Y-AXIS
  3 X
    X
    X
    X
  2 X
    X
    X
  1 X
    X
    X
    XXXXXXXXXXXXXXXXXXXXXXXXXXXXXXXXXXXXXXXXXXXXX
    0    1    2    3    4    5    6    7
                  X-AXIS
```

17. Write a program to produce as output the following conversion tables:

CONVERSION TABLES:
CENTIMETERS TO INCHES

CM.	INCHES	CM.	INCHES	CM.	INCHES
1.0	.3937	11.0	4.3307	21.0	8.2677
2.0	.7874	12.0	4.7244	22.0	8.6614
3.0	1.1811	13.0	5.1181	23.0	9.0551
4.0	1.5748	14.0	5.5118	24.0	9.4488
5.0	1.9685	15.0	5.9055	25.0	9.8425
6.0	2.3622	16.0	6.2992	26.0	10.2362
7.0	2.7559	17.0	6.6929	27.0	10.6299
8.0	3.1496	18.0	7.0866	28.0	11.0236
9.0	3.5433	19.0	7.4803	29.0	11.4173
10.0	3.9370	20.0	7.8740	30.0	11.8110

18. A ball is positioned 10 feet above a circular table that is rotating in a counterclockwise direction at one revolution per minute. At time t=0 the leading edge of the hole is at the "12 o'clock" position. The ball is at the "3 o'clock" position. At time t, to be read from a data card, the ball is dropped. Write a program to determine if the ball will pass through the hole in the table. Have the computer print YES or NO.

19.*An airline operates among four terminals. The X and Y coordinates of each terminal are given on separate data cards. Write a program to determine the distance between terminals and report these distances by generating the table shown.

Terminal Coordinates

	X	Y
1	16.27	43.94
2	46.19	67.21
3	38.54	7.34
4	91.12	30.51

Terminal	1	2	3	4
1	0.00	37.90	42.84	76.05
2	37.90	0.00	60.36	58.01
3	42.84	60.39	0.00	57.46
4	76.05	58.01	57.46	0.00

20. A programming example in Chapter 5 involved determining how many times the number 5 appears in a data deck. Write the program again to include the elegant output suggested. Use statements early in the program to produce the headings. Use statements later in the program to generate the final message, "RUN COMPLETE: FINAL RESULT 3". Generate the intermediate output as well.

CARD BEING PROCESSED	VALUE READ FROM CARD	CONDITION OF COUNTER
1	6	0
2	1	0
3	5	1
4	2	1
18	7	2
19	5	3
20	3	3
RUN COMPLETE: FINAL RESULT 3		

21. A toy manufacturer is considering producing a computerized tic-tac-toe game. Write software that will produce the basic game board as suggested in the illustration.

```
                    x                   x
                    x                   x
                    x                   x
                    x                   x
xxxxxxxxxxxxxxxxxxxxxxxxxxxxxxxxxxxxxxxxxxxxx
                    x                   x
                    x                   x
                    x                   x
xxxxxxxxxxxxxxxxxxxxxxxxxxxxxxxxxxxxxxxxxxxxx
                    x                   x
                    x                   x
                    x                   x
                    x                   x
```

22. A computer is used to generate inventory reports for the National Guard. Each report is twenty to thirty pages long, and there are hundreds of reports generated on one computer run. We need a convenient way to separate one report from another.

Write a program to be used at the end of each report that will generate *two* pages of output as follows, which will serve as a means of separating the reports.

```
XXXXXXXXXXXXXXXXXXXXXXXXXXXXXXXXXXXXXX
XXXXXXXXXXXXXXXXXXXXXXXXXXXXXXXXXXXXXX
XX                                  XX
XX                                  XX
XX                                  XX
XX                                  XX
XX                                  XX
XX                                  XX
XX                                  XX
XX                                  XX
XX                                  XX
XX                                  XX
XX                                  XX
XX                                  XX
XXXXXXXXXXXXXXXXXXXXXXXXXXXXXXXXXXXXXX
XXXXXXXXXXXXXXXXXXXXXXXXXXXXXXXXXXXXXX
```

Additional Applications

Programming Example
List by Section Number

A data deck contains the names of students enrolled in a FORTRAN course. There are *four* sections of these students. All students in section 014 appear first in the deck, followed by the students in section 015, and so on. Write a program to provide a separate listing of the students in each section. (When the section number changes, go to the top of a new page and provide an appropriate heading.)

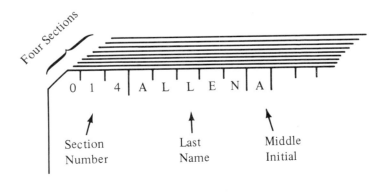

```
C..................................................................
C..   PURPOSE -   PROVIDE SEPARATE LIST OF NAMES              ...
C..               FOR EACH SECTION OF STUDENTS.               ...
C..................................................................
C
C                 -----IMPORTANT VARIABLES-----
C
C     --SECTN     SECTION NUMBER READ FROM CARD                  --
C     --NAME      NAME OF STUDENT
C     --MI        STUDENT'S MIDDLE INITIAL                       ::
C
C     --PRESNT    SECTION NUMBER PRESENTLY BEING PROCESSED       --
C
      INTEGER   SECTN, PRESNT
C
C                 SET PRESNT TO RIDICULOUS VALUE
C
      PRESNT = -999
C
C                 LOOP STARTS HERE
C
   10 READ(5,20,END=50)SECTN, NAME, MI
   20 FORMAT(I3,A6,A1)
C
C     IF(SECTN.NE.PRESNT) THEN
C
              WRITE(2,30)SECTN
   30         FORMAT(1H1,15X,'SECTION ',I3)
C
              PRESNT=SECTN
C
      ENDIF
C
      WRITE(2,40)NAME,MI
   40 FORMAT(5X,A6,4X,A1,1H.)
C
      GO TO 10
C
   50 STOP
      END
```

Programming Example
The Roll of the Dice

Two integer numbers appear as shown on a data card telling the "roll of the dice" in a crap game.

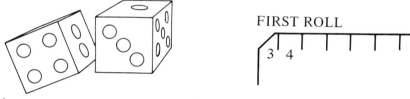

FIRST ROLL

Part A
IF this roll totals seven, issue the message:

FIRST ROLL   3 4   THE ROLL IS 7. YOU WIN.

IF this roll is other than seven (five for example), issue the message:

Part B Next Roll
If the first roll is other than seven, read additional data cards (like the first one) and issue messages such as:

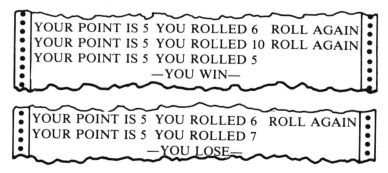

YOUR POINT IS 5 YOU ROLLED 6   ROLL AGAIN
YOUR POINT IS 5 YOU ROLLED 10 ROLL AGAIN
YOUR POINT IS 5 YOU ROLLED 5
                —YOU WIN—

YOUR POINT IS 5 YOU ROLLED 6   ROLL AGAIN
YOUR POINT IS 5 YOU ROLLED 7
                —YOU LOSE—

```
C.........................................................
C.:. PURPOSE -  SIMULATE ACTION IN A DICE GAME.        ::
C.........................................................
C
C                    -----IMPORTANT VARIABLES-----
C
C      --N1,N2  NUMBERS ON TWO DIE                      --
C      --TOTAL  SUM OF THESE NUMBERS                    --
C      --POINT  NUMBER SHOOTER IS TRYING TO GET         --
C
C      INTEGER TOTAL,POINT
C
C                    --- FIRST ROLL --
C
C      READ(5,10)N1,N2
   10  FORMAT(2I1)
C
C      TOTAL=N1+N2
C
C      IF(TOTAL.EQ.7)THEN
C
C                    WE HAVE A WINNER
C
C             WRITE(2,20)
   20        FORMAT(10X,'THE ROLL IS 7.   YOU WIN.')
C
C             STOP
C
C      ELSE
C
C             WRITE(2,30)TOTAL
   30        FORMAT(10X,'YOUR POINT IS ',I2,1H.)
C
C             POINT=TOTAL
C
C      ENDIF
C                    --- REMAINING ACTION ---
C
   40  READ(5,10)N1,N2
C
C      TOTAL=N1+N2
C
C      IF(TOTAL.EQ.POINT)THEN
C
C             WRITE(2,50)POINT,TOTAL
   50        FORMAT(10X,'YOUR POINT IS ',I2,' YOU ROLLED ',I2,
      1      /,20X,11H--YOU WIN--)
C
C             STOP
C
C      ENDIF
C
C      IF(TOTAL.EQ.7)THEN
C
C             WRITE(2,50)POINT,TOTAL
   60        FORMAT(10X,'YOUR POINT IS ',I2,' YOU ROLLED ',I2,
      1      /,20X,12H--YOU LOSE--)
C
C             STOP
C
C      ELSE
C
C             WRITE(2,70)POINT,TOTAL
   70        FORMAT(10X,'YOUR POINT IS ',I2,' YOU ROLLED ',I2,
      1      ' ROLL AGAIN')
C
C             GO TO 40
C
C      ENDIF
C
C      STOP
C
C      END
```

Programming Example
Computerized
Letters

A company specializes in "Computer Correspondence." It offers up to 90 different letters containing various business messages. Three typical letters appear in the next illustration . These letters are triggered from a data card that starts with a two-digit number code telling which message to generate. The next 60 columns give the name and address of the recipient. Two real values contain variables that must appear in the main body letter.

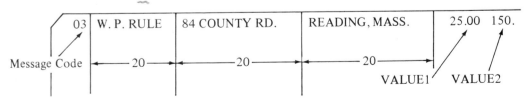

Write statements that would generate the three messages shown in the illustration.

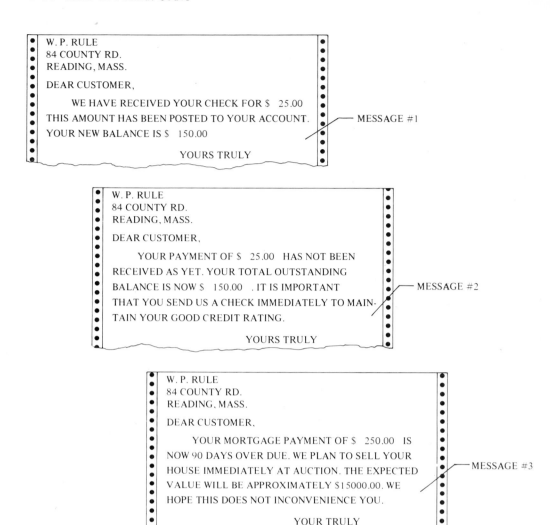

```
C••••••••••••••••••••••••••••••••••••••••••••••••••••••••••••••••••
C     PURPOSE- GENERATE VARIOUS BUSINESS LETTERS           ••
C••••••••••••••••••••••••••••••••••••••••••••••••••••••••••••••••••
C
C            -------IMPORTANT VARIABLES-------
C
C     --CODE                     NUMBER CODE TELLING WHICH
C                                LETTER TO PRODUCE
C     --NAME1,NAME2,NAME3,NAME4  PORTIONS OF RECIPIENTS
C                                NAME
C     --ST1,ST2,ST3,ST4          PORTIONS OF STREET A4DINbS
C     --TOWN1,TOWN2,TOWN3,TOWN4  PORTIONS OF TOWN ADDRESS
C     --VALUE1,VALUE2            VARIABLE NUMBERS IN MESSAGE
C
C     INTEGER CODE
C
      READ(5,100)CODE,NAME1,NAME2,NAME3,NAME4,ST1,ST2,ST3,
     1ST4,TOWN1,TOWN2,TOWN3,TOWN4,VALUE1,VALUE2
  100 FORMAT(I2,4A5,4A5,4A5,2F8.2)
C
C
C
C            PRODUCE ADDRESS AND OPENING SALUTATION
C
      WRITE(2,200)NAME1,NAME2,NAME3,NAME4
  200 FORMAT(1H1,5X,4A5)
      WRITE(2,201) ST1,ST2,ST3,ST4
  201 FORMAT(5X,4A5)
      WRITE(2,202)TOWN1,TOWN2,TOWN3,TOWN4
  202 FORMAT(5X,4A5,//)
      WRITE(2,203)
  203 FORMAT(5X,*DEAR CUSTOMER*,//)
C
```

```
C               USE COMPUTED GO TO
C
C      ........................................
C            GO TO (1,2,3,4,5,6,7,8,9,10,11,12),CODE
C      ........................................
C               SECTION FOR MESSAGE  1
C
    1 WRITE(2,101) VALUE1
  101 FORMAT(9X,*WE HAVE RECEIVED YOUR CHECK FOR $*,F8.2,*.*)
      WRITE(2,102)
  102 FORMAT(5X,*THIS AMOUNT HAS BEEN POSTED TO YOUR ACCOUNT*)
      WRITE(2,103)
  103 FORMAT(5X,*YOUR NEW BALANCE IS $*,F8.2,*.*,//)
      WRITE(2,104)
  104 FORMAT(22X,*YOURS TRULY*,//////)
C
      STOP
C
C               SECTION FOR MESSAGE 2
C
    2 WRITE(2,105)
  105 FORMAT(9X,*YOUR PAYMENT OF $*,F8.2,*HAS NOT BEEN*)

      WRITE(2,106)
  106 FORMAT(5X,*RECEIVED YET.  YOUR TOTAL OUTSTANDING*)
      STOP
      END
```

| **Programming Example** Shortest Tie-In | A community is serviced by a network of underground natural gas pipe lines. Points 1 through 6 represent possible points to tie into this system. |

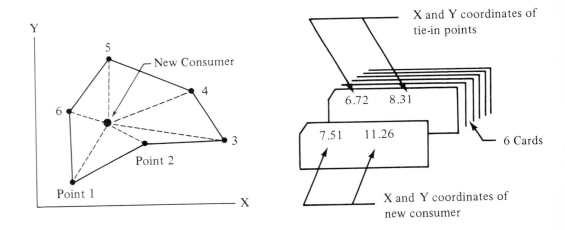

Given the X and Y coordinates of a new consumer, determine the closest point to tie into. The first card in the data deck describes the location of the new customer. Points 1 through 6 are described on the six cards that follow. Produce output as shown.

LOCATION OF NEW CUSTOMER		
X= 7.51		Y= 11.26
POINT	LOCATION	DISTANCE
1	X= 6.72 Y= 5.09	7.43
2	X=18.91 Y=12.26	14.47
3	X=25.37 Y=27.37	24.53
4	X= 4.22 Y=21.80	12.89
5	X= 1.04 Y=10.14	7.12
6	X=11.16 Y=10.01	4.21

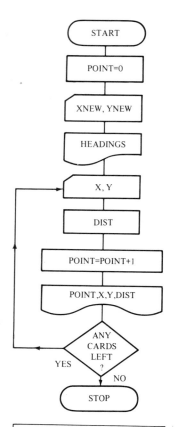

```
C...........................................................
C..    PURPOSE- TO COMPUTE CONNECTING DISTANCE BETWEEN   A  ..
C..          CUSTOMER AND SIX POSSIBLE TIE IN POINTS.       ..
C...........................................................
C
C          -------IMPORTANT VARIABLES------
C
C       +-XNEW      X COORDINATE OF THE NEW CUSTOMER       --
C       --YNEW      Y COORDINATE OF THE NEW CUSTOMER       --
C       --X         X COORDINATE OF POSSIBLE TIE IN POINTS --
C       --Y         Y COORDINATE OF POSSIBLE TIE IN POINT  --
C       --DIST      DISTANCE BETWEEN POINTS                --
C       --POINT     POINT COUNTER                          --
C
        INTEGER POINT
C
C                 ESTABLISH ALL INTIAL PARAMETERS
C
        POINT=0
C
        READ(5,11) XNEW,YNEW
     11 FORMAT(2F8.2)
C
        WRITE(2,12)
     12 FORMAT(1H1,40X,*LOCATION OF NEW CUSTOMER*)
        WRITE(2,13) XNEW,YNEW
     13 FORMAT(42X,2HX=,F9.2,10X,2HY=,F9.2,//)
        WRITE(2,14)
     14 FORMAT(20X,*POINT*,15X,*LOCATION*,15X,*DISTANCE*)
C
C                 ....LOOP ENTRY POINT....
C
     15 READ(5,11) X,Y
        DIST=((XNEW-X)**2+(YNEW-Y)**2)**0.5
        POINT=POINT+1
C
        WRITE(2,20) POINT,X,Y,DIST
     20 FORMAT(20X,I3,5X,2HX=,F9.2,2HY=,F9.2,10X,F9.2)
C
        IF(POINT.LT.6) GO TO 15
C
C                 ....LOOP ENDS HERE.....
C
        END
```

| **Programming Example**
Disaster At Sea
(Simple) | The X and Y coordinates of a disaster at sea are radioed to a control station. They are punched on a data card along with the X and Y location of the nearest point of land (all values expressed in miles). |

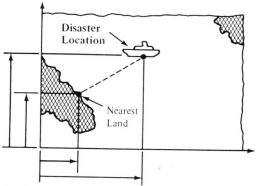

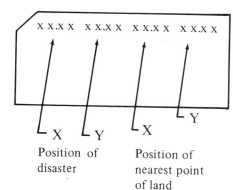

Write a program to determine and report the distance between the disaster and the nearest point of land.

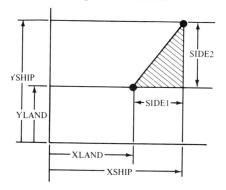

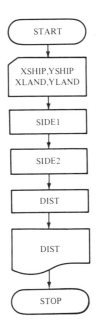

```
C....PURPOSE- COMPUTE THE DISTANCE BETWEEN A SHIP AND A LAND
C....          BASED RESCUE STATION.
C.............................................................
C
C              ------INPRORTANT VARIABLES-------
C
C      --XSHIP        X LOCATION OF SHIP                       --
C      --YSHIP        Y LOCATION OF SHIP                       --
C      --XLAND        X LOCATION OF RESCUE STATION             --
C      --YLAND        Y LOCATION OF RESCUE STATION             --
C      --DIST         COMPUTED DISTANCE BETWEEN TWO POINTS     --
C
       READ(5,10)XSHIP,YSHIP,XLAND,YLAND
C   10 FORMAT(4F8.2)
C
       SIDE1= XSHIP-XLAND
       SIDE2= YSHIP-YLAND
C
       DIST=(SIDE1**2+SIDE2**2)**0.5
C
       WRITE(2,20) DIST
C   20 FORMAT(1X,F12.2)
C
       STOP
       END
```

| Programming Example Disaster At Sea** (Complex) | Assume that the location of a number of ships in the disaster area is known. It is possible that the quickest rescue can be effected by one of these ships. A second card is added to the data deck. It contains a single integer telling how many ships are in the vicinity of the disaster. |

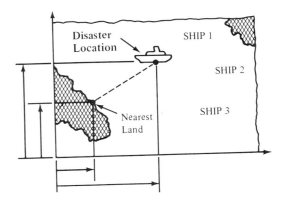

For each of these ships an additional card is added to the data deck to provide the following information about each possible rescue ship:

X	The approximate X and Y location of
Y	the rescue ship.
SPEED	The top speed of the ship (miles/hour).
HULL	Four-digit number representing the hull
NUMBER	number of the ship.

Write a more complex form of the last program, which will report the hull number and time required to reach the disaster, for all ships that can be on the scene in less than twelve hours. The complete data deck is shown on page 160.

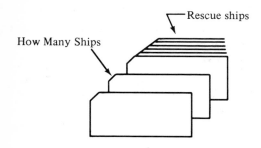

How Many Ships

Rescue ships

```
C.........................................................
C... PURPOSE- COMPUTE TIME FOR OTHER SHIPS TO ASSIST IN THE.
C...            RESCUE OPERATION.                          ..
C.........................................................
C
C        -----NEW INPORTANT VARIABLES----
C
C   --NSHIPS      NUMBER OF POSSIBLE RESCUE SHIPS     --
C   --XHELP       X COORDINATE OF POSSIBLE RESCUE SHIPS  --
C   --YHELP       Y COORDINATE OF POSSIBLE RESCUE SHIPS  --
C   --SPEED       MAXIMUM SPEED OF THIS SHIP           --
C   --TIME        TIME IT WILL TAKE SHIP TO ARRIVE ON SCENE-
C   --NHULL       IDENTIFYING HULL NUMBER OF THIS SHIP  --
C
C        .......READ PACK LEADER CARD.......
      READ(5,10) NSHIPS
10    FORMAT(I4)
C
C             LOOP ENTRY POINT
C
20    READ(5,30) XHELP,YHELP,SPEED,NHULL
30    FORMAT(3F12.2,I4)
C
      NSHIPS=NSHIPS-1
C
      DIST=((XHELP-XSHIP)**2+(YHELP-YSHIP)**2)**0.5
C
C          COMPUTE TIME FOR THIS SHIP TO GET ON SCENE
C
      TIME =DIST/SPEED
C
C             IS THIS FAST ENOUGH
C
      IF(TIME.LE.12.0)WRITE(2,40) NHULL,TIME
40    FORMAT(10X,I4,F7.2)
C
C             ANY CARDS REMAINING
C
      IF(NSHIPS.GT.0) GO TO 20
C
C             LOOP ENDS HERE
C
      STOP
      END
```

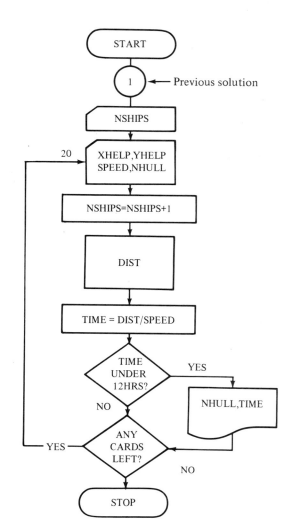

START

1 ← Previous solution

NSHIPS

20 → XHELP,YHELP SPEED,NHULL

NSHIPS=NSHIPS+1

DIST

TIME = DIST/SPEED

TIME UNDER 12HRS?   YES

NO

NHULL,TIME

ANY CARDS LEFT?   YES

NO

STOP

7 | More On Arithmetic Assignment Statements

There are several additional topics that should be covered to expand your understanding of the full potential of arithmetic assignment statements. Indexing statements, flags, accumulators, mixed mode operations and library functions are the new topics discussed in this chapter.

7.1 | Indexing Statements

There is a real mode counterpart to the techniques you have learned for creating an integer counter that starts at a preset value and advances through some orderly sequence.

Integer	Real
KOUNT=1	X= 1.0
KOUNT=KOUNT + 1	X=X+0.2
IF (KOUNT.LE.10)	IF(X.LE.10.0)

The statements on the right above set the initial value of the real variable, X, at 1.0. Each time the statement:

$$X = X + 0.2 \qquad \boxed{\text{INDEXING STATEMENT}}$$

is executed, the value of X will change (it increases by 0.2). The upper limit of X is controlled by the IF statement. This technique is used whenever we want a variable to take on a sequential series of values such as:

$$1.0 \quad 1.2 \quad 1.4 \quad 1.6...9.6 \quad 9.8 \quad 10.0$$

A typical application of this technique is shown in the following programming example.

Programming Example Math Tables	Write a program that controls the value of X so that it takes on the values shown on the left of the following table. For each value of X, compute and report X^2, X^3, $\sqrt{X}$, $\sqrt[3]{X}$, $1/X$. Make the output exactly as shown in the illustration.

161

One aspect of this program is to control the value of X so that it goes from 1.0 to 10.0 in steps of 0.1.

        X = 1.0
        X = X + 0.1
        IF(X.LE.10.0)

TABLE OF FUNCTIONAL VALUES					
X VALUE	X SQUARE	X CUBE	SQUARE ROOT	CUBE ROOT	RECIP- ROCAL
1.0	1.00	1.00	1.0000	1.0000	1.0000
1.1	1.21	1.33	1.0488	1.0323	0.9091
1.2	1.44	1.73	1.0954	1.0627	0.8333
1.3	1.69	2.20	1.1402	1.0914	0.7692
1.4	1.96	2.74	1.1832	1.1187	0.7143
1.5	2.25	3.37	1.2247	1.1447	0.6667
1.6	2.56	4.10	1.2649	1.1696	0.6250
1.7	2.89	4.91	1.3038	1.1935	0.5882
1.8	3.24	5.83	1.3416	1.2164	0.5556
1.9	3.61	6.86	1.3784	1.2386	0.5263
2.0	4.00	8.00	1.4142	1.2599	0.5000
9.6	92.16	884.74	3.0984	2.1253	0.1042
9.7	94.09	912.67	3.1145	2.1327	0.1031
9.8	96.04	941.19	3.1305	2.1400	0.1020
9.9	98.01	970.30	3.1464	2.1472	0.1010
10.0	100.00	1000.00	3.1623	2.1544	0.1000

Five arithmetic statements are needed to obtain the five functional values listed in the table. Since each line in the main body table contains six values (the value of X and five functional values), the output command WRITE must be followed by six variable names:

        ANS1 = X**2
        ANS2 = X**3
        ANS3 = X**0.5
        ANS4 = X**(1./3.)
        ANS5 = 1.0/X

        WRITE(2,7)X,ANS1,ANS2,ANS3,ANS4,ANS5

To spread the output evenly across the page, first determine the minimum F-code for each output quantity.

F4.1	F6.2	F7.2	F6.4	F6.4	F6.4

The field width of each of these codes should be increased by a fixed amount. Subtract the total columns required by these codes from the size of the output line. Dividing this number by 6 gives the value by which each field width may be increased without exceeding the line limit.

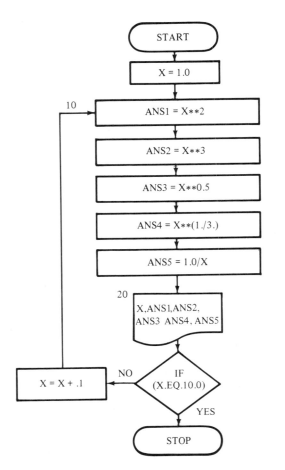

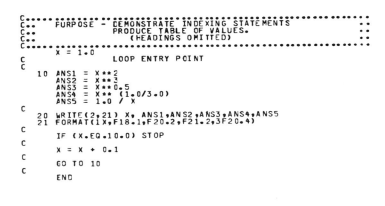

```
C........................................................
C..    PURPOSE - DEMONSTRATE INDEXING STATEMENTS        ..
C..             PRODUCE TABLE OF VALUES.                 ..
C..             (HEADINGS OMITTED)                       ..
C........................................................
      X = 1.0
C                  LOOP ENTRY POINT
C
   10 ANS1 = X**2
      ANS2 = X**3
      ANS3 = X**0.5
      ANS4 = X** (1.0/3.0)
      ANS5 = 1.0 / X
C
   20 WRITE(2,21) X, ANS1,ANS2,ANS3,ANS4,ANS5
   21 FORMAT(1X,F18.1,F20.2,F21.2,3F20.4)
C
      IF (X.EQ.10.0) STOP
C
      X = X + 0.1
C
      GO TO 10
C
      END
```

Indexing provides an opportunity to drive home an important point about real calculations. Take a look at the IF test used in the above problem. Would you be shocked to learn that the STOP statement will probably never be executed? The difficulty starts with the use of the number 0.1. It is an innocent-looking number, but that is because your mind is trained in the decimal system. In binary, the number 0.1 has no finite representation.

Decimal	*Binary*
0.1	.0001100110011001100011...

When this number is stored in memory, its value is diminished slightly (by an amount equal to the portion of the number truncated). This truncation error is magnified by the repeated execution of the statement:

$$X = X + .1$$

By the time X approaches 10.0, this statement has been executed ninety times. This causes an accumulation of the truncation error. As a result, the value of X is not precisely 10.0 but something like:

$$9.99999999999372$$

If you were to print this number, it would be displayed as 10.0, but that is because on output the number is usually *rounded*. In an IF test, X is taken at its true value. For this reason, the IF test:

$$IF(X.EQ.10.0)STOP$$

would not be evaluated as true. The statement should be rewritten as follows:

$$IF(X.GE.10.0)STOP$$

There is now a large range of values that will trigger the STOP statement.

Programming Style: ▌▌	Calculations involving real numbers are sus-
IF Tests Using ▌▌	ceptible to small errors that are usually of
Real Numbers — ▌▌	minor consequence. Such errors can some-
Use With Caution ▌▌	times have a serious effect in an IF test.

7.2 | Accumulators

You have seen arithmetic statements used in the following unique ways:

KOUNT = KOUNT + 1   X = X + .1

COUNTING   INDEXING

In both these uses, the quantity added or subtracted is a constant.
We now present a third type known as an accumulator:

SUM = SUM + X

ACCUMULATOR

When the quantity added or subtracted is a variable (in this case X), this statement is used to add up a string of numbers. For example, assume there is a series of data cards each containing a single real value called X. Figure 7.1 suggests the procedure for determining the sum of these X values.

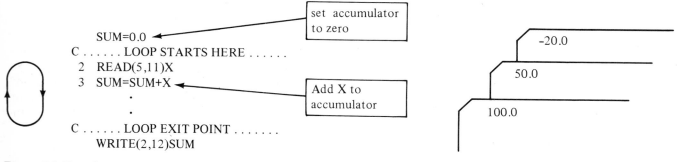

```
        SUM=0.0                    set accumulator
   C......LOOP STARTS HERE......   to zero
     2  READ(5,11)X
     3  SUM=SUM+X
        .                          Add X to
        .                          accumulator
   C......LOOP EXIT POINT.......
        WRITE(2,12)SUM
```

Figure 7.1 Use of Accumulators

Figure 7.2 First Few Cards

The statement:

SUM = 0.0

sets the initial value of the accumulator at zero before the loop is entered. (Just as a counter or indexing statement must be given an initial value, so too, must the accumulator be initialized). Inside the loop, the statement:

SUM = SUM + X

increases the contents of memory location SUM by the value of X read from a data card. Assume the first card contains the value 100.0 (see Figure 7.2). Statement 3 causes this value of X to be added to the accumulator (the number 0.0 and 100.0 are added together and the result sent to memory location SUM).
On the second time around the loop, the READ statement redefines X to 50.0, and the accumulator is reached again:

SUM = SUM + X
         ↑   ↖
       100.0   50.0

The values 100.0 and 50.0 are added together and the result (150.0) sent to SUM. The accumulator now holds the first two X values. On the next sweep X is –20.0 and SUM changes to 130.0.

A practical application of this type of statement would be to monitor bank transactions. Each deposit or withdrawal (X value) should cause an appropriate change in the individual's bank balance (SUM). This will be demonstrated in the next programming example. Accumulating statements are used to adjust inventory levels, balance checkbooks, etc.

7.3 | Flags

Programmers do strange things with arithmetic statements, one of which is pretending that they represent flags on a flag pole.

In programming, a flag is used to record if a particular event occurred. The general procedure is to set the condition of the flag at the beginning of the program by putting the flag in the down position. As the program is running, tests are made to determine if the event being monitored ever occurs. When the event occurs, the flag is raised. At the end of the program, the condition of the flag (up or down) provides the information needed. For example, we will soon be processing the deposits and withdrawals made to a checking account for the purpose of providing a monthly statement. If, at any time during the month, the balance in the account drops below $100.00, a service charge of $2.00 is authorized.

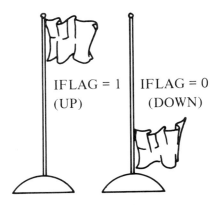

Figure 7.3 Flag Condition

Flags record an event: we need to know at the *end* of the program if something happened during the program, in this case, a low balance.

As the program starts, a zero is put in a memory location IFLAG, which means the flag is down (no low balance detected yet). As the various deposits or withdrawals are posted, each new balance is tested to see if the balance is above $100.00. If a low balance is detected, the flag is raised:

IF(BALNCE.LT.100.00)IFLAG=1

After all the transactions are posted, a test is made to determine if an additional $2.00 service charge is appropriate.

IF(IFLAG.EQ.1)BALNCE=BALNCE–2.00

Notice that this is considerably different from writing:

IF(BALNCE.LT.100.00)BALNCE=BALNCE–2.00

at the end of the program. Using this IF test, only one value of BALNCE would be tested, namely, the one at the end of the month.

Programming Example	Write a program to produce monthly bank statements as suggested below.
Monthly Statement	

ACCOUNT NUMBER 12345

WILFRED P. RULE
84 COUNTY ROAD
READING, MASS.

BALANCE AS OF JUNE 1, 1980 . . . . 178.62

WITHDRAWAL 50.00   128.62
DEPOSIT 100.00   228.62
DEPOSIT 25.00   253.62
DEPOSIT 20.00   273.62
WITHDRAWAL 200.00   73.62

BALANCE AS OF JUNE 30, 1980 . . . . 73.62

CHARGE FOR BALANCE BELOW $100.00   2.00

FINAL BALANCE 71.62

The purpose of this problem is to pull together many of the programming techniques you have learned. Your ability to handle a "complex" problem has grown substantially. Each of the requirements outlined below will be explained as the solution is developed. The list is being presented to show the scope of problems you are presently capable of handling.

Requirements

#1 – CARRIAGE CONTROL	Cause the line printer to advance to the top of a page before each new depositor's transactions are processed.
#2 – SPECIAL HEADINGS	Produce headings at the top of the page that include the depositor's account number and mailing address.
#3 – FLAG FOR LOW BALANCE	Use a flag to detect the occurrence of a low balance during the month.
#4 – USE OF ACCUMU-LATOR	Use an accumulator to keep track of the depositor's balance as various deposits and withdrawals are made.
#5 – CHECK FOR CORRECT ACCOUNT NUMBER	Before posting a deposit or a withdrawal, make sure the transaction is being posted to the correct account.
#6 – DEPOSIT OR WITH-DRAWAL MESSAGE	When listing a transaction, include the message "DEPOSIT" or "WITH-DRAWAL," as appropriate.
#7 – APPLYING SERVICE CHARGE	Use flag to apply a $2.00 service charge if low-balance condition is encountered.

Each month a bank must issue a statement to its depositors such as the one shown. The program that generates this statement is not a simple one, but it is one that is within your capabilities to write. Assume that each customer is represented in the data deck by a series of cards as suggested here.

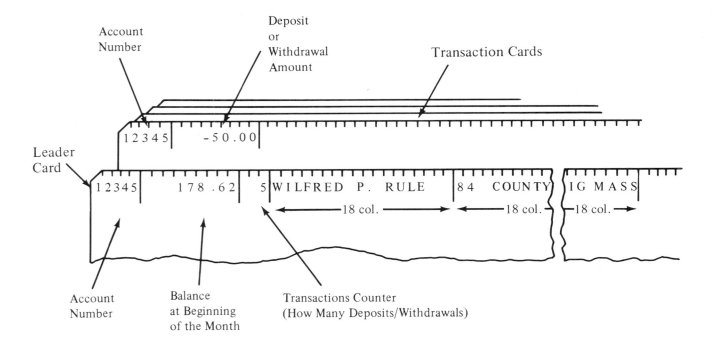

The first card is a leader card giving the customer's account number, the balance at the beginning of the month and a count of the number of transactions made during the month. The remainder of the card gives the depositor's name, street address and town address. Each of these last three items is assigned 18 columns.

Step 1: Getting the Headings

As the first step in the solution of this problem, read the leader card and transfer the information on it to the headings of the bank statement. The name, street address and town address each fills 18 columns, and so must be subdivided. If a maximum word size of A6 is assumed, each of the 18 columns would be divided into three parts. The variable names assigned are shown as part of the program documentation.

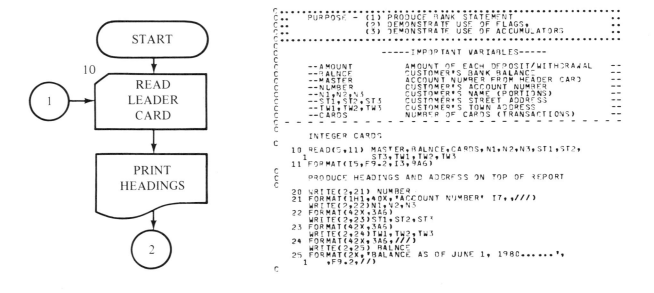

```
C......................................................
C..    PURPOSE -  (1) PRODUCE BANK STATEMENT        ..
C..               (2) DEMONSTRATE USE OF FLAGS,     ..
C..               (3) DEMONSTRATE USE OF ACCUMULATORS ..
C......................................................
C
C               -----IMPORTANT VARIABLES-----
C
C     --AMOUNT         AMOUNT OF EACH DEPOSIT/WITHDRAWAL  --
C     --BALNCE         CUSTOMER'S BANK BALANCE            --
C     --MASTER         ACCOUNT NUMBER FROM HEADER CARD    --
C     --NUMBER         CUSTOMER'S ACCOUNT NUMBER          --
C     --N1,N2,N3       CUSTOMER'S NAME (PORTIONS)         --
C     --ST1,ST2,ST3    CUSTOMER'S STREET ADDRESS          --
C     --TW1,TW2,TW3    CUSTOMER'S TOWN ADDRESS            --
C     --CARDS          NUMBER OF CARDS (TRANSACTIONS)     --
C
C
      INTEGER CARDS
C
   10 READ(5,11) MASTER,BALNCE,CARDS,N1,N2,N3,ST1,ST2,
     1           ST3,TW1,TW2,TW3
   11 FORMAT(I5,F9.2,I3,9A6)
C
C     PRODUCE HEADINGS AND ADDRESS ON TOP OF REPORT
C
   20 WRITE(2,21) NUMBER
   21 FORMAT(1H1,40X,'ACCOUNT NUMBER' I7,,///)
      WRITE(2,22)N1,N2,N3
   22 FORMAT(42X,3A6)
      WRITE(2,23)ST1,ST2,ST3
   23 FORMAT(42X,3A6)
      WRITE(2,24)TW1,TW2,TW3
   24 FORMAT(42X,3A6,///)
      WRITE(2,25) BALNCE
   25 FORMAT(2X,'BALANCE AS OF JUNE 1, 1980........',
     1      ,F9.2,//)
C
```

Step 2: Set Flag, and Process Transactions*

Prior to reading and processing any transaction card, set a flag to detect a low balance. Now enter the loop that processes each transaction. Inside the loop:

1. READ a transaction card,
2. decrement the card (transaction) counter,
3. see if the account number of the transaction card agrees with the number on the leader card (if it does not, print an error message "CARDS OUT OF ORDER" and stop the program),
4. otherwise update the balance to reflect the transaction,
5. post the transaction on the output sheet; use IF tests to determine if transaction is DEPOSIT or WITHDRAWAL (print message as appropriate),
6. see if new balance below minimum; if yes, raise the flag,
7. any more transactions to post?

When posting a transaction, one of two write statements is used. One includes the message "DEPOSIT" in the output line. The other includes the message "WITHDRAWAL." Keep the statements that process these two alternatives as close together as possible. Avoid jumping to one end of the program to handle one condition and to another point in the program to handle the alternative. This causes the program to become fragmented. Alternative actions should be kept together as much as possible.

Programming Style:
If the Logic Has
Several Alternatives,
Group Them

When writing a program with several closely-related alternatives in the logic, make an effort to group the alternative statements as close together as possible. It makes the program more compact and the logic easier to follow.

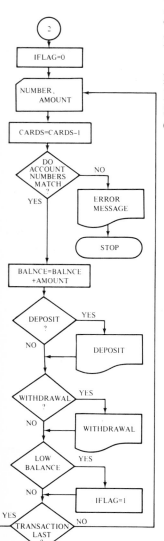

```
C
C                   IFLAG = 0
C
C                        LOOP ENTRY POINT
C
30   READ(5,31) NUMBER, AMOUNT
31   FORMAT(I5,F9.2)
C
     CARDS = CARDS - 1
C
     IF(NUMBER.EQ.MASTER) GO TO 20
C
C                    .....ERROR DETECTED.....
C
40   WRITE(2,41)
41   FORMAT(//////,2X,'CARDS ARE OUT OF ORDER')
C
     STOP
C
C                   NORMAL PROCESSING
C
50   BALNCE = BALNCE + AMOUNT
C
C                   IS THIS A DEPOSIT OR WITHDRAWAL
C
     IF (AMOUNT.LT.0.0) WRITE(2,61)AMOUNT,BALNCE
61   FORMAT(2X,'WITHDRAWAL...................',F9.2,15X,F12.2)
C
     IF(AMOUNT.GT.0.0) WRITE(2,62)AMOUNT,BALNCE
62   FORMAT(2X,'DEPOSIT......................',F9.2,15X,F12.2)
C
C                   CHECK FOR LOW BALANCE
C
     IF(BALNCE.LT.100.00) IFLAG = 1
C
C                   ANY TRANSACTIONS REMAINING
C
     IF(CARDS.GT.0) GO TO 30
C
C                   .....LOOP EXIT POINT.....
```

*There are a lot of activities to accomplish. Take them one at a time. Follow the flow diagram and read the explanation provided.

Step 3: Closing Balance

Having processed all the transaction cards, it is now necessary to post the closing balance. In the process, examine the flag to see if an additional charge of $2.00 is appropriate. If it is, the balance is decreased and the final balance posted.

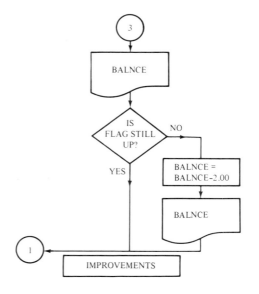

```
C        .....LOOP EXIT POINT.....
C
         WRITE(2,71) BALNCE
71  FORMAT(//,2X,'BALANCE AS OF JUNE 30, 1980' ,25X,F12.2)
C
C        CHECK FOR LOW BALANCE DURING MONTH
C-
      IF( IFLAG.EQ.0) THEN
C        LOW BALANCE DETECTED
C
         BALANCE = BALANCE - 2.00
C
80       WRITE(2,81)
81       FORMAT(//,2X,'CHARGE FOR BALANCE BELOW $100.00',27X,
     +        '$2.00',//)
C
      ENDIF
C
90    WRITE(2,91) BALNCE
91    FORMAT(14X,'FINAL BALANCE..................',F12.2)
C
         GO TO 10
         END
```

Improvements

This program could be improved in many ways. The dates of "JUNE 1, 1980" and "JUNE 30, 1980" change for each run of the program. They should not be part of the logic. An additional leader card could be used to specify these values.

This program is not equipped to handle an inactive account. The logic assumes at least one transaction card for each account. That is not reasonable. The whole idea of recording transactions on data cards (that must be sorted) is not realistic. Transactions should be recorded on a disc file, not data cards. The statements to read a disc file are not much different from the ones to read a card file. These statements are covered in Chapter 17.

7.4 | Top – Loop – Bottom

The various programming examples you have been dealing with exhibit a common and recurring structure. Statements appearing early in the program are executed once. They produce headings on output, establish initial values of counters or accumulators, set flags, etc. This frequently is referred to as the "initialization" section of the program.

The next group of statements are those that are executed over and over again. This is the loop portion of the program.

Ultimately, the loop is terminated and control passes to a final group of statements that accomplish the "wrap-up" activity. This part of the program computes and reports various summary results (final value of counters and accumulators).

Comment statements should be used to clearly display this basic structure.

Programming Style:
Display:
  Loop Entry Point
  Loop Exit Point

Show the basic structure of your program as clearly as possible. Isolate the initialization statements from those inside a loop. Show where the loop ends. Try to limit the number of exit points.

7.5   Mixed Mode Expressions

When the compiler starts processing an arithmetic assignment statement, the right-hand portion of the statement should be written in a consistent mode. All the terms (the constants and the variables) should be real or integer, but *not* a mixture. *Mixed modes should not occur within an expression.*

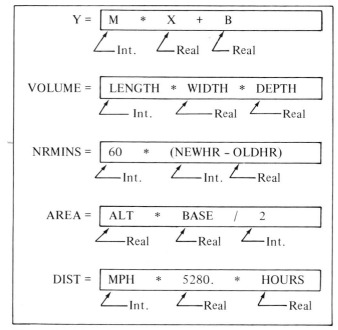

Figure 7.4 Mixed Mode Violations

You can save yourself a lot of difficulty by checking each expression to make sure it is written in a consistent mode. If you inadvertently forget a decimal point or are careless in naming a variable, most compilers will not "crash" your program. An attempt will be made to correct the error. The mixed expressions will be interpreted as described in the following examples.

Consider the processing of the statement:

AREA=1./3*RADIUS

The first operation performed is division. The compiler looks to the left and to the right of the divide operator to determine if this operation should be performed in the integer or real mode. (Note that the quantity to the left and right of the operational symbol (divide) are called operands.)

1. Real operands. If both values are real, division will be in the real mode.
2. Integer operands. If both values are integer, division will be in the integer mode.
3. Mixed operands. If the values are mixed, the integer will be converted to real and division will be in the real mode.

This means that the quantity 3 (integer) will be converted to 3.0 (real) and the statement will be processed as the programmer probably intended.

A less fortunate situation will result in the interpretation of the statement:

$$A = RADIUS**(1/3)$$

The first operation performed again is division (to clear out the expression inside parentheses). The values on either side of the divide operator are integer and, therefore, integer division takes place producing the value 0. This obviously is not the value intended. To compound the difficulties, it is possible that no error message will be given.

There are two ways to guard against this difficulty:

1. Write expressions in a consistent mode, and
2. Use test data to check for the correct interpretation of your equations.

FLOAT and IFIX

There are two special functions that are useful in avoiding mixed mode expressions:

FLOAT (integer argument)
IFIX (real argument)

The function FLOAT is used in a real expression to permit the appearance of an integer variable without a mixed mode error. Assume, for example, a program uses a counter called NYES. If the value of the counter is needed in a real expression, one solution is to make a real copy of the counter by the statement:

$$XYES = NYES$$

The quantity XYES now could be used in place of NYES. This can be accomplished more directly as follows:

$$AVE=FLOAT(NYES)/100.*FACTOR$$

The function FLOAT causes its integer argument NYES to be treated as a real value inside the real expression in which it is used.

The function IFIX accomplishes just the opposite action. It is used in integer expressions to permit the appearance of a real variable without incurring a mixed mode infraction. The statement:

$$I = M + 6*IFIX(ANS1)$$

uses the real variable ANS1 in an integer expression. The function IFIX causes its real argument ANS1 to be truncated and treated as an integer inside this expression.

It should be pointed out that it is only the expression portion of an arithmetic statement that should be written in a consistent mode. There is no requirement that the expression and the variable name to the left of the replacement operator be of the same mode. Statements such as:

$$J = X/3.+4.7 \quad or \quad X = (I+3)/(M-1)$$

are valid. The expression portion of each statement is in a consistent mode. The result of each calculation is sent to a memory location of the opposite mode. This is perfectly legal and was used in Chapter 5 to convert a student's grade into an integer for use as a selector value in a computed GO TO statement.

J = GRADE/10.

The Exception to the Rule

There is an exception to the rules concerning mixed mode expressions. It has to do with **exponentiation** (raising to a power). Under certain circumstances exponentiation can be accomplished by a repetitive multiplication process. At other times it is necessary to use logarithms. The programmer controls the method of computation by the mode used in expressing the exponent, as seen below:

$$\text{ANS} = X**3 \longleftarrow \text{integer}$$
$$\text{ANS} = X**3. \longleftarrow \text{real}$$

Specifying the exponent as a real value directs the computation to be accomplished by logarithms. If, however, the exponent is written in the integer mode, an entirely different method of evaluation is used. This involves a repetitive multiplication process that is usually faster and has other advantages, which we will cover shortly. The point now, however, is that the mode of the exponent is being used in a very special and unique way. For this reason, its mode can be opposite to that of the expression in which it appears without causing a mixed mode infraction. Accordingly, the following statements are not considered mixed mode:

AREA = PI*RADIUS**2
SCALE = 10.*X**(N–1)

The exception to the mixed mode rule: when exponentiation is involved, the power may be expressed as a real or an integer. There is another advantage to expressing the power as an integer value.

Y = Y**2

If the value of X is negative (like minus 4), repetitive multiplication will compute Y as +16. If the power had been specified as a real, the program would terminate immediately because this implies taking the log of a negative number, which is impossible.

Quiz#8   Arithmetic Assignment Statements

Part 1: Answer the following questions.
1. Why is there any difficulty about storing a simple decimal number such as the number 0.1?
2. The number stored in a memory location called X has the value:

9.999999823

How will that number be printed if an F6.2 code is used?
3. The number shown in question 2 appears in the following IF test:

IF(X.EQ.10.0)STOP

Explain why the STOP statement is not executed.
4. What is the purpose of a "FLAG"?
5. What is the purpose of an "ACCUMULATOR"?

6. Are "FLAGS" and "ACCUMULATORS" special hardware components?

7. The following statements are used to determine if a triangle is a *right* triangle. What is wrong with these statements?

> READ(5,10)SIDE1,SIDE2,HYPNUS
> VALUE=SQRT(SIDE1**2+SIDE2**2)
> IF(VALUE.EQ.HYPNUS)WRITE(2,*)'RIGHT TRIANGLE'

8. How should the statements in question 7 be written?

9. What is the purpose of the library function FLOAT?

10. Will both the mixed mode expressions shown below result in an error?

> Y=(X-6.)**(1/3)
> Y=(X-6)**(1.0/3)

Part 2: Write a Program (Is the Wheel Honest?)

11. When placing a bet at the roulette table, you may bet on the numbers 1 through 36. To test the honesty of the wheel, 200 spins are made and the winning number recorded on data cards. For our test we will divide these numbers into three groups:

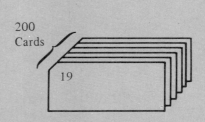

200 Cards

19

	NUMBER	ACTION
Low Numbers	1–12	32.6%
Middle Numbers	13–24	35.1%
High Numbers	25–36	32.3%

Write a program to determine what percent of the time a low number (1 to 12) came up and what percent of the time a high number (25 to 36) won.

Special: you have been playing the number 16 all night long. Is it true this number never came up?

Answers:

1. Computers generally deal in binary notation. A number that is easy to represent in decimal may not be easy to represent in binary.

2. ⌞⌞1,0,⌞0,0⌟   Rounding takes place.

3. No rounding is used in the evaluation of the "X=10.0" expression.

4. Determine at the end of a processing block if a particular event occurred during the processing activity.

5. To algebraically "add up" (accumulate) a string of numbers.

6. There is nothing special about these quantities except for the special way *the programmer* is using these variables.

7. Real IF tests are evaluated to many decimal place accuracy. If **VALUE** is just slightly different from HYPNUS, the equality will be rejected.

8. READ(5,10)SIDE1,SIDE2,HYPNUS
   VALUE=SQRT(SIDE1**2+SIDE2**2)   Absolute
   DIFF=ABS(VALUE-HYPNUS) ◄─────────────── Value
   IF(DIFF.LT.0.1)WRITE(2,*)'RIGHT TRIANGLE'   Function

   If the *difference* between VALUE and HYPNUS is less than 0.1, the triangle is assumed to be a right triangle.

9. To cause an integer value to be treated as a real in an expression:

> AVE=FLOAT(NYES)/FLOAT(NTOTAL)

10. The first statement will be in error. The expression (1/3) is integer and will be evaluated as zero.

11.
```
      C .............................................
      C       PURPOSE-CHECK THE HONESTY OF A ROULETTE. . . .
      C               WHEEL.
      C .............................................
      C                 —IMPORTANT VARIABLES—
      C
      C     —NUMBER  WINNING NUMBER
      C     —LOW     NUMBER OF TIMES LOW NUMBER WINS
      C     —HIGH    NUMBER OF TIMES HIGH NUMBER WINS
      C     —FLAG    FLAG TO DETERMINE IF 16 IS EVER
      C              A WINNER
      C     —CARDS   CARD COUNTER
      C
            INTEGER HIGH,FLAG,CARDS
      C
            CARDS=0
            FLAG=0
            LOW=0
            HIGH=0        . . . . .PROCESSING LOOP. . . . .
      10    READ(5,20)NUMBER
      20    FORMAT(I2)
      C
            IF(NUMBER.GE.1.AND.NUMBER.LE.12)LOW=LOW+1
      C
            IF(NUMBER.GE.25)HIGH=HIGH+1
      C
            IF(NUMBER.EQ.16)FLAG=1
      C
                  CARDS=CARDS+1
      C
                  IF(CARDS.LT.200)GO TO 10
      C
      C .............................................
            PCNTLO=FLOAT(LOW)/200.*100.
      C
            PCNTHI=FLOAT(HIGH)/200.*100.
      C
            WRITE(2,30)PCNTLO,PCNTHI
      30    FORMAT(1X.2F10.1)
      C
            IF(FLAG.EQ.0)WRITE(2,*)'YOUR NUMBER NEVER WON'
            IF(FLAG.EQ.1)WRITE(2,*)'YOUR NUMBER DID WIN'
            STOP
            END
```

7.6
Library Functions

Figure 7.5 shows a list of mathematical functions that are used so frequently in everyday computations that they are given special treatment in FORTRAN. By

Library Functions

Function	Function Name	Example	Statement
—square root	SQRT	$y=\sqrt{X-6}$	Y=SQRT(X-6.)
—sine	SIN	$y=R\sin\theta$	Y=R*SIN(THETA)
—cosine	COS	$x=R\cos\theta$	X=R*COS(THETA)
arc tangent	ATAN	$\theta=\tan^{-1}\left(\dfrac{Y}{X}\right)$	THETA=ATAN(Y/X)
arc tangent	ATAN2	$\theta=\tan^{-1}\left(\dfrac{Y}{X}\right)$	THETA=ATAN2(Y,X)

Note: Value of angles must be in radians

natural log	ALOG	$y=\ln X$	Y=ALOG(X)
common log	ALOG10	$y=\log_{10}(X+3)$	Y=ALOG10(X+3.)
—absolute value	ABS	$y=\lvert X-8\rvert$	Y=ABS(X-8.)
—exponential	EXP	$y=e^{x}-1$	Y=EXP(X)-1.

Figure 7.5 Commonly Used Library Functions

now you are familiar with the fact that these functions are implemented by software techniques. The coding necessary to evaluate each of those quantities has been written (usually in machine language) and stored on the system library. Much like reference books in a conventional library, these preprogrammed sets of instructions are stored in the processor available for use by the programmer whenever necessary. They are called **library functions**. Figure 7.5 is just a partial list of the more commonly used functions. A more exhaustive list is contained in the appendix on page 533.

Note that each function has a name that identifies to the processor which of the many functions the programmer wants to use. Immediately following the function name are parentheses containing what is called the argument(s) of the function. The following examples demonstrate that this argument can be a constant, a variable or an expression:

$$Y = SQRT(8.0) \qquad Y = SQRT(X) \qquad Y = SQRT(X**2+Y**2)$$

CONSTANT   VARIABLE   EXPRESSION

The rules for the form of an argument are quite liberal. An argument may even include another Library Function:

$$Y = SQRT(SIN(X))$$

Each of the functions in Figure 7.5 will be discussed separately, but for the moment let us examine how the computer processes an arithmetic statement involving several library functions. Consider the equation:

$$Y = \frac{1/4 \log_{10}(A+B)}{\sqrt{A}+\sqrt{B}}$$

The appropriate arithmetic statement would be:

$$Y = (ALOG10(A+B)/4.)/(SQRT(A)+SQRT(B))$$

In processing this statement, the compiler will eventually encounter the function name ALOG10. Since its argument is in the form of an expression, instructions will be generated as follows:

1. fetch a copy of memory location A and send it to the arithmetic unit;
2. fetch a copy of memory location B and send it to the arithmetic unit; and
3. add these values together.

At this point the argument of ALOG10 is considered reduced to a specific value, and what is needed now is a set of instructions telling how to work on this value (A+B) for the purpose of determining its common logarithm. These instructions will be provided by the system library.

The name ALOG10 is recognized as the name of a library function. Accordingly, a copy of the set of instructions associated with the name ALOG10 is taken from the library and inserted into your program. (If it takes a large number of instructions to define a function, it may be more efficient to transfer control to the instructions in the system library. These instructions would, of course, include a mechanism for linking back (returning) to your program.)

As processing of this statement continues, the library function SQRT is encountered *twice*. On each encounter, a copy of the instructions associated with the name SQRT will be taken from the library and inserted in your program. It is as simple as that.

SIN/COS

The two library functions provided for dealing with trigonometry problems are SIN and COS. Both require that the argument specifying the angle be expressed in *radians*. Here are 2 examples:

Equation	Statement
$y = \sin(45°)$	Y = SIN (45./57.3)
$y = \cos(x+30°)$	Y = COS((X+30.)/57.3)

The constant 57.3 is being used to convert angles specified in degrees to radians.

Any other trigonometric function (like tangent or secant) must be derived from SIN and COS by the programmer:

Equation	Statement
$y = \dfrac{\tan x}{4.}$	Y = (SIN(X/57.3)/COS(X/57.3))/4.
$y = CSC(25°)$	Y = 1./SIN(25./57.3)

ATAN/ATAN 2

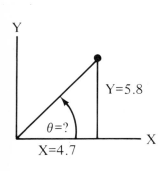

Arc functions are used when the sides of a triangle are known and we are asked to determine the angle. It is expressed mathematically as:

$$\theta = \tan^{-1}\left(\frac{Y}{X}\right)$$

In the example shown, both X and Y are positive so the angle theta (θ) will be in the first quadrant. Since Y is just a little larger than X, the angle will be larger than 45°, but remember the functions deal in *radians*.

```
        X = 4.7
        Y = 5.8
   THETA = ATAN (Y/X)
DEGREE = THETA*57.3
```

The angle returned by this function is between 0 to 90° if the argument is positive and between 0 and –90° if the argument is negative. This means you must determine the true quadrant yourself.

ATAN2 is a similar function but has the feature of keeping track of the correct quadrant. This library function has two arguments.

ATAN2(Y,X)

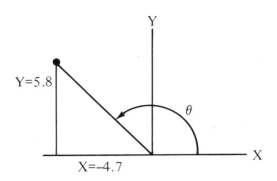

If the value of X and Y are as shown in the illustration, the angle could be determined by the statement:

$$\text{ANGLE} = 57.3 * \text{ATAN2}(5.8, -4.7)$$

When a library function requires multiple arguments, they appear inside the parentheses but separated by commas.

ALOG/ALOG10

When dealing with logs, there are two types: **common logs** (logs to the base 10) and **natural logs** (logs to the base e).
Some examples:

Equation	Statement
$y = \log_{10}(x+1)$	Y = ALOG10 (X+1.0)
$y = \ln(6)$	Y = ALOG (6.0)

ABS

The absolute value function is used to strip the sign from a value. If the value is negative, it is changed to positive. If it is already positive, no action is taken.
Examples:

Equation	Statement
$y = |x-6|$	Y = ABS (X–6.)
$y = \dfrac{\cos^2(X)}{|X|}$	Y = COS(X)**2/ABS(X)

EXP

This function is best displayed by showing several examples.

Equation	Statement
$y = e^x - 6$	Y = EXP(X)–6.
$y = \dfrac{e^x - e^{-x}}{2}$	Y = (EXP(X) – EXP (–X))/2.

7.7 | Other Functions

There are a few other library functions that may prove useful.

AMAX1	(A,B,C, . . .)	find maximum element of list of real arguments
AMIN1	(A,B,C, . . .)	find minimum element of list of real arguments
MAX0	(I,J,K,L, . .)	find maximum element of list of integer elements
MIN0	(I,J,K,L, . .)	find minimum element of list of integer elements

These functions allow for as many arguments as you want. They search for the largest or the smallest element. Notice that the name of the function is indicative of the mode of the value it returns.

7.8 | Data Statement

The portion of a program preceding any loop entry point frequently involves setting the initial value of many variables (counters and accumulators). This often requires a large number of relatively trivial statements. In the next program, for example, there are:

a) two counters (NLOW and NHIGH) that must be set at zero,
b) two accumulators (SUMLOW and SUMHI that must be cleared, and
c) a card counter that must be set at 100.

The DATA statement provides a quick and efficient method of assigning an initial value to each of a list of variables as suggested below.

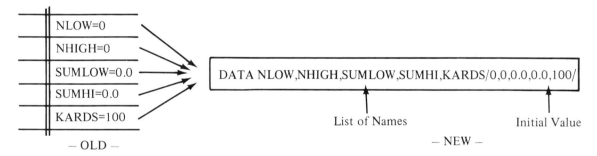

Notice the one-to-one matching of name to value. The usual restrictions apply; that is, the sequence of names must agree in number and mode with the sequence of constants appearing in the "initial value" list.

An alternate form of this statement is as follows:

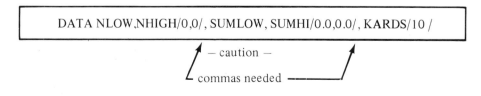

General Form

```
DATA list of names/list of values/
             or
DATA list₁ of names/list₁ of values/, list₂ of names/ list₂ of values/,
list₃ . . .
```

When the value to be assigned to a number of variables is the same, a repetition factor may be used in the initial value list as shown below.

DATA NLOW,NHIGH/2*0/,SUMLOW,SUMHI/2*0.0/

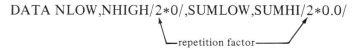

—repetition factor—

Review Exercises

1.*Does the statement:

$$X = SIDE\ 1 ** 2$$

represent a mixed mode infraction? Why not?

2. What is meant by the term "argument of a function"? In what form may the argument be given?

3. If your systems software only provides SIN and COS trigonometric functions, how are all the other trigonometric functions determined (for example, tangent)?

4.*In the statement:

$$Y = R * SIN\ (THETA)$$

how should the angle THETA be expressed? Degrees or radians?

5. A variable called X contains a negative number. Which of the following statements can be used to determine X cube? Explain.

$$Y = X ** 3.0$$
$$Y = X ** 3$$

6.*You have been told to exercise caution when using IF tests involving real numbers. Explain why the following STOP statement may not be executed even though the value of X is 25.0:

IF(SQRT(X).EQ.5.0)STOP

7. Describe two instances in which it would be necessary to use a "flag" while writing a program.

8. What are some typical activities that are accomplished in the "initialization" section of a program?

9.*What is the purpose of the DATA statement?

10. Write a DATA statement that makes use of a "repetition factor" in assigning the same value to two or more variables.

11. A data deck consists of 200 cards, each containing a dollar amount representing deposits or withdrawals at a bank. Negative values represent withdrawals. Positive values represent deposits. Determine how many deposits were made and the total value of these deposits. Provide similar information concerning the withdrawals.

12. Write a program to produce the table of trigonometric values shown.

	SIN	COS	TAN	COT	SEC	CSC
0.0	.0000	1.0000	.0000	–	1.0000	.0000
1.0	.0175	.9998	.0175	57.29	1.0002	57.14
2.0	.0349	.9994	.0349	28.64	1.0006	28.65
3.0	.0523	.9986	.0523	19.08	1.0014	19.12
178.0	.0349	.9994	.0349	28.64	1.0006	28.65
179.0	.0175	.9998	.0175	57.29	1.0002	57.14
180.0	.0000	1.0000	.0000	–	1.0000	.0000

13. The first portion of a data deck defines a list of X values punched one to a card. A leader card contains an integer telling how large the list is. The remainder of the data deck defines a second list of X values.

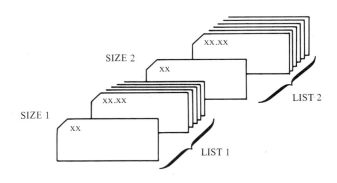

Determine and report the sum of X values in list 1 and list 2.

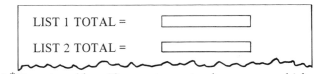

LIST 1 TOTAL =

LIST 2 TOTAL =

14.*Repeat problem 13 except report only one sum, whichever is the larger. Have the output appear as follows:

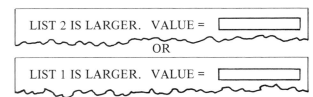

LIST 2 IS LARGER. VALUE =

OR

LIST 1 IS LARGER. VALUE =

15. The government is requiring that all new cars meet a minimum efficiency rating (like 25 miles/gallon) and

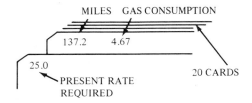

MILES GAS CONSUMPTION

137.2 4.67

25.0

PRESENT RATE REQUIRED

20 CARDS

that rating will be increased periodically. The first card in a data deck defines the present requirements; the next 20 cards give the results (miles driven and gas consumed) in twenty test runs on a specific model of car. Write a program that computes the mileage rating for each test run and compare each value with the government standard. Print as output one of two messages:

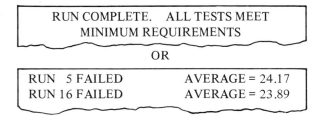

RUN COMPLETE. ALL TESTS MEET MINIMUM REQUIREMENTS

OR

| RUN 5 FAILED | AVERAGE = 24.17 |
| RUN 16 FAILED | AVERAGE = 23.89 |

16. Repeat problem 15 except consider the test unsuccessful if no more than 10% of the cars (2 cars) fall below the minimum imposed provided that the average "miles/gallon" for the 20 cars meet government standards. Have output appear as:

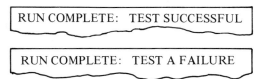

RUN COMPLETE: TEST SUCCESSFUL

RUN COMPLETE: TEST A FAILURE

Show what intermediate output values a cautious programmer would generate to assure the program is working well.

17. The navigator of a ship is asked to plot a proposed course change. The following information is provided:

 new heading: 135.0°
 proposed speed: 20.0 miles/hr.
 time on this course: 126.0 minutes

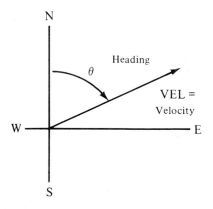

N

Heading

θ

VEL = Velocity

W   E

S

Write a program to read these three values from a data card and determine:

 a) total distance travelled
 b) N–S component
 c) E–W component

18. The first card in a data deck gives the magnitude and inclination (degrees) of a vector (V_1); a second data card gives the magnitude and inclination of a second vector (V_2).

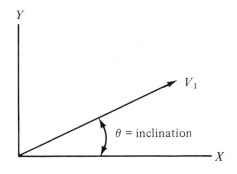

Y

V_1

θ = inclination

X

Part A: Write a program to determine the X and Y components of each vector.

| VECTOR 1 X-COMPONENT = | ☐ |
| VECTOR 2 X-COMPONENT = | ☐ |

| Y-COMPONENT = | ☐ |
| Y-COMPONENT = | ☐ |

Part B: Add statements to the program that will add the two X-components together in a memory location called SUMX. Add the two Y-components together and label this SUMY. Report these two values.

TOTAL X-COMPONENT = ☐

TOTAL Y-COMPONENT = ☐

Part C: Determine the magnitude and inclination of the vector V_R whose X and Y components are SUMX and SUMY. The total program will thereby compute the vector sum of V_1 and V_2.

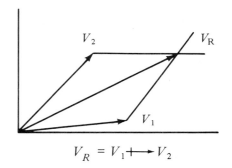

$$V_R = V_1 \longmapsto V_2$$

19. Repeat problem 18 except reverse the sign of the X and Y components of the second vector thereby accomplishing vector subtraction:

$$V_R = V_1 \rightarrow V_2$$

20. Combine the features of problem 18 and 19 into one program that involves a single data card:

CODE:
   1 = ADDITION
   2 = SUBTRACTION

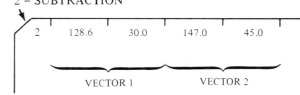

The first digit on this card determines if the two vectors are to be added or subtracted.

21.* Determine the minimum and maximum value of the equations shown between X = 1 and X = 10.

$$y = \log_{10}(x + 4) + |(x^3 - 64)|$$

22. Determine and report the X and Y value of 360 equally spaced points around the periphery of a circle of radius R (read from data). Cause a memory location called THETA to take on the following sequence of values:

$$0.0, 1.0, 2.0, 3.0, 4.0, \ldots 358.0, 359.0, 360.0$$

For each value of THETA compute X and Y from the equation:

$$X = R \cdot \text{COS}\theta$$
$$Y = R \cdot \text{SIN}\theta$$

23. We wish to evaluate the equation:

$$y = e^x(\ln(x + 1) - 4)$$

between two limits of X to be read from data:

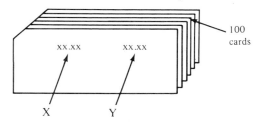

Write a program that reads these values and computes the total range of X they span. Divide this range by 100 defining a "stepping value." Set a memory location called X at XMIN, and then increase X by the computed "stepping value" until XMAX is reached. For each value compute and report Y.

24. Read 8 real numbers from a data card and report the largest and smallest value using the library functions shown on page 17.8.

25. A data deck consists of 100 cards, each containing the X and Y of successive points on a curve (values of X are sequential). Determine the average value of Y represented in this deck. Determine the largest difference in X between successive data points.

Additional Applications

| Programming Example |
| Folding a Number |
| 811 \| 249 \| 125 |
| Social Security Number |

Workers pay records are stored in a file cabinet using their social security numbers. To speed up the filing process it was decided to equip the cabinet with a series of folders numbered 000, 001, 002, 003. . .997, 998, 999 and to file records using only three digits of the workers social security numbers.

First Attempt:
   Initially, records were stored using the *first* 3 digits, but that procedure did not work well. Some folders had hundreds of records while others were empty, because of the way in which social security numbers are issued.

Second Attempt:
   The process was modified by shifting to the *last* 3 digits of the number, but the results were again not satisfactory.

Third Attempt:

Write a program to allow *all* digits to be used in generating the 3-digit filing number as follows:

(a) divide the 9 digit number into three equal parts;
(b) add these parts together;
(c) take the last three digits of this sum as the filing number.

This is called **folding the number.**

```
C.................................................................
C.. PURPOSE -  MODIFY A 9 DIGIT SOCIAL SECURITY NUMBER   ..
C..            AS DIRECTED.                               ..
C.................................................................
C
C               -----IMPORTANT VARIABLES-----
C
C  --N1,N2,N3  THREE EQUAL PARTS OF SOCIAL SECURITY     --
C              NUMBER
C  --SUM       SUM OF THESE PARTS                        --
C  --FILE      FILE NUMBER RESULTING FROM PROCESS        --
C
       INTEGER SUM, FILE
C
       READ(5,10)N1,N2,N3
    10 FORMAT(3I3)
C
       SUM=N1+N2+N3
```

Problem: The addition of these numbers may produce a four-digit result. When this happens we must determine the first digit and adjust the value of SUM appropriately.

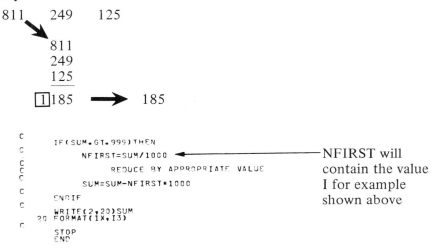

```
C      IF(SUM.GT.999)THEN
C         NFIRST=SUM/1000  ◄─────────────── NFIRST will
C            REDUCE BY APPROPRIATE VALUE         contain the value
C         SUM=SUM-NFIRST*1000                    1 for example
C      ENDIF                                     shown above
C      WRITE(2,20)SUM
   20 FORMAT(1X,I3)
C      STOP
       END
```

Programming Example Report Median Value (String of Five Digits)

To determine the median value of a string of numbers, it is first necessary to order the string (put values in numeric order). If the string consists of an odd number of values, the median is the middle number (see illustration below). If the string consists of an even number of values, the median is the average of the middle two numbers.

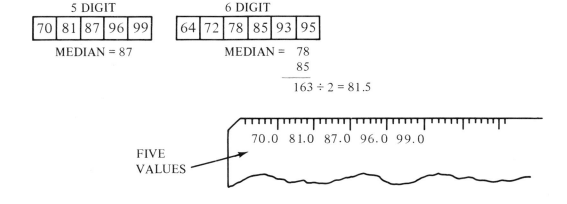

A data card consists of a string of five digits. Verify that these digits are in order, and then report the median value.

```
C.............................................................
C.:   PURPOSE -   VERIFY THE ORDER - REPORT THE MEDIAN      .:
C.............................................................
C
C                        -----IMPORTANT VARIABLES-----
C
C       --X1 TO X5   NUMBERS IN THE NUMBER SET            --
C
        READ(5,10)X1,X2,X3,X4,X5
    10  FORMAT(5F6.1)
C
        IF(X1.GT.X2)WRITE(2,*) ' FIRST TWO NUMBERS OUT OF ORDER'
C
        IF(X2.GT.X3)WRITE(2,*) ' SECOND AND THIRD NUMBER OUT OF ORDER'
C
        IF(X3.GT.X4)WRITE(2,*) ' THIRD AND FOURTH NUMBER OUT OF ORDER'
C
        IF(X4.GT.X5)WRITE(2,*) ' FOURTH AND FIFTH NUMBER OUT OF ORDER'
C
        WRITE(2,20)X3
    20  FORMAT(1X,F6.1)
C
        STOP
        END
```

Programming Example
Median Value
(General)

Write a more general program for reporting the median of a string of digits. The first card in the data deck provides an integer telling the size of the string (with the maximum number of elements being 9). Use a computed GO TO to reach one of two bodies of FORTRAN code to handle an even or odd set of elements.

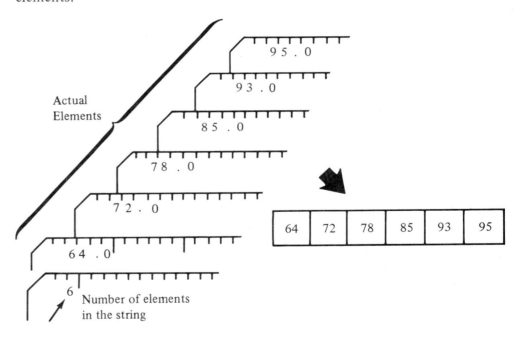

Actual
Elements

95 . 0

93 . 0

85 . 0

78 . 0

72 . 0

64 . 0

6 Number of elements
in the string

| 64 | 72 | 78 | 85 | 93 | 95 |

```
C.............................................................
C.:   PURPOSE -   FIND THE MEDIAN ELEMENT.              ..
C.............................................................
C                        -----IMPORTANT VARIABLES-----
C       --SIZE    INTEGER TELLING SIZE OF STRING           --
C       --XVALUE ELEMENTS OF THE STRING                    --
C       --MIDDLE INTEGER POINTING TO MIDDLE OF STRING      --
C
C       INTEGER SIZE
C
C       READ(5,10)SIZE
    10  FORMAT(I1)
C
        GO TO(1,2,1,2,1,2,1,2,1),SIZE
C
C               MODULE 1 - HANDLE ODD NUMBER OF ELEMENTS
C
    1   MIDDLE=SIZE/2+1
C
    20  READ(5,30)XVALUE
    30  FORMAT(F6.1)
C
C               ... IS THIS THE MEDIAN ...
C
        IF(SIZE.EQ.MIDDLE)THEN
```

```
C
              WRITE(2,40)XVALUE
   40         FORMAT(1X,F6.1)
C
C             STOP
C
    ELSE
C
              SIZE=SIZE-1
              GO TO 20
C
    ENDIF
C
C               MODULE 2 - HANDLE EVEN NUMBER OF ELEMENTS
C
    2 MIDDLE=SIZE/2
C
   50 READ(5,30)XVALUE
C
C               ... IS THIS ONE OF THE MIDDLE ELEMENTS ...
C
    IF(SIZE.EQ.MIDDLE)THEN
C
              FIRST=XVALUE
              READ(5,30)XVALUE
              SECOND=XVALUE
              VALUE=(FIRST+SECOND)/2.0
C
              WRITE(2,40)VALUE
         STOP
C
    ELSE
C
              SIZE=SIZE-1
              GO TO 50
C
    ENDIF
C
    END
```

| **Programming Example** Odd or Even |

Write a program to read an integer number from a data card and determine if the number is odd or even.

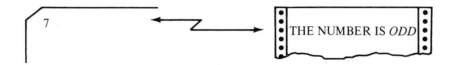

When an odd number is divided by 2 in the integer mode, truncation takes place. We can use this information as follows:

1. make a copy of the number,
2. divide the copy by 2
3. multiply the copy by 2

If the copy and the original number are now different, truncation has occurred, and the original number was odd.

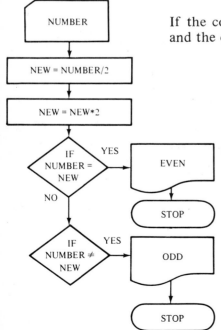

```
C............................................................
C..  PURPOSE - DETERMINE IF A NUMBER IS EVEN OR ODD       ..
C............................................................
C
   10 READ(5,11) NUMBER
   11 FORMAT(I2)
C
      NEW = NUMBER / 2
      NEW = NEW * 2
C
   21 IF(NEW.EQ.NUMBER) WRITE(2,21)
                        FORMAT(10X,'NUMBER IS EVEN')
C
   22 IF(NEW.NE.NUMBER) WRITE(2,22)
                        FORMAT(10X,'NUMBER IS ODD')
C
      STOP
      END
```

Programming Example
Polar to Cartesian

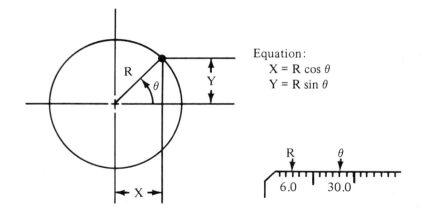

Equation:
$$X = R \cos \theta$$
$$Y = R \sin \theta$$

The location of the point can be specified in polar coordinates as follows:

Given: R = 6
$$\theta = 30°$$

The X and Y coordinates (cartesian) can be found by using the equations shown. Write a program to accept from data the polar coordinates of a point and compute the corresponding cartesian coordinates.

```
C.........................................................
C..   PURPOSE - CONVERT POLAR TO CARTESIAN COORDINATES.  ..
C.........................................................
C
C                    -----IMPORTANT VARIABLES-----
C
C      --R               RADIUS OF POINT                  --
C      --THETA           ANGLE (DEGREES)                  --
C      --X,Y             CARTESIAN COORDINATES OF POINT   --
C
       READ(5,10) RADIUS, THETA
    10 FORMAT(2F6.1)
C
       X = RADIUS*COS(THETA/57.3)
       Y = RADIUS*SIN(THETA/57.3)
C
       WRITE(2,20) X, Y
    20 FORMAT(3X,2HX=,F6.1,4X,2HY=,F6.1)
C
       STOP
       END
```

Programming Example
Either Way**
(see previous problem)

Given: R, θ	Given: X, Y
Req'd: X, Y	Req'd: R, θ

OR

$$X = R \cos \theta \qquad R = \sqrt{X^2 + Y^2}$$
$$Y = R \sin \theta \qquad \theta = \tan^{-1}(Y/X)$$

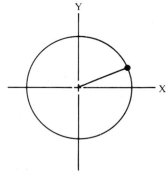

```
1        6.0          30.0
```

KODE   VALUE1   VALUE2

Write a program that can accept as input the polar coordinates of a point and compute the cartesian coordinates as output (KODE=1), or accept the cartesian coordinates and compute the corresponding polar coordinates (KODE=2).

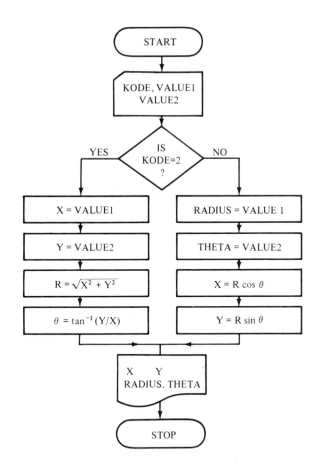

```
C.................................................................
C..    PURPOSE - CODE = 1  CONVERT TO CARTESIAN,          ..
C..              CODE = 2  CONVERT CARTESIAN TO POLAR,    ..
C.................................................................
C
C             -----IMPORTANT VARIABLES-----
C
C     --CODE          SELECTOR VALUE                      --
C     --X,Y           CARTESIAN VALUES                    --
C     --R,THETA       POLAR VALUES                        --
C     --VALUE1,VALUE2          VALUES READ FROM DATA CARD --
C
      INTEGER CODE
C
   10 READ(5,11)CODE, VALUE1, VALUE2
   11 FORMAT( I1,2F6.1)
C
C             TEST CODE VALUE
C
      IF(CODE.EQ.2) GO TO 20
C
C             CONVERT POLAR TO CARTESIAN
C
      RADIUS = VALUE1
      THETA = VALUE2
      X = RADIUS * COS(THETA /57.3)
      Y = RADIUS * SIN(THETA /57.3)
      GO TO 30
C
C             CONVERT CARTESIAN TO POLAR
C
   20 X = VALUE1
      Y = VALUE2
      RADIUS = SQRT(X**2+Y**2)
      THETA = ATAN2(Y,X)
C
C             OUTPUT MODULE
C
   30 WRITE(2,31) X, Y, RADIUS, THETA
   31 FORMAT(2X, 2HX=,F6.1,4X,2HY=,F6.1,4X,7HRADIUS=,F6.1,4X,
     1          6HTHETA=,F6.1)
C
      STOP
      END
```

Programming Example Poor Grades	The college board scores of 1000 randomly-selected students are to be analyzed to see if students from low-income families perform as well as students from affluent families. Determine:

    a) the number of students coming from families having incomes less than $8000,

    b) the average score achieved by this group,

    c) the number of students coming from families having incomes of $25,000 or more, and

    d) the average score achieved by this group.

COUNTERS

NLOW
NHIGH

ACCUMULATORS

SUMLOW
SUMHI

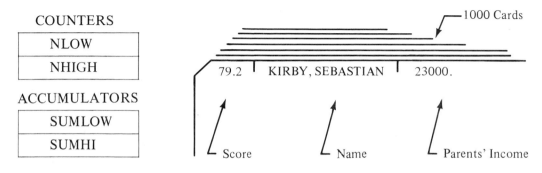

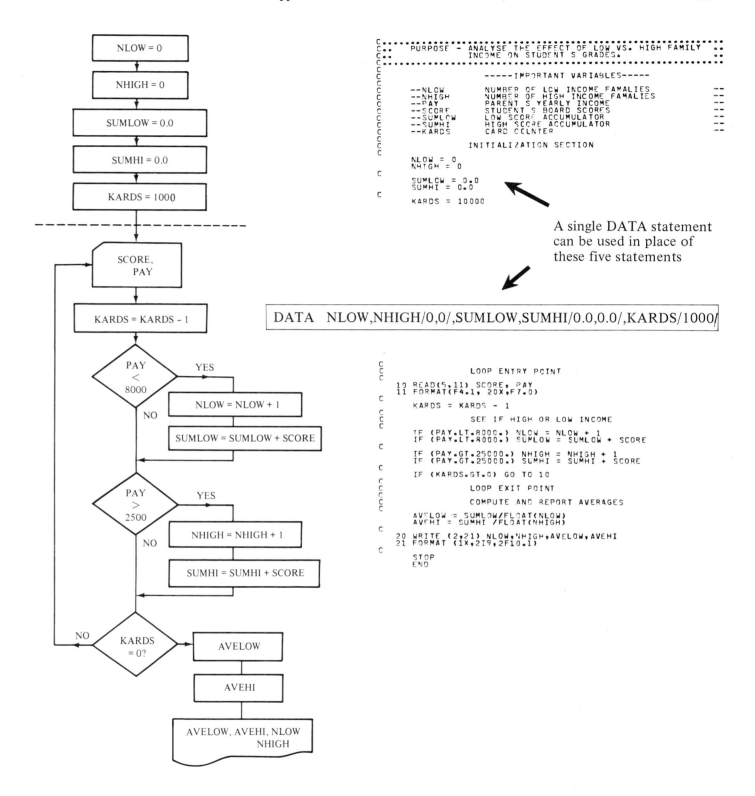

```
C....................................................................
C..  PURPOSE - ANALYSE THE EFFECT OF LOW VS. HIGH FAMILY  ..
C..            INCOME ON STUDENT S GRADES.                ..
C....................................................................
C
C               -----IMPORTANT VARIABLES-----
C
C      --NLOW      NUMBER OF LOW INCOME FAMALIES        --
C      --NHIGH     NUMBER OF HIGH INCOME FAMALIES       --
C      --PAY       PARENT S YEARLY INCOME               --
C      --SCORE     STUDENT S BOARD SCORES               --
C      --SUMLOW    LOW SCORE ACCUMULATOR                --
C      --SUMHI     HIGH SCORE ACCUMULATOR               --
C      --KARDS     CARD COUNTER                         --
C
C               INITIALIZATION SECTION
C
       NLOW = 0
       NHIGH = 0
C
       SUMLOW = 0.0
       SUMHI = 0.0
C
       KARDS = 10000
```

A single DATA statement
can be used in place of
these five statements

```
DATA   NLOW,NHIGH/0,0/,SUMLOW,SUMHI/0.0,0.0/,KARDS/1000/
```

```
C
C               LOOP ENTRY POINT
C
   10  READ(5,11) SCORE, PAY
   11  FORMAT(F4.1, 20X,F7.0)
C
       KARDS = KARDS - 1
C
C               SEE IF HIGH OR LOW INCOME
C
       IF (PAY.LT.8000.) NLOW = NLOW + 1
       IF (PAY.LT.8000.) SUMLOW = SUMLOW + SCORE
C
       IF (PAY.GT.25000.) NHIGH = NHIGH + 1
       IF (PAY.GT.25000.) SUMHI = SUMHI + SCORE
C
       IF (KARDS.GT.0) GO TO 10
C
C               LOOP EXIT POINT
C
C               COMPUTE AND REPORT AVERAGES
C
       AVELOW = SUMLOW/FLOAT(NLOW)
       AVEHI = SUMHI /FLOAT(NHIGH)
C
   20  WRITE (2,21) NLOW,NHIGH,AVELOW,AVEHI
   21  FORMAT (1X,2I9,2F10.1)
C
       STOP
       END
```

Programming Example
Trig Tables

The table shown was prepared for a math book. It gives trigonometric functions for angles between 0° and 90° at one degree increments. It has been decided to expand the table by using one-half degree increments (θ = 0.0, 0.5, 1.0, 1.5, 2.0, 2.5, etc.).

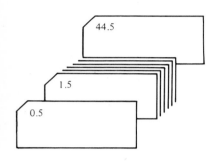

Degrees	sin	cos	tan	cot	
0°	.0000	1.000	.0000	—	90°
1°	.0175	.9998	.0175	57.29	89°
2°	.0349	.9994	.0349	28.64	88°
3°	.0523	.9986	.0524	19.08	87°
4°	.0698	.9976	.0699	14.30	86°
5°	.0872	.9962	.0875	11.43	85°
6°	.1045	.9945	.1051	9.514	84°
7°	.1219	.9925	.1228	8.144	
8°	.1392	.9903	.1405		
38°				1.280	52°
39°	.6293	.7771	.8098	1.235	51°
40°	.6428	.7660	.8391	1.192	50°
41°	.6561	.7547	.8693	1.150	49°
42°	.6691	.7431	.9004	1.111	48°
43°	.6820	.7314	.9325	1.072	47°
44°	.6947	.7193	.9657	1.036	46°
45°	.7071	.7071	1.000	1.000	45°
	cos	sin	ctn	tan	Degrees

Write a program to determine and report the *additional* values needed to expand the table. Report these values in a form similar to the existing table.

In developing the logic of this program, one of the first considerations is controlling a memory location (possibly called THETA) so that it will take on the desired sequence of values (0.5, 1.5, 2.5, . . . 44.5). One approach is to read values of THETA from data, but you now have a more direct way of controlling THETA (by an indexing statement).

```
C.............................................................
C..  PURPOSE - COMPUTE ADDITIONAL TRIGINOMETRIC VALUES TO  ..
C..            MAKE THE TABLE MORE COMPLETE.                ..
C.............................................................
C
C                 -----IMPORTANT VARIABLES-----
C
C     --THETA       ANGLE (IN DEGREES)                      --
C     --ANS1        FIRST OUTPUT VALUE - SINE VALUE          --
C     --ANS2        SECOND OUTPUT VALUE - COSINE VALUE       --
C     --ANS3        THIRD OUTPUT VALUE - TANGENT VALUE       --
C     --ANS4        COMPLEMENT OF THE ANGLE                  --
C     --COMP        COMPLEMENT OF ANGLE                      --
C
      THETA = 0.5
C
C               ....LOOP ENTRY POINT.....
C
   10 ANS1 = SIN(THETA/57.3)
      ANS2 = COS(THETA/57.3)
      ANS3 = ANS1/ANS2
      ANS4 = 1.0/ANS3
      COMP = 90.0 - THETA
C
C               PUBLISH LINE OF OUTPUT
C
      WRITE(2,20) THETA,ANS1,ANS2,ANS3,ANS4,COMP
   20 FORMAT(1X,F7.1,4F9.4,F7.1)
C
C               ADVANCE THETA
C
      THETA = THETA + 1.0
      IF(THETA.LT.90.0) GO TO 10
C
C               .....LOOP EXIT POINT.....
C
      STOP
      END
```

Programming Example
New Highway

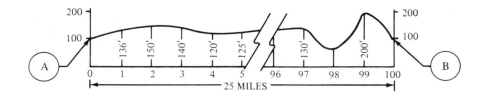

A 25-mile stretch of highway is being planned to connect point A and B shown above. The elevation of the land at 100 equally-spaced points along the route is determined and recorded on data cards. We are interested in locating those points along the highway where the change in elevation is excessive (greater than 20 ft.)

Read the first two data cards. If the change in elevation between these points is greater than 20 feet, report this as a trouble area.

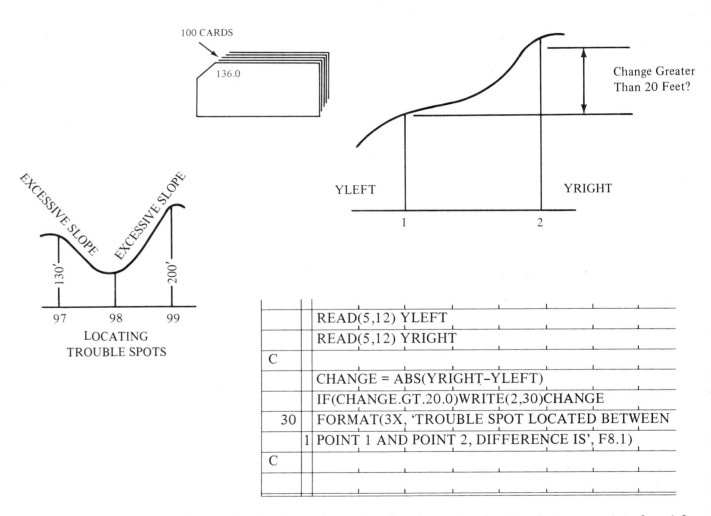

		READ(5,12) YLEFT
		READ(5,12) YRIGHT
C		
		CHANGE = ABS(YRIGHT−YLEFT)
		IF(CHANGE.GT.20.0)WRITE(2,30)CHANGE
30		FORMAT(3X, 'TROUBLE SPOT LOCATED BETWEEN
	1	POINT 1 AND POINT 2, DIFFERENCE IS', F8.1)
C		

Repeat this logic to determine the change in elevation between points 2 and 3, then between 3 and 4, etc. *Report any trouble spots.*

NOTE: Set a flag called IFLAG at the start of the program. If no trouble spots are located, use the flag to issue the printout "NO TROUBLE SPOTS LOCATED."

```
C..............................................................
C...  P URPOSE - LOCATE TROUBLE SPOTS ALONG A HIGHWAY.        ::
C..............................................................
C
C                     -----IMPORTANT VARIABLES-----
C
C      --POINT        INTEGER TELLING POINT IN HIGHWAY UNDER STUDY--
C      --NEXT         PCINT JUST BEYOND LOCATION POINT          --
C      --CHANGE       DIFFERENCE IN ELEVATION BETWEEN TWO POINTS --
C      --YLEFT        ELEVATION AT LOCATION POINT               --
C      --YRIGHT       ELEVATION AT LOCATION NEXT                --
C
       INTEGER POINT
C
       POINT = 1
       IFLAG = 0
C
C
       READ(5,10) YLEFT
   10  FORMAT(F5.1)
C
C              .....LOOP ENTRY POINT.....
C
   20  READ(5,10) YRIGHT
C
       CHANGE = ABS(YRIGHT - YLEFT)
C
       IF(CHANGE.GT.20.0) THEN
C
               NEXT = POINT + 1
               WRITE(2,30) POINT, NEXT, CHANGE
   30          FORMAT(3X,'TROUBLE SPOT LOCATED BETWEEN POINT ',I3,
      +             'AND POINT ',I3,' DIFFERENCE IS ',F8.1)
               IFLAG = 1
C
       ENDIF
C
C              ADVANCE POINT     REDEFINE YLEFT
C
       POINT = POINT + 1
       YLEFT = YRIGHT
C
       IF(POINT.LT.99) GO TO 20
C              .....LOOP EXIT POINT.....
C
       IF(IFLAG.EC.0) WRITE(2,40)
   40  FORMAT(3X,'NO TROUBLE SPOTS LOCATED*)
       STOP
       END
```

**Programming Example
Throw Darts**** A data deck consists of 1000 cards each containing two random numbers (numbers chosen by pure chance) whose values are between 0 and 1. Each pair of numbers will be used to specify the X and Y coordinates of where a dart landed when thrown at the target (to the right of the data deck). If these are truly random numbers, the darts will be evenly distributed throughout the target area.

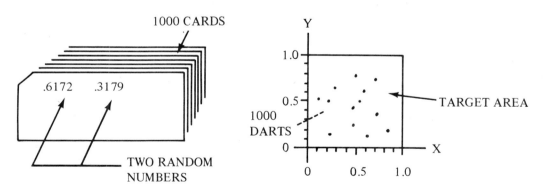

A more meaningful use of this technique is suggested by the illustration shown on page 191. It is 40 units tall and 12 units wide and contains the plot of the function:

$$y = X^2 + 12X$$

The area under this curve (the value of the integral) could be evaluated by again throwing darts and keeping track of the percentage of darts that fall below the curve. If 50% fall below the curve, the desired area is 50% of the 40-by-12 unit target area.

Consider some of the problems in writing a program to do all this. Each random number will have to be multiplied by 40 or 12 to compensate for the larger target area. Next, two counters will be needed (NYES and NNO) to keep track of how many darts fall above and below the curve. Finally, a means of

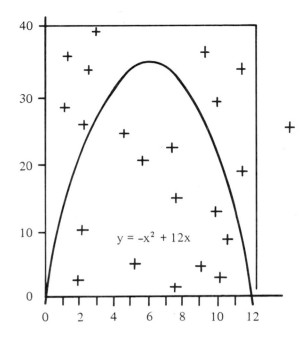

$$y = -x^2 + 12x$$

determining if a dart fell below the curve will have to be found. Use the following steps:

1. Substitute the X coordinate of the dart into the equation

$$y = -X^2 + 12X$$

2. Call this value YEQ
3. If the Y coordinate of the dart is greater than YEQ, the dart landed above the curve, and
4. If the Y coordinate of the dart is less than YEQ, the dart landed below the curve.

```
C............................................................
C..    PURPOSE - EVALUATE AN INTEGRAL BY RANDOM NUMBER       ..
C..              TECHNIQUE.                                  ..
C............................................................
C
C                    -----IMPORTANT VARIABLE-----
C     --NYES   NUMBER OF DARTS THAT FELL UNDER THE CURVE     --
C     --NNO    NUMBER OF DARTS THAT FELL ABOVE THE CURVE     --
C     --X      RANDOM NUMBER CONTROLLING X LOCATION OF DART  --
C     --Y      RANDOM NUMBER CONTROLLING Y LOCATION OF DART  --
C     --XDART  ACTUAL X LOCATION OF WHERE DART LANDED        --
C     --YDART  ACTUAL Y LOCATION OF WHERE DART LANDED        --
C     --YEQ    CUT OFF VALUE OF Y (FROM EQUATION)            --
C
      DATA NNO, NYES/ 0, 0/
C
C              LOOP ENTRY POINT
C
10         READ(5,11,END=25) X, Y
11         FORMAT(2F10.2)
C
C              SCALE THESE VALUES
C
      XDART = X * 12.0
      YDART = Y * 40.0
C
C              COMPUTE CUT OFF VALUE
C
      YEQ = XDART ** 2 + 12.0 * XDART
C
      IF(YDART.GT.YEQ) NNO = NNO +1
      IF(YDART.LT.YEQ) NYES = NYES +1
C
20    GO TO 10
C
C              ALL DARTS THROWN - COMPUTE AVERAGE
C
25    AVE = NYES / (NNO + NYES)
C
30    WRITE (2,31) AVE
31    FORMAT (10X,F10.2)
C
      STOP
      END
```

Take another look at statement 25. Is that the way it should be written? Using integer arithmetic will produce the value zero. The library function FLOAT is needed.

8 | Programming Style And Procedures

Most FORTRAN programs do not work correctly the first time they are run. Sometimes they do not work correctly on the second, third and fourth run. Up to half the time needed to produce a properly functioning program is spent on locating and correcting errors. One of the reasons for this is that programming is sufficiently complex to warrant a careful, methodical approach to solving each and every problem. Whimsical, off-the-top-of-the-head methods of solution are just not advisable.

The purpose of this chapter is to identify and organize the procedures that will increase the likelihood of a successful program. It may even be possible to have a successful run on the very first try.

8.1 | Structure Your Approach

There is no such thing as a standard method of solution. We would like nothing better than to provide a check-off list that, if rigidly followed, would guarantee success. On the other hand, there are specific steps that can be applied in an orderly fashion. Structure your approach to problem solving in the following way:

1. learn what steps and recommendations are available, and
2. apply these steps to each problem in an organized way.

Shown below is a list of recommendations that are particularly applicable in the early stages of defining a problem's algorithm.

Summary of Programming Style Recommendations

- Logic first — details later
  - Resist the temptation to start writing code immediately
    - Problem statement — do not start until you are sure
      - Get a firm grasp on the problem's input
        - Separate the familiar from the unfamiliar

The underlying theme of these recommendations is obvious. A solution must evolve slowly, after a series of refinements. The process starts by some top-level determinations as to exactly what the problem is all about and how it can be subdivided into a series of well-defined subtasks. Some students are exceptionally capable of performing this important management function. They are able to release themselves from the petty details of implementing a program and focus immediately on the broad strategies and plan of attack for the problem. These students have learned to fight one battle at a time – the big ones first, the little ones later (rather than all battles at once).

The end product of this phase of analysis is a less-than-perfect (and certainly not detailed) set of subtasks expressed in block diagram form (pseudocode). It is from this diagram that the refinement process begins. The only requirement imposed at this time is that no major operation be overlooked and omitted.

The next step is a simplification/familiarization process. Having identified the basic tasks (modules) that are involved in the solution, examine the flow of data *into and out of each module.* For many of these modules, you will have a good idea of how to accomplish the particular task involved. The various programming examples presented in this text should help in this regard. They have been presented to develop your experience in handling operations (tasks) that are frequently encountered in processing digital information.

There is a strong temptation to start writing FORTRAN code for these simpler modules. That is a mistake for several reasons:

1. It will take your attention away from the overall strategy of solving the problem.
2. Getting down to details this early may commit you to a method of solution that is good for this particular module but not best for the problem as a whole.
3. It is possible that you will wind up with several blocks of code that prove difficult to fit together.

Handling the Harder Modules

Do not expect to uncover a direct and simple solution to each and every module. The difficult modules will require further processing. Realize that this is just the first step in the solution. It is only important to get a clear identification of the *function* of each module at this time. The specific method of implementation comes later.

If you have difficulty identifying all the steps in a particular solution or if you want to verify the solutional steps you have already identified: *do a hand calculation of one or more typical applications of the algorithm.* This suggestion is being made to cut down on the number of abstractions you must face at any one time. It is easier to develop a "general" algorithm after several specific solutions have been worked out. It is part of the organized (structured) approach we are promoting.

8.2 | The Refinement Process

Programming Style
Algorithm Check List
(1) Detailed
(2) Exact
(3) Effective
(4) Efficient

Ultimately, an algorithm must be evolved that has the following features:

1. *Detailed:* each and every aspect of the problem solution must be identified, labelled and dealt with in detail. Special conditions that force alternative solutions or processing must be covered explicitly and integrated into the general solution.
2. *Exact:* the algorithm must be well-organized. It must present a methodical and unambiguous definition of what

factors affect the solution to the problem
and of how each of these factors are to
be handled (accommodated) as the solution progresses.

3. *Effective:* an algorithm must be based on
   sound mathematical or logical procedures
   that lead to a correct solution or a close
   approximation of the solution.

4. *Efficient:* an algorithm should express
   a closed solution to the problem. It
   should consist of a finite number of
   steps that converge on the final solution as rapidly as possible.

Transforming the existing block diagram into a completed algorithm having
the properties described above starts with a reexamination of the individual
blocks. For each block the following information has already been established:

a. what data this block receives as input,
b. what function (transform) takes place inside the block, and
c. what output is generated as a result of the transform.

If the block is relatively simple and within your ability to program, document its logic with a skeleton flow chart. This need not be a very elaborate
diagram. Just show the type of statements you plan to use and the expected
transfer of control within the block.

If a block is too difficult to program, it is either too big or not sufficiently
well defined. Try to sharpen your understanding of what function (transform)
is to take place inside the block. Attempt to further subdivide the block by listing a number of specific actions that must be taken to accomplish the block's
major function.

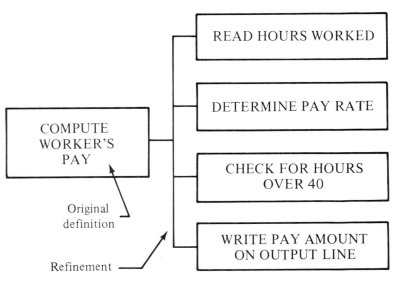

Figure 8.1 Refinement Process

If any of these blocks need further refinement, the breakdown would be
shown in a similar fashion (the diagram develops like the root of a tree). Ultimately, the process should bring the problem into clearer focus and result in
steps that are relatively simple to program.

The flow chart is the next step in the refinement process.

Programming Style
Flow Charts
(1) Top to Bottom
(2) Don't Jump
    Around
(3) Parallel Block
    Structure

A flow chart should start at the top of a page and basically flow to the bottom of the page in linear fashion. This should parallel the linear structure of the block diagram or pseudocode. Do not jump around any more than is necessary. Where binary or multiple decisions are made, set up parallel paths close to one another to highlight the logic.

In constructing a flow chart, keep a few things in mind. First, remember that there is no substitute for clarity. If you are wondering how to express the logic of an IF test, or the equation of an arithmetic statement, or the indexing of a counter — *use whatever method makes it clearer.*

Try to flow chart in the same "block form" used in developing the pseudocode. Generally speaking, these blocks will be one of three basic types (*processing* block, *decision* block, *loop* block).

A *processing* block consists of a fixed series of assignment statements that accomplish a sequence of calculations (data transforms).

A *decision* block contains alternative groups of statements as typified by the IF-THEN-ELSE construction.

A *loop* block is a group of statements that will be executed a number of times.

Use comment statements to make these blocks stand out as clearly as possible. Design the flow chart to move from one block to the other in a simple (linear) fashion. If possible:

1. Enter a block through the top statement only.
2. Exit the block through the last statement only.

Finally, do not expect a perfect flow chart on the first attempt. Keep an eraser handy. It is all part of the refinement process.

Summary of Programming Style Recommendations

- Use highly descriptive names for variables — keep a table
- Avoid tricks — do not get fancy
- Use comment statements — make them meaningful
- LOGICAL IF — Preferred
- Syntax — If you are not sure, look it up
- Parenthesize to avoid ambiguity
- Restrict the use of GO TO statements

The programming examples of this text have been written in a special way. Comment statements consisting of a blank line are used to highlight important parts of the program. Other comment statements separate various blocks of code and provide brief descriptions of their functions. Each program starts with statements that describe the purpose of the program and the names for all important variables.

Correct habits in writing clear and easy-to-follow FORTRAN codes are very important. They are called **programming style**. It is difficult for a student to fully appreciate the importance of programming style. For short programs, it may not be all that important. However, if you ever are required to make "updates" to a long program written by someone else, you will find programming style a life-saving feature. You are encouraged to develop a programming style of your own. Many times it makes the difference between "just a program" and "a first-class program."

Programming style starts when the individual statements are written out longhand on a coding form. Make them look as close to a computer listing as possible. Use capital letters. Be careful about spacing and indentation. Be generous in the use of comment statements, but make the comments as meaningful as possible. Check to make sure you have been consistent in the spelling of each variable name used.

8.3 Desk Check: An Important Step in the Refinement Process

The time spent carefully examining each line of code for missing commas, duplicate statement numbers, missing operators, etc., is called a **desk check**. This is the last phase in the refinement process. Now your attention should be totally focused on details. We have been concentrating on the avoidance of making *big* mistakes. Now is the time to be careful about making *little* ones — the so-called stupid mistakes. They are just as fatal.

A desk check should involve a very slow line-by-line examination of the program. Take your time and do a thorough, fastidious job. This phase of program preparation really is very important and should not be slighted.

Programming Style
Desk Check
(1) Syntax Scan
(2) Logic Scan
(3) Data Test

This is the stage of the programming effort where "details" are the most important item. Each line of code you have written should be scanned line by line for syntax errors, missing commas, unpaired parentheses, duplicate statement numbers, missing format statements, etc. This should not be a casual scan. Take the assignment seriously. A substantial number of compiler errors can be traced to an insufficient desk check of the program.

What follows next is a logic scan. To accomplish this, you assume the role of a computer. Examine the first statement in your program. Do what it tells you to do — nothing more and nothing less. Execute the next instruction exactly as you are told. If a calculation is involved, compute the value (as you're told) or approximate it. Put the value found in a box and label it. This may help you to detect errors in the logic of your program.

With the exception of the topics covered in the next section (debugging techniques), your program is ready for the ultimate test (presentation to the computer).

8.4 Debug Techniques

As repulsive as it may seem it is possible to go through the long and tedious procedures described in this chapter and still wind up with errors. Errors are an inevitable part of programming. Professional programmers build into their programs defensive mechanisms to cope with this annoyance. The basic tool is PRINT! PRINT! PRINT! PRINT!

Programming Style
Debug Techniques
(1) Echo Trace
(2) Arithmetic Trace
(3) Path (Logic)
    Trace

Programmers can do a lot to ease the job of error detection and isolation if they will dismiss an ego-inspired confidence that "all will go well" and adopt a more sensible defensive attitude in writing programs. The single most powerful weapon in defensive programming is temporary, intermediate printouts. They are used in three important ways.

Echo trace: An intermediate printout positioned after each input statement to display (echo) the values just read. The statement verifies that each data value has been read correctly.

Arithmetic trace: An intermediate printout positioned after a series of arithmetic operations. The statement is used to monitor the change in key variables as the program progresses.

Path trace: An intermediate printout positioned at the top or bottom of a block of code. The statement is used to signal that a specific block has been reached and thereby to show the basic path that a program is following.

The use of extra printouts can reduce the frustration of trying to locate an error in your program. These extra print statements almost guarantee firm control over the execution of a program. Omitting them leaves the programmer helpless and invites disaster.

A properly written program consists of well-defined modules or blocks of code. It is important to know if these blocks are being executed in the sequence intended. **Path traces** can provide this information. They consist of statements such as:

```
        WRITE(2,12)
    12  FORMAT(20X, 'PASSING CHECK POINT 1')
                    – OR –
        WRITE(2,13)
    13  FORMAT(20X, 'ENTERING BLOCK 3')
```

strategically placed throughout the program. Each block should have at least one trace statement. A more elaborate procedure is to include the value of key variables as part of the output message. This provides a combination of arithmetic and path trace features. The advantages of such safeguards are described below.

Assume your program aborts with the error message, "DIVIDE FAULT – DIVISION BY ZERO." Usually, there will be no clear indication of which statement caused the error. If there is only one WRITE statement at the end of the program, the error could be anywhere. If, on the other hand, you are using four or five path traces, the error is reasonably well isolated. The path trace will tell which blocks were executed successfully. You should be able to identify which block was the last entered before disaster struck.

If you still have difficulty locating the error, additional trace statements can be added to the block that is giving you trouble. This will pinpoint further the faulty statement. Another use of trace statements is described below.

Assume a program has been compiled and executed with test data, and the results are incorrect. If four or five combination path and arithmetic traces have been used, it is possible to examine these traces to see at what point the calculations went wrong. Each of these temporary printouts should indicate where in the program the print statement is located. The statement might include the message "PASSING STATEMENT 100" or "PASSING CHECK POINT 1." Usually, it is helpful to distinguish all the normal output from the temporary traces. One technique is to have the output of the trace statements appear on the right side of the output sheet and the normal output appear on the left, as shown below:

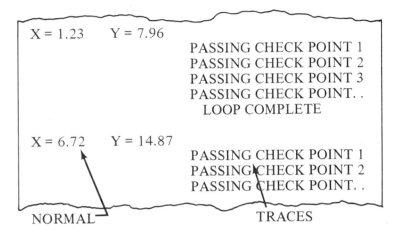

Another suggestion is to use multicolored statement cards for keypunching the trace statements during the preparation of your logic deck. Then they can be removed easily from the deck when the program is running correctly to get "clean" output (output without the traces).

When a program is exceptionally short, perhaps there is some justification for not going to all the extremes suggested in this section. If, after two trial runs of a program, errors still exist, your only recourse is to fall back on these debugging procedures. Nothing disturbs an instructor more than the following situation:

(1) Student complains he has been working for hours to get a program to run properly.
(2) Instructor looks at program and finds no ECHO traces, no ARITHMETIC traces, no PATH traces.

Space limitation prevents the inclusion of traces in each and every example program in this text. We will compromise by showing the technique periodically in the programming examples.

8.5 | Making Corrections

The following two recommendations are presented to set the stage for the way in which corrections to a program should be accomplished.

Programming Style ‖ If you have an error in your program, find
Trial-and-Error   out exactly what is causing it and correct it.
Correction: Do not just try something else. You will
Forget It   probably get deeper in trouble and surely
                     will become more confused. Error correction is an important part of your learning process. Take it seriously.

**Programming Style
Correct Them All —
Not One at a Time** ‖

If you are getting a series of errors, do not just change the first one you stumble upon and rerun the program. See if there is a pattern to your errors. Are they all coming from incorrect input/output operations? Is one error, early in the program, causing several errors later in the program? The important thing is to correct errors in batches, not one at a time. It is a more rewarding activity.

If you have followed the policy of using extra printouts, you should have a minimum amount of difficulty locating your error. However, there is one instance where the compiler can lead you astray with regard to pinpointing the location of an error.

The compiler will specifically state that an error exists in one statement when actually the error exists in the statement following. For example:

```
        READ(5,7) A, B, C
7   FORMAT(F8.1,F9.3,F9.4)
```
Error

The difficulty lies in the fact that the word FORMAT starts in column 6, not column 7. The F in column 6 will be interpreted as a continuation character, implying that the FORMAT statement is a continuation of the READ statement. The compiler, therefore, flags the READ statement as being an error.

Getting Help

If you are unable to understand a particular error, look for help, but be careful. Get professional help. Asking another student may or may not provide the answer. If that student starts a massive rewrite of your program, he is *not* doing you a service. Usually, there are people at the computation center trained to give you assistance. They are your best source of help. Bring your flow chart and any other documentation. If they see you have approached the problem in a professional (well-documented) way, you will get good help. If you bring a program with no flow chart, no listing of variable names, no comment statements and no printouts except the one at the end of the program. . .you will not get (and do not deserve) much help at all.

Quiz#9   Programming Style

Part 1: Answer the following questions.

1. Why should you resist the temptation to start writing FORTRAN code as the initial step in solving a problem?
2. An algorithm should be efficient. What does that mean?
3. A flow chart should show the flow of control from the top of a program to the bottom. As much as possible, that flow should be what?
4. What action should take place during a "desk check"?
5. When writing a module of FORTRAN code, what three basic types of processing blocks are recommended?
6. What one statement is most often carelessly used and causes an interruption of the desired linear flow of control?

7. A block of code should be entered at one point and exited from another point. Identify these points.

8. Why are highly descriptive variable names helpful?

9. What is wrong with having just one WRITE statement in your program?

10. What does the term "syntax" mean regarding a FORTRAN statement?

Part 2: Writing a Program (The MODE of a Set)

11. The mode of a set of numbers is the number that occurs most frequently in the set.

MODE

We have rolled a pair of dice 1000 times and recorded the results on the data cards shown. The sum of the two numbers on each card will range from a low of 2 to a high of 12. We would like to know the *mode* of these rolls.

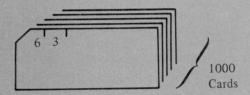

1000
Cards

You are given even money odds that the mode is the number 7 and four to one odds that the mode is the number 6 or 8. Which is it?

```
C . . . . . . . . . . . . . . . . . . . . . . . . . . . . . . . . . . . . . . . .
C  PURPOSE – DETERMINE IF THE MODE OF A SET. .
C            OF 1000 NUMBERS IS 6, 7 or 8.        . .
C . . . . . . . . . . . . . . . . . . . . . . . . . . . . . . . . . . . . . . . .
C
C                 – IMPORTANT VARIABLES –
C
C  –N1,N2  NUMBERS READ FROM EACH CARD
C  –NO6S   NUMBER OF 6'S ROLLED
C  –NO7S   NUMBER OF 7'S ROLLED
C  –NO8S   NUMBER OF 8'S ROLLED
C  –SUM    SUM OF N1 AND N2
```

Answers:

1. It diverts your attention away from the *overall* strategy of solving the problem.

2. The algorithm should reach a solution (or close approximation) as quickly as possible.

3. Linear.

4. Syntax Scan; Logic Scan; Data Scan.

5. Processing Block; Decision Block; Loop Block.

6. GO TO statement.

7. Enter at the top. Exit from the bottom.

8. It makes the program easier to read.

9. No help to locate (isolate) errors in program.

10. Has the statement been written correctly in a grammatical sense (according to the rules of FORTRAN).

11.
```
C                        —OTHER VARIABLES
C        —MODE           THE NUMBER 6,7,OR 8 (WHICHEVER
C                        OCCURRED MOST FREQUENTLY
C        —NUMBER         THE NUMBER OF TIMES THIS MODE
C                        VALUE APPEARED
C
C
         INTEGER SUM
C
         DATA/NO6S,NO7S,NO8S/3*0/
C
   10    READ(5,20,END=30)N1, N2
   20    FORMAT(2I1)
C
         SUM=N1+N2
C
         IF(SUM.EQ.6)NO6S=NO6S+1
         IF(SUM.EQ.7)NO7S=NO7S+1
         IF(SUM.EQ.8)NO8S=NO8S+1
C
         GO TO 10
C        **********************************
C        **          ALL DICE ROLLED          **
C        **********************************
C
   30    IF(NO6S.GT.NO7S)THEN
C
                        NUMBER=NO6S
                        MODE=6
         ELSE
                        NUMBER=NO7S
                        MODE=7
         ENDIF
C
C
         IF(NO8S.GT.NUMBER)THEN
                        NUMBER=NO8S
                        MODE=8
         ENDIF
C
C
         WRITE(2,40)MODE, NUMBER
   40    FORMAT(1X, 'THE MODE OF THE SET IS',I1,
  1                 'THAT NUMBER OCCURS', I4, 'TIMES.')
C
         STOP
         END
```

Review Exercises

1. When first addressing a problem, what are some of the steps that should be taken to make sure the problem solution evolves slowly and methodically?

2. At what point in a problem solution do the strategy concepts dominate the solution? In what form? When do the details come into play? In what form?

3.* What are some of the characteristics of a well-developed algorithm?

4. The process of step-wise refinement is suggested in the accompanying illustration. At what point should the refinement process be considered complete?

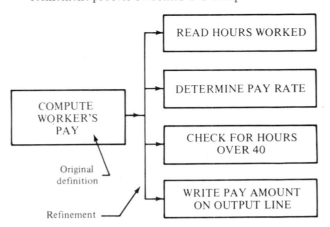

5. The flow chart of a properly structured program has well defined features. What are they?

6. In accomplishing a "DESK CHECK" of your program, what activities are involved? Describe the three separate types of errors that can be detected.

7.* What is the single most effective method of detecting and isolating errors that might occur in the running of your program?

8. What is the difference between an "ARITHMETIC TRACE" and a "PATH TRACE." Give specific examples of each.

9. How can the trace statements and the normal output be separated one from the other? How can the trace statements be removed from the logic deck easily?

10. Comment statements are useful to show the structure and documentation of a program. Describe at least three ways comment statements accomplish this important function.

11.* What is the purpose of indenting some statements? Give an example of when this technique would be used.

12. Give an explanation of the following programming style recommendations:

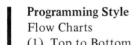

Programming Style
Separate the Familiar
From the Unfamiliar

Programming Style
Flow Charts
(1) Top to Bottom
(2) Don't Jump Around
(3) Parallel Block
Structure

Programming Style
Restrict the
Use of
GO TO Statements

13. When writing out your program longhand, how should the program be made to appear? What is the purpose of coding forms in this activity?

14.* What is a syntax error and when is the best time to catch such errors?

15. How do you locate execution errors in your program?

16. If a program has been compiled and has no execution errors, is this a guarantee that the program is correct? What else must be done to make sure the program is correct?

17. A program has been divided into a series of sub-tasks. For each task, a module of FORTRAN code will be written. What are the advantages of this modular approach?

18.* Most modules will be one of three basic types. What are these types?

19. Where should a module or block of code be entered? Where should it be exited?

20. Why is it more advisable to write FORTRAN code in easy-to-follow and relatively short steps as opposed to brief, highly concentrated code?

21. When a "desk check" is made of a program, what activities are involved?

22.* Describe a typical *execution* error. How do you know which statement in your program caused the error?

23. How can comment statements be used to make the various modules of a program easy to identify and understand? Give examples.

24.* When writing a program on a coding form, how should the program be made to appear?

Additional Applications

**Programming Example
Controlling Fuel
Deliveries**

The first card in a data deck lists the average temperatures for each day in a given week (7 values). Those values will be used to determine when heating fuel should be delivered to your home to run the furnace.

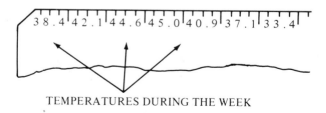

TEMPERATURES DURING THE WEEK

Each day the temperature is below 60°, your furnace will use some oil. When the temperature is one degree below 60°, that is called a "1-degree-fuel day." When the temperature is two degrees below 60°, it is called a "2-degree-fuel day."

Part A: Write statements that will determine the number of degree-fuel days experienced in the week reported.

After determining the amount of fuel needed during a given week, the fuel company uses a computer program to determine which of its customers are getting low on fuel oil.

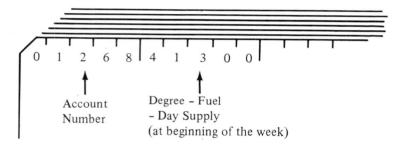

The remaining cards in the data deck give the account number and remaining fuel supply (in degree days) of customers of a local fuel dealer.

Part B: For each customer, subtract the fuel used due to the temperatures reported on the header card, thereby determining the present fuel supply. If any customer has less than 600 degree-days supply, mark that customer for a fuel delivery.

```
C..   PURPOSE -  COMPUTE NEW FUEL SUPPLIES - DETERMINE    ..
C..              WHO SHOULD GET DELIVERIES.                ::
C.....................................................::
C
C           -----IMPORTANT VARIABLES-----
C
C    --TEMP1 - TEMP7  TEMPERATURE ON EACH DAY OF THE WEEK --
C    --DDAY           DEGREE-FUEL-DAY FOR A PARTICULAR    --
C                     DAY OF THE WEEK                     --
C    --SUM            TOTAL DEGREE-DAYS FOR THE WEEK      --
C    --OLD            FUEL SUPPLY AT BEGINNING OF THE WEEK--
C    --NEW            FUEL SUPPLY AT THE END OF THE WEEK  --
C
     REAL NEW
C
     SUM=0.0
C
     READ(5,10)TEMP1,TEMP2,TEMP3,TEMP4,TEMP5,TEMP6,TEMP7
  10 FORMAT(7F4.1)
C
     IF(TEMP1.LT.60.)THEN
        DDAY=60.-TEMP1
        SUM=SUM+DDAY
     ENDIF
C
     IF(TEMP2.LT.60.)THEN
        DDAY=60.-TEMP2
        SUM=SUM+DDAY
     ENDIF
C
     IF(TEMP3.LT.60.)THEN
        DDAY=60.-TEMP3
        SUM=SUM+DDAY
     ENDIF
```

```
C
        IF(TEMP4.LT.60.)THEN
          DDAY=60.-TEMP4
          SUM=SUM+DDAY
        ENDIF
C
        IF(TEMP5.LT.60.)THEN
          DDAY=60.-TEMP5
          SUM=SUM+DDAY
        ENDIF
C
        IF(TEMP6.LT.60.)THEN
          DDAY=60.-TEMP6
          SUM=SUM+DDAY
        ENDIF
C
        IF(TEMP7.LT.60.)THEN
          DDAY=60.-TEMP7
          SUM=SUM+DDAY
        ENDIF
C
C
   20   READ(5,30,END=60)NUMBER,OLD
   30   FORMAT(I5,I5)
C
        NEW=OLD-SUM
C
        IF(NEW.GT.600.)WRITE(2,40)NUMBER,NEW
        IF(NEW.LT.600.)WRITE(2,41)NUMBER,NEW
C
   40   FORMAT(1X,I5,4X,I7)
   41   FORMAT(1X,I5,4X,I7,4X,'MAKE DELIVERY')
        GO TO 20
C
C
   60   STOP
        END
```

Programming Example Emergency Service

The fuel oil company of the previous problem must provide "Emergency Service" to your furnace if it breaks down on the weekend or on a holiday. The five names shown on the data card below provide this service on a *rotating basis*. This week Mr. Jones is on duty; next week it is Mr. Halpern.

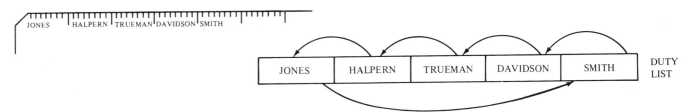

Write a program to read the five names into five different memory locations (NAME1 to NAME5). Have the program move all the names up one position and put the name at the front of the list to the back of the list.

```
C.....PURPOSE -  MOVE NAMES UP ONE POSITION TO           ..
C..             SHOW NEW DUTY LIST.                       ..
C.....
C     SPECIAL PROBLEM - IF WE MOVE JONES                  ..
C                TO THE END OF THE LIST USING             ..
C                THE STATEMENT NAME5=NAME1                ..
C                THIS WILL WIPE OUT THE NAME              ..
C                SMITH.                                   ..
C
C                -----IMPORTANT VARIABLES-----
C
C     --NAME1 TO   NAME OF PERSON IN POSITION 1            --
C     --NAME5      NAME OF PERSON IN POSITION 5            --
C     --HOLD       A MEMORY LOCATION TO HOLD THE           --
C                  FIRST NAME UNTIL ALL OTHER             --
C                  NAMES HAVE BEEN MOVED                  --
C
      INTEGER HOLD
C
      READ(5,10)NAME1,NAME2,NAME3,NAME4,NAME5
   10 FORMAT(5A8)
C
C                STORE FIRST NAME TEMPORARILY
C
      HOLD=NAME1
C
C                MOVE UP THE NAMES
C
      NAME1=NAME2
      NAME2=NAME3
      NAME3=NAME4
      NAME4=NAME5
C
C                NOW HANDLE LAST NAME
C
      NAME5=HOLD
C
      WRITE(2,20)NAME1,NAME2,NAME3,NAME4,NAME5
   20 FORMAT(1X,5(A8,3X))
      STOP
      END
```

Programming Example
Records by Date
(where in the file)

The Town Clerk's office records all transfers of deed titles on cards, which are then filed (sorted) according to the *date of transfer.*

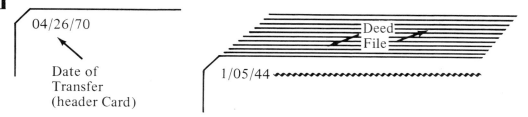

04/26/70

Date of
Transfer
(header Card)

Deed
File

1/05/44

We wish to find who was the legal owner of a piece of property on a certain date. Read a header telling the DATE OF TRANSFER and report where in the deeds file (that is on which cards) are listed the transfers for that date.

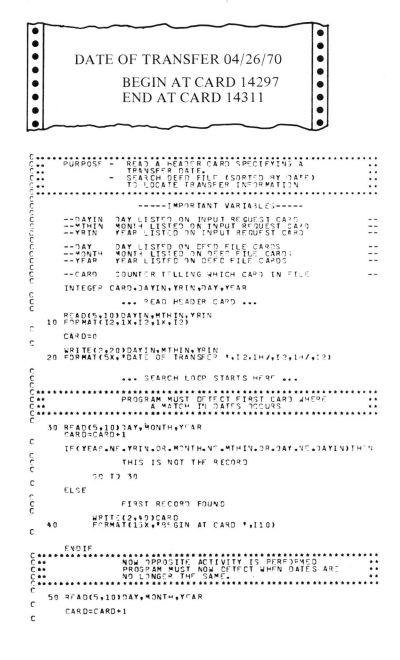

```
C  ....................................................................
C  ..   PURPOSE -   READ A HEADER CARD SPECIFYING A              ..
C  ..               TRANSFER DATE.                               ..
C  ..           -   SEARCH DEED FILE (SORTED BY DATE)            ..
C  ..               TO LOCATE TRANSFER INFORMATION               ..
C  ....................................................................
C
C                   -----IMPORTANT VARIABLES-----
C
C       --DAYIN    DAY LISTED ON INPUT REQUEST CARD              --
C       --MTHIN    MONTH LISTED ON INPUT REQUEST CARD            --
C       --YRIN     YEAR LISTED ON INPUT REQUEST CARD             --
C
C       --DAY      DAY LISTED ON DEED FILE CARDS                 --
C       --MONTH    MONTH LISTED ON DEED FILE CARDS               --
C       --YEAR     YEAR LISTED ON DEED FILE CARDS                --
C
C       --CARD     COUNTER TELLING WHICH CARD IN FILE            --
C
        INTEGER CARD,DAYIN,YRIN,DAY,YEAR
C
C                   ... READ HEADER CARD ...
C
        READ(5,10)DAYIN,MTHIN,YRIN
     10 FORMAT(I2,1X,I2,1X,I2)
C
        CARD=0
C
        WRITE(2,20)DAYIN,MTHIN,YRIN
     20 FORMAT(5X,'DATE OF TRANSFER ',I2,1H/,I2,1H/,I2)
C
C                   ... SEARCH LOOP STARTS HERE ...
C
C**********************************************************************
C**              PROGRAM MUST DETECT FIRST CARD WHERE            **
C**                  A MATCH IN DATES OCCURS                     **
C**********************************************************************
C
     30 READ(5,10)DAY,MONTH,YEAR
        CARD=CARD+1
C
        IF(YEAR.NE.YRIN.OR.MONTH.NE.MTHIN.OR.DAY.NE.DAYIN)THEN
C
C                     THIS IS NOT THE RECORD
C
                GO TO 30
C
        ELSE
C
C                     FIRST RECORD FOUND
C
                WRITE(2,40)CARD
     40         FORMAT(15X,'BEGIN AT CARD ',I10)
C
        ENDIF
C**********************************************************************
C**              NOW OPPOSITE ACTIVITY IS PERFORMED             **
C**              PROGRAM MUST NOW DETECT WHEN DATES ARE         **
C**              NO LONGER THE SAME.                            **
C**********************************************************************
C
     50 READ(5,10)DAY,MONTH,YEAR
C
        CARD=CARD+1
C
```

```
      C       IF(YEAR.EQ.YRIN.AND.MONTH.EG.MTHIN.AND.DAY.EQ.DAYIN)THEN
      C               THIS IS NOT THE RECORD
      C           GO TO 50
      C       ELSE
      C               - DATE CHANGED -
      C           CARD=CARD-1
      C           WRITE(2,60)CARD
          60       FORMAT(15X,'END AT CARD ',I10)
              STOP
      C       ENDIF
      C       END
```

Additional Applications: Review of Chapters 1-8

This completes the presentation of introductory topics that constitute the basics of programming. The following programming examples show some relatively advanced applications of the topics covered in Part 1. These case studies attempt to show the power of the language and the diverse and creative way in which it can be used to solve a cross-section of problems.

Programming Example
Limited Vector
Addition

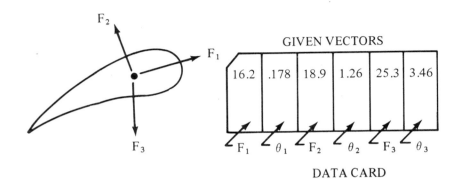

GIVEN VECTORS

| 16.2 | .178 | 18.9 | 1.26 | 25.3 | 3.46 |

DATA CARD

NOTE: ANGLES EXPRESSED
IN RADIANS

Here is the background of the problem:

Assume there is a repeated need to determine the sum of three force vectors acting on a wing profile. Because these are vector quantities, each force must be described by giving its magnitude and direction. In like fashion, the resultant or vector sum of these forces must be identified as to magnitude and direction.

The input consists of the three vectors described on a single data card, which gives F_1 followed by θ_1, followed by F_2, etc. Values of force are given in pounds; values of angles are given in radians.

Input Variables	
F1	Magnitude of the three
F2	input vectors (value in
F3	pounds).
ANG1	Angle (inclination) of
ANG2	three input vectors (value
ANG3	given in radians).

Because the forces are vector quantities, they may not be added directly but must:

a. be resolved into their X and Y components:

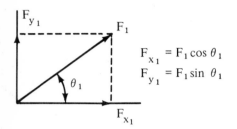
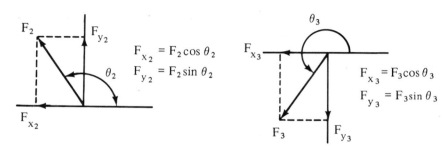

$F_{x_1} = F_1 \cos \theta_1$
$F_{y_1} = F_1 \sin \theta_1$

$F_{x_2} = F_2 \cos \theta_2$
$F_{y_2} = F_2 \sin \theta_2$

$F_{x_3} = F_3 \cos \theta_3$
$F_{y_3} = F_3 \sin \theta_3$

b. and then the X and Y components are added together:

$$\Sigma F_x = F_{x_1} + F_{x_2} + F_{x_3} \qquad \Sigma F_y = F_{y_1} + F_{y_2} + F_{y_3}$$

c. finally, the magnitude and inclination of the resultant is determined

$$R = \sqrt{(\Sigma F_x)^2 + (\Sigma F_y)^2}$$

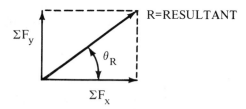

R=RESULTANT

Determination of angle: $\theta_R = \tan^{-1} \left(\dfrac{\Sigma F_y}{\Sigma F_x} \right)$

Internal Variables	
FX1 FX2 FX3	X-component of the three input vectors
FY1 FY2 FY3	Y-component of the three input vectors
SUMFX	Sum of the X-components
SUMFY	Sum of the Y-components

Output Variables	
R	Magnitude of Resultant
ANGR	Inclination of Resultant

The computer program for this problem follows the mathematics rather closely and also demonstrates descriptive variable naming and the use of comment cards (statements). The data card is read and a series of six arithmetic statements is used to resolve the vectors. The sum of all X components is then determined and stored as SUMFX. The sum of the Y components is similarly determined and stored as SUMFY. The resultant is then computed and the inclination of the resultant found. These are then printed.

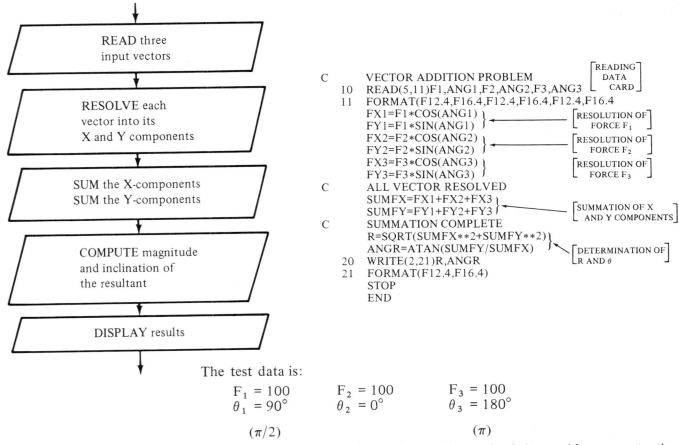

The test data is:

$$F_1 = 100 \qquad F_2 = 100 \qquad F_3 = 100$$
$$\theta_1 = 90° \qquad \theta_2 = 0° \qquad \theta_3 = 180°$$

$$(\pi/2) \qquad\qquad\qquad (\pi)$$

While the above program gets the problem solved, it provides no protection to the programmer if anything goes wrong. The program will be rewritten with the extra printouts that would supply the vital information to locate where and why the program failed.

```
C*********************************************
C    PURPOSE - ACCOMPLISH LIMITED VECTOR ADDITION.
C*********************************************
C
C          READ MAGNITUDE AND INCLINATION OF VECTORS
C                 (VERIFY BY ECHO CHECK)
C
      READ(5,5) F1,ANG1,F2,ANG2,F3,ANG3
    5 FORMAT(F12.4,F16.4,F12.4,F16.4,F12.4,F16.4)
      WRITE(2,10) F1,ANG1,F2,ANG2,F3,ANG3
   10 FORMAT(30X,'ECHO CHECK',6F16.4)
C
C          RESOLVE VECTORS INTO X AND Y COMPONENTS
C
      FX1 = F1 * COS(ANG1)
      FY1 = F1 * SIN(ANG1)
C
      FX2 = F2 * COS(ANG2)
      FY2 = F2 * SIN(ANG2)
C
      FX3 = F3 * COS(ANG3)
      FY3 = F3 * SIN(ANG3)
C
      WRITE(2,20) FX1,FY1,FX2,FY2,FX3,FY3
   20 FORMAT(30X,'CHECK POINT 1 - VECOTRS RESOLVED',/30X,6F16.4)
C
C          .........ADD X AND Y COMPONENTS........
C
      SUMFX = FX1 + FX2 + FX3
      SUMFY = FY1 + FY2 + FY3
C
      WRITE(2,30) SUMFX, SUMFY
   30 FORMAT(30X,'CHECK POINT 2 SUMFX =',F16.4,'SUMFY =',F16.4)
C
      R = SQRT(SUMFX**2 + SUMFY**2)
      ANGR = ATAN(SUMFY/SUMFX)
C
      WRITE(2,40) R, ANGR
   40 FORMAT(2X,'MAGNITUDE =',F16.4,' ANGLE =',F16.4,'RADIANS')
C
      STOP
      END
```

Programming Example
Vector Addition
Expanded

Expand the previous case study to add vectorially any number of coplanar force vectors and provide as output the magnitude and inclination of the resultant. Each vector is described on a single data card that gives the magnitude and inclination of the vector. The first card in the data deck, however, contains an integer number indicating how many vectors are to be added and, therefore, indicates how many data cards are in the main data deck.

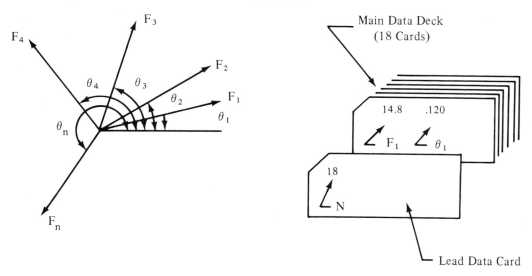

This program will be used to demonstrate the technique of dividing the total logic into a series of subtasks and then addressing those subtasks that are familiar to cut the problem down to size. The three groups of statements in the table below represent such a breakdown. Each group accomplishes the following subtasks:

GROUP 1: Deck Control
GROUP 2: Vector Resolution
GROUP 3: Accumulation of Components

Once the statements for these three groups are established, the remainder of the problem is relatively easy to handle.

Development of Program

GROUP 1 Deck Control	GROUP 2 Vector Resolution	GROUP 3 Accumulation of Components	COMPLETE PROGRAM
READ(5,10)N 10 FORMAT(I10)			READ(5,10)N 10 FORMAT(I10)
		SUMFX=0. SUMFY=0.	SUMFX=0. SUMFY=0.
	40 READ(5,41)F,ANG 41 FORMAT(2F16.4) 60 FX=F*COS(ANG) FY=F*SIN(ANG)		40 READ(5,41)F,ANG 41 FORMAT(2F16.4) 60 FX=F*COS(ANG) FY=F*SIN(ANG)
N = N - 1 IF(N.GT.0) GO TO 40		SUMFX=SUMFX+FX SUMFY=SUMFY+FY	SUMFX=SUMFX + FX SUMFY=SUMFY + FY N = N - 1 IF(N.GT.0)GO TO 40
		R=SQRT(SUMFX**2 +SUMFY**2)	R=SQRT(SUMFX**2 + SUMFY**2) ANGR=ATAN(SUMFY/SUMFX) 80 WRITE(2,81)R,ANGR STOP END

A program such as the one just written is not trivial, either in the programming concepts required or in the mathematics involved. If this program were to be made available for general use, it would overwhelm most users as it is now written. All programs should be accompanied by detailed documentation. The documented version of the program follows. It is written with tracer statements that should be removed as soon as the program is proven to work correctly.

```
C.......................................................................
C..   PURPOSE - GENERALIZED VECTOR ADDITION PROGRAM. ADD A  ..
C..      SERIES OF VECTORS. NUMBER OF VECTORS SPEC-  ..
C..      IFIED ON A LEADER CARD. VECTORS DESCRIBED   ..
C..      ON FOLLOWING DATA CARDS. EACH OF THESE CA-  ..
C..      CONTAIN TWO VALUES (MAGNITUDE FOLLOWED BY   ..
C..      INCLINATION OF THE VECTOR).                 ..
C.......................................................................
C
C              -----IMPORTANT VARIABLES-----
C
C      --F         MAGNITUDE OF EACH INPUT VECTOR          --
C      --ANG       INCLINATION OF INPUT VECTORS (RADIANS)  --
C      --N         NUMBER OF VECTORS (SUPPLIED ON LEADER CARD)
C      --FX,FY     X AND Y COMPONENTS OF EACH VECTOR       --
C      --SUMFX     SUMMATION OF ALL X COMPONENTS           --
C      --SUMFY     SUMMATION OF ALL Y COMPONENTS           --
C      --R         MAGNITUDE OF RESULTANT VECTOR           --
C      --ANGR      INCLINATION OF RESULTANT VECTOR         --
C
C              .....INITIALIZATION SECTION......
C
      READ(5,10) N
   10 FORMAT(I10)
C
      SUMFX = 0.0
      SUMFY = 0.0
C
C              .....LOOP ENTRY POINT.....
C
   40 READ(5,41) F, ANG
   41 FORMAT(2F16.4)
C
C          RESOLVE VECTORS      ACCUMULATE COMPONENTS
C
   60 FX = F * COS(ANG)
      FY = F * SIN(ANG)
C
      SUMFX = SUMFX + FX
      SUMFY = SUMFY + FY
C
      N = N - 1
C
      WRITE(2,70) FX,FY,SUMFX,SUMFY
   70 FORMAT(30X,'CHECK POINT 3   BOTTOM OF LOOP', 4F16.4)
C
      IF(N.GT.0) GO TO 40
C
C              .....LOOP ENDS HERE.....
C
      R = SQRT(SUMFX**2 + SUMFY**2)
      ANGR = ATAN(SUMFY/SUMFX)
C
   80 WRITE(2,81) R, ANGR
   81 FORMAT(10X,'MAGNITUDE =', F16.4,10X,'INCLINATION =' ,.4)
C
      STOP
      END
```

| Programming Example Tracking Problem | The initial position of a ship which is underway is given by X_0 and Y_0, its X and Y coordinates on a plotting chart. One minute later its position is X_1 and Y_1. Write a program to predict the track this ship will follow if it maintains course and speed. Determine at what distance and at what time it will pass closest to the lighthouse located at X_{LH}, Y_{LH}. The values $X_0, Y_0, X_1, Y_1, X_{LH}, Y_{LH}$ are given by the single data card shown. |

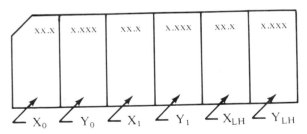

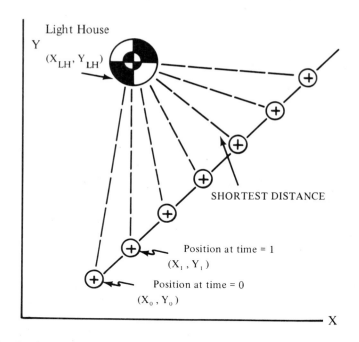

The logic of this problem will be easier to establish if a set of simplified input values (ship's position, lighthouse position) are assumed and a hand solution worked out. For example, assume the initial position of the ship is at the origin:

$$t = 0.0 \qquad X = 0.0 \quad Y = 0.0$$

| TIME | | POSITION |

If the ship moves to the position $X = 1.0$, $Y = 1.0$ in one minute, all future positions of the ship are easy to predict.

$$t = 1.0 \qquad X = 1.0 \quad Y = 1.0$$

| TIME | | POSITION |

Stationing the lighthouse at $X = 0.0$, $Y = 5.0$ makes the first (and subsequent) distance calculation easy to perform.

The basic point is that simplified data and a partial hand calculation will help make it easier to develop the generalized solution.

By comparing the ship's position at time = 1 minute and time = 0 minutes,

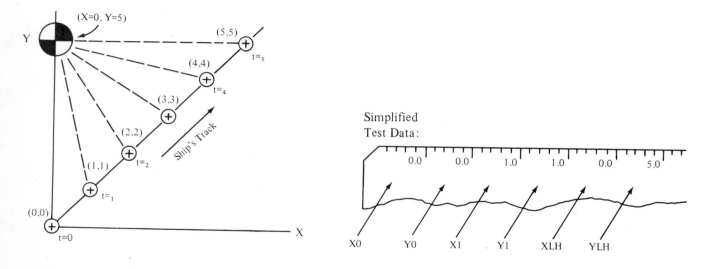

we can determine the change in X position and the change in Y position that the ship is able to accomplish in one minute.

$$\text{change in } X = \Delta X = X_1 - X_0$$
$$\text{change in } Y = \Delta Y = Y_1 - Y_0$$

The ship's position at any time "t" is given by

$$X = X_0 + t\Delta X$$
$$Y = Y_0 + t\Delta Y$$

The distance to the lighthouse at any time "t" is:

$$\text{DIST} = \sqrt{(X_{LH} - X)^2 + (Y_{LH} - Y)^2}$$

In order to predict future positions of the ship, the program uses a memory location called TIME to serve as a time clock. The statement:

TIME = 1.0

sets the clock with a value needed to calculate the first position. The statement:

TIME = TIME + 1.0

will advance the clock for future calculations.

A unique aspect of this program is the way in which it determines when the ship is closest to the lighthouse. It is done by comparing two sequential values of the distance to the lighthouse (DIST and DNEW).

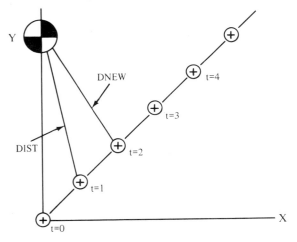

As the ship steams down its track, the distance to the lighthouse will become smaller and smaller (DNEW will be less than DIST). The minute any value of DNEW is larger than DIST, the ship has passed the closest point of approach. It is necessary to interrupt the calculation loop and report the value of DIST. This action is accomplished by the statements:

```
IF(DNEW.GE.DIST) THEN
        WRITE(2,41) DIST, TIME, X, Y
        STOP
ELSE
        TIME = TIME + 1.0
        GO TO 30
ENDIF
```

When these statements are first executed, the distance to the lighthouse at time $t = 1.0$ is stored in DIST and the distance at time $t = 2$ is stored in DNEW. Normally, DNEW should be smaller than DIST. The calculation loop will not be interrupted. The time clock will be advanced and control passed to statement 30 initiating another pass through the calculation loop. The pseudocode and flow chart describe the remainder of the problem's algorithm.

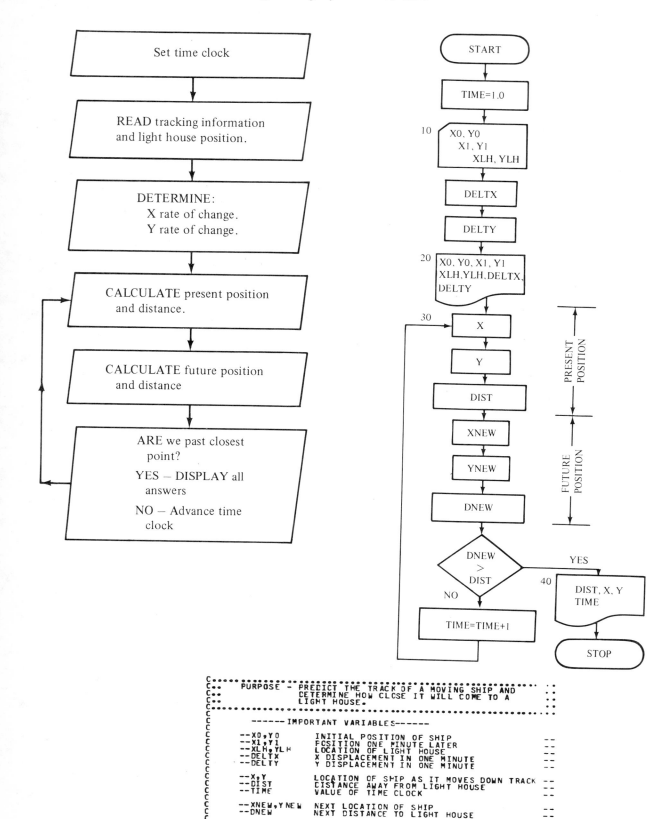

```
C.........................................................  ::
C..    PURPOSE - PREDICT THE TRACK OF A MOVING SHIP AND    ::
C..              DETERMINE HOW CLOSE IT WILL COME TO A      ::
C..              LIGHT HOUSE.                               ::
C.........................................................  ::
C
C          ------IMPORTANT VARIABLES------
C
C       --X0,Y0       INITIAL POSITION OF SHIP             --
C       --X1,Y1       POSITION ONE MINUTE LATER            --
C       --XLH,YLH     LOCATION OF LIGHT HOUSE              --
C       --DELTX       X DISPLACEMENT IN ONE MINUTE         --
C       --DELTY       Y DISPLACEMENT IN ONE MINUTE         --
C
C       --X,Y         LOCATION OF SHIP AS IT MOVES DOWN TRACK --
C       --DIST        DISTANCE AWAY FROM LIGHT HOUSE        --
C       --TIME        VALUE OF TIME CLOCK                   --
C
C       --XNEW,YNEW   NEXT LOCATION OF SHIP                 --
C       --DNEW        NEXT DISTANCE TO LIGHT HOUSE          --
C
C       ..........INITIALIZATION SECTION..........
C
       TIME = 1.0
C
   10  READ(5,11) X0,Y0,X1,Y1,XLH,YLH
   11  FORMAT(6F10.1)
C
       DELTX = X1 - X0
       DELTY = Y1 - Y0
C
```

```
      20 WRITE(2,21) XO,YO,X1,Y1,XLH,YLH,DELTX,DELTY
      21 FORMAT(1H1,2X,'INITIAL POSITION =',2F10.1,/,2X,'POSITIO
        1AT TIME T = 1',2F10.1,2X,'LIGHT HOUSE LOCATION =',2F10.
        2,2X,'RATE OF MOVEMENT =',2F10.1)
C
C......................................................
C....    LOOP ENTRY PCINT              .....
C......................................................
C
C                      COMPUTE PRESENT POSITION
C
      30 X = XO + TIME * DELTX
         Y = YO + TIME * DELTY
C
C
         DIST = SQRT((XLH-X)**2 + (YLH-Y)**2)
C
C                      COMPUTE FUTURE POSITION
C
         XNEW = XO + (TIME + 1.) * DELTX
         YNEW = YO + (TIME + 1.) * DELTY
         DNEW = SQRT((XLH-XNEW)**2 + (YLH-YNEW)**2)
C
C                      HAVE WE PASSED CLOSEST POINT OF APPROACH
C
C
         IF(DNEW.GE.DIST) THEN
C
C                          PASSED POINT
C
      40             WRITE(2,41) DIST, TIME, X, Y
      41             FORMAT(///,10X,'DISTANCE =',F10.1
        1                10X,'TIME OF CLOSEST APPROACH =',F10.1,10X,
        2                'OUR POSITION WILL BE',2F10.1)
                     STOP
C
         ELSE
C
C
C                          POINT STILL AHEAD OF US
C
                     TIME = TIME + 1.0
                     GO TO 30
C
         ENDIF
C
         END
```

Programming Example Optimal Shape	Very often the computer is used in the solution of design problems to allow the evaluation of many alternative design configurations and thereby permit the designer to select the best solution. The next problem is an exceptionally simplified example of this process.

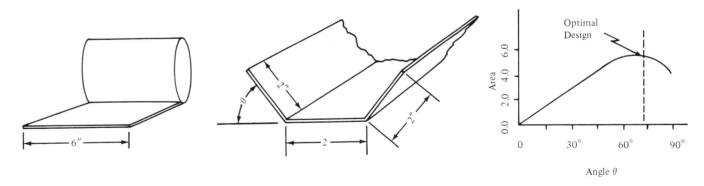

A 6″-wide roll of sheet metal is to be bent to form a trough for a rain gutter. The angle of bend, θ, affects the amount of liquid the trough is capable of handling. The computer will be used to determine the best shape for the trough. Assume the three sides of the trough are made equal (2″), determine what angle of bend, θ, gives the largest cross-sectional area.

The above graph shows the cross-sectional area of the trough for various angles of bend. When the sides are vertical ($\theta = 90°$), the cross-sectional area is 4 square inches. If θ is decreased slightly, the area increases. As θ is decreased further, the cross-sectional area continues to increase until a maximum value is reached (optimal shape). If θ is decreased beyond this point, the area decreases rapidly. When θ reaches zero, the trough is flat and the area is also zero. The maximum cross-section occurs somewhere between $\theta = 0°$ and $\theta = 90°$. The problem is to find where.

Working with a unit length of trough, we can divide the cross section into 3 simple shapes (one rectangle and two triangles). See the following object breakdown.

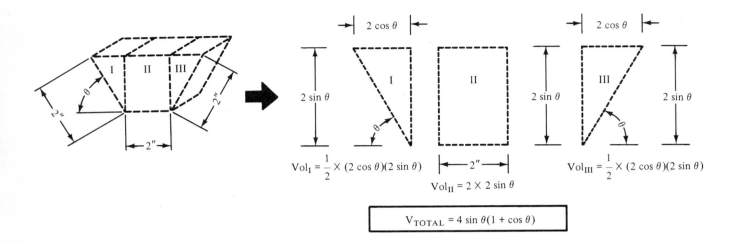

$$\text{Vol}_I = \frac{1}{2} \times (2 \cos \theta)(2 \sin \theta)$$

$$\text{Vol}_{II} = 2 \times 2 \sin \theta$$

$$\text{Vol}_{III} = \frac{1}{2} \times (2 \cos \theta)(2 \sin \theta)$$

$$V_{TOTAL} = 4 \sin \theta (1 + \cos \theta)$$

The above figure computes the volume of each of these individual shapes and presents an equation that expresses the total volume as a function of theta. We must evaluate this equation for various angles of theta. Write a program to evaluate the volume of this unit section of channel for various angles of θ. Start θ at 90° and decrease it by 1° increments until θ equals zero. For each value of θ, compute the volume.

Do not report all values of volume, but rather include statements in the program that will identify and report the largest volume (VMAX) and the corresponding angle (THEMX) only.

The program starts by giving an initial value to THETA, VMAX, and THEMX. Inside the loop, THETA is decremented and a new value of volume computed. If this value of volume is greater than VMAX, a redefinition takes place. Notice that the redefinition statements are indented to show they are under the control of the IF test:

```
IF   (VOL.GT.VMAX) THEN
        VMAX = VOL
        THEMX = THETA
ENDIF
```

**Programming Style
Indent to Show
Control Structure** ▌▌ Indenting statements to show the control structure of the program is a very important technique of programming style. The identation is a way of highlighting the program's organizational layout.

Notice that on each redefinition of VMAX it is necessary to redefine THEMX to save that value of THETA that produced this maximum value.

A final comment: those who know calculus realize that the maximum volume could be computed by taking the derivative of the volume equation with respect to θ and setting that equation equal to zero. This is a classical "minimum/maximum" calculation.

This higher-level mathematical procedure can be approximated by the simpler equations of the page 216 graph and the repeated procedures of this program.

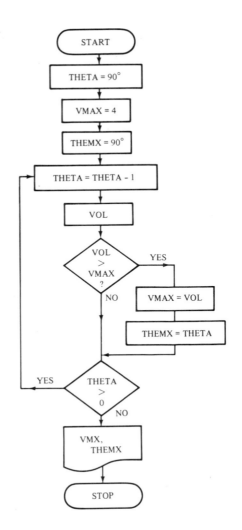

```
C..................................................................
C..    PURPOSE - OPTIMAL DESIGN PROBLEM.  DETERMINE MAXIMUM ..
C..           VOLUME OF CROSS SECTION OF RAIN GUTTER.       ..
C..................................................................
C
C               -----IMPORTANT VARIABLES-----
C
C       --VOL          VOLUME OF SECTION                    --
C       --THETA        ANGLE OF INCLINATION
C       --VMAX         LARGEST VOLUME DETECTED              --
C       --THEMX        ANGLE AT LARGEST VOLUME              --
C
C               ....INITIALIZATION SECTION....
C
       THETA = 90.0
       VMAX = 4.0
       THEMX = 90.0
C
C               ....LOOP ENTRY POINT....
C
   10  THETA = THETA - 1.0
       VOL = 4.*SIN(THETA/57.3)*(1.0+COS(THETA/57.3))
C
C       IF VOLUME JUST COMPUTED IS LARGER, REDEFINE VMAX
C
       IF(VOL.GT.VMAX) THEN
C
           VMAX = VOL
           THEMX = THETA
C
       ENDIF
C
   20  IF(THETA.GT.0.0) GO TO 10
C               .....LOOP EXIT POINT......
C
   30  WRITE(2,31) VMAX, THEMX
   31  FORMAT(1X,2F12.4)
C
       STOP
       END
```

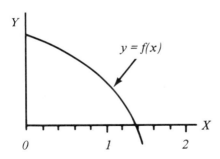

**Programming Example
Root Determination****

Write a program to determine the first positive root of the equation:

$$y = x^3 + 5x^2 - \ln(x + 1) + 12$$

Unlike the quadratic equation that was solved in Chapter 2, this equation cannot be solved by a simple formula such as:

$$x = \frac{-b \pm \sqrt{b^2 - 4ac}}{2a}$$

It can be solved, however, by a trial and error method.

This program is presented as the last case study because it places exceptional demands on the creativity of the programmer. The problem will be solved by "walking down" the X axis using large incrementing steps until we get close to the root. We then will use smaller stepping increments to get even closer to the root and then even smaller steps until we find the root to whatever accuracy we want.

At $X = 0$ the value of Y is positive and large, but as X increases, negative terms in the equation cause the value of Y to decrease until it crosses the X axis (the point of crossing is the root). This fact can be used to direct the solution of the problem.

Step 1   SET X at an initial value
of zero $X = 0.0$

Step 2	SET an incrementing value of 0.1	DELTX = 0.1
Step 3	INDEX X at this stepping rate until Y goes negative . . . We have passed the root.	Y=-X**3+5.*X**2-ALOG (X+10.)+12.0 IF(Y.LE.0.0)
Step 4	CORRECT for the "overshoot" by stepping back to the previous value of X.	X = X-DELTX
Step 5	DECREASE the stepping rate by a factor of ten	DELTX = DELTX/10.0
Step 6	REPEAT steps 3 through 5 (until the stepping rate is sufficiently accurate)	IF(DELTX.GT.ACC)GOTO3

Notice the statement that causes X to take a step backward when the root is "overshot" (Step 4). Notice the statement that cuts the stepping rate to a fraction of what it was before (Step 5).

The program has a single data card that describes how accurate the root is to be determined.

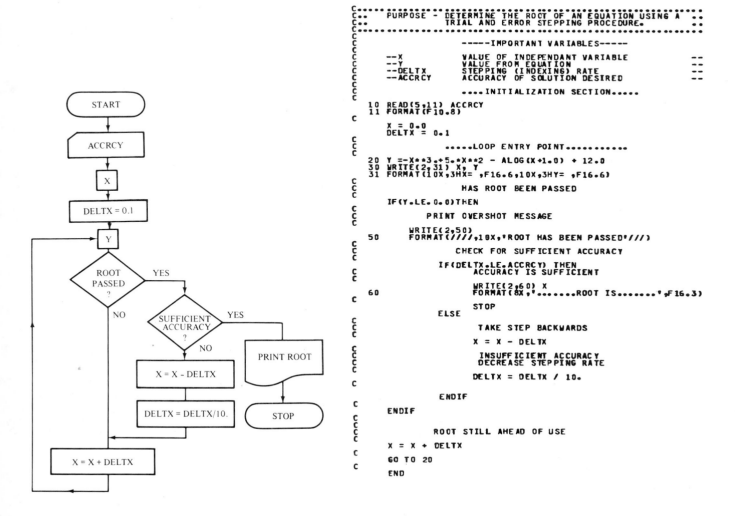

```
C..........................................................
C..  PURPOSE - DETERMINE THE ROOT OF AN EQUATION USING A  ..
C..            TRIAL AND ERROR STEPPING PROCEDURE.        ..
C..........................................................
C
C               -----IMPORTANT VARIABLES-----
C
C    --X              VALUE OF INDEPENDANT VARIABLE      --
C    --Y              VALUE FROM EQUATION                --
C    --DELTX          STEPPING (INDEXING) RATE           --
C    --ACCRCY         ACCURACY OF SOLUTION DESIRED        --
C
C               ....INITIALIZATION SECTION.....
   10 READ(5,11) ACCRCY
   11 FORMAT(F10.8)
C
      X = 0.0
      DELTX = 0.1
C
C               .....LOOP ENTRY POINT...........
   20 Y =-X**3.+5.*X**2 - ALOG(X+1.0) + 12.0
   30 WRITE(2,31) X, Y
   31 FORMAT(10X,3HX= ,F16.6,10X,3HY= ,F16.6)
C
C               HAS ROOT BEEN PASSED
C
      IF(Y.LE.0.0)THEN
C
C                   PRINT OVERSHOT MESSAGE
C
      WRITE(2,50)
   50     FORMAT(////,10X,'ROOT HAS BEEN PASSED'////)
C
C                   CHECK FOR SUFFICIENT ACCURACY
C
          IF(DELTX.LE.ACCRCY) THEN
C                   ACCURACY IS SUFFICIENT
C
          WRITE(2,60) X
   60         FORMAT(8X,'........ROOT IS........',F16.3)
C
          STOP
      ELSE
C
C                   TAKE STEP BACKWARDS
C
          X = X - DELTX
C
C                   INSUFFICIENT ACCURACY
C                   DECREASE STEPPING RATE
C
          DELTX = DELTX / 10.
C
      ENDIF
C
      ENDIF
C
C               ROOT STILL AHEAD OF USE
C
      X = X + DELTX
C
      GO TO 20
C
      END
```

The output sheet for this problem is shown below. It shows the stepping procedure, the step backs and the final solutional value.

Notice that X is incremented at a rate of 0.1 until X reaches 1.4 when Y turns negative. Incrementing then changes to 0.01 until an overshoot occurs at 1.33. In all, there are four overshoots and four refinements of DELTX.

```
X=           0              Y=      12.000000
X=        .100000          Y=      11.953690
X=        .200000          Y=      12.009678
X=        .300000          Y=      12.160636
X=        .400000          Y=      12.399528
X=        .500000          Y=      12.719535
X=        .600000          Y=      13.113996
X=        .700000          Y=      13.576372


X=        .800000          Y=      14.100213
X=        .900000          Y=      14.679146
X=       1.000000          Y=      15.306853
X=       1.100000          Y=      15.977063
X=       1.200000          Y=      16.683543
X=       1.300000          Y=      17.420091
X=       1.400000          Y=      18.180531
X=       1.500000          Y=      18.958709
X=       1.600000          Y=      19.748469
X=       1.700000          Y=      20.543748
X=       1.800000          Y=      21.338381
X=       1.900000          Y=      22.126289
X=       2.000000          Y=      22.901388
X=       2.100000          Y=      23.657598
X=       2.200000          Y=      24.388849
X=       2.300000          Y=      25.089078
X=       2.400000          Y=      25.752225
X=       2.500000          Y=      26.372237
X=       2.600000          Y=      26.943066
X=       2.700000          Y=      27.458667
X=       2.800000          Y=      27.912999
X=       2.900000          Y=      28.300023
X=       3.000000          Y=      28.613706
X=       3.100000          Y=      28.848013
X=       3.200000          Y=      28.996915
X=       3.300000          Y=      29.054385
X=       3.400000          Y=      29.014395
X=       3.500000          Y=      28.870923
X=       3.600000          Y=      28.617944
X=       3.700000          Y=      28.249437
X=       3.800000          Y=      27.759384
X=       3.900000          Y=      27.141765
X=       4.000000          Y=      26.390562
X=       4.100000          Y=      25.499759
X=       4.200000          Y=      24.463341
X=       4.300000          Y=      23.275293
X=       4.400000          Y=      21.929601
X=       4.500000          Y=      20.420252
X=       4.600000          Y=      18.741233
X=       4.700000          Y=      16.886534
X=       4.800000          Y=      14.850142
X=       4.900000          Y=      12.626048
X=       5.000000          Y=      10.208241
X=       5.100000          Y=       7.590711
X=       5.200000          Y=       4.757451
X=       5.300000          Y=       1.732450
X=       5.400000          Y=      -1.520298
```

ROOT HAS BEEN PASSED

```
X=       5.310000          Y=       1.417073
X=       5.320000          Y=       1.099513
X=       5.330000          Y=        .779763
X=       5.340000          Y=        .457817
X=       5.350000          Y=        .133670


X=       5.360000          Y=       -.192684
```

ROOT HAS BEEN PASSED

```
X=       5.351000          Y=        .101134
X=       5.352000          Y=        .068576
X=       5.353000          Y=        .035996
X=       5.354000          Y=        .003394
X=       5.355000          Y=       -.029231
```

ROOT HAS BEEN PASSED

```
X =         5.354100        Y =        -.000132
X =         5.354200        Y =        -.003130


ROOT HAS BEEN PASSED

X =         5.354110        Y =        -.000194


ROOT HAS BEEN PASSED

........ROOT IS.........        5.354110
```

9 | Introduction to DO Statements and Subscripted Variables

The introductory phase of computer programming is over. You are about to take a rather substantial step forward in the complexity and type of problem you will be able to solve. We are going to become involved in what students call "real data crunching." These new problems will have two basic characteristics:

1. the amount of data associated with the problem will be relatively large;
2. the data must be stored in such a way that it can be processed over and over again, not just once.

A typical problem may ask, for example, that a thousand values of X be read and a search made to find and report the largest value. When this assignment is complete, you will be asked to search for the next largest value and report it, then the next largest value, and so on.

Problems such as this require a considerable amount of looping and, therefore, an easier method of loop control will be defined – **the DO statement**. A better way of storing and addressing data will also be presented, called **subscripted variables**.

9.1 | Purpose of the DO Statement

One of the most important features of the computer is its ability to accomplish *iterative* calculations: that is, to *repeat* a series of operations again and again. Iteration is controlled most efficiently by the DO statement and, for this reason, the DO statement is considered one of the most powerful statements in FORTRAN. Before delving into the full use of the "DO," its properties will be examined in its most elementary setting.

Stating the Problem

These properties can be shown by presenting three solutions to a simple problem. Each solution represents a successively higher level of programming. We need to find the average of twenty examination grades punched as input on data cards.

$$AVE = \frac{\sum_{i=1}^{20} X_i}{20}$$

This problem involves twenty student grades. It is undoubtedly stretching the definition but, as an introduction to the topic, these grades will be referred to as the **data base**.

9.2   1st Level Solution: The Hard Way

In the 1st level solution we will attempt to show how difficult it is to deal with even a small data base using the old conventional methods.

1st LEVEL SOLUTION
READ (5,7) X1,X2,X3,X4,X5,X6,X7,X8, X9,X10,X11,X12,X13,X14,X15, X16,X17,X18,X19,X20
SUM = X1+X2+X3+X4+X5+X6+X7+X8+ X9+X10+X11+X12+X13+X14+X15 +X16+X17+X18+X19+X20
15   AVE = SUM / 20

The awkward aspect of this solution is that each time we deal with the data base a long list of variable names must be written. Twenty names are required following the command READ and are required again in the arithmetic expression defining SUM. Obviously, this method of addressing the data base is intolerable, and the situation would be even worse if 200 or 2000 grades were involved.

Before going on to the next solutions, it should be noted, however, that the data base of this problem is intact (no values are lost). Because twenty different variable names have been used, twenty memory locations have been assigned, and all the examination grades are in memory. All that is needed is a better way of referencing those variables — one that does not involve so much writing.

Using an Accumulator

The 2nd and 3rd level solutions will set up a loop that iteratively executes two statements:

```
READ(5,8) X
SUM = SUM + X
```

The memory location SUM is being used as an *accumulator* (Chapter 7), and on each execution of the loop a value of X will be read from input and added to the accumulator.

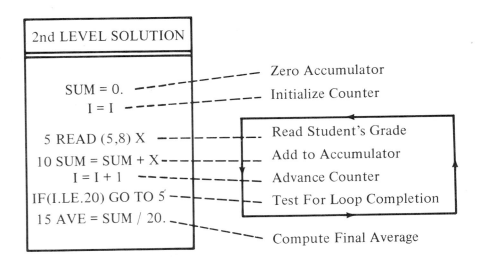

Statements Needed For Loop Control

One important aspect of this solution is the fact that it takes three statements to accomplish the desired loop control:

I = 1   statement needed to set the initial value of the loop counter.

I = I + 1   statement needed to advance the loop counter when an iteration of the loop is completed.

IF (I.LE.20)   statement used to test the loop counter with respect to some upper limit, in this case 20.

If iteration (looping) occurs as frequently as suggested, a more efficient method is needed. The obvious solution is to design a single statement that incorporates the important features of the three statements now being used. The new statement is called a **DO statement**.

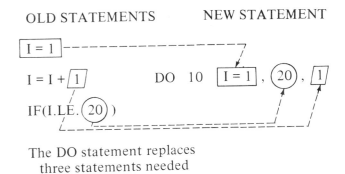

The DO statement replaces
three statements needed
previously

Figure 9.1 Formation of The DO Statement

The appearance of a DO statement signals a request for automatic loop control. The DO statement is placed at the top of any group of statements that are to be iteratively executed.

The DO statement has two very definite advantages, namely:

(1) it sets up loop control more efficiently, and
(2) it more clearly identifies the top or entry point of a loop the programmer is establishing.

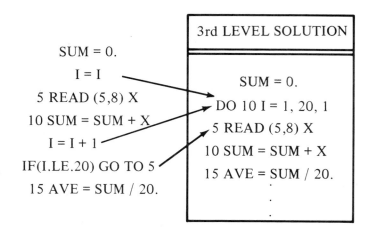

Parts of the DO Statement

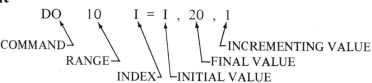

Figure 9.2 Parts of a DO Statement

To define the bottom of a loop, it is necessary to number the last statement in the loop. That number is then included as part of the DO statement. It is the number immediately following the command DO.

The command DO identifies the type of control statement being used and signals the need for automatic loop control. It is followed by a number (in this case, statement number 10) which defines the range of the statements to be included as part of the loop. The remaining items (parameters) are those features abstracted from the three statements used in the *2nd* level solution. While this is by no means a complete explanation of the DO statement, it will allow reasonable understanding of the 3rd level solution.

9.3 | Details of the 3rd Level Solution

C			. . . .
C			PURPOSE – DEMONSTRATE USE OF DO STATEMENT. . . .
C			THIRD LEVEL SOLUTION . . . .
C			. . . .
C			
			SUM = 0.0
C			
			DO 10 I = 1,20,1
C			
	5		READ(5,8) X
	8		FORMAT(F9.2)
	10		SUM = SUM + X
C			
	15		AVE = SUM / 20.0

Figure 9.3 The 3rd Level Solution

This solution starts by setting SUM equal to zero. The DO statement is then reached. When this statement is executed, the integer variable I is created and made equal to 1. The range of the DO (all statements up to and including statement 10) is established and all other DO parameters identified.

One other very important activity takes place. The DO statement will establish its own *independent* "trip" counter. For this particular problem, the behavior of this counter and the behavior of the index I are identical. Very shortly, however, we will be writing DO statements in which the index is a real variable and one or more of the parameters are real expressions. For example, it is possible to have a DO statement in which the incrementing value is specified as 0.1 or 0.25. For this reason, each time a DO statement is executed the parameters of the DO are automatically examined to determine *how many* iterations are needed to satisfy the DO. By "satisfy" we mean take the index from its initial value to the final value using the incrementing rate specified.

Once inside the loop, control passes to statement 5 and then to statement 10. Because statement 10 is the last statement in the range of the DO loop, it acts as a barrier preventing control from passing on to statement 15. In addition to serving as a barrier, statement 10 has another important function. Each time this statement is reached, it signals that another iteration of the DO loop has been completed. This affects both the internal trip counter and the index I. For example, when statement 10 is reached for the first time, the index I will be advanced from 1 to 2. The same thing happens to the trip counter indicating that the next iteration of the loop will be the second iteration.

Control is passed back to the top of the loop and the trip counter is tested. If its value does not exceed 20, another pass through the loop is permitted. The end result is that statements 5 and 10 are executed twenty times. Each execution causes a new value of X to be read from data and added to memory location SUM. On the last pass through the loop, the index I and the trip counter have the value 20. When statement 10 is reached, both counters will advance to 21. Now, when control passes to the top of the loop, the trip counter will be tested and evaluated as too large. The DO loop is considered satisfied and control is sent to the first statement after the range of the DO loop to statement 15.

Status of the Data Base

We have been somewhat preoccupied with the loop control associated with the 2nd and 3rd level solution of this problem. There is another important item to be considered, namely, the change in the status of our data base (i.e., the twenty examination grades). Since we now have only one variable name called *X*, there is only one memory location assigned. When the DO loop is completed, only one value of grade is known — the last one. The data base has been lost. For the simple problem we are dealing with now, this loss is of no importance. Very shortly, however, we will be dealing with problems where a loss such as this would be disastrous.

The problems assigned thus far have been carefully selected. They are ones that can be solved by a single examination of the data. The problem just solved is a typical example.

If the data base must be processed several times, we must find some way of retaining all the data (as was accomplished in the first-level solution) but without the long drawn-out writing hassle. The method of accomplishing this is covered in section 9.7.

9.4   The DO Statement-General

Let us take another look at the various parts of a DO Statement.

DO 35   K = 4, 104, 2

Command	DO	The command DO calls out iteration-READ AS: SET UP A LOOP STRUCTURE THAT INCLUDES ALL STATEMENTS THAT FOLLOW UP TO AND INCLUDING STATEMENT NUMBER _____.
Range	35	The RANGE of the DO includes the statements that are to be executed repeatedly. The last statement must be identified by number, and this statement number follows the command DO.
Index	K	Each DO statement has associated with it an INDEX. Frequently, this INDEX is an integer variable used by the programmer to keep track of the number of times the statements within the RANGE have been executed.
Initial Value	4	The programmer may exercise considerable control over the indexing variable. He may dictate its INITIAL VALUE, i.e., its value on the first execution of the statements in the range of the DO.
Final Value	104	This is the last value the INDEX should have, i.e., the value of the index on the last iteration of the loop.
Indexing Increment	2	A final control over the INDEX is obtained by an ability to specify how much the INDEX is to increase upon each execution of the statements in the range of the DO — in this case, by 2. *If no value is specified, the indexing increment is understood to be 1.*

Figure 9.4 DO Statements — General

    The DO statement shown above is in its most elementary form. Prior to the acceptance of the FORTRAN '77 standards, there were many restrictions imposed on the DO statement. The index had to be an integer variable. The initial, final and indexing values had to be constant or simple variables — expressions were not allowed. Indexing by a negative or fractional value was not permitted. These restrictions no longer apply and allow considerable flexibility in the way in which this statement can be formed.

    The following shows some of the variations the DO statement may have.

DO 20,KING = 1, 40	Statements up to and including statement 20 are to be executed forty times — first with KING=1, then with KING=2, etc. Variation: The omission of the indexing increment causes the increment to be one. There is an optional comma after the RANGE parameter.
DO 8 JOB = 2, N, 3	The index JOB has an initial value of 2, then 5, then 8, etc. The upper limit of index JOB is N. Variation: The "Final Value" is specified as a variable.

DO 12 M = I, LOVE, K	Index M has an initial value of I, then I+K, then I+2K, etc. The upper limit of index M is LOVE. Variation: The "Initial," "Final" and "Incrementing" values are variables.
DO 106 JOB = 40, 2, –2	Statements up to and including statement 106 are to be executed 20 times, first with JOB=40, then with JOB=38, then 36, then 34, etc. Variation: Index JOB is being controlled to have only even values beginning with 40 and ending with 2.
DO 8 X = –10., B– 3., 0.1	Index X has an initial value of –10.0, then –9.9, then –9.8, etc. The upper limit of the index is to be B–3. Variation: The index is real, the initial value is negative, the final value is an expression.

9.5 | The CONTINUE Statement

When reading a block of FORTRAN code, it is very important to be able to distinguish those statements that are inside a loop and those that are not. The DO statement very clearly defines the top of a loop. It is important to show the bottom of the loop with equal clarity. This can be accomplished by the CONTINUE statement.

The CONTINUE statement is used for one purpose only, namely, to end a DO loop. It is a "null" or "do nothing" statement in the sense that no hardware is called into play when this statement is executed. It does have the important feature of focusing attention on where the DO loop ends. Actually, there is another reason for making the last statement in the range of a DO the CONTINUE statement. Without going into detail at this time, the last statement in the range of a DO loop can be a READ or WRITE or arithmetic statement. The last statement may *not* be an IF or GO TO or other control statement. By using the CONtinue statement, you automatically avoid any such difficulties.

One other technique can be used to emphasize a loop structure. All statements associated with the loop except the first and last statements (the DO and the CONTINUE) are usually indented. Our 3rd level solution should be revised to look like this:

```
        SUM = 0.0
C
        DO 20 I = 1, 20, 1
C
          READ(5,10) X
   10     FORMAT(F9.2)
          SUM = SUM + X
C
   20   CONTINUE
C
        AVE = SUM / 20.
        END
```

Programming Style
For Clarity, Indent
Loop Statements

Use the technique of indenting statements inside a loop. This shows more clearly those statements controlled by the DO.

9.6 | Use of the Index

You have seen how the DO statement can be written to provide an index whose primary purpose is to count the number of times a series of statements is executed. Frequently, the index is used for another important purpose. It can be used to provide a subscript when it becomes necessary to subscript a variable.

On those occasions when it is necessary to retain all the values associated with a data base, we can implement a procedure that closely parallels the variable-naming technique used in the 1st level solution. Recall that twenty variables had the basic name X but with some added characteristic such as a 1, a 2 or a 3, etc., to distinguish one X value from another.

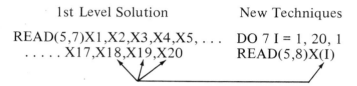

1st Level Solution	New Techniques
READ(5,7)X1,X2,X3,X4,X5, . . .	DO 7 I = 1, 20, 1
. . . . . X17,X18,X19,X20	READ(5,8)X(I)

Figure 9.5 Different Naming Techniques

The index of a DO statement can be combined with the variable name X to provide this distinguishing characteristic as suggested at the right of Figure 9.5. The variable

X(I)
       subscript
       provider

uses the DO loop's index I to provide a number following the variable X. Using this technique, it is possible to have all the advantages of the 1st level solution with all the efficiencies of the 2nd and 3rd level solutions. Let us go over this again.

9.7 | Subscripting a Variable

The whole notion of when and how to subscript a variable will take some time to develop. When a subscript is needed, however, it can be provided by the index of a DO. FORTRAN allows a variable name to be followed by a pair of parentheses enclosing an integer constant or variable, which serves as a subscript. This integer subscript frequently is provided by the *index* of a DO statement. Shown below are permissible forms of subscripted variables.

X(1)	X(20)	X(I)	NUMBER (35)
VALUE (J+1)	GRADE (200)	Y(K)	

When subscripting takes place, the identity of each element of the data base is retained:

DO 7 I = 1, 20	DO 7 I = 1, 20
7 READ (5,8) X	7 READ (5, 8) X(I)
IDENTITY LOST	IDENTITY RETAINED

Figure 9.6 Subscripting a Variable

In the READ statement on the right, the index I provides a subscript so that values of X will be read and stored as:

$$X(1); X(2); X(3); \ldots X(19); X(20)$$

Collectively, these values of X are called an **array**. The term array implies that a large number of variables are to be stored under a common name (in this case, the name X).

   Caution: When an array is to be stored in memory, the programmer must first declare how many memory locations are needed to accommodate the various elements of the array, i.e., he must give the size of the array. This is accomplished by a DIMENSION statement:

$$DIMENSION\ X(20)$$

This statement will be formally presented in Chapter 10.

9.8 | When is Subscripting Necessary?

It is important to know when and when not to subscript a variable. Unnecessary subscripting complicates your program and is wasteful of memory. Basically, a variable is subscripted if the statement of the problem requires more than one examination of the problem's data base. Take, for example, the problem of determining the average of 20 examination grades. As presently stated, no subscripting is necessary. By adding a slight complication to the problem, we can set up a situation that forces subscripting of the variable X.

| Programming Example |
| Scale The Grades |

Compute the average of twenty examination grades. *If the average is less than 60, adjust each grade so that the class average will be 75,* otherwise, let the average stand as is. In this problem, one examination of all the data is necessary before the class average can be determined. If, at that time, the average is low (below 60), another examination of the data is going to be required in order to give each student the extra points necessary to bring the average up to 75. If input was on magnetic tape, we could rewind the tape and get another look at the data. This is not possible with card input, so the obvious alternative is to store the data base as a subscripted variable (an array). In this subscripted form, the data base becomes remarkably easy to deal with. For example, assume the class average turns out to be 50 and you must give each student 25 extra points to bring the average up to 75. Using the old 1st level solution methods of storing the grades, it would take 20 arithmetic statements to accomplish this:

$$
\begin{aligned}
X1 &= X1 + 25.0 \\
X2 &= X2 + 25.0 \\
X3 &= X3 + 25.0 \\
X4 &= X4 + 25.0 \\
X5 &= X5 + 25.0 \\
&\quad \cdot \qquad \cdot \qquad \cdot \\
&\quad \cdot \qquad \cdot \qquad \cdot \\
&\quad \cdot \qquad \cdot \qquad \cdot \\
&\quad \cdot \qquad \cdot \qquad \cdot \\
X19 &= X19 + 25.0 \\
X20 &= X20 + 25.0
\end{aligned}
$$

With the data base stored as a subscripted variable, the task becomes almost trivial.

$$\text{DO 9 I} = 1, 20$$
$$X(I) = X(I) + 25.0 \qquad \text{Remember}$$
$$9 \ \ \text{CONTINUE} \underleftarrow{\hspace{1.5cm}} \text{To Indent}$$

The complete solution to the problem is now presented. The only new variable used is the quantity ADD, which will contain the extra points needed to bring the class average up to 75.

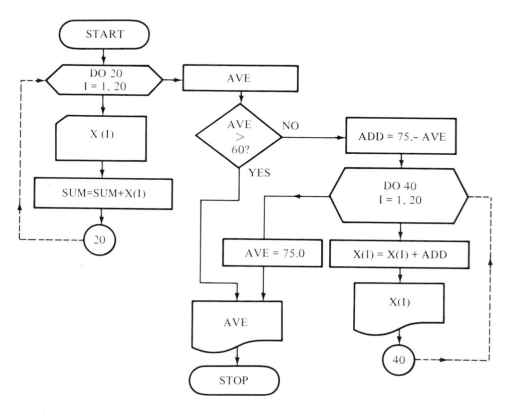

The first DO loop is used to read and accumulate the grades. A second DO loop may be executed if it is necessary to adjust and print the new grades.

```
C
      DIMENSION X(20)
C
      SUM = 0.0
C
      DO 20 I = 1, 20, 1         ─── READS VALUES OF X - RETAINS THEM
      READ(5,10) X(I)                IN SUBSCRIPTED FORM
10    FORMAT(F6.3)
      SUM = SUM + X(I)
20 CONTINUE
C
      AVE = SUM / 20.            ─── AVERAGE IS COMPUTED AND COMPARED WITH
      IF(AVE.GE.60.0) GO TO 50       60 - TO SEE IF CORRECTION IS NEEDED
C
C       .....SCALE GRADES IF NECESSARY......
C
C     ADD = 75.0 - AVE          ─── SCALING FACTOR IS APPLIED
      DO 40 I = 1, 20, 1             TO ALL VALUES OF X
      X(I) = X(I) + ADD
      WRITE(2,30) I, X(I)
30    FORMAT(I10,F12.2)         ─── ALL VALUES OF X ARE PRINTED
40 CONTINUE
C
      AVE = 75.0
C
C       .....TERMINATION SECTION............  ─── AVERAGE IS PRINTED
C
50 WRITE(2,60) AVE
60 FORMAT(10X,'THE AVERAGE SCORE IS ',F12.2)
      STOP
      END
```

Quiz#10 DO Statement

Part 1: Answer the following questions.

1. What is the primary purpose of the DO statement?
2. When manipulating a subscripted variable, how is the INDEX of a DO loop helpful?
3. Do all compilers use a "trip counter"?
4. How do the trip counter and the INDEX differ in their behavior?
5. What is the purpose of the CONTINUE statement?
6. What is the purpose of a DIMENSION statement?
7. When is subscripting of a variable necessary?
8. Must the subscript of a variable always be a variable? Can it be a constant?
9. What is the purpose of indenting the statements inside a DO loop?
10. How is the last statement in the range of a DO loop identified?

Part 2: Writing a Program (First or Second Half)

11. Each card in a data deck contains a single value to be called X.

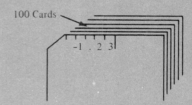

(a) Read the cards and store the values in an array called X.
(b) Verify that the array has been read correctly by printing every tenth element of the array.
(c) Elements of the array are supposed to be in ascending order of magnitude. Verify that this is true.
(d) If a value of X equal to 52.7 was to be placed in the array, would it belong in the *first half* or the *second half* of the array?

Answers:

1. To control looping.
2. It can be used to provide a subscript.
3. No. Older compilers are controlled by the index.
4. The trip counter is an integer quantity, while the index may be real.
5. To define the bottom of a DO loop.
6. To warn the compiler that a variable is to be subscripted and tell how much room in memory is needed to store all the elements of the array.
7. If more than one examination of the values in the data base is needed. To allow repeated processing.
8. It may be constant, a variable or an expression.
9. To show that the statements are under the control of the DO statement.
10. The statement is numbered and that number appears after the command DO.
11. C . . . .
    C   PURPOSE–PERFORM VARIOUS OPERATIONS ON A. . .
    C   ONE-DIMENSIONAL ARRAY.

```
C . . . . . . . . . . . . . . . . . . . . . . . . . . . . . . . . . . . . . . . . . . . . . . . . . . . . . .
      DIMENSION X(100)
C     . . . . .READING THE ARRAY. . . . .
      DO 20 I = 1, 100, 1
            READ(5,10) X(I)
   10       FORMAT(F6.2)
   20 CONTINUE
C
C     . . . .EVERY TENTH ELEMENT. . . .
C
      DO 40 I = 10, 100, 10
            WRITE(2,30) X(I)
   30       FORMAT(1X,F6.2)
   40 CONTINUE
C
C     . . . . .ASCENDING ORDER CHECK. . . . .
C
      DO 60 I = 2, 100, 1
            IF(X(I).LT.X(I-1)) WRITE(2,50)
   50                   FORMAT(1X, 'ELEMENT OUT OF ORDER')
   60 CONTINUE
C
C     . . . .FIRST OR SECOND HALF. . . . . . .
C
      XNEW = 52.7
C
      IF(XNEW.GT.X(1).AND.XNEW.LT.X(50)) THEN
            WRITE(2,70)
            FORMAT(1X, 'NEW VALUE BELONGS IN FIRST HALF')
   70 ENDIF
C
      IF(XNEW.GT.X(50).AND.XNEW.LT.X(100)) THEN
            WRITE(2,80)
   80       FORMAT(1X.'NEW VALUE BELONGS IN SECOND HALF')
      ENDIF
C
      STOP
      END
```

9.9

Problems Dealing with Large Arrays

The purpose of this section is to suggest other problems that require the use of subscripted variables. It is too early to get involved in writing complete problems, however. The examples that follow show situations that involve large data bases requiring the subscripting of a variable. After reading this section, you should be more comfortable when dealing with this new type of variable.

Multiple Choice Exam

A professor gives a multiple choice exam having 60 questions. There are 5 possible responses (1, 2, 3, 4 or 5) to each question, and the student must select the correct one. The exams are to be scored by the computer.

A leader card is prepared giving the correct answers as provided by the professor (60I1-code). The remaining cards represent the responses given by students. Determine how many questions each student answered correctly.

At any given time, it is necessary to compare the 60 integer values representing the correct answers and 60 integer values representing the students' answers. We must, therefore, reserve two blocks of memory.

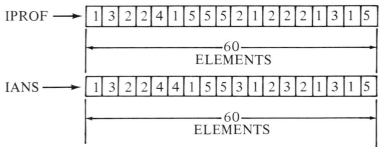

Figure 9.7 Display of Data Base

The variable name IPROF is used to represent the integer values provided by the professor and the name IANS to represent the integer answers provided by the students. These are subscripted variables, of course, each having 60 elements. To compare all 60 answers, a simple DO loop is established. Corresponding elements of the two data strings are compared. If they match, a counter is advanced.

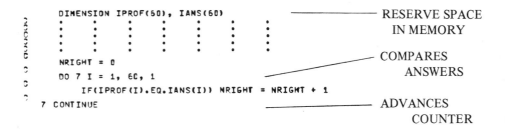

Notice the statement at the top of this program segment. It appeared in the previous program. Any time a subscripted variable is used in a program, the computer must be warned. It needs to know how much memory is needed to store this variable: that is, it needs to know the size or dimension of that variable.

| **Programming Example** |
| Hit or Miss |

In a psychological experiment a subject is given a controlled amount of a drug. To determine the effect of that drug on the subject, she is asked to fire at a moving target, and her average error is computed. Assume that the X and Y coordinates of the target position for 100 shots are recorded on data cards followed by cards giving the X and Y coordinates of the subject response. If we select the

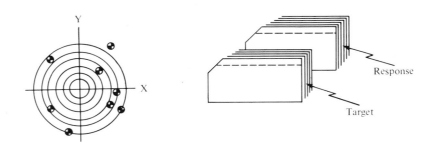

name XT and YT for the target locations and XR and YR for the response locations, the appropriate DIMENSION statement would be:

DIMENSION XT(100),YT(100),XR(100),YR(100)

This would set up four subscripted variables each having 100 elements, or memory locations.

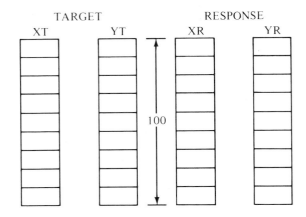

The following program segment computes the average error for all 100 shots.

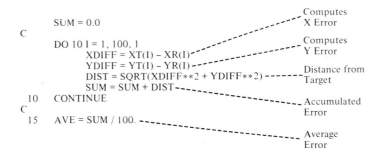

Programming Example
Starting Classes

A university has problems at the beginning of every school year with some classes being too big and some being too small. Three weeks before the term starts, each professor is asked to fill out a card for each course being taught telling the course number and the maximum number of students that can be accommodated in the course. Assume 1,000 courses are being offered (see Professors' Cards).

A week before class the students sign up for their courses and the count is tallied forming the second portion of the data deck. Each of these cards gives a course number and the number of students that plan to take the course.

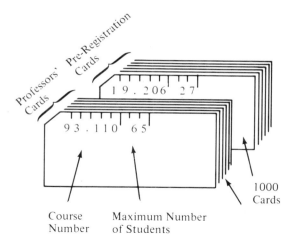

Course   Maximum Number
Number   of Students

Find all courses that are oversubscribed (too many students) and those courses that are undersubscribed (less than 10 students preregistered).

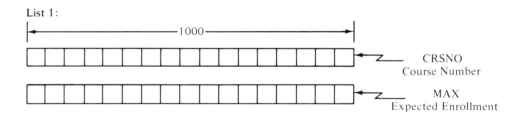

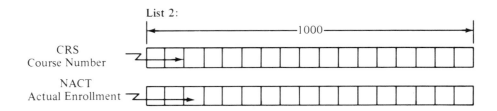

It is possible to read the first 1,000 professors' cards and store them in memory. We then can read a *single* preregistration card (using the *simple* variables CRS and NACT). If NACT is less than 10, the course is undersubscribed. If NACT is, let's say, 45, we would now have to search the professor's LIST1 cards (i.e. the data base) to see if the course is oversubscribed. This involves comparing the simple variable CRS with each element of CRSNO until a "hit" is made (CRS and one of the elements of CRSNO are the same). We would then compare NACT with the corresponding element of MAX.

This completed, we could read the next preregistration card and repeat the process. Not subscripting LIST 2 variables saves nearly 50% of memory space.

Output should appear as follows:

```
OVERSUBSCRIBED                          UNDERSCRIBED

                                        09.116  8  STUDENTS
                                        10.003  7  STUDENTS
11.115  16  STUDENTS TOO MANY
                                        11.126  3  STUDENTS
12.113   8  STUDENTS TOO MANY
12.414  12  STUDENTS TOO MANY           15.002  2  STUDENTS
                                        15.116  9  STUDENTS
            —                                    —
            —                                    —
            —                                    —
            —                                    —
```

This represents a list of courses that need attention. The majority of courses will neither be oversubscribed nor undersubscribed and, therefore, will not appear on the output sheet.

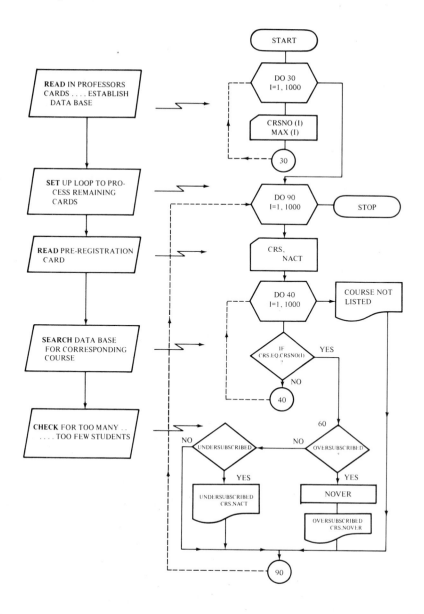

```
C ..........................................................
C       PURPOSE - EXAMINE ALL COURSE ENROLLMENTS. DETERMINE  ..
C            THE COURSES THAT ARE EITHER OVERSUBSCRIBED      ..
C            OR UNDERSUBSCRIBED.                             ..
C ..........................................................
C
C            -----IMPORTANT VARIABLES-----
C
C    --CRSNO      ARRAY OF COURSE NUMBERS (PROFESSOR CARD) --
C    --MAX        ARRAY OF MAXIMUM ENROLLMENT NUMBERS       --
C    --CRS        INDIVIDUAL COURSE NUMBERS (REGISTRAR CARD)-
C    --NACT       ACTUAL ENROLLMENT IN THAT COURSE (SIMPLE --
C                 VARIABLE)                                 --
C
      DIMENSION CRSNO(1000), MAX(1000)
C
C                 PUT HEADINGS AT THE TOP OF THE SHEET
C
      WRITE(2,1)
   10 FORMAT(1H1,//,10X,'OVERSUBSCRIBED',40X,'UNDERSUBSCRIBED')
C
C       .....ESTABLISH DATA BASE......
C
      DO 30 I = 1, 1000
      READ(5,20) CRSNO(I), MAX(I)
   20 FORMAT(F6.3,I3)
   30 CONTINUE
C
C            PROCESSING LOOP STARTS HERE
C
      DO 90 I = 1, 1000
      READ(5,20) CRS, NACT
C            SEARCH DATA BASE FOR THIS COURSE
      DO 40 J = 1, 1000
      IF(CRS.EQ.CRSNO(I)) GO TO 60
   40 CONTINUE
C
C            IF DO LOOP COMPLETED, COURSE NOT LISTED
C            IN THE DATA BASE
C
      WRITE(2,50) CRS
   50 FORMAT(10X,'COURSE NUMBER ',F7.3,' NOT LISTED')
      GO TO 90
C
C            COURSE LOCATED - CHECK ENROLLMENT
C
   60 IF(NACT.GT.MAX(I)) THEN
      NOVER = NACT - MAX(I)
      WRITE(2,70) CRS, NOVER
   70 FORMAT(10X,F6.3,'STUDENTS TOO MANY')
      ENDIF
C
C            CHECK FOR COURSE UNDERSUBSCRIBED
C
      IF(NACT.LT.10) THEN
C
      WRITE(2,80) CRS, NACT
   80 FORMAT(65X,F6.3,5X,I6,' STUDENTS')
      ENDIF
C
   90 CONTINUE
C
      STOP
      END
```

Review Exercises

1. When the data associated with a problem must be examined (processed) several times;
   - (a) Why must the data be transferred from cards and stored in an alternative form?
   - (b) What is this alternative form?

2. Must the subscript for a subscripted variable always be provided by the index of a DO statement?

3.*The statement:

    DO 40 KOUNT = 100, 200, 2

   is the equivalent (replaces) three simple statements. What are they?

4. The last statement in the range of a DO loop should not be an IF or a GO TO. What statement should be used?

5.*When trying to decide if a variable should be subscripted, what factors are taken into consideration?

6. Describe a problem that requires several examinations of the data base before a final result can be ascertained.

7.*An array called X has 100 elements and has been read from the data cards. Write statements that make a copy of this array. The duplicate array is to be called XCOPY.

8. If you were required to program the solution to question 7, one of the first statements needed in your program would be:

    DIMENSION X(100), XCOPY(100)

   What is this statement needed for?

9.*An array called X has been read by the following statements:

    DIMENSION X(40)
    DO 10 I = 1, 40, 1
        READ (5,20) X(I)
    10 CONTINUE

   The values of X are then used in the following way:

    SUM = 0.0
    DO 30 I = 1, 40, 1
        SUM = SUM + X
    30 CONTINUE

   What is wrong with the way in which elements of the

array X are being referenced?

10. Describe the array produced by the following statements:

$$\text{DIMENSION X(50)}$$
$$\text{DO 10 I} = 1, 49, 2$$
$$X(I) = -I$$
$$X(I+1) = 0.0$$
$$10 \quad \text{CONTINUE}$$

11. A data deck contains 100 cards and each card gives a part number and the present selling price of that part.

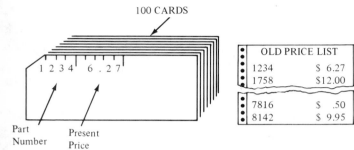

Part Number   Present Price

The selling price is to be increased according to one of two equations:

Equation 1 — Straight 10% increase

Equation 2 — 10% increase for parts selling at under $5.00
8% increase for parts selling at $5.00 or over

Write a program to produce a new price list according to equation 1 and then another price list according to equation 2.

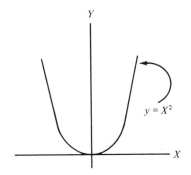

12. For the data base associated with problem 11, determine how many parts will have a selling price under $10.00 if equation 1 is used for the proposed price advance.

13.* The problem is to plot the parabolic curve shown.

$y = X^2$

Write a program to generate a table of X–Y values to facilitate the plotting. Let X assume values from −20 to +20 in increments of 0.1.

(a) Using an IF statement   (b) Using a DO loop

14. A data deck consists of 10 cards. Each card gives a real value called A, followed by another real value called B. Write a program to read these values and compute X according to the equation:

$$X = \sum_{i=1}^{10} (A_i^2 - B_i^2)$$

15. Repeat problem 14, except that the number of cards in the data deck is given by a leader card on which is a single integer value describing how many cards follow. That is, compute:

$$X = \sum_{i=1}^{n} (A_i^2 - B_i^2)$$

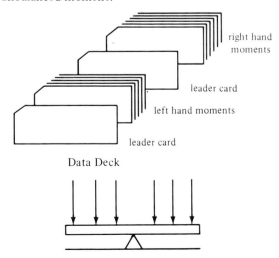

16.* A beam is pivoted in the center and is acted upon by a series of forces. The problem is to determine the unbalanced moment acting (which way the beam tilts). Each force is described by a separate data card giving the magnitude of the force and its distance from the fulcrum. All forces acting to the left of the fulcrum are grouped together and preceded by a leader card which lists an integer value describing how many forces are acting. The forces to the right of the fulcrum are similarly grouped and identified. Print as output the unbalanced moment.

Is it necessary to subscript the forces and distances in this problem?

17. A data deck consists of 1000 cards. Each card contains four integer values representing census information for a person as follows:

   1. Census number   J   (1 to 1000)
   2. Age   K
   3. Sex   L   (1=male; 2=female)
   4. Marital status   M   (1=single; 2=married; 3=widowed; 4=divorced)

   Write a program to print out the census number of all girls that are single and between the ages of 16 and 21.

18. If the number of girls in the age category defined in problem 17 is less than 200, increase the upper limit of age from 21 to 22 and print out the census number of girls that should be added to the list determined in problem 17.

19. You are given an extremely large data deck that represents a bank's transactions for a one-month period. Each customer is represented in the data deck as follows:

   a) A leader card giving customer account number, N; previous balance, BAL; followed by the number of transactions for the month, M.

   b) This is followed by M data cards, one for each deposit (a + value) or withdrawal (a - value).

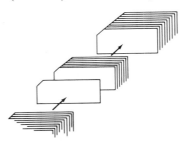

Write a program to compute the new balance for each customer, and if it is under 500 dollars, deduct a service charge of 1 dollar. Report as output each account number and its final balance. Plan on a trailer card containing 0's in all fields.

20. One pound of air has been compressed to a pressure of 100 p.s.i.a. and a volume of 10 cubic inches. It is

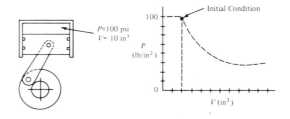

allowed to expand at constant temperature to a volume of 100 cubic inches. Write a program to obtain

data for plotting this expansion.

$$PV = CONSTANT$$

21. A particle moves from A to B with harmonic motion in N seconds. Distance A–B and time N are to be read from data cards. Write a program to compute the distance the particle is from A in one-second increments.

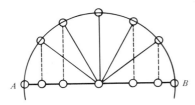

22. Particle 1 is in circular orbit about a center located at $X=4$, $Y=10$. The particle is rotating in a counter-clockwise direction. It makes one revolution every 10 minutes, starting from the position shown. Particle 2

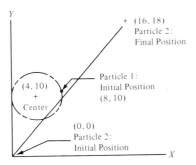

starts at a position $X=0$; $Y=0$ and reaches a final position of $X=16$; $Y=18$ in one hour. When are particles 1 and 2 closest to each other?

23.*This pulley system is used to raise a 1000 lb. weight.

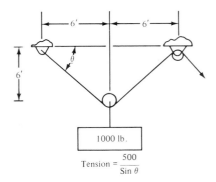

$$Tension = \frac{500}{Sin\ \theta}$$

For the position shown, the tension in the cable is $500\sqrt{2}$ lbs. As the weight is raised, this tension increases. How high can the weight be raised if the maximum tension is limited to 2000 lbs? Use a DO loop to compute and report the tension in the cable for each inch the weight is raised.

24. A submarine is travelling on a course of 045° at 20 miles per hour testing communication equipment. At 0800 the range and bearing of five stationary transmitting stations is recorded on data cards. (Bearing

is the clockwise angle measured from the vessel's direction of travel.)

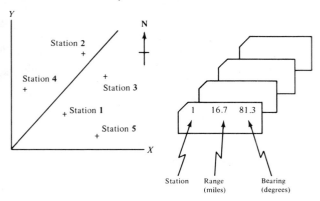

The submarine submerges at 0810. Write a program to compute and report the range and bearing of these stations at 10-minute increments for 4 hours.

25. Repeat problem 24, but report the range and bearing of the nearest station only. Identify by number the nearest station.

26. Repeat problem 24 under the following conditions: The maximum effective underwater transmitting range is 200 miles. Write a program to print as output those times in the four-hour period that the submarine will experience a communication blackout.

27. A $x=0$, the expression:

$$y = \left(\frac{1 - \cos^2 x}{4x^2} \right)$$

has the value 0/0, which is indeterminate. Write a program to evaluate y for $x=.1; .01; .001; \ldots; .000001$. In this way the programmer can determine the value y approaches as x approaches zero.

Additional Applications

Programming Example
Dealing with Arrays

The last quiz performed some basic operations on a one-dimensional array called X. The array X was read from data and statements were written to verify that the array was sorted in ascending order of magnitude. Continue processing this array as described below.

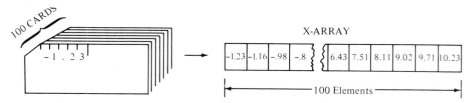

Part A:

Determine the average value of the first 10 elements of this array and the average of the last 10 elements.

```
      SUM=0.0
C
      DO 10 I=1,10,1
          SUM=SUM+X(I)
10 CONTINUE
C
      AVE=SUM/10.
C
      WRITE(2,20)AVE
20 FORMAT(1X,F10.4)
C
```

```
      SUM=0.0
C
      DO 30 I=91,100,1
          SUM=SUM+X(I)
30 CONTINUE
C
      AVE=SUM/10.
C
      WRITE(2,20)AVE
C
```

Part B:

The first element of this array is negative. At what point in the array do the positive values start (remember, array is in ascending order of magnitude).

```
      DO 50 I=1,100,1
C
          IF(X(I).GT.0.0)THEN
              WRITE(2,40)I
40            FORMAT(1X,I3)
              STOP
          ENDIF
C
50    CONTINUE
C
      STOP
      END
```

Part C:

What is the average value of the negative numbers? What is the average value of the positive numbers?

(STUDENT EXERCISE)

Part D:

We wish to add an element to the 100 values of X defining the present array (see new data card).

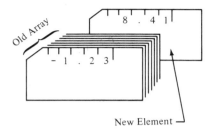

Compare this new element with the first and last element of the old array. Print one of three messages:

NEW ELEMENT BELONGS AT BEGINNING OF ARRAY

NEW ELEMENT BELONGS AT END OF ARRAY

NEW ELEMENT BELONGS INSIDE THE ARRAY

Note:

If the new element belongs inside the array, determine where in the array it belongs.

NEW ELEMENT BELONGS IN POSITION 16.

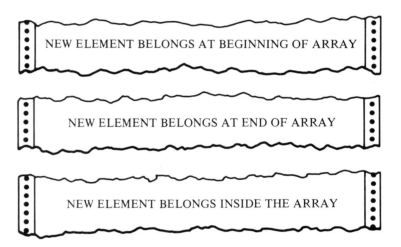

```
      DIMENSION X(100)
C
      DO 20 I=1,100,1
        READ(5,10)X(I)
10        FORMAT(F6.2)
20    CONTINUE
C
      READ(5,10)XNEW
C
      IF(XNEW.LT.X(1)) WRITE(2,30)
30    FORMAT(1X,'NEW ELEMENT BELONGS AT BEGINNING OF ARRAY')
C
      IF(XNEW.GT.X(100)) WRITE(2,40)
40    FORMAT(1X,'NEW ELEMENT BELONGS AT END OF ARRAY')
C
      IF(XNEW.GE.X(1).AND.XNEW.LE.X(100)) THEN
C
        WRITE(2,50)
50      FORMAT(1X,'NEW ELEMENT BELONGS INSIDE ARRAY')
C
```

```
C                      LOCATE WHERE IN ARRAY XNEW BELONGS
           DO 70 I = 1, 100, 1
C
              IF(X(I).GT.XNEW)THEN
                 LOCATN=I
                 WRITE(2,60)LOCATN
60               FORMAT(1X,'NEW ELEMENT BELONGS IN POSITION ',I4)
                 STOP
C
              ENDIF
C
70         CONTINUE
C
        ENDIF
C
C
C               IF DO SATISFIED - XNEW BELONGS ON END
C
        WRITE(2,80)
80      FORMAT(1X,'NEW ELEMENT BELONGS IN POSITION 101')
C
        STOP
        END
```

| **Programming Example** Group by Age | Read the name and age of 100 people from a data deck containing 100 cards like this one: |

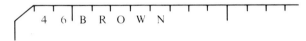

Form a one-dimensional array called NAME and a one-dimensional array called AGE.

Search the arrays for people between the ages of 20 and 30. List the names of people in this age group. Provide a second list of people between 31 and 40.

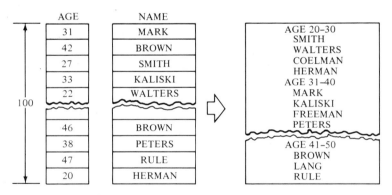

Provide a final list of people between 41 and 50.

```
C...........................................................
C..    PURPOSE -  PROVIDE THREE LISTS OF NAMES           ..
C...........................................................
C
        DIMENSION AGE(100),NAME(100)
C
C
        DO 20 I=1,100
           READ(5,10)AGE(I),NAME(I)
10         FORMAT(F2.0,A8)
20      CONTINUE
C
C          ......GENERATE FIRST LIST......
C
        WRITE(2,30)
30      FORMAT(1H1,20X,'AGE 20 - 30')
C
        DO 50 I=1,100
           IF(AGE(I).GE.20..AND.AGE(I).LE.30.)WRITE(2,40)NAME(I)
40         FORMAT(25X,A8)
50      CONTINUE
C
C          ......GENERATE SECOND LIST......
C
        WRITE(2,60)
60      FORMAT(1H1,20X,'AGE 31 - 40')
C
        DO 70 I=1,100
           IF(AGE(I).GE.31..AND.AGE(I).LE.40.)WRITE(2,40)NAME(I)
70      CONTINUE
C
C          ......GENERATE THIRD LIST......
C
        WRITE(2,80)
80      FORMAT(1H1,20X,'AGE 41 - 50')
C
        DO 90 I=1,100
           IF(AGE(I).GE.41..AND.AGE(I).LE.50.)WRITE(2,40)NAME(I)
90      CONTINUE
C
        STOP
        END
```

<table>
<tr><td>Programming Example
Typical Transactions
1. Unit Price Change
2. Ship Customer's
   Order</td><td>Our company sells 400 different automotive parts. Each part is described on a data card as follows:</td></tr>
</table>

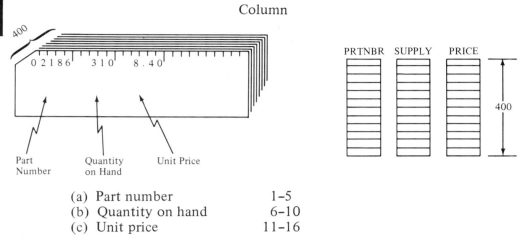

(a) Part number	1–5
(b) Quantity on hand	6–10
(c) Unit price	11–16

Part A: Read the Data Base

Write statements to read the information on these cards and store this data base as three one-dimensional arrays.

Part B: Unit Price Change

From time to time it is necessary to change the unit price that one or more parts should sell for. The next group of cards in the data deck has a header card telling how many parts are to be given a new selling price. For each card that follows, search the data base for that part and change the appropriate element of the array PRICE.

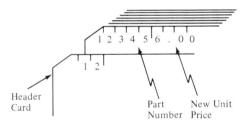

Part C: Orders Received

The final portion of the data deck represents orders received from various customers. The first card shown represents an order of 100 parts (Part Number 23456). For each order placed, reduce the quantity on hand of this part by the number of units needed to fill this order. If we do not have a sufficient supply to fill this order, print an appropriate message.

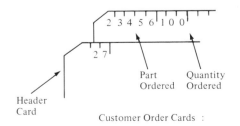

Customer Order Cards :

```
C...........PURPOSE - READ DATA BASE - PROCESS TWO TRANSACTIONS...
C..              A PRICE CHANGE      AN ORDER RECEIVED ..
C...............................................................
C
C                    -----IMPORTANT VARIABLES-----
C
C       --PRTNBR    PART NUMBER - ARRAY FROM DATA        --
C       --SUPPLY    NUMBER OF THESE PARTS ON HAND        --
C       --PRICE     UNIT PRICE OF THESE PARTS            --
C
C       --PARTTR    PART NUMBER INVOLVED IN TRANSACTION  --
C       --CHANGE    NEW PRICE READ FROM TRANSACTION CARD --
C       --ORDERD    NUMBER OF PARTS ORDERED
C
        DIMENSION PRTNBR(400),SUPPLY(400),PRICE(400)
C
C                    --- READ DATA BASE ---
C
        DO 20 I=1,400
C
            READ(5,10)PRTNBR(I),SUPPLY(I),PRICE(I)
   10       FORMAT(I5,I5,F6.2)
C
   20   CONTINUE
C.
C.............PROCESS UNIT PRICE CHANGES...............
C...............................................................
C
C               READ HEADER CARD
C
        READ(5,30) N
   30   FORMAT(I3)
C
        DO 100 I = 1, N
C
            READ(5,40) PARTTR, CHANGE
   40       FORMAT(I5,F6.2)
C
C           FIND PART.....CHANGE PRICE
C
            DO 50 K = 1, 400
C
                IF(PARTTR.EQ.PRTNBR(K)) THEN
                    PRICE(K) = CHANGE
                ENDIF
   50       CONTINUE
C
  100   CONTINUE
C
C..........      PROCESS ORDERS RECEIVED............
C...............................................................
C
        READ(5,30) N
C
        DO 200 I = 1, N
C
            READ(5,110) PARTTR, ORDERD
  110       FORMAT(I5,I3)
C
C           FIND PART IN DATA BASE
C
            DO 120 K = 1, 400
C
                IF(PARTTR.EQ.PRTNBR(K)) GO TO 130
C
  120       CONTINUE
C
C           PART FOUND - CHECK SUPPLY
C
  130       IF(SUPPLY(K).GE.ORDERD) THEN
C
                SUPPLY(K) = SUPPLY(K) - ORDERD
                WRITE(2,140) I
  140           FORMAT(1X,'TRANSACTION NUMBER',I3,
     1          'PROCESSED')
C
            ELSE
C
                WRITE(2,150) I
  150           FORMAT(1X,'TRANSACTION NUMBER',I3,
     1          'NOT PROCESSED DUE TO INSUFFICIENT SUPPLY')
C
            ENDIF
C
  200   CONTINUE
C
        STOP
        END
C.............TEST PROGRAM.........TEST PROGRAM..........
C.. PURPOSE - A SHORT (DRIVER) PROGRAM TO TEST THE ACCUR-..
C...............................................................
C
        ANG1 = TAN(45.0)
        ANG2 = TAN(30.0)
        ANG3 = TAN(0.0)
        WRITE(2,10) ANG1, ANG2, ANG3
   10   FORMAT(1X, 3F16.6)
C
        STOP
        END
```

Efficiency Considerations:

The DO loop used to process the "unit price" changes would be considered an inefficient loop because iteration (looping) continues *after* the part has been located in the data base. If, for example, the part we were looking for was the first part listed in the data base, the price of that part would be changed and 399 additional passes through the loop would follow.

In contrast, the loop used to process the searching of the data base when "processing orders" is more efficient. Iteration is interrupted the minute the part is found in the data base.

| **Programming Example** | A complicated data deck consists of N groups of cards. The value of N is given |
| Double Leader Cards | on the first card of the data deck and can be considered as the *first* or *master* |

leader card.

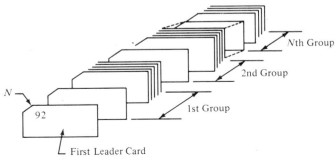

A second leader card appears at the head of each of the groups and tells how many of the cards that follow belong to that group. Finally, each of the remaining cards in the group lists a single value of X.

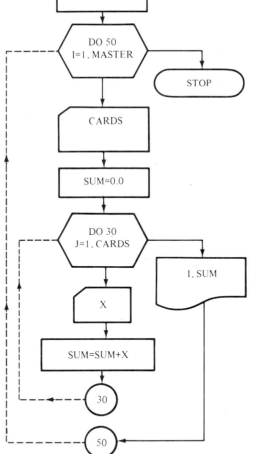

```
C.........................................................
C..  PURPOSE - DEMONSTRATE COMPLEX DECK CONTROL  ..
C..           (DOUBLE LEADER CARD)               ..
C.........................................................
C
C                -----IMPORTANT VARIABLES-----
C
C     --MASTER    NUMBER ON MASTER LEADER CARD   --
C                 (NUMBER OF GROUPS)             --
C     --CARDS     GROUP LEADER CARD VALUE        --
C     --X         VALUE ON INDIVIDUAL CARD       --
C     --SUMX      ACCUMULATED VALUES OF X        --
C
C                 READ MASTER LEADER CARD
C                 (HOW MANY GROUPS OF CARDS)
C
      INTEGER CARDS
C
   10 READ(5,11) MASTER
   11 FORMAT(I5)
C
C                 SET UP OUTER DO LOOP
C
      DO 50 I = 1, MASTER
C
C                 READ GROUP LEADER CARD
C
      READ (5,11) CARDS
      SUMX = 0.0
C
C                 ESTABLISH INNER LOOP
C
      DO 30 J = 1, CARDS
   20    READ(5,21) X
   21    FORMAT(F12.2)
         SUMX = SUMX + X
   30 CONTINUE
   40 WRITE (2,41) I, SUMX
   41 FORMAT(1X,I7,F12.2)
   50 CONTINUE
C
C                 INNER LOOP ENDS HERE
C
      STOP
      END
```

| **Programming Example** | A data deck consists of 600 cards, each containing three real values (X, Y, and Z). |
| Data Sampling | It is necessary to examine these values, but there are too many to warrant look- |

ing at each and every card. Set up a data sampling technique that prints out the information on every tenth data card only.

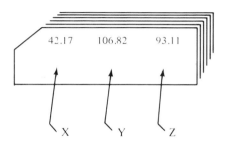

One possible procedure is to set up a DO loop that executes a READ statement 9 times but doesn't do anything with the values read. Following the DO loop, a READ/PRINT combination of statements could be used.

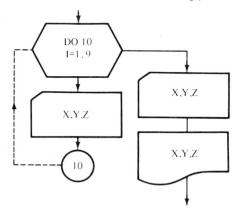

C	PURPOSE – CLEAR OUT NINE CARDS, PRINT VALUES
C	ON TENTH CARD
C	
	DO 10 I = 1 , 9
5	READ (5,6) X, Y, Z
6	FORMAT(3F12.2)
10	CONTINUE
C	
	READ(5,6) X, Y, Z
15	WRITE (2,16) X, Y, Z
16	FORMAT(3X,3F14.2)
C	

If the above is repeated 60 times, the desired data sampling will be achieved. All that remains is to set up an outer DO loop as shown below.

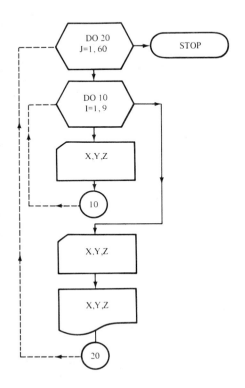

```
C.......PURPOSE - REPEAT CODE WRITTEN ABOVE 60 TIMES.........
C...                                                      ..
C.........................................................
C                    SET UP OUTER DO LOOP
C          DO 20 J = 1, 60
C
C                    READ NINE CARDS (NO PRINT OUT)
C
                     DO 10 I = 1, 9
     5                 READ(5,6)  X,Y,Z
     6                 FORMAT(3F12.2)
    10               CONTINUE
C
C                    READ AND PRINT TENTH CARD VALUES
C
                     READ(5,6)  X, Y, Z
    15               WRITE (2,16)  X, Y, Z
    16               FORMAT (3X, 3F14.2)
C
    20 CONTINUE
C
          STOP
          END
```

Programming Example Separate Courses by Major	Each card in a data deck gives the course number and the number of students enrolled in a particular course.

Write a program to search the data deck for all courses whose number

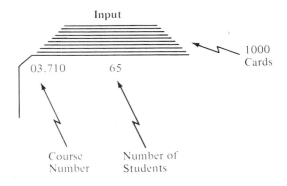

Input

1000 Cards

03.710   65

Course Number   Number of Students

Output

Course	Number
01.824	18
01.173	72
01.242	36
Course	Number
02.010	106
02.724	12
02.865	33
02.729	64
Course	Number
03.445	19
03.191	58

starts with the digits 01. Print these courses and their enrollments on a separate sheet of output.

When this is complete, make a search for all courses that start with the number 02. These starting numbers tell which department is giving the course.

Continue this search and print activity until you reach the 93 series, which is the largest department number course possible.

The data base:

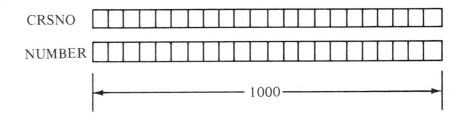

CRSNO

NUMBER

|← 1000 →|

Part A: Search for 01 series courses only

The basic procedure will be to examine each course number and convert the number to an integer. If that integer is 01, we have found a course number that should be printed out.

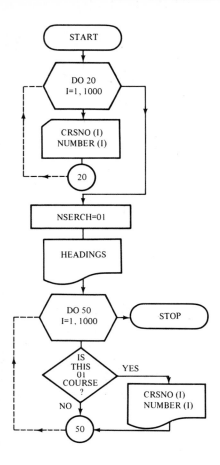

```
C....................................................
C..     PURPOSE - READ AND STORE DATA BASE REPRESENTING 1000 ..
C..          COURSES AND THEIR STUDENT ENROLLMENT.        ..
C..     ------------------------------------------        ..
C..          SEARCH FOR COURSES THAT START WITH 01        ..
C....................................................
C
C               -----IMPORTANT VARIABLES-----
C
C         --CRSNO      ARRAY OF COURSE NUMBERS           --
C         --NUMBER     ARRAY OF STUDENT ENROLLMENTS      --
C         --NSERCH     COURSE NUMBER BEING SEARCHED FOR (01)  --
C
      DIMENSION CRSNO(1000), NUMBER(1000)
C
C               READ DATA BASE
C
      DO 20 I = 1, 1000
10        READ(5,11) CRSNO(I), NUMBER(I)
11        FORMAT(F6.3,I3)
20    CONTINUE
C
C               SET SEARCH VALUE       START SEARCH
C
      NSERCH = 01
C
30    WRITE (2,31)
31    FORMAT(1H1,20X,'COURSE',10X,'NUMBER')
C
C               LOOP ENTRY POINT
C
      DO 50 I = 1, 1000
C
          M = CRSNO(I)
40        IF(M.EQ.NSERCH)WRITE(2,41) CRSNO(I),NUMBER(I)
41        FORMAT(10X,F6.3,13X,I3)
C
50    CONTINUE
C
      STOP
      END
```

Part B: Search for 01 through 93 series

The logic of this part is merely to set up an outer DO loop that will conduct search after search after search through the data base.

As has happened before, once the logic for solving one typical search through the problem is complete, it is only necessary to establish an outer DO loop so that repetitive applications of the logic are applied to the data base. In this case this means setting up a DO loop that will search for courses in department 02, 03, 04 .... 92, 93.

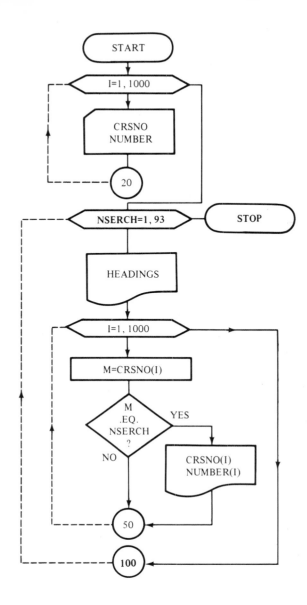

```
C:::::::::::::::::::::::::::::::::::::::::::::::::::::::::::::::::
C::    PURPOSE - PROVIDE A SEPARATE LISTING OF ALL COURSES   ::
C::              BEING OFFERED BY EACH DEPARTMENT.            ::
C::              (SEE LIST IN PREVIOUS EXAMPLE)              :
C:::::::::::::::::::::::::::::::::::::::::::::::::::::::::::::::::
C
C
      DIMENSION CRSNO(1000), NUMBER(1000)
C
C             READ DATA BASE
C
      DO 20 I = 1, 1000
10      READ(5,11) CRSNO(I), NUMBER(I)
11      FORMAT(F6.3,I3)
20 CONTINUE
C
C             SET UP OUTER DO LOOP
C
      DO 100 NSERCH = 1, 93
C
C             PRODUCE HEADINGS
C
30      WRITE(2,31)
31      FORMAT(1H1,20X,'COURSE' 10X,'NUMBER')
C
C             SET UP INNER DO TO SEARCH DATA BASE
C
      DO 50 I = 1, 1000
        M = CRSNO(I)
40      IF(M.EQ.NSERCH) WRITE(2,41)CRSNO(I),NUMBER(I)
41                      FORMAT(10X,F6.3,I25)
50      CONTINUE
C
C             .....THIS COMPLETES THE SEARCH......
C
100 CONTINUE
C
      STOP
      END
```

Programming Example Drunk Drivers	To keep drunks off the road, a new ignition lock is being developed that displays a four digit number and requires the operator to respond by punching in the same four digit number. Responding correctly three times in a row allows the car to be started.

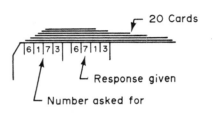

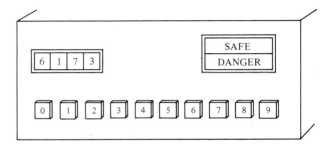

To test the system, a drunk is given 20 chances to beat the device

Problem Statement:

Write a program that determines if he ever makes three correct responses in a row. Output should be one of the messages:

(a) HE BEAT THE SYSTEM
(b) HE COULD NOT BEAT THE SYSTEM

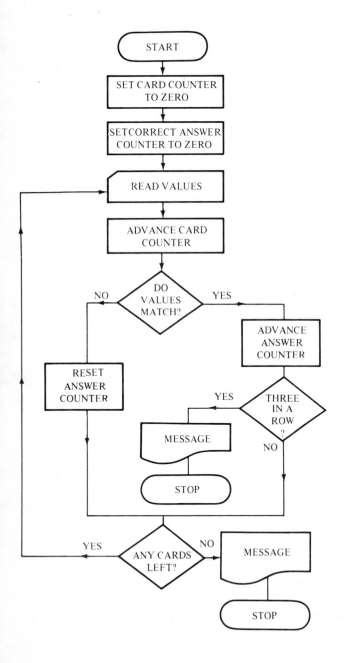

```
C.....................................................
C.. PURPOSE - TEST NEW IGNITION SYSTEM PERFORMANCE   :
C.....................................................
C
C                -----IMPORTANT VARIABLES-----
C
C      --NGOOD   CORRECT ANSWER COUNTER              --
C      --KARDS   CARD COUNTER                        --
C      --NWANT   NUMBER CALLED FOR                   --
C      --NGIVEN  NUMBER GIVEN IN RESPONSE            --
C
       DATA NGOOD, KARDS / 0, 0/
C
   10  READ (5,11) NWANT,NGIVEN
   11  FORMAT (2I5)
C
       KARDS = KARDS + 1
C
                TEST FOR CORRECT RESPONSE
C
       IF(NWANT.EQ.NGIVEN) THEN
C
                CORRECT ANSWER SECTION
C
       NGOOD = NGOOD + 1
C
            IF(NGOOD.EQ.3) THEN
C
                SYSTEM HAS BEEN BEATEN
C
                    WRITE (2,21)
   21               FORMAT(10X,'HE BEAT THE SYSTEM')
                    STOP
            ENDIF
C
       ELSE
C
                WRONG ANSWER - RESET COUNTERS
C
            NGOOD = 0
       ENDIF
C
                ANY CARDS REMAINING
C
       IF(KARDS.LT. 20) GO TO 10
C
   30  WRITE (2,31)
   31  FORMAT(10X,'HE COULD NOT BEAT SYSTEM')
C
       STOP
       END
```

Note: This problem does *not* require subscripting any variable. If you have used subscripted variables you have made the problem more difficult to solve than necessary. Be careful about this. Before subscripting ask yourself the question, "Is it really necessary?"

10 | Forming a Data Base

Chapters 1–8 of this text dealt with relatively simple problems in which all the input could be represented by simple variables. Your ability to handle these problems will make it an easy matter to write programs that operate on larger, more complex, masses of data. As you might anticipate, these problems will make frequent use of subscripted variables. For this reason, we will now present a more detailed discussion of this topic.

10.1 | Various Forms of the Data Base

Figure 10.1 shows some of the many options available for storing data. When only one value is involved, only one memory location is needed and a simple variable is used. The next option is to link a series of memory locations together, forming a singly subscripted variable. Problems requiring this form of storage were shown in the last chapter. This arrangement of data is graphically depicted as a string to convey its one-dimensional form or layout.

Sometimes an input variable will be basically two-dimensional in form, like these:

    (a) depth of water in the area surrounding an off-shore drilling sight,
    (b) radiation levels in the vicinity of a nuclear reactor,
    (c) distribution of population in a high crime district.

This information (depth, radiation, population) essentially maps itself on a two-dimensional surface. To represent this input, it is possible to organize a sequence of memory locations as if they were not just one string but a number of strings stacked one on top of the other. This produces a two-dimensional or block effect.

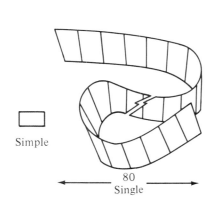

Simple

80
Single

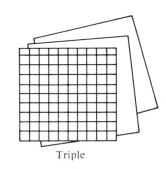

80

200

Double

Triple

Figure 10.1 Various Data Forms

Each string becomes one row of the data base that can be identified by a single variable name followed by two subscripts. It is called a **doubly subscripted variable**.

The vast majority of problems do not involve input any more complicated than the forms just described. A program that deals with weather predictions might possibly need to store the 3-dimensional temperature and 3-dimensional pressure distribution in the atmosphere. Figure 10.1 suggests that this would be like having a number of two-dimensional arrays (blocks) stacked one behind the other like pages in a book. This would involve a subscripted variable having three subscripts.

Which Form Should I Use?

There usually is no difficulty deciding which form is best suited for storing the data associated with a given problem. Let us take a specific example to show how the choice is made. Assume you are going to operate a computer dating service. Each participant is asked to complete an 80-question questionnaire in which each question requires a multiple-choice response of 1 through 9. This generates a data base consisting of 80 separate values, and it is necessary to request 80 integer memory locations to hold the data.

DIMENSION IDATA (80)

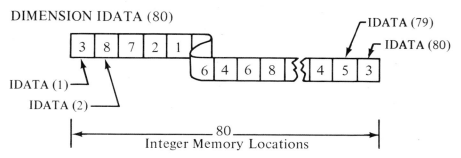

Figure 10.2 Single Subscript

Information stored this way is often referred to as a **vector** or a **one-dimensional array** of values.

This form of storage exactly suits the situation and allows the programmer easy control over the data base.

The answer to question 23 is in memory location IDATA(23).
The answer to question 48 is in memory location IDATA(48).
"   " 67 "   " IDATA(67).
"   " 79 "   " IDATA(79).

To demonstrate the next higher level of data complexity, assume that 200 people have volunteered for the dating service project. The number of data values has just increased:

$$200 \times 80 = 16000$$

participants   questions   data values

One solution might be to expand the DIMENSION statement to provide additional room for the data, but this will prove to be inconvenient:

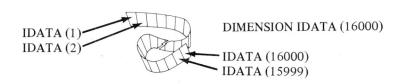

DIMENSION IDATA (16000)

Awkward Representation

If someone asks what is stored in memory location IDATA (79), the answer is easy: the response of person 1 to question 79. On the other hand, if someone asks what's in memory location IDATA (1472), the answer is less obvious. We need a better way of storing the data.

Assume that the data base represents responses made by females. We would like a string of 80 memory locations to represent the responses given by girl 1, a string of 80 memory locations to represent the responses given by girl 2; and so on, to a string of 80 memory locations to represent the responses given by girl 200. As suggested previously, it is possible to think of each of these 80-location strings as being positioned one on top of the other, forming row after row of values (one for each girl).

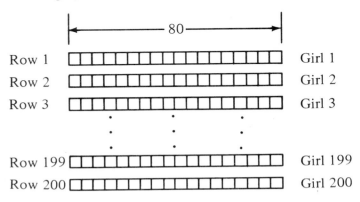

By using a slightly different DIMENSION statement:

DIMENSION IDATA (200, 80)

double subscript

we in effect ask that the 16000 memory locations be broken down into 200 segments or rows each containing 80 memory locations. Internally the data is in one long string, but you can deal with it just as if it were in block form as shown in Figure 10.3.

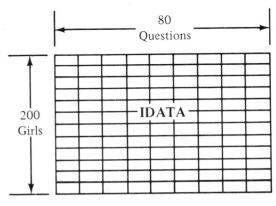

Figure 10.3 Double Subscript

All 16000 memory locations have the name IDATA, but individual elements of IDATA must be qualified by a double subscript:

IDATA (1, 80)
IDATA (16, 5)
IDATA (200, 1)

For reasons to be explained shortly, the first subscript tells which row (girl) gave the response and the second subscript tells which question. The important point is that this block or 2-dimensional form is a better way of representing the data base and is available in FORTRAN.* Data stored in this way is often called a **matrix** or **two-dimensional array**.

10.2 | Choose the Simplest Form Possible

Always store data in the simplest form possible. Stated another way: don't subscript unless it's absolutely necessary. When you *do* subscript, don't use any more complicated form than necessary. Just because a problem involves a considerable amount of data doesn't mean that subscripting is inevitable. Ask yourself the question, "How much of the data must be in memory at any one time?" The answer to this question decrees to what extent subscripting is necessary. Beginning programmers often get into a lot of trouble because they subscript everything in sight.

If subscripting is required, the next decision is, "Should you use single or double subscripts?" This is usually revealed by the statement of the problem. For example, an airline reservation problem may talk about a data deck containing the names of people booked on any one of 147 different flights operated by the company with each flight capable of accommodating up to 216 passengers.

If the problem requires all names to be in memory at once, the choice of a double subscript is obvious.

DIMENSION NAME (147,216)

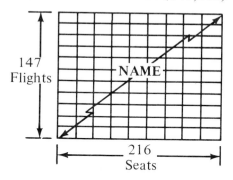

If a careful reading of the problem reveals that all that is wanted is an alphabetical list of the passengers on each flight, all names need not be in memory at any one time (only those associated with a single flight). We can decrease considerably the amount of memory needed.

DIMENSION NAME (216)

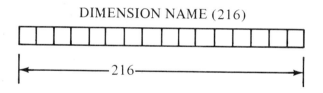

*The FORTRAN '77 standards require the subset language compiler to accommodate one-, two- and three-dimensional arrays. The full language compiler must be able to accommodate arrays with up to seven subscripts.

The problem can be solved by reading the names of passengers on flight 1 and sorting them. After printing the output, read the names associated with the next flight; sort and print, etc.

10.3 | Other Typical Uses

By now, you should begin to recognize the frequency with which subscripted variables are used to represent all but the most trivial problems. To fully appreciate how computers can be used to solve a diverse cross-section of problems, it will be necessary to suggest other more complex applications of subscripted variables.

Returning to the airlines problem, consider all the additional information that might be needed to monitor the scheduling of arrivals and departures of these planes.

Dispatcher's Office

For each of the 147 flights we might need information on:

(a) Time of departure
(b) Point of departure
(c) Time of arrival
(d) Destination
(e) Pilot's name, and so on.

SCHEDULING INFORMATION

TIME	START	ARRIVE	DEST	PILOT
12:35	BOST	12.58	MAINE	RULE
6:10	NEW	6:50	BOST	LANG
9:42	L.A.	11:00	CHIC	BROWN
21:30	DEN.	23:55	N.J.	JONES
16:44	N.Y.	17:30	BOST	HALPIN
2:00	CHIC	5:15	L.A.	WALK
7:45	SANF	9:12	PORT	HERTE
6:18	PORT	10:45	N.Y.	FINK

(147)

This scheduling information could be stored as a series of one-dimensional arrays, each 147 long.

DIMENSION TIME (147), START (147), ARRIVE (147), DEST (147), PILOT (147)

Control Tower

People in the control tower are faced with a different situation, namely keeping track of all the aircraft stacked up waiting to land and others waiting in line ready to taxi onto the runway. The first plane ready to land might be a 747, American Airlines flight 102. The next plane is Delta flight 16, a DC–10. Each

	INBOUND		OUTBOUND	
	CARRIER	FLIGHT NO. – TYPE	CARRIER	FLIGHT NO. – TYPE
1	AMERICAN	102-747	WESTERN	224-DC6
2	DELTA	16-DC10	AMERICAN	001-747
3	EASTERN	214-707	ALLEGHENY	194-707
4	PACIFIC	013-DC9	DELTA	613-DC10
5	T.W.A.	102-707	AMERICAN	014-727
6	DELTA	408-747	EXECUTIVE	016-LEAR
7	PAN. AM.	011-727		
8	SWISSAIR	183-747		

time one of these planes lands or takes off, the information contained in these arrays would have to be "moved up one" to represent the new situation (we will solve this problem later).

Stock Market

Consider all the information associated with monitoring transactions on the stock market. As each stock is traded, the number of shares involved must be added to the previous share traded to determine the total volume of sales. The stock's selling price is recorded and then compared to see if that price is higher than it has ever been recently (last 12 months) or lower than it has been recently. At the end of the day these data are summarized to give the total volume of sales, number of new highs, number of new lows, number of gains of the day, number of losses on this day.

NAME	VOLUME (No. of shares)	HIGH	LOW	LAST
AM. MOT.	13617	44.75	36.10	38.47
ALCOA	491310	25.50	19.25	22.91
BAXTER	1720	87.16	62.30	67.72
DOW CHEM.	61721	27.08	9.41	12.85
.	.	.	.	.
.	.	.	.	.
.	.	.	.	.
.	.	.	.	.
U.S. STEEL	31286	47.25	35.00	39.42
XEROX	1017	60.87	41.93	52.56
ZEBART	391571	8.41	6.37	7.72

Construction

A 25-mile stretch of highway is being planned to connect two points (A and B) on either side of the mountain. The computer can be used to:

(a) estimate cost of construction,

(b) evaluate different route configurations, and
(c) identify dangerous sections of the roadway.

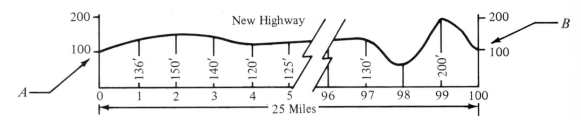

We must somehow provide a description of the mountain to the computer. As a start, the elevation of the mountain at 100 equally-spaced points between *A* and *B* is determined and formed into a one-dimensional array called ELEV.

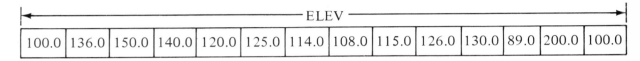

ELEV													
100.0	136.0	150.0	140.0	120.0	125.0	114.0	108.0	115.0	126.0	130.0	89.0	200.0	100.0

Comparing the adjacent elements of this array approximates the slope of the terrain. Sections that were excessively steep would thereby be identified.

It is usually necessary to provide a better description of the terrain to the computer, since the one-dimensional array gives only one profile. A topographic map or aerial photograph could be used. Here the land surface is divided into a large number of equally-spaced grid points and the elevation at each point in the grid is determined. If the grid spacing is such that there are 100 rows in the grid and 100 columns, we are talking about a two-dimensional array of elevations.

DIMENSION ELEV (100,100)

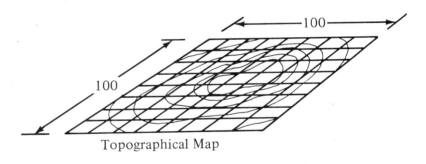

Topographical Map

Input/Output of Arrays

One of the first adjustments you must make in dealing with subscripted variables is in the special input/output statements they require. Because there are usually so much data involved, a typical data card will be packed with the maximum information. Take for example the 80-question questionnaire we have been talking about. Since each question has a single-integer response, the answer to all 80 questions can be recorded on one data card using an 80I1 format code. Attempting to read 80 values from a single card will be a new experience.

If these answers are to be stored in a one-dimensional array called DATA, we must:

(a) issue a *single* command READ, and
(b) follow the command READ by 80 variable names, IDATA(1), IDATA(2), . . . IDATA(79), IDATA(80).

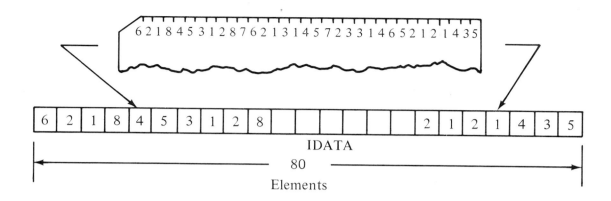

IDATA

80

Elements

The statements below show a READ operation that may appear to satisfy the above requirements, but it does not. There are two major errors: the command READ is executed 80 times, and only one name appears after the command READ. That is just the opposite of what is needed. These statements would attempt to read 80 cards, and only one value would be taken from each card.

```
        DIMENSION IDATA (80)
        DO 7 I=1,80,1
              READ(5,10)IDATA(I) ←—Incorrect Read
   10         FORMAT(80I1)
    7   CONTINUE
```

ERROR-ERROR-ERROR-ERROR-ERROR-ERROR-ERROR

To understand the correct READ procedure it is necessary to review some of the features associated with the DO statement, namely:

(1) creating an indexing variable name,
(2) setting its initial value,
(3) setting its final value, and
(4) controlling the incrementing rate.

```
DO 7  | I = 1, 100, 2
DO 3  | JOB = 2, 20, 1      —INDEX Control Features
DO 21 | M = 1, 500
```

These index control features are allowed in conjunction with statements other than the DO statment. They are allowed in READ/WRITE statements to provide a subscript so that the names IDATA(1), IDATA(2), IDATA(3) . . . IDATA(79), IDATA(80), can be expressed in a "shorthand" fashion.

READ(5,10)(IDATA(I), I=1,80,1)

INDEX
Control
Feature

The above single READ command is in effect followed by a list of 80 names. These names are written in a special way. The generalized name IDATA(I) is used, which is then followed by those parameters that cause I to cycle from 1 to 80. This feature is called an **implied DO index**.

READ(5,10)(IDATA(I), I=1,80)
is equivalent to
READ(5,10)IDATA(1), IDATA(2), IDATA(3), IDATA(4) . . .
IDATA(78), IDATA(79), IDATA(80)

This is admittedly a somewhat advanced technique and will require additional explanation. The topic of subscripted variables is being presented in steps. The first step is to learn why and how subscripted variables are used in programming. That step is completed. The next step is to learn how to form READ/WRITE statements for transferring large arrays to and from memory. The next programming examples will concentrate on that one topic only.

10.5   Additional Examples

Recall the data base associated with the "HIT or MISS" problem in the preceding chapter (page 234). There are 1000 X, Y values defining the location of the response made (4000 values in all). These values could be punched on the data cards in several possible ways. Each different arrangement would require a different READ statement.

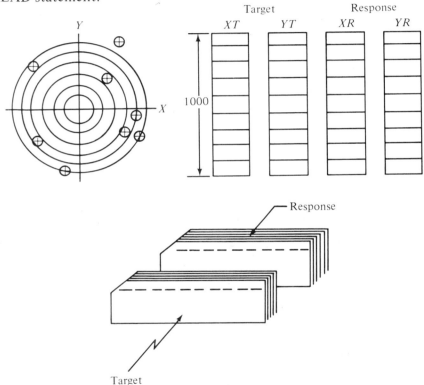

Target Values First

In the discussion that follows, all values are to be expressed using an F8.2 code. Assume as the first arrangement of data that all target values are given first followed by all the response positions.

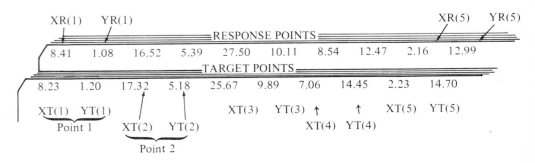

Since each card defines 5 points, it will take 200 cards to define the target positions, followed by 200 cards to define the response positions.

You are now faced with the problem of writing READ statements that will generate a sequence of variable names that match the sequence in which the data is being presented. The best approach is to either recite verbally or write out longhand the first and last few names of each sequence needed. To receive the target array, the sequence is:

$$XT(1),YT(1),XT(2),YT(2) \ldots XT(999),YT(999),XT(1000),YT(1000)$$

To receive the response array, the sequence is:

$$XR(1),YR(1),XR(2),YR(2) \ldots YR(999),YR(999),XR(1000),YR(1000)$$

To generate the same sequence of names, but in shorthand fashion, you merely resort to the use of an index inside a READ statement as follows:

```
READ(5,9) (XT(I),YT(I),  I = 1, 1000)
READ(5,9) (XR(I),YR(I), I = 1, 1000)
```

It is worthwhile reviewing this procedure because it represents an orderly way in which READ/WRITE statements can be written to transfer large data bases to and from memory.

1. Examine the deck and see in what sequence the individual values are being presented.
2. Either recite verbally or write out longhand enough of the variable names required so that the pattern or sequence is well defined.
3. Duplicate this sequence by writing the names in a general form (one that references an INDEX).
4. Control the INDEX to cycle through the appropriate range of values.

To show how efficient this operation can be, the whole data base could be read by a single READ statement as follows:

```
READ(5,9) (XT(I),YT(I), I = 1, 1000) , (XR(I)YR(I), I = 1, 1000)
```

This statement shows that it is possible to reset the index whenever it is necessary to start a new list of names. This particular READ statement is the equivalent of the command READ followed by 4000 names.

Alternating Values

Another possible arrangement of data is to present a target position, followed by a response position, followed by a target position, etc.

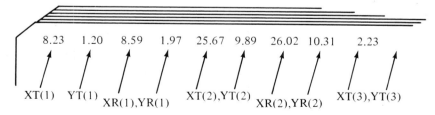

The sequence of names needed to process this arrangement of data is:

XT(1),YT(1),XR(1),YR(1),XT(2),YT(2),XR(2)...

. . . . XT(999),YT(999),XR(999),YR(999),XT(1000),YT(1000),

XR(1000),YR(1000)

The corresponding READ statement would be:

```
READ(5,9) (XT(I),YT(I),XR(I),YR(I), I = 1, 1000)
```

FORMAT Control

Now let's examine the role of the FORMAT statement in all of this READ activity. In the past there has always been a match in the number of names in the READ statement and the number of codes in the FORMAT statement. When massive data transfers are involved, it is more typical for the number of names to far exceed the data that could be punched on a single card. When this happens, the FORMAT statement is only expected to describe one typical card with the understanding that many cards of this format description probably will be needed to input the data base. The operation starts by matching the first variable name with the first format code. The second name is matched with the second code, the third name with the third code, and so on.

9   FORMAT (10F8.2)

When the tenth name and tenth code are matched, the end parenthesis of the format statement is reached. This says, in effect, there is no more data on this card. If there are names still left in the READ statement, the read operation is not considered finished. Additional cards will be read automatically until all names following the command READ have been loaded. In this operation the READ statement dominates, not the FORMAT. Technically, each time the end parenthesis of the FORMAT statement is reached, a new data card will be read automatically. The format statement will be scanned backwards until the first open parenthesis is detected and the format codes in between will be repeated.

10.6 | Reading Two-Dimensional Arrays

The process of reading a two-dimensional array is basically the same except that two subscripts are involved. Below is a group of three simultaneous equations. What is the best way of representing these equations?

$$\text{EQ. 1} \quad 9.0X_1 \quad + \quad 6.5X_2 \quad + \quad 3.5X_3 \quad = \quad 27.75$$
$$\text{EQ. 2} \quad 4.5X_1 \quad + \quad 2.2X_2 \quad + \quad 1.5X_3 \quad = \quad 10.50$$
$$\text{EQ. 3} \quad 6.7X_1 \quad + \quad 3.0X_2 \quad + \quad 1.0X_3 \quad = \quad 12.25$$

Notice that the coefficients preceding each X term are just naturally distributed in a two-dimensional fashion. The statement:

DIMENSION A(3,3)

gives these coefficients the common name A and allows individual elements of A to be addressed by a double subscript.

The only remaining values needed to define these equations are the three right-hand constants. The statement:

DIMENSION C(3)

sets up a one-dimensional array called C to store these values.

Array [A]   Array {C}

column

$$\begin{bmatrix} A_{11} & A_{12} & A_{13} \\ A_{21} & A_{22} & A_{23} \\ A_{31} & A_{32} & A_{33} \end{bmatrix} \text{row} \qquad \begin{bmatrix} C_1 \\ C_2 \\ C_3 \end{bmatrix}$$

$$\begin{bmatrix} 9.0 & 6.5 & 3.5 \\ 4.5 & 2.2 & 1.5 \\ 6.7 & 3.0 & 1.0 \end{bmatrix} \qquad \begin{bmatrix} 27.75 \\ 10.50 \\ 12.25 \end{bmatrix}$$

When dealing with a two-dimensional array, the first subscript tells what *row* the element is in; the second subscript gives the *column* position.

$$A_{2,3}$$

column position
row position

Applying this notation to our simultaneous equations, the element referenced above is in equation 2. It is the coefficient preceding X_3. Double subscripts allow the programmer an easy way to deal with a two-dimensional data base. For example, assume you are asked to print out the terms associated with equation 3. The appropriate WRITE statement would be:

WRITE(2,2)A(3,1),A(3,2),A(3,3),C(3)

If you were told to multiply each term in equation 2 by 6.7, the statements would be:

```
    DO  7 I = 1,3
        A(2,I) = 6.7*A(2,I)
 7  CONTINUE
    C(2) = C(2)*6.7
```

The point being made is that dealing with a doubly-subscripted variable is really not that difficult.

Forming Arrays From Data Cards

Assume the original set of three equations is punched on cards as shown in Figure 10.5(a).

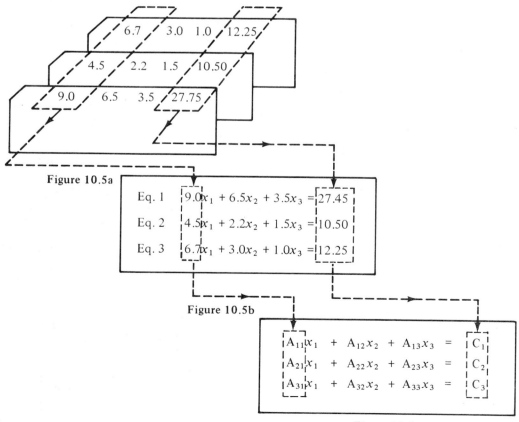

Figure 10.5a

Eq. 1 $9.0x_1 + 6.5x_2 + 3.5x_3 = 27.45$

Eq. 2 $4.5x_1 + 2.2x_2 + 1.5x_3 = 10.50$

Eq. 3 $6.7x_1 + 3.0x_2 + 1.0x_3 = 12.25$

Figure 10.5b

$A_{11}x_1 + A_{12}x_2 + A_{13}x_3 = C_1$

$A_{21}x_1 + A_{22}x_2 + A_{23}x_3 = C_2$

$A_{31}x_1 + A_{32}x_2 + A_{33}x_3 = C_3$

Figure 10.5c

Each card represents one equation by giving the coefficients of X_1, X_2, X_3 and the constant C in that order. Write a program that reads these cards and forms the array A and the array C in memory. The command READ will be executed three times to process the three cards. On each execution we are back to the same old problem: *defining a sequence of variable names that match the sequence of values appearing on that card.*

```
C
      DIMENSION A(3,3),C(3)
C
C         ESTABLISH LOOP TO READ THREE CARDS
C
      DO 20 I = 1, 3
      READ(5,10)A(I,1),A(I,2),A(I,3),C(I)
   10 FORMAT(4F15.2)
   20 CONTINUE
C
C         ECHO CHECK SELECTED ELEMENTS
      WRITE(2,10)A(1,3),A(3,2),A(2,1),C(2)
      STOP
      END
```

Consider the position of the above READ statement. It is inside a DO loop whose index is I. The command READ will be executed three times in rapid succession. On the first execution, I will have the value 1. The names in the list of the READ statement will be interpreted as A(1,1), A(1,2), A(1,3) and C(1).

Note: when a subscript appears other than as an integer constant, A(I,1) for example, the subscript is evaluated before the name is read. That is, the element of A we are reading is A(1,1) or A(2,1) or A(3,1) depending on the value of I. The names A(I,J) and A(L,M) may be identical names referring to the same element. This is true when:

(a) I has the same value as L; and
(b) J has the same value as M.

Returning to the READ statement in the DO loop, on the second execution of the loop I equals 2 and the names in the list of the READ statement are identified as A(2,1), A(2,2), A(2,3), and C(2).

The WRITE statement is used to sample elements of A and C to randomly check the proper storage of the two arrays. The FORMAT statement is used for both the READ and WRITE statements. Finally, the first statement of this program is a DIMENSION statement needed because A and C are arrays.

10.7   Arrays in FORTRAN

Arrays are groups of related numbers. In math/science applications, an array contains a group of real numbers or a group of integer numbers but usually not a mixture of each. The mode of these numbers is reflected by the array name. To name the array we follow the same rules for naming a non-subscripted variable. This name is followed by a pair of parentheses enclosing the subscripts. A one-dimensional array requires a single subscript. Two- and three- dimensional arrays require multiple subscripts separated by commas. You will usually find it convenient to express a subscript as either a simple integer constant or an integer variable. Occasionally, however, a subscript may take on a slightly more complex form, namely, an integer mode arithmetic expression such as:

$$A (\underbrace{I + 2}) \text{ or } A (\underbrace{2 * I - 6})$$
$$\text{Integer Expression}$$

Some compilers restrict the complexity of the expression used to define a subscript. The permitted forms are shown in Figure 10.6. The FORTRAN '77 standards are much more permissive and allow almost any form of expression including array elements and function references.

Subscript Form	General Form	Example
Constant	(C)	A(6)
Variable	(V)	A(I)
Expression		
1. variable plus a constant	(V+C)	A(I+6)
2. variable minus a constant	(V–C)	A(I–6)
3. constant times a variable	(C∗V)	A(6∗I)
4. constant times a variable plus a second constant	(C∗V+D)	A(6∗I+2)
5. constant times a variable minus a second constant	(C∗V–D)	A(6∗I–2)

Figure 10.6 Possible Subscript Restrictions

When dealing with a subscripted variable, the value of a subscript is usually a positive, non-zero value. Zero and negative subscripts are not very common. The new standards make it possible to have subscripts of this form, but such usage will not be shown in this text.

10.8 | The DIMENSION Statement

Whenever a program uses a subscripted variable, the compiler must be informed through the use of one or more DIMENSION statements. A DIMENSION statement must appear at the very beginning of the program, usually before the first executable statement. It directs the computer to allocate sufficient memory space for the storage of all arrays by providing the following information:

1. The names of variables to be subscripted.
2. The number of subscripts each will have.
3. The guaranteed maximum value of each subscript.

Consider the following DIMENSION statement:

DIMENSION A(10,12), B(10),X(12,25)

This statement informs the computer that:

1. A, B, and X are subscripted variables.
2. B is declared as a one-dimensional array, while A and X are two-dimensional arrays.
3. There are 10 possible elements in the array B; therefore, 10 positions in memory will be needed to store this array.

    Array A may have up to 10 rows and 12 columns, which will require 120 positions in memory to store this array.

    Array X has a maximum of 12 rows and 25 columns requiring 300 positions in memory for storage.

As a consequence of this dimension statement, 430 memory locations are set aside to store these arrays.

One word of caution: whenever a subscripted variable appears in a program, the value of its subscript must not exceed that given in the DIMENSION statement; the DIMENSION statement expresses a guarantee on the maximum values of all subscripts in the program.

Figure 10.7 shows other DIMENSION statements and indicates the information they convey.

DIMENSION NUM(9,5), A(8)	NUM is a two dimensional array of integer numbers. A is a one dimensional array consisting of up to eight real numbers.
DIMENSION X(25), Y(25), Z(25), I(50)	X, Y, Z and I are one dimensional arrays, I is an integer array. 125 positions in memory are needed to store these arrays. The subscripts of arrays X, Y and Z may not exceed 25. I's subscripts may not exceed 50.
DIMENSION M(6, 10, 4)	M is a three dimensional array. It consists of 4 planes. Each plane holds a 6 x 10 group of numbers (6 rows and 10 columns.

Figure 10.7 Example DIMENSION Statements

Type statements discussed in Chapter 3 may also serve the same purpose as a DIMENSION statement. For example, the statement:

REAL ITEM (100)

accomplishes two actions: it declares ITEM to be a real name, and it sets up 100 memory locations for this variable, i.e. makes ITEM a one-dimensional array of 100 elements.

The value expressing the size of an array in a DIMENSION statement must be an *integer constant:*

DIMENSION A (10,3) , C(100)

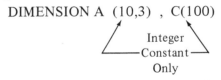

Integer
—Constant—
Only

Variables or expressions are *not* allowed. The reason for this is that the array size is needed during the compiling of the program (to control how much memory is to be allocated for each array). At compiling time, the computer can translate an expression, but it cannot *evaluate* the expression. Evaluation is possible only when the program is executed. *The subscripts appearing in the main program should not exceed the value declared in the DIMENSION statement.*

The storing of arrays consumes vital memory space, and care must be exercised not to exceed available memory capacity.

Once an array has been identified in a DIMENSION statement as a one-, two-, or three-dimensional array, all other reference to this array must be consistent. If an array is declared to be a two-dimensional array in a DIMENSION statement and later in the main program the array is referred to as a one-dimensional array, an error will result.

10.9
Non-Executable Statements

Most FORTRAN statements are called executable because they cause the activation of one or more hardware components. A limited number of statements are more passive in nature. They belong to the SPECIFICATION group described in Chapter 1. These statements supply supportive information needed by the compiler to effectively translate the executable statement. This usually means providing bookkeeping details such as how to interpret the various columns on a data card or how much room is needed to hold variables other than simple variables.

The DIMENSION and FORMAT statements fall into this "nonexecutable" classification. Because of the special nature of these statements, they should not be referenced by a branching instruction (IF or GO TO) statement. For the same reason, such a statement should not be the last one in the range of a DO loop. The nonexecutable feature of a FORMAT statement is what allows the placement of this statement to be rather flexible. It can appear almost anywhere in a program. A FORMAT statement is only used to assist in the execution of some READ/WRITE operation.

A complete list of nonexecutable statements is given in Appendix D.

Quiz #11   Subscripting a Variable

Part 1: Answer the following questions.

1. Correct the following statement:

    It makes no difference if you store an array as a one, two or three dimensional array. They are all just as easy to work with.

2. How many rows are there in the array ITEM:

    DIMENSION ITEM (100,50)

3. When reading arrays with many elements, the list of names is often written with an IMPLIED DO index. Give an example.

4. Does the FORMAT statement used when reading an array describe the whole array, one element of the array, or one unit record defining the array?

5. What is wrong with the following statements:

    ```
    DO   20 I-1,100
             READ(5,10)X(I)
    10       FORMAT(10F8.2)
    20       CONTINUE
    ```

6. What is wrong with the following DIMENSION statement:

    DIMENSION X (N,M)

7. Define a nonexecutable statement.

8. If the size of an array A varies as follows:

    (a) sometimes there are 60 elements
    (b) sometimes there are only 10 elements
    (c) once in a while there are 120 elements

    What must the DIMENSION statement look like?

9. Is it possible for the two elements of the array A shown below to be the same?

    A(M)   A(N)

10. What is wrong with the following statements.

    ```
    DIMENSION A(200)
    READ(5,10)(A(I),I=1,300)
    ```

Part 2: Writing a Program

11. The price of 200 stocks at the beginning and end of a report period are listed on the cards shown.

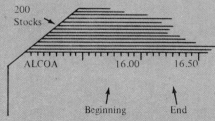

(a) Provide a list of all stocks that increased 10% or more in value.

(b) Provide a list of all stocks that decreased 10% or more in value.

Answers:

1. Arrays should be stored in the simplest form possible. One-dimensional is easier to deal with than two-dimensional.

2. 100.

3. READ(5,10)(GRADE(I),I=1,80)

   ∠Implied DO INDEX

4. Describes one unit record.

5. Only one name following command READ, but 10F8.2 code in FORMAT statement.

6. Size of array must be specified as *constants*.

7. Belongs to SPECIFICATION group. Supplies supportive information. Does not cause the execution of a hardware component.

8. DIMENSION A(120).

9. Yes, when M is equal to N.

10. Subscript exceeds value specified in DIMENSION statement.

11.
```
C . . . . . . . . . . . . . . . . . . . . . . . . .
C      PURPOSE-PROVIDE A LIST OF WINNERS. . . .
C                PROVIDE A LIST OF LOSERS. . . . .
C . . . . . . . . . . . . . . . . . . . . . . . . .
                -IMPORTANT VARIABLES-
C
C      -NAME    ARRAY OF STOCK NAMES
C      -BEGIN   PRICE AT START OF REPORT PERIOD
C      -END     PRICE AT END OF REPORT PERIOD
C
       DIMENSION NAME(200),BEGIN(200),END(200)
C
C
C
       READ(5,10)(NAME(I),BEGIN(I),END(I),I=1,200)
   10  FORMAT(A8,2F7.2)
C
       WRITE(2,20)
   20  FORMAT(40X,'LIST OF WINNERS',///)
C
       DO 40 I=1,200
            CHANGE=END(I)-BEGIN(I)
            IF(CHANGE.GT.BEGIN(I)*0.10)WRITE(2,30)NAME(I)
   30            FORMAT(45X,A8)
   40  CONTINUE
C
C
       WRITE(2,50)
   50  FORMAT(40X,'LIST OF LOSERS',///)
C
       DO 60 I=1,200
            CHANGE=END(I)-BEGIN(I)
            IF(CHANGE.LT.0.0.AND.ABS(CHANGE).GT.BEGIN(I)*0.10)
                 WRITE(2,30)NAME(I)
   60  CONTINUE
C
       STOP
       END
```

10.10 | Some Practice with Subscripted Variables

The next step in dealing with subscripted variables is to perform basic mathematical operations with them. This usually means setting up a loop structure in which each element of a data base contributes some small value toward the final solution.

Programming Example
Locating the Center
of Gravity

A missile has 1000 component parts. Each part is identified by a data card giving part weight (W_n) and part location (X_n) from the tip of the missile.

Write a program to read 1000 data cards and form a one-dimensional array called W and a one-dimensional array called X, each containing 1000 elements.

When the arrays are formed, write a program to determine the total weight of the missile:

$$\text{WEIGHT} = W_1 + W_2 + W_3 + W_4 + \ldots + W_{998} + W_{999} + W_{1000} = \Sigma W$$

Next, multiply each weight by the corresponding value of X to determine the individual moments (force times distance) each weight imposes on the missile.

$$\text{MOMENT} = W_1 X_1 + W_2 X_2 + W_3 X_3 + \ldots + W_{999} X_{999} + W_{1000} X_{1000} = \Sigma WX$$

Finally, divide the total moment by the total weight and determine the location of the center of gravity of the missile.

$$\frac{\text{CENTER OF}}{\text{GRAVITY}} = \frac{W_1 X_1 + W_2 X_2 + W_3 X_3 + \ldots + W_{1000} X_{1000}}{W_1 + W_2 + W_3 + \ldots + W_{1000}} = \frac{\Sigma WX}{\Sigma W}$$

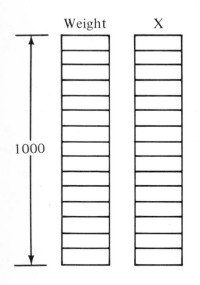

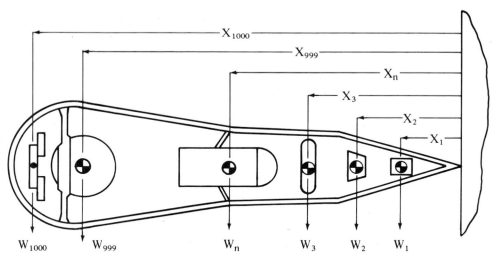

```
C..... PURPOSE - READ AN ARRAY OF WEIGHT VALUES AND AN ARRAY..
C..              OF LOCATIONS DESCRIBING THE DISTRIBUTION    ..
C..              OF COMPONENTS IN A MISSILE                  ..
C..                                                          ..
C..              DETERMINE THE TOTAL WEIGHT OF THE MISSILE   ..
C..              AND THE LOCATION OF ITS CENTER OF GRAVITY   ..
C...........................................................
C
C               -----IMPORTANT VARIABLES-----
C
C     --WEIGHT  ARRAY OF COMPONENT WEIGHTS (LBS.)          --
C     --X       ARRAY OF COMPONENT LOCATIONS (IN.)         --
C     --SUMW    ACCUMULATOR (TOTAL WEIGHT)                 --
C     --SUMM    ACCUMULATOR (TOTAL MOMENT)                 --
C     --CG      SIMPLE VARIABLE TELLING LOCATION OF THE     --
C               CENTER OF GRAVITY                          --
C
C               RESERVE ROOM IN MEMORY FOR THE TWO ARRAYS
C
      DIMENSION   WEIGHT(1000), X(1000)
C
      DO 10 I = 1, 1000
         READ(5,5) WEIGHT(I), X(I)
    5    FORMAT(2F12.2)
   10 CONTINUE
C
```

```
C                       INITIALIZE VALUE OF TWO ACCUMULATORS
C
      SUMW = 0.0
      SUMM = 0.0
C
C                       LOOP ENTRY POINT
C
      DO 20 I = 1, 1000
         SUMW = SUMW + WEIGHT(I)
         SUMM = SUMM + WEIGHT(I) * X(I)
 20 CONTINUE
C
C                       LOOP EXIT POINT
C
      CG = SUMM / SUMW
C
      WRITE(2,30) SUMW, CG
 30   FORMAT (10X, 'TOTAL WEIGHT = ', F14.2, 10X,
     +        'CENTER OF GRAVITY = ',F14.2)
C
      STOP
      END
```

Programming Example
Stock Market

At the beginning of each trading day the name of 1200 stocks and their previous highest and lowest trading prices are read from the data cards shown. It takes 20 columns to represent any one stock so that 4 stocks can be represented on one card.

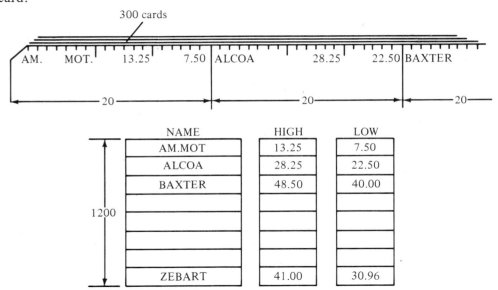

Part A: Establish the data base

Write statements that will read and store this information in memory.

```
C.................................................
C   PURPOSE – ESTABLISH DATA BASE FOR STOCK MARKET PROBLEM
C.................................................
C                     –IMPORTANT VARIABLES–
C   –NAME      ARRAY OF STOCK NAMES
C   –HIGH      ARRAY OF HIGHEST SELLING PRICE FOR EACH STOCK
C   –LOW       ARRAY OF LOWEST SELLING PRICE FOR EACH STOCK
C
C           PROVIDE ROOM IN MEMORY FOR DATA BASE
      DIMENSION NAME(1200), HIGH(1200)
      REAL LOW(1200)
C
C
      READ(5, 1)(NAME(I),HIGH(I),LOW(I), I = 1, 1200)
    1 FORMAT(A8,2F6.2,A8,2F6.2,A8,2F6.A8,2F6.2)
```

Part B: Read transaction card. . .locate stock in data base

Now that the data base is established, let's examine a typical operation that might be performed on the data base, namely, an update operation.

The remaining cards in the deck represent transactions made on the floor of the stock exchange. Each time a stock is bought or sold, the name of that stock is recorded on a data card along with the number of shares traded and the price per share.

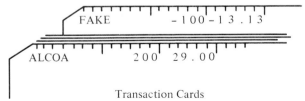

Transaction Cards

The end of the deck is signalled by a trailer card. We want to write statements that will READ the first transaction card and locate where in the data base information on this stock is located.

```
C....................................................
C..   PURPOSE - READ TRANSACTION CARD. LOCATE STOCK BEING  ..
C..              TRADED IN THE DATA BASE                    ..
C....................................................
C
C                -----IMPORTANT VARIABLES-----
C
C      --NAMETR   NAME OF STOCK BEING TRADED            --
C      --NSHARE   NUMBER OF SHARES BEING TRADED         --
C      --PRICE    PRICE STOCK TRADED FOR                --
C               (ALL SIMPLE VARIABLES)                  --
C
   10 READ(5,11) NAMETR, NSHARE, PRICE
   11 FORMAT(A8,I6,F6.2)
C
C              SEARCH ARRAY OF NAMES FOR THIS STOCK
C
      DO 20 I = 1, 1200
C
         IF(NAMETR.EQ.NAME(I)) GO TO 40
C
   20 CONTINUE
C
C
C         IF DO LOOP COMPLETED, STOCK NOT LISTED
C
   30 WRITE(2,31) NAMETR
   31 FORMAT(1X,A8,' THIS STOCK NOT LISTED IN DATA BASE.')
C
      STOP
C
C         STOCK FOUND, SUBSCRIPT 'I' TELLS WHERE
C
   40 WRITE(2,41) I
   41 FORMAT(3X,'THIS STOCK IS LOCATED IN POSITION',I4)
      STOP
      END
```

Part C: New highs/new lows

Now that the stock has been located, write statements that will test the price the stock traded for and determine if that stock hit a new high or a new low for the year. If either event occurs, change the corresponding element of the array HIGH or the array LOW as appropriate.

IF(PRICE.GT.HIGH(I)) HIGH(I) = PRICE
IF(PRICE.LT.LOW(I)) LOW(I) = PRICE

Having processed one transaction card, the logic would be repeated for all the transaction cards. When the trailer card is reached, you would print the data base in its latest updated form.

Part D: Summary information

After all the transaction cards are processed, you are asked to provide the following summary information regarding the day's stock market performance:

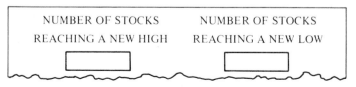

To provide this information it is necessary to make a copy of the array HIGH and the array LOW before processing any transaction cards. When the trailer card is reached, we will compare the updated HIGH and LOW arrays with their original condition and see how many elements changed.

```
C..........................................................
C..    PURPOSE - PROVIDE ADDITIONAL ROOM IN MEMORY FOR THE ..
C..              COPIES NEEDED, THEN DEFINE THESE ELEMENTS  ..
C..              AS EQUAL TO THOSE READ FROM DATA.          ..
C..........................................................
C
C               -----IMPORTANT VARIABLES-----
C
C      --HICOPY   DUPLICATE OF ARRAY HIGH                    --
C      --LOCOPY   DUPLICATE OF ARRAY LOW                     --
C      --NHIGH    NUMBER OF STOCKS REACHING NEW HIGHS        --
C      --NLOWS    NUMBER OF STOCKS REACHING NEW LOWS         --
C
       DIMENSION NAME(1200), HIGH(1200), HICOPY(1200)
C
       REAL LOW(1200), LOCOPY(1200)
C
C               READ DATA BASE
C
    20 READ(5,21)(NAME(I),HIGH(I),LOW(I),I=1,1200)
C
    21 FORMAT(A8,2F6.2,A8,2F6.2,A8,2F6.2,A8,2F6.2)
C
C               SET UP LOOP AND MAKE COPY OF TWO ARRAYS
C
       DO 30 I=1,1200
C
            HICOPY(I) = HIGH(I)
            LOCOPY(I) = LOW(I)
C
    30 CONTINUE
C
C..              DETERMINIE NUMBER OF NEW HIGHS           ..
C..              NUMBER OF NEW LOWS                       ..
C
       NHIGH = 0
       NLOWS = 0
C
       DO 40 I = 1, 1200
C
            IF(HIGH(I).GT.HICOPY(I)) NHIGH = NHIGH + 1
            IF(LOW(I).LT.LOCOPY(I)) NLOWS = NLOWS + 1
C
    40 CONTINUE
C
       STOP
       END
```

Combining all these features produces a long and involved program. Mastering these short applications of subscripted variables is of more immediate importance just now . . . the long problems can come later.

| **Programming Example** Move Up One | A one-dimensional array called LAND has twenty elements and represents the landing sequence at a busy airport. Each element uses a six character alphanumeric symbol to represent the airline and flight number of each aircraft in the landing pattern. |

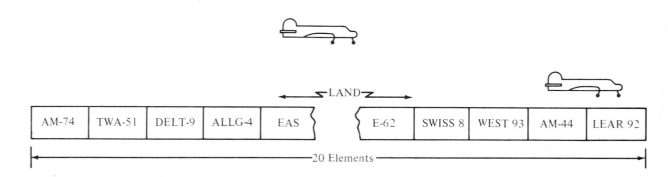

Part A: Read in

Write statements to READ the elements of this array from data cards (one per card — 20 cards) and form the array LAND. Display this waiting list as suggested below. Notice that two aircraft are given per line of output. On line one is aircraft 1 and aircraft 11. On the next line it is aircraft 2 and aircraft 12.

WAITING LIST			
NO.	SYMBOL	NO.	SYMBOL
1	AM-74	11	SWISS2
2	TWA-51	12	DELT63
3	DELT-9	13	LEAR15
4	ALLG-4	14	AM-49
9	TWA-08	19	AM-44
10	EXEC15	20	LEAR92

```
C.....................................................
C..   PURPOSE - READ A ONE-DIMENSIONAL ARRAY REPRESENTING ..
C..             LANDING AIRCRAFT - DISPLAY AS REQUESTED.   ..
C.....................................................
C
C                   -----IMPORTANT VARIABLES-----
C
C     --LAND    ARRAY OF CODED INFORMATION                --
C     --I       SUBSCRIPT FOR LEFT HAND COLUMN            --
C     --M       SUBSCRIPT FOR RIGHT HAND COLUMN           --
C
      DIMENSION LAND(20)
C
      READ(5,10) (LAND(I),I=1,20)
   10 FORMAT(A6)
C
      WRITE(2,20)
   20 FORMAT(1H1, 40X,'WAITING LIST')
      WRITE(2,30)
   30 FORMAT(4X,3HNO.,3X,6HSYMBOL,8X,3HNO.,6HSYMBOL,//)
C
C                   DISPLAY ELEMENTS OF ARRAY
C
      DO 50 I = 1,10
         M = I + 10
         WRITE(2,40) I, LAND(I), M, LAND(M)
   40 FORMAT(6X,I3,3X,A6,8X,I3,3X,A6)
   50 CONTINUE
C
```

Part B: Move elements

Write statements that will advance each element of the array up one position (a plane has landed). Read the next data card (card 21) and place that symbol in the last position.

```
C.....................................................
C..   PURPOSE - MOVE EACH ELEMENT UP ONE. FILL LAST    ..
C..             ELEMENT WITH THE NEXT AIRCRAFT WAITING. ..
C.....................................................
C
C                   -----IMPORTANT VARIABLES-----
C
C     --NEXT     SIMPLE VARIABLE- NEXT AIRCRAFT IN DECK  --
C
C                 MOVE EACH ELEMENT UP ONE POSITION
C
      DO 60 I = 1,19
         LAND(I) = LAND(I+1)
   60 CONTINUE
C
      READ(5,20) NEXT
   70 LAND(20) = NEXT
C
      STOP
      END
```

Review Exercises

1.*The simplest way in which information can be stored is as a simple variable. In order of complexity, describe the other alternative ways of storing information.

2. What is meant by the term "vector"?

3. When a variable is doubly subscripted, it is considered as having a number of rows and a number of columns. Which subscript provides the row descriptor? (First or second?)

4.*The following DO loop defines a one-dimensional array called X having 400 elements:

$$\text{DO 20 I} = 1,400$$
$$\text{READ(5,10)X(I)}$$
$$10 \qquad \text{FORMAT(F12.2)}$$
$$20 \quad \text{CONTINUE}$$

Write a READ statement that uses an implied DO index that is the equivalent of the statements shown above.

5. Write statements that will define a matrix of size 10 by 10, each element having a value equal to the sum of its row and column position.

6.*The following statements contain an error:

$$M=6$$
$$N=4$$
$$\text{DIMENSION ARRAY(M,N)}$$

What is the error?

7. Describe the allocation of memory associated with the following DIMENSION statement:

$$\text{DIMENSION A(10,10),B(200),C(6)}$$

8. Provide the definition of a problem that requires the use of a one-dimensional array called NAME and a one-dimensional array called AMOUNT.

9.*When reading large arrays, is it necessary for the number of codes in the FORMAT statement to match the number of names following the command READ in the input statement?

10. What does the term "non-executable" statement mean? Give several examples.

11. Twenty values of X are punched on a single data card using a 20F4.1 format code. Read this array of X values and determine the sum of the even elements and the sum of the odd elements of the array.

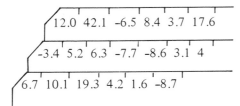

ARRAY X

12. A data deck consists of three cards similar to the card described in problem 11.

Use these cards to define three arrays called X1, X2 and X3. Now define an array called BIG, each element of which is the largest of the corresponding elements of X1, X2 and X3.

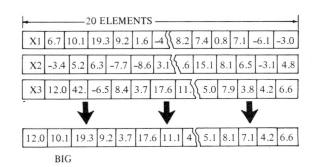

BIG

13.*Determine the average value of each of the arrays in problem 12 (arrays X1, X2 and X3). Now report how much each element of an array is above or below this average value.

14. The shape of a turbine shaft is defined by an array of X values and an array of R values. The shaft is considered to be a connected series of cylinders where each R value defines the radius of a cylinder and each X value defines its height or thickness.

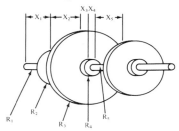

If each array contains 200 elements and the shaft is made of steel (density = 0.3 lb/in^3), determine the weight of the shaft.

15. Repeat problem 14 except that the number of elements in each array is a number N, which is less than 200. The value of N is given by a lead data card as shown. Determine the weight and center of gravity of the shaft.

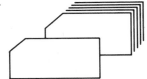

16.*An array called X has 100 elements that are in ascending order of magnitude. Define an array Y whose elements are the same as the elements of X except in descending order. Y(1) will have the value of X(100), Y(2) will have the value of X(99), etc.

17. The name, gross income and federal taxes paid of 1000 suspected tax evaders are stored as three one-dimensional arrays as shown.

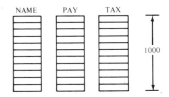

Determine what percentage of this group earned over $80,000 and paid less than $1,000 in taxes.

18. Expand the analysis of the data described in problem 17 to provide the following information:

| | Tax Paid | | | | |
	No tax paid	>$500	>$1000	>$2000	>$3000
Earned over $80,000 →					

19. The equation:

$$y = x^5 - 3x^3 \, 6x - 1$$

is to be analyzed between $X = X_{initial}$ and $X = X_{last}$. Write a program to evelute the equation at 100 equally spaced points between these limits of X (to be read from data).

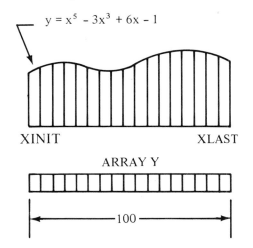

ARRAY Y

Each value of Y thus obtained is to form an element of a one-dimensional array to be called Y.

20.*An array called X has 100 elements which are in ascending order of magnitude. Values of X are punched 10 values per card using a 10F8.1 code. Read this array and then *remove element 50*, that is, the element that was in position 51 should now be in position 50, the element in position 52 should be in position 51, and so on.

21. Repeat problem 20 except that an element is to be *added* to the array called X. Read this additional element from a data card. Locate where in the array this element belongs. Starting at the end of the array, move elements up one position to make room for this new element. Finally, position the new element in the array and print the array.

22. The government monitors the price of 200 food items on a month-to-month basis. The array called START gives the cost of each item at the beginning of the year. Arrays PRICE1, PRICE2 and PRICE3 give the price of these items at the end of the first, second and third months of the year.

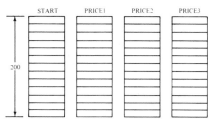

(a) How many items increased in cost for three consecutive months?
(b) How many items sold for less in the third month than they did at the beginning of the year?
(c) Determine the average increase in the cost of food during month one, month 2, month 3.

23. An array called X has 100 elements (10 rows and 10 columns) and represents the radiation level surrounding a nuclear power plant. Values of X appear on data cards, one per card, in row order.

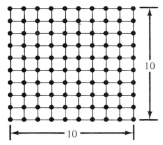

(a) Determine the average radiation level around the perimeter of the plant.
(b) Determine the average level inside the perimeter.

24. The elements of X in problem 23 are divided into four quadrants as shown in the accompanying illustration.

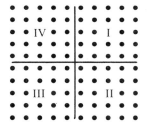

Determine the average radiation level in each quadrant.

25.*LIST1 and LIST2 are both arrays of integer numbers. We wish to know if any number in LIST1 also appears in LIST2.

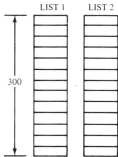

Determine if the first number in LIST1 appears anywhere in LIST2. Output should be the message:

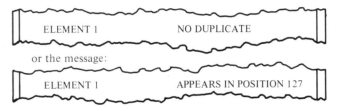

or the message:

26. Repeat the search accomplished in problem 25 for each element in LIST1.

27. An array called CARS has 5 rows and 5 columns and is used to keep track of the number of police cars in various sectors of a large metropolitan city.

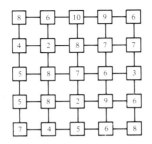

Design an algorithm to account for a car leaving one sector and entering another.

28. For the array shown in problem 27, design an algorithm to tell how many cars are in a given sector and all the sectors immediately adjacent to this sector.

29. A parcel of land 150 ft. by 100 ft. is divided into 10 ft. squares, and the elevation (above sea level) of each square is determined. Use these elevations to form a two-dimensional array called A. Values of A are punched on data cards one to a card in row order (see figure below).

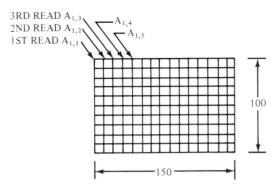

30. After forming the array A in problem 29, determine the average elevation of the land.

31. By comparing adjacent elements of array A in problem 29, it is possible to determine the local slope of the ground. Write a program to determine the maximum grade or slope of the land. (This is a reasonably difficult program for a beginner to write.)

32. Arrays A and B are both two-dimensional, having 9 rows and 10 columns. Assume these arrays have already been read from data. Write a program to compare each element of A with the corresponding element of B and print the larger of the two elements.

33.*Repeat problem 32, but use the larger of the two corresponding elements to form an element of an array to be called C. Array C will be the same size as A or B, and each element of C will be equal to or greater than the corresponding element in A or B.

34.*A two-dimensional array called M is to have 10 rows and 10 columns. All elements of M have the value 0, except those on the "main diagonal." Elements of the main diagonal are those whose row and column numbers are identical. These elements are each to have value 1. Write a program to form this array. Values of M are *not* to be read from data.

$$\begin{bmatrix} 1 & 0 & 0 & 0 & 0 & 0 & 0 & 0 & 0 & 0 \\ 0 & 1 & 0 & 0 & 0 & 0 & 0 & 0 & 0 & 0 \\ 0 & 0 & 1 & 0 & 0 & 0 & 0 & 0 & 0 & 0 \\ 0 & 0 & 0 & 1 & 0 & 0 & 0 & 0 & 0 & 0 \\ 0 & 0 & 0 & 0 & 1 & 0 & 0 & 0 & 0 & 0 \\ 0 & 0 & 0 & 0 & 0 & 1 & 0 & 0 & 0 & 0 \\ 0 & 0 & 0 & 0 & 0 & 0 & 1 & 0 & 0 & 0 \\ 0 & 0 & 0 & 0 & 0 & 0 & 0 & 1 & 0 & 0 \\ 0 & 0 & 0 & 0 & 0 & 0 & 0 & 0 & 1 & 0 \\ 0 & 0 & 0 & 0 & 0 & 0 & 0 & 0 & 0 & 1 \end{bmatrix}$$

Additional Applications

| Programming Example Cargo Loading | Each card of a data deck describes a piece of cargo to be loaded on an airplane. The first two numbers on each data card indicate the weight of the item and the number of the cargo bay (1, 2, or 3) it has been assigned to. Write a program to |

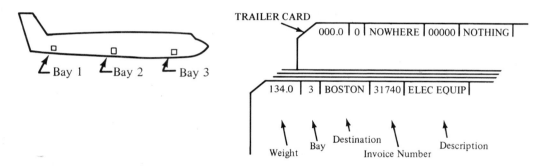

TRAILER CARD

000.0 | 0 | NOWHERE | 00000 | NOTHING

134.0 | 3 | BOSTON | 31740 | ELEC EQUIP

Weight   Bay   Destination   Invoice Number   Description

determine how many pieces of cargo are represented in the data deck and the total weight of this cargo. Also compute the weight of cargo in each of the three cargo bays.

```
C.............................................................
C..    PURPOSE - DETERMINE THE LOAD DISTRIBUTION ON A PLANE  ..
C.............................................................
C
C             -----IMPORTANT VARIABLES-----
C
C
C      --WEIGHT   WEIGHT OF EACH PIECE OF CARGO              --
C      --BAYNBR   NUMBER OF THE CARGO BAY                    --
C      --SUMWT    ARRAY OF TOTAL WEIGHT ACCUMULATORS         --
C                 SUMWT(1) = WEIGHT IN BAY 1                 --
C                 SUMWT(2) = WEIGHT IN BAY 2                 --
C                 SUMWT(3) = WEIGHT IN BAY 3                 --
C      --NCARGO   NUMBER OF PIECES IN TOTAL CARGO            --
C
       DIMENSION SUMWT(3)
       INTEGER BAYNBR
C
C          .....INITIALIZATION SECTION.....
C
       NCARGO = 0
C
C             ZERO ALL ACCUMULATORS
C
       DO 10 I = 1,3
          SUMWT(I) = 0.0
   10  CONTINUE
C
C          .....PROCESSING LOOP.....
C
   20  READ(5,21) WEIGHT, BAYNBR
   21  FORMAT(F5.1,I1)
C
C             TEST FOR TRAILER
C
       IF (WEIGHT.EQ.0.0) GO TO 40
C
C          .....CARD NOT TRAILER....ADVANCE COUNTER.....
C
       NCARGO = NCARGO + 1
C
C             USE BAY NUMBER TO ADVANCE APPROPRIATE
C             ACCUMULATOR
C.............................................................
   30           SUMWT(BAYNBR) = SUMWT(BAYNBR) + WEIGHT
C.............................................................
       GO TO 20
C
C             ALL CARDS PROCESSED
C
   40  TOTAL = SUMWT(1) + SUMWT(2) + SUMWT(3)
       WRITE(2,50)NCARGO,TOTAL,SUMWT(1),SUMWT(2),SUMWT(3)
   50  FORMAT (1X,I12,4(10X,F12.1))
       STOP
       END
```

Note: The selection of which accumulator to advance could have been accomplished by three IF statements:

$$\text{IF(BAYNBR.EQ.1)SUMWT(1) = SUMWT(1) + WEIGHT}$$
$$\text{IF(BAYNBR.EQ.2)SUMWT(2) = SUMWT(2) + WEIGHT}$$
$$\text{IF(BAYNBR.EQ.3)SUMWT(3) = SUMWT(3) + WEIGHT}$$

Statement 30 does all this testing with only one statement. We will use a similar statement to save rather exhaustive testing (100 tests) in the next programming example.

Programming Example
Frequency Charts

The array called IGRADE has 1000 elements. Scores on a college entrance exam are to be stored in the array.

The scores are punched on 250 data cards, four elements per card.

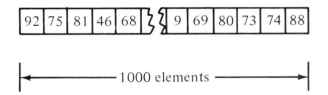

|←————————— 1000 elements —————————→|

Part A:

Read the scores off the data cards and store them in the IGRADE array.

```
        DIMENSION IGRADE(1000)
C       ....READ VALUES FOUR PER CARD
        DO 10 = 1, 1000, 4
           READ(5,5)IGRADE(I),IGRADE(I+1)
   +       IGRADE(I+2),IGRADE(I+3)
  5        FORMAT(4I8)
 10     CONTINUE
```

                                    or

```
        DIMENSION IGRADE(1000)
C ...... USE MORE EFFICIENT READ STATEMENT
C
        READ(5,5)(IGRADE(I),I=1,1000,1
C
  5  FORMAT(4I8)
```

Part B:

The ultimate goal of this program is to obtain a chart that shows the distribution of grades on the exam. It is technically called a **frequency chart**. It tells how many people scored 100, how many scored 99, etc. To start, we would like to know what was the highest score and what was the lowest score, i.e., what was the *range* of scores.

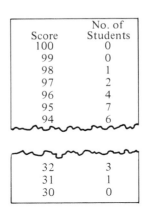

```
C       ....FIND RANGE OF SCORES.......
        IBIG = IGRADE(1)
        ISMALL = IGRADE(1)
        DO 20 I = 2, 1000
           IF(IGRADE(I).GT.IBIG) IBIG = IGRADE(I)
           IF(IGRADE(I).LT.ISMALL) ISMALL = IGRADE(I)
 20     CONTINUE
```

Part C:

Go through the array IGRADE and determine how many students scored the highest grade, next highest grade, and so on.

To accomplish this requirement, a 100 element array of frequency counters called IFREQ will be set up to function as follows: IFREQ(100) will count how many students scored 100; IFREQ(99) will count the 99's; IFREQ(98) will count the 98's; etc. These statements set up the IFREQ array and initialize its elements at 0.

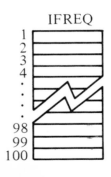

```
C       .....ZERO OUT ALL COUNTERS.......
        DIMENSION IFREQ (100)
        DO 30I = 1, 100
           IFREQ(I) = 0
 30     CONTINUE
```

One possible (but unreasonably long) approach to counting the frequency of grades is this:

```
C        ......THE HARD WAY.......THE HARD WAY.......
         DO 40 I = 1, 1000
              IF(IGRADE(I).EQ.1)IFREQ(1) = IFREQ(1) + 1
              IF(IGRADE(I).EQ.2)IFREQ(2) = IFREQ(2) + 1
              IF(IGRADE(I).EQ.3)IFREQ(3) = IFREQ(3) + 1
                      .            .            .
                      .            .            .
                      .            .            .
              IF(IGRADE(I).EQ.99)IFREQ(99) = IFREQ(99) + 1
              IF(IGRADE(I).EQ.100)IFREQ(100)=IFREQ(100)+ 1
```

The previous approach would have resulted in 100 IF statements. An obviously more efficient scheme would be this:

```
C        .....THE EASY WAY,....THE EASY WAY.......
C
         DO 40 I = 1, 100
              K = IGRADE(I)
              IFREQ(K) = IFREQ(K) + 1
      40   CONTINUE
```

Part D:

Produce the frequency chart that has been suggested. The chart should start at the highest grade and end at the lowest grade.

Score	No. of Students
98	1
97	2
96	4
95	7
94	6
37	3
36	0
35	2

```
C........................................................
C..    PURPOSE - PROVIDE A FREQUENCY CHART OF EXAM SCORES ..
C..              STARTING WITH THE HIGHEST SCORE AND ENDING ..
C..              WITH THE LOWEST SCORE                     ..
C........................................................
C
C           -----IMPORTANT VARIABLES-----
C
C      --IGRADE   ARRAY OF 1000 EXAM SCORES          --
C      --IBIG     HIGHEST GRADE ACHIEVED ON EXAM     --
C      --ISMALL   LOWEST GRADE ACHIEVED ON EXAM      --
C      --IFEREQ   AN ARRAY OF COUNTERS               --
C                 IFREQ(100) = HOW MANY SCORED 100
C                 IFREQ(99)  = HOW MANY SCORED  99
C                 IFREQ(98)  = HOW MANY SCORED  98
C
       DIMENSION IGRADE(1000), IFREQ(100)
C
C           .....READ DATA BASE....EXAM SCORES.....
C
       DO 10 I = 1,1000,4
C
           READ(5,5)IGRADE(I),IGRADE(I+1),IGRADE(I+2),IGRADE(I+3)
      5    FORMAT(4I8)
C
      10 CONTINUE
C
C           .....DETERMINE RANGE OF GRADES.....
C
       IBIG = IGRADE(1)
       ISMALL = IGRADE(1)
C
       DO 20 I= 2,1000
C
           IF(IGRADE(I).GT.IBIG)IBIG = IGRADE(I)
           IF(IGRADE(I).LT.ISMALL)ISMALL = IGRADE(I)
C
      20 CONTINUE
C
C           .....ZERO FREQUENCY ARRAY.....
C
       DO 30 I=1,100
C
           IFREQ(I) = 0
C
      30 CONTINUE
C
C           .....PROCESSING LOOP STARTS HERE.....
C
       DO 40 I= 1,1000
C
           K = IGRADE(I)
           IFREQ(K) = IFREQ(K) + 1
C
      40 CONTINUE
C
C           .....OUTPUT VALUES STARTING AT THE TOP.....
C
      50 WRITE(2,51) IBIG, IFREQ(IBIG)
      51 FORMAT(1X, 2I20)
C
```

```
C       .....DECREMENT IBIG AND TEST AGAINST ISMALL.....
C
        IBIG = IBIG - 1
        IF(IBIG.GE.ISMALL) GO TO 50
C
        STOP
        END
```

Programming Example
Pollution Control

The pollution level for the first 28 days of each month in the year 1972 have been measured and are to be formed into a two-dimensional array called BAD72 having 28 rows and 12 columns. These values are on data cards, 10 values per card, in column order according to a 10F8.2 code.

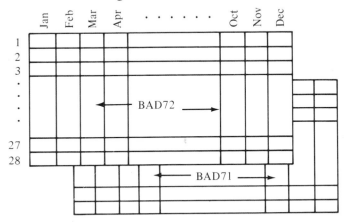

A similar set of data cards have been prepared for 1971. Their contents are to be stored in an array called BAD71.

Data Deck:

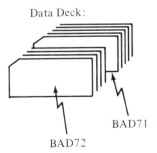

BAD72   BAD71

Part A:

Write statements that read in the data and form the arrays BAD72 and BAD71.

```
C
        DIMENSION BAD72(28,12),BAD71(28,12)
C
        READ(5,6)((BAD71(I,J),I=1,28),J=1,12)
        READ(5,6)((BAD72(K,J),K=1,28),J=1,12)
      6 FORMAT (10F8.2)
```

Part B:

Write statements that compute the average pollution level for the month of February, 1971.

```
C
        SUM =0.0
C
        DO 10 I=1,28
        SUM = SUM + BAD71(I,2)
     10 CONTINUE
C
        AVE = SUM/28.
C
```

Part C:

Write statements that compute and report the average for each month of the year 1972.

```
C              DO 20 J=1,12
C                 SUM = 0.0
C                 DO 30 K=1,28
C                    SUM = SUM + BAD72(K,J)
C        30       CONTINUE
C                 AVE = SUM/28.
C                 WRITE(2,40)AVE
C        40       FORMAT(1X,F6.2)
C        20 CONTINUE
C              END
```

Final Program:

Write a complete program to compute all the averages suggested in the simulated output sheet shown.

POLLUTION REPORT	1971	1972
AVERAGE POLLUTION LEVEL FOR JAN.	4.62	5.73
AVERAGE POLLUTION LEVEL FOR FEB.	3.93	6.08
AVERAGE POLLUTION LEVEL FOR MAR.	3.70	4.81
AVERAGE POLLUTION LEVEL FOR APR.	4.55	5.64
AVERAGE POLLUTION LEVEL FOR MAY	5.19	6.22
AVERAGE POLLUTION LEVEL FOR JUNE	4.09	5.17
AVERAGE POLLUTION LEVEL FOR JULY	4.42	5.38
AVERAGE POLLUTION LEVEL FOR AUG.	4.93	5.11
AVERAGE POLLUTION LEVEL FOR SEP.	5.20	6.31
AVERAGE POLLUTION LEVEL FOR OCT.	5.00	6.19
AVERAGE POLLUTION LEVEL FOR NOV.	5.61	6.72
AVERAGE POLLUTION LEVEL FOR DEC.	6.11	7.43

To obtain the months of the year on the output sheet as shown, they were first read in A-Format from a data card such as:

```
Jan.  Feb. Mar.  Apr.  May  June  July  Aug.  Sep.  Oct.  Nov.  Dec.
```

These values are stored as a one-dimensional array called MONTH containing 12 elements to be used later in the program in output statement 9.

```
C.........PURPOSE - PRODUCE MONTHLY COMPARISON OF POLUTION.......
C..                 LEVELS                                    ::
C..                 FOR YEARS 1971 AND 1972                   ::
C...........................................................::
C
C                  -----IMPORTANT VARIABL E-----
C
      DIMENSION BAD72(28,12),BAD71(28,12),MONTH(12)
C                  READ IN DATA BASE
      READ(5,5) ((BAD72(I,J),I=1,28),J=1,12)
      READ(5,5) ((BAD71(I,J),I=1,28),J=1,12)
    5 FORMAT(10F8.2)
C                  READ MONTHS OF YEAR FROM CARD AT END OF DEC5
      READ(5,10) (MONTH(I),I=1,12)
   10 FORMAT(12A4)
C                  PUT HEADINGS ON OUTPUT SHEET
      WRITE(2,15)
   15 FORMAT(1H1,19X,16HPOLLUTION REPORT,18X,4H1971,12X,
     +4H1972,///)
C
C                  OUTER COMPUTATIONAL LOOP
      DO 40 J = 1, 12
         SUM71 = 0.0
         SUM72 = 0.0
C
         DO 20 I = 1, 28
            SUM71 = SUM71 + BAD71(I,J)
            SUM72 = SUM72 + BAD72(I,J)
   20    CONTINUE
C
         AVE71 = SUM71/28.
         AVE72 = SUM72/28.
C
```

```
      WRITE(2,30)MONTH(J), AVE71,AVE72
   30 FORMAT(10X,@AVERAGE POLLUTION LEVEL FOR@,A4,10X,
     1F6.2,10X,F6.2)
   40 CONTINUE
C
      STOP
      END
```

Programming Example
Half Interval Search**

A relationship between X and Y has been established experimentally by the 64 data points shown. A table of these X,Y values has been stored in the computer as a one-dimensional array called X and a one-dimensional array called Y, each containing 64 elements.

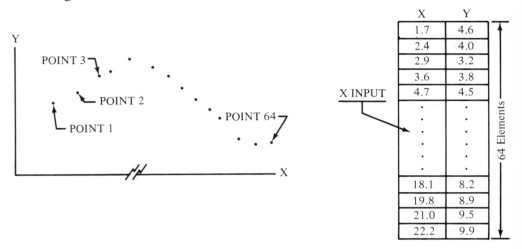

X	Y
1.7	4.6
2.4	4.0
2.9	3.2
3.6	3.8
4.7	4.5
.	.
.	.
.	.
.	.
18.1	8.2
19.8	8.9
21.0	9.5
22.2	9.9

64 Elements

Assume it is necessary to enter the table and see if a specific value of X is listed in the table and to print the corresponding value of Y if it does.

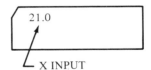

21.0 — X INPUT

Part A:

Write a series of statements that will read XINPUT from a data card and determine if it falls within the range of the table. If it does not, print the message "NOT IN THE RANGE OF THE TABLE."

```
C..........................................................
C::    PURPOSE - PROGRAM SEGMENT TO SEE IF A VALUE LIES   ::
C::            WITHIN THE RANGE OF A TABLE                 ::
C..........................................................
C
      READ(5,10)XINPUT
   10 FORMAT(F8.2)
C
C         IS VALUE TOO LOW
C
      IF(XINPUT.LT.X(1)) WRITE(2,20)
   20 FORMAT(10X,21HNOT IN RANGE OF TABLE)
C
C         IS VALUE TOO HIGH
C
      IF(XINPUT.GT.X(64))WRITE(2,20)
C
      STOP
      END
```

Part B:

Assuming XINPUT falls in the range of the table, it is now necessary to search for it. One method is to start at X(1) and move down the table sequentially. If XINPUT is 21.0 (a value way at the end of the table), this will be a long search. A better method (the half interval search) starts by determining if XINPUT lies in the upper or lower half of the table. This immediately eliminates 32 elements of the table. Write statements that do this.

```
C          IS VALUE IN FIRST HALF OF TABLE?
           IF(XINPUT.LT.X(32))WRITE (2,24)
  24            FORMAT(10X,24HPOINT LIES IN FIRST HALF)
C
C          IS VALUE IN SECOND HALF OF TABLE?
           IF(XINPUT.GE.X(32)) WRITE(2,25)
  25            FORMAT(10X,25HPOINT LIES IN SECOND HALF)
```

Part C:

The technique continues by dividing each surviving interval into two parts. The convergence is very rapid. The table below shows how many elements remain in the interval after each pass. The maximum number of passes is 6.

Write a complete program that will keep dividing the table into smaller and smaller "halves" until the value is located. The variables START, END, and MIDDLE will be used to define the interval that remains to be divided in half on the next pass of the logic.

PASS 1	REMAINING INTERVAL SIZE	32
2		16
3		8
4		4
5		2
6		1

```
C...............................................................
C..   PURPOSE - DEMONSTRATE BASIC TECHNIQUE OF HALF           ..
C..            INTERVAL SEARCH                                 ..
C...............................................................
C
C               -----IMPORTANT VARIABLES-----
C
C   --START    SUBSCRIPT OF FIRST ELEMENT OF REMAINING HALF
C   --END      SUBSCRIPT OF LAST ELEMENT OF REMAINING HALF--
C   --MIDDLE   SUBSCRIPT OF MIDDLE ELEMENT OF REMAINING   --
C
      DIMENSION X(64)
      INTEGER START, END
C
      READ(5,75) (X(I),I=1,64)
   75 FORMAT(10F8.2)
C
      READ(5,50) XINPUT
   50 FORMAT(F12.2)
C
C               ESTABLISH INITIAL LIMITS OF TABLE
      START = 1
      END = 64
      MIDDLE = 32
C
C               VALUE SHOULD BE FOUND IN 6 PASSES
C
      DO 100 I = 1,6
C
      IF(XINPUT.LT.X(MIDDLE)) THEN
C               VALUE IN FIRST HALF OF TABLE
C               ADJUST SEARCH PARAMETERS ACCORDINGLY
C
          END = MIDDLE
C
      ELSE
C               VALUE IN SECOND HALF OF TABLE
C
          START = MIDDLE
C
      ENDIF
C               REDEFINE MIDDLE OF TABLE
C
          MIDDLE = START + (END-START)/2
C
C               VALUE FOUND YET
C
      IF(XINPUT.EQ.X(START)) GO TO 140
C
  100 CONTINUE
C
  140 WRITE(2,150)X(START),START
  150 FORMAT(1X,F8.2,10X,I2)
```

Caution: This program represents an extremely simplified version of a complex algorithm. The program uses a convenient number of tabular values to show how the algorithm works. A program that accommodates a *variable* number of tabular values would be considerably more difficult to write.

11 Further Information on DO Loops

Introduction: DO Loops and Control Statements

Thus far, DO loops have been described in a more or less isolated way, that is, standing by themselves. Now they will be studied with respect to other control statements. It is important that these *other control statements* not subvert or disrupt the loop control function assigned to a DO statement. Possible conflicts can be avoided if you will keep the following in mind:

(1) Whenever a DO statement is executed, the index and loop counter associated with the DO are set at their initial value.
(2) Whenever the last statement of a DO is executed, the index and loop counter are advanced (incremented).

Proper loop control is in reality a matter of properly controlling the index and the loop counter. As you can see from (1) and (2) above, responsibility for this actually lies in the proper execution of the first and last statements of a DO loop.

The DO Statement

The DO statement should be used for but one purpose only: to enter a DO loop. Whenever control is passed to this statement (either from statement above, below or *inside* the DO loop), the assumption is that you want to *initiate* looping. The index and loop counter are then assigned their appropriate *initial* value.

The Last Statement

The last statement is used for one purpose only: to signal that the present iteration of the loop is completed and that the index and trip counter* should be incremented appropriately.

---

*In some compilers, only the index is used to control the DO loop. That is, no trip counter is used. For these compilers, the execution of the last statement causes both the incrementing and *testing* of the index. For compilers using a trip counter, testing is done at the top of the DO.

Very shortly you will be writing relatively complex programs that may involve one or more DO loops. Your program will also include IF statements and GO TO statements. When writing these latter control statements, the IF's and the GO TO's, make sure they do not conflict with the loop control you have established by your DO statements. The following rules are a way of assuring that these control statements do not interfere with the proper indexing of a DO loop.

11.2 | Rule 1

Control may not be passed from statements outside the range of a DO to statements inside the range of the DO. A DO loop must be entered through the DO STATEMENT ONLY.

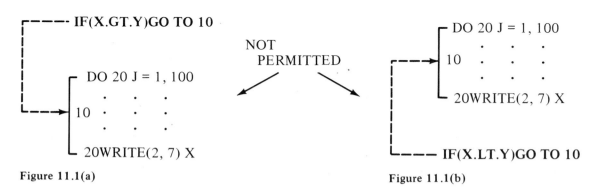

Figure 11.1(a)   Figure 11.1(b)

Transfer of control as shown in Figure 11.1(a) and (b) avoids the DO statement. This means that the computer is in the middle of a DO loop and the INDEX, its initial value, its test value, etc., have not been defined. Statement 20 has not been declared as the last statement in the range of the DO. Without this information, the DO loop cannot function properly.

11.3 | Rule 2

Control may be passed from statements inside the range of the DO to statements outside the range of the DO.

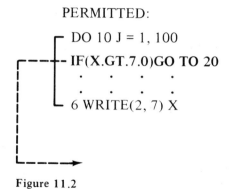

Figure 11.2

Control can be passed from statements inside the DO to statements outside the DO by what is called a **premature exit**. Very often it is necessary to know during which pass (iteration) of the loop exit took place. For this reason, the value of the INDEX at the time of exit is retained in memory and is available to the programmer. This feature was used in the stock problem in Chapter 10 when we set up a DO loop to search an array of stock names to find where a particular stock was listed. As soon as a match was found, the DO loop was exited and the value of the INDEX told us where the stock was located in the data base.

After a normal completion of a DO loop, however, the value of the INDEX usually will be one greater than the test value.

11.4 | Rule 3

Control may be passed from statements inside the DO to other statements inside the DO loop, but all branches thus formed must ultimately reach the last statement in the range of the DO.

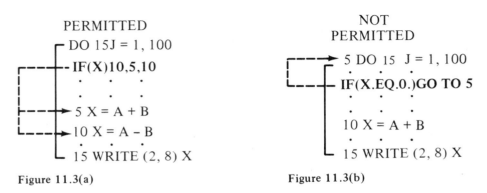

Figure 11.3(a)   Figure 11.3(b)

Once inside a DO loop, the intent is to execute a series of statements that need not be a *fixed* series. Control statements may be used inside the loop to allow branching. Proper indexing can be achieved only if each branch ultimately reaches the last statement in the range of the DO. Execution of this statement triggers the incrementing of the INDEX and the TRIP COUNTER.

Look at the IF statement in Figure 11.3(b). It will disrupt normal indexing. Each time a zero value of X is found (assume on the 15th execution), control will be passed to statement 5, the DO statement. This will cause the value of the index to reset itself back to its initial value of 1, and the value of the trip counter will be reset. This probably is not desired. Control should have been passed to the bottom of the DO loop. This would cause the advancing of J (not a reset).

11.5 | Rule 4

The fourth rule to remember is that the last statement in the range of a DO may not be a control statement. Use the CONTINUE statement instead. The last statement in the range of a DO can be a READ or WRITE statement, and it can be an arithmetic statement. **It should not be a control statement.** The last statement

NOT
PERMITTED

DO 10 J = 1, 100
. . . .

. . . .
5 WRITE(2,8) X
. . . .

. . . .
10 IF(X.LT.0.)GO TO 5

Figure 11.4(a)

PERMITTED
DO 10 J = 1, 100
. . . .

. . . .

. . . .

. . . .

. . . .
10 CONTINUE

Figure 11.4(b)

already has an implied control function:

 (a) increment the index, and
 (b) increment the trip counter.

Here are some illegal last statements:

 IF(X.GT.8.0) GO TO 9
 IF(A.LT.B) STOP
 GO TO (8,18,7,6,14),M

These statements set up a contradictory set of control instructions that interfere with the functioning of the DO loop.

 To avoid the possibility of conflicting instructions, the last statement in the range of a DO loop must *not* be a control statement. This restriction can be easily circumvented by always using the CONTINUE statement as the last statement.

11.6 | CONTINUE Statement

The CONTINUE statement is specifically designed to serve as the last statement in the range of a DO loop when the use of any other statement (a control statement) would violate Rule 4. The CONTINUE statement is a null statement. It does not cause any computation to be performed; it does not itself cause transfer of control. Its basic function is to assure (protect) the proper behavior of the index. It has the added advantage of clearly defining the bottom of the DO.

11.7 | Rule 5

Older compilers do not use a trip counter to control iteration but instead use the value of the index to determine whether or not looping should continue. For these compilers a special restriction must be imposed: **The programmer may not redefine or alter in any way the index or any of its parameters once inside the DO loop.** This is Rule 5.

 Compilers that conform to the FORTRAN '77 standards use a trip counter for loop control, and Rule 5 shown in Figure 11.5 does not apply. Statements inside the loop can, for example, redefine the index or the test value. These changes will not affect, however, the number of times the loop is iterated (the trip count). That value is determined when the DO loop is entered, and, once the DO statement is passed, it is under the control of the system software, not the programmer.

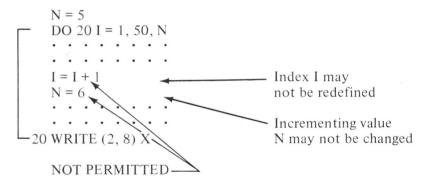

Figure 11.5

11.8 | Rule 6

The nesting of one DO loop inside another is permitted. Overlapping DO loops is not allowed.

DO loops may be nested. That is, one loop may lie inside another (as is the case in Figure 11.6(a)). Several loops may terminate on the same statement (as shown in Figure 11.6(b)). What is not allowed is *overlapping*. The inner DO loop of Figure 11.6(c) does not lie wholly inside the range of the outer DO loop. The loops overlap one another. This configuration is not allowed.

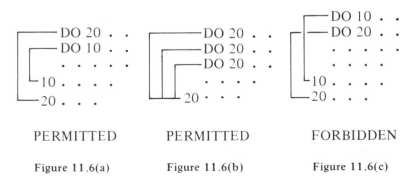

PERMITTED

Figure 11.6(a)

PERMITTED

Figure 11.6(b)

FORBIDDEN

Figure 11.6(c)

11.9 | Behavior of the Index in Nested DO's

Consider the nest of DO's shown in Figure 11.7. When the first DO statement is executed, the value of I is set equal to 1. Executing the second DO statement sets the value of J equal to 1, and the program continues until statement 10 is reached. This completes the first execution of all statements in the range of the *inner* DO. When statement 10 is reached, J is indexed to value 2 and control

Figure 11.7 Nest of DO's

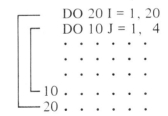

For each indexing of the outer DO, the inner DO will index from its initial to its test value.

passes to the top of the inner DO. Execution of statements inside the inner DO continues (four iterations) until J reaches its test value. Control is then allowed to pass statement 10, reaching statement 20 for the first time. Since this is the last statement of the *outer* DO, the index I is advanced to 2. The trip counter of the outer DO will be incremented. Control then passes to the top of the outer DO. Because this is a DO statement, its index J is reset to 1 and the inner loop counter is set to its initial value.

Looping continues until the inner DO is once again satisfied. Control passes statement 10 reaching statement 20. I changes from 2 to 3, and the outer trip counter is updated. Notice that the index of the inner DO is changing rapidly, while the index of the outer DO changes slowly.

The same sequence of indexing takes place for the "Nest of DO's" shown in Figure 11.8. When several DO loops end on the same statement, control is passed back to the top of the innermost uncompleted DO loop. Many programmers prefer to avoid using a single CONTINUE statement to terminate multiple DO loops. Instead, each loop is given its own CONTINUE statement to avoid any possible confusion.

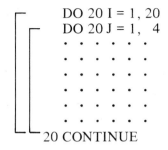

Figure 11.8 Similar Nest of DO's

| **Programming Example** Different Combinations |

Write a program to determine if any integer values of X, Y and Z satisfy the equation:

$$X^2 - 2Y^2 + 3Z = 0$$

between the limits:

$$X = 1 \text{ to } 10$$
$$Y = 1 \text{ to } 10$$
$$Z = 1 \text{ to } 10$$

This program requires one thousand ($10 \times 10 \times 10$) combinations of X, Y and Z to be tested. The nest of three DO loops will cycle X, Y and Z through the appropriate values. For each combination, the equation is evaluated and tested to see if its value is near zero (less than 0.1).

The real purpose of this example is to demonstrate how each index of the nested DO's behaves.

```
C.....................SEARCH FOR VALUES OF X, Y, AND Z THAT
C..     PURPOSE - SEARCH FOR VALUES OF X, Y, AND Z THAT
C..               SATISFY A GIVEN EQUATION (ARE ROOTS)
C.....................................................
C
C       DO 30 I = 1, 10, 1
C
C           DO 20 J = 1, 10, 1
C
C               DO 10 K = 1, 10, 1
                    X = I
                    Y = J
                    Z = K
C
                    VALUE = X**2 -2.0*Y**2 +3.0*Z
                    IF(ABS(VALUE).LE.0.1) GO TO 50
C
   10               CONTINUE
   20           CONTINUE
   30   CONTINUE
C
```

```
C
C                              NO ROOT FOUND
      WRITE(2,40)
   40 FORMAT(8X,@SEARCH COMPLETE, NO ROOT FOUND@)
C
      STOP
C
C                              SOLUTION FOUND
C
   50 WRITE(2,51) X, Y, Z
   51 FORMAT(8X,3HX= ,F9.1,3X,3HY= ,F9.1,3X,3HZ= ,F9.1)
C
      STOP
      END
```

The way these loops are written, subscript K cycles the fastest, the next fastest is J, while the subscript I cycles the slowest. On the first 10 iterations:

> I=1
> J=1
> K=1 to 10

On the next 10 iterations:

> I=1
> J=2
> K=1 to 10

Programming Example
Quality Control
(Sampling)

Transistors are purchased in case lots. A purchase of 100 cases is made. To assure reasonable uniformity of these parts, five transistors are selected at random from each case and inspected by a quality control engineer. The diameter, height, resistance, and so on, are measured and recorded on punched cards. This forms a data deck as shown in Figure 11.9.

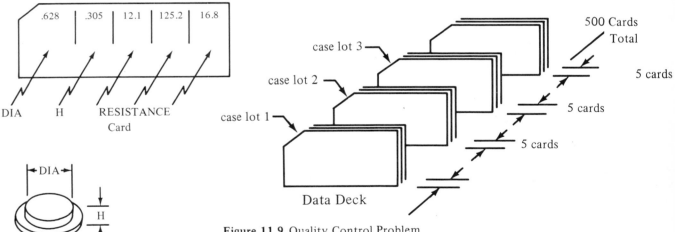

Figure 11.9 Quality Control Problem

The first five cards represent the tests performed on the five transistors selected from the first case lot. The next five cards represent the tests performed on the second case lot, and so on, for a total of 500 cards (representing 100 cases).

Write a program to determine the largest diameter transistor in each case lot of a 100–lot shipment.

This problem involves two DO loops, one (an inner DO loop) to control the reading of 5 cards representing each case lot and another loop (outer loop) to process all 100 cases. A test must be made inside the inner loop:

IF(DIA.GT.DIAMAX)

is also involved and must not interfere with proper loop control.

The purpose of this test is to transfer control to a pair of redefining statements each time a larger diameter transistor is processed. It is important that this transfer of control does not interfere or conflict with the operation of either the inner or outer loop control.

Output should appear as follows:

CASE 1 MAXIMUM DIAMETER IS 5.29 SAMPLE 3
CASE 2 MAXIMUM DIAMETER IS 5.31 SAMPLE 5
CASE 3 MAXIMUM DIAMETER IS 5.26 SAMPLE 2
CASE 4 MAXIMUM DIAMETER IS 5.33 SAMPLE 2

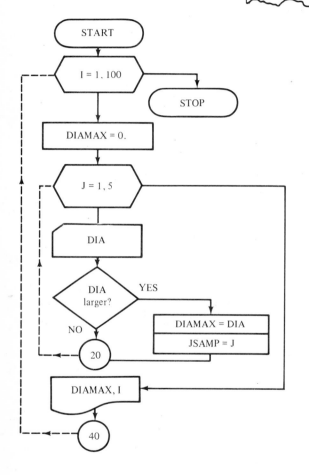

```
C ***** PURPOSE - SAMPLE FIVE TRANSISTORS FROM EACH   **
C **            CASE OF A 100 CASE SHIPMENT, REPORT.   **
C **            LARGEST TRANSISTOR IN EACH LOT.        **
C ************************************************************
C
C          -----IMPORTANT VARIABLES-----
C
C     --DIA       INDIVIDUAL TRANSISTOR DIAMETER    --
C     --DIAMAX    LARGEST DIAMETER WITHIN THE CASE  --
C     --I         INDEX FOR OUTER DO (WHICH CASE)   --
C     --J         INDEX FOR INNER DO (WHICH SAMPLE) --
C     --JSAMPL    WHICH SAMPLE IS THE LARGEST       --
C
      DO 40 I = 1, 100
C
          DIAMAX = 0.0
C
          DO 20 J = 1, 5
C
              READ(5,10) DIA
   10         FORMAT(F8.2)
C
              IF(DIA.GT.DIAMAX) THEN
C
                  DIAMAX = DIA
                  JSAMPL = J
C
              ENDIF
   20     CONTINUE
C
C              INNER LOOP COMPLETED
C
          WRITE(2,30) I, DIAMAX, JSAMPL
   30     FORMAT(3X,@CASE@,I4,3X,@MAXIMUM DIAMETER IS@
     +          ,F8.2,3X,@SAMPLE@,I3)
C
   40 CONTINUE
C
      STOP
      END
```

The index I identifies the lot being examined, the index J identifies the individual transistor within a given lot.

The outer DO will be executed 100 times, causing 100 executions of the WRITE statement. For each execution of the outer DO, the inner DO statements will be executed five times. These five executions read all the data cards of a given case lot and determine the largest diameter transistor of that lot.

11.10 Nested DO's and Two-Dimensional Arrays

When processing the information contained in a two-dimensional array, individual elements are addressed in one of two possible sequences:

1. *Row Order* — elements in row 1 are processed first, followed by the elements in row 2, followed by the elements in row 3, etc.
2. *Column Order* — elements in column 1 are processed first, followed by the elements in column 2, followed by the elements in column 3, etc.

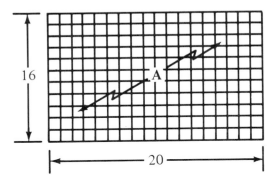

Figure 11.10 Typical Two-Dimensional Array

Subscript control for these activities is sometimes provided by nested DO statements.

Consider the array A shown in Figure 11.10. Assume we wish to find the sum of all these elements and a decision is made to process the array in row order (Figure 11.11a).

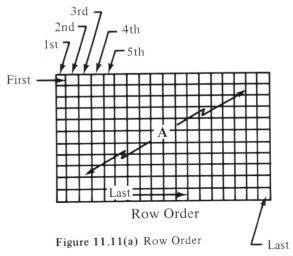

Row Order

Figure 11.11(a) Row Order

All the elements in row 1 will be processed, followed by all the elements in row 2 and so on until all rows are processed.
The following approach should be used.

Step 1: Process 1st row
Set up a DO loop to process all the elements in row 1 of the array only.

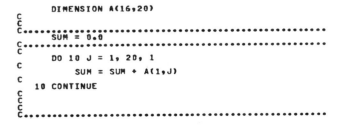

The sequence of variable names generated inside the loop is:

A(1,1), A(1,2), A(1,3), A(1,4). . .A(1,19), A(1,20)

The first subscript defines which row is being processed. Its value stays at one while the second subscript cycles through all the elements in that row.

Step 2: Process all rows

Now set up another DO loop, an outer loop, that repeats this "row processing" activity. . .process all 16 rows.

```
      SUM = 0.0
C.......................................................
C
      DO 20 I = 1, 16, 1
C
          DO 10 J = 1, 20, 1
C
              SUM = SUM + A(I,J)
C
   10     CONTINUE
C
   20 CONTINUE
```

There is one change to the statement inside the inner DO. The index I has been substituted for the constant 1 in the first subscript position. For the first 20 executions of this statement, I has the value 1, and the sequence of names is the same as in step 1. When statement 20 is reached, I advances to 2 (row 2 is to be processed next). J is set back to 1 and starts to cycle again. The elements of A are being accumulated in the sequence intended.

An Alternate Form of Processing: Column Order

There are times when the programmer has no choice as to what sequence in which to process an array. Assume, for example, you are told that the array A is punched on data cards, one value per card in *column* order.

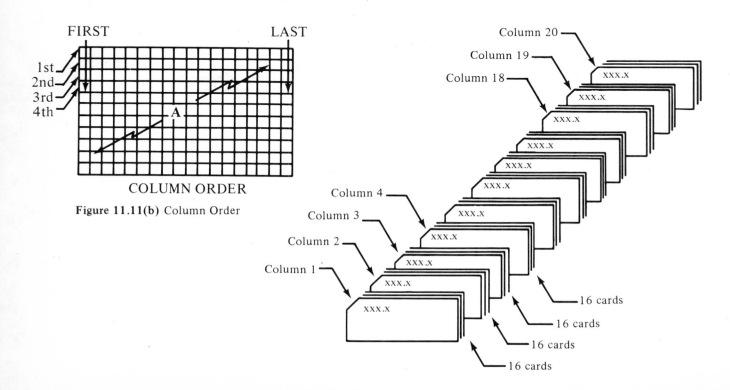

Figure 11.11(b) Column Order

All elements in column 1 of the array must be read first, followed by all the elements in column 2, and so on. As before, you are advised to handle the subscript control problem in steps. In this instance, we would first concentrate on setting up statements that read in column 1 of the array:

```
C
C..........................................................
      SUM = 0.0
C..........................................................
C
      DO 20 J = 1, 16, 1
C
          READ(5,10) A(J,1)
   10     FORMAT(F9.1)
C
          SUM = SUM + A(J,1)
C
   20 CONTINUE
C
```

The sequence of names being generated is:

A(1,1), A(2,1), A(3,1), A(4.1). . . . . .A(15,1), A(16,1)

Since the second subscript defines the column location, it should hold at 1 while the first subscript runs through the number of elements in a column (16 elements). Having this portion of the problem out of the way, an outer loop is set up to repeat this process for the remaining columns (20 in all). The constant 1 will be replaced by the index of this new loop as shown below.

```
      DIMENSION A(16,20)
C..........................................................
      SUM = 0.0
C..........................................................
C
      DO 30 J = 1, 20, 1
C
          DO 20 I = 1, 16, 1
C
              READ(5,10) A(I,J)
   10         FORMAT(F9.1)
              SUM = SUM + A(I,J)
C
   20     CONTINUE
C
   30 CONTINUE
```

Both DO loops could terminate on the same statement. The program has been written with two CONTINUE statements to avoid confusion.

Whenever you are dealing with double subscripts, go at things slowly. Determine if the data must be processed in row order or column order. Set up a statement that handles the first row or the first column only. Do not try to handle the total array all at once.

When these foundation statements are complete, *generalize them* by setting up an outer DO that processes *all* rows and *all* columns. This usually involves substituting the index of the outer DO where a constant was used before.

Obviously, punching one value per card is not very efficient. We will address the techniques of reading and printing data that is packed in what is called "high density" mode shortly.

11.11 | Review Questions

Each exercise that follows shows the way in which two or more DO loops are nested. Consider a transfer of control within these loops, and determine if any of these transfers violates the rules presented in this chapter.

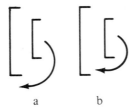

a   b

Example (a) shows a transfer of control from inside the inner DO, to statements outside the outer DO, which is allowed. The index of both the inner and outer DO will be retained in memory, as this is not a normal exit for both loops. Transfer of control as shown in example (b) is allowed.

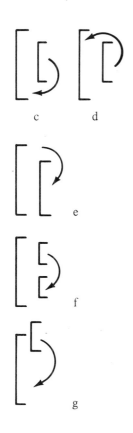

Transfer of control in examples (c) and (d) is allowed. With respect to the inner DO, control is being passed from inside the DO to statements outside the DO. This is allowed. With respect to the outer DO, control is being passed from statements inside the DO to other statements inside the DO. This is also allowed.

This example is *not* allowed on the basis that with respect to the inner DO, control is being passed from statements outside the loop to statements inside the loop. The DO statement of the inner loop is therefore not executed. This is not allowed.

This example is also not allowed. The second inner DO loop is entered improperly.

The overlapping of DO loops as shown is not allowed. The range of the inner DO must lie *wholly* within the range of the outer DO.

11.12 Input/Output of Large Arrays

When reading one-dimensional arrays, several methods of subscript control may be used. When the number of elements in the array is relatively small and when these elements are punched one per card, the READ statement in the Method 1 section of Figure 11.12 can be used. In this method the index of a DO loop provides the subscript.

If the number of elements in the array increases, we are more or less forced to pack as many elements as possible on each card and the READ statement of Method 2 is necessary. It has a self-contained index and allows the single command READ to be followed by a list of variable names that includes the names of the whole array.

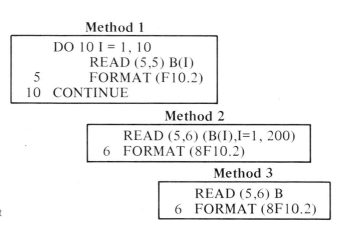

Figure 11.12 Forms of READ Statement

The Method 3 input statement has not been discussed before. It demonstrates an instance when the name of an array may appear without a subscript. When this form is used, it is understood that the *whole* array is being referenced. The compiler examines the DIMENSION statement, finds the size of the array, and sets up a mechanism to transfer all elements automatically. Beginning programmers are usually more comfortable providing a subscript and subscript control themselves.

Two-Dimensional Arrays

Figure 11.13 shows a similar sequence of input statements for two-dimensional arrays. Assume the data is presented in column order and we are again dealing with the array discussed in Section 11.11: $A(16,20)$.

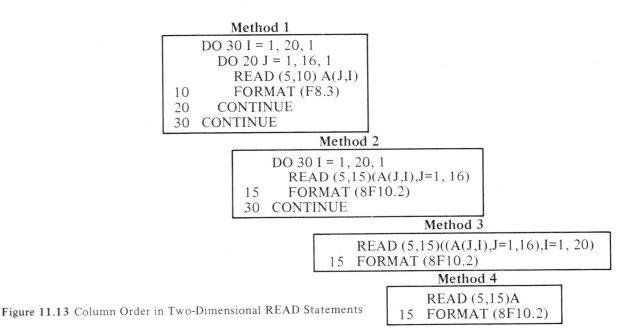

Method 1
```
         DO 30 I = 1, 20, 1
            DO 20 J = 1, 16, 1
               READ (5,10) A(J,I)
10             FORMAT (F8.3)
20          CONTINUE
30       CONTINUE
```

Method 2
```
         DO 30 I = 1, 20, 1
            READ (5,15)(A(J,I),J=1, 16)
15          FORMAT (8F10.2)
30       CONTINUE
```

Method 3
```
         READ (5,15)((A(J,I),J=1,16),I=1, 20)
15       FORMAT (8F10.2)
```

Method 4
```
         READ (5,15)A
15       FORMAT (8F10.2)
```

Figure 11.13 Column Order in Two-Dimensional READ Statements

Each method generates 320 names needed to process the whole array, but one method does it best.

Method 1 is not very realistic. Since there is only one name following the command READ, 320 data cards would be required. Method 2 is a little more efficient in that each execution of the command READ brings in one column of the matrix. There is an even more efficient READ statement, however. Method 3 is the preferred method. It executes a single command READ followed by all 320 names. The subscript J cycles between 1 and 16. The subscript I cycles between 1 and 20 (it is like a DO loop inside a DO loop). The index J is obviously the inner index (it cycles fast). The index I is the outer index (it cycles slowly). Take a minute to make sure you understand this. It is important.

Now let's turn things around. Assume the data is in row order. What should the READ statement look like?

```
READ(5,8)((A(J,I),I=1,20),J=1,16)
READ(5,8)((A(M,N),N=1,20),M=1,16)
```

Any statement where the second subscript cycles fast and the first cycles slowly is basically correct.

The READ statement in Method 4 causes the transfer of the whole array automatically. The array is transferred in column order. Transferring arrays by using READ/WRITE statements that have self-contained subscript control features is given a special name. It is called **implicit transfer** or **implied DO transfer**. Figure 11.14 shows other examples of this type of statement.

INPUT/OUTPUT STATEMENTS	EQUIVALENT DO STATEMENTS	MEANING
READ(5, 8)((X(I, J), J=1, 12), I=1, 10)	DO 15 I = 1, 10 DO 15 J = 1, 12 15 READ (5,7) X(I, J)	READ two dimensional array [X] in ROW order: $a_{1,1}$ $a_{1,2}$ $a_{1,3}$ ... $a_{1,11}$ $a_{1,12}$ $a_{2,1}$ $a_{2,2}$
WRITE (2,6) (A(I), I = 2, K, 2)	DO 18 I = 2, K, 2 18 WRITE (2,8) A(I)	PRINT all elements of one dimensional array [A] whose subscripts are even numbers and do not exceed value K.
WRITE (2,8) (A(I), B(I), I = 1, 10)	DO 9 I = 1, 10 9 WRITE (2,7) A(I), B(I)	PRINT elements of one dimensional array [A] and [B] as follows: $A_1 B_1 A_2 B_2 A_3 B_3$ ...
WRITE(2,8) (A(I), I=1, 10), (B(I), I=1, 10)	DO 9 I = 1, 10 9 WRITE (2,7) A(I) DO 10 I=1, 10 10 WRITE (2,7) B(I)	PRINT elements of a one dimensional array [A] and [B] as follows: $A_1 A_2 A_3$ ... $A_9 A_{10} B_1 B_2 B_3$ ... B_{10}

Figure 11.14 Additional Examples of Implicit Transfer

QUIZ#12 DO Loops

Part 1: Answer the following questions:

1. What two statements are used to control the trip counter and INDEX of a DO?

2. If control is allowed to pass to the DO statement while looping is in process, how does this affect the looping activity?

3. Why is it that an IF statement should not be used as the last statement in the range of a DO?

4. What statement should be used as the last statement?

5. If a DO loop is exited prematurely (before index reaches its final value) is the value of the index at the time of exit saved?

6. If branching takes place inside a DO loop, where should all paths ultimately pass control to?

7. Describe a nested DO.

8. If two DO loops are nested, the index of which DO changes faster?

9. Write statements to READ a two-dimensional array called A having 20 rows and 15 columns:

   (a) In row order

   (b) In column order

10. May more than one DO loop terminate on the same CONTINUE statement?

Part 2: Write a Program.

11.

	1	2	3	4	5	6	7	8	9
1	1	2	3	4	5	6	7	8	9
2	2	4	6	8	10	12	14	16	
3	3	6	9	12	15	18			
4	4	8	12	16	20				
5	5	10	15	20					45
6	6	12	18	24				48	54
7	7	14	21				49	56	63
8	8	16				48	56	64	72
9	9	18			45	54	63	72	81

A two-dimensional array called VALUES has 9 rows and 9 columns. Elements of the array value will be used to help children learn their multiplication tables.

Write a program to define all elements of VALUES (do not use read statement). Print the array in its natural order (ROW order).

Answers:

1. The first and last statement.

2. It is assumed that looping should be started all over again. The index is assigned its *initial* value.

3. The last statement already has a control assignment.

4. CONTINUE.

5. Yes.

6. The last statement (for proper indexing).

7. When the statements of one DO loop lie wholly inside the range of another DO.

8. The inner DO.

9. READ(5,10)((A(I,J),J=1,15),I=1,20)
   READ(5,10)((A(I,J),I=1,20),J=1,15)

10. Yes, but it is not considered good "style."

11.
```
C . . . . . . . . . . . . . . . . . . . . . . . . . . . . . . . . . . . . .
C       PURPOSE – GENERATE MULTIPLICATION TABLES . .
C . . . . . . . . . . . . . . . . . . . . . . . . . . . . . . . . . . . .
C                    – IMPORTANT VARIABLES –
C
C       –VALUES   TWO-DIMENSIONAL ARRAY (TABLE)
C       –IROW     INTEGER TELLING WHAT ROW
C       –ICOL     INTEGER TELLING WHAT COLUMN
C
        DIMENSION VALUES (9,9)
C
C       GENERATE FIRST ROW OF ARRAY
C                    (DEMONSTRATION ONLY)
        DO 10 ICOL=1,9
  10       VALUE(1,ICOL)=ICOL
        CONTINUE
C
C       GENERATE WHOLE ARRAY
C
        DO 40 IROW=1,9
C
            DO 30 ICOL=1,9
C
C                    VALUE(IROW,ICOL)=IROW*ICOL
  30    CONTINUE
C
  40    CONTINUE
C
        WRITE(2,50)((VALUE(IROW,ICOL),ICOL=1,9),IROW=1,9)
  50    FORMAT(1X,9F72.0)
C
        STOP
        END
```

Programming Example
Data Screening

In this problem we want to determine which elements of an array fall within a specified range and which do not. This process is called a **data screen**.

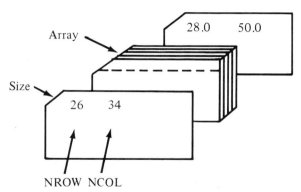

$$
\begin{matrix}
& & \text{Data} & \\
6.2 & 7.5 & 8.3 & 11.4 \\
14.3 & 6.2 & 18.4 & 7.6 \\
10.2 & 13.4 & -4.1 & 9.9 \\
3.6 & 4.7 & 8.9 & 12.1 \\
21.2 & 9.9 & 11.6 & 5.8
\end{matrix}
\qquad
\begin{matrix}
& & \text{Out} & \\
0.0 & 7.5 & 8.3 & 0.0 \\
0.0 & 0.0 & 0.0 & 7.6 \\
10.2 & 0.0 & 0.0 & 9.9 \\
0.0 & 0.0 & 8.9 & 0.0 \\
0.0 & 9.9 & 0.0 & 0.0
\end{matrix}
$$

The first card in a data deck gives two integer numbers telling the size of a two-dimensional array of real numbers to be called DATA. The first integer tells the number of rows. The second number tells the number of columns. The next sequence of data cards gives elements of the array DATA in row order, ten values per card (10F8.2). The maximum number of rows is 40. The maximum number of columns is 60.

Write statements that will read these cards and define the array DATA in memory.

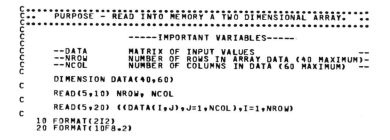

```
C...................................................................
C...  PURPOSE - READ INTO MEMORY A TWO DIMENSIONAL ARRAY.  ...
C...................................................................
C
C                    -----IMPORTANT VARIABLES-----
C
C          --DATA        MATRIX OF INPUT VALUES              --
C          --NROW        NUMBER OF ROWS IN ARRAY DATA (40 MAXIMUM)-
C          --NCOL        NUMBER OF COLUMNS IN DATA (60 MAXIMUM)  --
C
      DIMENSION DATA(40,60)
C
      READ(5,10) NROW, NCOL
C
      READ(5,20) ((DATA(I,J),J=1,NCOL),I=1,NROW)
C
   10 FORMAT(2I2)
   20 FORMAT(10F8.2)
```

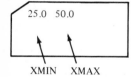

The DIMENSION statement declares DATA as a two-dimensional array of maximum size 40 rows, 60 columns. This size information must be given as integer constants! The READ statement finds out how large the array is for this run of the program.

The next READ statement brings in the whole array. Row order requires the second subscript to change fast and the first to change slowly. The test value for each index is the value read from the leader card.

Next, we are interested in knowing which elements of DATA fall between two limits (between 25.0 and 50.0, for example.) These limits are expressed on the last card in the data deck and are stored as XMIN and XMAX.

Write statements that will print all elements in row *one* of the matrix that fall within the specified (permitted) range (between XMIN and XMAX.)

```
C
C                      ......DETERMINE SIZE OF SCREEN......
C
      READ(5,20) XMIN, XMAX
   20 FORMAT(2F8.2)
C
C
C                      .....SEARCH ROW 1 OF THE INPUT DATA......
C
      DO 40 I = 1, NCOL
C
          IF(DATA(1,J).GE.XMIN.AND.DATA(1,J).LE.XMAX) THEN
C                          THIS VALUE IN PROPER RANGE
C                          WRITE(2,30) DATA(1,J)
   30                      FORMAT(F8.2)
C
          ENDIF
C
   40 CONTINUE
```

Last, write a complete program that examines each element of the array called DATA. Generate an array called OUT whose size is identical to DATA representing screened values. Elements of OUT are to be equal to elements of DATA except for those outside the specified limits. Set these elements of OUT equal to zero. Display OUT in its natural form (row order.)

```
C...................................................................
C..  PURPOSE - SCREEN AN ARRAY OF SIZE NROW BY NCOL AND         ..
C..            ELIMINATE (SET TO ZERO) ALL ELEMENTS THAT        ..
C..            FALL OUTSIDE A SPECIFIED RANGE (XMIN,XMAX)        ..
C...................................................................
C
C                      -----IMPORTANT VARIABLES-----
C
C     --DATA       MATRIX OF INPUT VALUES                       --
C     --OUT        MATRIX OF SCREENED VALUES                    --
C     --NROW       NUMBER OF ROWS IN BOTH ARRAYS                --
C     --NCOL       NUMBER OF COLUMNS IN BOTH ARRAYS             --
C     --XMIN       LOWER SCREEN VALUE                           --
C     --XMAX       UPPER SCREEN VALUE                           --
C
      DIMENSION DATA(40,60) , OUT(40,60)
C
C                      READ SIZE OF ARRAYS
C
      READ(5,10) NROW, NCOL
   10 FORMAT(2I2)
C
C                      .....ESTABLISH INPUT ARRAY........
C
      READ(5,20) ((DATA(I,J),J=1,NCOL),I=1,NROW)
   20 FORMAT(10F8.2)
C
C                      PICK UP SCREEN SIZE
C
      READ(5,20) XMIN, XMAX
C
      DO 30 I = 1, NROW
C
          DO 30 J = 1, NCOL
C
              IF(DATA(I,J).GE.XMIN.AND.DATA(I,J).LE.XMAX) THEN
C                          THIS VALUE WITHIN LIMITS
C                  OUT(I,J) = DATA(I,J)
C
              ELSE
C                          THIS VALUE OUTSIDE LIMITS
C                  OUT(I,J) = 0.0
C
              ENDIF
C
   30 CONTINUE
C
C                      ......DISPLAY SCREENED ARRAY......
C
      DO 50 I = 1, NROW
C
          WRITE(2,40) (OUT(I,J),J=1,NCOL)
   40     FORMAT(10F13.2)
C
   50 CONTINUE
C
      STOP
      END
```

Review Exercises

1.*What is meant by a *premature exit* of a DO loop? What value will the index have if any?

2. Once inside a DO loop, is there any way of increasing the number of iterations (trips) required to satisfy the DO?

3. When reading an array in column order, which subscript should cycle faster, the first or second subscript?

$$A(I, J)$$

with I labeled "First" and J labeled "Second"

4.*When reading a large two-dimensional array, is it necessary to provide subscript control (by an implied index for example)? If the answer is no, in what sequence will the array be read?

5. When addressing a specific element of an array, the subscript defining the desired element can be a constant, a variable or an expression. Is the same freedom allowed in specifying the size of an array in a DIMENSION statement?

6. In a modern compiler testing is accomplished at the top of a DO. With this in mind will the statements inside the following DO be executed if the value of N is 8?

$$DO \; 20 \; I = N, \; 6, \; 2$$

$$20 \quad CONTINUE$$

7.*In older compilers (those that do not use a trip counter), testing is made on the value of the index, but more importantly, testing is accomplished only when the *last* statement of the DO is reached. Based on this information, will the statements inside the loop shown in problem 6 be executed?

8. Providing a sequence of variable names following a command READ that matches the sequence in which data has been punched on cards is frequently a difficult task. Describe a procedure that will make this task less difficult, especially when dealing with two-dimensional arrays.

9. One of the common difficulties when dealing with nested DO loops is to get caught in an "endless" DO loop. An endless DO loop is one that for some reason is never satisfied. Give an example of such a situation.

10.*If a programmer inadvertently writes a program with an endless DO, does that mean the program executes indefinitely?

11. A two-dimensional array called A has 6 rows and 6 columns. Elements of A are punched on data cards one to a card. Write a program that uses a nest of DO statements (DO within a DO) to repeatedly execute the statement:

$$READ \; (5,7) \; A(I,J)$$

for the purpose of storing the array A. Elements of A appear on data cards in *row* order.

12. Repeat problem 11 except with the elements of array A appearing on the data cards in *column* order.

13. Repeat problem 11 except with the size of array A not being known in advance. A lead data card lists two integer numbers that specify the row and column size. These integers do not exceed 20.

14. For the array A described in problem 11, determine the sum of the elements appearing on the main diagonal (see the accompanying figure).

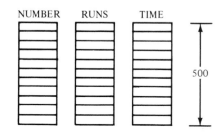

15.*For the array A described in problem 11, determine the sum of the interior elements of this array (see accompanying figure).

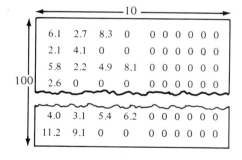

16. 500 students are using the same computer to run their programs. Each student is given an account number forming the array NUMBER. A student is allowed no more than 30 runs a week and no more than 100 minutes of CPU time. The arrays RUNS and TIME record how many runs and how much time each student has used thus far.

NUMBER	RUNS	TIME

500

Write an algorithm to read the account number of a student requesting to use the computer. Search the data base and determine if this student's program should be run.

17.*An array called DATA has 100 rows and 10 columns. Any row of DATA consists of a series of non-zero values, followed by a series of zero values.

|← 10 →|

6.1	2.7	8.3	0	0	0	0	0	0
2.1	4.1	0	0	0	0	0	0	0
5.8	2.2	4.9	8.1	0	0	0	0	0
2.6	0	0	0	0	0	0	0	0

| 4.0 | 3.1 | 5.4 | 6.2 | 0 | 0 | 0 | 0 | 0 |
| 11.2 | 9.1 | 0 | 0 | 0 | 0 | 0 | 0 | 0 |

100

Write a program to determine where the first zero value is located in each row.

18. A series of data cards represent values that are to be added to the array DATA of problem 17.

DATA

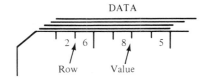

Each data card lists the value to be added and in what row it should go. Read each card and place the value on that card in the first "zero value" position of the row designated.

19. A two-dimensional array called TIME has 200 rows and 2 columns. Column 1 of this array represents the time a flight is scheduled to arrive at its destination. Column 2 represents the actual time it arrived at its destination.

TIME

16.42	16.44
8.29	8.28
10.59	11.06

200

12.00	12.16
4.10	4.31
8.49	9.03
1.15	1.09
2.36	2.36

Determine what percentage of the flights are more than 10 minutes late in arriving at their destinations.

20. To test if a person has extrasensory perception, a pair of dice is rolled 1000 times. The first two columns of array ROLL represent the number on each die for these rolls. Column 3 of the array ROLL represents the guess made by the subject being studied as to the total value of the two die. What percent of the time did the subject guess correctly?

ROLL

6	2	10
1	3	7
4	3	8
5	6	11

1000

5	6	2
2	5	8
1	4	9
3	5	7
5	1	6

21.*Make a table of values for $f(x)=e^x+X^2-12$ for X=0.0, 0.2, 0.4, 0.6, . . . continuing until f(x) becomes positive. How many values of X must be tried before f(x) becomes positive? Establish a DO loop to repeatedly evaluate f(x). Exit the DO when f(x) turns positive and report (as the only output) how many times the loop was iterated. If f(x) is still negative after 100 tries, so indicate and terminate the program.

22. A two-dimensional array called A has 10 rows and 20 columns. This array has been stored in memory. Write statements to determine if any element of array A is identically equal to zero. If any such element or elements are found, print as output their row and column position. If no zero element is found, print the message "ARRAY IS CLEAR."

23.*Write a program to determine all possible combinations of three integer values that multiplied together equal 30; i.e.,

$$2 \times 5 \times 3$$
$$1 \times 15 \times 2$$
$$1 \times 30 \times 1$$

24. A one-dimensional array called X and a one-dimensional array called Y each have 10 elements. Corresponding elements of these arrays represent the X and Y coordinates of a molecule (there are ten molecules). Write a program to form a two-dimensional array called DIST, each element of which represents the distance from one molecule to another; i.e., $DIST_{2,3}$ represents the distance between molecule 2 and molecule 3.

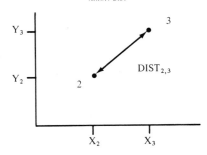

Test the program by assuming the coordinates of the ten molecules are:

$$X_1=1.0 \quad X_2=2.0 \quad X_3=3.0 \quad X_4=4.0 \ldots X_9=9.0 \quad X_{10}=10.0$$
$$Y_1=1.0 \quad Y_2=2.0 \quad Y_3=3.0 \quad Y_4=4.0 \ldots Y_9=9.0 \quad Y_{10}=10.0$$

Using this test data, print the array DIST in the usual rectangular pattern (10 rows of 10 elements each).

Inspect the output. The distance between molecules 2 and 3 should be equal to the square root of two and should be the same as the distance between molecules 3 and 2.

25.*After forming the array DIST in problem 24, write a program to compute the average distance between molecules (the average value of the elements in array DIST except those on the main diagonal).

26. Arrays A and C represent three simultaneous equations.

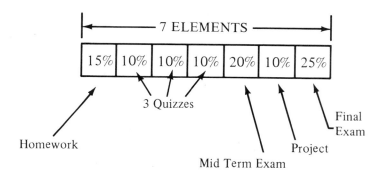

27. Write a program to modify the equations and therefore the arrays of problem 26. Each equation is to be divided by the coefficient of X_1 in that equation. This means that all terms in row 1 are to be divided by $A_{1,1}$. All terms in row 2 are to be divided by $A_{2,1}$. This will form arrays APRIM and CPRIM similar to A and C except that the first element in each row of APRIM will have the value 1.0. This would be the first step in solving these simultaneous equations.

Also (column context):

Write a program to determine if all the equations represented by these arrays are independent; i.e., one equation is not a constant multiple of another.

Additional Applications

Programming Example
Weighting Factors

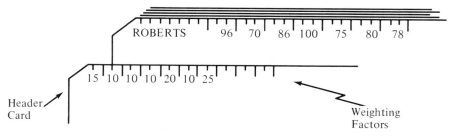

A one-dimensional array called FACTOR has 7 elements telling the relative importance of homework, quizzes and other items in computing a student's grade in a computer course. These values are punched on a header card.

The remaining cards in the deck give a student's name and the grades he or she achieved on each of the 7 items (the maximum score on each is 100).

Write a program to determine the student's final grade based on these weighting factors.

```
C.............................................................
C..    PURPOSE -   DETERMINE STUDENT GRADE BASED ON         ..
C..                CERTAIN WEIGHTING FACTORS.               ..
C.............................................................
C
C                      -----IMPORTANT VARIABLES-----
C
C      --FACTOR    ARRAY OF PERCENTILES                    --
C      --GRADE     ARRAY OF SCORES                         --
C      --NAME      STUDENT@S NAME                          --
C      --FINAL     STUDENT@S FIANL GRADE IN THE COURSE     --
C
C      DIMENSION FACTOR(7),GRADE(7)
C
C                   .... READ HEADER CARD ....
C
   10 READ(5,20)(FACTOR(I),I=1,7)
   20 FORMAT(7F2.0)
C
C                   .... PROCESSING LOOP STARTS HERE ....
C
      READ(2,30,END=100)NAME,(GRADE(I),I=1,7)
   30 FORMAT(A8,7F3.0)
C
      SUM=0.0
C
      DO 40 I=1,7
         SUM=SUM+GRADE(I)*FACTOR(I)/100.
   40 CONTINUE
C
      FINAL=SUM
C
      WRITE(2,50)NAME,FINAL
   50 FORMAT(1X,A8,10X,F8.1)
C
      GO TO 10
C
C
  100 STOP
      END
```

**Programming Example
Row Exchange**

When dealing with two-dimensional arrays, it is frequently necessary to exchange two rows in the array.

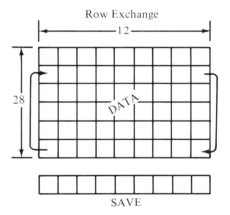

Part A:

Read an array called DATA whose size is 28 by 14. Elements of DATA are punched 8 per card in column order.

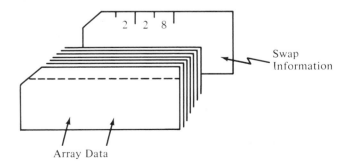

Part B:

Read a card at the end of the data deck defining which two rows are to be exchanged (for the card shown, row 2 and row 28). Accomplish this swap by first making a copy of one of these rows (row 2 for example) in a one-dimension array called SAVE. You may then move the other row involved in the transfer (row 28 for example) into its new position without losing any elements of the array DATA due to redefinition. Finally, use the vector SAVE to complete the exchange.

```
C................................................................
C..    PURPOSE -   PERFORM TYPICAL OPERATION ON A TWO           ..
C..                DIMENSIONAL ARRAY.                           ..
C................................................................
C
C                   -----IMPORTANT VARIABLES-----
C
C      --DATA       NAME OF DATA BASE
C      --N1,N2      NUMBER OF TWO ROWS INVOLVED IN SWAP          --
C      --SAVE       ONE-DIMENSIONAL ARRAY USED                   --
C                   FOR TEMPORARY STORAGE                        --
C
       DIMENSION DATA(28,12),SAVE(12)
C
C
       READ(5,10)((DATA(I,J),I=1,28),J=1,12)
    10 FORMAT(8F10.1)
C
C                   .... READ ROWS TO BE SWAPPED ....
C
       READ(5,20)N1,N2
    20 FORMAT(2I2)
C
C                   .... MOVE ELEMENTS FROM ROW N1
C                        TO ARRAY SAVE ....
C
       DO 30 I=1,12
          SAVE(I)=DATA(N1,I)
    30 CONTINUE
C
C                   .... MOVE ROW N2 TO ROW N1 ....
C
       DO 40 I=1,12
          DATA(N1,I)=DATA(N2,I)
    40 CONTINUE
C
C                   .... MOVE N1 (NOW IN SAVE) TO N2 ....
C
       DO 50 I=1,12
          DATA(N2,I)=SAVE(I)
    50 CONTINUE
C
       WRITE(2,60)((DATA(I,J),J=1,12),I=1,28)
    60 FORMAT(1X,12F10.1)
C
       STOP
       END
```

| **Programming Example** Sales Forecasting | A manufacturer of large computer systems is attempting to predict how many units it can expect to sell next year by analyzing sales over the last two years. |

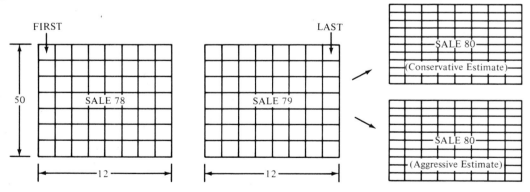

The number of units sold in each state has been reported by the regional sales manager on a monthly basis. These values form the arrays SALE78 and SALE79. Values for these arrays are provided in column order with the January 1978 sales given first and the December 1979 sales given last.

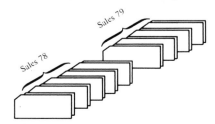

Model 1: (Conservative Estimate)

A conservative estimate of next year's sales is obtained by simply averaging the units sold in 1978 and in 1979 to get the expected sales in '80.

Model 2: (Aggressive Estimate)

A more aggressive model would be obtained by comparing sales in '78 and '79.

      (a) If sales went up by X number of units, expect that sales will go up by twice that number next year.

      (b) If sales went down by X number of units, expect that sales will only decrease by half that number next year.

Compute and display sales projections for next year using both models.

```
C::::::::::::::::::::::::::::::::::::::::::::::::::::::::::::::::
C::   PURPOSE - FORCAST SALES BASED ON TWO DIFFERENT MODELS::
C::::::::::::::::::::::::::::::::::::::::::::::::::::::::::::::::
C
C           -----IMPORTANT VARIABLES--------
C
C        --SALE78      PAST SALES FIGURE YEAR 1978          --
C        --SALE79      PAST SALES FIGURE YEAR 1979          --
C        --SALE80      PROJECTED SALES   YEAR 1980          --
C        ........ALL ARE TWO DIMENSIONAL ARRAYS..........
C        --NLAST       INCREASE OR DECREASE OF SALES 1978 TO 1979
C        --NAVE        AVERAGE UNITS SOLD 1978 TO 1979       --
C        --NNEW        EXPECTED INCREASE OR DECREASE NEXT YEAR --
C
         DIMENSION  SALE78(50,12),SALE79(50,12),SALE80(50,12)
         INTEGER SALE78, SALE79, SALE80
C
C
C        .........READ   PAST   SALES   FIGURES.................
C
         READ(5,10)((SALE78(I,J),I=1,50),J=1,12)
         READ(5,10)((SALE79(I,J),I=1,50),J=1,12)
      10 FORMAT(10I8)
C
C        ..........MODEL   1   PROJECTIONS.................
C
         DO 30 I = 1, 50
C
            DO 20 J = 1, 12
C
C              COMPUTE AVERAGE FOR TWO YEARS
               NAVE = (SALE78(I,J) + SALE79(I,J))/2
               SALE80(I,J) = NAVE
C
      20       CONTINUE
      30 CONTINUE
C
         DO 50 I = 1, 50
C
            WRITE(2,40) (SALE80(I,J),J=1,12)
      40       FORMAT(3X,12I10)
C
      50 CONTINUE
C
C        ..........MODEL   2   PROJECTIONS.................
C
         DO 70 I = 1, 50
C
            DO 60 J = 1, 12
C
C              WHAT WAS SALES INCREASE OR DECREASE
C
               NLAST = SALE79(I,J) - SALE78(I,J)
               IF(NLAST.GT.0) NNEW = SALE79(I,J) + 2*NLAST
               IF(NLAST.LE.0) NNEW = SALE79(I,J) - NLAST/2
               SALE80(I,J) = NNEW
C
      60       CONTINUE
C
      70 CONTINUE
C
         DO 80 I = 1, 50
C
            WRITE(2,40) (SALE80(I,J),J=1,12)
C
      80 CONTINUE
C
         STOP
         END
```

Programming Example
Data Reduction

A programmer must be prepared to provide output in several different forms. While the detailed output of the array SALE80 of the previous example is probably useful at lower levels of management, senior level supervisors usually need "summary" information that is not as overpowering. This involves the concept of **data reduction**.

Summarize the information contained in each *column* of array SALE80 by computing a one-dimensional array called MONTH having 12 elements and representing sales expectations for each month in 1980.

In like fashion, summarize the information contained in each *row* of SALE80 by computing a one-dimensional array called STATES having 50 elements. This

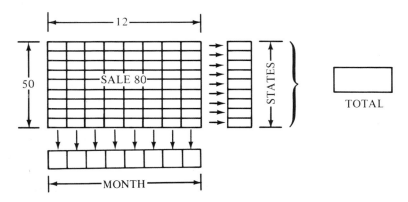

will define yearly sales expectations for each state. Provide these as separate outputs.

Finally, compute a simple variable called TOTAL representing the sum of all the elements in each array — the total sales expectations. Only the new or updated statements are shown below.

```
C
C
C       .....NEW MEMORY ALLOCATION.....FOR SUMMARY VALUES.....
C       DIMENSION MONTH(12), STATES(50)
C           .           .           .
C           .           .           .
C           .           .           .
C       .........DETERMINE SALES EXPECTATION FOR EACH MONTH.....
C       DO 80 I = 1, 12
C           MONTH(I) = 0.0
C           DO 70 J = 1,50
C               MONTH(I) = MONTH(I) + SALES80(J,I)
C   70      CONTINUE
C   80 CONTINUE
C
C           DISPLAY ARRAY MONTH
C       WRITE(2,90)
C   90 FORMAT(1H1,20X,@MONTHLY SUMMARY FIGURES@)
C
C       WRITE(2,91) (MONTH(I),I=1,12)
C   91 FORMAT(3X,I10)
C       ..............................................
C       ......   COMPUTE SUMMARY BY STATE   .........
C       ..............................................
C
C               EXERCISE FOR STUDENT
C
C       ..............................................
C       ........   COMPUTE FINAL TOTAL FIGURES   ......
C       ..............................................
C       TOTAL = 0.0
C       DO 100 I = 1, 12
C           TOTAL = TOTAL + MONTH(I)
C  100 CONTINUE
C       WRITE(2,110) TOTAL
```

Programming Example Graphical Output — Histograms (Bar Graphs)

When the amount of numerical information generated by a program becomes very great, the person who must make some decisions based upon it often feels overwhelmed by the pages upon pages of numbers before him. He is unable to visualize any interrelationships within so vast a display of results. He is "unable to see the forest for the trees."

The solution to such a problem lies in the field of graphical output. If we can cause the computer to display our results in the form of a graph, rather than on sheets and sheets of countless numbers, our ability to gain understanding of those results is greatly improved.

Although there does exist a whole family of X–Y Plotters specifically designed for producing line drawings (and requiring special software packages to operate), it is possible to produce simple graphs on the programmer's old familiar friend, the line printer. The simplest form of graphical output is exemplified by the *bar graph* or *histogram.*

We want to read in a deck of 250 data cards each containing four college entrance exam scores (for a total of 1000 scores) and print out a histogram showing graphically the number of examinees who earned each of the 100 possible scores (from 1 to 100). The histogram is to have the following format:

Grade	Frequency	
100	0	
99	1	*
98	0	
97	2	**
96	3	***
95	2	**
94	4	****
93	6	******
92	5	*****
91	7	*******
90	10	**********
89	9	*********
88	15	***************
etc.	etc.	etc.

Solution: in programming example "Frequency Charts" on page 277, the following code was developed to generate a one-dimensional array called IFREQ having 100 elements. Each element of IFREQ has an integer value telling how many students scored that particular grade. IFREQ(100) tells how many students scored 100. We are going to use this value, IFREQ(100), to determine how many stars or asterisks to print out opposite the number 100 on the histogram.

```
      DIMENSION IGRADE(1000), IFREQ(100)
C
      READ(5,5) (IGRADE(I),I=1,1000)
    5 FORMAT(4I8)
C
      DO 10 K = 1, 100
C
          IFREQ(K) = 0
C
   10 CONTINUE
C
      DO 20 I = 1, 1000
C
          K = IGRADE(I)
          IFREQ(K) = IFREQ(K) + 1
C
   20 CONTINUE
C
```

The next move in this problem is to establish a one-dimensional array called STAR having 100 elements. Array STAR will have a single alphanumeric character in each location, namely "*".

STAR (100 Elements)

INTEGER STAR(100)
DATA STAR/100*1H*/

You will remember that the DATA statement is used to set certain constants in a program. In this case the constant is an array of 100 elements and the DATA statement mentions the name of the array and loads 100 asterisks into the array.

The last important step in this solution is as follows. We will transfer each element in array IFREQ to a memory location LENGTH and then use this variable in an implied DO of the following WRITE statement:

$$WRITE(2,40)(STAR(I),I=1,LENGTH)$$

This will cause a number of elements of STAR to be printed. The number of elements is equal to the number of students that scored a particular grade.

```
C
C         ......SET UP STAR ARRAY......
C
          INTEGER STAR(100)
          DATA STAR/100*1H*/
C
C
C         .....GENERATE LINES OF OUTPUT.....
C
          NGRADE = 100
   30 LENGTH = IFREQ(NGRADE)
C
C...............................................
          WRITE(2,40) NGRADE,LENGTH,(STAR(I),I=1,LENGTH)
   40 FORMAT(2X,I3,6X,I3,6X,100A1)
C...............................................
C
          NGRADE = NGRADE - 1
          IF(NGRADE.GT.0) GO TO 30
C
          STOP
          END
```

While it is more common to use the DATA statement to load numeric constants into memory, the DATA statement is this time loading what is called a character or HOLLERITH constant in memory.

12

Complex/Logical/
Double Precision Variables

For the programming done so far, two types of variables (real and integer) have satisfied our needs reasonably well. The importance of these two basic types of variables is indicated by the fact that on some FORTRAN* systems they are the only types of variables permitted. Most FORTRAN compilers, however, allow other types, which are the subject of this chapter. For example, a *complex* variable will be introduced for use in storing and manipulating complex numbers. A *double-precision* variable will be presented, which permits values to be determined and stored to at least twice the usual accuracy. Finally, a *logical* variable will be described.

From now on, variable names appearing in a program are no longer just real or integer variable names. The name may represent a complex value, a double precision value or a logical value. It, therefore, will be necessary to declare early in the program all names used to represent these new types of variables. This is the purpose of **explicit type statements**.

12.1 Explicit Type Statements

The statements shown in Figure 12.1 are explicit type statements. Notice that for each type of variable (real, integer, complex, double precision, logical) there is a corresponding type statement that explicitly declares those names the programmer has chosen to be associated with each type of variable.

Explicit Type Statements
INTEGER X, ABLE, DER
REAL M, N, ISEC
DOUBLE PRECISION A, B, VALUE, C
COMPLEX XONE, XTWO
LOGICAL A1, A2, A3, D5, REM

Figure 12.1 Example of Explicit Type Statements

*The FORTRAN '77 standards define the features of:

    (a) the full language, and
    (b) a subset language.

Complex and double-precision variables are not part of the subset language.

As described in Chapter 3, integer and real values can be declared in two ways: explicitly or implicitly. Implicit definition describes the method of using the first letter of a variable name to declare it as either integer or real. Explicit definition, on the other hand, is accomplished by an explicit type statement that overrides (takes precedence over) the implicit definition.

Any name representing a double precision, complex or logical variable must be declared in an appropriate type statement. This is the only way of declaring these names.

$$\left.\begin{array}{r}\text{DOUBLE PRECISION} \\ \text{COMPLEX} \\ \text{LOGICAL}\end{array}\right\} \quad \begin{array}{l}\text{Names must be} \\ \text{declared by a} \\ \text{type statement}\end{array}$$

All type statements must be placed early in the source program so that the type statement precedes the first use of the variable name. It should also be noted that the resulting assignment of names is permanent for the remainder of that program. Once the type of a variable has been declared in a type statement, it may not be subsequently changed. Finally, a name may not appear in two different type statements. The name "SETS," for example, may be declared to be an integer variable name or a complex variable name, but not both.

12.2 | Variations in Compilers

At several points in this text, we have commented on minor variations in the way in which FORTRAN is implemented by various computers. These variations result from a difference in word size, memory capacity and type of machine language instructions available on a particular system.

Prior to the FORTRAN '77 standards, these variations were rather extensive. Smaller systems would limit the number of continuation cards allowed, the number of letters in a variable name, the type of input/output statements permitted, the form of subscripted variables, etc. These variations are known as **system characteristics** and are usually published in tabular form as suggested in Figure 12.2.

	IBM 704 (8k)	IBM 360 Level D	CDC 3600
Maximum number of continuation cards allowed	4	19	No limit
Maximum magnitude of integer constants allowed	$2^{35}-1$	$2^{31}-1$	$2^{47}-1$
Maximum digits of a real constant (mantissa size)	9	7	11
Maximum digits of a double precision constant		16	25
Maximum statement number allow	99999	9999	99

Figure 12.2 System Characteristics

These variations cause problems of portability (running a program on more than one system).

The effect of the new standards will be to minimize these variations. All compilers eventually will be made to meet one of two levels of certification:

1. *Full* language features (to be implemented on large systems).
2. *Subset* language features (to be implemented on smaller systems).

Double precision and complex variables are features available in the full language but not in the subset. A detailed description of the difference between the full and subset language is presented in Appendix F.

12.3 | Double Precision Values

A double precision value is very much like a real value except that more space in memory is allocated for storing double precision values. The usual practice is to string two real memory locations together to form one double precision memory location. The resulting mantissa size for a double precision variable is usually at least twice that of a real variable.

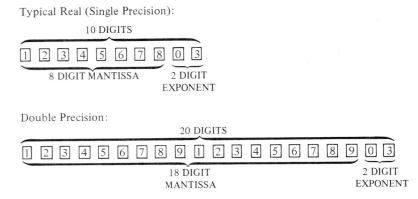

Figure 12.3 Typical Double Precision Word Size

Figure 12.3 shows the internal storage of a real number in a computer using a 10-digit word size (8-digit mantissa and a 2-digit exponent). Also shown is the internal storage of the same number in double precision form, using a 20-digit word size (18-digit mantissa and a 2-digit exponent).

One obvious use of double precision is to obtain more accurate solutions. Often a program is written, compiled and checked using real variables and constants until the program has proven itself. Then values are transformed into double precision form, and the program is run again to obtain more accurate results.

Another use of double precision is to reduce round-off errors. Consider the two real numbers stored in memory locations A and B of Figure 12.4. If these numbers are added and the result stored in real location C, the number stored in location C is identical to the number stored in memory location A.

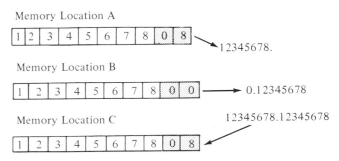

Figure 12.4 How Round-Off Errors are Generated

This has happened because the true result of this addition is a 16-digit number, but memory location C can accommodate only the first 8 digits. The remainder, 0.12345678, is called the round-off error, and the value stored in C is inaccurate by this amount. This error has resulted because A is so large compared to B. If the value as now stored in C is used in subsequent calculations, the effect of this error can grow.

Most calculations suffer from errors, but if this error is in the 8th or 9th decimal place of a value, the error is not serious. However, any result that is obtained after a long sequence of operations (each with its own error) may suffer from an accumulation of errors (error build-up). One way to reduce these errors is to use double precision.

There is a strong similarity between the way in which real and double precision expressions are formed. The description that follows will be easier to understand if this similarity is kept in mind.

Double Precision Constants

A double precision constant can be written just like a real number expressed in E-notation, except that the letter D is used instead of the letter E.

Double Precision Constants	
Constant	Meaning
0.15967D + 04	(1596.7)
0.923716534487D – 02	(.00923716534487)
–1483767.5421D00	(–1483767.5421)
8.3D02	(830.)
1.34D4	(13400.)
–16.D – 8	(–0.00000016)

The mantissa may contain from one to 16 digits written with a decimal point (located as desired) followed by the letter D and an exponent in integer form. This exponent indicates the power of ten by which the mantissa is to be multiplied. An alternate way of expressing a double precision constant is as a real number (written without an exponent) containing a sign and at least ten significant digits, as with these two examples.

–32.916752434   +627383.0691

Just as a real constant is distinguished from an integer constant by the presence or absence of a decimal point, there must be some unique feature to distinguish a double precision constant. That feature is the appearance of ten or more digits when specifying the constant.

Double Precision Variables

A double precision variable is formed by creating a name (according to the usual rules for naming a variable) and then declaring this name as being a double precision variable by using the appropriate explicit type statement.

DOUBLE PRECISION A, VALUE, ITEM, XRAY

Double precision variables may appear in the lists of input/output statements. When this happens, double precision numbers will be read from an input record (data card) or will be written on an output record. This READ/WRITE operation must be controlled by a FORMAT statement. The general form of the code describing double precision numbers is:

Fw.d.   **Fw.d.** if the number appears without an exponent

Dw.d.   **Dw.d.** if the number appears with an exponent as
described in the previous paragraphs.

This input/output procedure for double precision values will be demonstrated in the next case study.

A double precision constant(s) or variable(s) may appear in any arithmetic expression in exactly the same way that a real constant(s) or variable(s) appears. Further, single precision (real) and double precision values may appear in the *same* arithmetic expression.

When defining the mode of any arithmetic operation, the compiler looks to the left and right of the operational symbol at the operands involved.

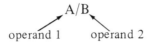

operand 1   operand 2

If one is real and the other is double precision, the operation will be performed in double precision. The remaining rules for forming double precision expressions are the same as the rules for single precision (real) expressions. The operational symbols (*,/,+,-,**) are the same. The hierarchy of operation, use of parentheses and mixed mode restrictions are the same.

It should be clearly understood that the use of single precision (real) values in a double precision expression may or may not imply inaccuracy. Take, for example, the number

1.24

Just because there are only 3 digits in the number does not mean it can be stored with complete accuracy in a single precision (real) memory location. The method of internal representation (storage) must be considered. If this number is stored in binary (base 2), octal (base 8) or hexadecimal (base 16), it may not have finite representation. On the other hand, numbers like 124. or 6297. could be stored in single precision form with complete accuracy.

Double Precision Library Functions

Library functions such as SIN, COS, SQRT, etc., which have been used in the past, evaluate the desired function to single precision accuracy. Double precision calculations involving these functions will require their evaluation to a higher degree of accuracy — to double precision accuracy. For this reason, the following double precision functions have been created.*

DSIN   DLOG
DCOS   DSQRT
DATAN   DABS

The argument(s) of these functions must be double precision quantities. The value returned is double precision.

---

*It may not be necessary to use the special functions just described. The FORTRAN '77 standards have defined what is called a **generic function**. A generic function returns a value consistent with the mode of the argument(s) used when evoking the function. For example, the generic library functions SIN, COS, SQRT, etc., can accept a real, double precision or complex argument. They will return a real, double precision or complex value depending on which type of argument was used.

12.4 | Use of Double Precision

<table>
<tr><td>**Programming Example**
Double Precision
Addition</td><td>Write a program to read the data card shown and to determine the sum of the values listed.</td></tr>
</table>

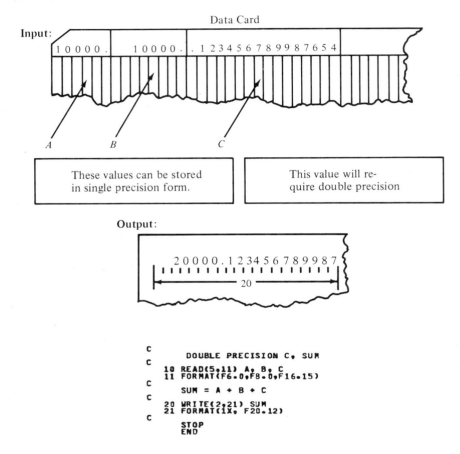

Examining the data card, we see that values A and B can be stored in single precision form, but C will require double precision. When A is added to B (in statement 10), single precision accuracy is used. The next add operation will be accomplished in double precision because of the appearance of the double precision variable C. To preserve this accuracy, the result should be stored (assigned) to a double precision memory location. For this reason, both C and SUM are declared as double precision values by the TYPE statement "DOUBLE PRECISION C, SUM."

<table>
<tr><td>**Programming Example**
Approximating A
Volume</td><td>Write a program to approximate the volume obtained by revolving the line y=f(x) about the x axis between the limits x=0 and x=6 (see Figure 12.5).</td></tr>
</table>

One approximation would be to form a series of cylinders of thickness ΔX ($\Delta V = \pi r^2 \Delta X$) and to sum these volumes. If the number of such cylinders is large, the "omitted volume" (see Figure 12.5) will be small, thereby reducing the error of the approximation. The theories of calculus would suggest we make Δx infinitely small to obtain the best approximation.

While increasing the number of cylinders reduces the geometric error of the approximation, it will, at the same time, increase the number of calculations that

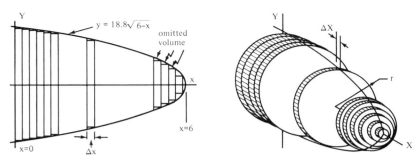

Figure 12.5 Approximation by a Series of Cylinders

must be performed. The student has been cautioned to avoid this situation: **any result that is obtained after a long sequence of operations (each with its own error) may suffer from an accumulation of errors (error build-up).**

Causing Δx to be excessively small can create a problem as the vertex of the solid is approached (x approaches 6). The volume already determined is large in relation to the volume of each cylinder yet to be accounted for. The effect of adding a small number to a large number has been demonstrated earlier.

For the reasons just stated, the following program employs double precision calculations where necessary.

```
C....................................................................
C..   PURPOSE - DEMONSTRATE DOUBLE PRECISION CALCULATIONS. ..
C....................................................................
C
C              -----IMPORTANT VARIABLES-----
C
C     --RAD         RADIUS (DOUBLE PRECISION)              --
C     --SUMV        SUM OF THE VOLUMES                     --
C     --VOL         VOLUME OF AN INDIVIDUAL CYLINDER       --
C
      DOUBLE PRECISION SUMV, X, RAD, VOL, DELTX
C
C            .....INITIALIZATION SECTION......
C
      DELTX = 0.01
      SUMV = 0.0
      X = DELTX
C
C              LOOP ENTRY POINT
C
   10 RAD = 18.8 * DSQRT(6.0 - X)
      VOL = 3.14159265358979 * RAD**2 * 0.01
C
      SUMV = SUMV + VOL
      X = X + DELTX
      IF(X.LT.6.0) GO TO 10
C
C            .....LOOP TERMINATES HERE.....
C
   20 WRITE(2,21) VOL
   21 FORMAT(1X,'VOLUME = ',F20.6)
C
      STOP
      END
```

The first series of statements are comment statements. The next statement declares SUMV, X, RAD and VOL as double precision. SUMV and VOL must be double precision variables so that each value of volume may be stored and accumulated to a high degree of accuracy. The accuracy to which the volume, VOL, can be determined depends on the accuracy to which the radius, RAD, is computed. The variable RAD, therefore, must be double precision. Finally, X is made double precision so that the argument of the square root function appearing in statement 11 will be a double precision value.

Method of Solution:

SUMV accumulates individual values of volume (VOL) generated as X moves from the origin to the vertex of the solid in increments of 0.01 (DELTX). The radius of each cylinder is obtained by substituting the value of X into the equation:

$$y = 18.8\sqrt{6-X}$$

12.5 | Complex Values

Complex numbers of the form (a+bi) occur frequently in mathematics. They consist of an ordered pair of real numbers (a and b) the latter of which is combined with the quantity "i", which has the property: $i^2 = -1$. Complex numbers can be used to represent vectors (see Figure 12.6).

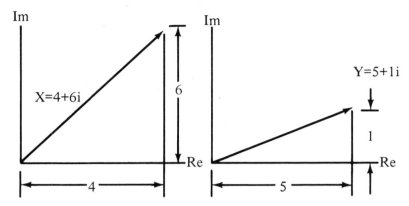

Figure 12.6 Vector Representation of Complex Numbers

The addition of complex numbers is defined as:

Addition: (a+bi) + (c+di) = (a+c) + (b+d)i

Applying this definition to X and Y of Figure 12.6:

    Z = X + Y
      = (4+6i) + (5+1i)
    Z = (9 + 7i)

The result if the complex number Z whose meaning is shown in Figure 12.7. It is the **resultant** (vector sum) of the system.

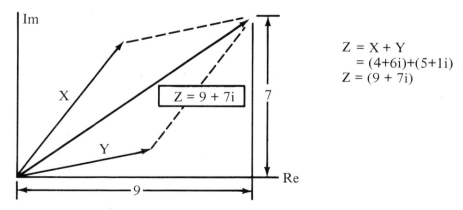

Figure 12.7 Vector Representation of the Resultant

The preceding example demonstrates that the arithmetic manipulation of complex numbers involves the identification and manipulation of the real and imaginary parts of these numbers. To facilitate this, "full language" compilers have been written to allow the direct storage and direct mathematical manipulation of complex values.

Specifically, if a variable is declared in a TYPE statement as a COMPLEX variable, that variable name will identify two consecutive floating point locations in memory in which the real and imaginary parts of the complex number are stored.

The real and imaginary parts are identified by a single name. In addition, if that variable name appears in an arithmetic expression, the operational symbols (+,−,*,/,etc.) will be understood to mean complex addition, complex subtraction, complex multiplication, etc.

Consider the following program segment.

```
      PROGRAM FIRST (INPUT,OUTPUT,TAPE5=INPUT,TAPE2=OUTPUT)
C.........................................................
C..    PURPOSE - PROGRAM SEGMENT TO ADD VECTORS X AND Y PRO- ..
C                 DUCING RESULTANT VECTOR Z.              ..
C.........................................................
C
      COMPLEX X, Y, Z
C
C                    READ COMPLEX VALUES FROM DATA
C
   10 READ(5,11) X, Y
C                 DATA CARD CONTAINS FOUR VALUES
   11 FORMAT(4F10.2)
C
C                    COMPLEX ADDITION THEN ACCOMPLISHED
C
      Z = X + Y
C
   20 WRITE(2,21) Z
   21 FORMAT(1X,2F10.2)
C
      STOP
      END
```

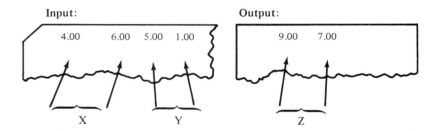

Input:

4.00   6.00   5.00   1.00

X   Y

Output:

9.00   7.00

Z

The TYPE statement is used to identify X, Y and Z as the names of complex variables. The READ statement is executed next. While there are only two names in the list of this READ statement, four values will be read from data because X and Y have been declared as complex quantities. The statement:

$$Z = X + Y$$

will result in the formation of the complex value Z through the complex addition of X and Y. The operational symbol + is interpreted as complex addition because X and Y are complex quantities. This program segment computes the vector Z shown in Figure 12.7.

Complex Constants

A **complex constant** is formed by specifying two floating point numbers enclosed in parentheses and separated by a comma. These values represent the real and imaginary parts of the complex constant.

Example		Meaning
(6.00,	5.20)	6.00 + 5.20i
(-4.82,	16.06)	-4.82 + 16.06i
(0.00,	4.00)	0.00 + 4.00i
(5.17,	0.00)	5.17 + 0.00i
(2.00E+02,	4.10)	200.00 + 4.10i

Complex Variables

A **complex variable** is formed by creating a name (according to the usual rules for naming a variable) and then declaring that name a complex value by using the appropriate TYPE statement.
For example:

    COMPLEX X, BRN, SUM
    COMPLEX A1, A2, A3
    COMPLEX X, Y

Input/Output

INPUT/OUTPUT of complex values is accomplished in the same way real values are transferred to and from memory, except that: the appearance of a complex variable name in the list of a READ/WRITE statement causes the transfer of *two floating point numbers* (the real and imaginary parts).

The controlling format statement must provide separate specifications describing each part of the complex number.

Arithmetic Expressions

Arithmetic operations involving complex numbers require special attention. The rules governing the addition, subtraction, multiplication and division of complex numbers are shown in Figure 12.8.

ADDITION	$(a+bi) + (c+di) = (a+c) + (b+d)i$
SUBTRACTION	$(a+bi) - (c+di) = (a-c) + (b-d)i$
MULTIPLICATION	$(a+bi) \times (c+di) = (ac-bd) + (bc+ad)i$
DIVISION	$(a+bi) \div (c+di) = \dfrac{(ac+bd) + (bc-ad)i}{c^2 + d^2}$

Figure 12.8 Mathematics of Complex Operations

These operations are the ones that occur most frequently in arithmetic expressions involving complex quantities.

A complex expression defines a sequence of arithmetic operations to be performed involving complex constants, complex variables, real constants, and real variables. Integer values may only appear as subscripts or as exponents.

Examples of complex expressions are:

    COMPLEX Z, A, B, SUM, X

(1) Z = (5.28, -6.15) * (7.56, 2.28)   (4) SUM = A + B + Z
(2) B = Z - (2.26, 3.39)   (5) X = CSQRT ((4.0, 3.0))
(3) A = (B/Z)**2

While the formation of a complex expression is similar to the formation of a real expression, certain differences do exist. These are outlined as follows:

(a) A complex quantity may only be raised to an integer power: real and complex values may not be used as the exponent of a complex expression.

(b) The result of a complex expression is a complex value and must be stored as such. If the right hand side of an arithmetic statement is a complex expression, the variable on the left hand side should be a complex variable.

(c) Complex variables have their own library functions, which are described in Figure 12.9.

Name	Purpose	Remarks
CABS	Computes the absolute value of a complex number.	Argument is a single complex quantity. The result is a real value.
CMPLX	Transforms two real values into a single complex quantity.	Arguments are two real values. The result is a complex number.
REAL	Separates and returns just the *real* portion of a complex number.	Argument is a complex value. The result is a floating point number.
AIMAG	Separates and returns just the *imaginary* portion of a complex number.	Argument is a complex value. The result is a floating point number.
CONJG	Produces the conjugate of its complex argument.	Argument and Result are both complex quantities.
CEXP	e^Z	Argument and
CLOG	$\ln Z$	Result are both
CSIN	$\sin Z$	
CCOS	$\cos Z$	complex quantities.
CSQRT	$\sqrt{Z}$	

Figure 12.9 Table of Complex Library Functions*

Some of these library functions require additional explanation.

CABS:

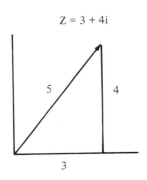

*Generic Library Functions may be available. See discussion in section 12.4.

The absolute value of a complex quantity is interpreted as the length of the vector representing the complex value. The argument of this function is a complex value. The result is a floating point number representing the physical length of the vector.

$$X = CABS (Z) \quad or \quad X = CABS ((3.0, 4.0))*$$

Floating Point — Complex   Floating Point — Complex

Both of the above expressions would result in the computation and storage of the floating point number 5 in memory location X.

CMPLX:

The function is designed to receive two floating point arguments as input and to form a single complex value from these. For example.

$$Z = CMPLX (3.0, 4.0) - CMPLX (A, B)$$

Complex Variable   Floating Point Constants   Floating Point Variable

The function CMPLX is used twice to form two complex values. The floating point constants (3.0 and 4.0) are used to form one complex value; the floating point variables (A and B) are used to form the second value. These are then subtracted (complex subtraction) producing a complex result which is stored in Z.

REAL and AIMAG:

There are occasions when it is necessary to determine just the real or just the imaginary part of a complex value. This can be accomplished by using the REAL or AIMAG function. These functions receive a complex value as arguments and produce a single floating point value (the real or imaginary part) as output.

12.6 | Use of Complex Values

**Programming Example
Analysis of a
Mechanism**

Complex numbers can be used in the design and analysis of mechanisms such as the one shown in Figure 12.10. As depicted, the mechanism consists of a series of links. The length and angular position of each link is described on a data card (see Figure 12.11, center column). The first step in the solution will be to convert these input values (length and angle) into vectors expressed in complex notation. These vectors are shown in the last column of Figure 12.11.

Write a program to read the data cards shown in Figure 12.11 (containing real values) and form the complex quantities AB, BC and CD. Determine the distance between center A and pin D of the mechanism (add vectors AB, BC and CD and compute the absolute value).

The program for this problem will proceed as follows:

1. Read the radius and inclination of each link from data;

---

*The argument of a function must be enclosed in parentheses. A complex constant consists of two numbers enclosed in parentheses. If the argument is a complex constant, two pairs of parentheses are needed.

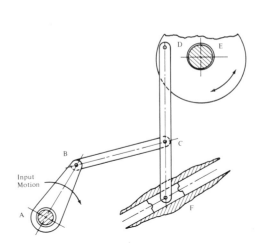

Figure 12.10 Mechanical Linkage

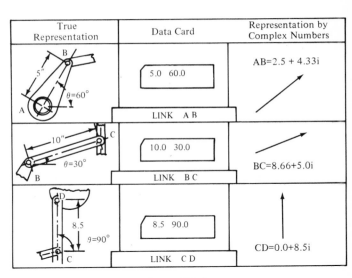

Figure 12.11 Representation of Links

2. Compute two floating point numbers representing the real and imaginary portions of the equivalent complex number representation (statements 20 and 30);
3. Call the library function CMPLX to create the complex equivalent using the two floating point numbers described above as arguments;
4. Having accomplished this transformation, perform complex addition to determine the desired distance;
5. Call the library function CABS to convert the complex representation of the desired distance to a real (absolute) value.

```
C...................................................................
C..    PURPOSE - DEMONSTRATE THE USE OF COMPLEX VARIABLES       ..
C..              DETERMINE THE POSITION OF OUTPUT CRANK.        ..
C...................................................................
C
C                    -----IMPORTANT VARIABLES-----
C
C     --RE         REAL COMPONENT OF COMPLEX NUMBER          --
C     --IM         IMAGINARY PART OF COMPLEX NUMBER          --
C     --N          LINKAGE COUNTER                           --
C     --AB,BC,CD   COMPLEX NUMBERS REPRESENTING THE POSIT-   --
C                  ION OF LINKS AB, BC, AND CD RESPECTIVELY--
C
      COMPLEX AB, BC, CD, SUMD
      REAL IM
C
      N = 0
C
C                 .....LOOP ENTRY POINT.....
C
   10 READ(5,11) R, THETA
   11 FORMAT(2F12.6)
      N = N + 1
C
C                 COMPUTE REAL AND IMAGINARY PARTS
C
   20 RE = R * COS(THETA/57.3)
   30 IM = R * SIN(THETA/57.3)
C
      IF(N.EQ.1) AB = CMPLX(RE,IM)
      IF(N.EQ.2) BC = CMPLX(RE,IM)
      IF(N.EQ.3) CD = CMPLX(RE,IM)
C
      IF(N.LT.3) GO TO 10
C
C                 .....LOOP TERMINATES HERE.......
C
C                 COMPLEX ADDITION OF VECTORS
C
   40 SUMD = AB + BC + CD
      DIST=CABS(SUMD)
C
   50 WRITE(2,51) DIST
   51 FORMAT(1X,E20.7)
C
      STOP
      END
```

| Programming Example AC Circuit Analysis | Complex numbers are used in ac circuit analysis. While the current, voltage, and resistance of a dc circuit can be represented by real numbers, these same quantities require complex representation in ac circuit analysis. Similarly, all calculations (such as the application of Ohm's law) will require complex arithmetic. |

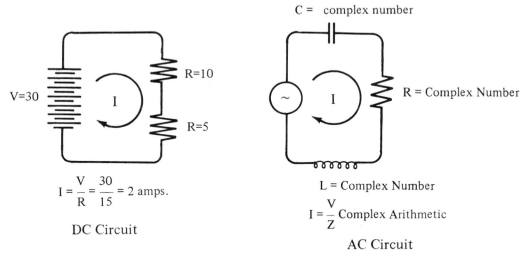

Figure 12.12 AC and DC Circuit Analysis

The effect of a capacitance, resistance, or inductance in an ac circuit is shown in Figure 12.13.

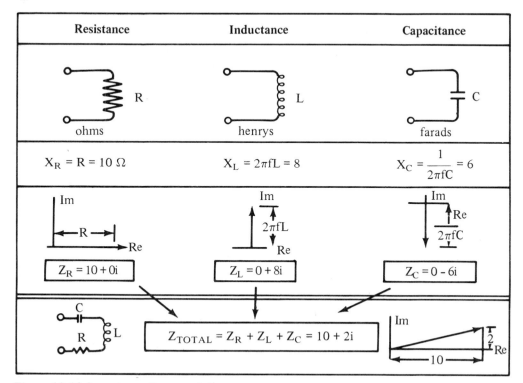

Figure 12.13 Impedance Representation

Given the values of R, L, and C for series circuit, the floating point quantities X_R, X_L, and X_C may be computed. They, however, may not be added directly because of the phase (angular) differences. The complex quantitites Z_R, Z_L, and Z_C must first be formed and then the total impedance of the circuit can be computed. This impedance is used to relate to the current, I, and the voltage, V, according to the equation:

$$I = \frac{V}{Z}$$

This equation affords an opportunity to describe the physical significance of complex division for the purpose of making the next example more meaningful.

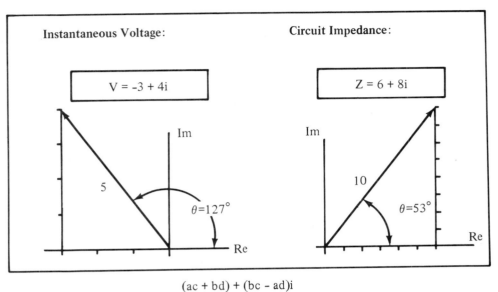

Division: $(a + bi) \div (c + di) = \dfrac{(ac + bd) + (bc - ad)i}{c^2 + d^2}$

Figure 12.14 Computation of Instantaneous Current

The division of two complex numbers such as V and Z produces a complex result, I, whose magnitude (absolute value) equals the magnitude of V divided by the magnitude of Z and whose inclination θ_I equals the inclination of V minus the inclination of $Z(\theta_v - \theta_z)$. The magnitude of V is 5 and θ_v equals $127°$. The magnitude of Z is 10 and θ_z equals $53°$. The magnitude of I=0.5 and θ_I equals $74°$.

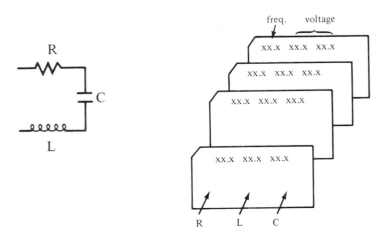

The following program reads a leader card, which specifies values for R, L, and C in the circuit shown. Each of the three remaining data cards specifies a frequency (real number) and the instantaneous voltage (complex number) that is applied to the circuit. For each frequency the program:

(a) computes X_R, X_C, and X_L (real values), and
(b) transforms these to their complex equivalent Z_R, Z_C, Z_L;
(c) the total impedance, Z, is determined, and
(d) the instantaneous current is determined and reported.

V	Voltage (complex)
L	Inductance (real)
I	Current (complex)
IABS	Current (absolute value)
ZR, ZC, ZL	Various Impedances (complex)
ZTOTL	Total Impedance
F	Frequency

```
C......................................................
C..    PURPOSE - APPLY COMPLEX MATHEMATICS TO THE SOLUTION ..
C..              OF AN A.C. CIRCUIT ANALYSIS PROBLEM.        ..
C......................................................
C
C                    -----IMPORTANT VARIABLES-----
C                       (SEE ACCOMPANYING TABLE)
C
      COMPLEX V, I, ZR, ZC, ZL, ZTOTAL
      REAL L, IABS
C
      N = 0
C                        DEFINE CIRCUIT PARAMETERS
   10 READ(5,11) R, L, C
   11 FORMAT(3F12.4)
C
C                        .....LOOP ENTRY POINT.....
C
   20 READ(5,11) F, V
C
C                        DETERMINE CIRCUIT IMPEDANCE
      XR = R
      XL = 2.0 * 3.1416 * F * L
      XC = 1.0 / (2.0 * 3.1416 * F * C)
C
C                        CONVERT TO COMPLEX NOTATION
C
      ZR = CMPLX( XR, 0.0 )
      ZC = CMPLX( 0.0, -XC )
      ZL = CMPLX( 0.0, XL )
C
C                        ACCOMPLISH COMPLEX ADDITION
C
      ZTOTAL = ZR + ZC + ZL
C
C                        ACCOMPLISH COMPLEX DIVISION
C
      I = V / ZTOTAL
      IABS = CABS( I )
   30 WRITE(2,31) I, IABS
   31 FORMAT(1X, 3E20.6)
C
      N = N + 1
      IF(N.LT.3) GO TO 20
C
C                        .....LOOP TERMINATION POINT.....
C
      STOP
      END
```

12.7 | Logical Variables

So far the applications of the FORTRAN language have been restricted to those problems that readily lend themselves to exact numerical solution. Double precision and complex variables were obviously developed to augment the computing capability and convenience of the FORTRAN language in handling certain problems within this broad category.

Attention must now be turned, however, to problems that are characteristic in that they do not lend themselves to exact numerical representation. Problems in medical diagnosis, personnel selection or analysis (identification) of chemical compounds fall into this category. Most typically, the solution to these problems must be based on the yes/no answers to such questions as:

1. Is blood pressure above normal?
2. Does the compound dissolve in sulfuric acid?
3. Is the applicant's I.Q. greater than 120 but less than 140?

Analysis of these problems is closely tied to two-value (Boolean) logic. Logical variables, constants, expressions and IF statements have been developed to give the FORTRAN language a convenient means of storing and manipulating the "yes/no" or "true/false" information typical of these problems.

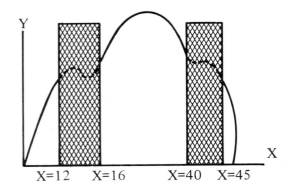

Figure 12.15 Representation of Wanted Data

To provide a concrete example of the use of logical variables as implemented in FORTRAN, consider the curve shown in Figure 12.15. The relationship between X and Y is well established except in the two shaded areas shown. Each value of X appearing in a program must be analyzed to determine:

(a) Is X greater than 12 but less than 16?
(b) Is X greater than 40 but less than or equal to 45?

If the answer to question (a) or (b) is true, special processing is necessary and control must be passed to statement 100.

   With the features to be described in this section, the logical variables A and B can be created by the statement:

   LOGICAL A, B

and these variables can be assigned the value "true" or "false" by the logical assignment statements:

   A = X . GT. 12.0 .AND. X .LT. 16.0
   B = X .GT. 40.0 .AND. X .LE. 45.0

Variables A and B will now contain the answers to questions (a) and (b). Finally, a logical IF statement is available to accomplish the desired transfer of control if either A or B has the value "true":

   IF (A .OR. B) GO TO 100

   While the logic of this example problem is not overpowering, consider the problems suggested in Figure 12.16. Two data cards have been specially prepared.

   Card 1 contains the results of a series of tests performed on an unknown chemical compound for the purpose of determining its composition. The compound may be dissolved by various acids, subjected to flame and precipitant tests, and so on, with the results recorded on the data card; T indicates true (or yes) and F indicates false (or no). Card 2 shows a profile of a naval officer's qualifications. He may or may not be a qualified officer of the deck, CIC officer, etc. In either example, it is possible to read the logical data on these cards and store the information in memory. Logical expressions can then be written to compare

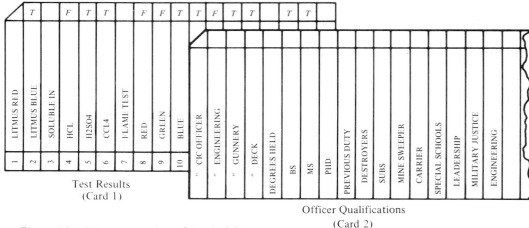

Figure 12.16 Representation of Logical Data

the stored information with desired or established standards. For example, on card 1 a T in columns 1, 12, 18 and 20 and an F in columns 6, 15, 19 and 21 may identify the compound as a nitrate.

Logical Constants / Variables

Logical variables are permitted by most FORTRAN compilers. The names of variables used to represent logical values must be declared in a LOGICAL type statement.

>   LOGICAL X, Y, Z, A, BIT

These variables can be assigned the value "true" or "false" by the LOGICAL assignment statements:

>   X = .TRUE.
>   Y = .FALSE.

where the quantities .TRUE. and .FALSE. are logical constants.

Variables can also be assigned values from data by INPUT statements such as:

>   READ (5,3) X, Y, Z, A, BIT
>   3   FORMAT (L5, L6, L1, L9, L1)

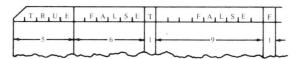

Figure 12.17 Representation of Logical Data

The general form of the format code controlling the INPUT/OUTPUT of logical quantities is:

>   Lw

where w specifies field width. On input, the first non-blank character within each specified field should be the letter T or F to indicate true or false. The remaining characters, if any, are of no importance. If the field is blank, the value false is assigned.

The data cards shown below convey the same meaning as the card in Figure 12.17.

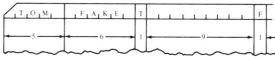

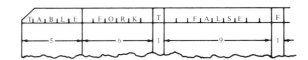

On output, only the letter T or F will be printed right justified in the specified field.

Logical Expressions

Logical expressions can be compared to arithmetic expressions in that both are used to specify a sequence or series of basic operations to be performed on various constants and variables. While the basic arithmetic operations are +, −, *, /, etc., the basic logical operations are:

.NOT.   .AND.   .OR.

These operations are made meaningful by the examples to follow. The logical expression:

A .AND. B

combines the logical variables A and B. The expression will have the value true if both A and B are true, otherwise the expression is false.

For example:

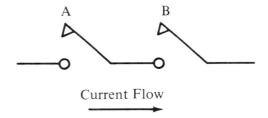

Current Flow

Switch A and switch B are in series. The state of each switch can be represented by a logical variable (A and B). An open switch has the value false; a closed switch has the value true. The logical expression, A .AND. B, tests to see if current will flow for the existing positions of the two switches.

The logical expression:

A .OR. B

combines the logical variables A and B. The expression will have the value true if either A or B (or both) have the value true.

For example:

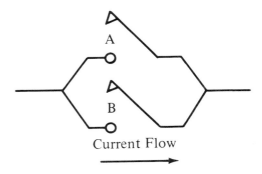

Current Flow

Switch A and switch B are in parallel such that current can flow if either switch A or switch B is closed. This is described by the expression A .OR. B.

The logical operation .NOT. is used to reverse the logical value. Recall the officer qualification card shown in Figure 12.16. Let logical variables A and B store the information as to whether the officer is qualified in engineering and whether he has had submarine duty. Further, assume there existed a need for an engineering officer who had not yet had submarine experience. The logical expression

A .AND. . NOT. B

expresses the desired logic. This expression will have the value true if A is true and B if false. If B is false, .NOT. B is true (since it reverses the logical value).

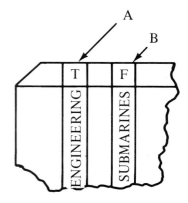

In the following examples of logical expressions, A has the value true; B has the value false; T has the value true; and F has the value false.

Expression	Value
.NOT. A	false
B .AND. F	false
B .OR. .NOT. F	true
A .AND. F .AND. B	false
A .OR. B .OR. F	true
A .AND. B .OR. F	false

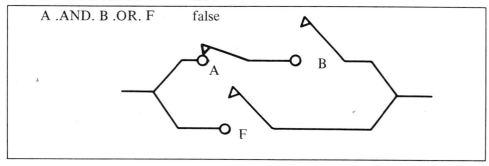

Problem: A, B and F represent the state of three switches in the circuit shown.

Write a logical expression telling under what conditions current will flow in the circuit.

Relational Operation Symbols

In some situations, numerical values may be available to establish a true/false relationship. In the following table are shown the available relational operators and their equivalent mathematical symbols.

Table of Relational Operators

Relational Operation Symbol	Meaning	Mathematical Symbol
.GT.	greater than	$>$
.GE.	greater than or equal to	$\geqslant$
.EQ.	equal to	$=$
.LT.	less than	$<$
.LE.	less than or equal to	$\leqslant$
.NE.	does not equal	$\neq$

These symbols may be used with real, double precision, or integer values as described in the following examples:

LET A = 1.0; B = 2.0; N = 10

Logical Expression	Value
A .GT. B	false
N .LE. 10	true
B .NE. 3.0	true
1.6D03 .LT. B	false
(A**4-5.) .EQ. (B/10.)	false
(A .GT. B) .AND. (B .EQ. 2.0)	false

The use of parentheses in the last two examples suggests that a hierarchy of operations exists. This hierarchy now involves arithmetic, logical, and relational operators, and is shown in the next table.

Hierarchy of Operations

Arithmetic First	**
	*, /
	+, −
Logical Last	.GT., .GE., .EQ., .LT., .LE., .NE.
	.NOT.
	.AND.
	.OR.

Left to right in cases of equal priority.

Each line on the table represents a different level. For example, multiplication and division will be performed before addition and subtraction. The logical operators .AND. will be performed before .OR. On the basis of this, are any of the parentheses in the last two examples in Figure 12.18 needed?*

Logical Assignment Statements

A **logical assignment statement** specifies a sequence of operations to be performed for the purpose of evaluating a logical expression. The true/false result

*No, but the policy of using parentheses when in doubt still applies.

is then assigned a location in memory identified by the logical variable name appearing on the left side of the statement.

In the following examples:

A = 1.0; B = 2.0; T = TRUE; F = FALSE and I = 10

LOGICAL T, F, X, Y, Z

X = A .GT. 6.2 .OR. .NOT. T	X is false
X = A .LT. 6.2 .AND. .NOT. T	X is false
X = A .LT. 6.2 .AND. T	X is true
Y = 6. 7D08/B .GE. A .AND. T	Y is true
Y = 6. 7D08/B .GE. A .OR. T	Y is true
Y = 6. 7D08/B .GE. A .AND. .NOT. T	Y is false
Z = I – 4 .GT. (I – 6) ** 2	Z is false
Z = A**I – 1 .EQ. B	Z is false
Z = .NOT. (A .GT. B)	

Review Exercises

1. Integer and real variables may be defined either implicitly or explicitly. Is this true for complex, double precision and logical variables?

2. If a calculation is to be performed to double precision accuracy, does that mean that all values (constants and variables) in the defining expression must be stored in the double precision mode?

3.*What is the difference between the library functions SIN and DSIN? Which would evaluate more terms in the approximating series expansion?

4. What is the purpose of the library function CABS? Describe the input argument(s). Describe the output to this function.

5. What is meant by a "generic" function? How does a generic function determine what type of argument to return?

6.*May a variable that has been declared as a double precision one early in a program be later redefined as a logical or complex variable?

7. In the hierarchy of operations which are accomplished first logical or arithmetic operations?

8. Describe the type of problem in which logical variables might be used.

9. In order for a round-off error to occur, an operation must be performed in which one of the operands is very large and the other operand is very small. Describe a situation where this might happen.

10. Evaluate the first twenty terms of the following equation for X=50.0:

$$Y = X + \frac{2}{X^2} + \frac{3}{X^3} + \frac{4}{X^4} + \frac{5}{X^5} + \frac{6}{X^6} + \cdots$$

Report the value of each term as a separate item. Report along with this value the sum of all terms in the equation up to and including this term. Repeat the process using double precision.

11.*A job has been offered that pays one cent the first week but doubles the salary each week: that is, \$.01 the first week \$.02 the second week, \$.04 the third week. . .$\frac{\$2^{n-1}}{100}$ in the nth week. Write a program that will determine and report the salary for each week and the salary paid to date for 50 weeks. Use double precision to obtain the accuracy needed for Income Tax purposes.

12. Write a program to determine accurately the probability of being dealt a perfect bridge hand. This may be represented by:

$$\frac{13!(52-13)!}{52!} = \text{Probability}$$

13. Write a program to determine the value of $\int_1^{10} e^x dx$, i.e., the area under the curve $Y=e^x$ from 1 to 10. Use the trapezoidal approximation:

$$A = \frac{\Delta x}{2} (Y_1 + 2Y_2 + 2Y_3 \cdots + 2Y_{n-1} + Y_n)$$

Let $\Delta x = .05$ and use both real and double precision variables. Compare answers.

14. A data deck consists of 10 cards, each containing 2 floating point values representing the real and complex portion of a vector. Write a program to determine the length of the largest vector appearing in the deck.

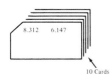

8.312   6.147

10 Cards

15.*Arm AB rotates about A, and wheel BC rotates about B. For the position shown:
  (a) Express the position of point B as a complex number.
  (b) Express the position of point C as a complex number.

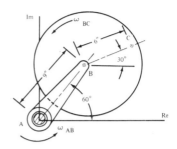

If both AB and BC rotate at one revolution per minute, report the position of B and C at one-second intervals starting from the present position.

16.*A computerized dating service operates in the following way. The true and false responses of a female client are compared with the true and false responses made by all the men participating in this service (see data deck shown). The first five digits represent the identification number. The remainder of the card contains the responses to questions. Write a program to read the first data card (representing a female) and then search the remaining data cards for the identification numbers of compatible males (i.e., those who answered 70 out of 75 questions the same way).

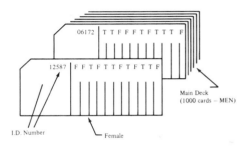

Additional Applications

Programming Example
Using a Logical Flag

A data deck consists of 40 cards each containing the X and Y coordinates of a point. All points should lie in the first quadrant (positive X and positive Y). Process these cards and print out one of the two messages shown below.

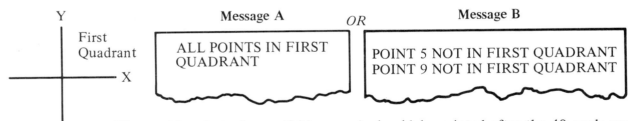

The problem is to know if Message A should be printed after the 40 cards are processed. Try setting a logical memory location called FLAG equal to .TRUE. early in the program. Then, if any point lies outside the first quadrant, report that point and execute the statement:

FLAG = .FALSE.

This pulls down the flag that was run up the pole at the beginning of the program. An IF statement now can be used at the end of the program (see statement 14) to check the condition of the flag (up or down) and execute or not execute Message A.

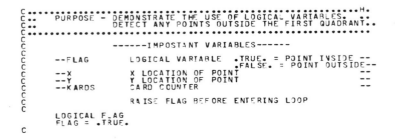

```
C
C              KARDS = 0
C
C                         LOOP ENTRY POINT
C
   10 READ(5,11) X, Y
   11 FORMAT(2F5.1)
C
      KARDS = KARDS + 1
C
C                      CHECK LOCATION OF POINT
C
      IF(X.LT.0.0.OR.Y.LT.0.0) THEN
          FLAG = .FALSE.
          WRITE(2,20) KARDS
   20     FORMAT(8X,'POINT',I4,'NOT IN FIRST QUADRANT')
C
      ENDIF
C
C                      ANY CARDS REMAINING
C
      IF(KARDS.LT.40) GO TO 10
C                      LOOP EXIT POINT
C
C                      SEE IF MESSAGE A APPROPRIATE
C
      IF(FLAG) WRITE(2,30)
   30          FORMAT(8X,'ALL POINTS IN FIRST QUADRANT')
C
      STOP
      END
```

Programming Example
Resultant Force

Input:

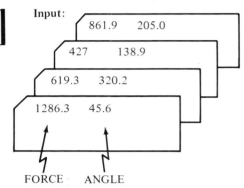

FORCE   ANGLE

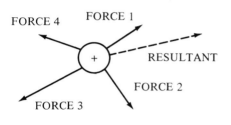

Four forces are applied to a small ring. The magnitude of each force is described on a data card (angle specified in degrees 0 to 360). Determine the resultant of these forces. Express the resultant in two ways:

    (a) standard representation (magnitude and inclination), and
    (b) complex representation (real and imaginary component).

```
C.....................................................
C..   PURPOSE - EXAMPLE OF USING COMPLEX VARIABLES   ..
C.....................................................
C
      COMPLEX FORCE1, FORCE2, FORCE3, FORCE4, RESULT
C
C              CONVERT INPUT TO COMPLEX NOTATION
C
      READ(5,10) F1, ANG1
   10 FORMAT (2F9.1)
      FORCE1 = CMPLX (F1*COS(ANG1/57.3),F1*SIN(ANG1/57.3))
C
      READ(5,10) F2, ANG2
      FORCE2 = CMPLX (F2*COS(ANG2/57.3),F2*SIN(ANG2/57.3))
C
      READ(5,10) F3, ANG3
      FORCE3 = CMPLX (F3*COS(ANG3/57.3),F3*SIN(ANG3/57.3))
C
      READ(5,10) F4, ANG4
      FORCE4 = CMPLX (F4*COS(ANG4/57.3),F4*SIN(ANG4/57.3))
C
C          ADD VECTORS OBTAIN RESULTANT
C
      RESULT = FORCE1 + FORCE2 + FORCE3 + FORCE4
      WRITE (2,20) RESULT
   20 FORMAT(2X,'COMPLEX REPRESENTATION OF RESULTANT.....'10X,
     1'REAL PART = ',F9.1,10X,'IMAGINARY PART =',F9.1)
C
C              CONVERT RESULTANT TO STANDARD FORM
C
      FORCE = CABS (RESULT)
C
      X = REAL (RESULT)
      Y = AIMAG(RESULT)
      ANGLE = ATAN(Y/X)*57.3
C
```

```
        WRITE (2,30) FORCE, ANGLE
     30 FORMAT(2X,'THE MAGNITUDE OF THE RESULTANT IS ',F9.1,
      1    'THE INCLINATION IS ',F9.1)
C
        STOP
        END
```

<table>
<tr><td>**Programming Example**
Financial Aid (Question Analysis)</td><td>Each data card shows a series of true/false answers given to 16 questions that are used to determine if a person qualifies for financial aid.</td></tr>
</table>

Input:

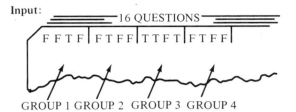

GROUP 1 GROUP 2 GROUP 3 GROUP 4

The questions are categorized into four groups consisting of four questions each. The applicant must respond "true" to at least one question in each group to qualify. Write a program to process each card and respond with the message APPLICANT QUALIFIES or APPLICANT DOES NOT QUALIFY.

```
C.....................................................
C..  PURPOSE - DEMONSTRATE THE USE OF LOGICAL VARIABLES TO..
C..             ANALYSE TRUE/FALSE (BINARY) INFORMATION.  ..
C.....................................................
C
C
        LOGICAL X1,X2,X3,X4,X5,X6,X7,X8,X9,X10,X11,X12,X13,
       +        X14,X15,X16
C
        LOGICAL GROUP1, GROUP2, GROUP3, GROUP4
C
C
     10 READ(5,11)X1,X2,X3,X4,X5,X6,X7,X8,X9,X10,X11,X12,X13,
       +          X14,X15,X16
     11 FORMAT(16L1)
C
C              TEST GROUP 1 SET
C
        IF(X1.OR.X2.OR.X3.OR.X4) THEN
           GROUP1 = .TRUE.
        ELSE
           GROUP1 = .FALSE.
        ENDIF
C
C              TEST GROUP 2 SET
C
        IF(X5.OR.X6.OR.X7.OR.X8) THEN
           GROUP2 = .TRUE.
        ELSE
           GROUP2 = .FALSE.
        ENDIF
C
C              TEST GROUP 3 SET
C
        IF (X9.OR.X10.OR.X11.OR.X12) THEN
           GROUP3 = .TRUE.
        ELSE
           GROUP3 = .FALSE.
        ENDIF
C
C              TEST GROUP 4 SET
C
        IF(X13.OR.X14.OR.X15.OR.X16) THEN
           GROUP4 = .TRUE.
        ELSE
           GROUP4 = .FALSE.
        ENDIF
C
C
C      .....................................
C      .............  TEST TOTAL GROUPS  ......
C      .....................................
C
        IF(GROUP1.AND.GROUP2.AND.GROUP3.AND.GROUP4) THEN
C
     20    WRITE(2,21)
     21    FORMAT(7X,'APPLICANT QUALIFIES')
C
        ELSE
C
     30    WRITE(2,31)
     31    FORMAT(7X,'APPLICANT DOES NOT QUALIFY')
C
        ENDIF
C
C              LOOP STOPS HERE
C
        GO TO 10
        STOP
        END
```

| Programming Example |
| Water Bill |

A data card gives the water meter reading of a customer at the beginning and end of the month. The number in column 1 indicates if this is an industrial or residential user.

Input:

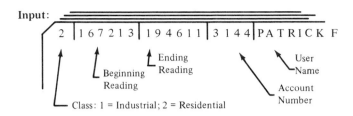

Industrial users are charged a flat rate of 0.5¢/gallon. Residential users pay 0.8¢/gallon until they reach 5000 gallons. The rate then changes to 0.6¢/gallon for all additional use.

Write statements that will determine and report a correct water bill for both types of users. Plan on a trailer card containing 0's in all fields.

Special situation:

Usually, the gallons of water consumed can be determined by subtracting the "end" and "beginning" meter readings. There is a single exception, however, and that is when the meter passes through its maximum value (999999) and moves on to 000000. This is called **meter-go-round**.

Include statements in your program to detect this situation and take appropriate corrective action.

```
C...........................................................
C..   PURPOSE - COMPUTE WATER BILL.                       ::
C...........................................................
C
C          ------IMPORTANT VARIABLES------
C
C     --NBEGIN    METER READING AT BEGINNING OF PERIOD    --
C     --NEND      METER READING AT THE END OF PERIOD      --
C     --NACCT     ACCOUNT NUMBER                          --
C     --CLASS     CLASS CODE                              --
C                   1 = INDUSTRIAL                        --
C                   2 = RESIDENTIAL                       --
C     --GAL       GALLONS OF WATER CONSUMED               --
C
      INTEGER CLASS
C
   10 READ(5,11) CLASS, NBEGIN, NEND, NACCT
   11 FORMAT(I1,2I6,I5)
C
C                    TEST FOR TRAILER CARD
C
      IF(NACCT.EQ.0) STOP
C
C                    HAS METER PASSED 999999
C                    IF YES CORRECT END READING
C
      IF(NEND.LT.NBEGIN) NEND = NEND + 1000000
C
C                    CALCULATE GALLONS AND REPORT BILL
C
      GAL = NEND - NBEGIN
C
C                    IF INDUSTRIAL USER APPLY FLAT RATE
C                    (0.5 CENTS PER GALLON)
C
      IF(CLASS.EQ.1) BILL = GAL * .005
C
C                    IF RESIDENTIAL USER CHECK FOR LOW USE
C                    (RATE =  0.8 CENTS PER GALLON)
C
      IF(CLASS.EQ.2.AND.GAL.LT.5000.) BILL = GAL * .008
C
C                    IF RESIDENTIAL AND OVER 5000 GALLONS
C
   20 IF(CLASS.EQ.2.AND.GAL.GE.5000.) BILL = 5000. * .008
     1                                 +(GAL - 5000.) * .006
C
      WRITE(2,31) NACCT, BILL
   31 FORMAT(10X,I5,10X,F9.2)
C
      GO TO 10
C
      END
```

13 | Functions/Subroutines/ Subprograms

In the early days of computers, the major technological advances concentrated pretty much on hardware development. We needed faster machines that could process several programs at once. We needed more memory and higher transfer rates. Costs had to be reduced. The situation today is considerably different. The majority of new advances are software oriented. The cost of hardware has become almost trivial, while the cost of programming and program management is skyrocketing. Why is this?

A textbook deals with relatively simple programs requiring 20 to 25 lines of FORTRAN code. Government and industry, on the other hand, have problems requiring up to 20 or 25 *thousand* lines of code. Teams of programmers and years of program development are involved. When programs are this large, certain new techniques are needed to handle them. These new techniques are the subject covered in this chapter. Just as subscripted variables provided an efficient means of dealing with high volumes of data, **subprogramming** will allow us to deal efficiently with problems having large volumes of complex, interrelated (and often repeated) FORTRAN code.

Subprogramming involves the concept of dividing a program's algorithm into manageable parts (modules) where each part will accomplish a subsidiary task of the overall problem. Each of these parts (subprograms) can be written, compiled and tested *independently,* making error detection, verification and program management much more efficient.

Each subprogram can even be written by a different person, if necessary.

Assume, for example, that you are involved in a large scientific project, and as part of the overall programming effort it is necessary to solve several large sets of simultaneous equations (such as those in Chapter 10). Subprogramming techniques will allow you to write the FORTRAN code necessary to accomplish this subsidiary task. When the code is written, it can be compiled as a separate item and tested independently. When the subprogram is found to be working correctly, it can easily be merged with other subprograms for use by the main program. This will prove to be an invaluable "divide and conquer" technique so important to modern software development. Further, as more and more subprograms (like your simultaneous equation one) are written, we start to develop a library of subprograms that considerably broaden our computational capabilities. We develop what is called a **software library**.

13.1 | Types of Subprograms

Subprograms fall into two basic categories: **FUNCTION subprograms** and **SUBROUTINE subprograms**. If the purpose of a subprogram is to compute or define a *single* value (like the root of an equation or the tangent of an angle or the area under a curve), a FUNCTION subprogram usually is used. When a subprogram has to compute or define more than one value, a SUBROUTINE subprogram should be used.

There is a strong similarity between writing a main program and defining a subprogram. Figure 13.1 demonstrates this point by writing (side by side) the FORTRAN code for computing the tangent of an angle, first as a program and then as a FUNCTION subprogram.

Program   **Subprogram**

```
      READ(5,10) X                      FUNCTION TAN (X)
C     ....CONVERT TO RADIANS....   C     ....CONVERT TO RADIANS....
C     THETA = X / 57.3             C     THETA = X / 57.3
C                                  C
C     TAN = SIN(THETA)/COS(THETA)  C     TAN = SIN(THETA)/COS(THETA)
      .........................          .........................
      WRITE(2,20) TAN                    RETURN
      STOP                               END
      END
```

Figure 13.1 Subprogram Conversion

Very shortly, we will explore in detail the difference between a program and a subprogram, but for the moment notice the following:

1. The subprogram has a title statement as its first statement. It declares the type and name of the subprogram.
2. The subprogram does not use a READ statement to define the input value X or a WRITE statement to output the value TAN.
3. The subprogram uses a RETURN statement in place of the STOP statement used in the main program.

Of these three differences, the easiest to explain is why a RETURN statement is used in place of a STOP statement.

Execution of a STOP statement signals that the program is completed; there are no more statements to execute; and the CPU (central processing unit) is released. While it is not impossible for a subprogram to issue a STOP instruction, that is an activity more typically accomplished in the main program. The subprogram is supposedly written to determine some intermediate value. When this value is found, we must somehow pass control from statements in the subprogram back to statements in the main or invoking program. That is what the RETURN statement accomplishes.

Differences Between Programs and Subprograms

Difference No. 1: the STOP statement does not normally appear in a subprogram. In place of the STOP statement, use the RETURN statement. It accomplishes the control transfer you want without releasing the CPU (stopping execution.)

Difference No. 2: READ and WRITE statements may appear inside a subprogram, but they are not the conventional and most convenient way to provide input/output to a subprogram. The next difference is that data values usually are not communicated to or from a subprogram by READ/WRITE operations. There is reason for this. Consider how inconvenient it would be if the subprogram SIN or SQRT contained READ or WRITE statements. Each time you wanted to use these functions, a data card would be required and extraneous (unwanted) lines of output generated.

The more conventional way of passing information to a subprogram is by using an argument list. In Figure 13.1, the input value X is passed to subprogram

TAN as an argument. The idea of communicating values by using one or more arguments is not new to you. You have done it before many times when communicating with library functions such as:

SIN(X)   ALOG10(B)   ATAN2(X,Y)

└─Input   └─Input   └─Input
Argument   Argument   Arguments

Difference No. 3: A subprogram must have a title or identification statement that declares the type of subprogram, the name of the subprogram and the parameters of the subprogram. When defining a subprogram, the title or identification statement is required as the first statement. We already have indicated that this statement declares the name of the subprogram and tells whether it is a FUNCTION subprogram or a SUBROUTINE subprogram. The title statement serves one more purpose: it defines the value(s) that must be provided as input for the subprogram to operate on.

FUNCTION   TAN   (X)

Type   Name   Argument
                       List

The variable name or names appearing in the argument list define the number and mode of the input values that must be provided in order to initiate the subprogram.

It may be easier for you to understand the argument list this way. Whatever variable names you previously would place after the command READ to provide input to a main program, these same names will now appear in the argument list to provide input to the subprogram. The normal procedure is to allow the main program to define (READ if necessary) all the input values and then pass them to the subprogram through the argument list. These input values are more correctly called the **parameters** of the subprogram. They are the names used in the definition of the subprogram. The term ARGUMENT is used for the corresponding variable names used by the invoking program.

Output from a function subprogram is transmitted through the function name. The name declared in the title statement of a function subprogram serves *two* purposes:

1. It is the *name* or title given to the block of FORTRAN code that defines the function, and
2. It is the *name* of a memory location in the invoking or using program that will be loaded each time the block of code is executed.

An *example* of this is as follows. The name TAN identifies the series of statements that compute this trigonometric value, and it is also the name of a memory location (in the main program) that will be loaded each time these statements are executed.

Because the name of a function subprogram serves as a **carrier** (holds the output generated by the subprogram), that name must be given a value somewhere inside the subprogram (usually by an assignment statement). This means that the name TAN must appear again somewhere between the title statement and the RETURN statement. This is the way the output of a function subprogram is transmitted back to the invoking program.

The title statement has already been described in some detail. It must be the first statement in the subprogram.

13.2 Driver (Test) Program

Now that we have written (defined) our first subprogram, the next step is to write a short main program (driver) that will test its correct performance. If the subprogram is found to be working correctly, we can release it for general use in whatever large program it was intended for.

Subprogram TAN used
(tested) three times

Output test results

Release CPU

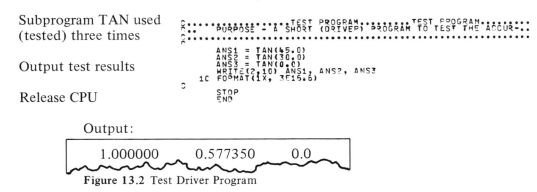

```
C.............TEST PROGRAM............TEST PROGRAM.........
C..  PURPOSE : A SHORT (DRIVER) PROGRAM TO TEST THE ACCUR-..
C.....................................................
      ANS1 = TAN(45.0)
      ANS2 = TAN(30.0)
      ANS3 = TAN(0.0)
      WRITE(2,10) ANS1, ANS2, ANS3
   10 FORMAT(1X, 3E16.6)
C
      STOP
      END
```

Output:

    1.000000   0.577350   0.0

Figure 13.2 Test Driver Program

The statements in Figure 13.2 are merely a brief main program that uses subprogram TAN three times. While the sample test data is not as extensive as it should be, it is sufficient to detect any major flaw.

Deck Layout

When one or more subprograms are used in solving a problem, the usual procedure is to place the statements defining each subprogram immediately after the statements defining the main program. As usual, the last item will be the data deck, and control cards may be needed to separate the various entities.

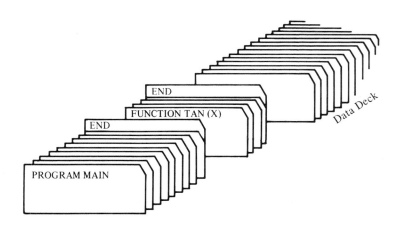

The main program and the various subprograms will be listed and compiled separately. If no compiling errors are detected, the execution process starts by passing control to the first statement in the main program. Whenever the name of one of your subprograms appears in the main program, control immediately leaves the main program and passes to statements inside the subprogram. These statements are executed until a RETURN statement is reached. At that time control passes back to the main (invoking) program.

For the driver program shown in Figure 13.2, that process takes place three times. Each time the function TAN appears in the main program, the argument enclosed in parentheses is passed to the subprogram. The subprogram operates on this value until the quantity TAN is defined. A RETURN statement is then reached, which passes control back to the main program where TAN is used to define ANS1, ANS2 or ANS3. A WRITE statement displays all these values and the STOP statement is executed. The program terminates.

13.3 Root of An Equation

We have dealt almost exclusively with functions that have a single variable in its argument or parameter list. A problem requiring a larger list is now presented.

Write a FUNCTION subprogram that determines *one* root of a quadratic equation.

General Form: $ax^2 + bx + c = 0$

Basic Equation: $\text{root} = \dfrac{-b + \sqrt{b^2 - 4ac}}{2a}$

For the moment only one root will be determined. That accomplished, the solution can be expanded to include both roots, thereby forcing a conversion to a SUBROUTINE subprogram.

As a means of demonstrating that a subprogram *can* contain a READ or WRITE statement, assume the following additional requirement is imposed: if the equation does not have real roots, issue the following error message:

> INSIDE FUNCTION SUBPROGRAM ROOT1 . . . .
>
> IMAGINARY ROOTS DETECTED . . . .

Do not attempt any further calculation.

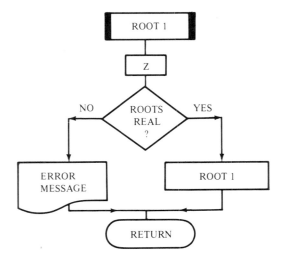

```
FUNCTION ROOT1 (A, B, C)
C
C    PURPOSE - DETERMINE ONE OF THE ROOTS OF A QUAD-
C              RATIC EQUATION.  DEMONSTRATE AN ARG-
C              UMENT LIST HAVING MORE THAN ONE
C              ARGUMENT.
C
C    --ROOT1      NAME OF FUNCTION SUBPROGRAM --
C    --A,B,C      COEFFICIENTS DEFINING THE EQUATION
C
C         TEST FOR REAL OR IMAGINARY ROOTS
C
      Z = B**2 -4.0*A*C
C
      IF(Z.GE.0.0) THEN
C
C            ROOTS ARE REAL
C
          ROOT1 = (-B+SQRT(Z))/(2.0*A)
          RETURN
C
      ELSE
C
C            ROOTS ARE IMAGINARY
C
          WRITE(2,10)
   10     FORMAT(2X,'INSIDE FUNCTION ROOT1....',/,
     +           12X,'IMAGINARY ROOTS DETECTED....')
C
          RETURN
C
      ENDIF
C
      END
```

The parameter list in the title statement declares that three real values are needed to initiate this subprogram. These arguments (parameters) are separated by commas. A statement inside the subprogram uses these parameters to define the value Z. The variable Z is called a **local variable** meaning that it is an intermediate quantity needed or used by the subprogram in the computational process.

Z is tested to determine if an imaginary root is involved. If the root is imaginary, an error message is generated. If the root is real, the variable ROOT1 (which is also the name of the function) is defined, after which control is returned to the using program.

13.4 | Converting to a Subroutine

If both roots of the quadratic equation are wanted, the easiest solution is to convert to a SUBROUTINE subprogram. The first modification is in the title statement. It would now be:

$$\text{SUBROUTINE ROOTS (A,B,C,ROOT1,ROOT2)}$$

$$\underbrace{\hspace{2cm}}_{\text{Sending}} \underbrace{\hspace{2.5cm}}_{\text{Receiving}}$$

The most noticeable difference in this title statement (other than the word SUBROUTINE) is that the argument list contains both input (sending) and output (receiving) variable names. Since a subroutine is expected to return more than one output value, the name of the subroutine is used for identification purposes *only*. It is *not* used to hold any of the output values. Names associated with the output of a subroutine simply are added to the parameter list. The complete subroutine now would be:

```
C       SUBROUTINE ROOTS (A,B,C,ROOT1,ROOT2)
C
C       PURPOSE - COMPUTE BOTH ROOTS OF EQUATION.  DEMONSTRATE
C                 SUBROUTINE SUBPROGRAM AND SHOW THE DIFFERENCE
C                 IN THE ARGUMENT LIST OF THIS TYPE OF SUBPRO-
C                 GRAM.
C
C       --A,B,C         INPUT PARAMETERS DEFINING THE EQUATION  --
C       --ROOT1         OUTPUT DEFINING ONE OF THE ROOTS        --
C       --ROOT2         OUTPUT DEFINING THE OTHER ROOT          --
C
C       -----TEST FOR REAL OR IMAGINARY ROOTS-----
C
        Z = B**2 -4.0*A*C
C
        IF(Z.GE.0.0) THEN
C
C            BOTH ROOTS ARE REAL
C
             ROOT1 = (-B+SQRT(Z))/(2.0*A)
             ROOT2 = (-B-SQRT(Z))/(2.0*A)
C
             RETURN
        ELSE
C
C            ROOTS ARE IMAGINARY
C
             WRITE(2,10)
10           FORMAT(2X,'INSIDE SUBROUTINE ROOTS.....',/,
      +           12X,'ROOTS ARE IMAGINARY......')
C
             RETURN
C
        ENDIF
        END
```

As you can see, the difference in defining a subroutine and a function subprogram is not substantial. It is basically the matter of providing additional entries in the parameter list of the subroutine to accommodate more than one output value.

13.5 | Formal Definitions

Now that you have a general understanding of subprogramming, we present some tighter, more formal definitions. It is important for you to know that there actually are four types of subprograms in FORTRAN.

Types of Subprograms

1. Library Functions
2. Arithmetic Statement Functions
3. Function Subprograms
4. Subroutine Subprograms

Library functions are the easiest to understand and the simplest to use. They represent a series of predefined function subprograms that are provided as part of the compiler/processor software. The list of library functions available on your system is provided in its reference manual. They cover the more common mathematical operations. If the mathematics you want to perform are not available as a library function, it is possible to design a "home-made" function by means of one of the other three types of subprograms.

If you are computing a single value and that value can be determined by a *single arithmetic statement,* there is a special function subprogram available. It is called the **arithmetic statement function** subprogram. Because this type of subprogram is so brief (consisting of only one arithmetic statement), it is handled in a special way. It does not require a separate block of code and a title statement. It does not require a RETURN statement or an END statement. This type of subprogram is merged more simply into the using or evoking program as will be shown shortly.

If you are computing a single value but many statements are needed, the FUNCTION subprogram would be used. Finally, if many values are to be computed (obviously requiring many statements), the SUBROUTINE subprogram is most appropriate.

13.6 | Definition vs. Use

There are two distinctly different operations involved when dealing with any subprogram:

1. Definition
2. Use

We have been concentrating on the definition of a subprogram, which starts by writing the title statement. The next step is to write the defining code. During this process, the programmer selects variable names, statement numbers and sequence of statements with all the freedom previously used when writing a main program.

If you decide to number some of the statements in your subprogram using the numbers 10, 20 and 30, you need not be concerned that some other subprogram or that the main program might be using these same statement numbers.

If you use the variable names X and Y in defining your subprogram, the names X and Y can be used by other subprograms (or by the main program) to represent entirely different variables and *no conflict will arise.* Each X and Y will have its own memory location. When you use the name X in your subprogram, you will get the X memory location tied to your subprogram and not some other X value. The reason for this is that each subprogram is *independent* of either the main program or any other subprogram. The END statement appearing as the last statement in each block of code signals the compiler to treat the block as a separate entity. It is to have its own statement numbers, its own variable name table, its own object code. **It is to be compiled separately.**

When a number of subprograms have been written and individually tested, all of them can be put together as shown in Figure 13.3.

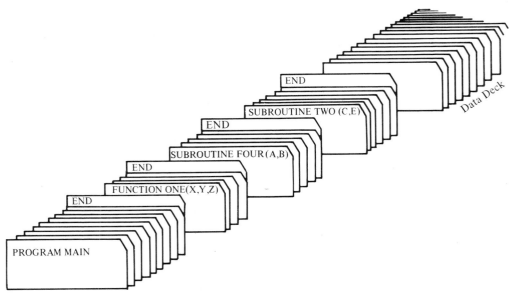

Figure 13.3 Deck Configuration

Using a Subprogram

Now that you see how to *define* a subprogram, it is necessary to start talking about the very much separate and distinctly different activity of *using* a program. In the case of FUNCTION subprograms, very little additional explanation will be needed. Using a SUBROUTINE subprogram, however, is something you have not seen before and will require considerable explanation. Since there is no numeric value associated with the name of a subroutine, the subroutine name is not used in arithmetic statements in the same way a function subprogram is used. A separate **CALL statement** is necessary, the details of which we will cover shortly.

A CALL statement can appear almost anywhere. One subroutine can CALL another (which could, in turn, CALL another). A CALL statement can appear inside a FUNCTION subprogram. About the only restriction imposed is that a subprogram cannot CALL itself. Realize however, that a CALL involves a transfer of control, and that transfer should be shown in the simplest most easy-to-follow way.

A Structured Approach

As the complexity of a program increases, there must be an increase in the *disciplined approach* you use in writing the program. You must learn to modularize your solution, that is, identify the program in terms of a number of related subtasks. Each of these subtasks can then be written as a somewhat independent (isolated) subprogram, usually a subroutine.

The main program is then given the responsibility for making CALLs to the various subroutines as they are needed. In this way, the main program takes on a supervisory or executive role and does not become involved in any of the petty calculations. If the main program is primarily responsible for making sequential calls to the various subprograms, it becomes almost like an organizational chart, showing in what order the various modules (subprograms) are used in the overall solution of the problem.

In the problems that follow, the main program will:

1. Control or supervise *the input* and storage of data values. (Establish the problem's data base.)
2. Make successive *calls* to the various subprograms. (Pass data to subprograms. . .receive data from subprograms.)
3. *Output* important values and generate any final reports.

Some of these functions even can be assigned to a subprogram, but, for the moment, let the main program handle the input, output, and most of the calls. Let the subprograms do all the work.

Transfer of Values

When a subprogram is used, the variables supplied as input by the invoking program (those in the argument list) must be coupled (bound) to the corresponding variable names used in the definition of the subprogram (those in the parameter list). The coupling process is accomplished in two different ways: **substitution by value** and **substitution by address**. Both methods will be described in detail in Chapter 14. In one case, the present value of an input variable (variable defined in the invoking program) is passed to the subprogram. In the second (and more frequently used) method, an address is passed. It tells which memory location in the invoking program holds the value wanted by the subprogram. In either method, there should be a consistency in number and mode between the variable names in the argument list and the parameter list. If the parameter list calls for a one-dimensional array of real numbers in its *defining* statement, the using program must oblige by providing a one-dimensional array of real numbers when the subprogram is *used*. Any variation almost surely will result in an error.

There are a few other things to learn before you can use a subprogram effectively, but these considerations will be deferred just a little longer.

13.7 | Arithmetic Statement Function (In Detail)

The arithmetic statement function has a great deal in common with library functions. It returns only *one* value to the point in the program where it was used. Depending on the mode of its name, that value will be either real or integer. The function can have one argument or many arguments. Once it has been properly defined *within a block of code* (a main program or a subprogram), it can be used in arithmetic expressions *within that particular block of code only*! You might say, it has "local" meaning (meaning within the block). All other subprograms have "global" meaning (can be used by all blocks).

The name of this function must conform to the same rules used for naming a variable:

1. No more than six characters.
2. The first character must be a letter and all other characters restricted to letters and numbers.
3. If the first letter is I, J, K, L, M or N, it is an integer function and will return an integer result; otherwise, it is a real function.

The need for this type of subprogram might develop in the following way. Assume you are writing a program or subprogram where two equations keep cropping up.

$$\text{Equation 1: } f(x,y) = \frac{x^4 - y^4}{xy} - 1 \qquad \text{Equation 2: } f(x,y) = \frac{(x-y)^4}{xy} - 1$$

It is an annoyance to keep writing these equations over and over each time they occur, so you elect to set up two arithmetic statement functions called EQ1 and EQ2. The defining statements would be:

EQ1(X,Y) = (X**4–Y**4)/(X*Y)–1.0
EQ2(X,Y) = (X–Y)**4/(X*Y)–1.0

 └─Name └─Dummy Arguments └─Defining Expression

These defining statements must appear at the top of the block of code they are to be used in (before any executable statement in that block). These statements show the function names, arguments and method of evaluation (how to compute the function based on the input arguments provided).

With these definitions established, statements such as:

ANS1 = EQ1(3.0,4.0) – EQ2(3.0,4.0)

can be written. Wherever X and Y appear in the definition of these functions, the values 3.0 and 4.0 will be substituted. Equation 1 is evaluated, then Equation 2. The difference is stored as ANS1.

Figure 13.4 shows several other arithmetic statement function definitions.

```
TAN(X) = SIN(X/57.3)/COS(X/57.3)
SIND(X) = SIN(X/57.3)
COSD(X) = COS(X/57.3)
SECD(X) = 1.0/COS(X/57.3)
CSCD(X) = 1.0/SIN(X/57.3)
```

Figure 13.4 Sample Arithmetic Statement Function

The first defines a function called TAN that has a single argument called X. The defining arithmetic expression shows how to use X to compute a value, which you should recognize as the tangent of X. This is a quicker way of doing what we did in Figure 13.1. Both techniques result in a function called TAN, but the one in Figure 13.4 could only be used in the block of code in which this defining statement occurred. It would have local meaning only. The one defined in Figure 13.1 (a function subprogram) could be used by any block of code.

The next four examples in Figure 13.4 could be used in a program that dealt with several trigonometry problems. They not only provide a secant and cosecant function, but also functions where the argument is in degrees, not radians.

Conflicting Names

What happens if you inadvertently name an arithmetic statement function the same as a library function? This situation should be avoided. In most systems, your definition will take precedence. It is a matter of how the compiler does its searching. If it searches for subprograms you have defined before those predefined by the processor, your error will be corrected.

As a final example, take a look at these two definitions:

ROOT1 (A,B,C) = (–B+SQRT(B**2–4.*A*C))/(2.*A)
ROOT2 (A,B,C) = (–B–SQRT(B**2–4.*A*C))/(2.*A)

We opened this chapter by determining these roots in FUNCTION subprograms. They then were combined into a SUBROUTINE subprogram. Now we are using an ARITHMETIC STATEMENT subprogram. All three forms are allowed in FORTRAN. Each has certain advantages over the other. This latter form is the quickest and easiest to define, but it is not global. The subroutine is more complex to define, but it is global and can include internal checking for imaginary roots.

Rules for Defining the Arithmetic Statement Function
Example: ROOT2 (A,B,C) = (–B–SQRT(B**2–4.*A*C))/(2.*A)

Name—⌐   Parameter List—↗   Defining Expression——↘

The Name: ROOT2

> The name must obey the rules for naming a variable and be consistent with the mode of the value it is to supply.

The Parameters: A,B,C

> 1. These are the defining parameters. They are **dummy variables** (explanation follows in section 13.9).
> 2. They are separated by commas when more than one.
> 3. They are enclosed in parentheses.
> 4. Subscripted variables are not allowed as parameters in the definition. (Only simple variables can be used.)

The Defining Expression: (–B–SQRT(B**2–4.*A*C))/(2.*A)

> 1. It establishes a relationship among the parameters.
> 2. It may include constants, variables other than parameters, library functions and other defined subprograms whose definition precedes this one.
> 3. It may not include subscripted variables in definition.

Special Location

As mentioned before, the unique nature of this subprogram (only one statement long) allows special positioning of its defining statement. It is located in the declarative portion of the program or subprogram in which it is to be used. The declarative portion is that part that lies before the first executable statement in the program. This defining statement is itself a non-executable statement; it just provides a definition. Other statements that are found in the declarative portion include REAL, INTEGER, DIMENSION, etc. (See Appendix D for a complete list and preferred sequence of presentation.)

13.8 | Dummy Variables

The defining parameters (variables) of this type of function are *not* true variables in that they do not cause the assignment of new memory locations. They are called **dummy variables** and simply serve to establish a relationship between each variable name's position in the parameter list and its position or positions within the defining expression. They are *place holders.* Since these defining variables are providing positional information only, they should be simple variables. Subscripted variables are not allowed in the definition.

When the function is used, the situation is entirely different. In the place of each defining (dummy) variable, a specific constant, the name of a variable (simple or subscripted) or an expression may be used. Remember the consistency requirements: **the arguments in the using statement must agree in number, order and mode (but not in *name*) with the arguments in the defining statement or subprogram.**

Using Different Names

Beginning programmers do not like the idea of using one set of variable names when defining a function and another set of names when using it. It is regarded as a purposeless confusion factor. "I don't care what they say," the programmer grumbles, "to avoid confusion, I'm always going to use the same names in the argument list that were used in the parameter list when the function was defined."

The point is well taken. When there is nothing to be gained in a different name, confusion *can* be avoided by using identical names. There are times, however, when this isn't practical. The library function SIN is probably *defined* in terms of a parameter called X. It would be a serious handicap if all *uses* of this function required X as an argument. We want more flexibility than that. The obvious solution is to allow any value when the function is used and to represent that value by the name X in the definition.

There are times when the name of the argument and the name of the corresponding parameter *must* be different.

Consider a main program that must deal with three quadratic equations. A value of A, B, and C is needed to define each equation. Accordingly the names A1, B1, and C1 are used to define the first equation; and A2, B2, and C2 are used to define the second equation; and A3, B3, and C3 are used to define the third equation.

Equation 1	Equation 2	Equation 3
A_1 B_1 C_1	A_2 B_2 C_2	A_3 B_3 C_3
$3x^2 + 6.5x - 7.2$	$5.8x_1 - 3.6x_2 - 2.9$	$4.0x^2 - 2.0x - 18.3$

The arithmetic statement subprograms we were dealing with a minute ago can now be used for solving these equations as follows:

$$\text{ROOT1 (A,B,C)} = (-B + SQRT(B**2 - 4.*A*C))/(2.*A)$$
$$\text{ROOT2 (A,B,C)} = (-B - SQRT(B**2 - 4.*A*C))/(2.*A)$$

To find the desired roots, it is only necessary to substitute a set of the new coefficients (A1, B1, and C1 for example) in place of those used in the definition.

$$\text{ANS1} = \text{ROOT1(A1, B1, C1)}$$
$$\text{ANS2} = \text{ROOT2(A1, B1, C1)}$$

$$\text{ANS3} = \text{ROOT1(A2, B2, C2)}$$
$$\text{ANS4} = \text{ROOT2(A2, B2, C2)}$$

$$\text{ANS5} = \text{ROOT1(A3, B3, C3)}$$
$$\text{ANS6} = \text{ROOT2(A3, B3, C3)}$$

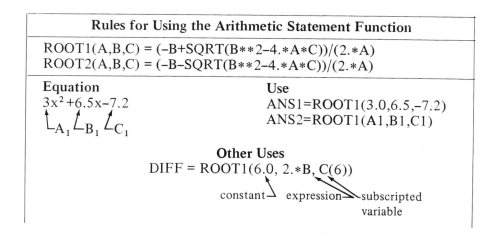

Rules for Using the Arithmetic Statement Function
ROOT1(A,B,C) = (–B+SQRT(B**2–4.*A*C))/(2.*A) ROOT2(A,B,C) = (–B–SQRT(B**2–4.*A*C))/(2.*A)

Equation	Use
$3x^2 + 6.5x - 7.2$ A_1 B_1 C_1	ANS1=ROOT1(3.0,6.5,–7.2) ANS2=ROOT1(A1,B1,C1)

Other Uses
$$\text{DIFF} = \text{ROOT1(6.0, 2.*B, C(6))}$$

constant — expression — subscripted variable

> **The Arguments:**
>   1. They are program variables (i.e., not dummies). They must agree in number, order, and mode with the arguments in the defining statement, but their actual names need not agree.
>   2. They may be subscripted variables.
>   3. They may be expressions.
>   4. They may be constants.

13.9 | The Function Subprogram

When the topic of FUNCTION subprograms was first introduced, somewhat trivial examples were given so as not to obscure how they operate. It is time to show their true potential by developing more substantial applications. In the process, the topic of defining vs. using arguments will be discussed in more detail.

Assume you have just been hired by a group that is involved in graphically displaying data. You are constantly being given a series of X and Y values and required to plot them (either by hand or by a computer-controlled plotter). The values are almost always too big or too small to plot directly. The first operation is to scale the data (determine a factor by which each value must be multiplied so that the data fits on the specified plotting surface).

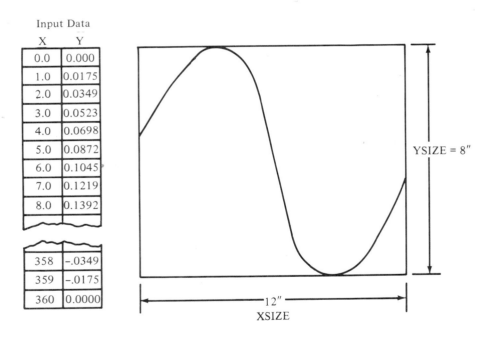

Input Data

X	Y
0.0	0.000
1.0	0.0175
2.0	0.0349
3.0	0.0523
4.0	0.0698
5.0	0.0872
6.0	0.1045
7.0	0.1219
8.0	0.1392
358	-.0349
359	-.0175
360	0.0000

Figure 13.5 Typical Graphical Plot

As a simple example, assume you have been asked to plot the X-Y values representing a sine curve (Figure 13.5). They are to be plotted so that the physical height of the plot (YSIZE) is 8 inches and the width (XSIZE) is 12 inches. Since the largest value of Y is +1 and the smallest value is –1, plotting Y directly would give a plot 2 inches in height, and, therefore, a scale factor of 4.0 is needed. The values of X range from 0.0 to 360. and these values will have to be scaled also — in this case, scaled down.

When processing unfamiliar data, it would be necessary to search for the largest value, search for the smallest value, define the range and then compute the scale factor. This is just the type of assignment a subprogram is designed to accomplish.

You need to write a FUNCTION subprogram called SCALE that receives as input:

ARRAY — the name of a one-dimensional array of data to be scaled.

NSIZE — an integer telling the number of elements in this ARRAY.

SIZE — the physical size (in inches) of the plotting surface.

The purpose of this subprogram is to compute a single real value called SCALE. This is the value that all elements in ARRAY should be multiplied by to get the data in a form that can be plotted directly.*

For the moment, assume that the maximum size of the input vector ARRAY is 1000 elements. Of course, the subprogram should be able to handle arrays of varying size, and that is the reason for the parameter NSIZE. Inside subprogram SCALE the data will be scanned to determine the largest and smallest element. Once these are known, the scale factor is computed by simple division.

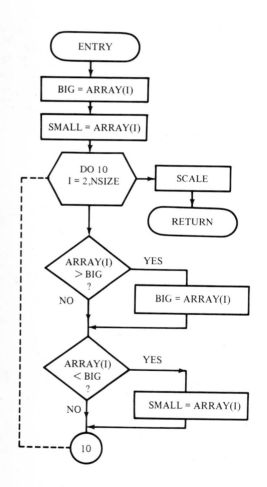

```
      FUNCTION SCALE (ARRAY, NSIZE, SIZE)
C.........................................................
C..    PURPOSE - SEARCH A ONE DIMENSIONAL ARRAY (VECTOR) AND..
C..              DETERMINE A SCALE FACTOR TO ALLOW THE DATA ..
C..              TO BE PLOTTED WITHIN A SPECIFIC AREA.      ..
C.........................................................
C
C              -----IMPORTANT VARIABLES-----
C
C     --ARRAY      ARRAY OF DATA TO BE SEARCHED           --
C     --NSIZE      NUMBER OF ELEMENTS IN ARRAY (1000 MAX) --
C     --BIG SMALL  LARGEST AND SMALLEST ELEMENT OF ARRAY  --
C
      DIMENSION ARRAY(1000)
C
C              INITIATE SEARCH ACTIVITY
C
      BIG = ARRAY(1)
      SMALL = ARRAY(1)
C
      DO 10 I = 2, NSIZE
C
         IF(ARRAY(I).GT.BIG) BIG = ARRAY(I)
         IF(ARRAY(I).LT.SMALL) SMALL = ARRAY(I)
C
   10 CONTINUE
C
C              COMPUTE SCALE FACTOR
C
      SCALE = SIZE / (BIG - SMALL)
C
      RETURN
      END
```

In the process of testing this subroutine, we can give a specific example of the requirement that arguments in the *using* statement must agree in number, type, order and mode with those established in the definition statement.

*To adjust the values of Y as required in Figure 13.5, the value of SCALE would be 4.0.

The test data will be X-Y values representing a sine curve (the data shown in Figure 13.5). These values are easily generated inside the main or driver program by statements such as:

```
C:::::PURPOSE - MAIN PROGRAM TO TEST THE EFFECTIVENESS OF
C::             FUNCTION SCALE. TEST DATA WILL BE SINE CURVE.
C...................................................
C            -----IMPORTANT VARIABLES-----
C
C    --X      ARRAY OF 361 VALUES REPRESENTING ANGLES    --
C                             (0 TO 360)
C    --Y      ARRAY OF 361 VALUES REPRESENTING SIN(X)    --
      DIMENSION X(361), Y(361)
C
C            SET UP LOOP TO DEFINE BOTH ARRAYS
C
      DO 10 I = 1, 361
C
         X(I) = FLOAT(I-1)
         Y(I) = SIN(X(I)/57.3)
C
   10 CONTINUE
```

The following statements invoke function SCALE twice: once to get the X-scale factor and once to get the Y-scale factor.

```
C
C
   20 XSCALE = SCALE(X, 361, 12.0)
C
C
   30 YSCALE = SCALE(Y, 361, 8.0)
C
```

In both these examples, the first argument is a real one-dimensional array, the second is a simple integer, and the last is a simple real variable. When the name X appears in the first use of SCALE, the name X and the name ARRAY are linked. The next time SCALE is used, the name Y is linked to the name ARRAY.

Now that the two scale factors are known, statements in the main (or driver) program can be written to modify each value of array X and array Y so that the elements of each can be plotted directly.

```
C
C         ......SCALE BOTH ARRAYS.......
C
      DO 40 I = 1, 361
C
         X(I) = X(I) * XSCALE
         Y(I) = Y(I) * YSCALE
C
   40 CONTINUE
C
C            ALL ELEMENTS ARE READY FOR PLOTTING
C
```

Passing an Array Name

This is the first time you have seen the name of an array passed as an argument. There is nothing terribly difficult about this except that an inexperienced programmer is tempted to put a subscript after the array's name:

```
C
   50 XSCALE = SCALE(X(I), 361, 12.0)
C
      STOP
      END
```

Incorrect Use of Subscript

(Most often you get in trouble when you do *not* provide a subscript. Here, you get in trouble if you do.) When a subscript is provided after the name of an array, you are no longer referencing the whole array, just one element of the array. An array name followed by a subscript is the equivalent of a simple variable.

The point then is this. If the subprogram asks for the whole array, *give the name only*. If a subscript is provided, the corresponding defining argument must be a simple variable.

13.10 | Defining and Using Arguments

For every different variable name appearing in a main program, the compiler automatically assigns a memory location for that variable and uses a variable name table to keep track of where in memory each value is located (its address). In the case of subscripted variables, the table records only where the first element is located. It is called the **base address** of the array. All other elements of the array can be found using this base address.

Variables in a subprogram are handled pretty much in the same way. Each subprogram has its own variable name table, and, as each new variable occurs, a new memory location is assigned and posted in the table.

Exception: variables that appear in the argument list (its parameters) are not treated in exactly the same way. They are listed in the variable name table, but they are not assigned addresses (locations in memory) of their own. Instead, they wait to take on the *address* of the variable they are to be related to in the calling program. This means that BIG or SMALL have their own memory location, but the names ARRAY, NSIZE and SIZE do not. The name ARRAY will pick up the base address of the array X on the first use of SCALE and the base address of Y on the second call. While we need this feature to couple the two programs, a definite danger is involved. The subprogram now is able to get directly at memory locations that are supposed to be under the control of (assigned to) the main program only. This could lead to difficulties.

A statement such as:

ARRAY (10) = 0.0

appearing in the subprogram in effect zeroes out the tenth element of X or the tenth element of Y in the main program.

A clever programmer can use this information to change many values in the invoking program when a function is called (not just the single value associated with the function name). For example, the whole array X could be modified in one call to the function SCALE. All you would have to do is modify each element of ARRAY and you are thereby modifying the X array. Any variable in the argument list is vulnerable to redefinition in this way.

This is not a recommended procedure. If the original intent is to modify more than one variable, a subroutine should be used. The purpose of this explanation is to issue a warning. When defining a subprogram, be careful in making charges to any variables in the parameter list. These charges have a direct effect on the corresponding variable in the invoking program. It may be convenient to think about some variables (parameters) as input variables or output variables, but both are capable of modifying memory locations in the using program because of the way in which correspondence of arguments is being accomplished (substitution by address), *any* argument is subject to change.

There is one last comment on this programming example. Based on what you have just been told, it would be possible to establish the identity of vector ARRAY in the subprogram by using the following DIMENSION statement:

FUNCTION SCALE(ARRAY,NSIZE,SIZE)
DIMENSION ARRAY(1)

Room For Base Address Only

This DIMENSION statement establishes the fact that ARRAY is a subscripted variable and provides sufficient room for accepting the base address of the one-dimensional array of the calling program. The reason for pointing this out is that this technique is often used in commercially prepared subprograms as will be shown in Chapter 15. When you see a DIMENSION statement like this for the first time, you might well be concerned that an error has been made and that the array is too small.

Warning:

When passing multidimensional arrays, it is necessary to pass more than just the base address of the array. For this reason, the technique used above only applies for one-dimensional arrays.

Quiz #13 Subprograms

Part 1: Answer the following questions.

1. Why is subprogramming so important when writing exceptionally large, complex programs?
2. Does the RETURN statement accomplish the same action that the STOP statement does?
3. Usually, input and output to a subprogram is accomplished by other than READ/WRITE operations. Explain.
4. The name of a FUNCTION subprogram serves two purposes. What are they?
5. What is a "Test Driver" program? What is it used for?
6. Describe the difference between the argument list of a FUNCTION and a SUBROUTINE subprogram.
7. What are the four types of subprograms allowed in FORTRAN?
8. Variable names used in a subprogram are said to be *independent* of variable names used in the main or other subprograms. What does this mean to you, the programmer?
9. What is the purpose of a CALL statement?
10. What are the rules for naming a subprogram?

Part 2: Writing a Subprogram (Median Value).

A FUNCTION subprogram called MEDIAN receives as input arguments:

> ARRAY – a one-dimensional array of values sorted in ascending order of magnitude.
>
> NSIZE – an integer telling the size of ARRAY (maximum value to be 100)

The subprogram verifies that ARRAY has been sorted properly and then returns the median value of the array – the middle element.

Answers:

1. Allows a large program to be divided into smaller, more manageable parts.
2. No. The STOP statement terminates execution and releases the central processing unit. The RETURN passes control back to the evoking program.
3. INPUT/OUTPUT is accomplished by the argument list.
4. Identifies the body of FORTRAN code defining the function. Identifies a memory location that receives the output of the function.

5. A short main program that sends test data to a sub-program to see if the subprogram is working properly.

6. The subroutine has both input and output arguments. The function subprogram has only input arguments.

7. Library functions   Arithmetic statement functions
   Function subprogram   Subroutine subprogram

8. You may create variable names without being concerned that the same name is used in any other program.

9. To evoke a SUBROUTINE subprogram.

10. The same as for naming a variable.

11.
```
C . . . . . . . . . . . . . . . . . . . . . . . . . . . . . .
C      PURPOSE – DETERMINE THE MEDIAN OF . .
C          AN ARRAY OF SORTED NUMBERS . . . .
C . . . . . . . . . . . . . . . . . . . . . . . . . . . . . .
C
       FUNCTION MEDIAN (ARRAY,NSIZE)
C
       DIMENSION ARRAY (100)
C
C         VERIFY ARRAY SORTED CORRECTLY
C
       DO 20 I=2,NSIZE
          IF(ARRAY(I-1).GT.ARRAY(I))THEN
             WRITE(2,10)
   10        FORMAT(10X,'ARRAY NOT SORTED
             CORRECTLY')
             RETURN
          ENDIF
   20 CONTINUE
C
C         IS NSIZE AN ODD NUMBER
C
       TEST=NSIZE/2*2-NSIZE
C
       IF(TEST.NE.0.0)THEN
          . . .NSIZE IS ODD NUMBER. . .
          MIDDLE=NSIZE/2+1
          MEDIAN=ARRAY(MIDDLE)
       ELSE
C         . . .NSIZE IS EVEN NUMBER. . .
          MEDIAN=(ARRAY(NSIZE/2)+ARRAY
          (NSIZE/2+1))/2.
       ENDIF
C
       RETURN
C
       END
```

13.11 | The Subroutine Subprogram

The subroutine subprogram is a most useful type of subprogram because it is specifically designed to handle more complex problems requiring the return of many values to the evoking program. The whole concept of software package development would not be possible without this basic building block.

As you will recall, the argument list of a subroutine contains both sending and receiving variables. These serve as "carriers" of values needed to initiate the subroutine and *clearly* return the output of the subroutine. In constructing the argument list:

SUBROUTINE ROOTS(A, B, C, ROOT1, ROOT2)

INPUT   OUTPUT

many programmers list the input or sending arguments first, followed by the output or receiving arguments. This is just a matter of style, but it makes things clearer and easier to follow. These arguments are like the arguments in a function subprogram. They are not assigned memory locations of their own, but, rather, assume the address of the corresponding memory locations used when the subprogram is evoked. The same warning applies. Changing any of these variables (input or output) causes changes in the evoking program.

Perhaps this is a good time to get a few things straight. The more capable student (and sometimes the more devious student) will say, "There is no such thing as an input or output argument. They are all the same." "I can compute many values inside a function and return them to the using program. What do I need a subroutine for?"

The cost of software is as high as it is because some people cannot resist the temptation to be tricky. They will do such things as use a variable as an input argument and then use it to hold output also. All these things are possible but, in the long run, not very smart.

Keep it Simple

We are about to write a large, somewhat involved program. It should be written as clearly and as simply as possible. People who get exceptionally clever when writing any program probably do not have any more errors than anyone else, but these errors are often much more difficult to track down.

13.12 | Use of a Subroutine

To evoke (use) a subroutine subprogram, a separate CALL statement is needed.

CALL ROOTS (6.0,7.2,–1.0, FIRST, SECOND)

The word CALL is followed by the name of the subprogram being evoked. This is followed by the argument list. In those positions where input or sending values are required, a constant, defined variable or expression may appear. In those positions where output or receiving values are required, you put the name of the memory locations in the invoking program that is to be loaded as a result of this call. The CALL statement shown above will load memory locations FIRST and SECOND with the two roots to the equation:

$$6x^2 + 7.2x - 1.0 = 0$$

As part of the definition of a subroutine, there should be considerable documentation provided to make the use of this routine as easy as possible. The required input arguments and their position in the argument list should be shown. The same for output arguments. The purpose of the routine should be stated, and sometimes a typical CALL statement is shown. This can be accomplished by a series of comment statements as will be shown in the next programming example.

**Programming Example
Correct the Exams**

A professor gives a multiple choice exam. To each question there are 5 possible responses (1, 2, 3, 4 or 5) and the student must select the correct response.

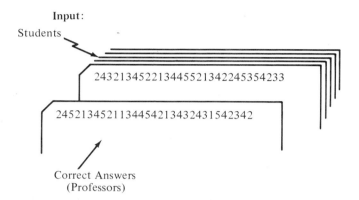

Write a subroutine called **GRADER** that compares the answers given by a student and the answers given by the professor to determine:

(a) Number correct
(b) Number wrong
(c) Score this student achieved

The subroutine should be able to process exams of varying length (i.e., number of questions.)

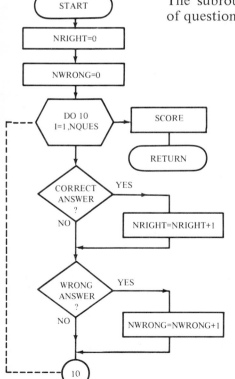

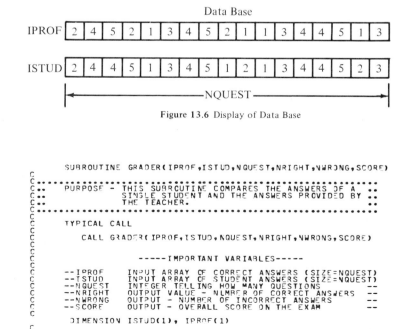

Figure 13.6 Display of Data Base

```
C          ....CLEAR ALL COUNTERS.....
C
      NRIGHT = 0
      NWRONG = 0
C
C          ......LOOP ENTRY POINT........
C
      DO 10 I = 1, NQUEST
C
          IF(ISTUD(I).EQ.IPROF(I)) NRIGHT = NRIGHT + 1
          IF(ISTUD(I).NE.IPROF(I)) NWRONG = NWRONG + 1
C
   10 CONTINUE
C
C          .....COMPUTE AVERAGE......
C
      SCORE = FLOAT(NRIGHT)/FLOAT(NQUEST)*100.
C
      RETURN
      END
```

Use of Grader

Subroutine GRADER will now be used to score two exams. The first card in the data deck indicates the number of questions and the number of students who have taken the first exam. The next card gives the correct answers to this exam. The student answers follow.

A second set of cards describe Exam 2 in a similar fashion. Assume that the number of questions and the number of students are different.

Write a main program to process both exams. Assume that the maximum number of questions is 80.

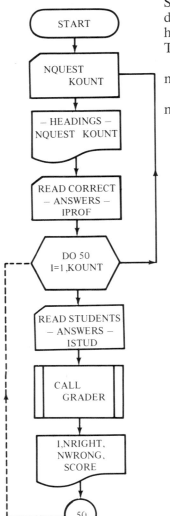

Use of Grader

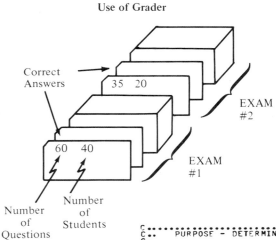

```
C..............................................................
C..   PURPOSE - DETERMINE THE SCORES OF EACH STUDENT.        ..
C..                                                          ..
C..           - SHOW EXECUTIVE BEHAVIOR OF MAIN PROGRAM.     ..
C..............................................................
C
C          -----NEW VARIABLE---------
C
C  --KOUNT      NUMBER OF STUDENTS TAKING THIS EXAM       --
      DIMENSION IPROF(80), ISTUD(80)
C
    5 READ(5,10) NQUEST, KOUNT
   10 FORMAT(2I4)
C
      WRITE(2,20) NQUEST, KOUNT
   20 FORMAT(1H1,10X,'NUMBER OF QUESTIONS IS ',I4,10X,
     1          'NUMBER OF STUDENTS IS ',I4,///)
C
C          .....ESTABLISH ARRAY OF CORRECT ANSWERS.....
C
      READ(5,30) (IPROF(I),I=1,NQUEST)
   30 FORMAT(80I1)
C
C          .....LOOP ENTRY POINT.....
C
      DO 50 I = 1, KOUNT
          READ(5,10) (ISTUD(J),J=1,NQUEST)
          CALL GRADER(IPROF,ISTUD,NQUEST,NRIGHT,NWRONG,SCORE)
C
          WRITE(2,40) I, NRIGHT, NWRONG, SCORE
   40     FORMAT(2X,'STUDENT NUMBER ',I4,4X,'NUMBER CORRECT ',
     1      I4,4X,'NUMBER WRONG ',I4,'AVERAGE SCORE =',F8.2)
C
   50 CONTINUE
C
C          .....PROCESSING COMPLETE.....PROCESS NEXT EXAM.....
C
      GO TO 5
      STOP
      END
```

This main program reads the input data, makes successive calls to subroutine GRADER, and controls the output of the final results. Names in the main program and in the subprogram have been made identical. These names could, of course, be different (see next example). In the main program, the arrays IPROF and ISTUD must be of sufficient size to take in the largest number of questions possible. In the subroutine, these arrays are dimensioned at one (that is, each array adds the answers of only one student).

Notice the new symbol in the flow chart. The processing box with thick vertical sides is frequently used to represent the use of a subroutine subprogram.

It would be nice if each student could get a list of the questions he or she failed to answer correctly as well as the correct answers. This could be accomplished inside subroutine GRADER. It might be nice if each student got a sheet of output with the professor's answers across the top, with the student's answers directly below, with the wrong responses suitably marked, and with the final SCORE printed at the bottom. The student is invited to expand subroutine GRADER appropriately to accomplish these tasks.

| Programming Example |
| A Large Scale Problem |
| (Aircraft Controller) |

To demonstrate the more complex use of subroutines, we are going to become aircraft controllers at a busy airport. Our responsibility is to keep track of where aircraft are on a radar screen, how close they are getting to each other, and to issue appropriate warnings and corrective action if they get too close. This will be a complicated task so we will break it into parts, each accomplished by a separate subroutine.

Subroutine TRACK

One of the first problems will be to track the planes on radar (for the moment we will ignore altitude variations). Accordingly, a subroutine TRACK is to be written whose input arguments are the X and Y position of an aircraft when first sighted (X0,Y0) and its position one minute later (X1,Y1). (This is like the lighthouse tracking problem in chapter 8.) The subprogram will use the four input values to predict the flight path of the plane. We want the output to be a vector XARRAY and a vector YARRAY, each containing 60 elements representing the expected X-Y positions of the plane at one-minute intervals for the next 60 minutes. Once subroutine TRACK is defined, we will test it twice. The first test will simulate a National Airlines flight departing from the airport, and the second test will simulate an American Airlines flight passing nearby. The input test data has been specifically chosen to allow easy recognition of the path both these planes will have.

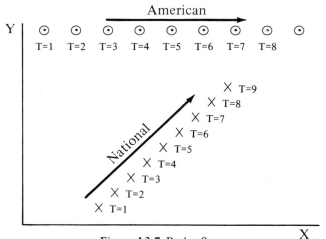

Figure 13.7 Radar Screen

The first input test data will be:

TIME=0   TIME=1

X0 = 0.0   X1 = 1.0
Y0 = 0.0   Y1 = 1.0

The output of this call is to represent a
National Airlines plane.

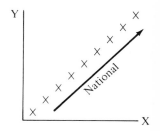

The second test data will be:

TIME=0   TIME=1

X0 = 0.0   X1 = 1.0
Y0 = 20.0   Y1 = 20.0

The output of this call will represent the
American Airlines plane.

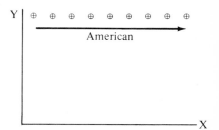

By making two calls to TRACK, we are computing four vectors representing the X-Y paths of two different aircraft on the radar screen. These positions
can be displayed on the screen to assist the controller, but they will serve another
important purpose in the next subroutine.

Subroutine CPA

The purpose of tracking these planes is to determine how close they will
get to each other if they maintain course and speed. A little mental computation will reveal that these planes are on a collision course if they are at the same
altitude. The minimum distance at which they will pass is called CPA (closest
point of approach). Write a subroutine with the same name (CPA) that receives
as input the projected path of two planes, and determine how close they will
get to each other and when that will happen.

Inside subroutine CPA, compute a one-dimensional array called DIST
representing the separating distances of the planes (again assuming the same altitude) at one-minute intervals for 60 minutes. Have subroutine CPA search
DIST for its minimum element (call it SMALL) and the position of this element
(subscript) in the array (call it ITIME). SMALL will tell how close the planes
get to each other. ITIME will tell how many minutes into the flight this will
take place.

Subroutine WARNING

If the value of SMALL is less than one mile, a possible dangerous situation
is developing. The altitude of the two aircraft should be verified by radar or by
voice communication or both. A warning message should be issued and, if the
separating altitude turns out to be less than 1000 feet, a course change, speed
change or altitude change made. Finally, the whole process should be repeated
to assure safe passing of these two planes. This could be accomplished by subroutine WARNING.

There are any number of additional tasks that could be involved, but we already have a sizable job in front of us.

Writing Subroutine TRACK

Given:

X0,Y0 — X and Y locations at time 0.
X1,Y1 — X and Y locations at time 1.

Required:

XARRAY — X and Y locations for next 60 minutes.
YARRAY

The first calculation inside subroutine TRACK is to determine the change in X for the first minute of flight and store that value as DELTAX. The corresponding change in Y should be determined and stored as DELTAY. To determine where the aircraft will be, let us say five minutes into the flight, it will be 5 times DELTAX and DELTAY away from where it was originally sighted.

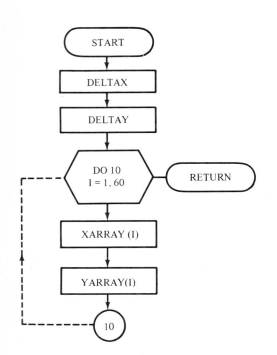

```
C
C:: PURPOSE - PREDICT THE FLIGHT PATH OF AN AIRCRAFT   ::
C::              BASED ON TWO SIGHTINGS.                ::
C
      SUBROUTINE  TRACK(X0,Y0,X1,Y1,XARRAY,YARRAY)
C
C              -----IMPORTANT VARIABLES-----
C
C     --X0,Y0     LOCATION OF AIRCRAFT WHEN FIRST SIGHTED --
C     --X1,Y1     LOCATION OF AIRCRAFT ONE-MINUTE LATER   --
C
C     -    -      -    -      -    -      -    -      -
C
C     --XARRAY    OUTPUT LOCATION ARRAY....X AND Y LOCAT- --
C     --YARRAY    IONS FOR A 60 MINUTE PERIOD.            --
C
      DIMENSION XARRAY(1), YARRAY(1)
C
C              ....COMPUTE RATE INFORMATION.....
C
      DELTAX = X1 - X0
      DELTAY = Y1 - Y0
C
C              DEFINE ELEMENTS OF OUTPUT ARRAY
C
      DO 10 I = 1, 60
         XARRAY(I) = X0 + FLOAT(I) * DELTAX
         YARRAY(I) = Y0 + FLOAT(I) * DELTAY
C
   10 CONTINUE
C
      RETURN
      END
```

The next step in the solution is to write a main program that calls TRACK twice: once for the National flight and once for the American flight. Recognizing that both flight paths will be needed for the next phase of the problem (writing and testing CPA), the main program must provide room in memory to store both flight paths.

The output should appear as follows:

NATIONAL		AMERICAN	
X	Y	X	Y
1.0	1.0	1.0	20.0
2.0	2.0	2.0	20.0
3.0	3.0	3.0	20.0
4.0	4.0	4.0	20.0
5.0	5.0	5.0	20.0
59.0	59.0	59.0	20.0
60.0	60.0	60.0	20.0

```
C...........................................................
C... PURPOSE - MAIN PROGRAM TO DEFINE THE FLIGHT PATH OF  ..
C...            TWO AIRCRAFT.                              ..
C...........................................................
C
C                   -----IMPORTANT VARIABLES-----
C
C      --XNAT       ARRAY OF X-POSITIONS (NATIONAL FLIGHT)  --
C      --YNAT       ARRAY OF Y-POSITIONS (NATIONAL FLIGHT)  --
C      --XAM        ARRAY OF Y-POSITIONS (AMERICAN FLIGHT)  --
C      --YAM        ARRAY OF Y-POSITIONS (AMERICAN FLIGHT)  --
C
       DIMENSION XNAT(60), YNAT(60), XAM(60), YAM(60)
C
C              -----DEFINE NATIONAL ARRAY-----
C
       CALL TRACK(0.0, 0.0, 1.0, 1.0, XNAT, YNAT)
C
C              -----DEFINE AMERICAN ARRAY-----
C
       CALL TRACK(0.0, 20.0, 1.0, 20.0, XAM, YAM)
C
       WRITE(2,10)
    10 FORMAT(1H1,3X,'NATIONAL',50X,'AMERICAN',///)
C
       WRITE(2,11)
    11 FORMAT(4X,'X',12X,'Y',45X,'X',12X,'Y',//)
C
C              DUMP ARRAYS
C
       WRITE(2,12)(XNAT(I),YNAT(I),XAM(I),YAM(I),I=1,60)
    12 FORMAT(1X,2F10.1,44X,2F10.1)
C
       STOP
       END
```

On the first call to TRACK, the four input arguments are specified as constants. Then the names XNAT and YNAT are specified, which are both array names. These are the memory locations the subprogram will be loading as a result of this first call to TRACK. On the second call to TRACK, the one-dimensional arrays XAM and YAM are defined.

Writing Subroutine CPA

Under the direction of the main program (it is acting like a supervisor) subroutine CPA will be passed the data generated by the two calls to subroutine TRACK. We will use subroutine CPA to suggest how several different programmers can be involved in writing different portions of a large program.

Assume for a moment that you have been completely isolated from any part of this problem description. You know nothing about a National or American Airlines flight — the fact that they are on a collision path or any of the variable names or calculations that have taken place thus far. All you have been told is that you will be given a number of arrays defining the position of two aircraft at one-minute intervals. You are told to use this information to produce an array defining the separating distance between the aircraft at each interval. You are further asked to determine the smallest element of this array and its position (location) in the array.

As you start to solve your part of the problem, you have the right to give the four input arrays any variable names you choose. Since you are dealing with the 60 X,Y values of two different planes, it is possible you would select names as follows:

DIMENSION X1(60),Y1(60),X2(60),Y2(60)

Even though the variable names X1 and Y1 have been used in another block of code (they are simple variables in subroutine TRACK), this is of no concern to you. *Any names you choose while writing CPA will be independent of any other names in other subprograms.*

Figure 13.8 shows how the distance between the two (test) aircraft keeps decreasing. The computation of any one value of DIST (like at time T = 10) is a relatively simple one. The difference in X location of the two aircraft is computed (and called SIDE1) and the difference in the Y location of the two aircraft is computed (and called SIDE2). Squaring these sides and taking the square root will compute one of the elements of the array DIST.

After sixty distances are computed, we will search array DIST for the smallest value and its position in the array.

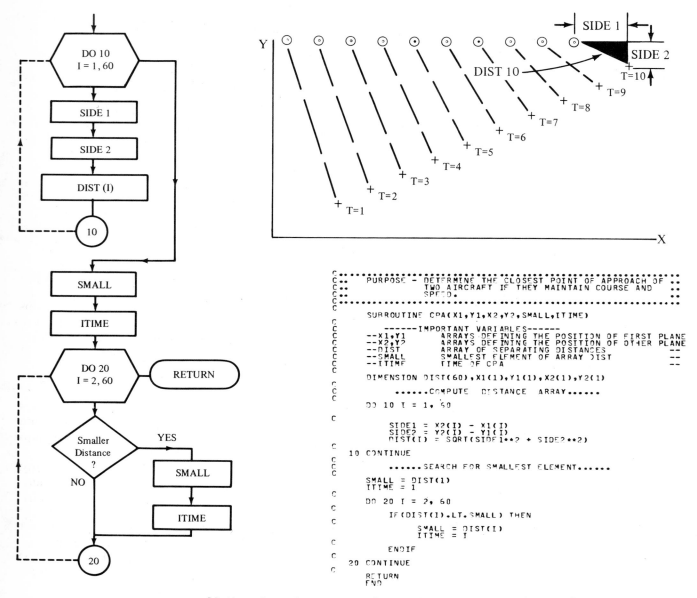

```
C.........................................................
C..  PURPOSE - DETERMINE THE CLOSEST POINT OF APPROACH OF  ..
C..           TWO AIRCRAFT IF THEY MAINTAIN COURSE AND     ..
C..           SPEED.                                       ..
C.........................................................
      SUBROUTINE CPA(X1,Y1,X2,Y2,SMALL,ITIME)

C      ------IMPORTANT VARIABLES------
C    --X1,Y1      ARRAYS DEFINING THE POSITION OF FIRST PLANE
C    --X2,Y2      ARRAYS DEFINING THE POSITION OF OTHER PLANE
C    --DIST       ARRAY OF SEPARATING DISTANCES           --
C    --SMALL      SMALLEST ELEMENT OF ARRAY DIST          --
C    --ITIME      TIME OF CPA                             --

      DIMENSION DIST(60),X1(1),Y1(1),X2(1),Y2(1)
C
C          ......COMPUTE  DISTANCE  ARRAY......
C
      DO 10 I = 1, 60
C
          SIDE1 = X2(I) - X1(I)
          SIDE2 = Y2(I) - Y1(I)
          DIST(I) = SQRT(SIDE1**2 + SIDE2**2)
   10 CONTINUE
C
C          ......SEARCH FOR SMALLEST ELEMENT......
C
      SMALL = DIST(1)
      ITIME = 1
C
      DO 20 I = 2, 60
C
          IF(DIST(I).LT.SMALL) THEN
C
              SMALL = DIST(I)
              ITIME = I
C
          ENDIF
C
   20 CONTINUE
C
      RETURN
      END
```

Notice that the array called DIST is dimensioned as having 60 elements while all the other arrays are dimensioned at one. Do you know why? The array DIST is not a parameter. It is a block of memory used inside of CPA to hold sixty intermediate values. All the other arrays are parameters. For the sake of programming style, it would really be better to dimension all the arrays to a value of 60.

Statements can now be added to the main program that will pass the arrays representing the flight paths of the National and American flights to subroutine CPA.

```
C.........................................................
C..  PURPOSE - SHOW STATEMENTS IN MAIN PROGRAM THAT PASS   ..
C..           FLIGHT PATH INFORMATION TO SUBROUTINE CPA    ..
C..           AND THEN RECEIVES OUTPUT FROM CPA.           ..
C.........................................................
      DIMENSION XNAT(60),YNAT(60),XAM(60),YAM(60)
C
   10 CALL TRACK(0.0,0.0,1.0,1.0,XNAT,YNAT)
   20 CALL TRACK(0.0,20.0,1.0,20.0,XAM,YAM)
C
C          .....PASS ARRAYS TO SUBROUTINE CPA.....
C
   30 CALL CPA(XNAT,YNAT,XAM,YAM,ANS,WHEN)
C
      WRITE(2,40) ANS, WHEN
   40 FORMAT(F12.2,I8)
C
      STOP
      END
```

If you understand argument transfer, you will see that subroutine CPA receives the base address of XNAT and YNAT that binds these arrays to the names X1 and Y1 (arrays). It also received XAM and YAM base addresses. When the RETURN statement in CPA is reached, a value called SMALL and a value called ITIME will have been defined. Each time these variable names are dealt with in the subprogram, memory locations ANS and IWHEN (locations in the main program) are defined.

An interesting feature of this problem is that in actual operation the initial X and Y positions are not read from data cards or typed on a terminal. A light pen is attached to the radar screen. The operator holds the light pen over the aircraft's position on the screen, and special electronics determine where on the screen the light pen is pointing. The X and Y of the pen is fed to the computer just as if a conventional READ statement had been executed.

We have carried this problem as far as we should, except that statements might be added to subroutine CPA that issue a special warning (in the form of a printout) if the value SMALL (minimum separating distance) is less than 1 mile.

The last few statements of CPA are repeated below with the extra print statement added.

```
C
C        DO 20 I = 2, 60
C           IF(DIST(I).LT.SMALL) THEN
               SMALL = DIST(I)
               TIME = I
C           ENDIF
C     20 CONTINUE
C
C        .....SEE IF PLANES ARE TOO CLOSE......
C        IF(SMALL.LT.1.0) WRITE(2,30) SMALL, TIME
      30 FORMAT(3X,'WARNING....WARNING....DISTANCE =',
     1          F5.1,' AT TIME =', I4)
C
         RETURN
         END
```

13.13 | Other Applications of Subprogramming

Do not get the impression that subprogramming is for scientific applications only. On the contrary, subroutines for business/data processing applications are equally extensive. It would be an easy matter to show other example subprograms that involve accounts payable, accounts receivable, inventory control, check writers, report generators, scheduling, preventative maintenance, insurance premium calculations, etc.

As part of the learning process, we have shown subroutines with complex argument lists and whose function is solely computational. By way of contrast, it is possible to write a subroutine with no argument list, whose sole function is to produce output. The output will be special headings that are to appear at the top of each page of a long report.

Computers are frequently used to generate reports in complex business and industrial settings. School Committee Reports, Auditory Reports, Profit and Loss Statements, Stolen Car Reports are just a few examples of information a computer can supply. To assist in this process, most management software systems have a group of subroutines that facilitate commonly occurring tasks in this effort. The subroutines are part of a software package called "report writer."

Assume that a large automotive dealership must keep track of all the sales within each of its several branch offices. Their sales must be broken down by date, salesman, sticker price, commissions, type of car, etc. A report generator can take this information and come up with a Sales Report at the end of the month, an Inventory Summary Sheet, a Sales Tax Report, etc. One report the salesman is always interested in lists his or her commissions. Assume that each page of such a report requires headings identifying the name of the company, and the address and telephone number of its home office. Below these page titles certain column headings such as "salesman name," "total sales," "vehicle description," "commissions," and so on, might be required. Repeating the WRITE and FORMAT statements each time they were needed would be a waste of time and effort. This is especially true because the FORMAT codes for this type of "dress up" output tend to be long and cumbersome. A far better approach would be to put the necessary WRITE/FORMAT statements in a subroutine called NEXTPG, for example, and simply CALL NEXTPG in the main program whenever necessary.

This process is suggested now and demonstrates that a SUBROUTINE subprogram can have *no argument list* at all. A FUNCTION subprogram, however, must have at least *one* argument.

```
       SUBROUTINE NEXTPG
C
C.......................................................
C..    PURPOSE - CAUSE THE PRINTING OF COMPLEX HEADING AT  ..
C..             THE TOP OF A NEW PAGE EACH TIME THE SUB-   ..
C..             PROGRAM IS CALLED.                         ..
C..                                                        ..
C..      -    -    -    -    -    -    -    -    -          ..
C..                                                        ..
C..         DEMONSTRATE A SUBROUTINE WITH NO ARGUMENTS  --
C.......................................................
C
       WRITE(2,10)
   10  FORMAT(1H1,40X,*QUALITY FORD DEALERSHIP*,///,40X,
      1        *BOSTON MASSACHUSETTS*,5X,*02113*,///,40X,
      2        *TELEPHONE 617-214-6300*,//)
C
C     ......PRODUCE COLUMN HEADINGS..........
C
       WRITE(2,20)
   20  FORMAT(////,5X,*SALESPERSON*,6X,*TOTAL SALES*, 5X,
      1        *COMMISSIONS*,6X,*TOTAL COMMISSIONS*,//)
C
       RETURN
       END
```

This subroutine would be used in the main report generator as suggested in Figure 13.8.

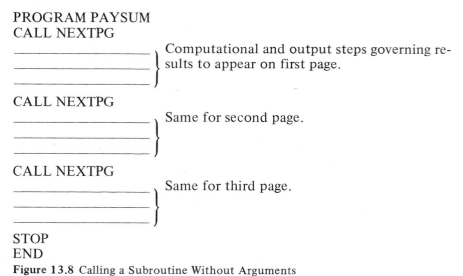

PROGRAM PAYSUM
CALL NEXTPG

$\left. \begin{array}{l} \rule{4cm}{0.4pt} \\ \rule{4cm}{0.4pt} \\ \rule{4cm}{0.4pt} \end{array} \right\}$ Computational and output steps governing results to appear on first page.

CALL NEXTPG

$\left. \begin{array}{l} \rule{4cm}{0.4pt} \\ \rule{4cm}{0.4pt} \\ \rule{4cm}{0.4pt} \end{array} \right\}$ Same for second page.

CALL NEXTPG

$\left. \begin{array}{l} \rule{4cm}{0.4pt} \\ \rule{4cm}{0.4pt} \\ \rule{4cm}{0.4pt} \end{array} \right\}$ Same for third page.

STOP
END

Figure 13.8 Calling a Subroutine Without Arguments

Review Exercises

1. Subprogramming involves the concept of dividing a program's algorithm into manageable parts or modules. Why are these modules described as being "more manageable"?

2.*Is a STOP statement absolutely forbidden in a subprogram?

3. The name of a FUNCTION subprogram serves a purpose not provided by the name of a SUBROUTINE subprogram. What is that purpose?

4. Explain how to test a subprogram you have written prior to merging it with many other subprograms in a large computer project.

5. Provide an example where it is necessary to have names in the argument list of the using statement different from the names in the parameter list of the defining statement of a subprogram.

6.*As the complexity of a computer project increases, the function of the main program is usually restricted to three major tasks. What are these tasks?

7. Discuss the terms "local" vs. "global". Give an example of each.

8.*Discuss the term "dummy variable" and show what is meant by "a place holder."

9. When passing the name of a whole array in an argument list, should a subscript follow the name of the array?

10.*Discuss the term "base address" as it applies to arrays. Why is this quantity so important when passing an array in an argument list?

11. Write a FUNCTION subprogram called KOUNT that will examine a one-dimensional array and determine how many times a specific value appears in the array:

> FUNCTION KOUNT (ARRAY, NSIZE, VALUE)
>
> ARRAY – Name of Array being searched
>
> NSIZE – Number of elements (size) of ARRAY
>
> VALUE – Specific value we are looking for.
>
> KOUNT – Number of times VALUE appears in ARRAY.

12. A one-dimensional array called X consists of whole numbers between 1.0 and 10.0:

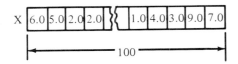

If the array X has 100 elements, use the subprogram in problem 11 to determine how many times the number 6.0 appears in the array.

13. Repeat problem 12, except determine how many times each of the whole numbers appears in the array. Report the number that occurs most frequently, i.e., the mode of the array.

14. Write a FUNCTION subprogram called BIG that will examine a one-dimensional array called DATA (of size NSIZE) and determine the largest element of array DATA.

15.*Write a FUNCTION subprogram called LOCATN that will examine the array called DATA of problem 14 and determine where the largest element of this array

is located, i.e., determine the subscript of the largest element.

16. Write a SUBROUTINE subprogram called BOTH that determines the two quantities requested in problems 14 and 15. That is, examine an array called DATA (of size NSIZE) and determine the largest element of the array and its location in the array:

> SUBROUTINE BOTH(DATA, NSIZE, BIG, LOCATN)

17.*The mechanism shown consists of a rotating crank, a connecting rod, and a piston. Crank R rotates at one revolution per second driving the piston P. The position of the piston is related to the position of the crank as follows:

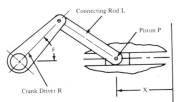

$$X = R (1. - \cos \theta)$$
$$+ L (1. - \sqrt{1. - (R/L)^2 \sin^2 \theta})$$

where $R = 12''$ X = Position of Piston
          $L = 24''$ θ = Position of Crank

Write an arithmetic statement function to compute X as a function of θ.

18. After the arithmetic statement function in problem 17 is defined, compute the position of the piston (the value of X) for θ equal to 0, 1, 2, 3, 4 . . . 358, 359, 360 degrees.

19.*The sine of an angle can be obtained by evaluating the series:

$$SIN(X) = X - \frac{X^3}{3!} + \frac{X^5}{5!} - \frac{X^7}{7!} + . . .$$

Write a subprogram to compute the first ten terms of this series. The argument of this function is to be X.

20. Write a subroutine to read a two-dimensional real array having N columns and M rows (N or M not to exceed 20) and determine the row and column position of the largest elements of the array.

21.*Write a subprogram to compute the area under any curve whose equation is of the form:

$$Y = X^A$$

between the limits $X_{initial}$ and X_{final}. Input arguments should be:

> (a) $X_{initial}$ (b) X_{final} (c) A

22. The equation

$$y = x^3 + 6x^2 + 10x - 12$$

is to be integrated from X = 0 to X = 10. The area under this curve is equal to the area under the curve

$y = x^3$ plus six times the area under the curve $y = x^2$; etc. Use the subprogram in problem 21 (several times) to evaluate the desired area.

23. Write a subprogram to determine all combinations of three integers whose product is N. N is an argument of the subprogram.

24. A projectile is fired with an initial velocity, $V_{initial}$ and travels at constant acceleration, a, for t seconds. Write a subprogram to determine the distance traveled.

$$S = V_{initial}\, t + \tfrac{1}{2} at^2$$

25. An aircraft fires a projectile at an initial velocity of 1000 ft/sec. This projectile is self-propelled and has an acceleration of 10 ft/sec^2. At firing time the speed of the aircraft is 800 ft/sec. The aircraft makes a 90° turn and accelerates at 16 ft/sec^2. Use the subprogram in problem 24 to determine when the aircraft and projectile are 10 miles apart.

26.*Write a subprogram to search a one-dimensional array and determine:

   (a) the largest element and its location if an integer variable M is positive, or
   (b) the smallest element and its location if the integer variable M is negative or zero.

Store the desired element in ELMT and its location in LOC. The array contains 100 elements. Arguments of the subprogram are the array and the integer variable M.

27. Each year every pilot working for an airline must take a test to evaluate his reaction time in performing 40 tasks. An array called TIME having 40 elements records a given pilot's performance on these tasks. The maximum time he is allowed is 12 seconds on any one task and 400 seconds for all 40 tasks.

Write a subroutine called TEST that receives the array TIME and returns the sum of the elements in array TIME as well as the number of elements that are less than 12.0.

28. Write a FUNCTION subprogram called AREA that will approximate the area under a curve. The curve is defined by a one-dimensional array called X and a one-dimensional array called Y (which are input arguments). The final input argument is NDIM, which tells how many data points there are and is the size of both arrays (NDIM not to exceed 100).

   (a) Write this program on the assumption that the points are equally spaced.
   (b) Write this program assuming the spacing between points is variable.

29. Write a subroutine that will divide each element in a specified row of a two-dimensional array by the real value XDIVID. Input arguments should be:

A	— The name of the array
NROW	— The number of rows in A
NCOL	— The number of columns in A
XDIVID	— The value to divide
NROWSP	— The row to be modified

Additional Applications

Programming Example Data Analysis (Standard Deviation)

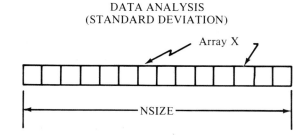

DATA ANALYSIS
(STANDARD DEVIATION)

Very often a series of data values will all be relatively close to one another in value. Any one element of an array X isn't much above or below the average value of X. An example of this is when an exam is given and all the students get about the same grade — the data values don't spread out very much.

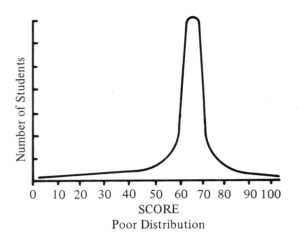

SCORE
Poor Distribution

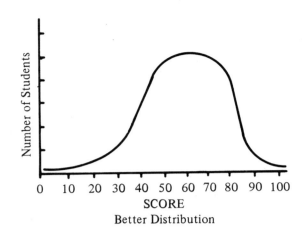

SCORE
Better Distribution

One way to determine how much the data spreads out is to compute the average value of the array X and then go back and compute the deviation of each element of X from this average value:

$$\text{Deviation}_i = |(X_i - X_{AVE})|$$

By summing up these individual deviations and dividing by the number of elements in array X, the value obtained is one way to express how much the data spreads out:

$$\text{Average Deviation} = \frac{\sum_{i=1}^{NSIZE} |(X_i - X_{AVE}|}{NSIZE}$$

Where: X_{AVE} = Average Value of Array X
         NSIZE = Number of Elements In Array X.

This is not the conventional way to determine the deviation of data. We will revise the calculation shortly.

```
C........................................................
C::  PURPOSE - EXAMINE AN ARRAY OF DATA VALUES.  FIND THE ::
C::           AVERAGE VALUE.  DETERMINE THE AVERAGE DEV-  ::
C::           IATION.                                     ::
C........................................................
C
C                  -----IMPORTANT VARIABLES-----
C
C       --X          ARRAY OF INPUT DATA                    --
C       --NSIZE      SIZE OF ARRAY (INPUT)                  --
C       --AVEX       AVERAGE VALUE OF ARRAY (INTERNAL)      --
C       --DEV        AVERAGE DEVIATION OF ARRAY (OUTPUT)    --
C
        DIMENSION X(1)
C
C                  COMPUTE AVERAGE VALUE OF ARRAY X
C
        SUM = 0.0
C
        DO 10 I = 1, NSIZE
C
            SUM = SUM + X(I)
C
   10   CONTINUE
C
        AVEX = SUM / FLOAT(NSIZE)
C
C                  COMPUTE AVERAGE DEVIATION
C
        SUM = 0.0
C
        DO 20 I = 1, NSIZE
C
            TERM = ABS(X(I) - AVEX)
            SUM = SUM + TERM
C
   20   CONTINUE
C
        DEV = SUM / FLOAT(NSIZE)
C
        RETURN
        END
```

The more accepted way to determine the dispersal of data is given by the equation:

$$\text{Standard Deviation} = \sqrt{\frac{(X_1 - X_{AVE})^2 + (X_2 - X_{AVE})^2 + \ldots + (X_n - X_{AVE})^2}{n-1}}$$

$$\text{Standard Deviation} = \sqrt{\frac{\displaystyle\sum_{i=1}^{NSIZE} (X_i - X_{AVE})^2}{NSIZE - 1}}$$

This equation requires each individual deviation to be squared before being accumulated. When this action is completed, exit the DO loop, compute the average value of these squared terms and take the square root of this average. The resulting value is defined as the standard deviation.

The section of code following the computation of the average value of the X array would now be slightly modified to obtain this new value.

```
C
C        AVEX = SUM / FLOAT(NSIZE)
C
C            ....COMPUTE STANDARD DEVIATION.....
C
C        SUM = 0.0
C
C        DO 20 I = 1, NSIZE
C            TERM = (X(I) - AVEX) ** 2
C            SUM = SUM + TERM
C    20   CONTINUE
C
C        DEV = SQRT(SUM / FLOAT(NSIZE - 1))
C        RETURN
         END
```

Programming Example
Data Screening

DATA SCREENING

$$
\begin{array}{c}
\text{Data In} \\
\begin{bmatrix}
6.2 & 7.5 & 8.3 & 11.4 \\
14.3 & 6.2 & 18.4 & 7.6 \\
10.2 & 13.4 & -4.1 & 9.9 \\
3.6 & 4.7 & 8.9 & 12.1 \\
21.2 & 9.9 & 11.6 & 5.8
\end{bmatrix}
\end{array}
\Longrightarrow
\begin{array}{c}
\text{Data Out} \\
\begin{bmatrix}
0.0 & 7.5 & 8.3 & 0.0 \\
0.0 & 0.0 & 0.0 & 7.6 \\
10.2 & 0.0 & 0.0 & 9.9 \\
0.0 & 0.0 & 8.9 & 0.0 \\
0.0 & 9.9 & 0.0 & 0.0
\end{bmatrix}
\end{array}
$$

Write a subroutine called SCREEN that will examine all the elements of a two-dimensional array of real numbers and set to 0 any element that does not lie within a specified range (between XMIN and XMAX inclusive). Arguments of subroutine SCREEN are to be:

Input:

DATA   A two-dimensional array to be screened, containing up to 20 rows and up to 20 columns.

NROW⎫
NCOL⎭   Integers specifying the actual number of rows and columns.

XMIN⎫
XMAX⎭   Two real numbers specifying the acceptable range of each element. In the above example, XMIN=7.5 and XMAX=10.2.

Output:

OUT   A two-dimensional output array of size NROW by NCOL containing the screened array.

Demonstrate the use of this subroutine in a main program that reads from data cards an array called HOT. The program is to pass the array to subroutine SCREEN and receive in return an array called COLD containing values in the range of 13.6 to 24.8 only. It should be set to handle HOT and COLD arrays of up to 20×20 elements in size, but should read from a header card the exact number of rows and columns to be processed in any particular run. The COLD array is to be printed after screening.

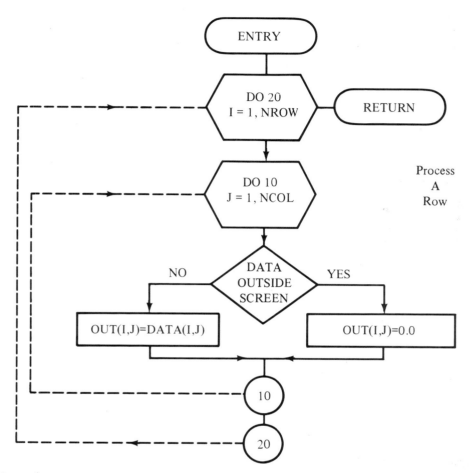

Subroutine:

```
C
      SUBROUTINE SCREEN(DATA,NROW,NCOL,XMIN,XMAX,OUT)
C.............................................................
C..   PURPOSE - SCREEN AN ARRAY CALLED DATA. GENERATE AN    ..
C..             OUTPUT ARRAY CALLED OUT HOLDING ALL THE     ..
C..             SCREENED VALUES.                            ..
C.............................................................
C
      DIMENSION DATA(20,20), OUT(20,20)
C
      THE SIZE OF THIS DIMENSION STATEMENT MUST AGREE IN SIZE
C     WITH THE DIMENSION STATEMENT IN THE MAIN PROGRAM.
C
C          PROCESS ARRAY IN ROW ORDER
C
      DO 20 I = 1, NROW
C
         DO 10 J = 1, NCOL
C
            IF(DATA(I,J).LT.XMIN.OR.DATA(I,J).GT.XMAX) THEN
C
C              DATA VALUE OUTSIDE SCREEN
C
                  OUT(I,J) = 0.0
C
            ELSE
C
C              DATA VALUE INSIDE SCREEN
C
                  OUT(I,J) = DATA(I,J)
C
            ENDIF
C
   10    CONTINUE
C
   20 CONTINUE
C
      RETURN
      END
```

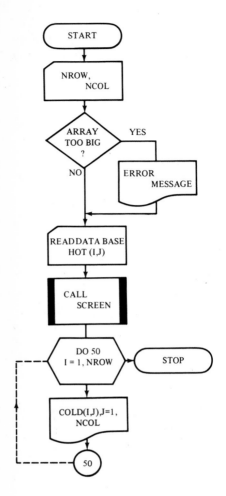

Main Program:

```
C.....................................................
C.. PURPOSE - DEMONSTRATE CALL TO SUBROUTINE SCREEN. ..
C.....................................................
C
      DIMENSION HOT(20,20), COLD(20,20)
C
C           ASSUME SIZE OF ARRAY SPECIFIED ON LEADER CARD
C
      READ(5,10) NROW, NCOL
   10 FORMAT(2I3)
C
C           MAKE SURE ARRAY IS NOT TOO BIG
C
      IF(NROW.GT.20.OR.NCOL.GT.20) WRITE(2,20)
   20     FORMAT(2X,'ERROR.....ERROR - SIZE TOO LARGE')
C
C           READ ELEMENTS OF INPUT ARRAY
C
      READ(5,30)((HOT(I,J),J=1,NCOL),I=1,NROW)
   30 FORMAT(20F4.1)
C
      CALL SCREEN(HOT,NROW,NCOL,13.6,24.8,COLD)
C
C           PRINT SCREENED ARRAY
C
      DO 50 I = 1, NROW
C
          WRITE(2,40)(COLD(I,J),J=1,NCOL)
   40     FORMAT(20F6.1)
C
   50 CONTINUE
C
      STOP
      END
```

Programming Example Searching Data	Write a subroutine called SEARCH that will receive as input arguments:

DATA   A one-dimensional array containing up to 100 elements.

N   An integer specifying the actual size of the array.

The purpose of this routine is to find the largest element in the array and to transfer it to the end of the array by swapping its position with the nth element of the array.

One technique is to compare the first element of the array with the last element. If the first is bigger, swap the two; if it is not, compare the second element with the last element; then the third with the last, etc.

This would involve an excessive number of swaps. A better technique is to search the array for the location of the largest element. When this element is located, swap it with the last element. Make sure you don't lose the value of the last element during the swap activity.

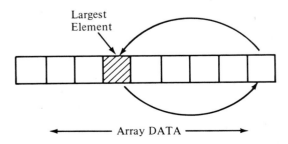

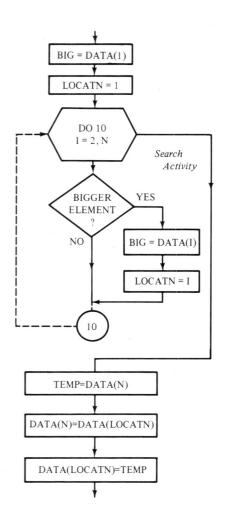

```
       SUBROUTINE SEARCH(DATA,N)
C
C....................................................................
C..:   PURPOSE - SEARCH AN ARRAY AND FIND THE LARGEST ELEMENT.:
C..:             MOVE THIS ELEMENT TO THE END OF THE ARRAY. :
C....................................................................
C
C               -----IMPORTANT VARIABLES-----
C
C      --DATA        NAME OF VECTOR ARRAY TO BE SEARCHED      --
C      --N           SIZE OF ARRAY DATA                       --
C
       DIMENSION DATA(1)
C
C       ASSUME FIRST ELEMENT IS THE LARGEST
C
       BIG = DATA(1)
       LOCATN = 1
C
C          SEARCH REMAINING ELEMENTS
C
       DO 10 I = 2, N
C
           IF(DATA(I).GT.BIG) THEN
               BIG = DATA(I)
               LOCATN = I
           ENDIF
C
    10 CONTINUE
C
C          SWAP STATEMENTS FOLLOW
C
       TEMP = DATA(N)
       DATA(N) = DATA(LOCATN)
       DATA(LOCATN) = TEMP
C
       RETURN
       END
```

SORTING DATA

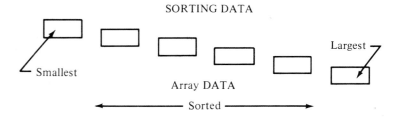

Array DATA

←————— Sorted —————→

| **Programming Example** Sorting Data | If an array called DATA had 60 elements and the previous subroutine, SEARCH, was called as follows: |

> CALL SEARCH(DATA,60)

the largest element of DATA should now be in position 60.

What would happen if a second call to SEARCH was made but with N indexed down by one to 59?

> CALL SEARCH(DATA,59)

Clearly, only the first 59 elements of DATA would be searched and the largest of these would be in position 59.

Problem Statement:

Write a subroutine called SORT that receives as input arguments:

DATA   A one-dimensional array containing up to 100 elements.

N   An integer specifying the actual size of the array.

This routine should sort elements of data in descending order of magnitude so that the smallest element is in position 1 and the largest element is in the nth position.

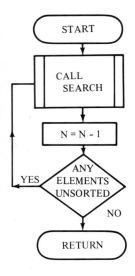

```
C
      SUBROUTINE SORT(DATA,N)
C.....................................................
C..   PURPOSE - MAKE SUCCESSIVE CALLS TO SUBROUTINE SEARCH  ..
C..                                                         ..
C..         - ON EACH CALL TO SORT, THE SIZE OF THE ARRAY.. ..
C..           WILL BE DECREASED BY ONE.  THE ARRAY WILL     ..
C..           EVENTUALLY BE TOTALLY SORTED.                 ..
C.....................................................
C
      DIMENSION DATA(1)
C
   10 CALL SEARCH(DATA,N)
C
      N = N - 1
C
C        ANY MORE ELEMENTS TO SORT
C
      IF(N.GT.1) GO TO 10
C
C        ARRAY COMPLETELY SORTED
C
      RETURN
      END
```

14 Additional Subprogramming Facilities

14.1 Consistency of Size—Multidimensional Arrays

We have presented numerous examples in which one-dimensional arrays have been passed as arguments between the using and defining subprogram. Because of the simple way in which one-dimensional arrays are stored in memory, using them as arguments is a relatively straightforward process. It just involves passing of the "base address" of the array.

The storage of multidimensional arrays (two-dimensional and three-dimensional) is not as simple, and passing them as arguments is more complicated in that the following restriction is imposed:

When multidimensional arrays are passed as arguments, the *size* of the array in the using program must be the *same* as the *size* of the array in the defining program.

This means that the array B of the program shown on the right of Figure 14.1 could not be used as an argument to supply values for an array called A in the subroutine SCALE because they are of different size. One is 3 by 3, the other is 10 by 10.

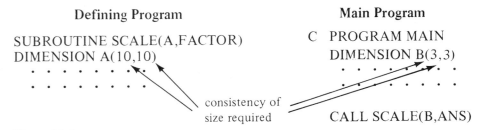

Defining Program

```
SUBROUTINE SCALE(A,FACTOR)
DIMENSION A(10,10)
  . . . . . . . . .
  . . . . . . . .
```

Main Program

```
C  PROGRAM MAIN
     DIMENSION B(3,3)
     . . . . . . . .
```

consistency of size required

```
     CALL SCALE(B,ANS)
```

Figure 14.1

Stated another way, subroutine SCALE (as presently written) can only process arrays of a fixed size, namely, 10 by 10. This would be a serious obstacle if it were not for the fact that DIMENSION statements describing arrays of a subprogram are allowed to have two special forms. You will recall that in a main program only *integer constants* are permitted when specifying the size (maximum subscript) of an array. The same restriction will be applied to DIMENSION statements used in a subprogram if the purpose of the DIMENSION statement is to reserve large areas of memory needed for *local* variables of that subprogram.

MAIN PROGRAM RESTRICTION

DIMENSION A(10, 10), B(16, 14) C (20)

Integer Constants

Arrays that are *arguments* do not fall in this category and are not bound by this restriction. For these variables there is no need to set up large areas of memory of their own. These variables will share the areas established by the DIMENSION statement in the evoking (using) program. Under these special circumstances, a DIMENSION statement need only show that a particular variable represents a subscripted quantity. For each of these variables, only the following information is needed:

1. the base address of the corresponding array in the calling program, and
2. the size of the array if the array is multidimensional (number of rows, number of columns, for example).

Under these conditions, the size of these arrays can be expressed as *integer variables* provided that these integer variables are defined in the argument list of the subprogram.

This is just the relief needed to meet the "SAME SIZE" requirements imposed on multidimensional arrays. The procedure is to use a DIMENSION statement that specifies the array size using variables like M or N. These names are added to the list of arguments with the requirement that their values be defined when the CALL is made. The end result is that both arrays appear to be of the same size (see the programming example that follows). By defining M or N, the subprogram can locate where beyond the base address a particular element of a two-dimensional array is located. These **adjustable dimensions** provide a convenient way to satisfy the consistency of size requirements.

DIMENSION A(M,N), OUT(14, 12) D(N)

Integer variable allowed
if array is an argument

Note: a second method is available on some systems that is even more direct in obtaining this "matching of size" condition:

DIMENSION A(∗,∗), OUT(∗,∗), D(∗)

It involves placing an asterisk in place of size descriptions. The appearance of the asterisk causes the compiler to examine the DIMENSION statement of the calling program to define the information (SIZE) usually supplied in that position.

Programming Example
Scale a Matrix

It is getting more and more difficult these days to avoid problems involving matrix operations. One of the simpler operations is to **scale a matrix**. This merely means to multiply each element of a two-dimensional array by a specific value like 2.0 or 3.8 or 1.6 (the scale factor). By writing a subroutine to accomplish this operation, we will be dealing with a relatively simple subprogram but one that requires the two-dimensional matrix to be consistent in size with the evoking program.

To be effective, this subroutine must be capable of accepting matrices of varying sizes. Write a subroutine called SCALE that receives as input:

A   the name of the matrix
NROW   the number of rows in the matrix

NCOL   the number of columns in the matrix

FACTOR the value by which each element is to be multiplied

Output of this subroutine will be the modified form of the array A. To test this subroutine, we will write a main program that scales two different arrays.

```
      SUBROUTINE SCALE (A,NROW,NCOL,FACTOR)
C
C...................................................
C.... PURPOSE - TO SCALE A MATRIX OF SIZE NROW BY NCOL. ..
C...................................................
C
C                 -----IMPORTANT VARIABLES-----
C
C       --A         THE MATRIX TO BE SCALED (INPUT)    --
C       --NROW      NUMBER OF ROWS IN MATRIX A         --
C       --NCOL      NUMBER OF COLUMNS IN MATRIX A      --
C       --FACTOR    THE SCALING FACTOR                 --
C
C           ....THE OUTPUT IS THE SCALED MATRIX A......
C
C            EXAMPLE OF VARIABLE DIMENSION
C
      DIMENSION A(NROW,NCOL)
C
      DO 10 I = 1, NROW
C
         DO 20 J = 1, NCOL
C
            A(I,J) = A(I,J) * FACTOR
C
   20    CONTINUE
C
   10 CONTINUE
C
      RETURN
      END
```

The first is array B of size 3 by 3. Each element of B will be set at 2.0 and a scale factor of 4.0 used. The second array, array C, will be a 4 by 5 array. Each element will be set at –1.0, and the scale factor will be –8.0. If subroutine SCALE works properly, all elements in both arrays will wind up with the value 8.0.

Input:

ARRAY B
Size: 3 by 3

2.0	2.0	2.0
2.0	2.0	2.0
2.0	2.0	2.0

ARRAY C
Size: 4 by 5

–1.0	–1.0	–1.0	–1.0	–1.0
–1.0	–1.0	–1.0	–1.0	–1.0
–1.0	–1.0	–1.0	–1.0	–1.0
–1.0	–1.0	–1.0	–1.0	–1.0

Output:

Scale Factor 4.0

8.0	8.0	8.0
8.0	8.0	8.0
8.0	8.0	8.0

Scale Factor –8.0

8.0	8.0	8.0	8.0	8.0
8.0	8.0	8.0	8.0	8.0
8.0	8.0	8.0	8.0	8.0

```
C...................................................
C.... PURPOSE - A MAIN PROGRAM THAT TESTS SUBROUTINE SCALE. ..
C..                                                  ..
C..          - THE PROGRAM GENERATES TWO SETS OF TEST DATA, ..
C..            AND THEN MAKES TWO CALLS TO SUBROUTINE SCALE...
C...................................................
C
C                 -----IMPORTANT VARIABLES-----
C
C       --B         FIRST TEST ARRAY...SIZE (3 BY 3)...ALL  --
C                   VALUES OF ARRAY B INITIALLY SET AT 2.0  --
C                                                           --
C       --C         SECOND TEST ARRAY...SIZE (4 BY 5)...ALL --
C                   VALUES OF ARRAY C INITIALLY SET AT -1.0 --
C
      DIMENSION B(3,3), C(4,5)
C
            DEFINE ALL ELEMENTS OF ARRAY B
```

```
C
C           DO 10 I = 1, 3
C              DO 10 J = 1, 3
C                 B(I,J) = 2.0
C       10 CONTINUE
C
C       ...........................................
C       ........ FIRST CALL TO SCALE ..............
C       ...........................................
C
C          CALL SCALE(B,3,3,4.0)
C              DISPLAY SCALED ARRAY
C          WRITE(2,20) ((B(I,J),J=1,3),I=1,3)
        20 FORMAT(3X,3F12.1)
C
C                 DEFINE ALL ELEMENTS OF ARRAY C
C          DO 30 I = 1, 4
C             DO 30 J = 1, 5
C                C(I,J) = -1.0
C       30 CONTINUE
C       ...........................................
C       ........ MAKE SECOND CALL TO SCALE ........
C       ...........................................
C          CALL SCALE(C,4,5,-8.0)
C              DISPLAY SCALED ARRAY
C
C          WRITE(2,40) ((C(I,J),J=1,5),I=1,4)
        40 FORMAT(3X,5F12.1)
C
           STOP
           END
```

14.2   Understanding Array Storage

Subprogramming has many advantages that we will continue to exploit in detail. For a moment, however, we must at least suggest a serious disadvantage: **the concept of subprogramming involves the sharing of memory, which can be dangerous.**

To understand the full implications of this warning, you must know how the computer stores two-dimensional arrays. The following presentations show how a 3 by 3 array called B is stored internally and how a 10 by 10 array called A is stored. We then will show what would happen if these arrays were linked in a subprogram.

Recall, if you will, the arrays suggested in Figure 14.1 (repeated below).

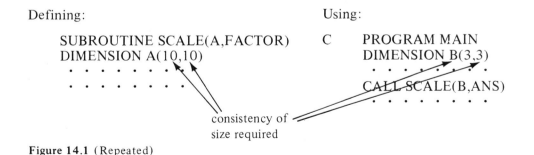

Defining:

        SUBROUTINE SCALE(A,FACTOR)
        DIMENSION A(10,10)
        · · · · · · · ·
        · · · · · · · ·

Using:

        C   PROGRAM MAIN
              DIMENSION B(3,3)
              · · · · · · ·
              CALL SCALE(B,ANS)
              · · · · · · ·

consistency of
size required

Figure 14.1 (Repeated)

If a main program declares a two-dimensional array of size 3 by 3, nine consecutive memory locations are assigned to hold this array. The first 3 locations will hold column 1 of the array, the next 3 locations will hold column 2 and the last 3 will hold column 3. That is, the array is stored *in column order*.

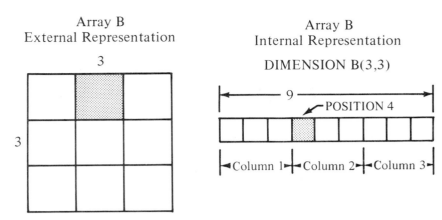

Figure 14.2 Illustration of Column Order Storage

Each time any element of this array is referenced, it is necessary to determine where in the string of nine memory locations this particular element is located. Take, as an example, the element:

B (1,2)

Since it is the first element of column 2, it is located in the fourth memory location. Remember, we are storing in column order.

Now consider the array A of the subprogram that is declared to be of size 10 by 10. If this array was assigned a memory location of its own, the first 10 locations would hold column 1 of the array, the next 10 locations would hold column 2, etc.

An element such as:

A (1,2)

would be 11 elements beyond the base address.

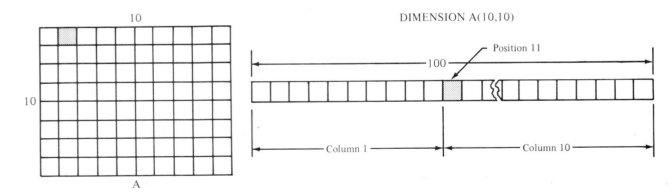

Do you see why these arrays cannot be equated? If the arrays were both the same size, A (1,2) and B (1,2) would be referencing the same elements of the two arrays. When the dimension statements are different, this is not true. A (1,2) is referencing a memory location 11 positions into the array, but the array (in the main program) is only 9 elements long. You would be referencing a memory location two positions beyond array B. If the statement:

A (1,2) = 0.0

was made, some variable two locations beyond array B would be redefined. Errors like this are rather sophisticated in nature and sometimes very difficult to find.

Using subprograms requires a better understanding of memory management because of this "sharing of memory" effect.

14.3

The Equivalence Statement

The EQUIVALENCE statement is a nonexecutable statement that allows the programmer to exercise control over the assignment of memory locations. The EQUIVALENCE statement allows a single memory location to be identified by more than one variable name. How would one use this feature? Assume a program (or subprogram) has been written, and that the programmer has inadvertently used the names IMAX, MAX and IBIG to represent the same value. It would be desirable to correct this error without rewriting all the statements that involve those variable names. The correction can be accomplished by adding (usually in the declarative section) the EQUIVALENCE statement:

EQUIVALENCE (IMAX,MAX,IBIG)

This causes the three variable names contained within the parentheses to refer to a single memory location, thereby correcting the error. The name IMAX, MAX and IBIG all will point, so to speak, to the same memory location.

An equivalence can be set up between more than one group of names. The statement:

EQUIVALENCE (IMAX,MAX,IBIG), (X,Y,Z), (D,E)

First Group   Second Group   Third Group

establishes the names IMAX, MAX and IBIG as being equivalent, while the names X, Y and Z are another group of names equated. Finally, D and E are made equivalent to each other. *The names within each pair of parentheses are equated to each other.*

The EQUIVALENCE statement can be used in an entirely different way. Assume that A, B and C represent rather large arrays within a program, but that only one

DIMENSION A(100), B(100), C(100)

of these arrays is needed at any given time in the program. The array A may be in active use early in the program. The array B is needed only for a short time in the middle of the program and array C is needed late in the program. We describe this situation by saying there is "no overlap in need" for these arrays. A single set of 100 memory locations could be used to store all values but referenced by three different names, thereby conserving memory. It is possible to establish an equivalence between these arrays by the statements:

DIMENSION A(100), B(100), C(100)
EQUIVALENCE (A(1), B(1), C(1))

While it appears that the equivalence statement is equating only three variables (the first element of each array), actually, the effect is much larger. Arrays are always stored in successive memory locations. This is accomplished automatically by the compiler. Aligning or equating the first element of these arrays automatically aligns or equates the remaining elements of the arrays. This relationship is shown in Figure 14.2. The shaded location is the only location referred to in the EQUIVALENCE statement.

|←———————————— 100 Memory Locations ————————————→|

A(1)	A(2)	A(3)	A(4)	A(5)	A(6)	A(7)	A		A(96)	A(97)	A(98)	A(99)	A(100)
B(1)	B(2)	B(3)	B(4)	B(5)	B(6)	B(7)	B(8)		B(96)	B(97)	B(98)	B(99)	B(100)
C(1)	C(2)	C(3)	C(4)	C(5)	C(6)	C(7)	C(8)		C(96)	C(97)	C(98)	C(99)	C(100)

Figure 14.4 Equating Whole Arrays

Using this technique has reduced the amount of memory consumed from 300 to 100.

While it is true we could go back and use a single variable name for all arrays (like A), this would involve rewriting the program and would reduce the ease and clarity with which the program can be read.

One does not often preplan the equating of large arrays. It most often happens on an after-the-fact basis, namely, when a program will not fit into the memory space available. It is then that the programmer starts shopping around to see what space can be saved. This is one method of making the program shorter.

The following example is offered to reinforce or clarify the alignment procedure that takes place when subscripted variables appear in EQUIVALENCE statements.

DIMENSION A(5), B(4), C(2)
EQUIVALENCE (A(3), B(2), C(1))

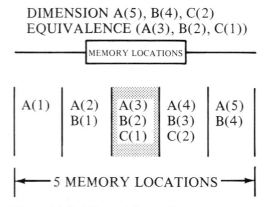

Figure 14.5 A Second Example

The arrays A, B and C are declared as being of size 5, 4 and 2 respectively. The equivalence statement aligns A(3), B(2) and C(1) as the shaded block shows. Then all other elements are positioned as shown. After this aligning, the variables A(4), B(3) and C(2) all refer to the same memory location.

A final reminder: when referencing a subscripted variable in an EQUIVA-LENCE statement, the subscript must be expressed as a constant.

14.4 The COMMON Statement

The EQUIVALENCE statement coordinates variable naming within a single program or subprogram. The COMMON statement allows the coordination of variable naming between a main program and one or more subprograms. It can be used (1) to conserve memory and (2) to allow the sharing of data by means other than an argument list.

Most computers reserve a specific amount of memory for the running of a program. The compiler uses this block of memory in the following way. Starting at the beginning of the block, memory is allocated sequentially to the variables and arrays of the main program and then to those of the various subprograms. The variable names used within each subprogram to identify these locations are, of course, independent of each other.

Normally, when this is completed, there will be some unused memory at the end of the block. We will take advantage of this to set up a special segment of memory, which starts at the end of the block and works forward. This area is called **COMMON storage** and is under your control through the use of the COM-MON statement. This area is unique in that it is accessible to any of the subprograms and to the main program (it can be shared) by evoking the COMMON statement and then declaring what names the sequential memory locations in this area are to be assigned. The statement:

COMMON A,X,BOY,I │ In the Main Program │

appearing in the main program says, in effect, that the main program intends to participate in the sharing of common storage. It declares the names A, X, BOY and I as those to be used in the main program to reference the first four locations in common storage.

The statement:

COMMON B,Y,GIRL,M │ In the Subprogram │

appearing in a subprogram indicates that this subprogram will also share these four memory locations, but that they are to be called B, Y, GIRL and M in this subprogram.

If, at any time in the main program, the variables A or X or I are defined, the corresponding locations in common storage are loaded, and, as a consequence, the variables B or Y or M in the subprogram will automatically become defined (known). On the other hand, defining B or Y or GIRL in the subprogram automatically defines A or X or BOY in the main program. A second subroutine could participate in the sharing process by using the statement:

COMMON X1, Y1, Y2, J

It now has access to these four locations in common storage using the names that the subprogram finds most appropriate, namely, X1, Y1, Y2 and J. If it becomes necessary, COMMON storage can be expanded.

Returning to the main program, consider these statements:

Old	**New**
COMMON A,X,BOY,I	COMMON A,X,BOY,I
	COMMON OUT(100),SALES(60)

The appearance of the second COMMON statement has extended common storage. In addition to the four original memory locations, 160 more real memory locations have been added on. The first 100 of these is an array called OUT followed by 60 locations to be called SALES.

This allocation of memory could have been accomplished by a single COMMON statement as follows:

DIMENSION OUT(100),SALES(60)
COMMON A,X,BOY,I,OUT,SALES

When constructing the list of variable names following the word COMMON in a program or the various subprograms that share common storage, a consistency of *mode* must be observed. The last COMMON statement declares that the first three locations in common storage are to be real in mode, followed by a single integer mode, followed by 160 real locations. You may, of course, set up any pattern of reals and integers you want, but once established: *all other COMMON statements must conform to the same pattern.*

The correspondence in mode consistence is displayed in the following example:

Main Program	**Subprogram**
DIMENSION J(4),X(35)	DIMENSION A(10),B(25)
COMMON J,X	COMMON K,L,M,N,A,B

Both lists of names declare that the first four locations in common storage are to be treated as integers and the next 35 as real.

Notice that it is possible to declare the size of arrays within the COMMON statement and eliminate the DIMENSION statement. The previous statement could be written more efficiently as:

Main Program	Subprogram
COMMON J(4),X(35)	COMMON K,L,M,N,A(10),B(25)

J(1) in the main program is identified as K in the subprogram. J(2) is identified as L, etc. Since the "address determination" for a subscripted variable takes longer than for a simple variable, the subprogram is accessing data more quickly than the main program.

Both the EQUIVALENCE and COMMON statements are nonexecutable statements and are best positioned in the declarative block of your program (those before any executable statement).

14.5 | Advantages of Common Storage

It should be obvious that the EQUIVALENT statement is *local* in nature and can be used to conserve memory within a given program or subprogram. The COMMON statement is said to be *global* and can be used to conserve memory between the main program and its subprograms. This is because the appearance of each COMMON statement does not cause the allocation of additional memory. It just allows the same area in common storage to be called by different names.

Common storage has another and perhaps more important application. Values that must be shared by a program and various subprograms do not have to be passed using an argument list. These values can be placed in common storage (usually by the main program) and then used or accessed by the various subprograms. In complex problems, the argument list tends to become long and cumbersome. The argument list can be made more manageable (i.e. reduced in size) by placing some of the variables in common storage. In the case of a subroutine, the argument list can even be eliminated altogether. A function subprogram, however, must have at least one argument. Using common storage to pass arguments of a subprogram is called **implicit transfer of arguments**.

The next programming example involves a large data base that must be accessible to four or five subroutines. These subroutines accomplish various tasks associated with an airlines reservation problem. Because the people using these routines will have little or no programming experience, it is essential that the argument list be as simple and as small as possible. Accordingly, the data base is stored in common storage. Each subroutine can access the information in the data base, but the name of the data base does not have to be a part of any argument list.

In large projects where many subprograms are involved, each with a different argument list, those arguments that the subprograms have in common are usually placed in common storage. The other arguments (those unique to each subprogram) are left in the argument list.

Programming Example Airline Reservation	An airline operates 128 flights each week and for simplicity's sake we will assume all flights have a seating capacity of 214 seats. As part of an "airlines reservation program," we must keep track of the names of passengers booked on each flight and what seat they have been assigned.

These names will be stored in an array called RESERV forming a large data base that will be operated on (shared) by several subroutines.

Each row of the array called RESERV is to represent a given flight. Each of the 214 elements in any row represents a seat on that flight. An element will

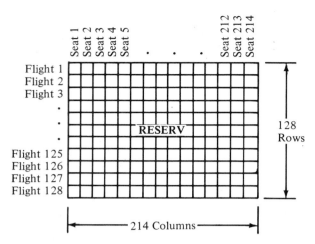

either contain the name of the passenger booked on that flight (and in that seat), or it will contain the word "EMPTY" (to signal the seat is available). The word size of each memory location is assumed to be 8 characters in length.

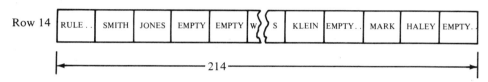

Figure 14.6 Typical Row in the Data Base

Part A: Any Seats Left on a Given Flight?

One of the subroutines we will be writing should be able to examine any row of the data base and determine how many seats are still unreserved (empty) for that specific flight, assuming the array RESERV already has been read and placed in common storage.

Write a subroutine called AVAIL that has a single input argument, FLIGHT. This number tells which flight a passenger is asking information about. For the moment, have this subroutine return a single argument, NSEATS, telling how many seats are still available.

This subroutine will examine one row of the data base to see if any of the elements contain the word EMPTY. Since each element contains 8 alphabetic characters, we need to know if the 8 characters are 'EMPTY_ _ _'. This will be accomplished by an IF test, but in a slightly new way: using an alphabetic constant.

Testing a Numeric Quantity:

    IF(X.EQ.12.0) KOUNT=KOUNT+1

     Numeric Constant

Testing an Alphabetic Quantity:

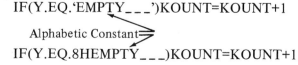

     IF(Y.EQ.'EMPTY_ _ _')KOUNT=KOUNT+1

      Alphabetic Constant

     IF(Y.EQ.8HEMPTY_ _ _)KOUNT=KOUNT+1

    Figure 14.7 Two Types of IF Statements

The IF tests shown in Figure 14.7 are of two distinctly different types. You are more familiar with the first IF test shown. It tests to see if the memory location X contains the *numeric* value 12.0. The other IF tests are used to see if the memory location Y contains a specific *alphabetic* value, namely 'EMPTY___'. The presence of quotation marks or H-code identifies an alphabetic constant as being the object of this IF test.*

```
C.....................................................
C..   PURPOSE - DEMONSTRATE THE USE OF COMMON STORAGE. ..
C..             DETERMINE THE NUMBER OF EMPTY SEATS ON A ..
C..             SPECIFIC FLIGHT.                         ..
C.....................................................
C
C                -----IMPORTANT VARIABLES-----
C
C     --RESERV    DATA BASE OF NAMES (IN COMMON STORAGE)  --
C     --FLIGHT    NUMBER OF FLIGHT BEING SEARCHED         --
C     --NSEATS    NUMBER OF EMPTY SEATS ON THAT FLIGHT    --
C
      COMMON RESERV (128,214)
C
      INTEGER FLIGHT
C
      NSEATS = 0
C
C           SET UP LOOP TO SEARCH ROW FLIGHT
C
      DO 10 I = 1, 214
C
        IF(RESERV(FLIGHT,I).EQ.'EMPTY   ')NSEATS = NSEATS + 1
C
   10 CONTINUE
C
      RETURN
      END
```

Part B: Getting Specific Seat Numbers

If there are sufficient seats on a flight, the next step is to determine the specific seat numbers of unreserved seats. This is to be accomplished by subroutine SEATS. Its input arguments are:

FLIGHT   — the flight we are booking.

NUMBER — the number of seats we want.

NSTART   — where in the plane the search for empty seats should start.

The last argument allows the passenger to locate approximately where in the plane he or she would like to sit.

Subroutine SEATS should print as output *twice* the number of seat numbers being requested to give the passenger a choice.

```
      SUBROUTINE SEATS(FLIGHT,NUMBER,NSTART)
C
C.....................................................
C..   PURPOSE - PRINT OUT AVAILABLE (EMPTY) SEATS ON A ..
C..             SPECIFIC FLIGHT STARTING WITH SEAT NUMBER ..
C..             NSTART.                                   ..
C.....................................................
C
C                ------NEW VARIABLES----------
C
C     --NUMBER    NUMBER OF SEATS REQUESTED              --
C     --NSTART    WHERE IN PLANE SEARCH STARTS FROM      --
C
      COMMON RESERV (128,214)
C
      INTEGER FLIGHT
C
C           SEARCH LOOP STARTS HERE
C
      DO 20 I = NSTART, 214
C
        IF(RESERV(FLIGHT,I).EQ.'EMPTY   ') THEN
          WRITE(2,10) I
   10     FORMAT(1X,I6)
C
          NUMBER = NUMBER - 1
          IF(NUMBER.EQ.0) RETURN
C
        ENDIF
C
   20 CONTINUE
C
      WRITE(2,30)
   30 FORMAT(10X,'THESE ARE THE ONLY SEATS AVAILABLE')
C
      RETURN
      END
```

*Without the quotation marks, EMPTY would be interpreted as the name of a simple variable.

Part C: Reserving Seats

The next subroutine to be written is called SOLD. It allows the booking agent to reserve specific seats. We will make the subroutine conversational in mode in that all the agent must do is enter the statement "CALL SOLD" and control will pass to the subroutine, which will then give directions for providing the necessary input. This assumes that the input/output is via terminals.

```
C
C
C...............................................
C..   PURPOSE - DEMONSTRATE CONVERSATIONAL MODE   ..
C..            PROGRAMMING. BOOK INDIVIDUAL        ..
C..            SEATS ON THE AIRCRAFT.              ..
C...............................................
C
C      COMMON RESERV(128,214)
C
C      INTEGER FLIGHT
C
       WRITE(2,10)
   10  FORMAT(3X,'ENTER THE FLIGHT NUMBER')      ①
C
       READ(5,11) FLIGHT
   11  FORMAT(I3)
C
       WRITE(2,12)
   12  FORMAT(3X,'ENTER PASSENGER NAME')         ②
C
       READ(5,13) PASNGR
   13  FORMAT(A8)
C
C          READ SEAT NUMBERS
C
   20  WRITE(2,21)
   21  FORMAT(3X,'TYPE IN SEAT NUMBERS ONE PER LINE',   ③
      1     'WHEN NO MORE SEATS NEEDED TYPE 999')
C
       READ(5,11) N
       IF(N.EQ.999) RETURN
C
C          BOOK PASSENGER NAME INTO DATA BASE
C
       RESERV(FLIGHT,N) = PASNGR             ④
C
       GO TO 20
C
       END
```

① Requesting Flight Number

② Requesting Passenger's Name

③ Requesting Seat Number

④ Making Reservation

Many other subroutines would be needed to complete this package. When a flight departs, it would be necessary to change all elements in one row of the data base to 'EMPTY___' to set up for future booking of this flight. Passengers often try to shift from one flight to another or have to cancel out. All these can be written by separate subroutines that operate on the data base stored in common storage.

14.6 Labelled Common

We have shown that common storage can be used to share large arrays with one or more subprograms. Common can also be used to avoid long argument lists between subprograms. Common storage is so useful, especially when a large number of subprograms are involved, that it has been found advisable to allow the programmer to set up more than one area of common storage. These areas will be similar to the common storage just described (to be called **unlabelled common** from now on) except that they must be given an identifying name and are, therefore, called **labelled common**. The statement:

COMMON/A/X, Y, Z(10)

creates a labelled common storage area named A. It assigns the names X and Y to the first two locations in the area and the name Z to the next ten areas (Z is a subscripted variable). If the statement:

COMMON/A/C, D, B(10)

appears in the subprogram, it will identify the variable names used by that program to identify successive memory locations in common storage A.

It is possible to identify memory locations in both labelled and unlabelled common with a single common statement. Consider the following statements:

Main Program:

COMMON A, B, C/Z1/D, E, F(10)/Z2/M, N

Subprogram:

COMMON R, S, T/Z1/U, V, W(10)/Z2/I, J

The first portion of these statements declares the names to be used in identifying the first three locations in unlabelled common storage. The name A in the main program and the name R in the subprogram both identify the first location in unlabelled common storage. The next sequence of names identifies locations in labelled common Z1. This labelled common area has twelve locations containing two nonsubscripted variables, followed by a one-dimensional array called F in the main program and W in the subprogram. Finally, labelled common Z2 is created containing two integer locations.

14.7 | The EXTERNAL Statement

Until now, the names appearing in an argument list of a subprogram have represented numeric values exclusively — they represent simple variables or arrays. A name in the argument list of a subprogram can, however, represent an entirely different quantity; it can represent the *name of another subprogram*. The implication is that one subprogram needs information contained within the other subprogram to function properly.

Assume you have been asked to write a subroutine called AREA:

SUBROUTINE AREA(XLEFT,XRIGHT,Y,ANS)

The purpose of this subroutine is to determine the area under a curve between two limits of X defined by XLEFT and XRIGHT.

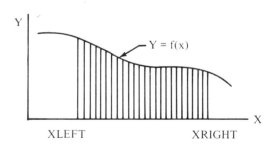

The argument ANS returns the computed area to the calling program. The remaining argument, Y, is used to define the curve. The curve may be known in two possible ways:

1. as a series of data points, or
2. as an equation.

If the curve is defined by a series of data points (by an array called Y), we would use a DIMENSION statement to show the special attribute of the name Y — to show it is an array.

If the curve is defined by an equation, we are allowed to define a function subprogram containing that equation, give it the name Y and include it in the argument list of subroutine AREA (just as we did before). We must again somehow show the special attribute of the name Y — to show it is the name of a subprogram. The EXTERNAL statement serves that purpose:

EXTERNAL Y

As a specific example, assume we are dealing with a curve whose equation is:

$$y = x^6 - x^2 + \ln(x+4)$$

The new procedure would suggest setting up the following function subprogram:

```
      FUNCTION Y (X)
C.....PURPOSE - TO HOLD THE EQUATION OF THE CURVE.
C
      Y = X**6 -X**2 + ALOG(X+4.0)
      RETURN
      END
```

We now write subroutine AREA, which is capable of receiving this function name (in the 3rd argument position) and of computing the area. The method of solution will be to:

1. divide the span of X into 100 equal parts,

$$\Delta X = \frac{(XRIGHT - XLEFT)}{100}$$

2. starting at XLEFT, evaluate the equation at each point in the span (by repeatedly invoking the function subprogram Y); and,
3. determine the average value of the equation in the span and multiply this by (XRIGHT - XLEFT). This will approximate the area.

```
      SUBROUTINE AREA (XLEFT,XRIGHT,Y,ANS)
C.....ARGUMENT Y IS THE NAME OF A FUNCTION SUBPROGRAM THAT
C              EXPRESSES THE EQUATION WE ARE DEALING WITH.
C
      DELTX = (XRIGHT - XLEFT) / 100.
      SUM = 0.0
      X = XLEFT
      DO 10 I = 1, 101
    5    SUM = SUM + Y(X)
         X = X + DELTX
   10 CONTINUE
      AVEVAL = SUM / 101.
      ANS = AVEVAL * (XRIGHT - XLEFT)
      RETURN
      END
```

Statement 5 is the key to the whole procedure. It invokes the subprogram Y for various values of X. Each time this statement is reached, control passes to the function subprogram to evaluate the equation. Had we placed our equation inside subroutine AREA, statement 5 would appear as follows:

```
5 SUM=SUM+X**6-X**2+ALOG(X+4.)
```

The resulting area would be the same, but the subroutine would no longer be general. Placing the specific equation inside subroutine AREA destroys its effectiveness. It becomes almost worthless. Allowing the equation to be referenced by the name Y (the name of a subprogram external to AREA) makes the subroutine invaluable.

Having written subroutine AREA, we would want to test it. Figure 14.8 shows two exceptionally simple curves that might be used:

1. A straight line passing through the origin whose slope is $45°$.

Equation: $y = x$

2. A horizontal line whose y value is constant.

Equation: $y = constant = 8$

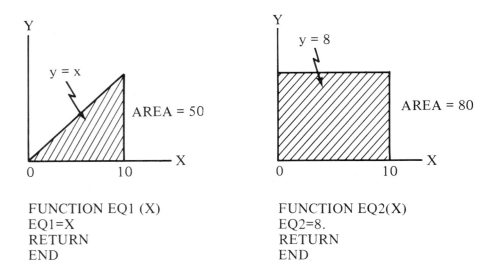

FUNCTION EQ1 (X)   FUNCTION EQ2(X)
EQ1=X   EQ2=8.
RETURN   RETURN
END   END

Figure 14.8 Testing by Using Two Simple Areas

Because we have two curves, we must set up two function subprograms as shown. One is called EQ1. The other is called EQ2. By choosing equally simple limits on x, say 0.0 and 10.0, we can compute the areas by inspection. For the triangle it is 50. For the rectangle it is 80.

Subroutine AREA
called twice

```
      C     MAIN PROGRAM TO TEST SUBROUTINE AREA
            EXTERNAL EQ1, EQ2
            CALL AREA (0.0, 10.0, EQ1, ANS1)
            CALL AREA (0.0, 10.0, EQ2, ANS2)
            WRITE(2,10) ANS1, ANS2
      10    FORMAT(1X,2E16.4)
            STOP
            END
```

Defines first
equation

```
            FUNCTION EQ1 (X)
      C     DEFINE 45 DEGREE LINE
            EQ1 = X
            RETURN
            END
```

Defines second
equation

```
            FUNCTION EQ2 (X)
      C     DEFINE HORIZONTAL LINE
            EQ2 = 8.0
            RETURN
            END
```

We call subroutine AREA twice. On the first call the name EQ1 is placed in the third argument position so that our first test equation will be evaluated. The name EQ1 will be identified with the name Y in the definition. On the second call to AREA, the name EQ2 will be substituted so that the second function subprogram will be linked to Y.

You have learned that the DIMENSION statement is used to warn the compiler that certain variable names are special in that they represent arrays. The names representing subprograms are also special, and we warn the compiler through the use of the EXTERNAL statement. This statement appears at the top of the test program and declares EQ1 and EQ2 as the names of subprograms external to the main program.

The EXTERNAL statement is needed whenever a CALL is made to a subprogram that has within its argument list the name of another (external) subprogram.

Programming Example
Merge Two Lists

LIST1 and LIST2 are both arrays of integer numbers. Each list has been sorted (smallest element first, largest element last). The size of each list is specified by an integer variable, NSIZE1 and NSIZE2.

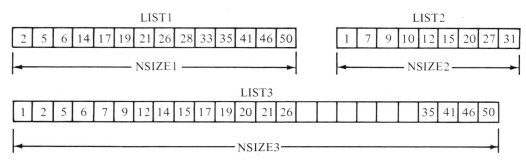

Write a subroutine called MERGE that will merge these two arrays into a single list of sorted numbers.

The logic of the subroutine is to compare the first element of LIST1 and LIST2. If the LIST1 element is smaller:

1. move that element into LIST3, and
2. advance the LIST1 and LIST3 subscript.

If the LIST2 element is the smaller:

1. move that element into LIST3, and
2. advance the LIST2 and LIST3 subscripts.

Continue this basic process until either LIST1 or LIST2 is depleted. When one list becomes depleted, pass control to statements that will "dump" the remainder of the other list directly into LIST3.

```
C ....................................................
C ... PURPOSE  MERGE TWO SORTED LISTS INTO A SINGLE (COMBINED)
C ...          SORTED LIST.
C ....................................................
C
C            -----IMPORTANT VARIABLES-----
C
C     --LIST1       NAME OF FIRST SORTED LIST              --
C     --L1          SUBSCRIPT USED WHEN DEALING WITH LIST1 --
C     --LIST2       NAME OF SECOND SORTED LIST             --
C     --L2          SUBSCRIPT USED WHEN DEALING WITH LIST2 --
C     --LIST3       NAME OF COMBINED (OUTPUT) LIST         --
C     --L3          SUBSCRIPT USED WHEN DEALING WITH LIST3 --
C
      DIMENSION LIST1(1), LIST2(1), LIST3(1)
C
      SET INITIAL VALUE OF INPUT ARRAY SUBSCRIPTS
C
      L1 = 1
      L2 = 1
C
C           LOOP ENTRY POINT
C
      DO 10 L3 = 1, NSIZE1 + NSIZE2, 1
C
         DETERMINE WHICH LIST HAS SMALLEST ELEMENT
C
         IF(LIST1(L1).LT.LIST2(L2)) THEN
C
            TAKE VALUE FROM LIST1
C
            LIST3(L3) = LIST1(L1)
            L1 = L1 + 1
C
         ELSE
C
            TAKE VALUE FROM LIST2
C
            LIST3(L3) = LIST2(L2)
            L2 = L2 + 1
C
         ENDIF
C
         SEE IF EITHER LIST IS DEPLETED
C
         IF(L1.GT.NSIZE1) GO TO 20
         IF(L2.GT.NSIZE2) GO TO 40
C
   10 CONTINUE
C
      RETURN
C
C ....................................................
C ..... THIS SECTION HANDLES LIST1 ..................
C .....          DEPLETION SITUATION ................
```

```
 C
2C  DO 30 I3 = L3, NSIZE1 + NSIZE2, 1
 C       DUMP REMAINDER OF LIST2 INTO LIST3
            LIST3(I3) = LIST2(L2)
            L2 = L2 + 1
 C
3C  CONTINUE
    RETURN
 C
 C........THIS SECTION HANDLES LIST2..........
 C.........   DEPLETION SITUATION   ..........
 C
4C  DO 50 I3 = L3, NSIZE1 + NSIZE2, 1
 C       DUMP REMAINDER OF LIST1 INTO LIST3
            LIST3(L3) = LIST1(L1)
            L1 = L1 + 1
 C
5C  CONTINUE
    RETURN
    END
```

Review Exercises

1. Does the "consistency in size" requirement in arrays that are passed as arguments apply to all arrays?

2. What are some of the ways in which this "consistency of size" requirement is satisfied when arrays are shared?

3.*A two-dimensional array called A is 5 by 4 in size. Describe how this array is stored in memory. In what position is the element A(3, 2) located?

4. Up until now, the size of an array as expressed in a DIMENSION statement must be provided as an integer *constant*. Under what circumstances can the size be expressed as a variable?

5.*An array used in a subprogram is described as a "local" array. Describe what that means. What restrictions apply to the DIMENSION statement declaring the size of this array?

6. A memory location in common storage may be known by different variable names in various subprograms. How is this accomplished?

7. Describe two situations that might require the use of the EQUIVALENCE statement.

8.*Several subprograms have argument lists that are very long. A number of arguments appear in each of the several argument lists. Describe how these argument lists can be made shorter.

9. The DIMENSION statement is used to declare that a variable name represents the name of an array and not a simple variable. What statement is used to declare that a name represents the name of a subprogram?

10.*Until now, an argument list consists of a sequence of simple variables or the names of arrays. Now an argument list may contain the name of a "user supplied" subprogram. Why is this new type of argument needed? Give an example.

11. A company is divided into twenty different divisions each manufacturing the same item. A one-dimensional

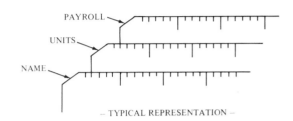

– TYPICAL REPRESENTATION –

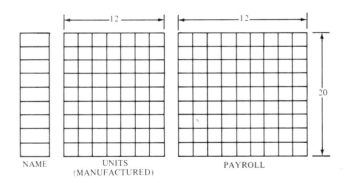

array called NAME identifies the name of the supervisor of each department. For each department a monthly record of the production output of that department is kept (units manufactured each month). The array UNITS holds this information. The cost of labor to produce these units in each department is also recorded on a monthly basis forming another two-dimensional array. Write a subroutine to read the information described above and place it in common storage. Each division is represented in the data deck as follows:

Card 1 – Name of supervisor	A6
Card 2 – Number of units produced	12I6
Card 3 – Monthly payroll	12F6.0

12. Using the data base established in problem 11, write a subroutine called NUMBER that computes the number of units manufactured by each department for the year.

13. Repeat problem 12 except have the subroutine NUM-BER report the units manufactured by the most productive department first (give supervisor's name and units manufactured), then the next most productive department, and so on.

14. Write a subroutine that will compute the variation in *unit cost* to produce the items described in problem 11. This subroutine should compute a two-dimensional array called COST having 20 rows and 12 columns. Elements of COST are obtained by dividing each department's monthly payroll by the units produced. The array COST should then be searched for the largest and smallest elements.

15. A two-dimensional array called A has 14 rows and 28 columns. Write a subroutine called CHANGE that will examine the elements in column 1 of each row of array A and determine which of these elements is the largest. The row containing this largest element is to be moved to the top of the array (do a row swap).

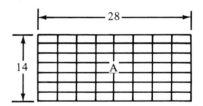

16. Repeat problem 15 except that the size of array A is to be variable.

17. A subroutine called ROOTS receives three input arguments.

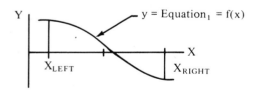

The first argument is the name of a user-supplied function subprogram containing the equation we are trying to find the root of. A typical example is:

```
FUNCTION Y(X)
Y = X**6-ALOG(X)*X**4
RETURN
END
```

The remaining two arguments are XLEFT and XRIGHT defining the interval of the expected root. Have subroutine ROOTS determine and report the value of the equation at X_{LEFT}, X_{RIGHT} and halfway between these two values.

18.*In problem 17, if the value of the equation at X_{LEFT} and at the midpoint have a different algebraic sign, the root lies to the left of the midpoint. If the value of the

equation at the midpoint and at X_{RIGHT} have a different algebraic sign, the root lies to the right of the midpoint. Expand subroutine ROOTS to issue one of two messages:

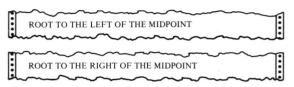

19. Problem 18 does not account for the possibility that the algebraic sign of the equation will be the same at all three test points (no root in the interval).
Expand subroutine ROOTS to accommodate this possibility.

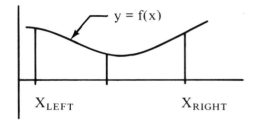

20. A unit matrix is by definition a square matrix (number of rows equals number of columns) in which elements on the main diagonal have the value 1.0. All other elements have the value 0.0. Write a subroutine called TEST that will receive as input an array called A and determine if A is a unit matrix. The output of TEST should be one of two messages:

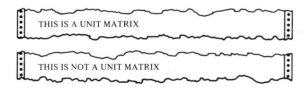

21. A series of data points are represented by a one-dimensional array called X and a one-dimensional array called Y.

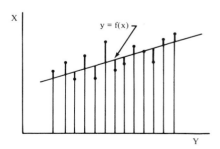

These points are to be compared to the equation of a straight line defined inside a usersupplied FUNCTION subprogram called EQ; as in this typical example:

```
FUNCTION EQ(X)
EQ = 6.72*X+1.43
RETURN
END
```

Write a subprogram to determine how many points lie above the line and how many points lie below the line.

22. For each point in problem 21 determine the distance that the point lies above or below the line. Report each distance and the average error of these points.

23.*An array A has NROW rows and NCOL columns. Each row of this array is to be scaled (multiplied by a value).

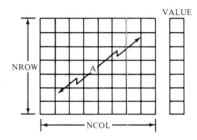

The scale factor for each row is defined by a one-dimensional array called VALUE.

Write a subroutine called SCALE that redefines all elements of array A as described above.

24. A user-supplied SUBROUTINE subprogram defines two equations that are both functions of X, as in this typical example:

```
SUBROUTINE Y (X,EQ1,EQ2)
EQ1 = X**3-1.4*X**2-4.
EQ2 = X**2-9.6*X+1.4
RETURN
END
```

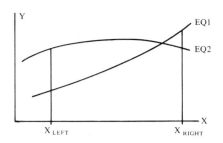

We are interested in knowing which of the two equations has the larger value at the two test points (X_{LEFT} and X_{RIGHT}). Write a subprogram called TEST that determines the desired information. Have subprogram TEST print a message such as:

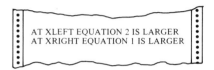

AT XLEFT EQUATION 2 IS LARGER
AT XRIGHT EQUATION 1 IS LARGER

25. Repeat problem 24, except that we do not want any printout. Instead of the printout, load a memory location called MLEFT with the value 1 or 2 depending on which equation is larger at XLEFT. Load a memory location MRIGHT with the value 1 or 2 depending on which equation is larger at XRIGHT.

26. If MLEFT and MRIGHT hold different numbers after a call to subroutine TEST, the two equations cross over (intersect) within the interval XLEFT and XRIGHT. Expand subroutine TEST to search for this point of intersection.

Additional Applications

| Programming Example |
| Data Boundaries |
| (Specific) |

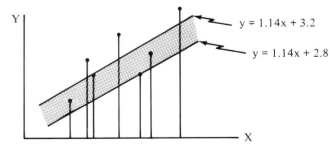

$y = 1.14x + 3.2$

$y = 1.14x + 2.8$

An array called X and an array called Y define a series of data points. We are interested in knowing how many of these points are bounded (lie inside) the two straight lines shown above.

Write a SUBROUTINE called BOUND that receives as input:

XARRAY   Array of X Values (Data Points),
YARRAY   Array of Y Values (Data Points),
NSIZE   Number of Elements (Data Points)

Determine how many points lie inside the bounds specified by the two straight lines.

```
C.............................................................
C..    PURPOSE -   DETERMINE IF DATA POINTS LIE WITHIN        ::
C..                SPECIFIC BOUNDS.                           ::
C.............................................................
C
C
      DIMENSION XARRAY(NSIZE),YARRAY(NSIZE)
C
      INSIDE=0
C
      DO 10 I=1,NSIZE
C
          YMAX=1.14*XARRAY(I)+3.2
          YMIN=1.14*XARRAY(I)+2.8
C
          IF(YARRAY(I).LT.YMAX.AND.YARRAY(I).GT.YMIN)THEN
C
              INSIDE=INSIDE+1
C
          ENDIF
C
   10 CONTINUE
C
      PERCNT=FLOAT(INSIDE)/FLOAT(NSIZE)*100.
C
      RETURN
      END
```

Programming Example
Data Boundaries
(General)

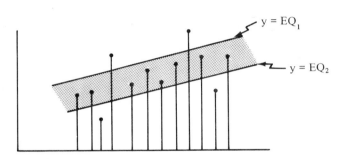

The two equations representing the data boundaries shown in the previous programming example change from time to time. Accordingly they are placed inside two FUNCTION subprograms as shown below.

```
FUNCTION EQ1(X)
EQ1 = 1.14 *X + 3.2
RETURN
END

FUNCTION EQ2(X)
EQ2 = 1.14 *X + 2.8
RETURN
END
```

Rewrite SUBROUTINE BOUND to accept the name of these two FUNCTIONS in its argument list and process the data points as before.

```
      SUBROUTINE BOUND(XARRAY,YARRAY,NSIZE,EQ1,EQ2,INSIDE,PERCNT)
C
      EXTERNAL EQ1,EQ2
C
      DIMENSION XARRAY(NSIZE),YARRAY(NSIZE)
C
      INSIDE=0
C
      DO 10 I=1,NSIZE
          YMAX=EQ1(XARRAY(I))
          YMIN=EQ2(XARRAY(I))
          IF(YARRAY(I).LT.YMAX.AND.YARRAY(I).GT.YMIN)THEN
              INSIDE=INSIDE+1
          ENDIF
C
   10 CONTINUE
C
      PERCNT=FLOAT(INSIDE)/FLOAT(NSIZE)*100.
C
      RETURN
      END
```

Programming Example
Symmetric Array
(Partial Check)

ARRAY

1.1	2.2	3.3	4.4	5.5	6.6	7.7
2.2	2.6	2.8	3.0	3.2	3.4	3.6
3.3	2.8	-5.2	-5.0	-4.8	-4.6	-4.4
4.4	3.0	-5.0	-0.4	-0.4	-0.2	-0.0
5.5	3.2	-4.8	-0.4	4.3	4.1	3.9
6.6	3.4	-4.6	-0.2	4.1	8.7	8.9
7.7	3.6	-4.4	-0.0	3.9	8.9	2.1

A two dimensional array is said to be symmetric if:

    (a) the number of rows equals the number of columns (a square matrix) and,

    (b) elements above and below the main diagonal have the same value:

$$A(M,N) = A(N,M)$$

Write a subprogram called TEST that receives the following input:

    A   Name of array to be checked.
    NROW Number of rows in array A.
    NCOL Number of columns in array A.

Subroutine TEST should attempt to determine if array A is symmetric as follows:

Size Error:

    If the number of rows does not equal the number of columns, reject the array immediately.

Some Elements:

    Check the elements in row 1 of the array to see if they equal the elements in column 1 of the array. If all elements are equal, issue the message "MAYBE."

```
      SUBROUTINE TEST(A,NROW,NCOL)
C
C.....................................................
C..   PURPOSE -   MAKE A PARTIAL CHECK TO SEE IF     ..
C..               AN ARRAY IS SYMETRIC.             ..
C.....................................................
C
      DIMENSION A(NROW,NCOL)
C
C
      IF(NROW.NE.NCOL)THEN
C
          WRITE(2,10)
   10     FORMAT(1X,'ARRAY NOT SYMETRIC - SIZE ERROR')
          RETURN
C
      ENDIF
C
C           CHECK ROW/COLUMN 1
C
      DO 30 I=1,NROW
C
          IF(A(I,1).NE.A(1,I))THEN
              WRITE(2,20)
   20         FORMAT(1X,'ARRAY NOT SYMETRIC - ELEMENTS NOT EQUAL')
              RETURN
C
          ENDIF
C
   30 CONTINUE
C
      WRITE(2,40)
   40 FORMAT(1X,'MAYBE')
C
      RETURN
      END
```

Programming Example
Symmetric Array
(General)

Write subroutine TEST to check all elements of array A (all rows against all columns).

ARRAY A

1.1	2.2	3.3	4.4	5.5	6.6	7.7
2.2	2.6	2.8	3.0	3.2	3.4	3.6
3.3	2.8	−5.2	−5.0	−4.8	−4.6	−4.4
4.4	3.0	−5.0	−0.4	−0.4	−0.2	−0.0
5.5	3.2	−4.8	−0.4	4.3	4.1	3.9
6.6	3.4	−4.6	−0.2	4.1	8.7	8.9
7.7	3.6	−4.4	−0.0	3.9	8.9	2.1

```
C..........................................................
C..     PURPOSE -   MAKE GENERAL TEST TO SEE IF AN        ::
C..                 ARRAY IS SYMETRIC.                    ::
C..........................................................
C
        DIMENSION A(NROW,NCOL)
C
        IF(NROW.NE.NCOL)THEN
C
            WRITE(2,10)
   10       FORMAT(1X,'ARRAY NOT SYMETRIC - SIZE ERROR')
            RETURN
C
        ENDIF
C
C...................... SET UP OUTER DO LOOP ................
C..........................................................
C
C
C
C...................... INDEX M TELLS WHICH ROW ............
C...................... IS BEING CHECKED AGAINST ..........
C...................... WHICH COLUMN ......................
C..........................................................
C
        DO 40 M=1,NROW
C
            DO 30 I=M,NROW
C
                IF(A(I,M).NE.A(M,I))THEN
                    WRITE(2,20)
   20               FORMAT(1X,'ARRAY  NOT  SYMETRIC'
     1                    ,' ELEMENTS NNOT EQUAL')
                    RETURN
C
                ENDIF
C
   30       CONTINUE
C
   40   CONTINUE
C
C              .... ALL ELEMENTS CHECKED ....
C
        WRITE(2,50)
   50   FORMAT(1X,'ARRAY IS SYMETRIC')
C
        RETURN
        END
```

| **Programming Example**
Largest Value | We wish to know which of two equations has the largest value between two limits of X (between XINIT and XFINAL).
Write a subroutine that received as input: |

XINIT   Initial value of interval.
XFINAL   Final value of interval.
EQ1   Function subprogram holding first equation.
EQ2   Function subprogram holding second equation.

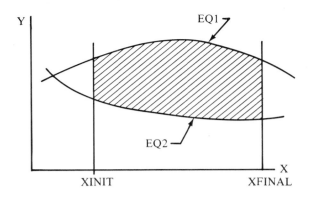

The output of this subroutine should be:

BIGY   Largest value in interval.
X   Value of X for largest Y.
NUMBER Integer (1 or 2) telling which equation gives largest value.

```
C ...................................................
C ..   PURPOSE -  FIND LARGEST VALUE OF Y           ::
C ...................................................
C
      EXTERNAL EQ1,EQ2
C
C              DIVIDE INTERVAL INTO 100 EQUAL PARTS
C
      DELTX=(XFINAL-XINIT)/100.
C
C              DEFINE Y AT START FOR BOTH EQUATIONS
C
      Y1=EQ1(XINIT)
      Y2=EQ2(XINIT)
C
      X=XINIT
C
C              PROCESSING LOOP STARTS HERE
C
      DO 10 I=1,101
C
C              ... CHECK FIRST EQUATION ...
C
      YNEW=EQ1(X)
C
      IF(YNEW.GE.Y1)THEN
              Y1=YNEW
              X1=X
      ENDIF
C
C              ... CHECK SECOND EQUATION ...
C
      YNEW=EQ2(X)
C
      IF(YNEW.GE.Y2)THEN
              Y2=YNEW
              X2=X
      ENDIF
C
      X=X+DELTX
C
   10 CONTINUE
C
C              DETERMINE WHICH EQUATION HAS LARGER Y
C
      IF(Y1.GT.Y2)THEN
              BIGY=Y1
              X=X1
              NUMBER=1
      ELSE
              BIGY=Y2
              X=X2
              NUMBER=2
C
      ENDIF
C
      RETURN
      END
```

15

Use of Large Software Packages

Unless you become a professional programmer, the chances are that from now on you will become less involved in *writing* subprograms and more involved in *using* them. In this chapter we will show how the various subprograms of several typical software packages are organized and documented. We will try to convey the tremendous scope of these packages and explain how to use them.

The experience you have gained in writing just a few subprograms of your own will make this a relatively easy task. As powerful as these software packages are, just remember, they aren't much more than a collection of FORTRAN subroutines. As such you must be prepared to provide input in two basic forms.

The majority of routines operate on pure numeric data. Accordingly the documentation will ask you to define certain *variables* and *arrays*. These will then be passed as input. This represents the first and most frequent form of input. A second group of subprograms on occasion may require an equation as input. When this happens, you will be told to write a "user supplied" subprogram that holds this alternative form of input and to pass the name of that subprogram in an argument list. This is the same procedure used in the last chapter to pass an equation to subroutine AREA. This is the second basic form of input.

15.1 | Typical Software

All computer centers maintain a file of commonly used arithmetic functions and problem algorithms to accomplish a wide variety of mathematical operations. In the early days of computers, these files were rather modest in scope and were not considered very powerful. Today the situation is entirely different. The importance of providing quality software to support existing hardware systems has been recognized and hundreds of man-years of effort have been expended to organize, code, and test a powerful and comprehensive group of subprograms. A partial list includes subprograms to:

(a) solve linear and non-linear equations;
(b) solve systems of simultaneous equations;
(c) integrate and differentiate equations;
(d) analyze raw data (find mean, average, variance, standard deviation, minimum value, maximum value, etc.);

(e) tabulate data and determine correlation coefficients;

(f) do factor analysis of data and compute eigenvalues;

(g) solve numerically both differential and partial differential equations;

(h) do curve fitting and curve smoothing (i.e., generate an equation to satisfy a series of data points);

(i) do matrix operations (such as add, subtract, multiply, divide, invert, transpose, etc.);

(j) do regression analysis, time series, and develop non-parametric statistics on data.

This list is presented not to overwhelm you, but to show how extensive and complete these software packages are. As formidable as this list may be, it represents only a part of the software development that is going on today. Many special interest groups such as business, banking, and management have developed large scale "discipline-oriented" software to facilitate the extensive use of computers in their particular areas of interest. Deposits and withdrawals, interest calculations, check processing, mortgage payments, payroll control, accounts receivable, accounts payable are just a few of the many day-to-day business activities accomplished by an interconnected group of subroutines.

Engineers and architects bring the power of the computer to bear on problems such as highway design, stress analysis of structures, plant layout, numeric control of machinery, maintenance scheduling and a variety of activities too numerous to mention. Social scientists have software systems to simulate and analyze urban networks and population distributions. Medical researchers use software packages to assist in diagnostic evaluations, complex equipment control and other health care treatment problems.

Development of software is a multi-billion dollar business.

15.2 | A Look at Software Documentation

To make the individual subroutines of a software package as easy to use as possible, careful attention has been given to provide clear and uniform documentation within each routine. This documentation will tell you:

(a) what the purpose of the subroutine is,

(b) what arguments it needs,

(c) which are input, which are output,

(d) how the subprogram should be called,

(e) what method of solution is used,

(f) any special requirements or limitations.

Within any package, the documentation is *consistent*. That is, the documentation for any one routine is the same as for all others.

In the last chapter, we wrote a subroutine called AREA that computed the area under a curve between two limits of X. This process is known in calculus as computing the integral of a function. The following subroutine is taken from the I.B.M. Scientific Subroutine Package and is used to show typical documentation. This subroutine is much more sophisticated than our subroutine AREA, but the similarity is sufficient to help you follow its documentation.

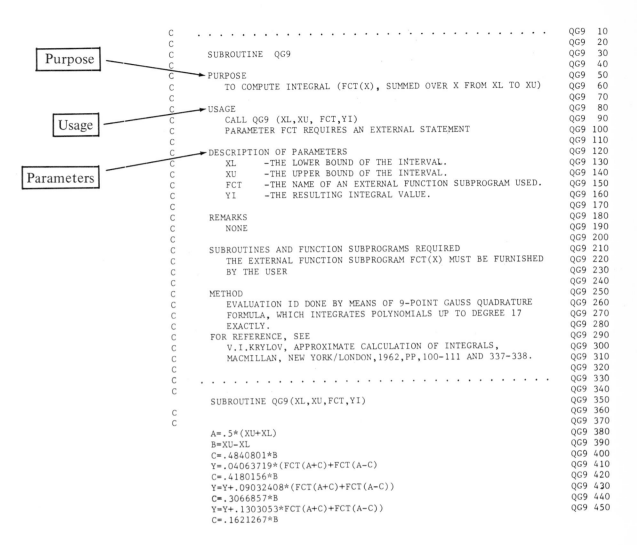

Figure 15.1 Integration Routine

In the USAGE section, you are shown how to make a call to this subroutine, i.e. how the argument list is constructed. To further help you, each of the parameters on this list is explained in more detail in the section called DESCRIPTION OF PARAMETERS.

This subroutine is one of those that must be passed an equation to operate on. Notice the extreme effort that is made to make sure you handle this properly. In the PARAMETER section you are told that an external subprogram is needed. In the USAGE section you are reminded to use an EXTERNAL statement in the calling program. Finally, in the section entitled SUBROUTINES AND FUNCTION SUBPROGRAMS REQUIRED you are told the type of subprogram the user must supply and what argument list should be used.

*Reprinted from H20-0205-0 "System/360 Scientific Subroutine Package" © 1966. courtesy of IBM Corporation.

To demonstrate the use of this subroutine, assume that we wish to determine the integral of the equation:

$$y = e^x - \frac{\ln (x^2 + 1)}{X}$$

between X=5 and X=10. Two blocks of code would be required. The first is the main or calling program.

```
C ...........................................................
C.. PURPOSE - MAIN PROGRAM THAT DEMONSTRATES HOW TO MAKE  ..
C..          A CALL TO SUBROUTINE QG9 (IBM-SSP).          ..
C ...........................................................
C
      EXTERNAL Y
C
      CALL QG9(5.0,10.0,Y,ANSWER)
C
      WRITE(2,10) ANSWER
   10 FORMAT(3X,'ANSWER =',F16.4)
C
      STOP
      END
```

Notice how extremely easy to is to take advantage of this prewritten routine.

The second item that must be supplied is the FUNCTION subprogram holding the specific equation to be integrated. We have chosen to use the name Y, for that subprogram.

```
C
      FUNCTION Y(X)
C
C ...........................................................
C.. PURPOSE - THIS IS A DEFINITION OF THE SUBPROGRAM      ..
C..          REQUESTED BY QG9.  THIS SUBPROGRAM HOLDS     ..
C..          THE EQUATION THAT IS TO BE INTEGRATED.       ..
C ...........................................................
C
      Y = EXP(X) - ALOG(X**2 + 1.0) / X
C
      RETURN
      END
```

When using one of the routines of a software package, it is usually necessary to signal which software package is being used. This is accomplished by one or more control cards. They are placed in front of the program deck and provide direction as to where to search for the specific subroutine that is being called within the main program, but is not supplied in the program deck. These control cards vary from installation to installation. Your computer center will provide instructors for preparing these cards. We will now look at another subroutine in the IBM software package to point out the similarity in documentation.

15.3 | Subroutine SIMQ

Subroutine SIMQ is used to find the solution to simultaneous equations such as:

Eq. 1 $9.0X_1 + 6.5X_2 + 3.5X_3 = 27.75$
Eq. 2 $4.5X_1 + 2.2X_2 + 1.5X_3 = 10.50$
Eq. 3 $6.7X_1 + 3.0X_2 + 1.0X_3 = 12.25$

Figure 15.2 Simultaneous Equation Set

Before reading the documentation of SIMQ, it would help to anticipate what information must be passed to such a subroutine to solve equations of this form. Obviously the coefficient preceding each X term is needed, suggesting a two-dimensional array (matrix) possibly called A. The three right-hand coefficients are needed suggesting a one-dimensional array (vector) B. We must provide either the size of these arrays or an integer telling how many equations are in the set. With this as a start, let's look at SIMQ (see Figure 15.3).

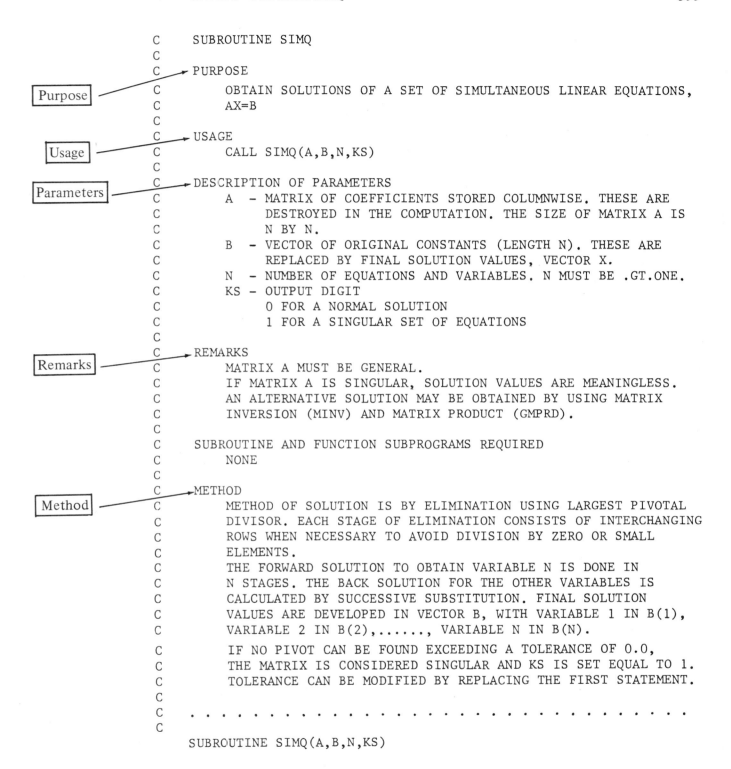

```
C       SUBROUTINE SIMQ
C
C       PURPOSE
C           OBTAIN SOLUTIONS OF A SET OF SIMULTANEOUS LINEAR EQUATIONS,
C           AX=B
C
C       USAGE
C           CALL SIMQ(A,B,N,KS)
C
C       DESCRIPTION OF PARAMETERS
C           A  - MATRIX OF COEFFICIENTS STORED COLUMNWISE. THESE ARE
C                DESTROYED IN THE COMPUTATION. THE SIZE OF MATRIX A IS
C                N BY N.
C           B  - VECTOR OF ORIGINAL CONSTANTS (LENGTH N). THESE ARE
C                REPLACED BY FINAL SOLUTION VALUES, VECTOR X.
C           N  - NUMBER OF EQUATIONS AND VARIABLES. N MUST BE .GT.ONE.
C           KS - OUTPUT DIGIT
C                0 FOR A NORMAL SOLUTION
C                1 FOR A SINGULAR SET OF EQUATIONS
C
C       REMARKS
C           MATRIX A MUST BE GENERAL.
C           IF MATRIX A IS SINGULAR, SOLUTION VALUES ARE MEANINGLESS.
C           AN ALTERNATIVE SOLUTION MAY BE OBTAINED BY USING MATRIX
C           INVERSION (MINV) AND MATRIX PRODUCT (GMPRD).
C
C       SUBROUTINE AND FUNCTION SUBPROGRAMS REQUIRED
C           NONE
C
C       METHOD
C           METHOD OF SOLUTION IS BY ELIMINATION USING LARGEST PIVOTAL
C           DIVISOR. EACH STAGE OF ELIMINATION CONSISTS OF INTERCHANGING
C           ROWS WHEN NECESSARY TO AVOID DIVISION BY ZERO OR SMALL
C           ELEMENTS.
C           THE FORWARD SOLUTION TO OBTAIN VARIABLE N IS DONE IN
C           N STAGES. THE BACK SOLUTION FOR THE OTHER VARIABLES IS
C           CALCULATED BY SUCCESSIVE SUBSTITUTION. FINAL SOLUTION
C           VALUES ARE DEVELOPED IN VECTOR B, WITH VARIABLE 1 IN B(1),
C           VARIABLE 2 IN B(2),......, VARIABLE N IN B(N).
C
C           IF NO PIVOT CAN BE FOUND EXCEEDING A TOLERANCE OF 0.0,
C           THE MATRIX IS CONSIDERED SINGULAR AND KS IS SET EQUAL TO 1.
C           TOLERANCE CAN BE MODIFIED BY REPLACING THE FIRST STATEMENT.
C
C       . . . . . . . . . . . . . . . . . . . . . . . . . . . . . .
C
        SUBROUTINE SIMQ(A,B,N,KS)
```

Figure 15.3 Subroutine SIMQ Documentation

First, examine the CALL statement and the description of parameters:

CALL SIMQ (A,B,N,KS)

Notice that we have predicted or anticipated the first three arguments. In the DESCRIPTION OF PARAMETERS, however, it is stated that the matrix A and the vector B are destroyed in the computation. The reason for this needs explaining.

One of the first steps in solving the problem is to get the coefficients preceding X_1 in all the equations to be the same. This is done by multiplying each row of matrix A (and an element of B) by an appropriate value. While this does not destroy the functional relationships expressed by these equations, it does destroy their original identity.

We are also told that the final solution values (X_1, X_2, X_3) replace the original values in vector B. Vector B is being used for both input and output. On input, B holds the right-hand constants. On output, it holds all the answers.

Usually, it is not necessary to preserve the identity of the original equations. All that are needed are the solution values. If the equations must be preserved, the obvious answer would be to make a copy of both arrays and feed these copies to SIMQ.

A Mailbox

The last argument, KS, is like a mailbox and is used to signal if a normal solution is being achieved. Statements inside SIMQ are constantly checking to see if anything is going wrong. If no difficulties are encountered, the number 0 will be loaded into memory location KS just before the RETURN statement is executed. This signals a normal solution.

If, however, the subroutine detects something has gone wrong (one equation is the exact multiple of another), a number other than 0 will be loaded into memory location KS using a statement such as:

KS = 1

and the RETURN statement executed immediately, terminating the solution. If a number other than 0 is returned in KS, a list of "disaster" codes is provided to match the number to the difficulties encountered. You then are told to ignore any other output values.

All software packages have some method of signaling the user when something has gone wrong. This is one of many techniques used.

The steps involved in writing the main program, which uses a typical predefined subroutine, are:

1. define the variables, arrays or subprograms requested as input in the description of parameters,
2. make the appropriate call,
3. check for a normal solution, and
4. output results or pass values to other subprograms.

Our original set of three equations could now be solved by the following main program:

```
C..........................................................
C..    PURPOSE - DEMONSTRATE CALL TO SUBROUTINE SIMQ (IBM-SSP).
C..              WHERE BASIC INPUT IS BY ARRAYS.
C..........................................................
C
       DIMENSION A(3,3), B(3)
C
C              READ EQUATIONS FROM DATA
C
       DO 20 I = 1, 3
C
          READ(5,10) A(I,1), A(I,2), A(I,3), B(I)
   10     FORMAT(4F12.2)
C
   20 CONTINUE
C
C      ..........................................
C              CALL SIMQ(A,B,3,MAIL)
C      ..........................................
C
C      CHECK MAIL FOR SUCCESSFUL SOLUTION
C
       WRITE(2,30) MAIL
   30 FORMAT(10X, I1)
C
       IF(MAIL.NE.0) STOP
C
C              PUBLISH SOLUTION VALUES
C
       WRITE(2,40) (B(I),I=1,3)
   40 FORMAT(10X,3F15.3)
C
       STOP
       END
C
```

15.4 | Other Software Packages (Conversational)

Consider yourself fortunate that you are competent in a computer language such as FORTRAN. Software packages are of two basic types. One type is for those who can program and one is for those who cannot. The packages that require no programming skill must compensate in some way. This can be achieved by making or incorporating a conversational feature inside the subprogram.

Consider the use of one such conversational subprogram called SIMULEQN in solving another set of simultaneous equations:

$$3x + 2y + 1z = 3$$
$$5x - 3y + 2z = -3$$
$$4x + 16y + 5z = 27$$

After logging in on the remote console, the interactive feature is initiated by typing the key word:

SIMULEQN

The console responds with the message:

DO YOU WANT INSTRUCTIONS (0=NO, 1=YES), WHICH?

If the programmer now answers:

YES

You have given an incorrect response and the console patiently replies:

ILLEGAL INPUT. RETYPE?

After giving an acceptable response of 1, the following documentation is presented on the console. A complete set of instructions is provided followed by an example set of equations and the input that would be supplied for this example set.

```
SIMULEQN

DO YOU WANT INSTRUCTIONS (0=NO, 1=YES), WHICH? YES ILLE-
GAL INPUT. RETYPE ?1

SIMULEQN SOLVES SYSTEMS OF N LINEAR EQUATIONS IN N UN-
KNOWNS. ALL DATA IS ENTERED BY NUMBERED DATA STATE-
MENTS. THE FIRST DATA STATEMENT MUST BE NUMBERED 10,
AND MUST SPECIFY THE NUMBER OF SYSTEMS TO BE SOLVED
AND THE NUMBER OF EQUATIONS (AND HENCE THE NUMBER OF
VARIABLES) IN THE SYSTEM.

DATA STATEMENTS NUMBERED FROM 11 TO 99 AS REQUIRED
ARE USED TO ENTER THE COEFFICIENTS AND RIGHT-HAND SIDE
CONSTANTS.
ENTER THE COEFFICIENT MATRIX, BY ROWS, AND THEN THE
RIGHT-HAND SIDE CONSTANT TERMS. THIS PROGRAM IS SLOW.
IF ADDITIONAL CASES WITH THE SAME COEFFICIENT MATRIX
BUT DIFFERENT RIGHT SIDES ARE TO BE RUN, THEY WILL BE
RUN AT ONCE BY SIMPLY ENTERING ADDITIONAL RIGHT-HAND
CONSTANT TERMS.

FOR EXAMPLE, THE TWO SYSTEMS:
   3X + 5Y - 2Z =  9     3X + 5Y - 2Z = 19
   7X +  Y      = -3     7X +  Y      = -3
    X - 7Y + 9Z = 14      X - 7Y + 9Z =  8
COULD BE SOLVED BY TYPING:

*10 DATA 2, 3
*11 DATA 3,5,-2,7,1,0,1,-7,9
*12 DATA 9,-3,14,19,-3,8
*RUN
```

```
*10 DATA 2, 3
*11 DATA 3,5,-2,7,1,0,1,-7,9
*12 DATA 9,-3,14,19,-3,8
*RUN
AFTER THE COMPUTER RESPONDS WITH READY AND AN ASTERISK
* ENTER YOUR DATA STATEMENT IMMEDIATELY FOLLOWING THE
ASTERISKS SUPPLIED, THEN TYPE RUN
```

Notice that a set of instructions is given, followed by sample input to clarify the responses required.

Responding to all this, the first input would be:

```
10 DATA 1,3
```

indicating a desire to solve one set of three equations. The statement:

```
11 DATA 3,2,1,5,-3,2,4,16,5
```

provides the coefficient array in row order. Finally, the right hand constants are supplied by:

```
12 DATA 3,-3,27
```

The subprogram takes over and the final results are presented as follows:

```
ready
*10 DATA 1,3
*11 DATA 3,2,1,5,-3,2,4,16,5
*12 DATA 3,-3,27
*RUN

S I M U L E Q N

SOLUTION FOR LINEAR SYSTEM OF ORDER      3

                           INDEX:
                 1               2               3
SOLUTION VECTOR FOR CASE      1

     -.3614458          1.337349        1.409639
PROOF OF SOLUTION FOR CASE   1

            3              -3              27
```

This example shows the documentation and use of another typical software package.

15.5 Output Alternatives

So far, we have concentrated on how to provide *input* to some of these software routines. Figures 15.4 through 15.8 now show some of the *output* options available within certain subprograms. Figure 15.4 shows the output of a statistical subroutine used to analyze the scores of 1000 students on a college entrance exam.

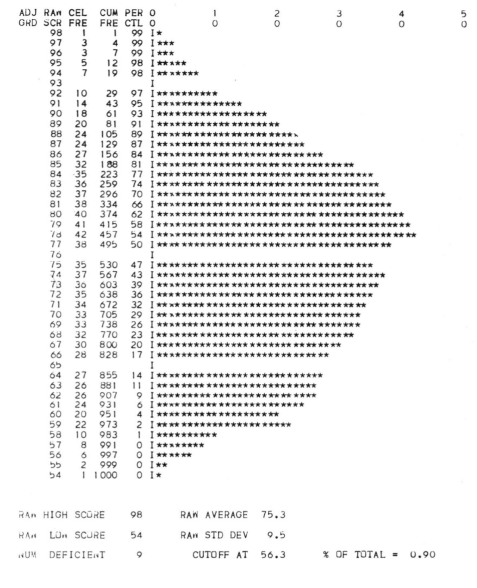

ADJ RAW GRD SCR	CEL FRE	CUM FRE	PER CTL	0 0	1 0	2 0	3 0	4 0	5 0
98	1	1	99	I*					
97	3	4	99	I***					
96	3	7	99	I***					
95	5	12	98	I*****					
94	7	19	98	I*******					
93				I					
92	10	29	97	I**********					
91	14	43	95	I**************					
90	18	61	93	I******************					
89	20	81	91	I********************					
88	24	105	89	I************************					
87	24	129	87	I************************					
86	27	156	84	I***************************					
85	32	188	81	I********************************					
84	35	223	77	I***********************************					
83	36	259	74	I************************************					
82	37	296	70	I*************************************					
81	38	334	66	I**************************************					
80	40	374	62	I**					
79	41	415	58	I***					
78	42	457	54	I**					
77	38	495	50	I**************************************					
76				I					
75	35	530	47	I***********************************					
74	37	567	43	I*************************************					
73	36	603	39	I************************************					
72	35	638	36	I***********************************					
71	34	672	32	I**********************************					
70	33	705	29	I*********************************					
69	33	738	26	I*********************************					
68	32	770	23	I********************************					
67	30	800	20	I******************************					
66	28	828	17	I****************************					
65				I					
64	27	855	14	I***************************					
63	26	881	11	I**************************					
62	26	907	9	I**************************					
61	24	931	6	I************************					
60	20	951	4	I********************					
59	22	973	2	I**********************					
58	10	983	1	I**********					
57	8	991	0	I********					
56	6	997	0	I******					
55	2	999	0	I**					
54	1	1000	0	I*					

RAW HIGH SCORE   98   RAW AVERAGE 75.3

RAW LOW SCORE   54   RAW STD DEV   9.5

NUM DEFICIENT   9   CUTOFF AT 56.3   % OF TOTAL = 0.90

DESCRIPTIVE STATISTICS

NUMBER OF OBSERVATIONS 1000
MEAN .... 7.534900E+01
MEDIAN .... 7.500000E+01
RANGE .... 4.400000E+01
UNADJUSTED VARIANCE .... 9.057687E+01
UNADJUSTED STANDARD DEVIATION .... 9.517188E+00
ADJUSTED VARIANCE .... 9.066754E+01
ADJUSTED STANDARD DEVIATION .... 9.521950E+00
SKEWNESS ....-6.200773E-06
KURTOSIS .... 2.153488E+00

Figure 15.4 Elegant Output

Notice the wealth of information presented. In addition to determining the highest, lowest, and average score, the subprogram determines and reports the mean, variance, standard deviation, and the skewness of distribution. The subprogram even generates a histogram. All this output results from a single call to a subroutine called HIST1.*

*Program developed for the U.S.M.A. Academic Computer Center system library by Mrs. Sylvia Sands of the U.S.M.A. staff.

Income vs. Grades

If the income of the students' parents is known, a tabulation of scores achieved vs. parents' income could be obtained by using a program called CROSSTABS**. The elegant output shown in Figure 15.5 is controlled almost entirely within the subprogram, the user providing just a few labels.

```
                      INCOME
                      I$5001-   $10001-   $15001-   $20001-   OVER      ROW
                      I$10000   $15000    $20000    $25000    $25001    TOTAL
                      I    2.00I    3.00I     4.00I     5.00I     6.00I
    GRADES       --------I--------I---------I----------I----------I---------I
                 1.00 I    3 I    43 I    23 I     0 I     0 I      69
    50-60             I  4.3 I  62.3 I  33.3 I   0.0 I   0.0 I     6.9
                 -I--------I--------I---------I---------I---------I
                 2.00 I    0 I    74 I   176 I     9 I     0 I     259
    61-70             I  0.0 I  28.6 I  68.0 I   3.5 I   0.0 I    25.9
                 -I--------I--------I---------I---------I---------I
                 3.00 I    0 I     0 I   157 I   181 I     0 I     338
    71-80             I  0.0 I   0.0 I  46.4 I  53.6 I   0.0 I    33.8
                 -I--------I--------I---------I---------I---------I
                 4.00 I    0 I     0 I     5 I   189 I    97 I     291
    81-90             I  0.0 I   0.0 I   1.7 I  64.9 I  33.3 I    29.1
                 -I--------I--------I---------I---------I---------I
                 5.00 I    0 I     0 I     0 I     5 I    38 I      43
    91-100            I  0.0 I   0.0 I   0.0 I  11.6 I  88.4 I     4.4
                 -I--------I--------I---------I---------I---------I
            COLUMN        3       117       361       384       135      1000
            TOTAL        .3      11.7      36.1      38.4      13.5     100.0
```

CHI SQUARE =   1070.67107   WITH 16 DEGREES OF FREEDOM
CRAMER≠S V =   .51737
CONTINGENCY COEFFICIENT =   .71907
KENDALL≠S TAU B =   .76551
KENDALL≠S TAU C =   .67805
GAMMA =   .96754
SOMER≠S D =   .78580

Figure 15.5 Typical SPSS Output

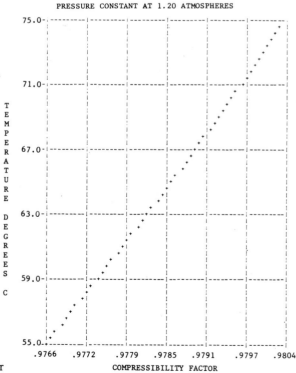

Figure 15.6 Graph Using On-Line Printer

*"Statistical Package for the Social Sciences" developed by Bent, Nie and Hull in conjunction with Stanford University.

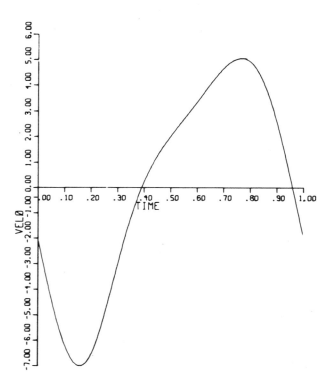

Figure 15.7 Graph Using CalComp Plotter*

Figure 15.6 shows the output of a subprogram used by chemical engineers to calculate the compressibility of a gas. The computer-aided solution includes graphical output (using the line printer) to plot the functional relationship determined.

Finally, there are a number of software packages that produce graphical output on special devices such as an incremental digital plotter. These routines are activated just like any others, i.e., by passing simple variables, subscripted variables, or user supplied subprograms. For example, the hidden lines in Figure 15.8 were generated by calls to the subroutine DASHLN:

CALL DASHLN(X1,Y1,X2,Y2)

whose arguments define the X and Y location of the beginning and end of the dashed line. The circles were drawn by subroutine SIMCIR:

CALL SIMCIR(X,Y,R)

whose argument list obviously specifies the location of the center of the circle and its radius.

*Reprinted from "Digital Computer Plotting" © 1969, courtesy of Professor Franklyn K. Brown, Northeastern University.

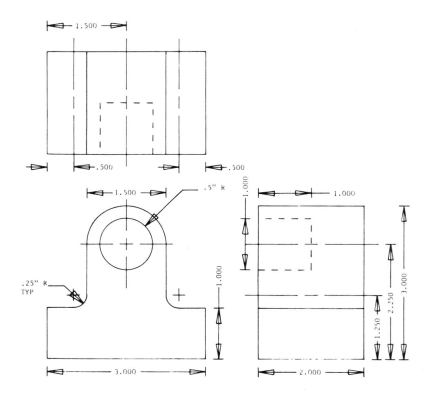

Figure 15.8 Multi-View Drawing*

15.6 | A Final Example: Numerical Methods

Not all subroutines are easy or safe to use. The examples given thus far have had relatively simple argument lists. The subroutine in this final example is more typical of what a complex argument list looks like.

There is another difficulty in using some subprograms, especially those involving complicated mathematics. Subprogramming involves a shift in responsibility for knowing the theory behind solving the problem. The person who writes a subprogram must know what he or she is doing, and *so should the user.* When that is not true, *trouble* cannot be far off.

Numerical methods is an area of mathematics concerned with finding better and more efficient ways of solving problems on a computer. For example, there ee basic numerical techniques for solving simultaneous equations (deter-mina..t, iteration, and elimination methods). One method may be very good if there are only a few equations involved. This same method would be deadly if 50 equations were to be solved. While some amount of warning is given in the documentation, it is generally dangerous to use a routine whose theory is un-known to the user.

*Reprinted from "Digital Computer Plotting" © 1969, courtesy of Professor Franklyn K. Brown, Northeastern University.

The Newton-Raphson Procedure

The problem that follows is typical of various numerical methods available in most software packages. It is the well known **Newton-Raphson procedure** for determining the roots of nonlinear equations. Early in this text a clumsy "trial and error" procedure was used: that of letting X take on a series of values (0.1, 0.2, 0.3, 0.4, etc.) hoping a root would be nearby (see Chapter 8). The programmer was essentially guessing at successive values of X to try.

It is possible to use the derivative or slope of an equation to come up with a better sequence of X values to try.

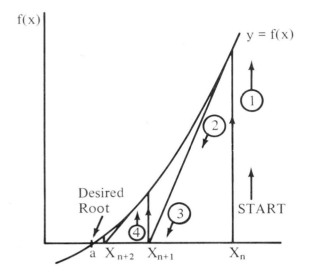

The method is:

1. Starting with some initial guess, X_n, determine Y (the value of equation at $X=X_n$).
2. At $X=X_n$ determine the derivative (slope) of the equation.
3. Extend this slope line until it crosses the X-axis. Use this intercept as the next value of X to try (X_{n+1}).
4. Repeat the process.

The root should be reached much faster because successive approximations to the root are *calculated*, not guessed at.

There are some dangers in using this method. If any of the values of X, developed in approaching the root, are in the vicinity of X_1 or X_2 of Figure 15.9, the slope or tangent line will not intersect the X axis.

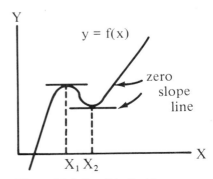

Figure 15.9 Possible Problems

If any value of X falls between X_1 and X_2, the slope or tangent line will intersect off to the right, which is not in the direction of the root.* These situations will exist if the value of the derivative is changing rapidly in the vicinity of the root, i.e., if the equation is not well behaved.

With this as background, consider the use of subroutine RTNI (Figure 15.10) for determining a root to the equation:

$$y = e^x - \ln(x^2 + 1) - \frac{1}{\sqrt{e^{-x} + 1}}$$

While the call to RTNI seems formidable, it is really not so bad.

CALL RTNI(X,F,DERF,FCT,XST,EPSI,IEND,IER)

Consider the last four arguments. XST is the initial guess needed to start the search; EPSI asks the degree of accuracy to which the root should be determined. If EPSI is set equal to 0.001, the method will be repeated until the root is known to this degree of accuracy. It may be impossible to obtain a solution to this degree of accuracy, so IEND specifies the maximum number of iterations to be performed. If the root has not been determined to the desired degree of accuracy after IEND cycles, then a value of 1 is given to IER to indicate this lack of convergency. If a near-zero slope occurs at any time, IER is given a value of 2.

```
C                                                                          RTNI 001
C ...................................................................      RTNI 002
C                                                                          RTNI 003
C       SUBROUTINE RTNI                                                    RTNI 004
C                                                                          RTNI 005
C       PURPOSE                                                            RTNI 006
C          TO SOLVE GENERAL NONLINEAR EQUATIONS OF THE FORM F(X) = 0       RTNI 007
C          BY MEANS OF NEWTON'S ITERATION METHOD.                          RTNI 008
C                                                                          RTNI 009
C       USAGE                                                              RTNI 010
C          CALL RTNI (X,F,DERF,FCT,XST,EPS,IEND,IER)                       RTNI 011
C          PARAMETER FCT REQUIRES AN EXTERNAL STATEMENT.                   RTNI 012
C                                                                          RTNI 013
C       DESCRIPTION OF PARAMETERS                                          RTNI 014
C          X      - RESULTANT ROOT OF EQUATION F(X) = 0.                   RTNI 015
C          F      - RESULTANT FUNCTION VALUE AT ROOT X.                    RTNI 016
C          DERF   - RESULTANT VALUE OF DERIVATIVE AT ROOT X.               RTNI 017
C          FCT    - NAME OF THE EXTERNAL SUBROUTINE USED.  IT COMPUTES     RTNI 018
C                   TO GIVEN ARGUMENT X FUNCTION VALUE F AND DERIVATIVE    RTNI 019
C                   DERF.  ITS PARAMETER LIST MUST BE X,F,DERF.            RTNI 020
C          XST    - INPUT VALUE WHICH SPECIFIES THE INITIAL GUESS OF THE   RTNI 021
C                   ROOT X.                                                RTNI 022
C          EPS    - INPUT VALUE WHICH SPECIFIES THE UPPER BOUND OF THE     RTNI 023
C                   ERROR OF RESULT X.                                     RTNI 024
C          IEND   - MAXIMUM NUMBER OF ITERATION STEPS SPECIFIED.           RTNI 025
C          IER    - RESULTANT ERROR PARAMETER CODED AS FOLLOWS             RTNI 026
C                   IER = 0 - NO ERROR,                                    RTNI 027
C                   IER = 1 - NO CONVERGENCE AFTER IEND ITERATION STEPS,   RTNI 028
C                   IER = 2 - AT ANY ITERATION STEP DERIVATIVE DERF WAS    RTNI 029
C                             EQUAL TO ZERO.                               RTNI 030
C                                                                          RTNI 031
C       REMARKS                                                            RTNI 032
C          THE PROCEDURE IS BYPASSED AND GIVES THE ERROR MESSAGE IER = 2   RTNI 033
C          IF AT ANY ITERATION STEP DERIVATIVE OF F(X) IS EQUAL TO 0.      RTNI 034
C          POSSIBLY THE PROCEDURE WOULD BE SUCESSFUL IF IT IS STARTED      RTNI 035
C          ONCE MORE WITH ANOTHER INITIAL GUESS XST.                       RTNI 036
C                                                                          RTNI 037
C       SUBROUTINES AND FUNCTION SUBPROGRAMS REQUIRED                      RTNI 038
C          THE EXTERNAL SUBROUTINE FCT(X, F, DERF) MUST BE FURNISHED       RTNI 039
C          BY THE USER.                                                    RTNI 040
C                                                                          RTNI 041
```

*RTNI will use a "mailbox" called IER to signal if difficulties are encountered while searching for the root.

```
C        METHOD                                                    RTNI  042
C           SOLUTION OF EQUATION F(X) = 0 IS DONE BY MEANS OF NEWTON'S  RTNI  043
C           ITERATION METHOD, WHICH STARTS AT THE INITIAL GUESS XST OF  RTNI  044
C           A ROOT X.  CONVERGENCE IS QUADRATIC IF THE DERIVATIVE OF    RTNI  045
C           F(X)AT ROOT X IS NOT EQUAL TO ZERO.  ONE ITERATION STEP     RTNI  046
C           REQUIRES ONE EVALUATION OF F(X).AND ONE EVALUATION OF THE   RTNI  047
C           DERIVATIVE OF F(X).  FOR TEST ON SATISFACTORY ACCURACY SEE  RTNI  048
C           FORMULAE (2) OF MATHEMATICAL DESCRIPTION.                   RTNI  049
C           FOR REFERENCE,   SEE R. ZURMUFHL, PRAKTISCHE MATHEMATIK FUER  RTNI  050
C           INGENIEURE UND PHYSIKER, SPRINGER, BERLIN/GOETTINGEN/       RTNI  051
C           HEIDELBERG, 1963,  PP. 12-17.                              RTNI  052
C                                                                       RTNI  053
C        .................................................;................  RTNI  054
C                                                                       RTNI  055
         SUBROUTINE RTNI(X, F, DERF, FCT, XST, EPS, IEND, IER)          RTNI  056
C                                                                       RTNI  057
C                                                                       RTNI  058
C        PREPARE ITERATION                                             RTNI  059
         IER = 0                                                       RTNI  060
         X = XST                                                       RTNI  061
         TOL = X                                                       RTNI  062

         CALL FCT(TOL, F, DERF)                                         RTNI  063
         TOLF = 100. * EPS                                             RTNI  064
C                                                                       RTNI  065
C                                                                       RTNI  066
C        START ITERATION LOOP                                          RTNI  067
         DO 6 I = 1, IEND                                              RTNI  068
         IF (F) 1, 7, 1                                                RTNI  069
C                                                                       RTNI  070
C        EQUATION    NOT SATISIFIED BY X                               RTNI  071
       1 IF (DERF) 2, 8, 2                                             RTNI  072
C                                                                       RTNI  073
C        ITERATION IS POSSIBLE                                         RTNI  074
       2 DX = F/DERF                                                   RTNI  075
         X = X - DX                                                    RTNI  076
         TOL = X                                                       RTNI  077
         CALL FCT(TOL, F, DERF)                                         RTNI  078
C                                                                       RTNI  079
C        TEST ON SATISFACTORY ACCURACY                                 RTNI  080
         TOL = EPS                                                     RTNI  081
         A = ABS(X)                                                    RTNI  082
         IF (A-1.) 4, 4, 3                                             RTNI  083
       3 TOL = TOL * A                                                 RTNI  084
       4 IF (ABS (DX) - TOL) 5, 5, 6                                   RTNI  085
       5 IF (ABS (F) - TOLF) 7, 7, 6                                   RTNI  086
       6 CONTINUE                                                      RTNI  087
C        END OF ITERATION LOOP                                         RTNI  088
C                                                                       RTNI  089
C                                                                       RTNI  090
C        NO CONVERGENCE AFTER IEND ITERATION STEPS.  ERROR RETURN.     RTNI  091
         IER = 1                                                       RTNI  092
       7 RETURN                                                        RTNI  093
C                                                                       RTNI  094
C        ERROR RETURN IN CASE OF ZERO DIVISOR                          RTNI  095
       8 IER = 2                                                       RTNI  096
         RETURN                                                        RTNI  097
         END                                                          RTNI  098
```

Figure 15.10 Root Determination Subroutine

This subroutine needs a USER SUPPLIED subprogram to obtain values and the derivative of the function for each new X value to be tried. The section entitled SUBROUTINES AND FUNCTION SUBPROGRAMS REQUIRED suggests that a subroutine called FCT be provided whose argument list includes the input value X and the output quantities F and DERF.

RTNI will compute successive values of X starting from XST. For each X, a call to FCT is made to determine F and DERF. On the last call to FCT, X will be the resulting approximation to the root. F will be the value of the function at that X value (usually F will be near zero) and DERF will be the derivative at this root.

To demonstrate the use of RTNI, the following main program and user-supplied subprogram are shown for the equation suggested before:

$$Y = e^x - \ln(x^2 + 1) - \frac{1}{\sqrt{e^{-x} + 1}}$$

```
C       MAIN PROGRAM
C
C       EXTERNAL FCT
C
        READ(5,10) XSTART
     10 FORMAT(F12.2)
C
        CALL RTNI(XROOT,Y,YPRIME,FCT,XSTART,0.0001,20,IER)
C
        WRITE(2,20) XROOT, Y, IER
     20 FORMAT(1H1,1X,2E18.6,I3)
C
        STOP
        END
        SUBROUTINE FCT(X, Y, YPRIME)
C
        Y = EXP(X)-ALOG(X**2+1.)-1./SQRT(EXP(-X)+1.)
     10 YPRIME = EXP(X)-2.*X/(X**2+1.)-EXP(-X)*.5*(EXP(-X)+1.)
       1     **(-1.5)
C
        RETURN
        END
```

If it proved too difficult to determine the derivative of the equation by calculus (see statement 10 in Subroutine FCT), a numerical technique could be used. Two adjacent values of Y would be computed and their difference divided by ΔX. Obviously this will affect the accuracy somewhat. How much? The answer lies in the field of Numerical Methods. Those who have a background in this field can give good estimates of the probable error. For the student who does not have such background, it is enough to know that this numerical technique would result in *some* degree of error and that all results should be used with caution.

Review Exercises

1. Describe some of the documentation provided by a typical software package to make the use of any one of its routines as straightforward as possible.

2.*What is meant by the term "discipline-oriented" software package?

3. Describe what functions are accomplished in the main program when using one or more of these prewritten subprograms.

4.*Most software routines use statements inside the subprogram to determine if the solution is progressing properly. Describe at least one method of signalling the user that something has gone wrong.

5. What are some of the features unique to software packages that are written for use with terminals and employ "conversational" features?

6. Describe some of the rather exotic output that is available from some of these software routines.

7. Some software routines, like SIMQ, destroy the identity of the equations the routine is solving. Why?

8.*How can the identity of the original equations described in exercise 7 be retained?

9. Describe some of the software routines that could be used to make the running of a hospital more efficient. Describe a discipline-oriented software package that might be used by a police department.

10. Write a subroutine subprogram that will sort a vector of real numbers. Provide documentation of this routine similar to that used in the I.B.M. Scientific Subroutine Package.

11. Repeat exercise 10 and provide a means of sorting the vector in either ascending or descending order depending on whether a variable called INMAIL has a value of 1 or 2.

12.*Write a subprogram that receives as input two sides of a right triangle and returns the size of the hypotenuse and angle "a" and angle "b" of the triangle.

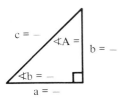

13. Generalize the subprogram in exercise 12 to receive alternate forms of input such as one side and the hypotenuse or one side and an angle. Carefully document this routine.

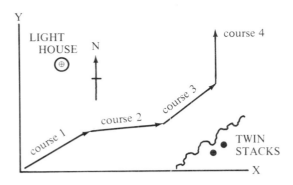

14. Devise one or more routines to be used on a merchant ship to assist in the navigation of that ship. For example, write a subroutine to receive as input a vector of course headings, a vector of times (number of minutes on each course heading) and a vector of speeds (ship's speed on each heading). Have the subroutine report the X and Y location of the ship at any time t.

15. Expand the subroutine in exercise 14 to provide as output the bearing at which certain landmarks will appear (like a lighthouse or twin smoke stacks) as the ship steams along its course.

16. Revise exercise 14 to allow for two additional input values, namely, the direction and speed of the current (flow of water that will set the vessel off course if not accounted for).

17.*Write a root determination routine that uses a *half-interval search* technique. This routine should receive as input: (1) the name of a user-supplied subprogram holding the equation whose root we are looking for: (2) XLEFT and XRIGHT defining the span of X within which the root lies. This routine should determine the sign of the function at XLEFT, XRIGHT

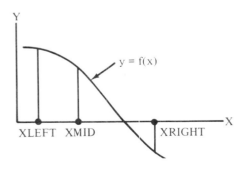

and at the midpoint of this span. With this information it is possible to determine if the root lies in the right or left half of the span. For example, if the root lies in the right half of the span, redefine XLEFT (give it the value of the present midpoint) and repeat the process.

18. Repeat exercise 17, except provide *two* methods of terminating the solution similar to those used in RTNI. That is, allow the user to stipulate:

   1. the degree of accuracy to be imposed on the root, or
   2. the maximum number of iterations of the half interval procedure to be used.

19. Repeat exercise 17, except provide means of determining if the solution runs into difficulties. The possible difficulties should include:

   1. No solution in the span designated,
   2. Solution terminated due to reaching maximum iterations, and
   3. Any other difficulty this procedure might encounter (give description).

20. Describe the difficulties that would be encountered if the procedures developed in exercise 17 were used for the functions shown below.

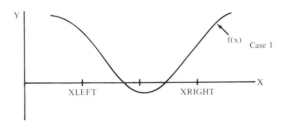

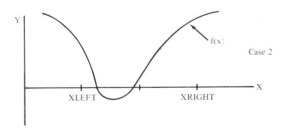

16 | Structured Programming

16.1 | Introduction

In many ways, the objectives of structured programming and the objectives of programming style are quite similar. Both attempt to bring a high order of discipline and organization into:

    (a) the way in which an algorithm is developed, and
    (b) the way in which FORTRAN code is written.

Structured programming, however, has a much broader, far reaching control over the way in which a program is written. Structured programming embodies the concept of rigid discipline at two distinct levels: program design and program implementation.

At the implementation level, structured programming places numerous restrictions on the way in which individual blocks of code may be written. First each block must be controlled in *length* (number of statements). A commonly accepted length is 60 lines, which will fit on one page of computer paper. Large blocks of complex code are just not allowed. Next, each block must conform to one of three permitted forms or *constructs:* sequence, decision or loop construct. The type of construct being used is declared by the first statement in the block. Each construct may be entered at one point only, *through the top statement,* and can have only one exit point, *the bottom statement.* Transfer of control within the block is severely restricted. It must be linear in fashion with no lateral transfers permitted. (The use of GO TO statements is all but forbidden.)

Programs written according to these tight restrictions are programs in which there are never any surprises, no wild detours, no unexpected branches. In structured programming everything is more precise, more controlled, more predictable. It is this aspect of structured programming that will be the main concern of this chapter.

At the program design level, structured programming provides an invaluable tool or methodology by which project managers can maintain a well-organized, highly efficient control over large-scale computer projects. It is sometimes difficult for student programmers to grasp the scope of complexities involved in even a modest computer project. As a result, they usually underestimate the importance of programming style and programming structure. There is a reason for this. A student is usually asked to solve a relatively small and well-defined problem. Because there is only one person involved in the assignment, there are no scheduling, coordinating or interface problems. The situation facing a project manager is considerably different. The problems are magnified a hundredfold.

413

Consider the following typical assignment:

Develop a software package to be used in screening the accuracy
of Federal Income Tax Returns for a six-state region.

Just attempting to identify the many subtasks involved in this project is a challenge in itself. For each task identified, a clear set of specifications must be written. These specifications must tell the number and size of the various data bases representing input to this module and what transformations are to be accomplished inside this module. A set of performance standards should be included that defines a number of sets of test data to which the module must satisfactorily respond. An estimate must be made of when in the production schedule work should be started on this module, and how many days or months will be needed to write and debug the module.

Because many modules will share the same data bases, a strict organizational control must be established. Transfer of control from one subprogram to another must be tightly regulated. It is at this point that the design implications of structured programming play a dominant role. Structured programming imposes a strict "top-down," "successive refinement" approach as explained below.

The Old Way: Bottom-Up Approach

Prior to the development of structured programming techniques, there was a tendency to use a somewhat "bottom-up" approach. Many of the simple (low level) modules of a project were written to "get things started." The more difficult modules were either set aside for the moment or given a deferred priority. Using this approach, a programmer may not know exactly when or where her particular module will be inserted into the overall program. Frequently, important design decisions were made that might have been correct for the little (low level) module being written but were totally incorrect as far as the overall project was concerned.

This approach invites all kinds of difficulties when it comes time to try to tie all the lower-level modules together into an integrated package. It often takes more time to find out why two modules will not run well together than it took to write the modules in the first place. The difficulty with the "bottom-up" approach is obvious: it addresses the problem of coordination too late in the project.

The New Way: Top-Down Approach

Structured programming forces organizational control to be defined at the beginning of a project. The function, input, output, and performance criteria for the top-level modules are defined first. From this a controlled series of successive refinements is applied to define equally tight specifications for a series of second- and third-level modules. At each level, more concern is given to describing the function of each module than to the FORTRAN code that might be used. An organization chart is produced. This chart resembles the ones used in large companies to show who reports to whom in the company. The top line shows the company president. The next line shows the vice presidents who report to the president. The next level shows who reports to each vice president.

The purpose of this chart and structured programming is to focus attention on matters of major importance at the beginning of the project, *not* at the end. Problem definition, coordinating and transfer of control, data base management, and performance criteria are considered from the outset. A disciplined, rather rigid approach is applied.

The use of a structured "top-down" method of program design is one of the more recent and interesting developments in programming. This chapter will deal with only one small aspect of this topic. It will identify those factors that are of importance to the individual programmer when writing small blocks of code to be used in some large project.

16.2 | Structured Programs

When programs are *not* structured, it is painfully obvious that each programmer is allowed to do his or her own thing. FORTRAN statements can be put together in any and all possible combinations. The size of a module can vary from just a few statements to hundreds of statements. Entry into the module and exit from the module can be almost anywhere. There is no attempt to isolate one module from another, and it is frequently difficult to tell where one module ends and another module begins. There is a single word for this set of conditions: chaos. Simply stated, structured programming is merely an attempt to bring some degree of order to what otherwise is a sea of confusion.

Structured programming starts by asking each programmer to build any block of code so that it matches one of a limited number of basic constructs. These constructs will represent the fundamental building blocks from which all programs are to be constructed. Each construct will have a **header statement** identifying where the construct starts and declaring which basic construct is being used. It will have a **terminating statement** to show clearly where the construct ends. Those familiar with structured programming will then immediately know what pattern of statements to expect inside this block of code.

Each construct will have a *single* entry point and a *single* exit point. As stated before, there should be no surprises in structured programming. A construct is entered through the first or header statement and exited from the last or terminal statement. Inside the construct the transfer of control is regulated to flow in linear fashion from the top statements to the bottom statements. Uncontrolled IF's and GO TO's are just not allowed. Branching, backtracking and premature exits (spaghetti logic) are not allowed. At first, you may find it difficult to adapt to the various restrictions. You probably will object to making your programs fit into a specific mold, but soon you will find that there is only a little loss in freedom and a considerable gain in clarity and readability of the program.

16.3 | IF-THEN-ELSE Construct*

In order to meet the objectives of structured FORTRAN it becomes necessary to expand (and thus improve) some of the control statements we have been using in the past, the first of which will be an extension of the logical IF. As the first improvement, we will allow a whole group of statements to be executed if the logical expression is true, not just *one* statement. Next, provisions will be made for the inclusion of an alternate group of statements to be executed if the logical expression is false. The statement is called the **IF-THEN-ELSE statement**. Notice that this control statement is not written on one continuous line. It consists of three parts:

1. *IF (logical expression) THEN* — the *header* portion used to identify the top of the construct and the type of construct.

*This statement was introduced in Chapter 5 but has not been used extensively because it may not be available in some compilers.

2. *ELSE* – a separator used to separate the "TRUE" statement group from the "FALSE" statement group.

3. *ENDIF* – the terminator that identifies where the construct ends.

Notice also the varying degrees of indentation used to emphasize the structure of this construct. The IF, ELSE and ENDIF are aligned, more or less forming an outer margin with the "TRUE" and "FALSE" statements aligned and indented to form an inner margin. Indentation makes the clarity of this structure stand out exceptionally clear and is dictated by programming style. It is not required by the FORTRAN compiler.

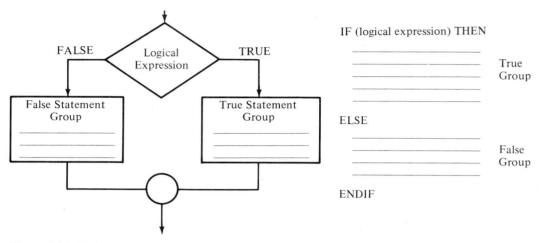

Figure 16.1 IF-THEN-ELSE Construct

Programming Example Quadratic Equation

The following example reads values of A, B and C from data that are the coefficients of a quadratic equation. If the roots are real, control passes to one set of instructions. If they are not, control passes to another set, but in a linear and more structured way.

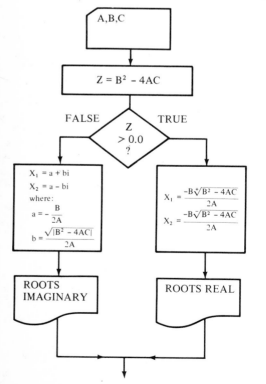

```
C
        READ(5,10) A, B, C
     10 FORMAT(3F7.2)
C
        Z = B**2-4.*A*C
C
        IF(Z.GE.0.) THEN
C
           XONE = (-B+SQRT(Z)) / (2.*A)
           XTWO = (-B+SQRT(Z)) / (2.*A)
C
           WRITE(2,20) XONE, XTWO
     20    FORMAT(2X, *ROOTS ARE REAL*,
        1  3HX1=,F8.3,5X, 3HX2=,F8.2)
C
C        ELSE
C
           X1REAL = -B / (2.*A)
           X1IMAG = SQRT(ABS(Z)) / (2.*A)
C
           X2REAL = X1REAL
           X2IMAG = -X1IMAG
C
           WRITE(2,30) X1REAL, X1IMAG,
        1  X2REAL, X2IMAG
     30    FORMAT(2X, *ROOTS IMAGINARY*,3HX1=,
        1  F8.3,3H  I,5X,3HX2=,
        2  2F8.3,1HI,5X,2F8.3,1HI)
C
        ENDIF
        STOP
        END
```

Programming Example
KOUNT Still Positive?

A memory location called KOUNT tells how many cards are left in a data deck. If the value of KOUNT is positive, READ another value of X from data and add it to an accumulator called SUM, otherwise PRINT the value of SUM and terminate the construct.

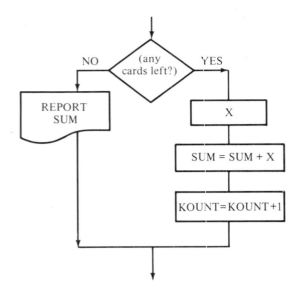

```
C
C          IF(KOUNT.GT.0)  THEN
      10        READ(5,10)  X
C               FORMAT(F8.2)
                KOUNT = KOUNT - 1
C               SUM = SUM + X
C          ELSE
      20        WRITE(2,20)  SUM
C               FORMAT(2X,'TOTAL  = ',F10.2)
C          ENDIF
C
```

Simulated IF-THEN-ELSE

Compilers that as yet have not been updated to conform to the FORTRAN 77 standards may not allow the IF-THEN-ELSE statement. The next programming example shows how to simulate this statement if necessary.

Programming Example
Which Number
Is Smaller?

Determine which of two values, A and B, is the larger and which is the smaller.

True Structure:

```
C
C
C
        IF(A.GT.B)  THEN
            BIG = A
            SMALL = B
        ELSE
            BIG = B
            SMALL = A
        ENDIF
C
```

Simulated:

```
C
        IF(A.GT.B)  GO TO 10
            GO TO 20
C
C .......TRUE  STATEMENT  GROUP.........
    10      BIG = A
            SMALL = B
            GO TO 30
C ........FALSE  STATEMENT  GROUP........
C
    20      BIG = B
            SMALL = A
C
    30  CONTINUE
C
```

The simulation is accomplished as follows. Position the "true" statements in a group and give the first statement in this group a number. Use a conventional IF statement at the top of this module to pass control to this group if the statement is true.

Position the "false" statements together (below the "true" group). Again number the first statement in this "false" group and use a GO TO statement immediately below the logical IF (header statement) to pass control to this group if the logical expression is false. The CONTINUE statement at the bottom of this block of code serves as the common exit point (to conform to the single entry/single exit restraint).

16.4 | Single Alternative IF (Abbreviated Form)

Figure 16.2 shows an abbreviated form of the IF-THEN-ELSE construct. In the situation shown, there is a group of statements to be executed if the logical IF is evaluated as "true," *but there is no "false" group* to be executed. This is called the **single alternative IF** in which the ELSE clause (or qualifying portion) is omitted from the construct.

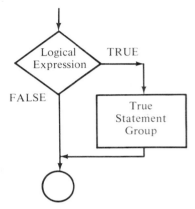

Figure 16.2 Single Alternative IF

| Programming Example
Find Larger/Smaller
Value (Repeated) | Determine which of two values, A and B, is the larger and which is the smaller. |

True Structure: Simulated Structure:

```
                                    C
        BIG = A                           BIG = A
        SMALL = B                         SMALL = B
        IF(B.GT.A) THEN                   IF(B.GT.A) GO TO 10
           BIG = B                         GO TO 30
           SMALL = A             10        BIG = B
        ENDIF                              SMALL = A
    C                               30 CONTINUE
    C
```

In the introduction to structured programming we talked about bringing order out of chaos. Notice how orderly the IF-THEN-ELSE construct is. Control passes from the top of the construct to the bottom without any unexpected and erratic jumps. The header statement alerts you to the possibility that one of two groups of statements is to be executed next. The location of each group is fixed. The true group comes first and the false group (if any) comes next. The end of the construct is clearly marked. This standardization of an acceptable or preferred framework in which FORTRAN code should be written is long overdue.

Exercises Using IF-THEN-ELSE

| Programming Example
#1 | Write an IF-THEN-ELSE construct to load a memory location called Y with the absolute value of X without calling the ABS function. |

```
C
C
      IF(X.GT.0.0) THEN
         Y = X
      ELSE
         Y = -X
      ENDIF
C
C
```

| Programming Example #2 | Write an IF-THEN-ELSE construct to determine how many points must be added to each student's grade to have a class average of at least 65. |

```
C
      IF(AVE.GT.65.0) THEN
         ADD = 0.0
      ELSE
         ADD = 65.0 - AVE
      ENDIF
C
```

| Programming Example #3 | If a variable called DOLLAR is positive, it represents a DEPOSIT. If it is negative, it is a WITHDRAWAL. Use an IF-THEN-ELSE construct to execute an appropriate output statement. |

```
C
C
      IF(DOLLAR.GT.0.0) THEN
         WRITE(2,10) DOLLAR
   10    FORMAT(1X,'DEPOSIT......',F8.2)
C
C
      ELSE
         WRITE(2,20) DOLLAR
   20    FORMAT(1X,'WITHDRAWAL...',F8.2)
C
      ENDIF
C
```

| Programming Example #4 | If two integer variables are equal (that is, the same), issue the message "YOUR ANSWER IS CORRECT" and advance a counter called NGOOD. IF they are not equal, issue the message "WRONG ANSWER – TRY AGAIN." |

```
C
      IF(M.EQ.N) THEN
C
         WRITE(2,10)
   10    FORMAT(1X,'YOUR ANSWER CORRECT')
         NGOOD = NGOOD + 1
C
      ELSE
C
         WRITE(2,20)
   20    FORMAT(1X,'WRONG ANSWER - TRY AGAIN')
C
      ENDIF
```

16.5 | Case Construct (Multiple Alternatives)

If a problem involves more than just a one- or two-way branch, it is called a **multiple alternative** or "case" problem. A typical example of this type of problem is deciding if a person should be given an A, B, C, D or F as a letter grade on an exam. Problems such as these require a *sequence* of logical decisions to be made. Accordingly, a series of IF statements will be written and presented in a "nested" fashion very much like DO statements are nested. The logical expressions are tested one after another. The first logical expression that is evaluated as true will cause the statements associated with that particular logical expression to be executed (the specific case has been located) and the construct terminated. No additional testing takes place. Control is then passed to the bottom of the construct.

This construct should be viewed as a simple extension of the basic IF-THEN-ELSE construct. It merely allows the ELSE clause to be followed by another logical IF test. This IF test is "nested" or subordinate to the IF test above it. Additional subordinate IF tests are used to cover each possible alternative (case) present. The general form would be:

ELSE IF (logical expression) THEN

When this construct is encountered, a test will be made for the first case, then the second, then the third, and so on. If none of the cases (logical IF ex-

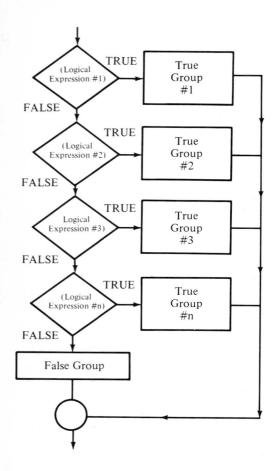

```
C
C
C           IF(GRADE.GE.90.0) THEN
C                   LETTER = 1HA
C           ELSE    IF(GRADE.GE.80.0) THEN
C                   LETTER = 1HB
C           ELSE    IF(GRADE.GE.70.0) THEN
C                   LETTER = 1HC
C           ELSE    IF(GRADE.GE.60.0) THEN
C                   LETTER = 1HD
C           ELSE
C                   LETTER = 1HF
C           ENDIF
```

pressions) is evaluated as "true," the final ELSE clause (followed by a corresponding "false" set of statements) will be executed if they are present. A single ENDIF statement shows the end of the construct.

IF (logical expression #1) THEN

⎫
⎬ True Group #1
⎭

ELSE IF (logical expression #2) THEN

⎫
⎬ True Group #2
⎭

ELSE IF (logical expression #3) THEN

⎫
⎬ True Group #3
⎭

.   .   .   .   .
.   .   .   .   .
.   .   .   .   .

ELSE IF (logical expression # n) THEN

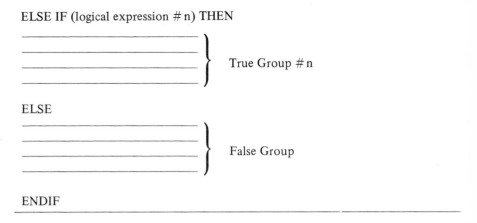

Figure 16.4 General Form of Multiple Alternatives

Only one group of statements will be executed: the statements associated with the first "true" expression. For this reason, the construct is sometimes called **the first-case construct.**

Programming Example
Which Equation?

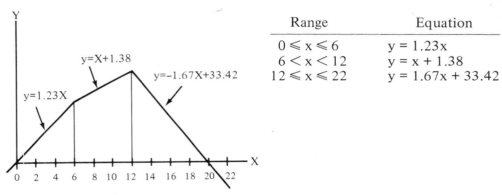

Range	Equation
$0 \leqslant x \leqslant 6$	$y = 1.23x$
$6 < x < 12$	$y = x + 1.38$
$12 \leqslant x \leqslant 22$	$y = 1.67x + 33.42$

Figure 16.3 Select the Correct Equation

A problem presented in Chapter 5 requires that one of three possible equations be used to evaluate Y, depending on the input value X. Use a first-case construct to determine and report the proper value of Y assuming that X lies somewhere between 0.0 and 22.0.

```
C..........................................................................
C..    PURPOSE - SELECT ONE OF THREE EQUATIONS.                   ..
C..            - DEMONSTRATE FIRST CASE CONSTRUCT.                ..
C..........................................................................
C
      READ(5,10) X
   10 FORMAT(F8.2)
C
      IF(X.GE.0.0.AND.X.LE.6.0) THEN
C
C                    USE EQUATION ONE
C
             Y = 1.23 * X
             WRITE(2,20) X, Y
   20        FORMAT(10X,'EQUATION ONE USED',2F9.1)
C
      ELSE  IF(X.LT.12.0) THEN
C
C                    USE EQUATION TWO
C
             Y = X + 1.38
             WRITE(2,30) X, Y
   30        FORMAT(10X,'EQUATION TWO USED',2F9.1)
C
      ELSE
C
C                    USE EQUATION THREE
C
             Y = -1.67 * X + 33.42
             WRITE(2,40) X, Y
   40        FORMAT(10X,'EQUATION THREE USED',2F9.1)
C
      ENDIF
C
      STOP
      END
```

Simulated Form

The multiple alternative IF can be simulated if necessary as shown in Figure 16.4. A flow chart is provided to help you follow the logic.

Simulated:

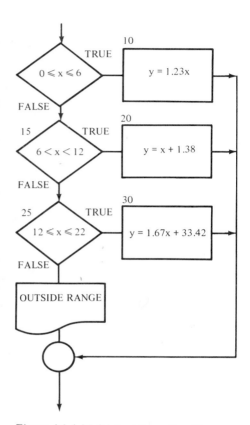

```
C
C
        IF(X.GE.0.0.AND.X.LE.6.0) GO TO 10
            GO TO 15
C
   10       Y = 1.23 * X
            GO TO 40
C
   15 IF(X.LT.12.0) GO TO 20
            GO TO 25
C
   20       Y = X + 1.38
            GO TO 40
C
   25 IF(X.LE.22) GO TO 30
            GO TO 35
C
   30       Y = -1.67 * X + 33.42
            GO TO 40
C
   35 WRITE(2,36)
   36 FORMAT(2X,'X OUTSIDE DEFINED RANGE')
C
C
   40 CONTINUE
      STOP
      END
```

Figure 16.4 Multiple-Alternative Construct

	Below	60's	70's	80's	Above
Programming Example Distribution of Grades	17	29	43	20	9

The examination grades of a large class are recorded on data cards, one per card. The last card is a trailer or sentinel card to identify the end of the deck. It contains a negative number.

Write a program segment to determine the distribution of grades. Determine those numbers needed for the table shown above.

This problem was covered in Chapter 5 and the variable names for the various counters were chosen as follows:

```
C
C        ------IMPORTANT VARIABLES------
C
C   --GRADE      EXAMINATION GRADE BEING PROCESSED       --
C   --NO90S      NUMBER OF STUDENTS SCORING 90 OR BETTER --
C   --NO80S      NUMBER OF STUDENTS SCORING IN THE 80'S  --
C   --NO70S      NUMBER OF STUDENTS SCORING IN THE 70'S  --
C   --NO60S      NUMBER OF STUDENTS SCORING IN THE 60'S  --
C   --NBELOW     NUMBER OF STUDENTS WHO FAILED           --
C
```

One of the important modules in this program is a block of code used to determine which one of five possible counters should be advanced because of the value of GRADE presently being processed. Since this module will be invoked for each grade processed, we will make it a subroutine subprogram.

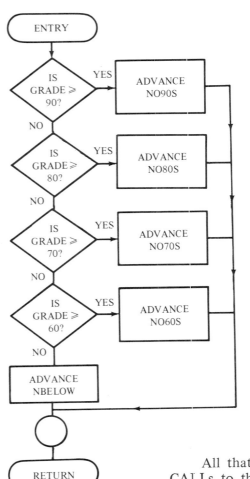

```
      SUBROUTINE COUNT (GRADE,NO90S,NO80S,NO70S,NO60S,NBELOW)
C
C
C     PURPOSE - DETERMINE THE NUMBER OF STUDENTS THAT
C               SCORED AN  A  -  B  -  C  -  D  -  F
C               ON AN EXAMINATION.
C
C
C
C        .......SET UP FIRST CASE CONSTRUCT......
C     IF(GRADE.GE.90.0) THEN
C
C          NO90S = NO90S + 1
C
C     ELSE   IF(GRADE.GE.80.0) THEN
C
C          NO80S = NO80S + 1
C
C     ELSE   IF(GRADE.GE.70.0) THEN
C
C     ELSE   IF(GRADE.GE.60.0) THEN
C
C          NO60S = NO60S + 1
C
C     ELSE
C
C          NBELOW = NBELOW + 1
C
C     ENDIF
C
      RETURN
      END
```

All that remains now is to set up a loop that reads data cards and makes CALLs to this subroutine until the trailer card is detected. The loop constructs allowed in structured FORTRAN are covered next.

16.6 | Loop Structures (WHILE Construct)

Loop structures that involve counting are controlled by the DO statement presented in Chapter 9. Very often, we do not know the exact number of times a loop should be repeated. A data deck that uses a trailer card is a typical example of this situation. A loop structure is needed that continues until a specific event occurs. The WHILE construct is a loop control statement that uses a logical expression to determine if statements within the range of the loop should be executed or not.

WHILE (logical expression) DO

_____
_____   } Loop
_____   Statements
_____
_____
_____
_____

END WHILE

The header statement contains the command WHILE followed by a logical expression, followed by the word DO.

Some examples:

WHILE (X.LT.6.5)DO
WHILE (GRADE.GE.0.0)DO
WHILE (IFLAG.EQ.1)DO
WHILE (A.GT.B.AND.C.EQ.4.)DO

Each time the statements within the loop are iterated, control passes back to the top of the loop, or more specifically, to the "logical expression" in the header statement. If the expression is still evaluated as true, another iteration will take place. If the expression is false, iteration ceases and control passes to the bottom of the construct, that is, to the statement following the ENDWHILE statement. If the logical expression is false when the WHILE statement is first executed, the loop will be terminated immediately without any of the loop statements being executed.

The advantages of this type of loop control are considerable. We are no longer tied to counters as the only means of loop control. Any variable or combination of variables can be used to control looping. Repetition of the loop can be dependent upon more than one event:

WHILE (BALNCE.GT.0.0.OR.IFLAG.NE.1) DO

Obviously, one of the variables chosen to control the loop must be subject to change (or update) within the loop. If this were not so, the loop would never end!

Programming Example
Trailer Card

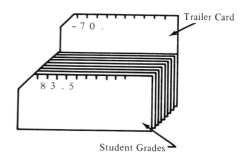

Trailer Card
- 7 0 .
8 3 . 5
Student Grades

Use the WHILE structure to CALL the subroutine COUNT of the previous programming example, but *only as long as there are meaningful cards in the data deck* (not the trailer).

```
C..............................................................
C..   PURPOSE - DEMONSTRATE LOOP CONTROL USING WHILE        ..
C..             STRUCTURE. LOOP TERMINATES WHEN TRAILER     ..
C..             CARD (NEGATIVE GRADE) IS DETECTED.          ..
C..............................................................
C
C           INITIALIZE ALL COUNTERS
      DATA NO90S,NO80S, NC70S, NO60S, NBELOW /5*0.0/
C
C           PROVIDE INITIAL READ STATEMENT
      READ(2,10) GRADE
   10 FORMAT(F5.1)
C
C     WHILE (GRADE.GT.0.0) DO
C           CALL COUNT (GRADE,NO90S,NO80S,NO70S,NO60S,NBELOW)
C
C           CHECK CORRECT BEHAVIOR CF ALL MEMORY LOCATIONS
      WRITE(2,20)GRADE,NO90S,NO80S,NO70S,NO60S,NBELOW
   20 FORMAT(4X,F5.1,5I7)
C
C           READ CARD FOR NEXT PASS
      READ(5,10) GRADE
C     ENDWHILE
C
C           PRINT OUT FINAL RESULTS
      WRITE(2,30)NO90S,NO80S,NO70S,NO60S,NBELOW
   30 FORMAT(1X,'FINAL RESULTS',5I8)
C
      STOP
      END
```

As long as the value of GRADE read from data is positive, the statements within the WHILE-controlled loop are executed. The reading of a negative value from the trailer card causes the looping to terminate.

16.7 | EXIT Statement

The rules you have learned with respect to the nesting of DO statements apply to the nesting of WHILE statements. They are both loop constructs. *Overlapping of loop constructs is not allowed.* One construct must lie wholly inside another. Structured entry and structured exit must be observed. A construct must be entered through the header statement, and exit is allowed only at the terminal statement.

This latter requirement: **you should exit a construct only through the terminal statement of that construct,** makes it necessary to provide a control statement that will cause an immediate transfer to the bottom of a construct and at the same time *terminate* the construct. The statement:

> EXIT

does precisely this. When used in a loop structure, it immediately stops the iteration process and passes control to the first executable statement below the loop terminator.

An alternate form of this statement is recommended. Some examples are:

> EXIT n
> EXIT 7
> EXIT 15

This alternate form allows the inclusion of a statement number following the word EXIT. This statement number identifies the terminator statement of the construct being exited.

| Programming Example |
| Posting Payments |

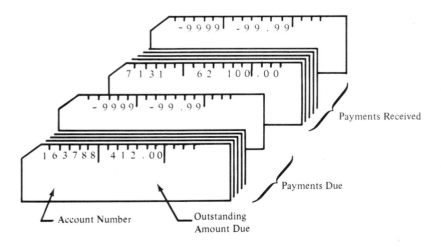

A charge card company maintains a file of accounts that have an outstanding balance. This is simulated by the first portion of the data deck shown above. Each card lists an account number and the amount due. The end of this portion of the data deck is signalled by a trailer card (negative account number) and this deck is less than 2000 cards in size.

Part A: READ IN

Using structured programming techniques, read these cards and form an array called NUMBER and an array called DUE. In the process load a memory location called KARDS with the number of accounts with money due the company (the size of the array DUE and NUMBER). Determine the total amount of money owed.

```
C....PURPOSE....DEMONSTRATE.STRUCTURED.PROGRAMMING............
C..                TECHNIQUES IN READING INITIAL DATA BASE.  ..
C.............................................................
C
C                     -----IMPORTANT VARIABLES-----
C
C       --NUMBER       VECTOR OF ACCOUNT NUMBERS              --
C       --DUE          VECTOR OF AMOUNT DUE VALUES            --
C       --KARDS        CARD COUNTER TELLING THE SIZE OF THE DECK-
C       DIMENSION NUMBER (2000), DUE(2000)
C
        SUM = 0.0
        KARDS = 1
C
        READ(5,10) NUMBER(KARDS), DUE(KARDS)
     10 FORMAT(I6, F7.2)
C
        WHILE (NUMBER(KARDS).GT.0) DO
C
             SUM = SUM + DUE(KARDS)
             KARDS = KARDS + 1
             READ(5,10) NUMBER(KARDS), DUE(KARDS)
C
        ENDWHILE
C
        WRITE(2,20) SUM, KARDS
C
             :    :    :    :
             :    :    :    :
```

Part B: Posting Payment

The remaining cards in the deck reflect payments made by various customers. The account number and the amount paid are listed. Another trailer card signals the end of this deck. Using structured programming, write statements that will read *one* of these cards, search the data base established in part A, and update the appropriate element of the array DUE.

```
C....PURPOSE.=.PROCESS.A.SINGLE.PAYMENT.CARD.(SEARCH.AND......
C..                UPDATE PROCEDURE).                         ..
C.............................................................
C
C                     -----IMPORTANT VARIABLES-----
C
C       --NPAID        ACCOUNT NUMBER OF CUSTOMER MAKING PAYMENT-
C       --PAID         DOLLAR AMOUNT RECEIVED FROM THIS CUSTOMER-
        READ(5,10) NPAID, PAID
C
        DO 30 I = 1, KARDS
C
             IF(NPAID.EQ.NUMBER(I)) THEN
C
                   CUSTOMER FOUND
C
                   DUE(I) = DUE(I) + PAID
C
                   WRITE(2,25) NPAID, PAID, DUE(I)
     25            FORMAT(5X,'ACCOUNT NUMBER',I7,3X,
     1             'AMOUNT RECEIVED',F12.2,'REMAINING BALANCE'
     2             F12.2)
C                        EXIT 30
             ENDIF
C
     30 CONTINUE
C
        STOP
        END
```

Notice that the EXIT statement allows a termination of the search loop as soon as the correct account number (customer) is found.

Part C: Posting All Payments

Part C demonstrates the need for a special (extra) READ statement needed to get the operation of a WHILE construct started. You are to process all payment cards. When this is complete, provide a list of all accounts that have an unpaid balance of $500.00 or more.

Loop control for processing payment cards will use a WHILE construct that executes the statements in part B as long as a positive account number is read from data. The header statement will be:

WHILE (NPAID.GT.0) DO

Because NPAID is the control variable, it must be defined when the construct is entered. This requires a READ statement above the construct in addition to the READ that will be needed inside the loop. Since the first READ is executed only once, it serves the function of more or less "priming the pump." That is, it gets things started.

```
C
C                          NOW PROCESS ALL THE PAYMENTS
C                          PROVIDE INITIAL READ STATEMENT
C
C          READ(5,10) NPAID, PAID
           WHILE (PAID.GT.0) DO
C              SET UP INNER SEARCH LOOP
C
C              DO 30 I = 1, KARDS
C                  IF(NPAID.EQ.NUMBER(I)) THEN
C                      DUE(I) = DUE(I) + PAID
C
                       WRITE(2,25) NPAID, PAID, DUE(I)
       25              FORMAT(5X,'ACCOUNT NUMBER',I7,3X,
        1              'AMOUNT RECEIVED',F12.2,'REMAINING BALANCE'
        2              F12.2)
C
C                      EXIT 30
C                  ENDIF
       30      CONTINUE
C
C              READ(5,10) NPAID, PAID
C
           ENDWHILE
C
C                          PRESENT FINAL LISTING
C
           DO 50 I = 1, KARDS
               IF(DUE(I).GE.500.00) WRITE(2,40)NUMBER(I), DUE(I)
       40      FORMAT(10X,I6, F8.2)
C
       50  CONTINUE
C
           STOP
           END
```

Notice that by using the natural control features of the various constructs, there is little need to execute explicit transfer instructions like the GO TO statement. There is no jumping around. Control passes more smoothly and more logically, from top to bottom.

16.8 | Closing

There are many more important aspects to structured programming than the basic constructs discussed in this chapter. Unfortunately these topics go beyond what should be covered in an introductory FORTRAN text. Obviously, structured programming attempts to reduce the amount of randomness in program design that has evolved in the absence of a set of standards and guidelines. The growth of software development cannot be continued successfully without a total commitment to the techniques embodied in the structured approach.

The topics presented in this chapter do represent an important start. Learning to confine your program or module design to one of the basic constructs, learning to execute structured entry and structured exit, learning to eliminate explicit transfer instructions (like the GO TO) are important first steps in improving program design.

Review Exercises

1.*What is the purpose of restricting the number of statements (lines of FORTRAN code) associated with any one module or block of code?

2. Describe a structured approach to the design of a large computer project.

3. Why is it important to design the top-level modules of a program before writing the lower-level modules?

4. What does the term "top-down" design mean with respect to designing an individual module of FORTRAN code?

5.*What is meant by a case (multiple alternative) construct?

6. What is the main advantage of the WHILE-DO construct over the standard DO construct?

7.*When entering one of the basic constructs allowed in structured programming, how do you know which type of construct you are dealing with?

8. What are some of the indications that a program is not well written or well structured?

9. What is the purpose of the EXIT statement?

10. Describe how to simulate an IF-THEN-ELSE construct.

11. Write a structured module of code that determines the largest of three real numbers, A, B or C.

12.*Write a structured module of code to determine how many elements of an integer array are odd and how many are even.

13. Write a structured module of code to determine the largest value of the function:

$$y = e^{x+3} - \ln(x^2 + 2) - 6$$

between the interval X_{LEFT} and X_{RIGHT}.

14. Write a structured module of code to determine if all elements of a one-dimensional array are positive. Have the module print one of two messages:

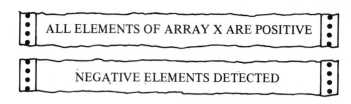

ALL ELEMENTS OF ARRAY X ARE POSITIVE

NEGATIVE ELEMENTS DETECTED

15.*Write a program to compute the average value and standard deviation of the numbers in each row of a two-dimensional array X. This array is 10 by 15 in size.

16. Write a program that will merge three lists of numbers (each list is sorted) into a single list until one of the lists is depleted.

17. A one-dimensional array called PAY has 100 elements and represents the annual salary of workers at a small machine shop. An array called OLD represents the pay of these workers last year. Determine the average increase of these workers and what percentage received an increase of greater than 7%.

18. A one-dimensional array called PAY is described in exercise 17. A one-dimensional array called NAME has 100 elements and holds the name of each worker. Generate an array called BIG that holds the name of all workers earning more than $30,000.00. How many elements are in array BIG?

17 | Magnetic Tape and Disc Operations

Up to this point in the text we have dealt exclusively with internal memory as a place to store data. Because their programs tend to be limited in size, students seldom, if ever, require more memory than is immediately available to them in the computer's central memory unit. Not so in the "real world" of computers. The amount of data manipulated by a typical industrial program is frequently so large that it will not all fit in memory at one time. It becomes necessary to divide the data into parts. The usual procedure is to place the various parts out on what is called an **auxiliary memory device** (a magnetic tape or disc, for example) and then provide a means of moving each part in and out of internal memory as it is needed.

As an introduction to this procedure, it is necessary to know how the features and limitations of internal memory compare to those of auxiliary storage devices. The most important feature of internal memory is *speed.* By speed we mean, for example, "How fast can a value be fetched from memory and made available for processing?" Internal memory has a very remarkable and unique feature: *each and every word of memory is directly addressable.* This means that no matter where a value is stored in internal memory it can be retrieved quickly and directly. The time it takes to access a word at the end of memory is the same as for a word stored at the beginning of memory. Because each word is individually addressable, there is no need to read any words preceding the one in which you are interested. Memory units designed with these features are called **random access memory.**

The material of this chapter will show that information stored on auxiliary memory devices cannot be retrieved as directly. The typical retrieval process starts with a relatively slow mechanical positioning activity to reach the approximate location of the information that is wanted. It is then necessary to initiate a search to find where at this location the desired information is located. Auxiliary storage devices, while somewhat slow, have a very definite advantage over internal memory in one important respect. They have an exceptionally high storage capacity, while internal memory is relatively low in the amount of information it can hold.

If this last remark seems rather strange to you, it is only because of the types of problems you have been dealing with so far. The illustration in Figure 17.1 depicts a situation you have as yet not been exposed to. The photo shows the huge data base associated with the administration of the Social Security Program in this country. The portion of this data base that can be in internal memory at any one time is almost insignificant. There do exist, however, data-based management techniques that, when properly employed, make it appear to the programmer that memory is virtually infinite in size.

429

Figure 17.1 The Tape Files of the Social Security Administration

This chapter deals with the storage and manipulation of files of data stored on tapes and discs, hereafter referred to simply as **tape files** or **disc files**. We will consider the five basic operations for manipulating a file:

(a) **File building,** or the transfer of data from another medium, usually cards, onto tape or disc.

(b) **Searching** the file for items of data that meet some desired criterion.

(c) **Updating,** which is the correction of old data and the purging of unwanted data.

(d) **Sorting,** or the rearrangement of the contents of the file in some desired order.

(e) **Merging,** or the combining of two old files into a single file so that within the new file all elements are in their proper respective order.

17.1
Direct Access Files

The most convenient auxiliary memory device is a **disc drive.** It consists of a number of discs attached to a common spindle that rotates at high speed (3600 revolutions per minute is a typical value). Each disc consists of up to 400 concentric tracks. Data is recorded on each track in groups of characters called **physical records.** A physical record is all the information written on the disc (track) during any one READ/WRITE operation. This could be the information associated with a single data card or all the information associated with several data cards.

Multiple READ/WRITE heads can address any track on any disc (the tracks do not have to be read sequentially). This means we have direct access to any physical record on the disc file. In this section we will show how to reserve (set up) an area of storage on one or more disc drive units. For each of these areas it is necessary to specify the number, type and length of the records to be stored

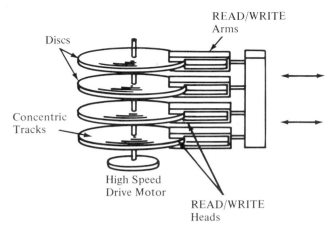

Figure 17.2 Typical Disc Drive

in that file. Based on this information, the operating system will determine how much **disc space** (number of concentric tracks) is required for the file. It will automatically do the bookkeeping of identifying which tracks on the disc are to be associated with your program. Then it will divide each track into segments where the size of each segment matches the length of the records you plan to put in the file. Each segment is assigned a number such that segment 1 holds record 1, segment 2 holds record 2, and so on.

Once the file has been built, the programmer may request a specific record from the file (record number 124, for example). The operating system will determine on which track and in which segment the specific record is located. The movable READ/WRITE arms will access the record and bring it into internal storage.

Defining the File

A specification statement called the DEFINE FILE statement is used to supply the information necessary to create a disc file. The statement:

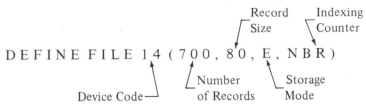

establishes a file on input/output device number 14 (a disc drive). The file has provisions for 700 records, each record containing 80 characters. These characters are in "EDITED" form (that is, they were read under the supervision of a FORMAT code). The integer variable NBR is to serve as an automatic indexing counter to facilitate reading and writing sequential records in the file.

General Form

DEFINE FILE

> 1. device code: identifies the disc drive* the file is to be associated with,

*Each input/output device has been assigned a number (device code) by the computation center. It is used to identify which piece of equipment to use in implementing a specific READ/WRITE operation.

2. length: an INTEGER CONSTANT telling the length of the file (maximum number of records in the file),
3. size: an INTEGER CONSTANT telling the size of each record (number of characters if in edited form or number of words if in unedited form),
4. mode: U = unedited (pure binary), E = edited (format coded),
5. index: an integer variable available to assist in READ/WRITE operations (such as the index of a DO statement).

The difference between the edited and unedited mode of storage is not difficult to understand. If a transfer of data is between one internal device and another (memory to disc, for example), the transfer is usually accomplished in pure binary (no editing involved). The pattern of 0's and 1's in any memory location is transferred directly to the disc, or vice versa, without any attempt to distinguish what type of information is being transferred (integer, real, alphabetic, etc.).

When the transfer is not totally internal (card reader to memory or memory to line printer), a FORMAT code is used to interpret the 0's and 1's so that they are in a form easily identified by humans (an edited form).

In building a disc file, the usual process is to read data cards (under format control) and load internal memory with 0's and 1's representing the values on the card. The READ statement will reference the card reader as the input device and provide the number of a supporting FORMAT statement. The next step is to transfer the pattern of 0's and 1's associated with these memory locations to disc causing the formation of the record on the disc file (an unedited transfer would be most efficient). We will use a WRITE statement that references the disc drive but does not provide a supporting FORMAT statement number. The mode of records stored in this form is declared by the letter U, meaning that storage is in the unedited form. When records are stored in the unedited mode, the size parameter (telling the size of a given record) is expressed in *words*. By words we mean how many memory locations are involved in the transfer.*

When a record of this form is retrieved from the disc file, the transfer of 0's and 1's is from disc to memory. The various internal memory locations are now reloaded with the same information as when the record was originally read from the card reader.

The last parameter in the DEFINE FILE statement is an index. This index is used to help in processing sequential records in a file. Whenever you READ or WRITE a record in the file, the value of the index will be one greater than the record now being processed.

Now we give some examples of DEFINE FILE statements:

A data card contains information about the academic standing of a student.

Example #1

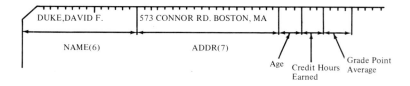

---

*If the record is to be transferred in edited form, the mode is declared by the letter E and the record size is specified in terms of the number of characters in the record.

Notice that the name and address fields on each card are relatively large and must be divided as suggested below.

Card Column	Information	Specification
1–24	Name	A24
25–42	Address	A28
43–45	Age	I3
46–48	Credit Hours Taken to Date	F3.0
49–52	Grade Point Average	F4.3

The card will be read from data using the following statement:

        READ(5,50)(NAME(I),I=1,6),(ADDR(I),I=1,7)AGE,CRDHR,GRDAV
    50 FORMAT(6A4,7A4,I3,F3.0,F4.3)

This READ statement will load 16 memory locations as follows:

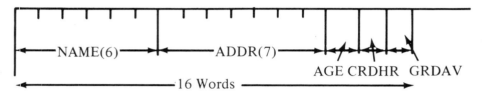

- 6 memory locations for the name.
- 7 memory locations for the address.
- one each for the age, credit hours taken and grade point average.

If the information from 2000 cards is to be placed in a disc file whose device code is 19, the following statement would be used:

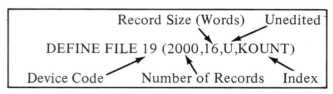

Example #2:

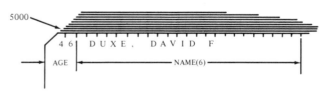

In the next chapter a sorting problem will deal with 5000 records each giving the name and age of a person:

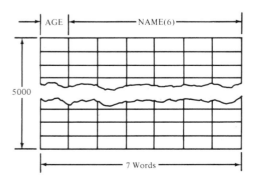

The statement:

DEFINE FILE 1 7 (5 0 0 0 , 7 , U , K)

could be used to provide room on disc drive 17 to hold the information associated with this file.

Input/Output

To access any individual record established by the last DEFINE FILE statement, we use a READ/WRITE statement specifically designed for direct access files:

READ (17′214) AGE, (NAME(I),I=1,6)

Device Number⟶ ⟵Record Number

WRITE (17′214) AGE, (NAME(I),I=1,6)

Had these records been established in the edited mode, the statements would be:

```
    READ (17′214,7) AGE, (NAME(I),I=1,6)
7   FORMAT (I3,6A4)
    WRITE (17′214,7) AGE, (NAME(I),I=1,6)
7   FORMAT (I3,6A4)
```

These READ/WRITE statements are the same as any other you have been dealing with, except that the device number is followed by the specific record to be accessed (record 214 in this instance). In each statement, the device number is that of the disc drive the file was established on and a format statement number, if any, appears in the usual place. The value defining which record to access is the only new feature. As you will soon see, it may be a constant, variable or expression.

Use of the Index

Once a file has been declared in a DEFINE FILE statement, the usual procedure is to read cards (records) from the data deck and place them one after another in the file. This can be accomplished by setting up a DO loop and using the index of the DO to position each record in the file. By position we mean, providing a number after the DEVICE NUMBER in the READ/WRITE statements used in direct access input/output. The number can also be provided by the index declared as part of the DEFINE FILE statement. Both of these techniques will be demonstrated in the next programming example.

Programming Example
Parking Permit

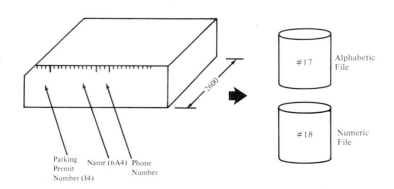

Each card in a data deck gives the name (6A4) and phone number (17) of a student who has a campus parking permit. The first number on the card is the permit number (I4). The cards are in alphabetical order. These cards will be used to build two different disc files:

> File #17 — Alphabetic File: records positioned in the file in alphabetic order.
>
> File #18 — Number File: records positioned in the file based on parking permit number.

To build File #17, we merely place records in the disc file in the same sequence they appear in the data deck. To build File #18, we will read each card and use the parking permit number on the card to control where that record is to be positioned in the file. This will order the file based on the permit number.

Example 1: Using a DO Loop

```
C.......................................................
C..   PURPOSE - BUILD FILE 17 (ALPHABETIC FILE) USING INDEX  ..
C..             OF DO STATEMENT TO POSITION THE RECORDS.     ..
C.......................................................
C
C                    -----IMPORTANT VARIABLES-----
C
C      --NAME        NAME OF STUDENT (SUBSCRIPTED VARIABLE)   --
C      --PHONE       PHONE NUMBER OF STUDENT                  --
C      --NUMBER      NUMBER ON PARKING PERMIT                 --
C
       INTEGER NAME(6), PHONE
C
       DEFINE FILE 17 (2600,8,U,KOUNT)
C
       DO 20 INDEX = 1, 2600
C
C                    READ A CARD FROM DATA DECK
C
           READ(5,10)NUMBER,(NAME(I),I=1,6),PHONE
   10      FORMAT(I4,6A4,I7)
C
C                    TRANSFER RECORD TO DISC FILE
C
           WRITE(17'INDEX) NUMBER,(NAME(I),I=1,6),PHONE
   20  CONTINUE
C
C      ........... FILE COMPLETE ..................
```

Example 2: An Alternate Method

Whenever a record is accessed on a disc file, the index of that file (established in the DEFINE FILE statement) is assigned a value that points to the next record in the file. If we read record 100, the index will be set at 101. If we write record 82, the index will be set at 83. This is useful when several records are to be dealt with sequentially, or a series of records are to be read until a specific value is found.

In the next programming example the index KOUNT (established in the DEFINE FILE 17 statement) will be used to position records sequentially into File #17. *KOUNT merely replaces the variable INDEX of the previous program.* As each card is read, however, it will be positioned in two files. The variable NUMBER (as read from each card) will be used to position records in File #18 (place them in numeric order).

```
C.......................................................
C..   PURPOSE - BUILD BOTH FILES  17-ALPHABETIC, 18-NUMERIC..
C.......................................................
C
       INTEGER NAME(6), PHONE
C
       DEFINE FILE 17 (2600,8,U,KOUNT)
       DEFINE FILE 18 (2600,8,U,NO)
C
       KOUNT = 1
C
       DO 20 INDEX = 1, 2600
C
C                    READ A CARD FROM DATA DECK
C
           READ(5,10) NUMBER,(NAME(I),I=1,6),PHONE
   10      FORMAT(I4,6A4,I7)
C
C                    TRANSFER RECORD TO DISC FILE 17
C
           WRITE(17'KOUNT)NUMBER,(NAME(I),I=1,6),PHONE
C
C                    TRANSFER RECORD TO DISC FILE 18
C
           WRITE(18'NUMBER)NUMBER,(NAME(I),I=1,6),PHONE
C
   20  CONTINUE
C
C
       STOP
       END
```

To obtain a listing of parking permits in numeric order, all that is required is to read file #18 sequentially and send a copy of each record to the printer.

```
C·····················································
C·· PURPOSE - PRINT LIST IN NUMERIC ORDER.          ··
C·····················································
C
      DO 40 INDEX = 1,2600
C
C           READ RECORD FROM DISC DILE
C
      READ(18'INDEX)NUMBER,(NAME(I),I=1,6),PHONE
C
C             DISPLAY RECORD ON LINE PRINTER
C
      WRITE(2,30)NUMBER,(NAME(I),I=1,6),PHONE
   30 FORMAT(4X,I4,4X,6A4,4X,I7)
C
   40 CONTINUE
C
      STOP
      END
```

File Key

Most disc files use some portion of the information within each record to tell where in the file the record is located. This is called the **KEY**. In the last problem, the parking permit number was the key. If you know the parking permit number, you know where the record is located. Without the key, a long search is involved. All problems do not have such a convenient key as the last problem did. This can lead to considerable difficulties as suggested in the next section.

Delete Code

Some portion of each record can be used to tell if that particular record is still active or not. If, for example, the student with parking permit number 1234 leaves school, it is possible to go to that record position and change the value of NUMBER to –1234 (a negative value). In this way, the sign of NUMBER serves as a "delete code." If NUMBER is positive, the record is active. If NUMBER is negative, the record has been deleted for some reason and should not be considered part of the file.

17.2 | Hashing

The file shown below is just the same as the "parking permit" file except that the parking permit number has been replaced by a social security number.

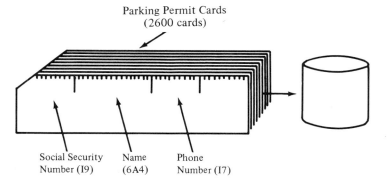

Parking Permit Cards
(2600 cards)

Social Security Number (I9)   Name (6A4)   Phone Number (I7)

A nine-digit social security number *cannot* be used directly to position records in a file. Any nine-digit number has almost one billion possible combinations of digits. It is just not realistic to set up a record position for each and every combination. Even if a file that large could be established, it would represent a hideous waste of facilities. If we were to place the 2600 parking permit records in a file that large, there would only be one active record in every 400,000 record positions (on the average).

While a social security number cannot be used directly to position a record, it can be used indirectly. It is a relatively simple matter to transform this nine-digit number into a number between 1 and 2600 (a hashing technique will be used). Then that number, the hash value, can be used to position the record. The tricky aspect, however, is to reduce the likelihood of several social security numbers resulting in the same hash value. This would mean that two or more records were vying for the *same* record position in the disc file. This situation is called a **collision**.

For this reason, it is usually necessary to establish a file space that is somewhat larger than the number of records that must be placed in the file. This reduces the likelihood of a collision. In the example that follows, the file will have 5200 record positions. This is twice the amount of space needed, but it makes the procedures easier to follow. Even at this high value, collisions are bound to occur and must be dealt with. Perhaps an overflow area can be established or the nearest empty record position used when a collision occurs.

Let us now examine how the hashing process works. Our ultimate goal is to randomly scatter the records within the now-enlarged file. One technique is to divide the social security number by a value equal to or just a little larger than the number of spaces available in the file:

$$\text{Hash} = \frac{\text{Social Security Number}}{5201}$$

Whatever value is thus obtained, we are only interested in the digits after the decimal point, the remainder.

Hash	Remainder
6.178429	.178429
2.936328	.936328
4.051067	.051067

If the divisor in the HASH equation (5201 in this case) is a prime number, this remainder will have a very useful property: it will be *evenly distributed* between the upper and lower limits it may have, namely, between .000001 and .999999. We can use this properly to distribute the records evenly throughout the file as follows: Multiply the remainder by the number of record positions in the file (and add 1*). Use this value to position the record (it is called the **hash address**).

Hash	Remainder	Final Adjust-ment (REMAIN 5200 + 1)*
6.178429	.178429	928
2.936328	.936328	4869
4.051067	.051067	266
0.543718	.543718	2828
8.742246	.742246	3860

HASH Address

*If the remainder was exceptionally small, this multiplication could result in the value zero, which should be translated into record position one.

The FORTRAN code to accomplish this could be written as follows:

Available Spaces

```
C
       HASH = SSN / 5201.0
C
C          DETERMINE REMAINDER
C
       IHASH = HASH
       REMAIN = HASH - FLOAT(IHASH)
C
C        USE THIS VALUE TO POSITION THE RECORD
C
       LOCATN = REMAIN * 5200 + 1
C
```

To actually implement a program that uses this hashing technique, it is not necessary to do your own hashing. There are system software routines that will do it for you. These routines also handle the problem of collisions. Manipulation of disc files is an exceptionally interesting topic but, unfortunately, beyond the scope of this introductory text.

17.3 | The Tape and Tape Drive

The magnetic tape used by computer systems is very similar to that used by the tape recorders and players found in so many homes and cars today. It is a plastic base tape coated with an iron oxide material and stored on reels. It is of better quality, however, than the tape used in homes; it is one inch wide and usually in reels of 2400 feet. There is a length of stronger, uncoated leader attached to both ends of the tape for the operator to use in threading the tape through the tape drive.

Tape drives are equipped with a single read/write and erase head. A tape drive contains all the other necessary mechanisms to provide for the movement

Figure 17.3 A Magnetic Tape Drive

of the tape at the proper speed in front of the read/write head. Information can be recorded on the tape only while it is in motion. The speed of that motion (approximately 100 inches/second) is very critical to the accurate recording and reading of information on the tape. Just after the tape's beginning leader and just before its trailing leader are adhesive metallic strips called the **load point** and **trailer markers**, respectively. Being metallic, the markers give the tape drive the ability to electrically detect the "official" beginning and ending of the tape. When an operator has mounted a reel of tape on the tape drive and threaded it, he pushes a button to turn control of the tape drive over to the CPU. As soon as the button is pushed, the tape is reeled forward until the drive detects the load point marker. Only after the marker has been located does the computer consider the tape ready for use. The load point marker also has the function of indicating where the tape drive should stop during a rewind. Complete unreeling of the tape is thereby prevented.

The trailer marker also serves as a warning device to mark the end of the usable portion of the tape. When a trailer marker is found during a data recording operation, the operator is informed to mount a new reel of tape.

As a safeguard against the accidental erasing of valuable data, each reel is equipped with a **write permit ring**. Unless that ring is in place on the reel at the time it is mounted on the tape drive, recording of new data on the tape is automatically prevented. "No ring, no write!" is how the saying goes.

One of the features that makes tape so desirable is the tremendous space saving it represents. The number of cards whose data can be stored on one reel of tape is naturally dependent on many factors. Under the worst conditions, however, a 2400-foot reel can store the data of roughly 22,000 cards — the contents of eleven card boxes.

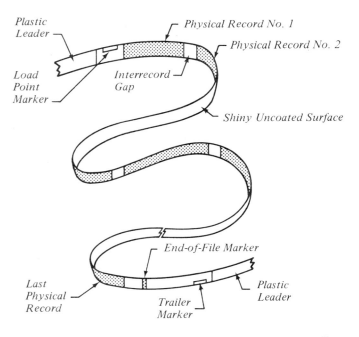

Figure 17.4 The Arrangement of a Data File on Magnetic Tape

The Arrangement of Data on Tape

Data is recorded on magnetic tape in groups of characters called **physical records**. As described in the section on discs, a physical record is all of the information that is written on the tape during any one movement of the tape. Thus, a physical record is the section of tape between two erased or unused portions of tape. The length of a physical record is determined by the amount of information the programmer instructs the computer to write each time the tape is accelerated to the required operating speed. A physical record could contain as little as the value of a single variable. It could contain a full data card's worth of values, or many data cards' worth of values (up to a maximum of all the values of variables in internal memory).

The only time a tape actually moves under the read/write heads is when the program directs a read or write operation or a rewind. At all other times the tape remains motionless. Prior to any read or write operation, the tape must be accelerated from zero velocity to in excess of 100 inches per second. In order for the characters to be properly spaced, the tape must be read or written on only when moving at full speed. The tape drive can bring the tape from a stop to full speed in 3/8 inch, and it can also bring the tape to a full stop in 3/8 inch. Therefore, any physical record that will be read or written in one operation must have 3/8 inch of blank tape on the leading end as a starting space, and 3/8 inch of blank tape after the last character as a stopping space. Since physical records come one after the other, the stopping space of one record adds to the starting space of the next to create a 3/4 inch total space known as the **inter-record gap** (IRG).

17.4 | Logical Records vs. Physical Records

A **physical record** is the group of characters that is read or written in one operation. A **logical record** is a set of pieces of information that logically belong together. A logical record might contain a student's name, social security number, data of birth, home address, and so on. The information contained on one data card is often considered to comprise one logical record.

It is possible to write a tape file program, in which one logical record (the contents of one data card) is put in every physical record. This is sometimes referred to as recording "card images" or "unit records" on tape. A data card with all 80 columns filled takes up less than 1/2 inch of space on magnetic tape. When one recalls that each physical record requires a 3/4 inch inter-record gap, it is clear that the "card image" approach wastes 60% of the reel of tape to empty inter-record gaps!

If two logical records (two cards) are included in one physical record, the data from both will be contained in less than one inch. One inch used with 3/4 inch wasted means only 44% of the reel will be unused. Recording three logical records in each physical record wastes only 33% of the reel.

Not only is the economical use of the tape a consideration here, but also the improvement of processing time. The more frequently the tape must be started and stopped in its reading of a given number of logical records, the more time that reading operation will consume. If three logical records are recorded in card-image form, the tape will have to be started and stopped three separate times. If all three are grouped into one physical record, the tape will have to be started and stopped only once.

Obviously, the more logical records that can be included in each physical record, the more efficient the operation will become. How far can this process of maximizing the length of physical records be carried? Recall that a physical record contains all the data that is recorded in one movement of the tape, and that the recording of a physical record on tape is triggered by a write command in the program. By this point in the text, it is second nature for the reader to know that if he tells the computer to write something on the line printer, the information that will be printed will come from internal memory. Likewise, if the programmer directs that something be written (recorded) on magnetic tape, the information to be recorded there will come from internal memory. This is why the point was made earlier about the maximum capacity of a physical record being equal to all the variables in memory. And this is where the quest for more and more logical records per physical record must stop: *when the total number of words in the logical records intended to be included in a single physical record threatens to exceed the number of words available for that purpose in internal memory.*

There exists one other constraint on the size of a physical record that on some occasions takes precedence. Every computer is limited by its hardware as to the maximum number of characters that may be transferred to or from a tape drive at one time, and therefore the maximum number of characters that may be in a single physical record. On one popular model, for example, that limit is roughly 5000 characters. The programmer must take the necessary precautions to assure that she does not attempt to exceed the character transfer limitations of her computer. Since the size of this limitation is so much a function of the individual computer's design, it will not be considered further in this text.

17.5 Files and the EOF Mark

To handle large quantities of data, computer installations assemble all the information that has common characteristics into a useful package called a **data file**. For example, the logical records pertaining to a class of college freshmen could be grouped together in a data file. Computer files may be stored in many ways: as boxes upon boxes of punched cards, or on reels of magnetic tape, or on a disc file.

No matter what the form of the file, the computer must have some way to identify the end of the file. A file of data cards is ended by a specially-punched **end-of-file (EOF) card** (colored red at many installations). A file of data on tape is ended by an EOF mark (see Figure 17.4). It is recorded on the tape following the last physical record, and separated from it by what is called an **EOF gap** (larger than the normal inter-record gap).

The programmer who creates the tape file must provide for the recording of the EOF mark. This is done by means of the ENDFILE statement discussed in the next section. During a read operation, if the computer finds that it has read the EOF mark, it will cause the same result as would occur if it were reading a data deck and read the EOF card: the program would terminate on a ran-out-of-data type error message.

17.6 Tape File Manipulation Verbs

WRITE (i,n) list	ENDFILE i
WRITE (i) list	REWIND i
READ (i,n) list	BACKSPACE i
READ (i) list	

The WRITE verb causes data to be written on the tape from memory. The READ verb causes data to be read off the tape and stored in memory. The word "list" in the examples above refers to the list of variable names normally associated with READ and WRITE statements. Both statements can be used with or without associated FORMAT statements. When a FORMAT statement is to be used, its number is placed in the location indicated by the letter "n".

The letter "i" is the device code. It is a one- or two-digit number or a variable indicating the device that is to respond to the command. It is the responsibility of the computer operator, and not the programmer, to establish an identity link between the various tape drives available at the moment and the device code used by the programmer. For the sake of simplifying further discussions, the device codes will be referred to from this point on as if they were "tape numbers."

ENDFILE i causes an EOF mark to be recorded on the tape on tape drive i.

REWIND i causes tape drive i to rewind its tape.

The BACKSPACE command, which causes a backward movement to the beginning of the previous physical record, can be used with tapes only under certain restrictions. In practice, these restrictions result in programmers using the command only in programs involving discs and seldom with tapes.

17.7 | Edited vs. "Pure Binary" Recording Formats

Information is stored on tapes in much the same way it is stored on discs, either in "pure binary" form or in a coded (edited) form. In either form the information is represented on the tape as small magnetic spots that are binary in nature. In the "pure binary" format the information is represented on the tape in much the same arrangement as it has in internal memory. The edited format more nearly resembles the arrangement of data on a punched card. Information stored in pure binary uses READ/WRITE statements that specify a device code (tape number) only. Information stored in edited form uses READ/WRITE statements that include reference to a FORMAT statement.

"EDITED" Input/Output Instructions	"PURE BINARY" Input/Output Instructions
WRITE(i,n)list	WRITE(i)list
READ(i,n)list	READ(i)list

You are familiar with the advantages of pure binary representation. The following describes when edited storage is advantageous.

Many computers are capable of processing many programs at once. As the intermediate results of each program are generated, it is impractical to send these results directly to the line printer. (There are too many programs in execution at any one time). As an alternative, these intermediate results are used to build an "output" file for each program (usually on discs but sometimes on tape). When the program ends, that file is sent to the line printer for processing. Information in the output file should be in the edited mode because then it can be transferred from the file to the printer more efficiently. A small program known as a **character dump** is used to literally dump the contents of the output file as rapidly as the printer can accept it. This transfer is accomplished very rapidly because the information in the file is in a coded or edited form and minimum conversion is required as it is passed to the printer.

17.8 | Unit Record Input/Output

Earlier in this chapter we referred to the practice of recording "card images" or "unit records" on tape. Even when this practice is used, only as much of a card as contains data is actually recorded on the tape. Recording a single logical record in every physical record, considered by many to be a wasteful use of tape length, would only be more wasteful if the empty portions of the data cards were also recorded. For that reason, the term "card images" is considered a misleading one. "Unit record" is preferred to describe the recording of one (hence the word "unit") logical record per physical record. ("Blocked records" is a term often used to describe recording more than one logical record per physical record.)

Edited input and output, because of its purpose, is in unit records. For example, information may be written on tape in edited form by using these statements:

$$\text{WRITE}(4,77)A,I,R$$
$$77 \quad \text{FORMAT}(F7.3,I3,F7.4)$$

A, I, and R are the variables whose values are to be recorded on the tape. The number 4 specifies the tape drive holding the tape upon which the computer is to write (record) the values. The number 77 specifies the FORMAT statement that is to govern the arrangement of the three values within the physical record which this WRITE statement will create. As a result of the above statements, tape 4 will have recorded upon it a physical record resembling the first 17 columns of a data card containing the characters 082.37552403.1416 (assuming A=82.375, I=524, and R=3.1416).

If tape 4 was rewound (by a REWIND 4 statement), the three values could be read back into memory using these statements:

$$\text{READ}(4,78)B,K,S$$
$$78 \quad \text{FORMAT}(F7.3,I3,F7.4)$$

This would result in the value 82.375 being assigned to B, 524 to K, and 3.1416 to S. Different variable names were used here to illustrate that, just as with data punched on data cards, variable names are not associated with the values on the tape. Also, the point was illustrated here that, just as with data cards, values must be read exactly as they have been recorded on the tape.

If only two variables were in the READ(4,78) statement, then the third value would have been lost, because the tape will always move to the next inter-record gap. This is analogous to reading a data card that contains more values than there are variables in the READ statement.

If more variables appeared in the READ(4,78) statement than there were values in the tape's physical record, a record-length error will occur as the computer "reads" the inter-record gap in its attempt to satisfy the READ(4,78) command. The program run is terminated whenever this occurs.

Although unit record input/output will be de-emphasized in this text, several vital points have been made in this section that apply to all forms of input and output with magnetic tape:

1. Values recorded on the tape must be retrieved (read) in exactly the same format and order in which they were recorded.
2. Values are recorded "naked" on tape, i.e., with no hint as to which variable name they originally belonged.
3. Physical records must be read in their entirety. Attempting to read less than a complete physical record results in lost data values. Attempting to read more than a complete physical record results in a fatal record-length error.
4. Before a programmer can use a tape as input to a program she is writing, she must know how the data was recorded on the tape.

17.9 "Pure Binary" Input/Output

Information is written (recorded) on tape in "pure binary" form by using statements such as this:

WRITE(3)A,B,C,D

The 3 means the information is to be recorded on tape 3. Note the absence of a number referencing an associated FORMAT statement.

As in the previous section, the four values could be read off the tape by first executing a REWIND 3 and then a statement of the form:

READ(3)E,F,G,H

Again, the four values, although now recorded on the tape in binary form, are in no way associated with specific variables. They can just as easily be read and given to E, F, G, and H as to A, B, C, and D.

17.10 Subscripted Input/Output in Binary Form

As has always been true with subscripted variables, it is possible to input or output entire arrays of data without specification of subscripts. This is possible because the FORTRAN compiler contains a built-in procedure for cycling subscripts if the user has not indicated any controlled cycling by the use of DO statements or implicit DO loops. When transferring data from internal memory to a file, it makes no difference if the array is transmitted in row order or column order, as long as the same transfer procedure is applied as the data are transferred from the file back to memory. The following partial program illustrates this point.

DIMENSION NAME(100,5),DOB(100),SSN(100)

WRITE(4)NAME,DOB,SSN

READ(4)NAME,DOB,SSN

STOP

As a result of the WRITE(4) statement, the entire 100x5 NAME array will be written on the tape followed by 100 dates of birth, followed by 100 social security numbers. The READ (4) will receive this information in exactly the same manner.

Now that the rudiments of magnetic tape procedures have been discussed, the five tape operations listed at the beginning of this chapter can be described.

17.11 Building a Data File on Tape

The process of building files on tape will be demonstrated by means of a programming example.*

*This file will be similar to the disc file used as an example of the DEFINE FILE statement.

Programming Example Student Registration

A university registrar wants to transfer a card file on all students to magnetic tape to cut down on its bulk. Presently, the file is made up of one card for each of the school's 15,564 students. Each card contains the following information:

Card Column	Information	Example	Specification
1–24	Name	Duke David F.	A24
25–52	Address	573 Connor Rd. Smallberg, SD	A28
53–61	Social Security Number	081325549	I9
62–63	Graduation Year	76(1976)	I2
64–65	Major	ME(Mech. Eng.)	A2
66–68	Credit Hours Taken to Date	124(124.)	F3.0
69–72	Grade Points Earned to Date	0412(412.)	F4.0
73–76	Grade Point Average	3323(3.323)	F4.3
77–80	Code	Blank except for final card in deck which will contain a 9999	I4

The solution:

The first decision to be made in this problem is what logical-record-to-physical-record ratio to use. As has been pointed out earlier, the fewer physical records that are on the tape, the fewer interrecord gaps and the less waste of tape there will be. The more logical records that can be fitted into each physical record, the larger each physical record will be, and fewer of them will be needed. Since a physical record is the amount of information that is written on the tape during one movement of the tape, its *maximum* size (that is to say, the *maximum* number of logical records that it can contain) is determined by the amount of memory that can be devoted to storing information destined for the physical record about to be written. The section of memory that the programmer decided to "dedicate" to the accumulation of information destined for each physical record is referred to as a **file buffer** area.

So the first question that must be answered is, "How much memory (in words) can be devoted to file buffers?" The answer to that question is usually arrived at by a simple scratch pad subtraction problem. From the computer center, the programmer finds out how many words of memory are going to be needed for the compiler program. Based upon experience, she estimates the number of words that will be used up by the program itself, and the remainder are the words that will be available for her file buffers. The following represents a typical computation:

```
  11000   words for the entire program
-  6000   words for the compiler program
 ───────
   5000
-  3000   words for the program itself
 ───────
   2000   words for file buffers and other
          program variables
```

Using this sample computation, it is now known that in the registrar's problem each physical record must be limited to 2000 words.

The logical records of this problem were described earlier. Each is determined to contain 19 words as shown below. The code field is not counted because it will not be recorded on the tape. Its only purpose is to provide a field in which a 9999 can be punched to signal the last card in the deck. Such a card often is referred to as a **sentinel card**. It contains nothing in any field except the code field and is placed at the back of the data deck to mark its end. To make use of the sentinel card, the programmer simply includes an IF(CODE.EQ. 9999) statement in his program immediately after the READ statement controlling the reading of cards. On all "real" data cards, the CODE field is left blank, so for them the value of CODE is zero.

Field	Specification	Words
Name	A24=6A4	6
Address	A28=7A4	7
S. S. N.	I9	1
Grad. Year	I2	1
Major	A2	1
C.H. to date	F3.0	1
G.P. to date	F4.0	1
G.P. average	F4.3	1
Code	I4	Not counted
Total Words		19*

The logical-to-physical-record ratio can now be calculated by use of this equation:

$$\frac{2000 \text{ words/PR}}{19 \text{ words/LR}} = 105 \text{ LR:PR} = 100 \text{ LR:PR}$$

Based upon the calculation, it is decided to use an LR:PR ratio of 100. Note that the figure 105 was rounded in the direction of safety to the next convenient lower round number. Rounding up might result in using more core memory than was available.

The complete program for building the registrar's tape file is shown below. The file buffer of 100 elements is set up by the DIMENSION statement. The real meat of the program is represented by the DO 30 loop, in which cards are read in groups of 100, their contents being stored in the proper slots in the buffer as they are read, and by the WRITE(15) statement, which causes the contents of the filled buffer to be recorded in one physical record on the tape.

```
C ••••••••••••••••••••••••••••••••••••••••••••••••••••••••••
C•• PURPOSE - BUILD A TAPE FILE (BLOCKING FACTOR IS 100 ••
C•• LOGICAL RECORDS PER PHYSICAL RECORD).
C NAME ADDR SSN GRADNYR MAJOR CREDHR GRADPT GRADAV
C (NAMES ON BUFFER AREA TO HOLD CONTENTS OF 100 CARDS)
C ----------------------------------------------------------
C --NR NUMBER OF RECORDS IN THE BUFFER AREA --
C THIS NUMBER IS PLACED AT THE END OF EACH --
C PHYSICAL RECORD TO SIGNAL HOW LARGE THE --
C THE PHYSICAL RECORD IS.
C --CODE VARIABLE USED TO PICK-UP 9999 FROM SENTINEL CARD
C
C (FILE BEING FORMED ON TAPE 15)
C
      DIMENSION NAME(100,6),ADDR(100,7),SSN(100),GRDNYR(100),
     1MAJOR(100),CREDHR(100),GRADPT(100),GRADAV(100)
C
      INTEGER ADDR, SSN, GRDNYR, CODE
C
C     BRING TAPE 15 TO STARTING POINT
C
      REWIND 15
C
C     ....START FILLING BUFFER AREA......
C
   10 NR = 0
C
      DO 30 I = 1, 100
C
C     READ INDIVIDUAL DATA CARD
1
      READ(5,20)(NAME(I,J),J=1,6),(ADDR(I,J),J=1,7),SSN(I)
     1,GRDNYR(I),MAJOR(I),CREDHR(I),GRADPT(I),GRADAV(I)
     2,CODE
   20 FORMAT(6A4,7A4,I9,I2,A2,F3.0,F4.0,F4.3,I4)
C
C     IS THIS THE SENTINEL CARD
C
      IF(CODE.EQ.9999) THEN
C     NO MORE CARDS TO PROCESS
C
C     WRITE PARTIALLY FILLED BUFFER ON TAPE
C
      IF(NR.NE.0)WRITE(15)NAME,ADDR,SSN,GRDNYR
     1,MAJOR,CREDHR,GRADPT,GRADAV,NR
C
```

```
                              END FILE 15
                              REWIND 15
                              STOP
        C
        C                ELSE
        C
        C                    CONTINUE PROCESSING
        C
                              NR = NR + 1
        C
        C                ENDIF
        C
            30 CONTINUE
        C
        C        ........BUFFER IS FILLED - DUMP TO TAPE............
        C
                 WRITE(15)NAME,ADDR,SSN,GRDNYR,MAJOR,CREDHR,GRADPT
                1          ,GRADAV,NR
        C...................................................................
        C
        C                    START BUILDING THE BUFFER AREA
                 GO TO 10
        C
        C
                 END
```

The variable NR is used to record at the tail end of each PR the exact number of LR's that are recorded in that PR. If there are 15,564 cards in the card file, then the first 155 PR's will all contain 100 LR's, but the 156th PR will contain only 64. This is necessary information for any program that must read the contents of the tape file.

The buffer area is filled with the information contained on the first 100 cards. When the DO loop is satisfied, the buffer area is dumped onto the tape. This process continues over and over again. Eventually, the sentinel card is detected. The partially-filled buffer area is dumped on the tape and the END OF FILE mark is placed on the tape.

Note the positioning of the REWIND statements. One appears at the beginning of the program to assure that the tape is in fact positioned at its load point marker before attempting to record anything on it. Another appears before the STOP statement so that when the program ends the computer operator will find the tape already rewound and ready for demounting. Graphically, the buffer area contains the information shown in Figure 17.5:

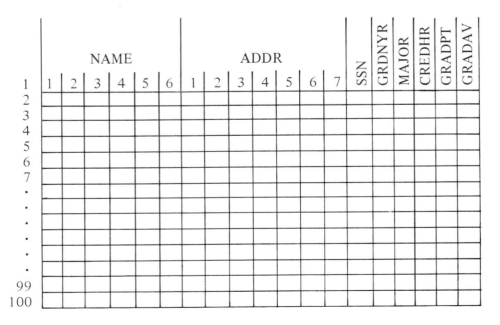

Figure 17.5 The File Buffer: Working Storage

Each physical record of the tape holds this information as suggested in Figure 17.6.

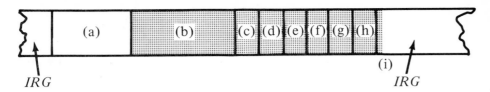

(a) All 600 elements of the NAME array.
(b) All 700 elements of the ADDR array.
(c) All 100 elements of the SSN array.
(d) All 100 elements of the GRDNYR array.
(e) All 100 elements of the MAJOR array.
(f) All 100 elements of the CREDHR array.
(g) All 100 elements of the GRADPT array.
(h) All 100 elements of the GRADAV array.
(i) The single variable NR, which tells how many LR's are recorded in this PR.

Figure 17.6 The Arrangement of Data Within Each Physical Record

The file-building operation can be summarized in these steps:

1. Decide on the LR:PR ratio.
2. Design the DIMENSION statement to establish a file buffer of the proper size.
3. Write the program to:
    (a) File the buffer with data from cards in correct size groups.
    (b) Transfer buffer loads of data to tape to create the PR's.
    (c) Tag the tail end of each PR with the number of LR's it contains.
    (d) Detect the sentinel card.

17.12
Reading Data From Tape Files

Aside from the obvious fact that data on tape is useless without a means of retrieving (or reading) it, the reading of tape files is important because it is fundamental to all remaining tape operations that are to be discussed. Again, a demonstrative problem will be used to describe the process.

We want to write statements that will read the registrar's tape file and transfer a copy to the line printer.

```
C     PURPOSE - READ TAPE FILE...MAKE COPY ON LINE PRINTER...
C
      DIMENSION NAME(100,6),ADDR(100,7),SSN(100),GRDNYR(100),
     1MAJOR(100),CREDHR(100),GRADPT(100),GRADAV(100)
      INTEGER ADDR, SSN, GRDNYR
C               MAKE SURE TAPE IS AT LOAD POINT
      REWIND 15
C        .......READ PHYSICAL RECORD............
C               (LOAD BUFFER FROM TAPE)
10    READ(15) NAME,ADDR,SSN,GRDNYR,MAJOR,CREDHR,GRADPT,
     1         GRADAV,NR
C        .......TRANSFER BUFFER TO OUTPUT......
      DO 30 I = 1, NR
         WRITE(2,20)(NAME(I,J),J=1,6),(ADDR(I,J),J=1,7),SSN(I),
     1           GRDNYR(I),MAJOR(I),CREDHR(I),GRADPT(I),
     2           GRADAV(I)
20       FORMAT(5X,6A4,5X,7A4,5X,I9,5X,I2,5X,A2,5X,F4.0,5X,
     1           F5.0,5X,F5.3)
30    CONTINUE
C        .......SEE IF END OF TAPE REACHED.........
      IF(EOFCKF(15).EQ.1) THEN
C               END OF FILE DETECTED
```

```
C
             REWIND 15
             STOP
C
     ELSE
C
                 GO TO 10
C
     ENDIF
C
     END
```

For the most part, the program is straightforward. The student is reminded of the purpose of the variable NR, as described in the previous section. Its value is found at the end of each PR in the form of a simple variable and represents the number of valid LR's that have been recorded in that PR. In this program NR will have a value of 100 in all PR's except the last. Note NR's use as a DO loop parameter in this program.

One other item peculiar to the programming necessary to read data off tape is the mandatory check for the EOF mark. The manner in which this is accomplished varies widely from system to system; however, it must be provided for in the program. In the method chosen for this programming example, a library function called EOFCKF(i) is used in a logical IF test. (The argument i of the function represents the tape number to which the test refers.) When the READ(15) command is executed, if an EOF mark is found (instead of a normal PR), EOFCKF will be given a value of 1. If a normal PR is found, EOFCKF will be given a value of 0. In this program when the EOF mark is found, the tape is rewound and the program is terminated.

17.13 | Searching

The problem demonstrated in the previous section, where the entire contents of a data file were read off tape and printed on the line printer, is in truth an unrealistic one. The more usual task facing a programmer is to retrieve and print only one or only a selected group of logical records that meet some predetermined criteria. To accomplish this a search is performed.

Suppose, for example, that the registrar had a social security number and wanted to know if the person to whom the number belonged was a registered student at his school. If the student was found to be registered, the registrar might ask for his name and address. The following printout shows the programming necessary to accomplish this search through the tape file.

```
      DIMENSION NAME(100,6),ADDR(100,7),SSN(100),GRDNYR(100),
     1MAJOR(100),CREDHR(100),GRADPT(100),GRADAV(100)
C
C
      INTEGER ADDR, SSN, GRDNYR, CODE
C
C
      READ(5,10) NSSN
   10 FORMAT(I9)
C
      REWIND 15
C
C
   20 READ(15)NAME,ADDR,SSN,GRDNYR,MAJOR,CREDHR,GRADPT,
     1       GRADAV,NR
C
C       SEARCH BUFFER FOR THIS RECORD
C
C
      DO 40 I = 1, NR
C
          IF(SSN(I).EQ.NSSN) THEN
C
C             RECORD FOUND
C
              WRITE(2,30)(NAME(I,J),J=1,6),(ADDR(I,J),J=1,7)
   30         FORMAT(5X,6A4,5X,7A4)
C
              REWIND 15
              STOP
C
          ENDIF
C
   40 CONTINUE
C
C     RECORD NOT IN THIS BLOCK
C
C       HAS END OF FILE MARK BEEN REACHED
C
      IF(EOFCKF(15).EQ.1) THEN
```

```
C
              WRITE(2,50)
    50        FORMAT(1X,20HSSN NOT IN TAPE FILE  )
C
              REWIND 15
              STOP
        ENDIF
C
C         CONTINUE SEARCH......READ ANOTHER PHYSICAL RECORD
C
        GO TO 20
C
        END
```

In this program the social security number to be searched for is read from a data card. The actual searching is performed by the DO 40 loop. If the social security number is found, statements are executed that result in the student's name and address being printed, the tape being rewound, and termination of the program. If the social security number is never found, the EOF mark will be detected, resulting in the execution of a WRITE statement where the failure of the search is reported, the tape is rewound, and the program terminated.

This type of search is called a **linear search** because there is a direct (or linear) relationship between the length of the file and the amount of time it takes to search through it. Linear searches are time-consuming because, on the average, approximately half the file must be examined before a desired record is found. Improvements in time can be realized if the variable in the file that is the basis of the search is in some known order. A **logarithmic search** technique (so named because the time of the search is proportional to the log of the table length) is widely used whenever the file is ordered. Despite its time advantage, it is useless if the file is unordered or when searches for groups of logical records are to be conducted, so this text has limited itself to discussing the slower, but more versatile, linear search technique.

17.14 Updating

The search operation is far more important in its role as a part of the updating procedure.

The process of **updating**, perhaps the most frequently used of the tape operations, is the process of correcting out-of-date information in the data file. In theory the process can be summed up by these steps:

1. Perform a search for the logical record containing the out-of-date information.
2. Correct the information.
3. Backspace the file to the beginning of the last physical record (which, of course, was the physical record containing the out-of-date logical record).
4. Write the physical record onto the file from the file buffer. This will overlay the old physical record (which contained the out-of-date information) with the new, corrected physical record.

These steps require the use of the BACKSPACE command, but that command is usually not permitted with tape, so the four steps must be modified. When performing an update on a tape file, it is necessary to involve two tapes. One is the original tape containing the out-of-date information, and the other is the tape that will contain the file in its updated form.

The steps involved in updating a tape file are these:

1. Perform a search operation to find the out-of-date logical record. As the search operation proceeds, transfer each physical record onto the new tape.
2. When the out-of-date logical record is found, correct its incorrect information before recording the physical record of which it was a part onto the new tape.
3. Complete the new tape file by recording on it the remaining physical records from the old tape.

An update program is demonstrated in the next printout. In this case the old tape is tape 15 and the new tape is tape 16. After rewinding both tapes, a data card is read containing the SSN of the student whose record is in need of updating. In statement 20, the first READ(15) statement, a physical record is read off the old tape. The DO 30 loop governs the search for the out-of-date logical record by looking for an exact match equality between the SSN of the student whose record must be updated and each of the SSN's in the file. If no match is found, a normal exit from the DO 30 loop is made, but, before returning to statement 20 to fetch the next physical record, the first WRITE(16) statement is executed to cause the physical record through which the search was just conducted to be recorded onto the new tape. This process of reading a physical record off the old tape into the buffer, searching through the buffer, and then recording that buffer-load onto the new tape is repeated over and over until the out-of-date logical record is found by the IF statement in the DO 30 loop. When that occurs, the proper elements of the logical record are corrected and the program branches to statement 50. At statement 50 a loop is commenced (consisting of the second WRITE(16) statement, the second READ(15) statement, and the "End of File Check" statement.) This loop will control the transfer of all remaining physical records from the old tape to the new tape. In the process of executing this last loop, when an EOF mark is detected on the old tape, the program drops down to statement 60 where an EOF mark is recorded on the new tape, both tapes are rewound, and the program is terminated.

```
C..........................................................
C..   PURPOSE - UPDATE A TAPE FILE      OLD FILE = 15      ..
C..                                     NEW FILE = 16      ..
C..........................................................
C
C              -----IMPORTANT VARIABLES-----
C
C      --NSSN      SEARCH VALUE - SOCIAL SECURITY NUMBER OF --
C                  STUDENT WHO HAS TAKEN ADDITIONAL COURSES --
C      --CRED      NUMBER OF ADDITIONAL CREDIT HOURS TAKEN   --
C      --GRAD      GRADE POINTS EARNED IN THESE COURSES      --
C
       DIMENSION NAME(100,6),ADDR(100,7),SSN(100),GRDNYR(100),
      1MAJOR(100),CREDHR(100),GRADPT(100),GRADAV(100)

       INTEGER ADDR, SSN, GRDNYR
C
C              ...BRING BOTH TAPES TO LOAD POINT .......
C
       REWIND 15
       REWIND 16
C
C              READ UPDATE INFORMATION
C
       READ(5,10) NSSN, CRED, GRAD
    10 FORMAT(I9,F4.0,F5.0)
C
C              LOAD BUFFER FROM OLD TAPE
C
    20 READ(15)NAME,ADDR,SSN,GRDNYR,MAJOR,CREDHR,GRADPT,
      1          GRADAV,NR
C
C     .....SEARCH BUFFER FOR NSSN RECORD.....
C
       DO 30 I = 1, NR
C
          IF(SSN(I).EQ.NSSN) THEN
C              ADD ADDITIONAL HOURS AND CREDITS
             CREDHR(I) = CREDHR(I) + CRED
             GRADPT(I) = GRADPT(I) + GRAD
C              COMPUTE NEW GRADE POINT AVERAGE
             GRADAV(I) = GRADPT(I) / CREDHR(I)
             GO TO 50
C
          ENDIF
C
    30 CONTINUE
C
C
C     WHEN DO LOOP SATISFIED,NSSN NOT IN THIS PHYSICAL RECORD
C              WRITE THIS PHYSICAL RECORD ON NEW TAPE
C
       WRITE(16)NAME,ADDR,SSN,GRDNYR,MAJOR,CREDHR,GRADPT,
      1          GRADAV,NR
C
C
C              TEST FOR END OF OLD TAPE
C
       IF(EOFCHF(15).EQ.1) THEN
C
          WRITE(2,40) NSSN
    40    FORMAT(2X,I9,' THIS SSN NOT IN FILE')
C
          END FILE 16
          REWIND 15
          REWIND 16
C
          STOP
C
       ELSE
C
C              CONTINUE      SEARCHING
C
          GO TO 20
C
       ENDIF
C
```

```
C
C
C     PURPOSE - THE PURPOSE OF THIS SECTION IS TO TRANSFER
C              RECORDS FROM THE OLD FILE TO THE NEW FILE
C
C
   50 WRITE(16)NAME,ADDR,SSN,GRDNYR,MAJOR,CREDHR,GRADPT,
     1          GRADAV,NR
C
C     IF(EOFCKF(15).NE.1) THEN
C
          READ(15)NAME,ADDR,SSN,GRDNYR,MAJOR,CREDHR,GRADPT,
     1          GRADAV,NR
          GO TO 50
C
      ENDIF
C
   60 END FILE 16
C
      REWIND 15
      REWIND 16
C
      STOP
      END
```

Review Exercises

1.*What are the essential differences between "internal" memory and "auxiliary" memory?

2. Describe the difference between a "direct access file" (disc file) and a "sequential access file" (tape file).

3. Describe a typical "file building" operation.

4.*When would it be most appropriate to store information on a disc file in the unedited (pure binary) form?

5. What is the purpose of the DEFINE FILE statement?

6. What is the purpose of a "file key"? Give an example.

7.*What is the purpose of a "delete code"?

8. What is "hashing" used for?

9. Describe the difference between a "logical" record and a "physical" record.

10.*Why are many physical records grouped together into a large logical record when these records are transferred to tapes?

11. What is the purpose of the ENDFILE statement?

12.*Describe the difference between the following WRITE statements:

    WRITE (2,10) A
    WRITE (4) A

13. What is a "buffer"?

14. Discuss the relative capacity of internal storage and the storage capacity provided by a tape or a disc.

15.*An automotive parts company stocks 8,000 to 10,000 types of small repair parts. The information on these parts is stored on data cards in the following fields:

Card Column	Information	Example	Specification
1–6	Part number	627398	I6
7–24	Part name	Discombobulator	A18
25–32	Cost of part	13.75	F8.2
33–35	Quantity on hand	17	I3
36–38	Quantity on order	3	I3
39–40	Location by dept.		I2
41–43	Location by bin		I3

Assuming a limitation of 5000 words of internal storage available for storage of data, write the DI-MENSION statement necessary to set up a file buffer for use in a program for storing this data in a magnetic tape file.

16. In the Lower Slobovian State Lottery, all lottery ticket purchases are recorded on a magnetic tape file in ascending numerical order by ticket number. The file is recorded with an LR:PR ratio of 250, and each logical record conforms with this description:

Field	Specification
Ticket Number	I6
Name of Ticket Holder	5A4
Address of Ticket Holder	6A4

The last item in each physical record is a simple integer value, which tells how many logical records it contains. At drawing time, the numbers of all tickets sold are placed in a barrel. The first, second, and third place winners are chosen by a blindfolded lottery official reaching into the barrel and drawing three numbers. The order of a number's being drawn dictates which prize it is for. Three data cards are prepared, each containing a ticket and prize number in this form:

Field	Specification	Example
Ticket No.	I6	421978
Prize No.	I1	1 = 1st Prize
		2 = 2nd Prize
		3 = 3rd Prize

A search for the name and address of the prize winners is to be performed. To ease the search procedure, the three data cards are also placed into ascending numerical order by ticket number.

Write the program to accomplish the search and to provide for the printing of output in the following form for each winner:

PRIZE NO. 2   TICKET NO. 666666
ALISON J. RULE
44 GRANITE AVE., RANGATANG, L.S.

(Note Printout may be in numerical order by ticket number.)

17. The First National Bank keeps all information on its mortgage accounts in magnetic tape files. Each logical record consists of the following fields:

Field	Specification
Account number	I7
Name of mortgagee	5A4
Address of mortgagee	6A4
Interest rate	F4.3
Amount of minimum monthly payment	F7.2
Unpaid balance of mortgage	F10.2

All logical records are recorded in the old tape in ascending numerical order by account number, using a blocking factor of 200 logical records per physical record. The last item in each physical record is a simple integer value which tells how many logical records it contains. The tape file is updated on the 15th of each month and contains data as of the most recent update. During the update operation, a data deck describing the mortgage payments received since the last update run is fed to the computer, each card containing information as follows:

Columns	Field	Specification
1–7	Account number	I7
8–14	Amount of actual payment	F7.2

The cards are also arranged in ascending numerical order by account number.

The update program compares account numbers in the tape with those on the cards. When an account is found on the tape that does not appear in the deck, a message is printed out on the line printer:

ACCOUNT NR. 8421734 MADE NO PAYMENT

When a match is found between the account number in the deck and an account number in the file, the amount of the actual payment is compared to the prescribed minimum monthly payment. If the actual payment was too small, a message is printed out on the line printer:

ACCOUNT NR. 8421734 PAID TOO LITTLE

and no update of that account's data is performed. If the amount paid is sufficient, the file's data is updated according to these equations:

Interest Due	$= 1/12 *$ Interest Rate $*$ Mortgage Balance
Principal Payment	$=$ Actual Payment $-$ Interest Due
New Mortgage Balance	$=$ Old Mortgage Balance $-$ Principal Payment

Write the program to perform this update operation. Plan on a trailer card containing 9999999 in the account number field.

18
Magnetic Tape Operations (Continued)

18.1 | Sorting

It was mentioned earlier that the time needed to search a file can be greatly reduced if the file is ordered. Multiple-record update operations are most efficiently accomplished when the file being updated is in order. The merging operation, to be discussed later, can only be performed on ordered files. When information is collected to form a data file, it is often not in the desired order. The sort operation is employed to rearrange the logical records of a data file into the desired order.

Unfortunately, it is only possible to perform the sort procedure on as much of the file as can reside in the file buffer, i.e., one physical record at a time. When a file of more than one physical record is encountered, the sort operation is performed independently on each physical record and then a merge operation is used to redistribute the logical records among the various physical records so as to achieve a completely ordered file. Merging is a topic to be covered later in this chapter, so this discussion of the sort operation must of necessity limit itself to that required for sorting single buffer loads of logical records.

There are a number of different sorting schemes, some more efficient than others, some demanding less internal storage space than others, some simpler than others. The "interchange" sort has been chosen for this discussion because it requires a minimum amount of additional internal storage and represents a good compromise between efficiency and simplicity.

The interchange sort works by comparing the first two adjacent elements in the file buffer being sorted and interchanging them if they are found to be out of order. When an interchange is necessary, it is accomplished as shown in the diagram below. The temporary (TEMP) storage location shown is necessitated by the "destructive write" feature of computer memory operations.

The 2nd and 3rd elements are then compared and interchanged (if necessary), followed by the 3rd and 4th elements, and so on, until one complete pass has been made through the file buffer. A sufficient number of passes is made through the buffer, the buffer becoming more and more ordered with each successive pass, until it is finally in the desired order. Figure 18.1 provides a simplified illustration of how the interchange sort functions by demonstrating its use in the sorting of a table of nine numbers.

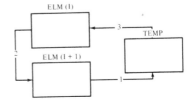

Item Number	Unsorted Table	After 1st Pass	After 2nd Pass	After 3rd Pass	After 4th Pass	After 5th Pass	After 6th Pass	After 7th Pass	After 8th Pass
1.	20	17	17	17	14	14	14	14	09
2.	17	20	20	14	17	17	17	09	14
3.	35	35	14	20	20	20	09	17	17
4.	41	14	35	28	22	09	20	20	20
5.	14	41	28	22	09	22	22	22	22
6.	76	28	22	09	28	28	28	28	28
7.	28	22	09	35	35	35	35	35	35
8.	22	09	41	41	41	41	41	41	41
9.	09	76	76	76	76	76	76	76	76

Brackets indicate how much of the table is completely sorted after each pass.

Figure 18.1 The Interchange Sort

Consider the following example of the sort of a short table with only four numbers. The variable NPASS will keep track of which pass is in progress, and CMPARE will keep track of which comparison is being performed. As was noted in Figure 18.1, the comparison and exchange process that is needed goes less and less farther through the table with each subsequent pass. This same phenomenon is also seen here.

| NPASS | 1 | 1 | 1 | 2 | 2 | 3 | |
CMPARE	1	2	3	1	2	1	Result
T	35	17	17	17	17	17	14
a	17	35	20	20	20	14	17
b l	20	20	35	14	14	20	20
e	14	14	14	35	35	35	35

The example above illustrates two important points:

1. The number of passes necessary is one less than the number of elements in the file.
2. The number of comparisons (and possible interchanges) necessary during each pass starts out equal to the number of passes and decreases by one with each successive pass. By taking advantage of this feature, the time to execute the sort is half of what it would otherwise be.

The program segment that would accomplish the sorting of the above example is as follows:

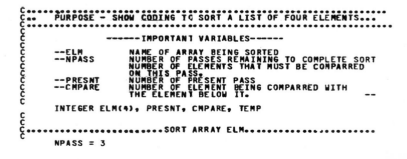

```
C..........................................................
C..  PURPOSE - SHOW CODING TO SORT A LIST OF FOUR ELEMENTS....
C..........................................................
C
C            ------IMPORTANT VARIABLES------
C
C      --ELM       NAME OF ARRAY BEING SORTED
C      --NPASS     NUMBER OF PASSES REMAINING TO COMPLETE SORT
C                  NUMBER OF ELEMENTS THAT MUST BE COMPARRED
C                  ON THIS PASS.
C      --PRESNT    NUMBER OF PRESENT PASS
C      --CMPARE    NUMBER OF ELEMENT BEING COMPARRED WITH
C                  THE ELEMENT BELOW IT.            --
C
C      INTEGER ELM(4), PRESNT, CMPARE, TEMP
C
C...................SORT ARRAY ELM...................
C
       NPASS = 3
```

```
C
C           DO 20 PRESNT = 1, 3
C
C               ON THIS PASS THE NUMBER OF ELEMENTS TO
C               BE COMPARRED IS NPASS.
C
C               DO 10 CMPARE = 1, NPASS
C
C                   SWAP ELEMENTS IF NECESSARY
C
C                   IF(ELM(CMPARE).GT.ELM(CMPARE+1)) THEN
C
                        TEMP = ELM(CMPARE+1)
                        ELM(CMPARE+1) = ELM(CMPARE)
                        ELM(CMPARE) = TEMP
C
C                   ENDIF
C   10          CONTINUE
C
C               THIS PASS COMPLETE....DECREMENT PASS COUNTER
C
C           NPASS = NPASS - 1
C   20   CONTINUE
C
```

These examples demonstrate the sorting of one-dimensional arrays. When faced with the sorting of a file buffer, the programmer is in fact sorting a two-dimensional array, each row of the array being one logical record from the file. The rule that governs here is, "Keep the logical record intact!" Although comparisons are made on only one of the logical record's many elements, when the decision is made that an interchange is necessary, the entire logical record with all its elements must be interchanged.

To illustrate this rule, consider the following program segment, which sorts a file buffer of NR logical records. Each logical record contains a student's name and age. The segment sorts the file according to age in ascending order (youngest first).

The elements being compared are the elements of AGE. Note that when in the IF test it is determined that an exchange is necessary, the AGE's and also the NAME's (all 6 elements) are interchanged. The logical record is "kept intact." Note also the innermost or DO 5 loop. It is necessitated by the fact that each NAME has six elements itself, each one of which must also be individually interchanged through TEMP.

```
        SUBROUTINE SORT (ELM,NPASS,FRESNT,CMPARE)
C
C
        INTEGER ELM(4), PRESNT, CMPARE, TEMP
C
C           COMPUTE NUMBER OF PASSES BASED ON NR
C
        NPASS = NR - 1
C
        DO 20 PRESNT = 1, NPASS
C
C               ON THIS PASS THE NUMBER OF ELEMENTS
C               TO BE COMPARRED IS NPASS
C
            DO 10 CMPARE = 1, NPASS
C
C               SWAP ROWS IF NECESSARY
C
                IF(AGE(CMPARE).GT.AGE(CMPARE+1)) THEN
C
C                   ...SWAP ELEMENT OF AGE FIRST......
C
                        TEMP = AGE(CMPARE)
                        AGE(CMPARE+1) = AGE(CMPARE)
                        AGE(CMPARE) = TEMP
C
C                   ....SWAP ALL 6 ELEMENTS OF NAME.......
C
                        DO 5 K = 1, 6
```

```
        C
                                    TEMP = NAME(CMPARE+1,K)
                                    NAME(CMPARE+1,K) = NAME(CMPARE,K)
                                    NAME(CMPARE,K) = TEMP
        C
        C    5              CONTINUE
        C
        C              ENDIF
        C
        C   10    CONTINUE
        C
        C        ........THIS PASS COMPLETE....DECREMENT PASS COUNTER
        C
                      NPASS = NPASS - 1
        C
            20 CONTINUE
```

Note:

The next two sections (18.2 Purging and 18.3 Merging) are somewhat advanced operations. These sections are important only to those who want to get heavily involved in tape/disc operations. The more casually interested student can skip these sections.

18.2 | Purging

The purging operation was described earlier as an update operation where the object is to completely eliminate out-of-date records from the file rather than to correct them. As an example, such an operation would be performed on the registrar's file every time a student dropped out of school. Like the update operation, purging a tape file requires the use of two tapes: an old tape and a new tape. Unlike the update operation, in purging, the two tapes may not share the same file buffer. Responsible for this complication is the fact that while logical records from the old file are being eliminated, the programmer must continue to provide for physical records on the new file that do not have any "holes" in them, and all of which (except the last) contain a full complement of logical records (100 in this example).

To solve this programming problem, two file buffers are used, one into which physical records from the Old Tape File will be loaded, from now on called the Old Buffer; and the other, called the New Buffer, in which logical records will be accumulated for recording in each physical record of the New Tape File.

The logic involved in the purging operation will be developed by means of flowcharts. In the flowcharts, the following abbreviations are used:

OTF = Old Tape File
OB = Old Buffer
NTF = New Tape File
NB = New Buffer

The expression "Fill OB" in the flowchart refers to the reading of the next physical record off the Old Tape File (which, of course moves the contents of that physical record into the Old Buffer). The expression "Dump NB" refers to the writing of the next physical record on the New Tape File from the New Buffer.

Variable names will be the same as in the first programming example except that the letter O will be added to the end of variables in the Old Buffer, and the letter N will be added to the end of variables in the New Buffer.

Old Buffer	New Buffer
NAMEO(100,6)	NAMEN(100,6)
ADDRO(100,7)	ADDRN(100,7)
SSNO(100)	SSNN(100)
etc.	etc.

For subscript control, the variables IO and IN will be used for the Old and New Buffer variables respectively.

The remark "Move logical record from OB to NB" refers to the action to be taken with a logical record that is not to be purged. It translates to statements of this form:

$$SSNN(IN) = SSNO(IO)$$
$$GRDYRN(IN) = GRDYRO(IO)$$
$$MAJORN(IN) = MAJORO(IO)$$

The basis for this flowchart development will be a programming example where the requirement is to purge from the registrar's file the logical record on a student who has withdrawn from school. The SSN of the student to be purged is to be read off a data card and given to the variable name SSNPRG.

Figure 18.2a shows a basic algorithm for purging.

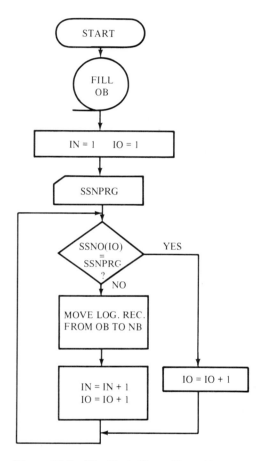

Figure 18.2a The Basic Purge Operation

Logical records are moved from the Old Buffer to the New Buffer until the SSN of the logical record to be purged is found. If and when it is found, it is not moved to the New Buffer. IO, the Old Buffer's subscript, is advanced while IN, the New Buffer's subscript, is held at its former value to wait for the next transfer of a nonpurged logical record. We will gradually build upon this basic flowchart to accommodate three special occurrences.

In Figure 18.2b an addition to the diagram is made. This addition provides the necessary logic to prevent "running out the bottom" of the Old Buffer. (The variables NRO and NRN perform the same functions for the Old and New Tape Files of this example as NR did for the single Tape Files of previous examples: it is recorded at the end of each physical record to indicate the number of logical records that are included in that physical record.) When all records currently in the Old Buffer have been processed, the value of IO will exceed NRO by one, because of the positioning of the IO=IO+1 statement. When this condition is detected, the next physical record is read from the Old Tape File into the Old Buffer, IO is reinitiated at 1, and processing of the Old Buffer is reinitiated "from the top."

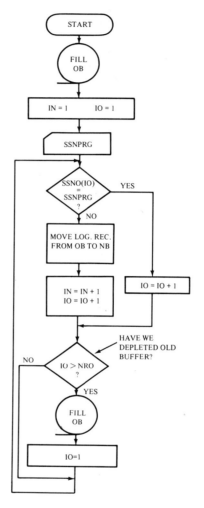

Figure 18.2b The Purge Operation: First Modification

The next event whose occurrence must be provided for is the filling of the New Buffer "to capacity." Figure 18.2c adds the necessary logic to provide for this event. In this example a desired New Buffer size of 100 is assumed. When IN is found to have a value greater than 100, the records currently in the New Buffer are written on the New Tape File as the next physical record. IN is then reinitiated at 1 to cause filling of the New Buffer to resume "from the top."

Figure 18.2d presents the complete flow diagram. Here provision has been made for the eventual detection of the EOF mark on the Old Tape File. When the EOF mark is detected on the Old Tape File, the contents of the New Buffer and an EOF mark are written on the New Tape File, and the program is terminated.

Figure 18.3 contains the program written from the complete purge flowchart. Statement numbers are shown on Figure 18.2d as an aid in correlating the flowchart with the program coding. This is a substantial program and it may take some time to trace through.

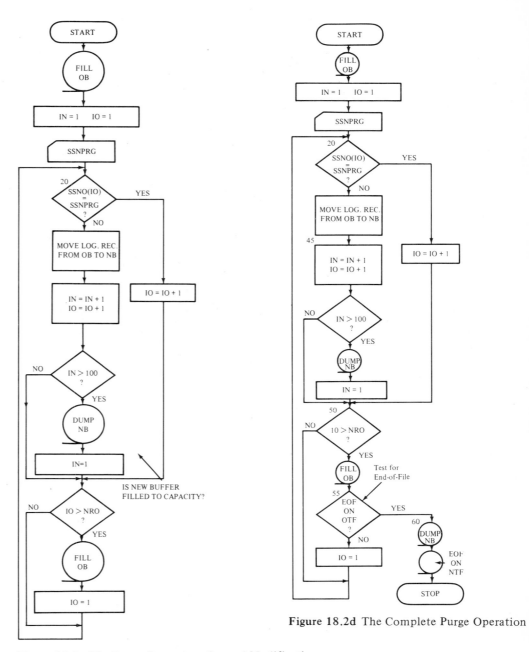

Figure 18.2c The Purge Operation: Second Modification

Figure 18.2d The Complete Purge Operation

```
C........................................................
C..   PURPOSE - PURGE A RECORD FROM A TAPE FILE - GENERATE ..
C..          NEW TAPE FILE FROM OLD TAPE FILE.           ..
C..          OLD FILE = 15,        NEW FILE = 16         ..
C........................................................
C
C            SET UP OLD AND NEW BUFFER AREAS
C
      DIMENSION NAMEO(100,6),ADDRO(100,7),SSNO(100),GRDYRO(100)
     1,MAJORO(100),CRDHRO(100),GRDPTO(100),GRDAVO(100)

      DIMENSION NAMEN(100,6),ADDRN(100,7),SSNN(100),GRDYRN(100)
     1,MAJORN(100),CRDHRN(100),GRDPTN(100),GRDAVN(100)
C
      INTEGER ARRDO, ADDRN, SSNO, SSNN, GRDYRO, GRDYRN
C
C            ....INITIALIZATION SECTION......
C            GET BOTH TAPES TO LOAD POINT
C
      REWIND 15
      REWIND 16
C
C            ....FILL OLD BUFFER....
C
      READ(15)NAMEO,ADDRO,SSNO,GRDYRO,MAJORO,CRDHRO,GRDPTO,
     1     GRDAVO,NRO
C
C            INITIALIZE BOTH SUBSCRIPTS
```

```
          IN = 1
          IO = 1
C
C                        READ IDENTIFIER OF RECORD TO BE PURGED
C
      READ(5,10) SSNPRG
   10 FORMAT(I9)
C
C.....  START PROCESSING INDIVIDUAL RECORDS FROM OLD FILE  ...
C
   20 IF(SSNO(IO).EQ.SSNPRG) THEN
C
C                    THIS RECORD DOES NOT
C                    BELONG IN NEW FILE
C
          IO = IO + 1
C
      ELSE         THIS RECORD BELONGS IN NEW FILE
C                  TRANSFER NAME FIRST
C
          DO 30 K = 1, 7
C
             NAMEN(IN,K) = NAMEO(IO,K)
C
   30     CONTINUE
C                  NOW TRANSFER REMAINDER OF RECORD
C
          DO 40 K = 1, 7
C
             ADDRN(IN,K) = ADDRO(IO,K)
C
   40     CONTINUE
C
          SSNN(IN) = SSNO(IO)
          GRDYRN(IN) = GRDYRO(IO)
          MAJORN(IN) = MAJORO(IO)
          CRDHRN(IN) = CRDHRO(IO)
          GRDPTN(IN) = GRDPTO(IO)
          GRDAVN(IN) = GRDAVO(IO)
C
          ....TRANSFER OF THIS RECORD COMPLETE.....
C
C.............................................................
C                  DO BOOKKEEPING WORK ON SUBSCRIPTS
   45             IN = IN + 1
                  IO = IO + 1
C
C                 ....IS OUTPUT BUFFER FILLED YET......
C
                  IF(IN.GT.100) THEN
C
                     NRN = 100
                     DUMP NEW BUFFER ON NEW TAPE
      1              WRITE(16)NAMEN,ADDRN,SSNN,GRDYRN,
                     MAJORN,CRDHRN,GRDPTN,GRDAVN,NRN
C
C                    RESET NEW BUFFER SUBSCRIPT
C
                     IN = 1
C
                  ENDIF
C
      ENDIF
C
C         ......IS OLD BUFFER DEPLETED YET
C
   50 IF(IO.GT.NRO) THEN
C
C             REFILL OLD BUFFER
C
      1       READ(15)NAMEO,ADDRO,SSNO,GRDYRO,MAJORO,CRDHRO,GRDPTO
              ,GRDAVO,NRO
C
C             CHECK FOR END OF FILE ON OLD TAPE
C
   55         IF(EOFCHF(15).EQ.1) THEN
C
C             HOW MANY RECORDS IN OUTPUT BUFFER
C
              NRN = IN - 1
              DUMP THESE RECORDS ON NEW TAPE AND TERMINATE
   60 1       WRITE(16)NAMEN,ADDRN,SSNN,GRDYRN,MAJORN,CRDHRN
              ,GRDPTN,GRDAVN,NRN
C
              END FILE 16
              REWIND 16
              REWIND 15
              STOP
C
          ELSE
C
              IO = 1
C
          ENDIF
C
      ENDIF
C
C.......................................................
C     PROCESS NEXT RECORD ......   REPEAT LOGIC ...........
C.......................................................
C
      GO TO 20
C
      END
```

STATEMENTS TO
TRANSFER A RECORD
TO NEW BUFFER

Figure 18.3

The Complete Purge Program

18.3 | Merging

The last file operation to be discussed is the merge operation. In the merge problem, the programmer must take a file of old data records (the Old Tape File) and a file of newly acquired data records (the Update Tape File), both files being in some known order. He is to produce from these two input files a New Tape File that will contain all the records of both input files in the proper order. In this operation, three buffer areas are needed, one for each tape file. As in the last section, the merge logic will be developed using a flowchart. The abbreviations introduced in the last section will be used in this flowchart, with these additions:

UTF = Update Tape File
UB = Update Buffer

All variable names associated with the Update Buffer will end in the letter U, and IU is the subscript to be used with that buffer.

In the programming example for which the flow diagram will be developed, the registrar has an update file of newly arrived students that he wishes to have merged with his old file. As must be the case in merge programs, it will be assumed that the Old Tape and Update Tape Files are recorded in some known order: i.e., SSN's in ascending numerical order.

Figure 18.4a shows a basic algorithm for merging. The SSN of the old file is compared with the SSN of the update file. If the old file's SSN is less, the Old Buffer's logical record is moved into the New Buffer, and the subscripts of the New and Old Buffers, IN and IO, are advanced by one. If the update file's SSN is less, the Update Buffer's logical record is moved into the New Buffer, and IN and IU are advanced by one.

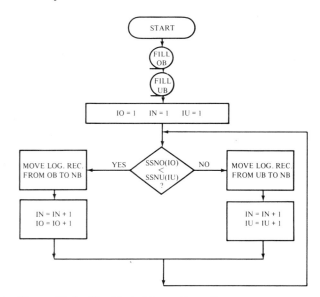

Figure 18.4a The Basic Merge Operation

In Figure 18.4b an addition is made to the basic diagram to provide the necessary logic for determining when the New Buffer is "filled to capacity." In this example as before, the desired buffer size of 100 logical records is assumed. When the New Buffer is full its contents are "dumped" onto the New Tape File. IN is reinitiated at 1 so that loading of the New Buffer will resume from the top.

In the next modification to the flowchart, shown in Figure 18.4c, exhaustion of the logical records in either the Old or the New Buffer is anticipated. When that occurs, the buffer is refilled from its tape and its subscript is reinitialized at 1.

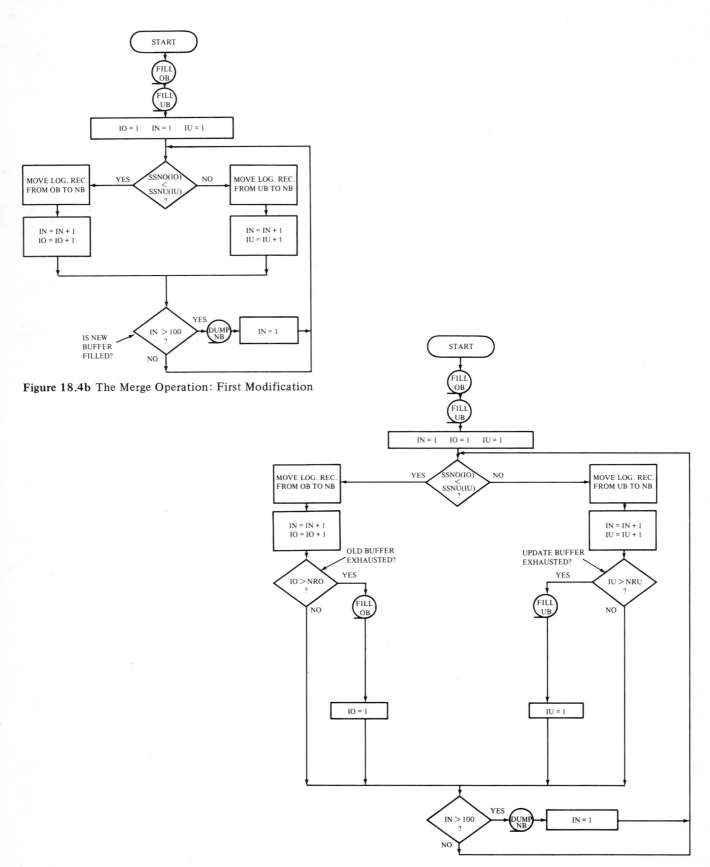

Figure 18.4b The Merge Operation: First Modification

Figure 18.4c The Merge Operation: Second Modification

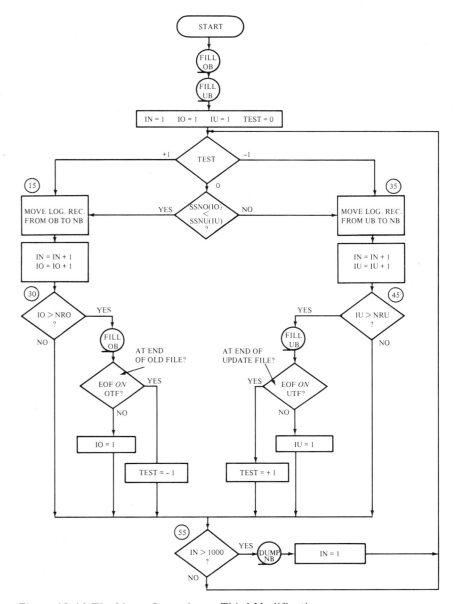

Figure 18.4d The Merge Operation — Third Modification

An addition must now be made to the diagram to provide for an occurrence of more than average complexity. If in the process of merging, an EOF mark is detected on the Update Tape File, all remaining records from the Old Tape File must be transferred directly to the New Tape File. On the other hand, if an EOF mark is first detected on the Old Tape File, all records remaining from the Update Tape File must be directly transferred. The flowchart must also be modified to avoid the comparison of SSN's, a meaningless operation under these circumstances. This problem is solved by the establishment of a variable called TEST whose value will have the following meanings:

TEST Value	Meaning
0	No EOF's found yet
+1	EOF found on UTF
−1	EOF found on OTF

The modifications to the flowchart made in Figure 18.4d introduce the variable TEST into the logic of the merge operation. At the top of the chart TEST is initialized at 0. Near the bottom of the chart TEST is given values of +1 or −1 according to whose EOF mark is first detected. Again near the top of the chart, TEST is examined to see which of its three possible values it has, and control is diverted to one of three paths as appropriate.

Figure 18.4e makes the final modification to the chart. It provides the answer to the question of what to do when, having already detected the EOF on the Update Tape File, the EOF on the Old Tape File is detected, or vice versa. When the second EOF is detected, the contents of the New Buffer and an EOF mark are written onto the New Tape File, and the program is terminated.

Figure 18.5 shows the program coding that results from the flowchart. Again, circled numbers have been added to the flowchart to make it easier to correlate diagram symbols with resulting program statements. The subroutines OBTONB and UBTONB called from the program are not included in the figure.

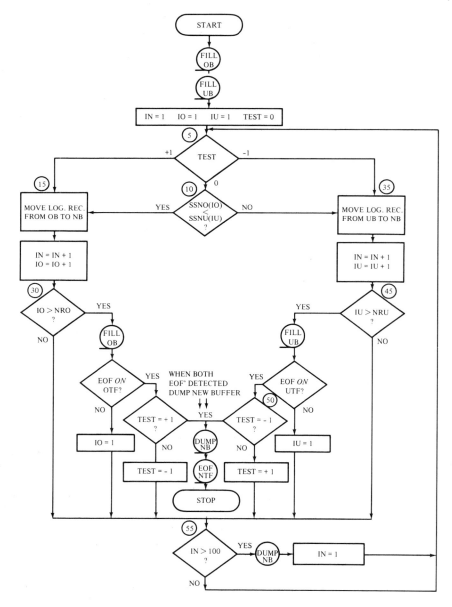

Figure 18.4e The Complete Merge Operation

Subroutine OBTONB would be the same as in the purge program of Figure 18.3. Subroutine UBTONB would be so very similar that its presentation here is felt unnecessary.

```
C................................................................
C..     PURPOSE - MERGE OLD FILE AND UPDATE FILE TO FORM NEW   ..
C..        FILE.                                               ..
C..           OLD FILE = 15 UPDATE FILE = 16 NEW FILE = 17     ..
C................................................................
C
        INTEGER NAMEO, ADDRU, ADDRO, SSNO, SSNU, SSNN
        INTEGER GRDYRO, GRDYRU, GRDYRN, TEST
C
C       .......... SET UP THREE BUFFER AREAS .....
        DIMENSION NAMEO(100,6),ADDRO(100,7),SSNO(100),GRDYRO(100)
       1,MAJORO(100),CRDHRO(100),GRDPTO(100),GRDAVO(100)
C
        DIMENSION NAMEU(100,6), ADDRU(100,7),SSNU(100),GRDYRU(100)
       1,MAJORU(100),CRDHRU(100),GRDPTU(100),GRDAVU(100)
C
        DIMENSION NAMEN(100,6),ADDRN(100,7),SSNN(100),GRDYRN(100)
       1,MAJORN(100),CRDHRN(100),GRDPTN(100),GRDAVN(100)
C
C
C       ............. GET ALL TAPES TO LOAD POINT .............
C
        REWIND 15
        REWIND 16
        REWIND 17
C
C       ...... FILL OLD BUFFER AND UPDATE BUFFER ..............
C
        READ(15)NAMEO,ADDRO,SSNO,GRDYRO,MAJORO,CRDHRO,GRDPTO,
       1        GRDAVO,NRO
C
        READ(16)NAMEU,ADDRU,SSNU,GRDYRU,MAJORU,CRDHRU,GRDPTU,
       1        GRDAVU,NRU
C
C       ..... INITIALIZATION SECTION .......
C
        IN = 1
        IO = 1
        IU = 1
C
        TEST = 0
C
C       ...... TOP OF LOOP ..... BRANCH ON TEST ........
C
    5   IF(TEST) 35, 10, 15
C
C................................................................
C........ COMPARE SOCIAL SECURITY NUMBERS ............
C................................................................
C
   10   IF(SSNO(IO).LT.SSNU(IU)) THEN
C
C           MOVE RECORD FROM OLD BUFFER TO NEW BUFFER
C
   15       DO 20 K = 1, 6
C
C               NAMEN(IN,K) = NAMEO(IO,K)
C
   20       CONTINUE
C
            DO 25 K = 1, 7
C
C               ADDRN(IN,K) = ADDRO(IO,K)
C
   25       CONTINUE
            SSNN(IN) = SSNO(IO)
            GRDYRN(IN) = GRDYRO(IO)
            MAJORN(IN) = MAJORO(IO)
            CRDHRN(IN) = CRDHRO(IO)
            GRDPTN(IN) = GRDPTO(IO)
            GRDAVN(IN) = GRDAVO(IO)
C
C           DO BOOKKEEPING ON OLD AND NEW SUBSCRIPTS
C
            IN = IN + 1
            IO = IO + 1
C
C           SEE IF OLD BUFFER DEPLETED BY THIS TRANSFER
C
   30       IF(IO.GT.NRO) THEN
C
C               REFILL OLD BUFFER
C
                READ(15)NAMEO,ADDRO,SSNO,GRDYRO,MAJORO,
       1                CRDHRO,GRDPTO,GRDAVO,NRO
C
C               .....END OF FILE DETECTED IN THIS READ
C
                IF(EOFCKF(15).EQ.1) THEN
C
C               ....YES...CHECK CONDITION OF OTHER TAPE
C
                    IF(TEST.EQ.+1) GO TO 60
C
                    TEST = -1
C
                ELSE
C
C               ......END OF FILE NOT DETECTED
C
                    IO = 1
C
                ENDIF
C
            ENDIF
C
C           SEE IF NEW BUFFER FILLED YET
C
            GO TO 55
C
C................................................................
C...... MOVEMENT OF RECORD FROM OLD BUFFER COMPLETED .....
C................................................................
```

```
C          ELSE
C
C                      MOVE RECORD FROM UPDATE BUFFER TO NEW BUFFER
C     35             DO 40 K = 1, 6
C                       NAMEN(IN,K) = NAMEU(IU,K)
C     40             CONTINUE
C
                     DO 42 K = 1, 7
C                       ADDRN(IN,K) = ADDRU(IU,K)
C     42             CONTINUE
                       SSNN(IN) = SSNU(IU)
                       GRDYRN(IN) = GRDYRU(IU)
                       MAJORN(IN) = MAJORU(IU)
                       CRDHRN(IN) = CRDHRU(IU)
                       GRDPTN(IN) = GRDPTU(IU)
                       GRDAVN(IN) = GRDAVU(IU)
C
C                      DO BOOKKEEPING WORK ON UPDATE AND NEW SUBSCRIPTS
                     IN = IN + 1
                     IU = IU + 1
C
C                      SEE IF UPDATE BUFFER DEPLETED BY THIS TRANSFER
C     45             IF(IU.GT.NRU) THEN
C
C                        REFILL UPDATE BUFFER
                       READ(16)NAMEU,ADDRU,SSNU,GRDYR,MAJORU,
     1                      CRDHRU,GRDPTU,GRDAVU,NRU
C
C                        ..... END OF FILE DETECTED ON THIS READ
                       IF(EOFCKF(16).EQ.1) THEN
C
C                        ......YES....CHECK CONDITION OF OTHER TAPE
C     50                 IF(TEST.EQ.-1) THEN
C
C                            END OF FILE DETECTED ON BOTH TAPES
C                            DUMP NEW BUFFER....STOP RUN
C
                           NRN = IN - 1
C
                           WRITE(17)NAMEN,ADDRN,SSNN,GRDYRN,
     1                        MAJORN,CRDHRN,GRDPTN,GRDAVN,NRN
C
                           END FILE 17
C
                           REWIND 15
                           REWIND 16
                           REWIND 17
C
                           STOP
C
C
C                        ELSE
C
                             TEST = +1
C
C                        ENDIF
C
                       ELSE
C                        .....END OF TAPE NOT DETECTED
C
                           IU = 1
C
                       ENDIF
C
                 ENDIF
C
C......................................................................
C..... MOVEMENT OF RECORD FROM UPDATE BUFFER IS NOW COMPLETE)
C......................................................................
C
C          ......SEE IF NEW BUFFER FILLED YET.....
     55   IF(IN.GT.100) THEN
C
               NRN = 100
               WRITE(17)NAMEN,ADDRN,SSNN,GRDYRN,MAJORN,CRDHRN,
     1             GRDPTN,GRDAVN,NRN
               IN = 1
C
          ENDIF
C
C.....................................................................
C      PROCESS NEW RECORD
C.....................................................................
C
          GO TO 5
          END
```

18.4 File Management

It would not have been incorrect to dub this chapter with the more lofty title, "File Management," for that is what it has been all about. The operations described are basic to the management of any massive file of data, regardless of the storage medium in which it is stored. The examples discussed, however, have all involved sequential files. This is one limitation of magnetic tape; it most frequently handles only sequential files. In searching for a record to print-out or update, the search routine must start at the beginning of the tape and move sequentially through the tape until it finds the record, a time-consuming process.

Magnetic discs give the programmer a considerable advantage because of their direct access capability. This becomes tremendously important in "real time" programs, such as those used by airlines to manage their flight reservations system. The feature of direct-access, disc-stored files is achieved at a considerably higher cost, however. That fact, along with the large number of applications where sequentially stored files are perfectly acceptable, accounts for the enduring popularity of the much less costly tape storage systems.

There is a final note with regard to both tape and disc files. In most examples of this chapter, programs were written with no provision for the possibility of faulty data cards. This was done solely in the interest of holding down the length of the programming examples, and not of demonstrating good programming technique. If ever the axiom, "Do as I say, not as I do!" applied, it applies in this instance. It is poor practice to assume that no errors will ever be made in the preparation of input data. It is incumbent upon the programmer to *assume* that mistakes *will* be made and to include steps in the program to cover that possibility.

Review Exercises

1. Describe an "interchange" sort. If there are 20 items to be sorted, how many passes would be needed?

2.*On each pass, must all 20 items be compared?

3. Why is it only possible to sort records that are in the buffer?

4.*In an update operation, why do we need both an old tape and a new tape?

5. Describe what is meant by the term "merging" as it applies to tape operations.

6. What is meant by the expression, "Keep the logical record intact"?

7. Describe a set of circumstances when a direct access (disc) file operation would be preferred over a tape file operation.

8.*Describe a set of circumstances under which a tape file operation would be preferred over a disc file system.

9. When is it more appropriate to store information on a file in the "edited" mode?

10.*When merging two files and an end-of-file mark is detected in one of the files, what should happen next?

11. The manager of the Atlanta 500 Speedway has been given a deck of 150 data cards containing qualifying data on all entries. Each card is organized as follows:

Card Col.	Item	Specification	Example
1–3	Car number	I3	187
4–13	Make	3A4	Oldsmobile
14–18	Qualifying speed	F5.1	162.2 (mph)

The deck is ordered by car numbers in ascending order. The capacity of the raceway cannot accommodate all entries. The track officials therefore want a listing from which they can easily identify the best qualifiers.

Write a program that will read the deck into memory, sort the data with fastest qualifier first, and print out the listing of all entries, fastest to slowest.

12. The State of Massachusetts licenses millions of automobiles annually. Assume that pertinent information regarding vehicles for one county have been stored in a tape file using a blocking factor of 500. Each logical record contains information as follows:

Field	Specification
License number	I7
Model year	I4
Make	3A4

A new law has been passed that declares that automobiles manufactured in or before 1936 are no longer to be licensed as automobiles, but instead as antiques. Write a program that reads the data off the old tape file and creates a new tape file from which all 1936 or earlier cars have been purged.

13.*The Telephone Company uses a computer to assist in the compilation of its phone book. All entries in the book are maintained as logical records in a tape file. The logical records are in alphabetical order by customer name and are blocked at 300 logical records per physical record. Each contains the following information.

Field	Specification
Customer name	5A4
Customer address	6A4
Phone number	I10

The last item in each physical record is a simple integer value, which tells how many logical records it contains. We want a program that will take the phone book tape file as input and produce from it a file containing all logical records in ascending numerical order by telephone number.

Obviously, a sort program is desired here, but a complication not heretofore encountered must now be faced: the sort is to be performed on a file containing more than one physical record. As mentioned earlier in the chapter, such a sort is accomplished by first sorting each physical record independently into the desired order, and then by performing repeated merge operations on the physical records to achieve proper ordering of the whole file.

The requirement of this problem is to write a program that will perform the sort on the phone book file so that each of its physical records is properly sorted internally.

14. This is a continuation of problem 13. To achieve sorting of the entire file across all physical records, repeated merge operations must be performed, using three tapes as outlined in the following table. As before, OTF refers to the Old (or original) Tape File. T16 refers to tape 16, and T17 refers to tape 17.

Operation	Old Buffer Input	Update Buffer Input	New Buffer Output
Initialize	1st PR from OTF	None	1st PR on T16
Merge 1	2nd PR from OTF	1st PR from T16	2 PR's on T17
Merge 2	3rd PR from OTF	1st PR from T17 2nd PR from T17	3 PR's on T16
Merge 3	4th PR from OTF	1st PR from T16 2nd PR from T16 3rd PR from T16	4 PR's on T17
Merge 4	5th PR from OTF	1st PR from T17 2nd PR from T17 3rd PR from T17 4th PR from T17	5 PR's on T16
Merge 5	6th PR from OTF	1st PR from T16 2nd PR from T16 3rd PR from T16 4th PR from T16 5th PR from T16	6 PR's on T17
Etc.	Etc.	Etc.	Etc.

Each of the individual merge operations indicated above will be substantially the same as described in the main body of the chapter. The only exception is that on each of these merges, the logic must not wait until the EOF mark is detected on the OTF to set TEST = -1, but rather it must set TEST = -1 as soon as IO>NRO. Note also that at the end of every individual merge operation, whichever tape (16 or 17) was serving as the output tape must be ENDFILE'd, and both tapes 16 and 17 must be rewound. The OTF must *not* be rewound until its EOF mark has been detected, and when that happens, the entire merge is completed.

A helpful provision of FORTRAN may be employed to ease the switching back and forth between tapes 16 and 17. FORTRAN allows the input/output device code to be an integer variable. As the program starts out, this coding might appear:

NTAPEA = 16
NTAPEB = 17

Whenever a PR is to be written on Tape 16, this statement may then be used:

WRITE (NTAPEA) NAMEN, IADDRN, NPHONN, NRN

Just prior to moving to start the next merge operation, these statements would be executed:

ITEMP   = NTAPEA
NTAPEA = NTAPEB
NTAPEB = ITEMP

Requirement: write the program to complete the sort of the phone book tape file.

19

Advanced Topics/Case Studies (Using Structured Programming)

19.1 | Processing Character Information

We have been dealing almost exclusively with the manipulation and modification of *numerical* values. It is time to cover a somewhat different set of operations, namely, those that operate on *character* information. This is not a totally new topic in that you have already used character constants to produce page headings and Hollerith messages in WRITE statements that generate elegant output. Another character constant:

"EMPTY___"

was used in the airline reservation problem to search for empty seats on an aircraft.

On several occasions we have read the name of a stock or the name and address of a customer (or company) and stored this character information in memory. It is now time to look into some of the details of how character information is processed. A statement such as:

READ(5,7) M
7   FORMAT(A4)

reserves a location in memory called M in which alphameric (character) information is stored. Because computers are only equipped to deal with numbers, each alphameric character will be represented internally by some number code. (Each character is assigned either a two-digit or three-digit number – see Figure 19.2.)

Figure 19.1 shows a data card containing the letters R, U, L and E. Assume this card is used to load memory location M. The A4 code in the FORMAT statement causes this sequence of four characters to be converted to a sequence of eight digits (assuming a two-digit code conversion) as suggested in this illustration. These numbers will be converted back to character form whenever a FORMAT statement calls for the conversion by the appearance of another A-code.

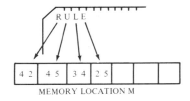

Figure 19.1 Typical Conversion Process

Each compiler uses a different character code but all are required* to have

*American National Standard Programming Language FORTRAN, X3.9–1978.

Character	Internal Code	Character	Internal Code	Character	Internal Code
Blank	00	R	42	,	51
A	21	S	43	.	52
B	22	T	44	)	53
C	23	U	45	(	54
D	24	V	46	+	55
E	25	W	47	;	56
F	26	X	50	*	57
G	27	Y	51	–	60

Figure 19.2 Typical Character Code

the following features:

(a) the number code for a blank is smaller than the code for any letter or any digit.

(b) letters in the alphabet must be in order, with the number code for the letter A the smallest.

(c) the number code for digits must be in order and precede the letters but not the blank.

This is called the **collating sequence**.

This method of number representation and the collating sequence should provide a good deal of insight as to how character manipulation is accomplished on the computer. Consider the internal representation of the following short words read from data under the content of an A3 format code.

Word	Internal Representation		
A C E	21	23	25
A C T	21	23	44
A R E	21	42	25
A T	21	44	00
B A R	22	21	42
D C	24	23	00
W E T	47	25	44

Figure 19.3 Internal Representation (A3 code)

Words beginning with an A have a smaller number code than words beginning with B. Words that are shorter than three letters are padded with blanks.

Alphabetic sorting can now be accomplished as follows: Read a group of words. Find the word with the smallest internal number code. Print it out in A-format. Look for the word with the next smallest number code. Print it out, etc. A problem in alphabetic sorting will be covered shortly.

19.2 | Simple Transfer

One of the more elementary character operations is a simple character string transfer. The data card in Figure 19.4 contains a name and address used in generating address labels for bulk mailing.

Input:

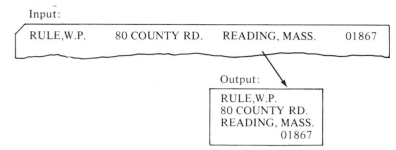

| RULE,W.P. | 80 COUNTY RD. | READING, MASS. | 01867 |

Output:

RULE,W.P.
80 COUNTY RD.
READING, MASS.
01867

Figure 19.4 Address Labels

This is typical of a string of alphameric data that is quite long, and more than one memory location will be needed to store it. One of two approaches can be used. The information on the card can be read using an 80A1 code:

```
DIMENSION INFO(80)
READ(5,7) (INFO(I),I=1,80)
7  FORMAT(80A1)
```

Assume the customer's name is in the first 20 columns of the card; followed by the street address in the next 20 columns; the town and state in the next 20 columns; followed by the zip code.

This character string can then be made to appear on four separate lines of the mailing label as follows:

```
WRITE(2,10) (INFO(I),I=1,80)
10  FORMAT(10X,20A1)
```

Each line will be indented ten spaces and contains 20 characters.

The alternate approach is to determine how many characters can be stored in a single memory location. This depends on the word size of the computer Different computers have different word sizes, but, by using a 4-character word size, you will find that your program will run on the overwhelming majority of computers. With this word size, we can pack the information more tightly by the statements:

```
DIMENSION INFO(20)
READ(5,7) (INFO(I),I=1,20)
7  FORMAT(20A4)
```

Figure 19.5 suggests how the information is being stored in the sequential elements of the array INFO (4 characters per element). The appropriate output statements would be:

```
WRITE(2,10) (INFO(I),I=1,20)
10  FORMAT(10X,5A4)
```

Usually character manipulation problems are more difficult than this and frequently require a good deal of subscript manipulation.

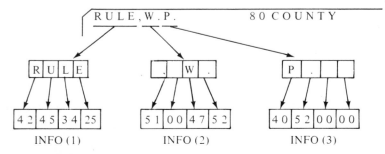

Figure 19.5 Packing Using A4 Code

Input: Output:

| BROWN, F.K.   124 POND ST. | | RULE,W.P. | FINKENAUR, R. | LANG, R.S. | BROWN, F.K. |

| **Programming Example** Four at a Time | Read the name and address from our consecutive cards, then print four address labels all at one time as suggested in the illustration. To solve this problem, we will store the character information on each card in four different arrays and then print a portion of each array to set the names four abreast. |

```
C.........................................................
C..     PURPOSE - READ ADDRESS INFORMATION FROM FOUR DATA ..
C..             CARDS AND GENERATE FOUR LABELS SIMULTAN-   ..
C..             EOUSLY.                                    ..
C.........................................................
C
C               -----IMPORTANT VARIABLES-----
C
C      --INFO1,INFO2      ARRAYS HOLDING CHARACTER INFORMATION
C      --INFO3,INFO4      ASSOCIATED WITH FOUR CARDS.      ..
C
       DIMENSION INFO1(20),INFO2(20),INFO3(20),INFO4(20)
C
C           .......READ FOUR CARDS AT A TIME......
    10 READ(5,20) INFO1, INFO2, INFO3, INFO4
    20 FORMAT(20A4)
C
C               OUTPUT ARRAYS IN PARALLEL
C
       WRITE(2,30)(INFO1(I),I=1,5),(INFO2(I),I=1,5),
      1           (INFO3(I),I=1,5),(INFO4(I),I=1,5)
       WRITE(2,30)(INFO1(I),I=6,10),(INFO2(I),I=6,10),
      1           (INFO3(I),I=6,10),(INFO4(I),I=6,10)
       WRITE(2,30)(INFO1(I),I=11,15),(INFO2(I),I=11,15),
      1           (INFO3(I),I=11,15),(INFO4(I),I=11,15),
       WRITE(2,30)(INFO1(I),I=16,20),(INFO2(I),I=16,20),
      1           (INFO3(I),I=16,20),(INFO4(I),I=16,20)
    30 FORMAT(10X,5A4,10X,5A4,10X,5A4,10X,5A4)
C
       GO TO 10
       END
```

The READ statement elects not to use subscript control on input. The mention of each array name causes the input of the whole data base (4 arrays, 20 elements in each). Four cards are read. The WRITE statements cause four labels to be printed, each separated by a 10-column margin.

19.3 | Character Strings and Logical IF's

After a memory location has been loaded with alphameric data (a character string) it becomes like any other memory location in that it contains a sequence of digits (numbers). While it is difficult to think of circumstances when these numbers would be added or subtracted in arithmetic operations, it is easy to see how we might test two such numbers to determine if one number is larger than (or equal to) another. Memory locations containing character information may appear in any logical expression — in a logical IF test for example.

The IF test operates on the digit strings in the usual way. However it would be best to store the character strings in *integer* memory locations.

The structure of a real memory location involves a mantissa portion and an exponent portion that cause difficulties when comparisons of character information are made. Further, the two strings being compared should be of the same length. It is reasonable to compare a single character to another to find which is lower in the collating sequence. Comparing a four-character string with another four-character string makes sense. Comparing a four-character string to a three-character string *does not* make sense. The 8-digit number (internal representation) of the first string will be larger than the 6-digit number of the second string (the characters involved notwithstanding).

Character Constant

The following IF tests are used to determine if a memory location holds the characters 'VET.' or 'EMPTY___'.

Character Constant

```
        IF(INFO(I).EQ.'VET.') WRITE(2,12)
   12   FORMAT(10X, 'PERSON BEING PROCESSED IS A VETERAN.')

        IF(RESERV(I,J).EQ.'EMPTY__') WRITE(2,8)
    8   FORMAT(2X, 'THIS SEAT IS EMPTY.')
```

Character Constant

The quantity 'VET.' and 'EMPTY___' are called **character constants**. The quotation marks instruct the compiler to set up a numeric constant that is the equivalent to the number code of the characters within the quotation marks.

This provides the ability to search for specific character values as information is being processed. In the next programming example we will look for the character constant VET., which indicates that the person being processed is a veteran.

| Programming Example |
| Is He a Veteran? |

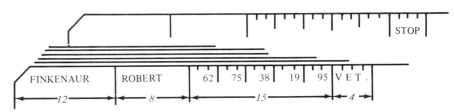

A large data deck contains information on people applying for positions in the postal service. Columns 1–12 give the applicant's last name; columns 13–20 give the first name. The next 15 columns give scores on five civil service exams. *The next 4 columns may contain the characters, VET.* Veterans are given 10 bonus points above the average score they achieved on these exams.

Process the cards shown. If the person is a veteran, add 10 points to the average and post the word VETERAN on the output sheet.

The last card in the data deck contains the letters *STOP* in the zone where the letters VET. normally appear. Use this to terminate the READ activity.

```
C..............................................................
C..    PURPOSE - EVALUATE SCORES ON CIVIL SERVICE EXAMS.  ..
C..            - PREFERENCE OF 10 POINTS GIVEN TO VETERANS. ..
C..............................................................
C
C              -----IMPORTANT VARIABLES-----
C
C      --NAME        ARRAY HOLDING APPLICANT NAME          --
C      --SCORE       ARRAY HOLDING 5 EXAM SCORES           --
C      --INFO        CHARACTER STRING - VET. = VETERAN     --
C                                     - STOP = TRAILER     --
C
       DIMENSION NAME(5), SCORE(5)
C
C      .....PROCESS FIRST EXAM TO ENTER WHILE CONSTRUCT.....
C                    (PRIME THE PUMP)
C
       READ(5,10) NAME, SCORE, INFO
   10  FORMAT(5A4, 5F3.0, A4)
C
C               LOOP ENTRY POINT
C
       WHILE (INFO.NE.'STOP') DO
C
           SUM=SCORE(1)+SCORE(2)+SCORE(3)+SCORE(4)+SCORE(5)
           AVE = SUM / 5.0
C
           IF(INFO.EQ.'VET.') THEN
C
                   ADD EXTRA POINTS
                   AVE = AVE + 10.0
                   WRITE(2,20) NAME, AVE
   20              FORMAT(2X, 5A4, 2X,'VETERAN',F8.1)
C
           ELSE
C
                   NO EXTRA POINTS
                   WRITE(2,30) NAME, AVE
   30              FORMAT(2X,5A4,9X,F8.1)
C
           ENDIF
C
               READ ADDITIONAL CARDS
           READ(5,10) NAME, SCORE, INFO
C
       ENDWHILE
C
       STOP
```

19.4 | Character Processing During Compilation

To give you some idea of how involved character processing can get, consider the problems handled by the compiler as each of your FORTRAN statements is processed. A table of key words (READ, WRITE, GO TO, WHILE, etc.) is used to detect which particular instruction is being given. Once the type is determined, each must be broken down into its component parts.

$$\underbrace{\text{WRITE} \quad \xleftarrow{\quad} (2,12) \xrightarrow{\quad} A,B,C}_{\text{component parts}}$$

This may involve searching for an open and a closed parenthesis and then extracting the two numbers inside.

The next programming examples suggest some simple operations that might be involved.

Programming Example
Where Does It End?

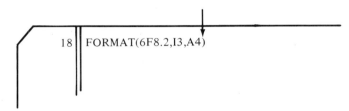

18 | FORMAT(6F8.2,I3,A4)

In the process of compiling a FORTRAN statement, assume that it is necessary to read a statement card (as if it was a data card) and determine in what column the statement ends. We can do this by storing the information on the card using an 80A1 code. We can then scan the card *backwards* until a non-blank character is detected.

```
C.....................................................
C..    PURPOSE - FIND IN WHAT COLUMN A STATEMENT ENDS.   ..
C.....................................................
C
C             -----IMPORTANT VARIABLES-----
C
C      --INPUT       ARRAY OF INPUT CHARACTERS (80A1)      ..
C      --NSIZE       OUTPUT VALUE - WHERE STATEMENT ENDS   ..
C      --BLANK       CHARACTER CONSTANT HOLDING A BLANK    ..
C
       DIMENSION INPUT (80)
       INTEGER BLANK
C
       DATA BLANK /1H /
C
C          READ 80 CHARACTERS FROM A CARD
C
       READ(5,10) INPUT
   10  FORMAT(80A1)
C
C          SEARCH STRING BACKWARDS
C
       DO 20 I = 80, 1, -1
C
          IF(INPUT(I).NE.BLANK) THEN
C
             NSIZE = I
             WRITE(2,15) NSIZE
   15        FORMAT(2X,'THIS STATEMENT ENDS IN COLUMN ',I3)
             STOP
C
          ENDIF
C
   20  CONTINUE
C
C          IF THIS DO LOOP SATISFIED CARD MUST HAVE BEEN BLANK
C
       WRITE(2,30)
   30  FORMAT(1X,'THE CARD WAS BLANK')
C
       STOP
       END
```

The data statement loads memory location BLANK with the number code of a blank. The structured DO allows reverse subscript control from 80 backwards. The first time a non-blank element of the array INPUT is detected, a WRITE statement displays the location of the first non-blank character and the STOP-statement (inside the loop) is executed. If no interruption of this loop takes place, the card must be blank. An appropriate output message is given and the program stops.

Blank characters embedded in a FORTRAN statement provide no useful information to the compiler.* These blanks are usually removed to facilitate a more compact storage of the statement. This involves examining each column of the statement card and transferring to memory only those non-blank characters detected.

Programming Example	Write a subroutine called CRUNCH that will receive the array called INPUT and

Programming Example
Removing All Blanks

Write a subroutine called CRUNCH that will receive the array called INPUT and its size (NSIZE). Remove all blanks from the string, forming an array called OUT. Return the size of OUT as the argument NOUT.

```
      SUBROUTINE CRUNCH (INPUT,NSIZE,OUTPUT)
C..........................................................
C..  PURPOSE - REPRODUCE INFORMATION FROM STATEMENT CARDS ..
C..            IN A HIGHLY CONDENSED FORM.               ..
C..........................................................
C
C               -----IMPORTANT VARIABLES-----
C
C     --INPUT       ARRAY OF INPUT CHARACTERS (80A1)      --
C     --NSIZE       NUMBER OF ACTIVE ELEMENTS IN ARRAY INPUT--
C     --OUTPUT      ARRAY OF CONDENSED CHARACTERS         --
C     --NOUT        NUMBER OF ELEMENTS IN ARRAY OUTPUT    --
C
      INTEGER INPUT(1), OUTPUT(1),BLANK
      DATA BLANK /1H /
C
C         INITIALIZE SUBSCRIPT OF OUTPUT ARRAY
C
      NOUT = 1
C
C     .....SEARCH AND TRANSFER IF NON-BLANK CHARACTER......
C
      DO 10 I = 1, NSIZE
C
         IF(INPUT(I).NE.BLANK) THEN
C
C               MOVE ELEMENT INTO OUTPUT ARRAY
C
            OUTPUT(NOUT) = INPUT(I)
C               ADVANCE SUBSCRIPT OF OUTPUT ARRAY
C
            NOUT = NOUT + 1
C
         ENDIF
C
   10 CONTINUE
C
C         .....PROCESSING COMPLETE - RESET ADVANCED SUBSCRIPT
C
      NOUT = NOUT - 1
C
      RETURN
      END
```

19.5 Alphabetic Sort

A more practical application of character manipulation is the alphabetic sorting of a list of names. This operation occurs so frequently that many advanced algorithms have been developed to accomplish the sort in an efficient, high-speed fashion. The method presented in this section is not very efficient, but it is relatively easy to follow.

We will accomplish the sort in two parts. The first part will deal with a list of names that is fixed in size (40 names) and will ask that the name with the largest number code be found and moved to the bottom of the list. For the list of names used, the name ZOTOS is the largest. It is moved from position 13 in the list to position 40.

Once the programming to accomplish this is complete, we will generalize the code to:
1. work with a list of variable size (NSIZE), and
2. employ a WHILE-DO loop structure to repeat the code until the list is fully sorted.

Programming Example
Sort: First Pass

A data deck contains the names of 40 students not in alphabetic order. These names are punched ten per card. For simplicity's sake, assume that the word

*In some languages a blank is used as a **delimeter**, which tells where something ends. FORTRAN does not make use of a blank as a delimiter.

size of the computer will accept 8 characters per word. Sort these names as follows:

Part A

Read the data deck and print the names, 10 per line.

CASWELL	GILMORE	OSMOND	...	KING	RULE
EPSTEIN	CLIFFORD	ZOTOS	...	RYDER	MACKEY
PENNEY	STUART	WALKER	...	VAUGHN	MARTIN
COHEN	SCHMIDT	BAILEY	...	FISHER	YOUNG

This step is used to allow the programmer to examine the original configuration of the data.

Part B

Find the name whose numerical equivalent is the largest. Print this name and its position in the array.

THE LARGEST NAME IS ZOTOS . IT IS IN POSITION 13 .

This step verifies that the largest name has been detected correctly.

Part C

Move this "largest name" to the end of the array, but be careful not to lose the name already in position 40.

Republish the array to see if the swap activity required above has been effective.

CASWELL	GILMORE	OSMOND	...	KING	RULE
EPSTEIN	CLIFFORD	YOUNG	...	RYDER	MACKEY
PENNEY	STUART	WALKER	...	VAUGHN	MARTIN
COHEN	SCHMIDT	BAILEY	...	FISHER	ZOTOS

```
C.............................................................
C..   PURPOSE - THIS PROGRAM WILL FIND THE LARGEST NAME IN  ..
C..             AN UNSORTED LIST OF 40 NAMES AND MOVE THAT  ..
C..             NAME TO THE BOTTOM OF THE LIST.             ..
C.............................................................
C
C              -----IMPORTANT VARIABLES-----
C
C      --NAME        VECTOR OF 40 STUDENT NAMES            --
C      --LARGE       LARGEST OF THE 40 NAMES               --
C      --LOC         LOCATION (SUBSCRIPT) OF LARGEST NAME  --
C
      DIMENSION NAME (40)
C
C         READ NAMES......PRINT FOR VERIFICATION
C
      READ(5,10)(NAME(I),I=1,40)
   10 FORMAT(10A8)
C
      WRITE(2,20)(NAME(I),I=1,40)
   20 FORMAT(10(4X,A8))
C
C         ASSUME FIRST NAME IS THE LARGEST
C
      LARGE = NAME(1)
      LOC = 1
C
C      ........PROCESS REMAINING NAMES........
C
      DO 30 I = 2, 40
C
C              IS THIS NAME LARGER
C
         IF(NAME(I).GT.LARGE) THEN
C
            LARGE = NAME(I)
            LOC = I
C
         ENDIF
C
   30 CONTINUE
C
C         ...PART B PRINT OUT...
C
      WRITE(2,40) LARGE, LOC
   40 FORMAT(///,10X,'THE LARGEST NAME IS',A8,
     1         'ITS POSITION IS ',I2)
C
C      ........SWAP NAMES,BE CAREFUL NOT TO LOSE THE LAST NAME...
C
      ICOPY = NAME(40)
      NAME(40) = LARGE
      NAME(LOC) = ICOPY
C
C      ........VERIFY THAT SWAP HAS TAKEN PLACE........
C
      WRITE(2,20)(NAME(I),I=1,40)
C
      STOP
      END
```

Part D

The program just completed can now be generalized. Wherever the specific value 40 appears, we will substitute the variable NSIZE. NSIZE tells how many elements of the input array are as yet unsorted. We make the statement:

NSIZE = 40

to start the program, but will reduce NSIZE by 1 each time a name is moved to the bottom of the list. A WHILE-DO construct is used to maintain looping until the list is totally sorted.

```
C...................................................................
C..   PURPOSE     THIS PROGRAM REPEATS THE LOGIC OF THE PRE-   ..
C..               VIOUS EXAMPLE PROBLEM TO COMPLETELY SORT     ..
C..               THE LIST OF 40 NAMES.                        ..
C...................................................................
C
C                    -----IMPORTANT VARIABLES-----
C
C        --NSIZE       SIZE OF LIST AS YET UNSORTED              --
C
C
C        DIMENSION NAME(40)
C
C        .....READ NAMES.....PRINT FOR VERIFICATION....
C
        READ(5,10)(NAME(I),I=1,40)
     10 FORMAT(10A8)
C
        WRITE(2,20)(NAME(I),I=1,40)
     20 FORMAT(10(4X,A8))
C
        NSIZE = 40
C
        WHILE (NSIZE.GT.1) DO
C
C              ASSUME FIRST NAME THE LARGEST
C
          LARGE = NAME(1)
          LOC = 1
C
C          .....PROCESS REMAINING NAMES....
C
            DO 30 I = 1, NSIZE
C
                IF(NAME(I).GT.LARGE) THEN
C
                    LARGE = NAME(I)
                    LOC = I
C
                ENDIF
     30     CONTINUE
C
C          ...........START SWAP ACTIVITY............
C
          ICOPY = NAME(NSIZE)
          NAME(NSIZE) = LARGE
          NAME(LOC) = ICOPY
C
C          ..............DECREASE SIZE OF UNSORTED LIST............
C
          NSIZE = NSIZE - 1
C
        ENDWHILE
C
C
C            PRINT OUT SORTED LIST
C
        WRITE(2,20) (NAME(I),I=1,40)
C
        STOP
        END
```

One substantial danger exists when storing a character string. It has to do with the fact that the left-most binary digit (bit) of a memory location is usually used to indicate if a memory location contains a positive or negative number. This is called the **sign bit** (zero indicates plus, one indicates minus.)

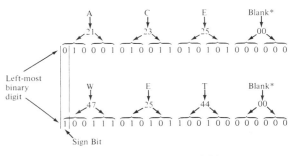

Figure 19.6 Binary Representation of Characters

*Unused portions of the word are filled with blanks.

19.6 | R-Code

When the two-digit number code for A is converted to binary and stored in memory, the left-most bit is a *zero*. When the two-digit number code for W is converted and stored, the left-most digit is a *one*. The memory location containing WET will be considered negative, while the location containing ACE is interpreted as positive.

This difficulty is easily avoided by using an alternate form of the A-format code, namely an R-format code of the form:

Rw

where R indicates alphameric data to be stored right-justified and w is the field width as before. This code results in a blank being stored in the left-most position (and therefore 0 in the left-most bit) if the programmer will limit the storage of alphameric characters to at least one fewer than the maximum number specified for his computer (3 in this case.)

19.7 Object Time Format

The use of conventional FORMAT statements forces a rigid demand on the form of the input data. It can appear in one and only one form: the form described by that FORMAT statement. This means that the data deck must be specifically tailored to match exactly the FORMAT description in the main program. This is not always convenient. Considerable flexibility in the appearance of the input data can be achieved if the FORMAT description of the data is allowed to appear as part of the *data deck*. This scheme is referred to as **object time format** and is described below.

A data card is shown in Figure 19.7.

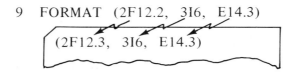

9   FORMAT (2F12.2, 3I6, E14.3)

(2F12.3, 3I6, E14.3)

Figure 19.7 Format Code on Data Cards

Notice that it contains the coded information usually associated with a FORMAT statement that would normally appear in the main program. This information can be read from the data card and stored as alphameric data by statements such as

        READ (5,7) (M(I), I = 1, 5)
    7   FORMAT (5A4)

The array (M) now holds format information, but this information has been read in at objective time.

Most compilers will now allow the array name containing the FORMAT codes (M, for example) to replace the FORMAT statement number that normally appears in a READ/WRITE statement, such as

        WRITE (2, M) X, Y, I, J, K, Z

Using this type of statement, it is possible to write a more general program in that the format of the data deck is not predefined (by statements in the main program,) but may be defined on each application of the program (by cards in the data deck.)

19.8 Evaluation of an Integral

The remainder of this chapter will show several programming examples that fall in the area called "numerical analysis." They attempt to show how the computer is used to solve relatively high level mathematical problems. These examples will provide an opportunity to demonstrate some of the new structured programming constructs we have just presented.

Programming Example
Evaluate an Integral
Write a program to evaluate the integral shown:

$$\int_{x=1}^{x=10} (x^2 + 2x + 3)dx$$

The value of this integral is first found by what is called a trapezoidal approximation, outlined below. We will then use a slightly more advanced method — Simpson's Rule — to gain a better approximation of the integral.

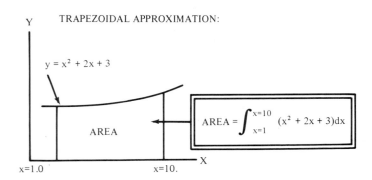

Step 1: Divide the total area under the curve into a number of small differential areas (thin strips, 0.1 inches wide).

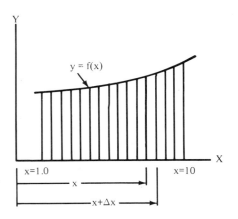

Step 2: The area of each strip can be approximated by the area of a trapezoid whose geometry is as shown in the accompanying figure. The values of Y and Y+ΔY are obtained by substituting X and X+ΔX respectively into a given equation.

$$\text{WIDTH} = \Delta X = 0.1$$
$$\text{AVERAGE HEIGHT} = \frac{(y + \Delta y) + (y)}{2}$$

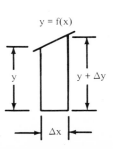

Step 3: Compute the area of each differential strip.

$$\Delta A = \frac{[(y + \Delta y) + y]}{2}\Delta X$$

Differential
Area

Area of
Trapezoid

Step 4: Determine the sum of these differential areas.

$$AREA = \Sigma \Delta A = \int_{x=1}^{x=10}(x^2 + 2x + 3)dx$$

The graphical depiction of what's being accomplished by this solution is shown in Figure 19.8. This is called the **trapezoidal method** because each of the differential areas is being evaluated as if it was a trapezoid.

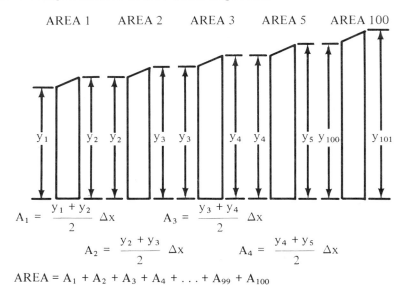

AREA 1   AREA 2   AREA 3   AREA 5   AREA 100

$$A_1 = \frac{y_1 + y_2}{2}\Delta x \qquad A_3 = \frac{y_3 + y_4}{2}\Delta x$$

$$A_2 = \frac{y_2 + y_3}{2}\Delta x \qquad A_4 = \frac{y_4 + y_5}{2}\Delta x$$

$$AREA = A_1 + A_2 + A_3 + A_4 + \ldots + A_{99} + A_{100}$$

$$EQ.\ 19.1 \quad AREA = \frac{1}{2}(y_1 + 2y_2 + 2y_3 + 2y_4 + 2y_5 + \ldots + 2y_{99} + 2y_{101} + y_{101})\ \Delta X$$

Figure 19.8 How Small Areas are Formed

```
C.........................................................
C..    PURPOSE - DETERMINE THE AREA UNDER A CURVE (INTEGRATE)..
C..              BY THE CLASSICAL TRAPEZOICAL APPROXIMATION  ..
C..              METHOD.                                     ..
C.........................................................
C
C                   -----IMPORTANT VARIABLES-----
C
C      --AREA        VALUE OF ACCUMULATED AREA            --
C      --X           VALUE OF INDEPENDENT VARIABLE        --
C      --YPLUS       VALUE OF Y AT X = X + DELTX          --
C------------------------------------------------------------
C
C          ....INITIALIZATION SECTION.....
C
       DATA AREA, DELTX / 0.0, 0.1 /
C
C          USE INDEX OF DO LOOP TO CONTROL X
C
       DO 10 X = 1.0, 10.0, 0.1
C
          Y = X**2 + 2.0*X + 3.0
          YPLUS = (X+DELTX)**2 + 2.0*(X+DELTX) + 3.0
          AREA = AREA + DELTX * (YPLUS + Y) / 2.0
C
    10 CONTINUE
C
       WRITE(2,20)
    20 FORMAT(1X,F20.4)
C
       STOP
       END
```

Improving the Program

Three major improvements should be made to this program to make it at all acceptable.

1. Reference to a specific equation will be removed. The value of the equation will be obtained by invoking a user-supplied function subprogram.
2. The limits of integration are made variable (read from a data card.)

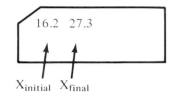

$X_{initial}$ X_{final}

3. A more accurate approximation technique will be used.

In the previous program the equation being integrated was approximated by a series of straight lines (first order equations.) If the curve (equation) is of second or higher order, an inaccuracy occurs as suggested in Figure 19.9. This error can be reduced by connecting any two points with a second order curve (a parabola) instead of a straight line. This reduces the approximation error and involves the concept of using a point upstream or downstream of the specific differential area to define the correct parabola to use. This is suggested in Figure 19.10 and when worked out mathematically requires the evaluation of an equation only slightly more complicated than the one used before (Eq 19.1 — Figure 19.8.)

$$\text{Eq 19.2: AREA} = \frac{\Delta X}{3}(Y_1 + 4Y_2 + 2Y_3 + 4Y_4 + \ldots$$
$$\ldots + 2Y_{99} + 4Y_{100} + Y_{101})$$

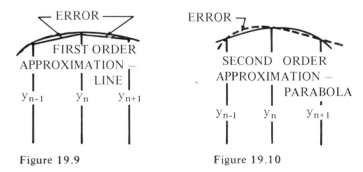

Figure 19.9   Figure 19.10

This method of approximation is called **Simpson's Rule.**

The procedure is:

(a) READ the data card defining the limits of integration $X_{initial}$ and X_{final}.
(b) Divide this interval into 100 strips of equal width (ΔX).
(c) Define an array called Y consisting of 101 elements by invoking the user-supplied program 101 times.
(d) Use this array as directed by equation 19.2 to determine the desired AREA (integral).

One of the complications in equation 19.2 is that all the even subscripted elements of Y should be multiplied by 4 and all the odd terms (except the first and last) should be multiplied by 2.

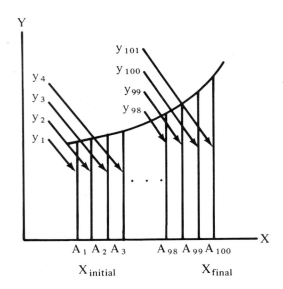

Figure 19.11 Dividing the Interval

```
C..................................................................
C.. PURPOSE - WRITE A MORE GENERAL INTEGRATION PROGRAM ..
C..          USING SIMPSON'S RULE OF APPROXIMATION.       ..
C..................................................................
C
C
C                -----IMPORTANT VARIABLES-----
C
C    --XINTL       INITIAL LIMIT OF INTEGRATION           --
C    --XFINL       FINAL LIMIT OF INTEGRATION             --
C    --DELTX       WIDTH OF DIFFERENTIAL AREAS            --
C    --EQ          USER SUPPLIED (EXTERNAL) FUNCTION      --
C                  SUBPROGRAM DEFINING THE FUNCTION.      --
C    --Y           ARRAY OF 101 ELEMENTS REPRESENTING THE --
C    --            EQUATION IN DIGITAL FORM.              --
C    --ODD         ACCUMULATOR OF MAJORITY OF ODD TERMS   --
C    --EVEN        ACCUMULATOR OF MAJORITY OF EVEN TERMS  --
C    --AREA        VALUE OF INTEGRAL
C
      DIMENSION Y(101)
C
      EXTERNAL EQ
C
C            DETERMINE LIMITS OF INTEGRATION
C
      READ(5,10) XINTL, XFINL
   10 FORMAT(2F10.2)
C
C            DEFINE ARRAY OF Y VALUES
C
      DELTX = (XFINL - XINTL) / 100.0
      X = XINTL
C
      DO 20 I = 1, 101
C
          Y(I) = EQ(X)
          X = X + DELTX
C
   20 CONTINUE
C
C        ACCUMULATE THE MAJORITY OF EVEN SUBSCRIPTED Y ELEMENTS
C
      EVEN = 0.0
C
      DO 30 I = 2, 100, 2
C
          EVEN = EVEN + Y(I)
C
   30 CONTINUE
C
C
C
C        ACCUMULATE THE MAJORITY OF ODD SUBSCRIPTED Y ELEMENTS
C
      ODD = 0.0
C
      DO 40 I = 3, 99, 2
C
          ODD = ODD + Y(I)
C
   40 CONTINUE
C
C            ADD IN THE FIRST AND LAST TERMS
C            (USE PROPER WEIGHTING FACTORS)
C
      AREA = DELTX/3.0*(Y(1)+4.0*EVEN+2.0*ODD+Y(101))
C
      WRITE(2,50) AREA
   50 FORMAT(1X,E20.5)
C
      STOP
      END
C
C
C..................................................................
C.. PURPOSE - USER SUPPLIED SUBPROGRAM DEFINING THE       ..
C..           EQUATION THAT IS TO BE INTEGRATED.          ..
C..................................................................
C
      FUNCTION EQ(X)
C
      EQ = X**2 + 2.0*X + 3.0
C
      RETURN
      END
```

Each equation to be integrated is placed inside the FUNCTION subprogram (supplied by the user) as suggested below.

19.9 | Simulation: Bouncing Ball

There is a large area of application in which the computer is made to simulate some complex model or situation. As an example of this usage, assume we are asked to determine under what conditions a ball fired into the chamber shown in Figure 19.12 will fall through the hole in the floor positioned as shown. A ball enters a chamber with an initial velocity V_0 = 10.0 ft./sec. acting at angle θ = 45°.

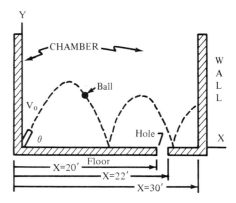

Figure 19.12 Bouncing Ball Problem

Interesting parts of this solution will be to determine the equation of motion of the ball; to determine when the ball is about to bounce off the floor; and to either redirect the motion of the ball if it doesn't hit the hole or signal a successful traverse if the ball does reach the hole.

Equations of Motion for Parts 1 and 2

Displacement:

$$\text{in X direction } X = V_{X_0} \cdot t \text{ (constant velocity)}$$
$$\text{in Y direction } Y = V_{Y_0} \cdot t - \frac{1}{2}gt^2 \text{ (constant acceleration)}$$

$$\text{where: } V_{X_0} = V_0 \cos \theta$$
$$V_{Y_0} = V_0 \sin \theta$$

Part 1:

Write a program to determine the X and Y coordinates of the ball at time increments of 0.01 seconds until the ball impacts with the floor for the first time.

First the initial velocity and entry angle of the ball (VZERO and ANGLE) are read from data. Then the X and Y components of this velocity are computed. All that remains now is to evaluate the displacement equation over and over again

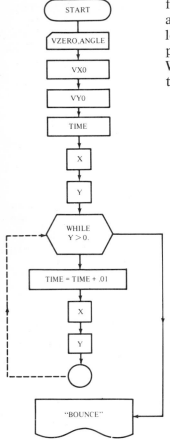

for various values of time. A memory location called TIME is created and given an initial value of 0.01. The first X and Y location values are computed. Memory location TIME is indexed by 0.01 and another X and Y value computed. This process continues as long as the ball is still in the air (Y has a positive value). When Y becomes zero or negative, looping is interrupted and control passes to the WRITE statements that give the time and location of this first bounce.

```
C.....................................................
C::..  PURPOSE - SIMULATE THE MOTION OF A BOUNCING BALL.  ..::
C.....................................................
C
C               -----IMPORTANT VARIABLES-----
C
C      --VZERO      INITIAL VELOCITY OF THE BALL          --
C      --ANGLE      ANGLE OF ENTRY                        --
C      --VXO        X COMPONENT OF INITIAL VELOCITY       --
C      --X          X POSITION OF THE BALL                --
C      --VYO        Y COMPONENT OF INITIAL VELOCITY       --
C      --Y          Y POSITION OF THE BALL                --
C
C      --TIME       TIME CLOCK                            --
C
C           DETERMINE X AND Y VELOCITY COMPONENTS
C
       READ(5,10) VZERO, ANGLE
   10  FORMAT(2F10.2)
C
       VXO = VZERO * COS(ANGLE / 57.3)
       VYO = VZERO * SIN(ANGLE / 57.3)
C
C          SET TIME CLOCK....COMPUTE INITIAL X AND Y VALUES
C
       TIME = 0.01
C
       X = VXO * TIME
       Y = VYO * TIME - 32.2 / 2.0 * TIME ** 2
C
C          ....ESTABLISH COMPUTATIONAL LOOP.....
C
       WHILE (Y.GT.0.0) DO
C
           TIME = TIME + 0.01
           X = VXO * TIME
           Y = VYO * TIME - 32.2 / 2.0 * TIME ** 2
C
       ENDWHILE
C
C          ....BALL HAS HIT THE FLOOR......
C
       WRITE(2,20) TIME
   20  FORMAT(2X,'BALL HAS HIT THE FLOOR.   TIME =',F6.2)
C
       WRITE(2,30) X, Y
   30  FORMAT(2X,'LOCATION IS X = ',F8.2,'Y = ',F8.2)
C
C
       STOP
       END
```

Part 2:

Expand the program to determine if the ball falls through the hole in the floor — assume an infinitely small ball. To improve accuracy, index time at a *slower* rate (0.001 sec.) when the ball is close to impact (Y≤1 ft.).

Two additional requirements have been imposed by the Part 2 solution. To obtain a more accurate solution when impact is imminent, the time clock (TIME) should be incremented at a slower rate, 0.001 seconds, when the ball is less than one foot off the floor. Therefore, these statements will be incorporated into the solution.

```
        IF(Y.GT.1.0) THEN
            TIME = TIME + 0.01
        ELSE
            TIME = TIME + 0.001
        ENDIF
```

We must also detect if the ball has by chance fallen into the hole.

```
        IF(X.GE.20.0.AND.X.LE.22.0) THEN
            WRITE(2,40)
   40       FORMAT(2X"BALL WENT IN THE HOLE")
        ELSE
            WRITE(2,41)
   41       FORMAT(2X, "JUST MAKING A BOUNCE")
        ENDIF
```

The flowchart and FORTRAN code are updated to incorporate these features.

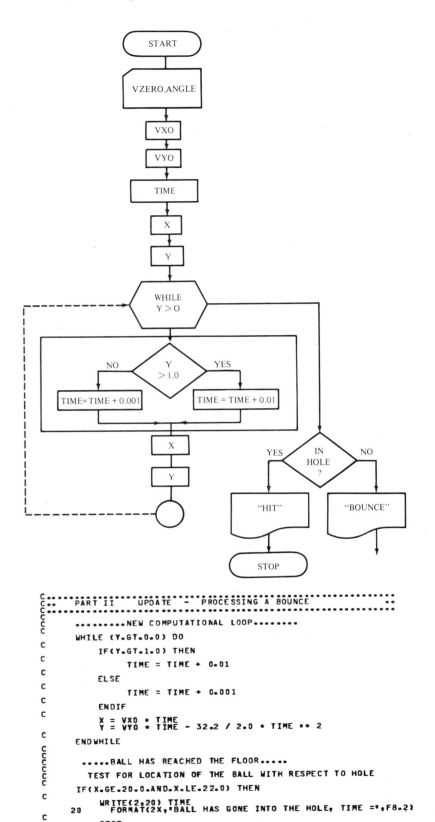

```
C.................................................................
C..     PART II    UPDATE  -   PROCESSING A BOUNCE           ..
C.................................................................
C
C        ........NEW COMPUTATIONAL LOOP........
C
        WHILE (Y.GT.0.0) DO
C
            IF(Y.GT.1.0) THEN
C
                    TIME = TIME + 0.01
C
            ELSE
C
                    TIME = TIME + 0.001
C
            ENDIF
            X = VXO * TIME
            Y = VYO * TIME - 32.2 / 2.0 * TIME ** 2
C
        ENDWHILE
C
C
C        .....BALL HAS REACHED THE FLOOR.....
C
C        TEST FOR LOCATION OF THE BALL WITH RESPECT TO HOLE
C
        IF(X.GE.20.0.AND.X.LE.22.0) THEN
C
            WRITE(2,20) TIME
    20      FORMAT(2X,'BALL HAS GONE INTO THE HOLE, TIME =',F8.2)
C
            STOP
C
        ELSE
C
            WRITE(2,21) TIME, X, Y
    21      FORMAT(2X,'BALL BOUNCED. TIME = ',F8.2,
    1           'LOCATION X=',F8.2,' Y= ',F8.2)
C
        ENDIF
C
        STOP
        END
```

Part 3:

If the ball does not pass through the hole, our program must account for a bounce (impact). The major adjustments are as follows:

(a) If the floor is assumed to be frictionless, the horizontal velocity is unaffected by impact. Displacement computations continue as before.

(b) The vertical velocity component must be reversed and decreased in magnitude by a value called the **coefficient of restitution.**

This part of the solution demonstrates a simple but very important method of analysis. It's called the **method of superposition.** The complex motion of this ball can be treated as one simple motion superimposed on another simple motion. The X motion is one of constant velocity. The computation of this motion remains the same throughout the problem.

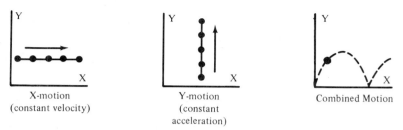

| X-motion | Y-motion | Combined Motion |
| (constant velocity) | (constant acceleration) | |

Figure 19.13 Analysis of Motion

We can now concentrate on the remaining more-complex Y motion. At each impact or bounce we must:

(a) compute the Y component of velocity prior to impact.

$$V_y = V_{y_0} - at$$

(b) change the sign (direction) of the velocity and decrease its magnitude (by 85% – coefficient of restitution.)

$$V_{y_0} = -.85 \cdot V_y$$

(c) set a new time clock (TNEW) back to zero on each impact (as if a new problem was starting all over again).

$$TNEW = 0.0$$

The statements to accomplish this will be:

```
C . . . . . . . . . . RECOMPUTE Y VELOCITY DUE TO IMPACT . . . . . .
C                             VELOCITY JUST PRIOR TO IMPACT
      VY = VYO – 32.2 * TNEW
C                             REVERSE AND DIMINISH VELOCITY
      VYO = –0.85*VY
C                             RESET TIME CLOCK
      TNEW = 0.0
```

These statements will be executed each time a bounce occurs. This allows for a continuous solution until the ball hits the far wall.

The problem must now use two time clocks. TIME is used for the X-motion calculations and runs continuously. TNEW is for the Y-motion calculations and is reset to zero each time a bounce takes place.

The complete program is now presented.

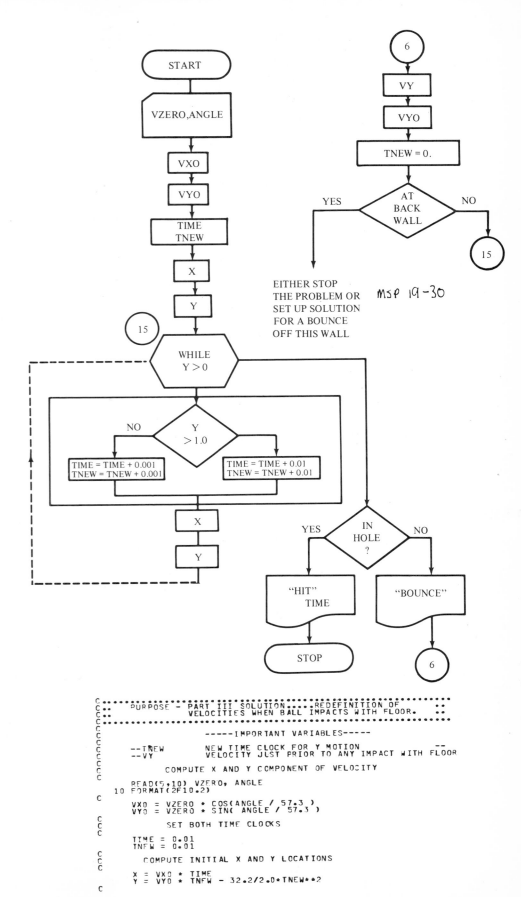

EITHER STOP
THE PROBLEM OR
SET UP SOLUTION
FOR A BOUNCE
OFF THIS WALL

MSP 19-30

```
C.............................................................
C..    PURPOSE - PART III SOLUTION.....REDEFINITION OF       ..
C..              VELOCITIES WHEN BALL IMPACTS WITH FLOOR.    ..
C.............................................................
C
C                   -----IMPORTANT VARIABLES-----
C
C
C    --TNEW           NEW TIME CLOCK FOR Y MOTION             --
C    --VY             VELOCITY JUST PRIOR TO ANY IMPACT WITH FLOOR
C
C             COMPUTE X AND Y COMPONENT OF VELOCITY
C
      READ(5,10) VZERO, ANGLE
   10 FORMAT(2F10.2)
C
      VXO = VZERO * COS(ANGLE / 57.3 )
      VYO = VZERO * SIN( ANGLE / 57.3 )
C
C             SET BOTH TIME CLOCKS
C
      TIME = 0.01
      TNEW = 0.01
C
C       COMPUTE INITIAL X AND Y LOCATIONS
C
      X = VXO * TIME
      Y = VYO * TNEW - 32.2/2.0*TNEW**2
C
```

```
C
C       .......SET UP COMPUTATIONAL LOOP........
C
     15 WHILE (Y.GT.0.0) DO
C
C          NEAR IMPACT
C
           IF(Y.GT.1.0) THEN
               TIME = TIME + 0.01
               TNEW = TNEW + 0.01
           ELSE
               TIME = TIME + 0.001
               TNEW = TNEW + 0.001
           ENDIF
C
C          .....COMPUTE BALL LOCATION.....
C
           X = VX0 * TIME
           Y = VY0 * TNEW - 32.2/2.0*TNEW**2
C
       ENDWHILE
C
C      .......BALL HAS REACHED THE FLOOR.......
C
       IF(X.GE.20.0.AND.X.LE.22.0) THEN
           WRITE(2,20) TIME
     20    FORMAT(2X,'BALL HAS GONE INTO THE HOLE, TOME =',F8.2)
C
           STOP
C
       ELSE
C
C          .......RECOMPUTE Y MOTION DUE TO IMPACT........
C              VELOCITY JUST PRIOR TO IMPACT
C
           VY = VY0 - 32.2 * TNEW
C
C              REVERSE AND DIMINISH VELOCITY
C
           VY0 =   0.85 * VY
C
C          RESET TIME CLOCK FOR Y MOTION
C
           TNEW = 0.0
C
C          .....HAS BALL REACHED THE FAR WALL YET.........
C
           IF(X.GT.30.0) THEN
               WRITE(2,30) TIME
     30        FORMAT(2X,'BALL AT BACK WALL. TIME =',F8.2)
C
               STOP
C
           ELSE
C
               GO TO 15
C
               ENDIF
C
       ENDIF
C
       STOP
       END
```

19.10

Solving Simultaneous Equations

The solution of simultaneous equations is another example of numerical methods. It provides a good opportunity to review operations dealing with two-dimensional arrays.

We will start by representing the equations in the following way:

$$
\left.
\begin{aligned}
a_{11}x_1 + a_{12}x_2 + a_{13}x_3 + \cdots + a_{1n}x_n &= c_1 \\
a_{21}x_1 + a_{22}x_2 + a_{23}x_3 + \cdots + a_{2n}x_n &= c_2 \\
a_{31}x_1 + a_{32}x_2 + a_{33}x_3 + \cdots + a_{3n}x_n &= c_3 \\
\cdots\cdots\cdots\cdots\cdots\cdots\cdots\cdots\cdots\cdots\cdots \\
a_{n1}x_1 + a_{n2}x_2 + a_{n3}x_3 + \cdots + a_{nn}x_n &= c_n
\end{aligned}
\right\} \text{EQ. 19.3}
$$

General Form of Equations

Coefficients preceding the terms in (X) were stored as a two-dimensional array called A. The right hand coefficients are stored as a one-dimensional array called C.

$$
[A] = \begin{bmatrix}
a_{11} & a_{12} & a_{13} & \cdots & a_{1n} \\
a_{21} & a_{22} & a_{23} & \cdots & a_{2n} \\
a_{31} & a_{32} & a_{33} & \cdots & a_{3n} \\
\cdots & \cdots & \cdots & \cdots & \cdots \\
a_{n1} & a_{n2} & a_{n3} & \cdots & a_{nn}
\end{bmatrix}
\qquad
[C] = \begin{bmatrix}
c_1 \\
c_2 \\
c_3 \\
\cdot \\
c_n
\end{bmatrix}
$$

The method of solving these equations will be easier to follow if we deal with a specific set of equations, namely the set introduced in Chapter 11.

$$\text{EQ. 1} \quad 9.0X_1 + 6.5X_2 + 3.5X_3 = 27.75$$

$$\text{EQ. 2} \quad 4.5X_1 + 2.2X_2 + 1.5X_3 = 10.50$$

$$\text{EQ. 3} \quad 6.7X_1 + 3.0X_2 + 1.0X_3 = 12.25$$

Figure 11.7 Repeated

Step 1:   First Reduction

This solution starts by eliminating X_1 from all equations except equation 1. In Figure 19.14 we obtain a new equation 2 in which the coefficient preceding X_1 is zero as follows:

(a) divide each term in equation 1 by 9.0 and then multiply by 4.5
(b) subtract each of these terms from the corresponding term in equation 2, to get the new equation 2 as shown here:

Write statements that will accomplish (a) and (b) above. In the process, redefine elements of array A and array C associated with equation 2, but not those associated with equation 1.

```
C...................................................
C..   PURPOSE - OBTAIN A NEW EQUATION NO. 2      ..
C...................................................
C
      FACTOR = 4.5 / 9.0
C
C     ......LOOP ENTRY POINT......
C
      DO 5 I = 1, 3, 1
C
          TERM = FACTOR * A(1,I)
          A(2,I) = A(2,I) - TERM
C
    5 CONTINUE
C
C     ......REDEFINE ELEMENT OF C......
C
          TERM = FACTOR * C(1)
          C(2) = C(2) - TERM
C
```

We can eliminate X_1 from equation 3 by an almost identical process.

This time terms in equation 1 are multiplied by $\dfrac{6.7}{9.0}$ and then subtracted from equation 3.

Write statements that will define a new equation 3, but deal with the general equation 3 of Figure 19.13 (not the specific equation shown above).

Block 1:

```
C
C.................................................................
C.. PURPOSE - OBTAIN A NEW EQUATION NO. 3 (GENERAL)            ..
C.................................................................
C
      FACTOR = A(1,3) / A(1,1)
C
C     .......LOOP ENTRY POINT.......
C
      DO 10 I = 1, NOEQS, 1
          TERM = FACTOR * A(1,I)
          A(3,I) = A(3,I) - TERM
C
   10 CONTINUE
C
C     ......REDEFINE ELEMENT OF C..........
C
          TERM = FACTOR * C(1)
          C(3) = C(3) - TERM
```

Notice that the multiplication factor is expressed in general terms and is equal to the coefficient of X_1 in the equation we are redefining divided by the coefficient of X_1 in equation 1. The only other difference is in the number of equations in the set. The variable NOEQS replaces the constant 3.

Repeating the code just written (BLOCK 1) for all the remaining equations will cause a redefinition of almost the whole array A and array C as follows:

$$\left.\begin{array}{l} a_{11}x_1 + a_{12}x_2 + a_{13}x_3 + \cdots + a_{1n}x_n = c_1 \\ O + a'_{22}x_2 + a'_{23}x_3 + \cdots + a'_{2n}x_n = c'_2 \\ O + a'_{32}x_2 + a'_{33}x_3 + \cdots + a'_{3n}x_n = c'_3 \\ \cdots\cdots\cdots\cdots\cdots\cdots\cdots\cdots\cdots\cdots\cdots \\ O + a'_{n2}x_2 + a'_{n3}x_3 + \cdots + a'_{nn}x_n = c'_n \end{array}\right\} \text{EQ. 19.4}$$

The FORTRAN code used to accomplish the large volume of computations involved is remarkably concise:

```
C
C...............................................................
C.. PURPOSE - ELIMINATE X1 FROM ALL EQUATIONS EXCEPT          ..
C..           EQUATION ONE.                                   ..
C...............................................................
C
C             REPEAT PREVIOUS LOGIC
C
C             DO 20 KOUNT = 2, NOEQS, 1
C
      FACTOR = A(1,KOUNT) / A(1,1)
C
C     .........INNER LOOP ENTRY POINT.........
C
      DO 10 I = 1, NOEQS
C
          TERM = FACTOR * A(1,I)
          A(KOUNT,I) = A(KOUNT,I) - TERM
C
   10 CONTINUE
C
C     ......REDEFINE ELEMENT OF C......
C
          C(KOUNT) = C(KOUNT) - TERM
C
   20                 CONTINUE
```

This new block of code has very efficiently eliminated X_1 from all equations (except equation 1) by setting the original code in a simple DO loop.

Step 2:   Further Reduction

The next move is to eliminate X_2 in all equations except equation 2, then eliminate X_3 from all equations except equation 3, and so on. All this will be accomplished by setting the code already written inside another DO loop. The end result will redefine arrays A and C as follows:

$$\left.\begin{array}{l} a''_{11}x_1 + O + O + O + \cdots + O = c''_1 \\ O + a''_{22}x_2 + O + O + \cdots + O = c''_2 \\ O + O + a''_{33}x_3 + O + \cdots + O = c''_3 \\ \cdots\cdots\cdots\cdots\cdots\cdots\cdots\cdots\cdots \\ O + O + O + O + \cdots + a''_{nn}x_n = c''_n \end{array}\right\} \text{Eq. 19.5}$$

Step 3:   Back Substitution

In this form all elements of A except those on the main diagonal are zero, which is convenient because any value of X can then be determined by simple division.

$$X_1 = \frac{C_1''}{a_{11}''}\,;\; X_2 = \frac{C_2''}{a_{22}''}\,;\; X_3 = \frac{C_3''}{a_{33}''}\,;\; \ldots \,;\; X_n = \frac{C_n''}{a_{nn}''}$$

These solution values would be obtained by the following statements:

```
C
C
C              BACK SUBSTITUTION FOR FINAL ANSWERS
C       DO 40 I = 1, NOEQS, 1
C           X(I) = C(I) / A(I,I)
C
           WRITE(2,30) X(I)
       30  FORMAT(20X,E20.6)
C
       40 CONTINUE
C
           STOP
           END
```

Implementing Step 2

To accomplish the logic in step 2, we start by letting equation 2 assume the dominant role previously played by equation 1. That is, equation 2 will be multiplied by various factors so that when subtracted from the other equations (1, 3, 4, 5, etc.) a new equation will be formed in which X_2 has been eliminated. X_2 is to be retained in equation 2 only. Equation 2 becomes what is called the **pivot equation**.

For example, to eliminate X_2 from equation 1, the multiplication factor is:

$$\frac{a_{12}}{a_{22}}$$

To eliminate X_2 from equation 3, the factor is:

$$\frac{a_{32}'}{a_{22}'}$$

In the program segment that follows, an integer variable called PIVOT is used to identify which equation is the PIVOT equation. When PIVOT is 1, equation 1 dominates the mathematics to eliminate X_1. When PIVOT is 2, equation 2 dominates and X_2 is being eliminated.

This programming is obviously getting rather complex. Without extensive documentation, it would be almost impossible to follow.

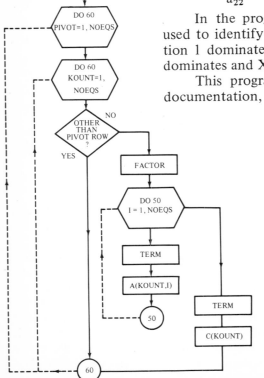

```
C.............................................................
C..  PURPOSE - SOLVE A SET OF LINEAR SIMULTANEOUS EQUATIONS.
C..
C.............................................................
C            -----IMPORTANT VARIABLES-----
C
C   --PIVOT      AN INTEGER TELLING WHICH EQUATION IS      --
C               THE PIVOT EQUATION
C
C   INTEGER PIVOT
C            SET UP OUTER MOST LOOP
C               (INDEX NAME IS PIVOT)
C   DO 60 PIVOT = 1, NOEQS
C       FOR EACH PIVOT EQUATION WE MUST PROCESS ALL OTHER
C       EQUATIONS EXCEPT THE PIVOT EQUATION TO ELIMINATE
C       X(PIVOT) FROM EACH OF THESE EQUATIONS.
C
C          DO 60 KOUNT = 1, NOEQS
C
C          WE ARE NOW AT THE INDIVIDUAL EQUATION LEVEL
C          AND MUST ASK THE QUESTION,'DOES KOUNT EQUAL
C          PIVOT'   IF YES - DO NOT REDUCE THIS EQUATION
C                   IF NO - REDUCE THIS EQUATION
```

```
C
C                                IF(KOUNT.NE.PIVOT) THEN
C                                     FACTOR = A(KOUNT,PIVOT)/A(PIVOT,PIVOT)
C                                     DO 50 I = 1, NOEQS
C
C                                        WE ARE NOW AT THE LEVEL OF MODIFYING
C                                        INDIVIDUAL TERMS IN THE EQUATION.
C
C                                        TERM = FACTOR * A(PIVOT,I)
                                         A(KOUNT,I) = A(KOUNT,I) - TERM
C       50                            CONTINUE
C
                                       TERM = FACTOR * C(PIVOT)
                                       C(KOUNT) = C(KOUNT) - TERM
C
       60 CONTINUE
C
C             .......BACK SUBSTITUTION SECTION........
C
C          DO 80 I = 1, NOEQS
C
             X(I) = C(I) / A(I,I)
             WRITE(2,70) X(I)
       70    FORMAT(20X,-20.6)
C
       80 CONTINUE
C
C....  CAUTION - THIS SOLUTION IS STILL NOT COMPLETE IN THAT..
C.           IT DOES NOT CHECK FOR THE CONDITION OF
C.           A(PIVOT,PIVOT) BEING EQUAL TO ZERO.  WHEN
C.           THIS CONDITION OCCURS A ROW SWAP IS
C..          NECESSARY.
C
          STOP
          END
```

No mention has been made of possible pitfalls in this solution. One very obvious one is the possibility of division by zero (or near zero) values. If any of the pivot terms (a_{11}, a'_{22}, a''_{33}) are zero, this solution "blows up." To avoid this, one might test any pivot term for a near zero value and accomplish an equation interchange if one is detected.

Another problem is the number of operations required as the number of equations increases. These and other aspects of the solution would be covered in a course called "*Numerical Analysis.*"

19.11 Curve Fitting

In this final case study, we will form a set of simultaneous equations the solution of which defines an equation that best represents a series of data points. This is called **curve fitting**.

The world of science and engineering is as much experimental in nature as it is analytic. It is often difficult to theoretically derive exact mathematical models (sets of equations) that correctly describe each and every situation or problem that needs solving. It is often necessary to resort to empirical methods and techniques. The design of a space capsule, for example, involves new and complex aerodynamic, structural, and thermodynamic relationships. It is fair to say that the state of the art in these fields does not provide exact theory to solve each new problem that occurs. In these situations, laboratory experimentation and test flights become an important aspect of the total design effort. This case study shows how the multiplicity of data values (that are typical of this empirical approach) can be reduced to a more convenient form, namely, reduced to an equation. This is called *curve fitting* and concentrates on generating equations (curves) that best represent the experimentally obtained data. This is an exceptionally powerful analytic tool.

An experiment is conducted (see Figure 19.14) and M data points are established. The X and Y coordinates of each point are recorded on a data card forming the data deck shown.

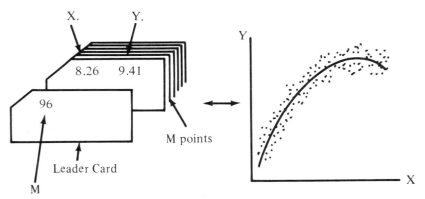

Figure 19.14 Experimentally Obtained Data

A leader card is added and declares the value of M (the number of data points.) It appears from plotting these values that a second-order polynomial of the form:

$$y = a_1 + a_2 x + a_3 x^2 \qquad\qquad \text{Eq. 19.6}$$

could be used to represent the data. It remains, however, to determine a_1, a_2, and a_3. By the method described in this section, it is possible to compute values of a_1, a_2, and a_3 that will best represent the given data. The strategy will be:

1. Establish what criterion is to be used in evaluating whether equation 19.6 effectively represents the data, i.e., write an equation that expresses the *error* or deviation between the observed data values and the values as given by equation 19.6.
2. Having derived this error equation, use the methods of calculus to make the error a minimum; that is, take the first derivative of the error equation and set it equal to zero.

Step 1:   Evaluation of Error

Consider the two typical data points shown in Figure 19.15.

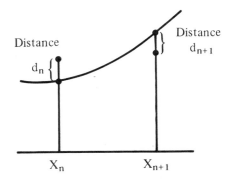

Figure 19.15 Definition of Error

The nth data point is a small distance above the curve. This distance is actually the difference in two Y values:

$$d = \text{Distance} = Y_{\text{Observed}} - Y_{\text{Equation}} \qquad \text{Eq. 19.7}$$

where: Y_{Observed} is the value of Y read from the nth data card and Y_{Equation} is obtained by substituting the value of X appearing on the nth data card into equation 19.6. At first glance, it appears that this distance could be used to represent the error. Notice, however, that the distance as given by equation 19.7 will have a negative value for points that fall below the curve and a positive value for points that fall above the curve. This would mean that the average error for two points such as shown in Figure 19.15 would be small even though the individual distances are large. This difficulty could be circumvented by using the absolute value of these distances, but this creates problems when an attempt is made to take derivatives of the error equation.

A simpler solution is to define the error as the *square* of the distances. This eliminates the sign difficulty and results in the so-called "method of least squares" fit. The following steps define and proceed to minimize this value. Let S be the sum of the squares of the individual distance:

$$S = d_1^2 + d_2^2 + d_3^2 + \ldots + d_m^2$$

$$S = \sum_{i=1}^{m} [Y_{\text{Observed}} - Y_{\text{Equation}}]^2$$

$$S = \sum_{i=1}^{m} [Y_{(i)} - a_1 - a_2 X_{(i)} - a_3 X_{(i)}^2]^2$$

To minimize this function (obtain the best fit) take its partial derivatives with respect to a_1, a_2, and a_3

$$\frac{\partial S}{\partial a_1} = \frac{\partial S}{\partial a_2} = \frac{\partial S}{\partial a_3} = 0$$

and set them equal to zero.

Step 2: Minimize Error

$$\left.\begin{aligned}
\frac{\partial S}{\partial a_1} &= -2 \sum_{i=1}^{m} [Y_{(i)} - a_1 - a_2 X_{(i)} - a_3 X_{(i)}^2] = 0 \\
\frac{\partial S}{\partial a_2} &= -2 \sum_{i=1}^{m} X_{(i)} [Y_{(i)} - a_1 - a_2 X_{(i)} - a_3 X_{(i)}^2] = 0 \\
\frac{\partial S}{\partial a_3} &= -2 \sum_{i=1}^{m} X_{(i)}^2 [Y_{(i)} - a_1 - a_2 X_{(i)} - a_3 X_{(i)}^2] = 0
\end{aligned}\right\} \text{Eq. 19.8}$$

The result is a set of three simultaneous equations written in terms of three unknown quantities (a_1, a_2, and a_3). Figure 19.16 shows these equations rearranged and set up to solve for the unknown a's. The 3 by 3 coefficient array is made up of various sums. For example, ΣX is the sum of all the X values appearing on the M data cards, and ΣX^2 is the sum of all the X values squared; etc. The computer will be able to evaluate these sums exceptionally well for the purpose of forming the two-dimensional coefficient array and the one-dimensional constant array. At this point the value of the computer makes itself evident. Not only can it be used to accomplish the tedious task of obtaining the various sums needed to form the coefficient and constant matrices, but it can then be used to solve these simultaneous equations by the methods of the previous case study.

$$Ma_1 + \Sigma X a_2 + \Sigma X^2 a_3 = \Sigma Y$$

$$\Sigma X a_1 + \Sigma X^2 a_2 + \Sigma X^3 a_3 = \Sigma XY$$

$$\Sigma X^2 a_1 + \Sigma X^3 a_2 + \Sigma X^4 a_3 = \Sigma X^2 Y$$

—————————OR—————————

$$\begin{bmatrix} M & \Sigma X & \Sigma X^2 \\ \Sigma X & \Sigma X^2 & \Sigma X^3 \\ \Sigma X^2 & \Sigma X^3 & \Sigma X^4 \end{bmatrix} \begin{Bmatrix} a_1 \\ a_2 \\ a_3 \end{Bmatrix} \begin{Bmatrix} \Sigma Y \\ \Sigma X Y \\ \Sigma X^2 Y \end{Bmatrix}$$

Coefficient   Unknowns
Matrix   Constants

Figure 19.16 Simultaneous Equations

Write statements that will determine ΣX; that is, write statements that will read the value of X from each data card and determine the sum of these values.

```
C...............................................................
C..   PURPOSE - DETERMINE ONE OF THE COEFFICIENTS  ..
C...............................................................
C
      SUMX = 0.0
      READ(5,10) M
C
      DO 30 I = 1, M
C
         READ(5,20) X, Y
         SUMX = SUMX + X
C
   30 CONTINUE
         :     :     :     :
C
```

Next, write statements that will determine all elements in the coefficient matrix: i.e., determine ΣX, ΣX^2, ΣX^3, ΣX^4.

In the program segment to follow, each value of X is read from the data deck. X^2, X^3, and X^4 are then determined. A subscripted variable called SUMX is used to accumulate these terms:

$$SUMX\ (1) = \Sigma X$$
$$SUMX\ (2) = \Sigma X^2$$
$$SUMX\ (3) = \Sigma X^3$$
$$SUMX\ (4) = \Sigma X^4$$

```
C.....................................................................
C...................................................................
C..   PURPOSE - DETERMINE ALL THE COEFFICIENTS            ..
C...................................................................
C
C            -------IMPORTANT VARIABLES-------
C
C      --M          NUMBER OF DATA POINTS               --
C      --X,Y        INDIVIDUAL DATA POINT VALUES        --
C      --SUMX(1)    SUMMATION OF X     TERMS            --
C      --SUMX(2)    SUMMATION OF X**2 TERMS             --
C      --SUMX(3)    SUMMATION OF X**3 TERMS             --
C      --SUMX(4)    SUMMATION OF X**4 TERMS             --
C
      DIMENSION SUMX(4)
C
C            ......SET EACH ACCUMULATOR TO ZERO......
C
      DO 10 I = 1,4
C
         SUMX(I) = 0.0
C
   10 CONTINUE
C
C            .........HOW MANY DATA POINTS........
C
      READ(2,20) M
   20 FORMAT(I4)
C            ....LOOP ENTRY POINT.....
C
      DO 40 KOUNT = 1, M, 1
C
         READ(5,30) X
   30    FORMAT(F10.2)
C
         SUMX(1) = SUMX(1) + X
         SUMX(2) = SUMX(2) + X**2
         SUMX(3) = SUMX(3) + X**3
         SUMX(4) = SUMX(4) + X**4
C
   40 CONTINUE
C
C
```

Form A Coefficient Matrix

It now remains to use the sums just computed to form a two-dimensional coefficient matrix as originally shown in Figure 19.16. Each element of the coefficient matrix (which will be called C) equals one of the elements in the one-dimensional array SUMX.

$$\begin{bmatrix} C_{11} & C_{12} & C_{13} \\ C_{21} & C_{22} & C_{23} \\ C_{31} & C_{32} & C_{33} \end{bmatrix} \qquad \begin{bmatrix} M & \Sigma X & \Sigma X^2 \\ \Sigma X & \Sigma X^2 & \Sigma X^3 \\ \Sigma X^2 & \Sigma X^3 & \Sigma X^4 \end{bmatrix}$$

You can determine which one by adding the two subscripts of C and subtracting 2.

$$\text{C (I, J)} \qquad\qquad \text{SUMX (K)}$$
$$K = I + J - 2$$

The following statement defines the two-dimensional array C using this relationship. When I and J are both 1, a special condition exists. C(1,1) equals M. This is easily handled by an IF test.

```
C
C
C        DO 80 I = 1, 3
C            DO 80 J = 1, 3
C                K = I + J - 2
C                IF (K.NE.0) THEN
                     C(I,J) = SUMX(K)
                 ELSE
                     C(1,1) = M
                 ENDIF
C        80 CONTINUE
```

Form A Right-Hand Constant

Finally to form the right-hand constants, statements similar to those used in forming the X sums are employed in the creation of the one-dimensional array CONST:

CONST (1) = ΣY
CONST (2) = ΣXY
CONST (3) = $\Sigma X^2 Y$

In the final solution that follows, module 1 will read the data and form the various sums. Module 2 will use these sums to define array C. Module 3 will solve the simultaneous equations this formed and print out the solution values — the A values defining the equation that fit the data.

```
C.............................................................
C..  PURPOSE - FIND THE BEST SECOND ORDER POLYNOMIAL TO     ::
C..             FIT THE DATA.                                ::
C.............................................................
C
C        -------NEW VARIABLES-------------
C
C      --CONTS(1)      SUM OF THE Y TERMS              --
C      --CONST(2)      SUM OF THE XY TERMS             --
C      --CONST(3)      SON OF THE X**2Y TERMS          --
C      --  A           ARRAY OF SOLUTION VALUES        --
C
       DIMENSION SUMX(4), C(3,3), CONST(3), A(3)
C
C                    MODULE 1
C
C        ...SET ALL ACCUMULATORS TC ZERO...
C      DO 10 I = 1, 4
C          SUMX(I) = 0.0
C   10 CONTINUE
C      DO 20 I = 1, 3
C          CONST(I) = 0.0
C   20 CONTINUE
C          HOW MANY DATA POINTS
C      READ(5,30) M
   30 FORMAT(I4)
C
```

```
C
C                ........LOOP ENTRY POINT........
C
      DO 50 KOUNT = 1, M, 1
C
           READ(5,40) X, Y
   40      FORMAT(2F10.2)
C
           SUMX(1) = SUMX(1) + X
           SUMX(2) = SUMX(2) + X**2
           SUMX(3) = SUMX(3) + X**3
           SUMX(4) = SUMX(4) + X**4
C
C                        ....NOW DEFINE CONST ARRAY.....
C
           CONST(1) = CONST(1) + Y
           CONST(2) = CONST(2) + X*Y
           CONST(3) = CONST(3) + X**2*Y
C
   50 CONTINUE
C
C                        MODULE 2
C
C
C                .....DIFINE COEFFICIENT ARRAY.....
C
      DO 70 I = 1, 3
C
         DO 60 J = 1, 3
C
            K = I + J - 2
C
            IF(K.NE.0) THEN
C
                 C(I,J) = SUMX(K)
C
            ELSE
C
                 C(1,1) = M
C
            ENDIF
C
   60       CONTINUE
   70 CONTINUE
C
C
C
C                        MODULE 3

      STOP
      END
```

$\Downarrow$

TO SIMULTANEOUS EQUATION PROGRAM
TO DETERMINE ARRAY OF A VALUES.

The program just completed will put the best second-order polynomial through the data points given. However, it may be that the data represents a third- or higher-order polynomial. If that was so, a poor fit would have been achieved. Curve fitting is a trial-and-error procedure. If a second-order curve does not represent the data very well, a higher-order curve is tried.

It is natural then to review this case study to accommodate higher-order polynomials. If the equations (coefficient and constant matrices) are examined for a fourth-order curve, a pattern can be detected.

$$Y = a_1 + a_2 x + a_3 x^2 + a_4 x^3 + a_5 x^4$$

$$\begin{bmatrix} M & \Sigma X & \Sigma X^2 & \Sigma X^3 & \Sigma X^4 \\ \Sigma X & \Sigma X^2 & \Sigma X^3 & \Sigma X^4 & \Sigma X^5 \\ \Sigma X^2 & \Sigma X^3 & \Sigma X^4 & \Sigma X^5 & \Sigma X^6 \\ \Sigma X^3 & \Sigma X^4 & \Sigma X^5 & \Sigma X^6 & \Sigma X^7 \\ \Sigma X^4 & \Sigma X^5 & \Sigma X^6 & \Sigma X^7 & \Sigma X^8 \end{bmatrix} \begin{Bmatrix} a_1 \\ a_2 \\ a_3 \\ a_4 \\ a_5 \end{Bmatrix} = \begin{Bmatrix} \Sigma Y \\ \Sigma XY \\ \Sigma X^2 Y \\ \Sigma X^3 Y \\ \Sigma X^4 Y \end{Bmatrix}$$

Observe the following:

    (a) If N is the order of the polynomial, there are N+1 values of A and N+1 simultaneous equations;

    (b) The maximum exponent of X in the summing terms is 2N. With this in mind, rewrite this case study allowing the reading of N (not to exceed 10) from the same leader card M is on, and form the coefficient and constant arrays.

Review Exercises

1. What is a "character constant"? Give an example.

2.*Describe how character information is stored.

3. What is meant by the term "collating sequence"?

4. Describe how this collating sequence provides an easy way to accomplish an alphabetic sort.

5.*Explain why a character string consisting of four characters should only be compared with a character string of equal length in an IF test.

6. When a character string is very long, describe how to break the string up to account for the word size of the machine.

7. Describe one or more typical character operations performed while your program is being compiled.

8. Prepare a data deck consisting of 10 cards. On half the cards put the word READ starting in column 7. On the other half put the word WRITE. Write a program to determine which cards contain the command READ.

9.*What is the purpose of object time format?

10. If an equation is defined by a series of Y values, explain how the area under this curve can be obtained with as little error as possible.

11.

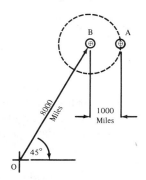

Planet A moves around planet B once every two hours. Planet B moves around center O once every hour. Simulate the motion of planet B at one-second intervals. Simulate the motion of planet A with respect to planet B. Add these two motions to determine the motion of planet A with respect to center O.

12. A train leaves point A travelling at 30 miles per hour but stops every ten minutes to pick up passengers

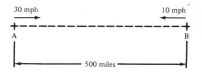

(one-minute stops). A train leaves point B travelling at 10 miles per hour (constant speed). Simulate the motion of both trains. Terminate the simulation when the trains meet.

13.*Write a program that accomplishes a straight line curve fit for M data points. That is, determine the best slope m and best y intercept b.

$$y = mx + b$$
$$\text{or}$$
$$y = a_1 + a_2 x$$

14.

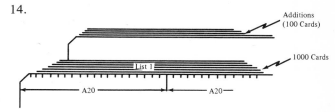

The mailing address of 1000 customers is recorded on data cards and constitutes a file called LIST1:

Columns	Information
1–20	Customer's Name
21–40	Customer's Street Address
41–60	Customer's Town Address
61–80	Customer's State Address

The next 100 cards represent similar information on customers that are to be added to the mailing list. Assume that neither LIST1 nor its additions is sorted.

Write a program to determine if the first name on the additions list appears anywhere in LIST1. If it does not, add this name to LIST1.

15. Repeat problem 14 for all names on the cards that represent possible additions.

16. After the new LIST1 is established, sort the list according to ZIP code (last 5 numbers in state address). Print the list.

20 | FORTRAN Programming With Time-Sharing

20.1 | Use of a Time-Share System

Most large computer systems are prepared to receive programs in two basic modes of submission: "batch" and "time shared." In the **batch mode**, the statements defining how to solve a program (the instruction deck) and the cards containing the input data (the data deck) are submitted all at once at the card reader. The name "batch" comes from the fact that the program is received as one large batch of cards.

An increasingly popular alternative method of program submission is through the use of a **time-sharing (TS) system**. Time sharing usually involves a large number of remote terminals located in various rooms and buildings but connected via telephone lines to the main computer. In the time-sharing mode, the computer responds to many different programs at any given time. This is accomplished by giving each program a small slice of the computer's CPU time on a regular, recurring basis. This "time slice" is provided so frequently that it appears to any programmer that he or she has the full attention of the computer system.

At one time this was a relatively complex and costly mode of operation. Responding to forty, fifty or sixty programs (all at one time) is bound to present

Figure 20.1 Programming in the TS Mode

problems. One problem is that it is impossible to keep this many programs in main memory all at one time. It just cannot hold them all. This means that each program must be stored on some auxiliary memory device (like a disc) and "rolled into" main memory just before the "slice of CPU time" is provided and "rolled out of" main memory when the time slice is over. These and many other problems have been solved, however. Today time sharing is a relatively inexpensive mode of operation. Terminals can be purchased or rented for a nominal cost. Further, the hardware and software at the computer end of the system (to control this "multiple input environment") has been developed and made cost effective. The day of "time sharing" has truly arrived.

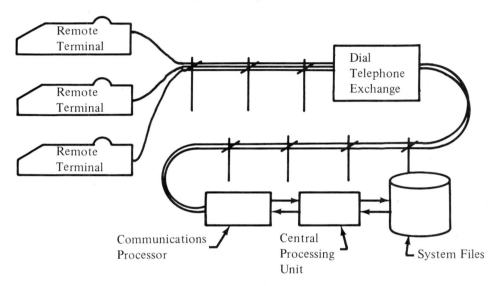

Figure 20.2 Diagram of a Time-Share System

The advantages of a time-sharing system are considerable. Results are obtained almost immediately. There are no long time delays between successive computer runs. Debugging a program is a lot easier because it is a continuous, uninterrupted operation. In time sharing the programmer and the computer are linked closer together. Because the terminal is both an input and output device, interactive or conversational mode dialogue can be achieved. All these features are not available in the batch mode.

There are several types of time-sharing terminals on the market today, but they all employ a keyboard device similar to a teletypewriter to provide input. On some units the programmer is provided with a typewritten copy of the program (and the output answers) on a sheet of paper. This is called a "hard copy" device. Other terminals are equipped with a TV picture tube on which the program and its results are presented in a video display. More elaborate models are equipped with an X–Y plotting capability so that interactive graphic output can be transmitted to and from the remote user.

Terminals that are in close proximity to the computer can be "hard wired" to the computer over telephone lines.

Some terminals have their own telephone dial as part of the keyboard. In this instance, the phone and "acoustic coupler" are an integral part of the terminal. More often the acoustic coupler is a separate device. In this arrangement, you will be instructed to dial the computer center on a standard phone, and, when you receive a "high pitched" tone, place the receiver in the acoustic coupler. Be careful to look for a sign on the acoustic coupler that tells which way the receiver should be placed. The sign usually reads, "cord end here." When proper contact has been established, some signal is usually provided (a small signal light with the word "Carrier" will come on).

Dials and Settings

Each terminal uses a set of dials, switches and display lights. It will be necessary for you to get "checked out" on the use of any particular unit. The following is a set of general instructions that may be helpful.

(a) **Power on**: look for a button or switch marked ON or POWER. It may be necessary to provide power to both the terminal and the acoustic coupler by separate switches.

(b) **Other settings**: look for knobs or a switch marked as follows. If you find any, be sure they are set like this:
PARITY: none or zero
DUPLEX: half
CR: on
ROLL: on

(c) **Baud rate**: the computer can communicate with the terminal at several different transmission rates called the baud rate. 110 baud is a low speed rate, 300 baud is a high speed rate. There will be a different phone number for each rate, and the baud rate setting on the acoustic coupler or terminal must *match* the baud rate of the phone number used. If garbage characters start to appear, you have the wrong baud rate setting.

(d) **Carriage return**: as you type any line on the terminal, you must hit the CARRIAGE RETURN (CR) button in order to transmit what you have typed to the computer. This button may be marked RETURN or NEW LINE on some terminals.

(e) **User number/password**: time-sharing users must have permanent files where they can store various programs on which they are working. Each user is supplied a number to identify the user's files. Any "sign-on" procedure will usually start by asking for this number and possibly a password used to protect the file.

Because each computer installation has a different "sign-on" procedure, it would serve no useful purpose to present an example of the statements and responses needed to tie into your computer over the terminal. Your instructor will provide this information.

20.2 | FORTRAN in the Time-Sharing Mode

There is very little difference between FORTRAN programming in the TS mode and FORTRAN programming in the batch mode. The rules of FORTRAN grammar are the same in either mode. There are some elementary procedural differences, however, and these are discussed in the paragraphs that follow.

Sign-On Procedures

These take the place of control cards, and they have the same purpose. Like control cards, their exact form is dictated by the individual computer center being used, so they are only mentioned here.

Line Numbers

TS FORTRAN requires that every line of a program be given a line number. Line numbers *do not* replace statement numbers, which must still be part of the program. Unlike statement numbers, line numbers *must* be in numeric order (usually assigned in intervals of 10).

At the end of a program, if it is necessary to add, correct or delete a line, the line is referenced by its **line number**. This action is called **EDITING the program**.

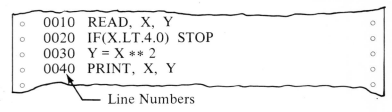

```
0010   READ, X, Y
0020   IF(X.LT.4.0) STOP
0030   Y = X ** 2
0040   PRINT, X, Y
```
—— Line Numbers

Free-Format Input and Output

Input of data and output of answers without the use of FORMAT statements is used quite frequently in TS FORTRAN. Output is achieved through the use of the PRINT command, and results are printed in E-format when they are real or I-format when they are integer. When free format output is being used, Hollerith characters may be printed by including them in the PRINT statement itself, bounded by quotation marks. (Formatted input and output are also available.)

Data Input During Execution

There is no counterpart to the data card in TS FORTRAN. When in the course of executing a program, a READ statement is encountered, the computer calls for input of the desired data by causing an = or a ? to be printed at the terminal. When the programmer sees this, she simply types in the data she knows is being called for. This feature of TS FORTRAN is what provides the key to interactive or conversational programming, to be discussed later.

Special TS Processing Commands

There are a special set of commands that are used only in the TS environment to tell the computer what processing is desired. The following is a sampling of typical TS commands.

RUN The programmer gives this command when she is finished typing her program and wants the computer to compile and execute it.

LIST The programmer has made some corrections to her program and wants to see if they were entered as she intended. She tells the computer to LIST the program in its most recent form.

SAVE As a TS user types a program, it is accumulated in an area of memory known as the **current** or **scratch file**. When the program is finished, if the programmer signs off without telling the computer to SAVE the program, it will be lost. If the command SAVE is issued, the program will be moved from the scratch file to the file associated with your user number and, thereby, will be saved for later use.

PURGE This command tells the computer to erase a program SAVE'd in your files. Unless you PURGE old programs, eventually your file area will become filled up, and there will be no room to SAVE new programs. The command PURGE allows you to "clean out" your file.

DONE The programmer is saying to the computer, "I am done with this program, but do not break contact with me. I have another program I would like to run."

BYE The programmer tells the computer that she is completely finished for this session. The computer will break contact with her.

An example TS program is shown in Figure 20.3. After a proper sign-on procedure, the computer goes into the "build mode"; that is, it assumes a posture ready to accept statements from the programmer as they are typed on the terminal. The asterisk at the beginning of each line was typed there "by the computer" and signifies that it is in the build mode. Note that the programmer has typed a line number immediately after the asterisk on every statement line, even on the line containing statement number 10. Remember, line numbers do not replace the need for statement numbers. This programmer has wisely assigned line numbers. Rather than choosing to use 1, 2, 3, 4, 5, etc., she has used 10, 20, 30, 40, 50, etc. By so doing, she has left herself the opportunity to insert statements into the program later without having to completely renumber every statement in the program. If, for example, she later desires to insert a statement between the IF and STOP statements, she will be able to do so by simply giving the new line a number between 60 and 70, such as 65.

The card column spacing of keypunching is not required when typing a TS program, but a space *is* required between the line number and the FORTRAN statement.

When the programmer has typed all statements of her program, she then types the command RUN and the program runs. Note that in this and in subsequent programming examples, when the computer sends the programmer a message, it appears on the terminal in lower-case letters. This is a feature available on some terminals.

```
*10 X = 1.0
*20 7 Y = X ** 2
*30 Z = X ** 3
*40 PRINT, X, Y, Z
*50 X = X + 1.0
*60 IF(X.LE.5.0)G) TO 7
*70 STOP
*80 END
*RUN
     1.0000000E+00    1.0000000E+00    1.0000000E+00
     2.0000000E+00    4.0000000E+00    8.0000000E+00
     3.0000000E+00    9.0000000E+00    2.7000000E+01
     4.0000000E+00    1.6000000E+01    6.4000000E+01
     5.0000000E+00    2.5000000E+01    1.2500000E+02
program stop at 70
*BYE
```

Figure 20.3   An Example TS Program

Error correction in TS is much easier than it is in batch mode. When typing a card on a keypunch, it is impossible to correct a typographical error without typing the card over again. Not so in TS. When typing a statement on a terminal, incorrectly typed characters can be "erased" or deleted by typing the character ← once for each character to be deleted. This is a character usually found on the right-hand side of the keyboard.

Lines as Typed at the Terminal	Lines as Understood by the Computer
*10 X = 1.9←0	*10 X = 1.0
*20 7 Y=XTRA←←←**2	*20 7 Y=X**2
*30 X = X***←3	*30 Z = X**3
*40 WR←←PRINT,XY←,Y,Z	*40 PRINT,X,Y,Z
*50 X = X +B←1.0	*50 X = X +1.0

Figure 20.4   Use of the Correction Character ←

Errors discovered by the programmer after she has passed the line containing them or errors that are pointed out to her by error messages can be corrected by simply retyping the omitted or incorrect lines correctly using the line number to indicate to the computer which statement she is inserting or correcting. Figure 20.5 demonstrates this feature being used.

```
*10 X=1.0
*20 7 Y–X**2
*30 PRINT,X,Y,Z
*40 X=X++1.0
*50 IF(X.LE.5.0)GO TO 7
*60 STOP
*70 END
*RUN
seq 20 unrecognizable statement
seq 40 illegal operator in context

*20 7 Y=X**2
*40 X=X+1.0
*25 Z=X**3
*05 PRINT, 'TABLE OF XYZ VALUES'
*LIST

05 PRINT, 'TABLE OF XYZ VALUES'
10 X=1.0
20 7 Y=X**2
25 Z=X**3
30 PRINT,X,Y,Z
40 X=X+1.0
50 IF(X.LE.5.0)GO TO 7
60 STOP
70 END
*RUN
TABLE OF XYZ VALUES
   1.0000000E+00   1.0000000E+00   1.0000000E+00
   2.0000000E+00   4.0000000E+00   8.0000000E+00
   3.0000000E+00   9.0000000E+00   2.7000000E+01
   4.0000000E+00   1.6000000E+01   6.4000000E+01
   5.0000000E+00   2.5000000É+01   1.2500000E+02
program stop at 60
*BYE
```

Figure 20.5 Correcting Errors in a TS Program

Notice that two statements are being corrected, a new PRINT statement added, and an omitted statement inserted between statements 20 and 30.

20.3 | Data Input in TS

As a demonstration of the functioning of the READ statement in a TS program, consider the sample program of Figure 20.6. In this sample, the user has written a program with which he can calculate the value of any positive quantity raised to any exponent.

His logic will result in the program stopping if a negative value is input for X, which he might do either accidentally or, more likely, when he runs out of input values and desires to stop execution. Notice the = at the beginning of every line of input data. That sign was printed there by the computer whenever it encountered the READ statement during program execution. In this manner it notified the programmer when it was ready for the data values to be input.

```
*10 5 READ,X,EXP
*20 IF(X.LT.0.0)STOP
*30 Y=Y**EXP
*40 PRINT,Y
*50 GO TO 5
*60 END
*RUN
= 5.0 3.0
   1.2500000E+02
= 312. 2.0
   9.7344000E+04
= -9.0
program stop at 20
*BYE
```

Figure 20.6 Input of Data to a TS Program

If only one value was typed after the equal sign and the carriage return activated, another equal sign would appear because insufficient input was provided.

20.4 | Saving a Program

As mentioned earlier, it is possible to cause a program to be saved in the system files for use at a later time through the use of the processing command SAVE. In Figure 20.7 the programmer, apparently a teacher, has set up a program to compute the average of an unknown number of exam grades. The program is set to handle up to 100 grades, but the exact number to be input during each run is to be given to the computer during execution. Grades are to be input in groups of five.

Particular attention is called to the SAVE statement. In addition to the command SAVE, it contains the file descriptor:

Every subscriber to a TS service is allowed a certain portion of the system files in which to store the programs he wishes to save. The group of programs he has stored is referred to as his **catalog**, and all his programs will have a common **catalog name**.

In order to provide a measure of protection to the programs in his catalog, the programmer assigns a PASSWORD to his catalog that must be given whenever one of his saved programs is called out for use.

Each of the programmer's saved programs must have its own unique FILE NAME.

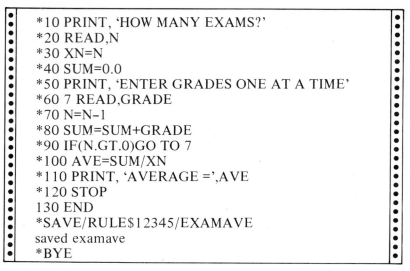

```
*10 PRINT, 'HOW MANY EXAMS?'
*20 READ,N
*30 XN=N
*40 SUM=0.0
*50 PRINT, 'ENTER GRADES ONE AT A TIME'
*60 7 READ,GRADE
*70 N=N-1
*80 SUM=SUM+GRADE
*90 IF(N.GT.0)GO TO 7
*100 AVE=SUM/XN
*110 PRINT, 'AVERAGE =',AVE
*120 STOP
130 END
*SAVE/RULE$12345/EXAMAVE
saved examave
*BYE
```

Figure 20.7 Saving a Program

20.5 | Using a Saved Program

In the last step of the sign-on procedure, the programmer is asked by the computer:

```
old or new?
```

In other words, is the programmer about to type in the statements of a brand new program, or is he about to run a program that he has already saved in the system files? In all programming examples given up to this time, the response would have been:

```
old or new?
NEW
```

If the programmer desires to run a program that he has saved, he replies with OLD and the file descriptor of the program he desires to run. For example:

```
old or new?
OLD/RULE$12345/EXAMAVE
```

Figure 20.8 shows how the programmer might then proceed to use the saved program EXAMAVE. In this case he has two sets of grades for which he needs averages: one set of 13 and one of 16. Notice that the computer reports "ready" followed by an asterisk on the next line when the saved program has been called out and is ready for use. The programmer then simply commands RUN.

In this case a clever assortment of additional PRINT commands included in the program will ensure that its user will not forget which data he is to input and when.

```
old or new?
OLD/RULES$12345/EXAMAVE
ready examave
*RUN
HOW MANY GRADES?
=10
ENTER GRADES ONE AT A TIME
=75
=100
=63
=74
=80
=95
=91
=42
=88
=90
AVERAGE = 7.9800000E+01
program stop at 120
*BYE
```

Figure 20.8 Using a Saved Program

20.6 | Interactive Programming

A principal feature of TS programming is the capability it provides to write interactive or conversational programs. These are often computer-aided instructional programs in which a remote terminal "asks" a series of questions, evaluates responses, and continues a dialogue with the user. Figure 20.9 demonstrates how

```
I CAN HELP YOU LEARN YOUR MULTIPLICATION TABLES.
WHICH TABLE WOULD YOU LIKE TO WORK ON?
=9
OK. WE WILL WORK ON THE 9 TIMES TABLE.
READY? HERE WE GO . . .
  9 TIMES 2
=18
CORRECT.
  9 TIMES 3
=27
CORRECT.
  9 TIMES 4
=32
WRONG. TRY AGAIN.
  9 TIMES 4
=34
WRONG AGAIN. STOP GUESSING.
  9 TIMES 4
=35
SORRY, BETTY
YOU ARE STILL GUESSING. STUDY YOUR 9 TIMES
TABLE AGAIN TONIGHT, AND COME BACK TO SEE ME
TOMORROW. BYE BYE.
program stop at 280
*BYE
```

Figure 20.9 An Interactive Program as Seen by the User

such a program might appear to a user. In this case the program is one to drill elementary school students in their multiplication tables.

Figure 20.10 shows the programming necessary to produce the computer-student "conversion" in Figure 20.9. Note the steps taken to interject a sense of personalization into the dialogue. This and all interactive programs involve three basic elements:

1. Large numbers of statements to cause output of complete English sentences that either ask questions or give instructions.
2. READ statements to demand responses from the user.
3. Logic to evaluate the responses and to branch to appropriate portions of the program depending on the correctness of the response.

The response evaluation logic need not always seek exact agreement between the student's response and the 100% correct answer.

```
old or new?
NEW
ready
*10 PRINT, 'WHAT IS YOUR NAME?'
*20 READ 5, NAME
*30 FORMAT(A8)
*40 PRINT 6,NAME
*50 6 FORMAT(' HELLO ',A8)
*60 PRINT, ' I CAN HELP YOU LEARN YOUR MULTIPLICATION TABLES'
*70 PRINT, 'WHICH TABLE WOULD YOU LIKE TO WORK ON?'
*80 READ,N
*90 PRINT, 'OK. WE WILL WORK ON THE ',N,' TIMES TABLE'
*100 PRINT, ' READY? HERE WE GO. . . . . . '
*110 K = 2
*120 7 NRBAD = 0
*130 10 PRINT,N, 'TIMES',K
*140 READ,IANS
*150 IF(IANS.EQ.N*K) GO TO 80
*160 NRBAD = NRBAD + 1
*170 IF(NRBAD.EQ.1) GO TO 11
*180 IF(NRBAD.EQ.2) GO TO 12
*190 IF(NRBAD.EQ.3) GO TO 13
*200 11 PRINT, ' WRONG. TRY AGAIN. '
*210 GO TO 10
*220 12 PRINT, ' WRONG. STOP GUESSING. '
*230 GO TO 10
*240 13 PRINT 14, NAME
*250 14 FORMAT (' SORRY ',A8)
*260 PRINT, ' YOU ARE STILL GUESSING. STUDY YOUR ' ,N, 'TIMES'
*270 PRINT, ' TABLE AGAIN TONIGHT AND COME BACK AND SEE ME'
*280 PRINT, ' TOMORROW. BYE, BYE'
*290 STOP
*300 80 PRINT, ' CORRECT. '
*310 80 K = K + 1
*320 IF(K.LE.12) GO TO 7
*330 STOP
*340 END
*SAVE/RULE$12345/MULTDRILL
saved multdrill
*BYE
```

Figure 20.10 An Interactive Program as Seen by Its Programmer

An interactive program to drill a student in the use of the slide rule, for example, could hardly expect the student to respond with precisely the same answer as the computer. The author of such a program would have to write the program to accept all answers that fall within a specified accuracy range of the correct answer.

Interactive programs are not limited to Math/Science related drill problems. Programs have been written to drill students in nearly every field from foreign languages to history. Responses from the student and correct answers loaded in the computer in this category of interactive programs must be in alphameric form, so exact matches between student response and correct answer *are* necessary in these applications.

As demonstrated in Chapter 15, these interactive techniques can be put to good use in writing software packages accessible over time-sharing systems.

20.7 | Saving Data

It is also possible to store data in a system file for use later. Use of saved data can spare the programmer from having to retype his data every time he runs a revised version of the program that uses that data. Figure 20.11 shows the essential steps involved in saving data by means of a simple example. The line numbers are not essential but are advisable. Without them, the programmer is unable to make reference to the line of data in which an error may have been made, or to insert an omitted line. The SAVE statement is in exactly the same form as before.

```
old or new?
NEW
ready
*10 25.2 32.4 71.1 49.8
*20 31.2 42.5 10.1 12.3
*30 08.4 72.9 42.1 21.4
*40 00.1 98.0 72.6 41.7
*50 84.0 79.6 21.4 10.9
*SAVE/RULE$12345/DATAFILE
saved datafile
*BYE
```

Figure 20.11 Saving a Data File

20.8 | Using Saved Data

In Figure 20.12, we outline the steps needed to access data that has been saved in order to use it in a new program. As shown, the GET command is necessary to cause the saved file of data to be made available to the program being run. As with all statements that make reference to material saved in the system files, the GET command must include the same file descriptor under which the file was saved. The READ statement in this case must be formatted. Note, however, that in place of the input/output device code number in the FORMAT statement, the file name is used. The 2X code in the FORMAT statement is necessary to cause the line number to be skipped as data values are being picked up from the lines of DATAFILE.

Figure 20.11 demonstrates how a saved program can be made to use a saved data file. The figure assumes that the program of Figure 20.10 has been saved under the file name DISTANCE.

```
old or new?
NEW
ready
*GET/RULE$12345/DATAFILE
*10 DO 5 I=1,5
*20 READ("DATAFILE",4)X1,Y1,X2,Y2
*30 4 FORMAT(2X,4F5.1)
*40 DIST=SQRT((X2-X1)**2+(Y2-Y1)**2)
*50 5 PRINT,DIST
*60 STOP
*70 END
*RUN
  4.9087371E+01
  3.6840874E+01
  6.1546243E+01
  9.1792919E+01
  9.2943262E+01
program stop at 60
*BYE
```

Figure 20.12 Using Saved Data

```
old or new?
OLD/RULE$12345/DISTANCE
ready distance
*GET/RULE$12345/DATAFILE
*RUN
  4.9087371E+01
  3.6840874E+01
  6.1546243E+01
  9.1792919E+01
  9.2943262E+01
program stop at 60
*BYE
```

Figure 20.13

20.9 Differences in Time-Sharing Systems

The information and examples presented in this chapter are based upon an actual TS system in operation today. The student must bear in mind, however, that just as there are differences in FORTRAN from computer to computer, there, likewise, exist differences among TS systems. All material presented on TS systems must, therefore, be viewed as representative and typical rather than as gospel.

Note: The programming examples that follow require understanding of DO loops and subscripted variables covered in Chapter 9-11. If you have not reached that point, do not attempt to follow the logic of these problems.

Additional Applications

Programming Example
Graphical Output: Curves of Mathematical Functions

At the end of Chapter 15, a programming example was given on the topic of Graphical Output. It described printing of histograms or bar graphs. This programming example is intended to demonstrate that the techniques used in obtaining Graphical Output on the line printer can be applied to output on remote terminals as well. It further demonstrates the next level of complexity in programming for Graphical Output: plotting of mathematical functions.

Requirement 1: Write a program to print a graph of the following function:

$$y = 1.3 + 3(x-1) - .25(x-1)^2$$

for values of x from 1 to 13 in increments of 1.

X	Y	KY
1.	1.3	1
2.	4.0	4
3.	6.3	6
4.	8.0	8
5.	9.3	9
6.	10.0	10
7.	10.3	10
8.	10.0	10
9.	9.3	9
10.	8.0	8
11.	6.3	6
12.	4.0	4
13.	1.3	1

The scheme involves a 15 element one-dimensional array called IPLOT, initially loaded with blanks. During each iteration of the program, one of the 13 X values is used to calculate a Y value, and the Y value is used (through subscript KY) to indicate which of IPLOT's elements is to be loaded with a *. Then the contents of the entire IPLOT array are printed. Consider first the table of X, Y, and KY values for this function, shown to the left.

Solution 1: The form of the output to be printed is shown below. Note that (typical of problems of this type) the y-axis runs across the printed page and the x-axis is parallel to the edge of the page. (The output has been turned 90° for ease of viewing in this text.)

```
*RUN
     0    5   10   15
  0++++++++++++++
  1+*
  2+   *
  3+     *
  4+       *
  5+        *
  6+         *
  7+         *
  8+         *
  9+        *
 10+       *
 11+     *
 12+   *
 13+*
program stop at 260
*BYE
```

Program 1: Note that the C (for comments) goes immediately after the line number.

```
old or new?
NEW
ready

*10C SET UP IPLOT ARRAY AND INITIALIZE ALL ELEMENTS
*20 C AS BLANKS.
*30 DIMENSION IPLOT(15)
*40 DO 3 K=1, 15
*50 3 IPLOT(K)=1H
*60C PRINT CALIBRATION VALUES FOR Y-AXIS
*70C USING IMPLIED DO LOOP.
*80 WRITE(2,5)(I,I=5,15,5)
*90 5 FORMAT(3X,1HO,3(3X,I2))
*100C PRINT Y-AXIS.
*110 WRITE(2,7)
*120 7 FORMAT(2X,1HO,16(1H+))
*130C ESTABLISH DO LOOP TO PLOT 13 POINTS.
*140 DO 10 I=1,13
*150 X=I
*160 Y=1.3+3.0*(X-1.)-0.25*(X-1.)**2
*170C PLACE * IN PROPER ELEMENT OF IPLOT.
*180 KY=Y
*190 IPLOT(KY)=1H*
*200C PRINT ONE LINE OF GRAPH.
*210 WRITE(2,6)I,(IPLOT(K),K=1,15)
*220 6 FORMAT(1X,I2,1H+,15A1)
*230C CLEAR * FROM IPLOT WITH BLANK.
*240 10 IPLOT (KY)=1H
*250 STOP
*260 END
*RUN
```

Requirement 2: Write a program to print a graph of the function
$$y = 15 \sin \theta$$
for values of θ from 10° to 360° in increments of 10°.

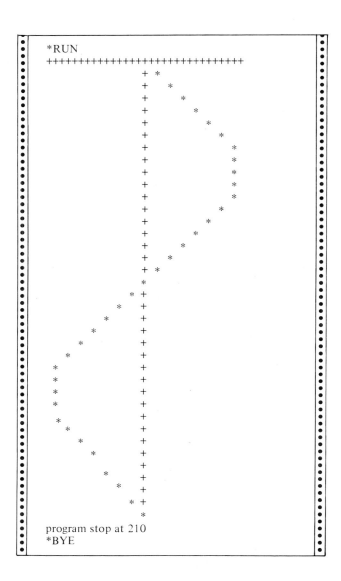

Solution 2: Two new problems are introduced by this requirement:

    (a) The function generates positive and negative values.

    (b) The horizontal axis should be scaled in order to keep it to a reasonable length.

    The form of the output will be as shown on the previous page. Again, the printout should be turned 90° from its orientation on the terminal for proper viewing; the space limitations have prevented that here.

In the y direction provision has been made for 15 positive values, 15 negative values, and 1 zero value. IPLOT must therefore be a 31-element array.

In the theta direction, plotting has been scaled down to 1 plotted point for every 10°, giving 36 points. Plotting at every 1° would have resulted in 360 points plotted and a theta axis ten times as long as this one.

Program 2:

```
*10 DIMENSION IPLOT(31)
*20 DO 3 K=1, 31
*30 3 IPLOT(K)=1H
*40C PRINT Y-AXIS.
*50 WRITE(2,6)
*60 6 FORMAT(1X,31(1H+))
*70C ESTABLISH DO LOOP TO PLOT 36 POINTS.
*80 DO 10 I=10, 360, 10
*90C LOAD CHARACTER FOR THETA AXIS.
*100 IPLOT(16)=1H+
*110C COMPUTE Y VALUE.
*120 THETA=I
*130 KY=15.*SIN(THETA/57.3)
*140C DISPLACE KY TO ALLOW FOR NEGATIVE Y VALUES.
*150 KY=KY+16
*160C REMAINDER SAME AS PROGRAM 1.
*170 IPLOT(KY)=1H*
*180 WRITE(2,7) (IPLOT(K),K=1, 31)
*190 7 FORMAT (1X,31A1)
*200 10 IPLOT(KY)=1H
*210 STOP
*220 END
*RUN
```

Review Exercises

1.*What does the term "batch mode processing" mean?

2. How can the computer respond to so many time-sharing users at any one time?

3. What are some of the advantages of programming in the time-sharing mode?

4.*What is meant by the term "hard copy"?

5. Distinguish between line numbers and statement numbers when programming in the time-sharing mode.

6. What is the difference between a "scratch" file and a "permanent" file?

7. Describe how to "erase" a character that you have typed incorrectly.

8.*How do you add a statement to your program?

9. How do you remove a statement from your program?

10. As part of the sign-on procedure, the programmer receives the following request:

old or new?

What information is being requested?

11. Describe how to build a data file.

12. Demonstrate the conversational mode feature of time-sharing by requesting a 5-digit security number (or a password) at the beginning of a program so that only those people knowing the number (or password) can use the program.

13. Repeat exercise 12 except give the person three tries at providing the number. If the proper number has not been given after three tries, issue the message "ILLEGAL USER" and terminate the program.

14. You have been working on a program for a class assignment. Assume the program is complete and you wish to eliminate it from your file. How is this done on your system?

15. Is column 1 the carriage control column for terminal output as it is in the batch mode?

16. Describe how to correct an error in a FORTRAN statement that was detected during the compilation of a program.

17. Describe the sign-on procedure at your installation.

18. If a FORTRAN statement is too long to fit on one line, describe how a second and third line can be identified as a "continuation" of this long first line.

System Characteristics

	Classification	Word Length (bits)	Main Storage	Major Compilers	Real Fraction	Real Exponent	Real Double	Internal Code
IBM								
SYSTEM 3	M	8	C,M	C,B,F	—	—	—	E
1130	M	16	C	F,R	—	—	—	E
360/40	SB	32	C	C,F,P	24	7	56	E
360/50	SB	32	C	C,F,P	24	7	56	E
370/series	GP	32	B,M	all	24	7	56	E
4300	GP	32	M	all	24	7	56	E
PDP								
11/45	M	16	C,M	C,B,F	24	8	56	A
11/60	M	16	M	C,B,F	24	8	56	A
11/70	M	16	C	C,B,F	24	8	56	A
CDC								
3000	M	24	C	C,F	36	11	—	B
6600	GP	60	C	all	48	11	—	B
CYB 170	GP	60	M,B	all	48	11	—	B
Univac								
1100	GP	36	C	all	27	8	60	A
90/70	GP	32	M	C,F,R	24	7		E

	Classification	Word Length (bits)	Main Storage	Major Compilers	Real Fraction	Real Exponent	Real Double	Internal Code
DEC								
10	GP	36	C	C,B,F	27	8	54	A
20	GP	36	C	all	27	8	62	A
Burrows								
1700	M	8	M	C,B,F	—	—	—	—
2800	M	16	M	C,B,F	—	—	—	B
6700	GP	48	M	all	39	6	78	E
7700	GP	48	M	all	39	6	78	E
Xerox								
SIGMA 6	GP	32	C	all	24	7	56	E
Honeywell								
60	GP	32	M	C,F,R	24	7	—	E
6000	GP	36	C,M	all	27	8	57	E
NCR								
C 101	M	8	C	C,B,F	24	7	—	A
200	GP	64	C	all	56	7	—	A
Data General								
ECLIPSE 130	M	16	C,M	F,B,A	16	5	—	A

Keys to chart categories:

Classification:
M = Mini-computer
SB = Small Business
GP = General Purpose

Main Storage:
C = Magnetic Core
M = Magnetic Oxide
   Semiconductor
B = Bipolar Transistor

Major Compilers:
C = COBOL   R = RPG
B = BASIC   P = PL1
F = FORTRAN   A = ALGOL

Internal Code:
B = BCD
E = EBCDIC
A = ASCHII

My Computer:

		Typical Value		
		16 bit	36 bit	60 bit
Maximum Size INTEGER		6 digits	11 digits	18 digits
Precision of REAL Variables		5 digits	9 digits	14 digits
Maximum Magnitude of REAL Variable		$10^{\pm 38}$	$10^{\pm 127}$	$10^{\pm 308}$
Number of Characters (A-code) per Word			4	8

B Use of the IBM 29 Card Punch

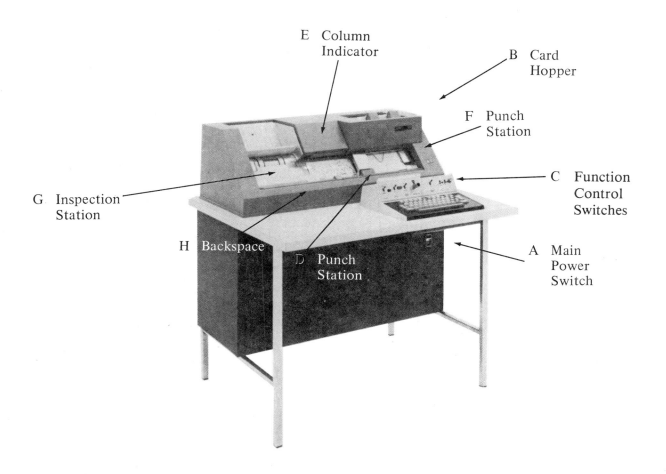

E Column Indicator

B Card Hopper

F Punch Station

C Function Control Switches

G Inspection Station

H Backspace

D Punch Station

A Main Power Switch

The IBM 29 Card Punch
(Courtesy of IBM Corporation)

518

Operating Instructions:

1. Turn on Main Power Switch (A) and allow 30 seconds to warm up.
2. Load Card Hopper (B) with blank cards.
3. There is a group of four Function Control Switches (C) centered over the keyboard. Usually these should be placed in the up position.
4. On the right hand side of the keyboard there is a key marked FEED. Press this key twice. This will cause cards to leave the card hopper and be positioned at the Punch Station (D).
5. You may now start typing the FORTRAN statement on the input data just as if you were dealing with a typewriter. One noticeable difference is that the punch head obscures your view of which column you are punching. That information is displayed by the Column Indicator (E), which is visible through a small window located at the top center of the keypunch.
6. When you have completed punching information on the card, locate the RELease key on the keyboard (it's just above the FEED key). Pressing the RELease key causes the card to pass from the punch station to the Inspection Station (G).
7. Examine the card and see if any error in keypunching has been made. Assume you have typed a faulty character in column 59. (Each column on the card is numbered to help locate your errors.)
8. Pushing the DUPlicate button (top row center) will cause the information on the card at the inspection station to be duplicated on the blank card at the Punch Station. Using this feature, an error can be corrected without retyping the whole card. The idea is to duplicate all columns other than those with an error (column 59 for example). When the column with the error is reached, use the key board to make the correct entry. *Don't forget to throw away the faulty card.*
9. A Backspace Key (H) is located below the Inspection Station and it causes the card to backspace if necessary. If you inadvertently go by the column in which you intended to punch information, the backspace key can be used.

Correcting A Single Card:

The procedures in steps 1–9 are used when there are many cards to be keypunched, i.e., when you first keypunch your program. To keypunch or correct a **single** card, it is more convenient to "**hand feed**" the cards involved.

1. Place the card to be corrected directly into the Inspection Station (G). There are slots at the top and bottom to permit the insertion of a card.
2. Place a blank card directly into the Punch Station (F).
3. Press the key marked REGister and start typing as described in step 4 of the operating instructions.

Answers to Selected Problems

Chapter 1, page 1

1. Both of these
3. Central Processing Unit
5. Add, subtract, multiply, divide
8. Punched holes
11. Magnetic tape
15. No
16. Yes
18. 101
21. Convert instructions to machine language
25. Translated into machine language
28. FORmula TRANslation

Chapter 2, page 21

2. Waits until compiling complete
4. END statement
7. Yes
9. No
11. No
14. Data may appear anywhere
18. Integer
21. Instruction deck; data deck
25. Number of digits one memory location can hold; no
32. Should start in column 7
34. Series of statements that are repeated several times
36. Use column 6 to signal continuation card(s)

Chapter 3, page 51

1. a
4. c
7. a
10. e
11. c or d
13. a

15. b
17. c or d
19. a
21. c or d
25. b
28. a or d

30. c
32. b
35. e
38. c
40. b

44. b
46. Do not cause multiplication
48. Innermost
51. Use parenthesis

Chapter 4, page 73

4. Data overflow (insufficient field width).
6. Column 1 — a blank.
9. Tell which input device to use.
13. Put blank in carriage control column.
17. Not true for integers.
18. Print data as soon as it is read to verify it has been read correctly.

Chapter 5, page 97

1. True and false.
4. False; False; True.
9. Use extra printouts to verify that program is progressing as intended.
12.*Transfers control to statement 20 when end of data deck detected.

```
13.        READ (5,10) X,Y
    10     FORMAT (2F6.1)
           DIST = (X**2+Y**2)**0.5
           WRITE (2,20) DIST
    20     FORMAT (1X,F10.2)
16.        INTEGER CARDS
           LARGE=0
           CARDS=0
    10     READ (5,20) AMOUNT
    20     FORMAT (F12.2)
           CARDS=CARDS+1
           IF(AMOUNT.LT.-200.00)
     1            LARGE=LARGE+1
           IF(CARDS.LT.50)GO TO 10
           WRITE (2,30) LARGE
    30     FORMAT (1X,I8)
```

```
        LARGE=0
40      READ (5,20) AMOUNT
        CARDS=CARDS+1
        IF(AMOUNT.LT.-200.00)
1               LARGE=LARGE+1
        IF(CARDS.LT.100)GO TO 40
        WRITE (2,30) LARGE
        STOP
        END
19.     READ (5,10) X1,Y1,X4,Y4
10      FORMAT (4F12.2)
        DELTX=(X4-X1)/3.0
        DELTY=(Y4-Y1)/3.0
        X2=X1+DELTX
        Y2=Y1+DELTY
        X3=X1+2.0*DELTX
        Y3=Y1+2.0*DELTY
        WRITE (2,40) X2,Y2,X3,Y3
40      FORMAT (1X,4F12.2)
        DIST12=((X2-X1)**2+(Y2-Y1)**2)**0.5
        DIST23=((X3-X2)**2+(Y3-Y2)**2)**0.5
        DIST34=((X4-X3)**2+(Y4-Y3)**2)**0.5
        WRITE(2,50)DIST12, DIST23, DIST34
50      FORMAT(1X, 3F12.2)
        STOP
        END
24.     INTEGER CARDS
        CARDS=0
10      READ(5,20)N1,N2
20      FORMAT(2I1)
        CARDS=CARDS+1
        IF(N1.EQ.6.AND.N2.EQ.6)THEN
            WRITE(2,30)CARDS
            FORMAT(1X,I3)
            STOP
        ENDIF
        IF(CARDS.LT.200) GO TO 10
        WRITE(2,*) 'BOX CARS NEVER ROLLED'
        STOP
        END
```

Chapter 6 , page 137

2. (a) Yes
   (b) Yes
   (c) XINIT
   (d) No
   (e) _ _ -20.76_ _ 14.2_ _ 4071.080
       _ _ _ 203.770_ _ _ _ _ 4
4.   -9999 to 99999*
         -.999999 to 9.999999
       -9999.9999 to 99999.999
         -999999 to 999999*
   Limited by exponent size only.
   *Size of integers is also restricted by processor.

8. Statements on the left. "1X" used to set carriage control character.

11. End parenthesis of FORMAT statement part of Hollerith field. FORMAT statement not terminated properly.

```
16.  5   FORMAT(20X,1HX)
    10   FORMAT(19X,2H1X)
    20   FORMAT(19X,2H2X)
    30   FORMAT(19X,2H3X)
    40   FORMAT(20X,42(1HX))
    50   FORMAT(20X,1HO,5X,1H1,5X,1H2,5X,1H3,
     1      5X,1H4,5X,1H5,5X,1H6,5X,1H7)
         WRITE(2,30)
         WRITE(2,5)
         WRITE(2,5)
         WRITE(2,5)
         WRITE(2,20)
         WRITE(2,5)
         WRITE(2,5)
         WRITE(2,5)
         WRITE(2,10)
         WRITE(2,5)
         WRITE(2,5)
         WRITE(2,5)
         WRITE(2,40)
         WRITE(2,50)
         STOP
         END
19.      READ(5,10)X1,Y1
         READ(5,10)X2,Y2
         READ(5,10)X3,Y3
         READ(5,10)X4,Y4
    10   FORMAT(2F10.2)
         WRITE(2,20)
    20   FORMAT(1H1,3X,*TERMINAL*,9X,1H1,9X,1H2,
     1      9X,1H3,9X,1H4)
         DIST11=0.00
         DIST12=((X2-X1)**2+(Y2-Y1)**2)**0.5
         DIST13=((X3-X1)**2+(Y3-Y1)**2)**0.5
         DIST14=((X4-X1)**2+(Y4-Y1)**2)**0.5
         WRITE(2,30)DIST11,DIST12,DIST13,DIST14
    30   FORMAT(8X,1H1,4X,4F10.2)
         DIST21=DIST12
         DIST22=0.00
         DIST23=((X3-X2)**2+(Y3-Y2)**2)**0.5
         DIST24=((X4-X2)**2+(Y4-Y2)**2)**0.5
         WRITE(2,40)DIST21,DIST22,DIST23,DIST24
    40   FORMAT(8X,1H2,4X,4F10.2)
         DIST31=DIST13
         DIST32=DIST23
         DIST33=0.00
         DIST34=((X4-X3)**2+(Y4-Y3)**2)**0.5
         WRITE(2,50)DIST31,DIST32,DIST33,DIST34
    50   FORMAT(8X,1H3,4X,4F10.2)
         DIST41=DIST14
```

```
              DIST42=DIST24
              DIST43=DIST34
              DIST44=0.00
              WRITE(2,60)DIST41,DIST42,DIST43,DIST44
      60      FORMAT(8X,1H4,4X,4F10.2)
              STOP
              END
```

Chapter 7, page 161

1. No, exponent may be real or integer when raising to a power

4. Radians

6. Real IF tests should be used with caution. If SQRT function (series approximation) results in 4.9999997, STOP will not be executed.

9. Set initial values to various memory locations.

14.
```
              READ(5,10)NSIZE1
      10      FORMAT(I2)
              SUM1=0.0
      20      READ(5,30)X
      30      FORMAT(F12.2)
              NSIZE1=NSIZE1-1
              SUM1=SUM1+X
              IF(NSIZE1.GT.0) GO TO 20
              READ(5,10)NSIZE2
              SUM2=0.0
      40      READ(5,30)X
              NSIZE2=NSIZE2-1
              SUM2=SUM2+X
              IF(NSIZE2.GT.0) GO TO 40
              IF(SUM1.GT.SUM2) THEN
                 WRITE(2,50)SUM1
      50      FORMAT(1X,*LIST1 IS LARGER.
              VALUE=*, F14.2)
              ELSE
                 WRITE(2,60)SUM2
      60      FORMAT(1X,*LIST 2 IS LARGER.
              VALUE=*,F14.2)
              ENDIF
              STOP
              END
```

21.
```
              X=1.0
              YMIN=ALOG10(X+4.0)+ABS(X**3-64.0)
              YMAX=ALOG10(X+4.0)+ABS(X**3-64.0)
      10      X=X+0.1
              Y=ALOG10(X+4.0)+ABS(X**3-64.0)
              IF(Y.GT.YMAX)YMAX=Y
              IF(Y.LT.YMIN)YMIN=Y
              IF(X.LT.10.0) GO TO 10
              WRITE(2,20)YMIN,YMAX
      20      FORMAT(1X,2F14.2)
              STOP
              END
```

Chapter 8, page 193

3. Detailed, exact, effective, efficient.

7. Extra print statements.

11. Show subordination. Statements that are subordinate to an IF test, for example.

14. Statement not written in proper form. Best detected during desk check.

18. Sequence, decision, loop.

22. Division by zero; trying to take the logarithm of a negative number; attempting to read when data deck is depleted. Many intermediate printouts.

24. Just as it looks when listed by the computer.

Chapter 9, page 221

3.
```
              KOUNT=100
              KOUNT=KOUNT+2
              IF(KOUNT.LE.200)
```

5. If more than one sequential examination of the values associated with this variable is needed, then the variable should be subscripted.

7.
```
              DO 10 I=1,100,1
                 XCOPY(I)=X(I)
      10      CONTINUE
```

9. In the statement SUM=SUM+X, the variable X is not subscripted.

13.
```
              DIMENSION X(401),Y(401)
              VALUE=-20.0
              I=1
      10      X(I)=VALUE
              Y(I)=VALUE**2
              VALUE=VALUE+0.1
              I=I+1
              IF(I.LE.401) GO TO 10

              DIMENSION X(401),Y(401)
              VALUE=-20.0
              DO 10 I=1,401,1
                 X(I)=VALUE
                 Y(I)=VALUE**2
                 VALUE=VALUE+0.1
      10      CONTINUE
```

16.
```
              SUMML=0.0
              SUMMR=0.0
              READ(5,10)NLEFT
      10      FORMAT(I3)
              DO 30 I=1,NLEFT
                 READ(10,20)F,X
      20      FORMAT(2F10.2)
                 SUMML=SUMML+F*X
      30      CONTINUE
              READ(5,10)NRIGHT
```

```
          DO 40 I=1,NRIGHT
             READ(10,20)F,X
             SUMMR=SUMMR+F*X
   40     CONTINUE
          RESULT=SUMMR-SUMML
          WRITE(2,50)RESULT
   50     FORMAT(1X,F12.2)
          STOP
          END
23.       XHIGH=0.0
          DO 20 L=1,72,1
             XHIGH=XHIGH+1.0
             TENS=500.*SQRT(36.+(6.-XHIGH/12.))
                /(6.-XHIGH/12.)
             IF(TENS.GE.2000.)THEN
                WRITE(2,10)TENS,XHIGH
                FORMAT(1X,F10.1,F10.2)
                STOP
             ENDIF
   20     CONTINUE
          END
```

Chapter 10, page 251

1. Vector (one-dimensional array). Matrix (two-dimensional array). Three-dimensional array, etc.

4. READ(5,10)(X(I),I=1,400,1)

6. Size of arrays must be specified as constants in DIMENSION statement.

9. No. FORMAT statement describes one *typical* unit record (card).

```
13.       DIMENSION X1(20),X2(20),X3(20)
          DATA SUM1,SUM2,SUM3/3*0.0/
          READ(5,5)(X1(I),I=1,20),(X2(I),I=1,20),
   1         (X3(I),I=1,20)
   5      FORMAT(20F4.1)
          DO 10 I=1,20,1
             SUM1=SUM1+X1(I)
             SUM2=SUM2+X2(I)
             SUM3=SUM3+X3(I)
   10     CONTINUE
          AVE1=SUM1/20.
          AVE2=SUM2/20.
          AVE3=SUM3/20.
          DO 30 I=1,20,1
             DIFF1=X1(I)-AVE1
             DIFF2=X2(I)-AVE2
             DIFF3=X3(I)-AVE3
             WRITE(2,20) I,DIFF1,DIFF2,DIFF3
   20     FORMAT(1X,I7,3F16.2)
   30     CONTINUE
          STOP
          END
```

```
16.       DIMENSION X(100),Y(100)
          READ(5,10)(X(I),I=1,100,1)
   10     FORMAT(10F8.1)
          DO 20 I=1,100,1
             K=101-I
             Y(I)=X(K)
   20     CONTINUE
          WRITE(2,10)(Y(I),I=1,100)
          STOP
          END
20.       DIMENSION X(100)
          READ(5,10)(X(I),I=1,100,1)
   10     FORMAT(10F8.1)
          DO 20 I=50,99
             X(I) = X(I+1)
   20     CONTINUE
          WRITE(2,30)(X(I),I=1,99)
   30     FORMAT(1X,10F10.1)
          STOP
          END
25.       DIMENSION LIST1(300),LIST2(300)
          READ(5,10)(LIST1(I),I=1,300),(LIST2(I),
             I=1,300)
          DO 30 I=1,300
             IF(LIST2(I).EQ.LIST1(1))THEN
                WRITE(2,20)I
   20     FORMAT(3X*ELEMENT 1 APPEARS IN
             POSITION*,I5)
          STOP
          ENDIF
   30     CONTINUE
          WRITE(2,40)
   40     FORMAT(3X,*ELEMENT 1 NO DUPLI-
             CATES*)
          STOP
          END
34.       DIMENSION M(10,10)
          DO 20 I=1,10,1
          DO 10 J=1,10,1
             IF(I.EQ.J)THEN
                M(I,J)=1
             ELSE
                M(I,J)=0
             ENDIF
   10     CONTINUE
   20     CONTINUE
```

Chapter 11, page 283

1. An exit of the DO loop prior to the loop counter (or index) reaching its upper limit. Index has value prevalent at time of exit.

4. No. Column order.

7. Yes. The loop statements will be executed once, irrespective of the initial value.

10. No. Most systems allow programmer to set an upper limit on the amount of time a program should be allowed to run. The program will terminate when that limit is reached.

15.
```
        SUM=0.0
        DO 20 IROW=2,5
        DO 10 ICOL=2,5
          SUM=SUM+A(IROW,ICOL)
10      CONTINUE
20      CONTINUE
```

17.
```
        DO 40 IROW=1,100
        DO 20 ICOL=1,10
          IF(DATA(IROW,ICOL).EQ.0) GO TO 30
20      CONTINUE
        WRITE(2,25)IROW
25      FORMAT(1X,*NO NON-ZERO ELEMENTS
                            IN ROW*,I4)
        GO TO 40
30      WRITE(2,35)IROW,ICOL
35      FORMAT(1X,2I8)
40      CONTINUE
```

21.
```
        X=0.0
        DO 10 I=1,100,1
          Y=EXP(X)+X**2-12.0
          IF(X.GT.0.0) THEN
            WRITE(2,5)I
5           FORMAT(1X,I3)
            STOP
          ENDIF
        X=X+0.2
10      CONTINUE
        WRITE(2,20)
20      FORMAT(1X,*100 TRIES. Y STILL NEGA-
        TIVE*)
        STOP
        END
```

23.
```
        DO 10 I=1,30
        DO 10 J=1,30
        DO 10 K=1,30
          M=I*J*K
          IF(M.EQ.30)WRITE(2,5)I,J,K
5         FORMAT(1X,3I7)
10      CONTINUE
        STOP
        END
```

Chapter 12, page 309

3. Since DSIN must be known to double precision accuracy, more terms are evaluated for this function.

6. Once a variable has been declared as a certain type, it must remain that type throughout the program.

11.
```
        DOUBLE PRECISION DSAL,SUM
        SUM=0.0
        DO 20 I=1,50
          DSAL=(2.**(I-1))/100.
          SUM=SUM+DSAL
          WRITE(2,10)I,DSAL,SUM
10      FORMAT(1X,I2,2D20.2)
20      CONTINUE
        STOP
        END
```

15.
```
        COMPLEX A,B,RESULT
        DATA THETA1,THETA2,DTHETA/60.,
        30.,6./
        INTEGER TIME
        TIME=1
10      XAB=9.0*COS(THETA1/57.3)
        YAB=9.0*SIN(THETA1/57.3)
        A=CMPLX(XAB,YAB)
        XBC=6.0*COS(THETA2/57.3)
        YBC=6.0*SIN(THETA2/57.3)
        B=CMPLX(XBC,YBC)
        RESULT=A+B
        X=REAL(RESULT)
        Y=AIMAG(RESULT)
        WRITE(2,20)I,X,Y,XAB,YAB
20      FORMAT(1X,I2,4F16.2)
        THETA1=THETA1+DTHETA
        THETA2=THETA2+DTHETA
        TIME=TIME+1
        IF(TIME.LE.60) GO TO 10
        STOP
        END
```

16.
```
        LOGICAL FEMALE(75),MALE(75)
        READ(5,10)IGIRL,(FEMALE(I),I=1,75)
10      FORMAT(I5,75L1)
20      NUMBER=0
30      READ(5,10,END=60)IBOY,(MALE(I),I=1,75)
        DO 40 I=1,75
          IF(MALE(I).EQ.FEMALE(I)) NUMBER=
          NUMBER+1
40      CONTINUE
        IF(NUMBER.GE.70)WRITE(2,50)IBOY
50      FORMAT(1X,I5)
        GO TO 20
60      STOP
        END
```

Chapter 13, page 335

2. No

6. Read input values. Make CALLS, print desired results

8. It is not assigned a memory location of its own nor does it pick up the address of another variable. It is merely a place holder that shows where in a calculation this quantity appears.

10. When a subprogram must examine the values of an array defined (known) in the calling program, the address of the first element of the array is passed from the calling program to the using program. This address is called the **base address** of the array.

15.
```
      FUNCTION LOCATN(DATA,NSIZE)
      BIG=DATA(1)
      LOCATN=1
      DO 10 I=2,NSIZE
        IF(DATA(I).GT.BIG) THEN
          BIG=DATA(I)
          LOCATN=I
        ENDIF
10    CONTINUE
      RETURN
      END
```

17.
```
      XPISTN(THETA)=R*(1.-COS(THETA))+L-
           L*SQRT(1.- (R*SIN(THETA)/L)**2)
```

19.
```
      FUNCTION SIN2(X)
      SIN2=0.0
      XSIGN=-1.0
      DO 20 I=1,19,2
        DENOM=1.0
        DO 10 K=1,I
          DENOM=DONOM*FLOAT(K)
10      CONTINUE
        XSIGN=XSIGN*(-1.0)
        TERM=XSIGN*X**I/DENOM
        SIN2=SIN2+TERM
20    CONTINUE
      RETURN
      END
```

21.
```
      FUNCTION AREA(A,XINIT,XFINL)
      DELTX=(XFINL-XINIT)/100.
      AREA=0.0
      DO 10 I=1,100,1
        Y=X**A
        X=X+DELTX
        YPLUS=X**A
        AREA=AREA+(Y+YPLUS)/2.XDELTX
10    CONTINUE
      RETURN
      END
```

26.
```
      SUBROUTINE SEARCH(M,A,ELMT,LOC)
      DIMENSION A(100)
      ELMT=A(1)
      LOC=1
      IF(M.GT.0) THEN
        DO 10 I=2,100
          IF(A(I).GT.ELMT) THEN
```

```
            ELMT=A(I)
            LOC=I
          ENDIF
10      CONTINUE
      ELSE
        DO 20 I=2,100
          IF(A(I).LT.ELMT) THEN
            ELMT=A(I)
            LOC=I
          ENDIF
20      CONTINUE
      ENDIF
      RETURN
      END
```

Chapter 14, page 371

3. Consumes twenty consecutive memory locations. The first 5 hold column 1 of the matrix. The last 5 hold column 4. It is in the 8th memory location.

5. This array is defined inside the subprogram only and is not shared with any other program (the array name does not appear in the argument list). Size of array must be defined by constants.

8. Place variables that are common to these subprograms in **COMMON** storage. These variables can then be eliminated from each argument list.

10. When it is necessary to pass information that is best represented by an equation. Area under a curve or root of an equation.

15.
```
      SUBROUTINE CHANGE(A)
      DIMENSION A(14,28)
      BIG=A(1,1)
      LOCATN=1
      DO 10 I=2,14
        IF(A(I,1).GT.BIG)) THEN
          BIG=A(I,1)
          LOCATN=I
        ENDIF
10    CONTINUE
      IF(LOCATN.EQ.1)RETURN
      DO 20 I=1,28,1
        TEMP=A(1,I)
        A(1,I)=A(LOCATN,I)
        A(LOCATN,I)=TEMP
20    CONTINUE
      RETURN
      END
```

18.
```
      SUBROUTINE ROOTS(Y,XLEFT,XRIGHT)
      EXTERNAL Y
      XMID=XLEFT+(XRIGHT-XLEFT)/2.0
      YLEFT=Y(XLEFT)
      YMID=Y(XMID)
      YRIGHT=Y(XRIGHT)
```

```
C       IF TWO VALUES OF Y HAVE THE SAME
C       SIGN, THE PRODUCT OF THESE VALUES
C       IS POSITIVE.
C               (PROBABLY NO ROOT IN THIS SPAN)
C       IF TWO VALUES OF Y HAVE OPPOSITE
C       SIGNS THE PRODUCT OF THESE VALUES
C       IS NEGATIVE.
C                       (ROOT IN THIS SPAN)
        PROD=YLEFT*YMID
        IF(PROD.LT.0.0) THEN
            WRITE(2,10)
   10       FORMAT(1X,*ROOT TO THE LEFT OF
                        THE MIDPOINT*)
            RETURN
        ENDIF
C
        PROD=YMID*YRIGHT
        IF(PROD.LT.0.0) THEN
            WRITE(2,20)
   20       FORMAT(1X,*ROOT TO THE RIGHT OF
                        THE MIDPOINT*)
            RETURN
        ENDIF
C
        WRITE(2,30)
   30   FORMAT(1X,*SIGN AT ALL THREE TEST
                    POINTS THE SAME*)
        RETURN
        END
23.     SUBROUTINE SCALE (A,NROW,NCOL,
                            VALUE)
        DIMENSION A(NROW,NCOL),VALUE
                            (NROW)
        DO 20 I=1,NROW
          FACTOR=VALUE(I)
          DO 10 J=1,NCOL
            A(I,J)=A(I,J)*FACTOR
   10     CONTINUE
   20   CONTINUE
        RETURN
        END
```

Chapter 15, page 395

2. A group of subprograms that accomplish repetitive activities associated with a particular professional occupation such as accounting, civil engineering, aircraft controlling, trucking, etc.

4. Using an integer argument that is given a value 0, 1, 2, 3 . . . , which conveys if the solution has progressed properly or encountered some difficulties.

8. Make a copy of the arrays and feed these copies to the subroutine.

```
12.     SUBROUTINE TRIG(A,B,C,ANGA,ANGB)
        C=SQRT(A**2+B**2)
```

```
        ANGA=ATAN(A/B)*57.3
        ANGB=90.0-ANGA
        RETURN
        END
17.     SUBROUTINE ROOTS(Y,XLEFT,YRIGHT,
                            XROOT,MAIL)
        EXTERNAL Y
        DO 100 LOOP=1,10,1
            XMID=XLEFT+(XRIGHT-XLEFT)/2.0
            YLEFT=Y(XLEFT)
            YMID=Y(XMID)
            YRIGHT=Y(XRIGHT)
C       IF TWO VALUES OF Y HAVE THE SAME
C       SIGN, THE PRODUCT OF THESE VALUES
C       IS POSITIVE (PROBABLY NO ROOT IN
C                       THIS SPAN)
C
C       IF TWO VALUES OF Y HAVE OPPOSITE
C       SIGN, THE PRODUCT IS NEGATIVE IN-
C       DICATING ROOT WITHIN THIS SPAN.
        PROD=YLEFT*YMID
        IF(PROD.LT.0.0)THEN
            XRIGHT=XMID
            GO TO 100
        ENDIF
C
        PROD=YMID*YRIGHT
        IF(PROD.LT.0.0) THEN
            XLEFT = XMID
            GO TO 100
        ENDIF
C       IF THIS POINT REACHED ALL Y VALUES
C       HAVE THE SAME SIGN
        MAIL=1
        RETURN
  100   CONTINUE
        MAIL=0
        XROOT=XMID
        RETURN
        END
```

Chapter 16, page 413

1. Limit the degree of complexity and number of actions accomplished in one unit of code.

5. A construct that must select and execute one of many very similar blocks of code.

7. The first statement in the construct reveals the type of construct.

```
12.     SUBROUTINE TEST (ARRAY,NSIZE,ODD,
        EVEN)
        INTEGER ARRAY (NSIZE), ODD,
        EVEN
        DATA ODD, EVEN/0,0/
C       IF AN INTEGER IS DIVIDED BY 2 AND
C       THEN MULTIPLIED BY 2(IN THE INTEGER
```

```
C     MODE), EVEN-VALUED INTEGERS ARE
C     NOT AFFECTED; ODD ARE.
      DO 10 I=1,NSIZE
        K=ARRAY(I)/2
        J=K*2
        IF(J.EQ.ARRAY(I))THEN
          EVEN=EVEN+1
        ELSE
          ODD=ODD+1
        ENDIF
10    CONTINUE
      RETURN
      END
```

15.
```
      DIMENSION X(10,15)
      READ(5,10)X
10    FORMAT(10F8.1)
      DO 50 IROW=1,10
      SUM=0.0
      DO 20 ICOL=1,15
        SUM=SUM+X(IROW,ICOL)
20    CONTINUE
      AVE=SUM/15.0
      SUM=0.0
      DO 30 ICOL-1,15
        SUM=SUM+(X(IROW,ICOL)-AVE)**2
30    CONTINUE
      DEV=SQRT(SUM/14.0)
      WRITE(2,40)DEV,AVE
40    FORMAT(1X,2F12.4)
50    CONTINUE
      STOP
      END
```

Chapter 17, page 429

1. Internal memory has fast access time but limited capacity. Auxiliary memory is slower but has very large capacity.

4. When the exchange of information is internal (not involving input or output device).

7. Signals that a record in a file is no longer active.

10. Cut down on the number of interrecord gaps.

12. The first involves an "edited" transfer requiring the use of a FORMAT statement to interpret the meaning of a memory location. The second is an "unedited" transfer. Information is written in pure binary (no FORMAT interpretation needed).

15. DIMENSION NRPT(450),NAME(450,5),COST(450), IQOH(450),IQORD(450),NRDEPT(450), NRBIN(450)

Chapter 18, page 455

2. No, number of passes decreases by one each time.

4. When a record on an "old" tape is to be updated or deleted, that record has already been read and most systems do not provide provision for "backing up"

the tape to make the necessary changes.

8. Speed of processing not critical. Large volume of active records in file.

10. Records associated with other file should be directly transferred onto output file.

13.
```
      DIMENSION NAME(300,5),IADDR(300,6)
      NPHONE(300)
      REWIND 15
      REWIND 16
10    READ(15)NAME,IADDR,NPHONE,NRLR
      WHILE(EOFCKF(15).NE.1)DO
      NP=NRLR-1
      NC=NP
      DO 50 IP=1,NP
      DO 40 IC=1,NC
        IF(NPHONE(IC).GT.NPHONE(IC+1))THEN
          ITEMP=NPHONE(IC+1)
          NPHONE(IC+1)=NPHONE(IC)
          NPHONE(IC)=ITEMP
          DO 20 K=1,5
            ITEMP=NAME(IC+1,K)
            NAME(IC+1,K)=NAME(IC,K)
            NAME(IC,K)=ITEMP
20        CONTINUE
          DO 30 K=1,6
            ITEMP=LADDR(IC+1,K)
            LADDR(IC+1,K)=LADDR(IC,K)
            LADDR(IC,K)=ITEMP
30        CONTINUE
40      CONTINUE
        NC=NC-1
50    CONTINUE
      WRITE(16)NAME,LADDR,NPHONE,NRLR
      END WHILE
60    ENDFILE 16
      REWIND 15
      REWIND 16
      STOP
      END
```

Chapter 19, page 471

2. Character information is stored according to a number code where each character is represented by a two- or three-digit number.

5. The character string that is the longer of the two will always have a larger value.

9. Allow the format of the data cards to be of variable configuration.

13.
```
      DIMENSION SUMX(2)'CONTS(2)
      DATA SUMX(1),SUMX(2),CONTS(1),
      CONTS(2)/4*0.0/
      READ(5,10)M
10    FORMAT(I4)
      DO 30 I=1,M
```

```
        READ(5,20)X,Y
20      FORMAT(2F12.2)
        SUMX(1)=SUMX(1)+X
        SUMX(2)=SUMX(2)+X**2
        CONTS(1)=CONTS(1)+Y
        CONTS(2)=CONTS(2)+X**Y
30      CONTINUE
        A1=(CONTS(1)*SUMX(2)-CONTS(2)*SUM
        X(1))
    1      /(FLOAT(M)*SUMX(2)-SUMX(1)**2)
        A2=(CONTS(1)-FLOAT(M)*A1)/SUMX(1)
        WRITE(2,40)A1,A2
40      FORMAT(1X,2F14.4)
        STOP
        END
```

Chapter 20, page 501

1. Submission of programs, usually by card input, where the program is entered all at once (as opposed to entering statements one at a time as in time-sharing).

4. Some time-sharing devices provide printed output on paper, while others provide output on a video screen. The output on paper is called **hard copy**.

8. Statements are usually entered with line numbers beginning with 10 and at intervals of 10 (10, 20, 30, 40, etc.). To add a statement you assign a number in between the numbers already assigned.

15. Yes

18. The time-share FORTRAN has a provision for a continuation column.

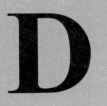

D | Non-Executable Statements

The following is a list of non-executable statements in the FORTRAN language.

BLOCK DATA	END	FUNCTION
COMMON	ENTRY	INTEGER
COMPLEX	EQUIVALENCE	LOGICAL
DATA	EXTERNAL	NAMELIST
DIMENSION	FORMAT	REAL
DOUBLE PRECISION		SUBROUTINE

Order of Specification Statements

Restrictions exist with respect to the placement of specification statements. These have been mentioned throughout the text. Adherence to the following order of these statements will satisfy all existing restrictions.

Type Statements	DATA Statement
EXTERNAL Statement	Arithmetic Function Defining Statements
DIMENSION Statement	Executable Statements
COMMON Statement	FORMAT Statement
EQUIVALENCE Statement	END Statement
NAMELIST Statement	

Comparison of Full vs. Subset Compilers

The following table identifies features that are common to both the full and subset compilers as defined by the FORTRAN–77 standards.

Assignment Statements:		INPUT/OUTPUT Statements:	
ARITHMETIC		READ, WRITE	
LOGIC		BACKSPACE, REWIND, ENDFILE	
CHARACTER		Direct access I/O	
CONTROL Statements:		End-of-file specifiers	
Unconditional GO TO		**Other:**	
Computed GO TO		DIMENSION	EQUIVALENCE
Assigned GO TO		COMMON	Named COMMON
		ASSIGN	CONTINUE
Arithmetic IF		EXTERNAL	FORMAT
Logical IF		STOP	END
		PAUSE	PROGRAM
IF-THEN-ELSE		FUNCTION	SUBROUTINE
ELSE IF		CALL	RETURN

The following table identifies those features that are available in the full and subset compilers as defined by the FORTRAN-77 standards.

	Subset Language	Full Language		Subset Language	Full Language
Data Types			**DO Statement**		
INTEGER	Yes	Yes	Negative incrementation	Yes	Yes
REAL	Yes	Yes	Real or double precision variable	No	Yes
DOUBLE PRECISION	No	Yes			
COMPLEX	No	Yes	Parameters as expressions	No	Yes
LOGICAL	No	Yes	**Expressions**		
CHARACTER	Yes	Yes	Mixed mode arithmetic expressions	Yes	Yes
Arrays					
Maximum dimensions	3	7	Relational and logical expressions	Yes	Yes
Adjustable dimensions	Yes	Yes	Generic functions	No	Yes
Lower bound of subscript other than unity.	No	Yes	Character functions	No	Yes
			Data Statement		
			Allowed	Yes	Yes
			Using implied DO	No	Yes

G | FORTRAN Library Functions

Trigonometric Functions

Generic Name	Function	Symbolic Form	Type of Argument	Type of Function	Definition
SIN	Trigonometric sine	SIN (X) DSIN (X) CSIN (X)	R D C	R D C	sine of X X is in radians
COS	Trigonometric cosine	COS (X) DCOS (X) CCOS (X)	R D C	R D C	cosine of X X is in radians
TAN	Trigonometric	TAN (X) DTAN (X)	R D	R D	tangent of X X is in radians
ASIN	Inverse sine function	ASIN (X) DASIN (X)	R D	R D	$\sin^{-1}$ (X) value
ACOS	Inverse cosine function	ACOS (X) DACOS (X)	R D	R D	$\cos^{-1}$ (X) value returned in radians
ATAN	Inverse tangent function	ATAN (X) DATAN (X)	R D	R D	$\tan^{-1}$ (X) value returned in radians
ATAN2	Inverse tangent function	ATAN2(X,Y) DATAN2(X,Y)	R D	R D	same as above except two arguments
SINH	Hyperbolic sine function	SINH (X) DSINH (X)	R D	R D	sinh (X)
COSH	Hyperbolic cosine function	COSH (X) DCOSH (X)	R D	R D	cosh (X)
TANH	Hyperbolic tangent function	TANH (X) DTANH (X)	R D	R D	tanh (X)

Arithmetic Functions

Generic Name	Function	Symbolic Form	Type of Argument	Type of Function	Definition
SQRT	Square root	SQRT (X) DSQRT (X) CSQRT (X)	R D C	R D C	$\sqrt{x} = x^{1/2}$ $X \geqslant 0$

EXP	Exponential	EXP (X)	R	R	e^x
		DEXP (X)	D	D	
		CEXP (X)	C	C	
ABS	Absolute value	IABS (M)	I	I	$\|X\|$ Absolute value
		ABS (X)	R	R	function.
		DABS (X)	D	D	
		CABS (X)	C	C	
LOG 10	Common logarithm	ALOG10 (X)	R	R	$\log_{10}(X)$
		DLOG10 (X)	D	D	
LOG	Natural logarithm	ALOG (X)	R	R	
		DLOG (X)	D	D	$\log_e(X)$
		CLOG (X)	C	C	$\ln(X)$
MAX	Largest element in argument list	AMAX0(I,J, . . .)	I	R	Returns largest element in argument list of two or more elements
		AMAX1(X,Y, . . .)	R	R	
		MAX0(I,J, . . .)	I	I	
		MAX1(X,Y . . .)	R	I	
		DMAX1(X,Y . . .)	D	D	
MIN	Smallest element in argument list	AMIN0(I,J, . . .)	I	R	Returns smallest element in argument list of two or more elements
		AMIN1(X,Y, . . .)	R	R	
		MIN0(I,J, . . .)	I	I	
		MIN1(X,Y, . . .)	R	I	
		DMIN1(X,Y, . . .)	D	D	
MOD	Remainder from division of two arguments	MOD (I,J)	I	I	Modular arithmetic, remainder of division of X by Y.
		AMOD (X,Y)	R	R	
		DMOD (X,Y)	D	D	
INT	Truncation.	INT (X)	R	I	Drops the fractional part of X and returns the whole number portion.
		AINT (X)	R	R	
		DINT (X)	D	I	
ANINT	Nearest whole number	ANINT (X)	R	R	Nearest whole number.
		DNINT (X)	D	D	
NINT	Nearest integer	NINT (X)	R	I	Nearest integer number.
		IDINT (X)	D	I	

Other Functions

REAL — determines the real part of a complex argument.

AIMAG — determines the imaginary part of a complex argument.

CONJ — defines the conjugate of a complex function.

SIN — transfer of sign of first argument to second argument.

ISIGN — same as above except integer arguments.

DSIGN — same as above except double precision arguments.

DIM — produce positive difference between two real arguments.

IDIM — same as above except integer arguments.

FLOAT — converts integer argument to real.

LEN — determines the length of a character string.

INDEX — determines the position of a substring "a_1" in a string "a_2".

ICHAR — value (position) of a character in the collating sequence.

CHAR — the character corresponding to the value (position) of the argument in the collating sequence.

ERF — computes an error function:

$$\frac{2}{\sqrt{\pi}} \int_0^x e^{-u^2}\, du$$

GAMMA — computes gamma function:

$$\int_0^\infty u^{x-1} e^{-u}\, du$$

Index